MW01626828

LOUIS CARL BRUNO HÉROUX

AUBREY BEARDSLEY

JAMES ENSOR

JOSEF KUGLER

FRITZ HEGENBART

CHRISTIAN BEHRENS

ARNOLD BÖCKLIN

ADOLF MÜNZER

FRANCISCO DE GOYA

VIKTOR MÜLLER

THÉOPHILE ALEXANDRE STEINLEN

FRANZ VON STUCK

ODILON REDON

GUSTAV KLIMT

AUGUST BRÖMSE

FÉLICIEN ROPS

FRANZ VON BAYROS

HEINRICH KLEY

WILHELM LIST

ALFRED KUBIN

in dialogue

LUCIEN LÉVY-DHURMER

GEORGES ANTOINE ROCHEGROSSE

MAX KLINGER

CARL MOLL

GUSTAVE MOREAU

KARL MEDIZ

RICHARD LUKSCH

EDVARD MUNCH

BERTRAM HARTMAN

RUDOLPH HÖLBE

KLEMENS BROSCH

SASCHA SCHNEIDER

JOSEF ENGELHART

FERNAND KHNOPFF

OTTO GREINER

FERDINAND FREIHERR VON REZNIČEK

HUGO HÖPPENER (FIDUS)

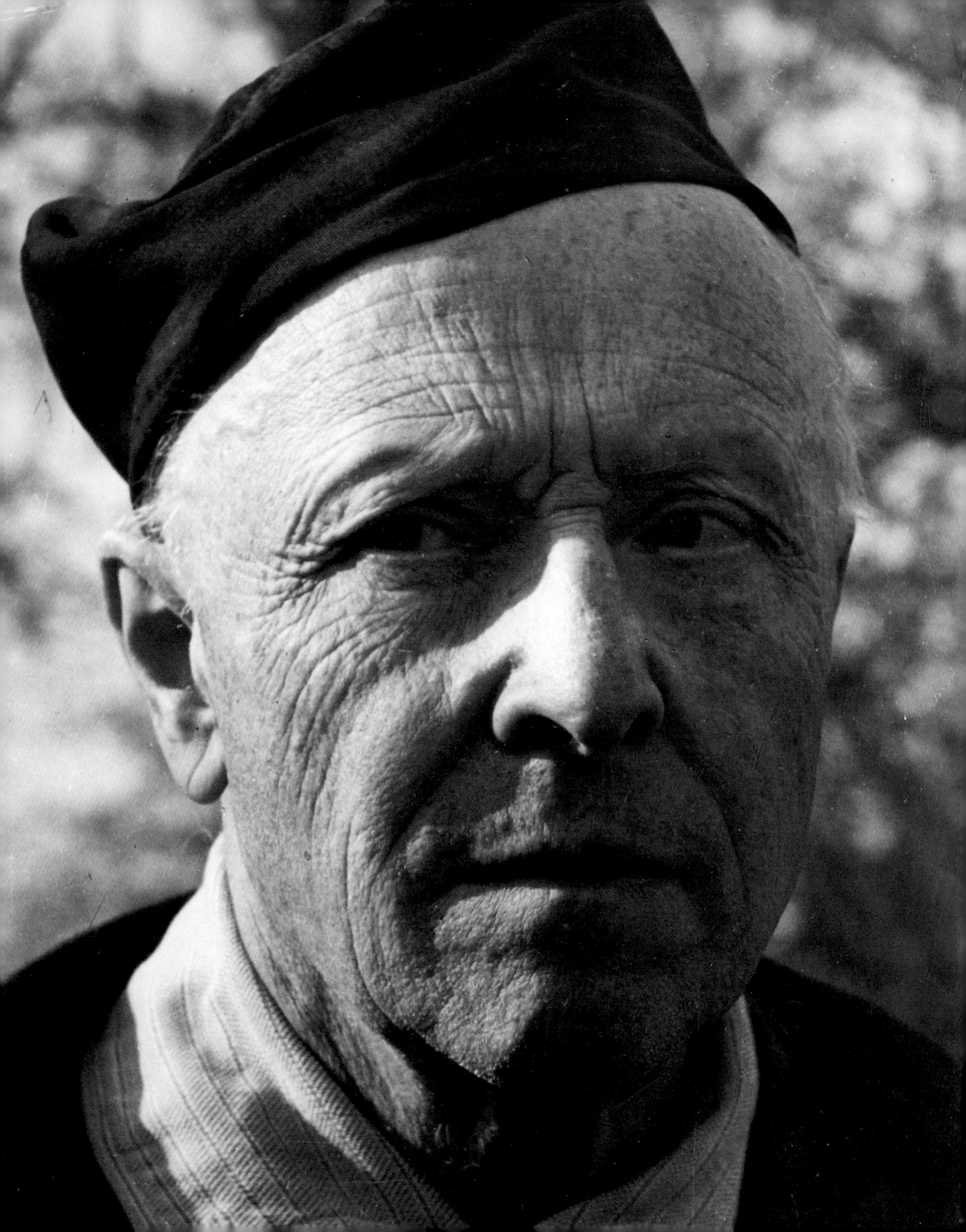

ALFRED KUBIN

Confessions of a Tortured Soul

Editor
Hans-Peter Wipplinger

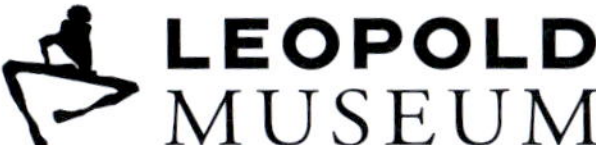

Verlag der Buchhandlung Walther und Franz König, Köln

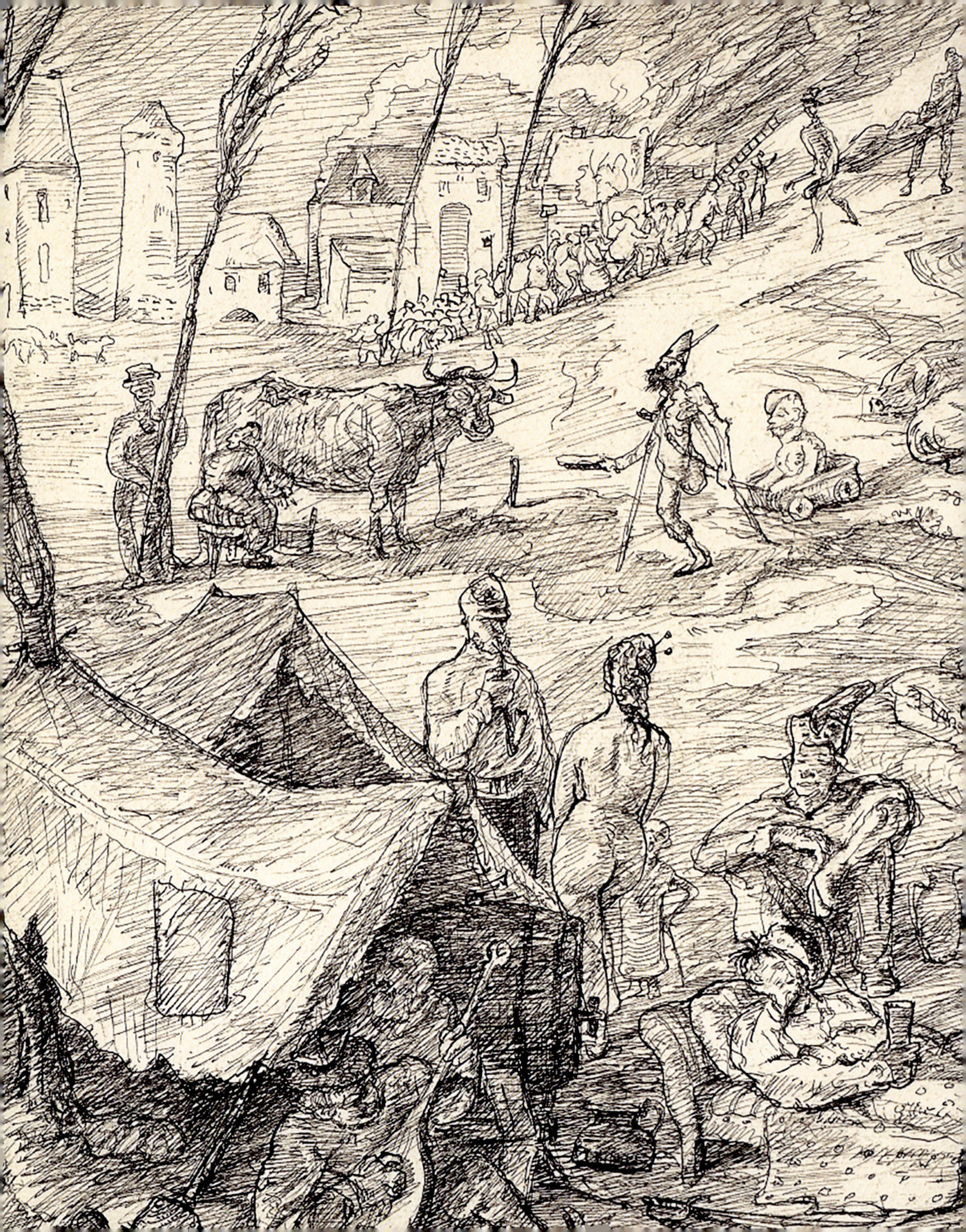

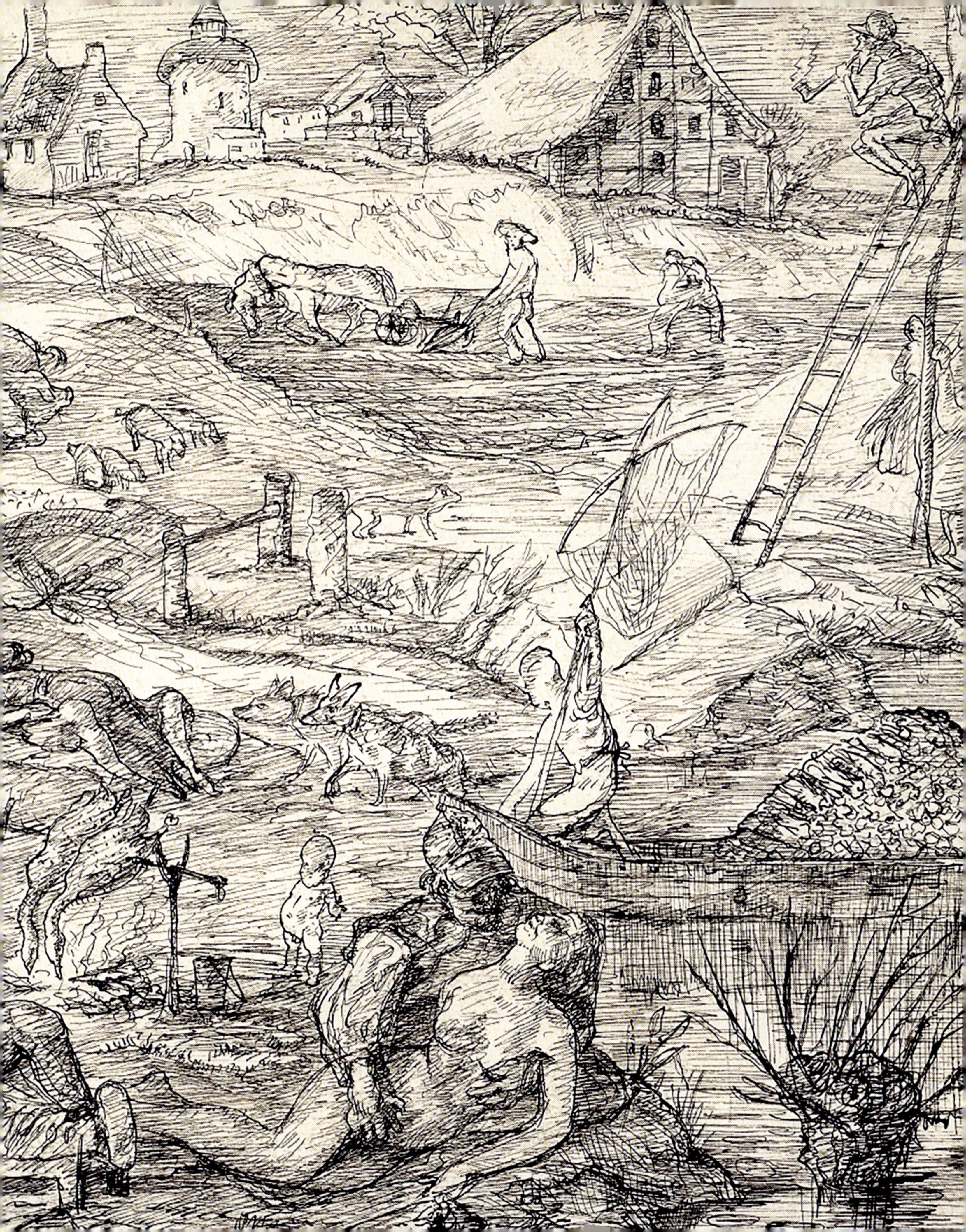

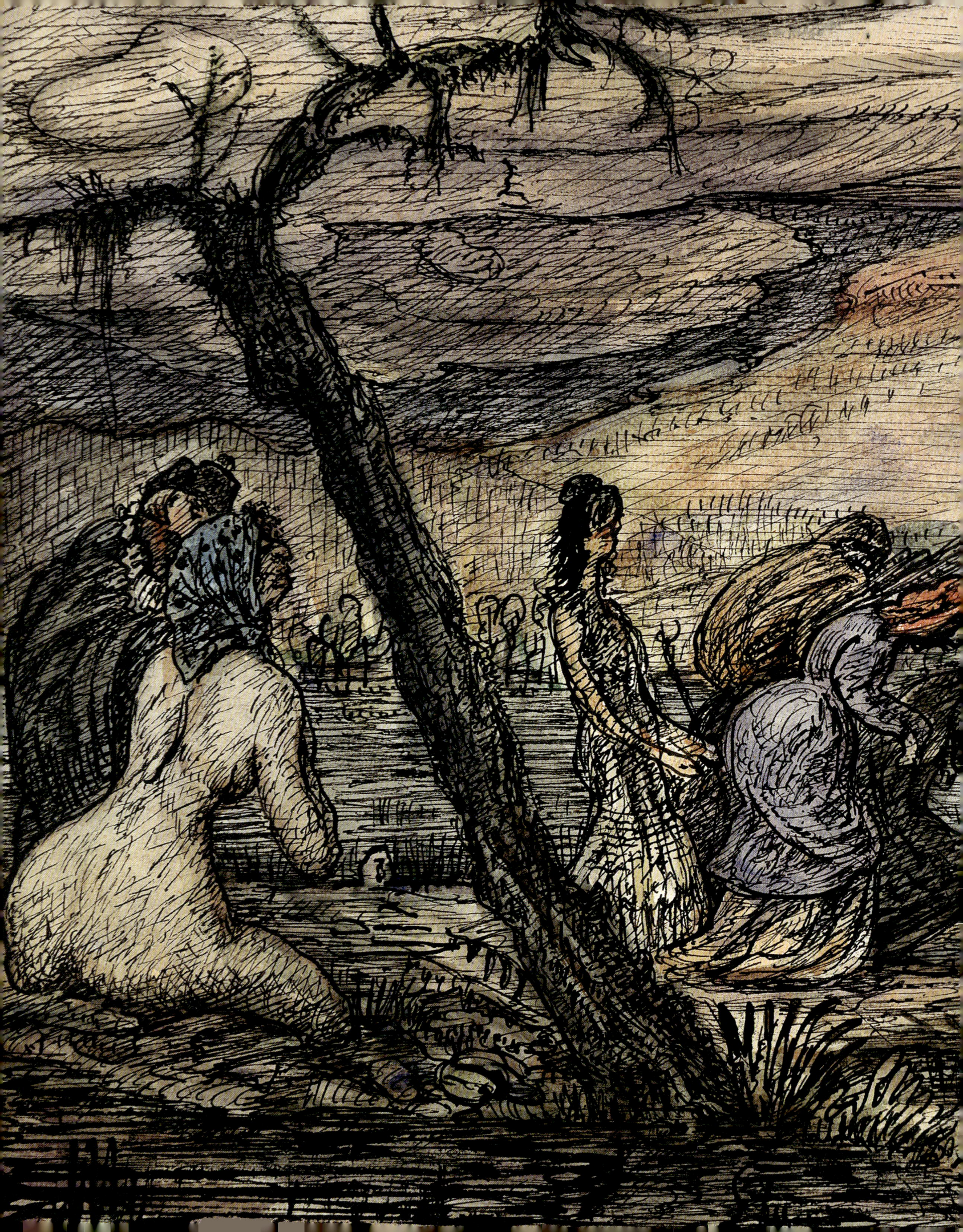

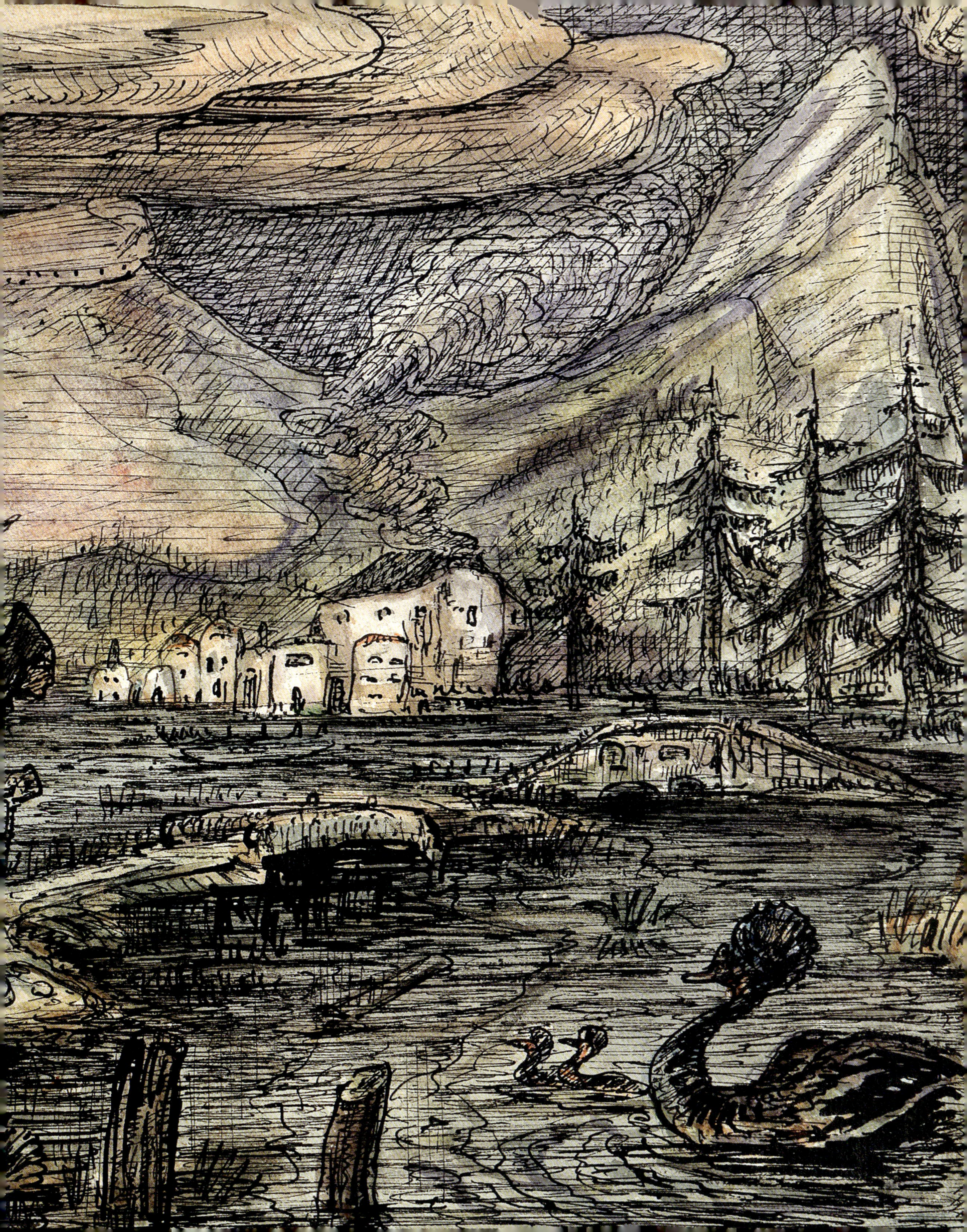

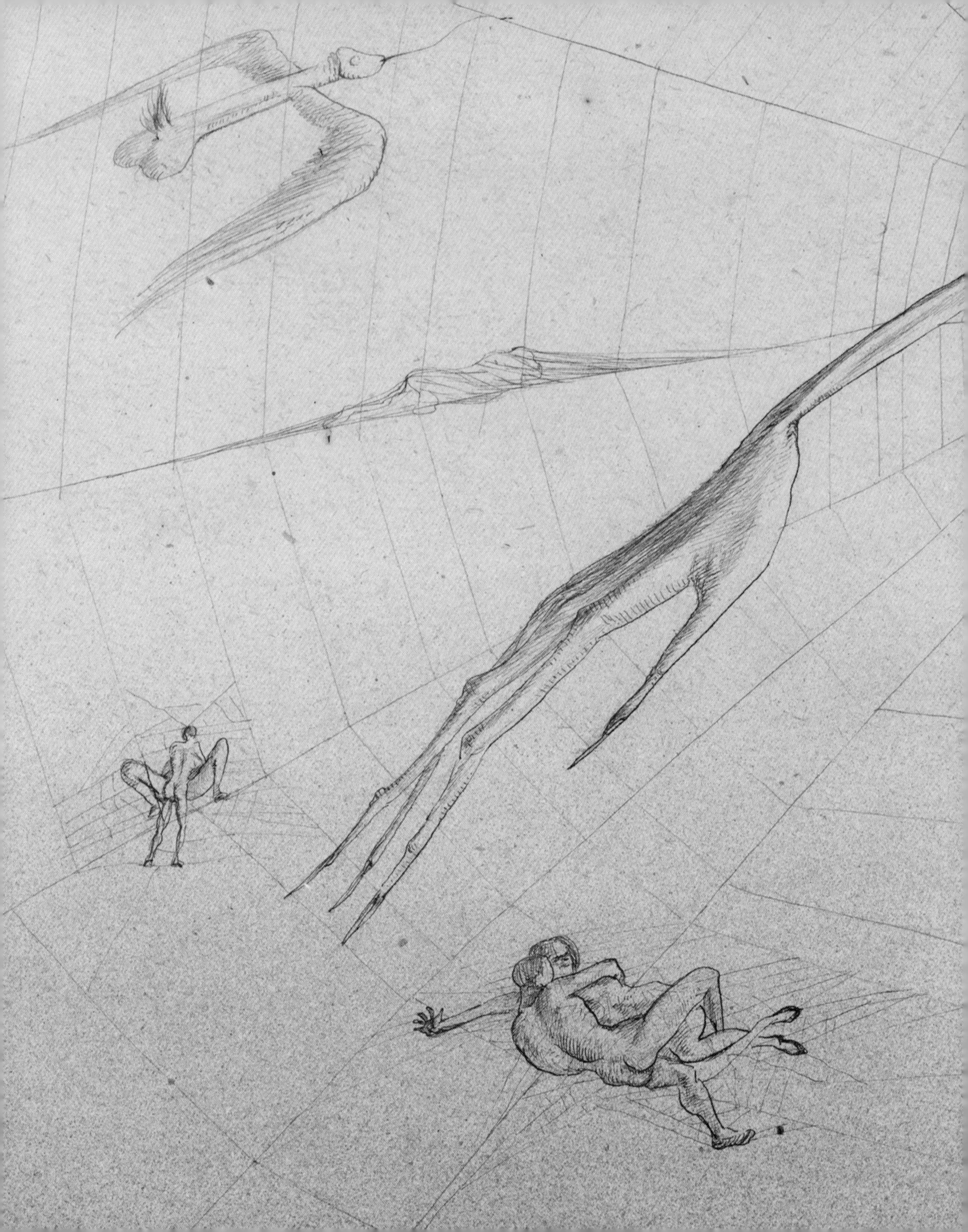

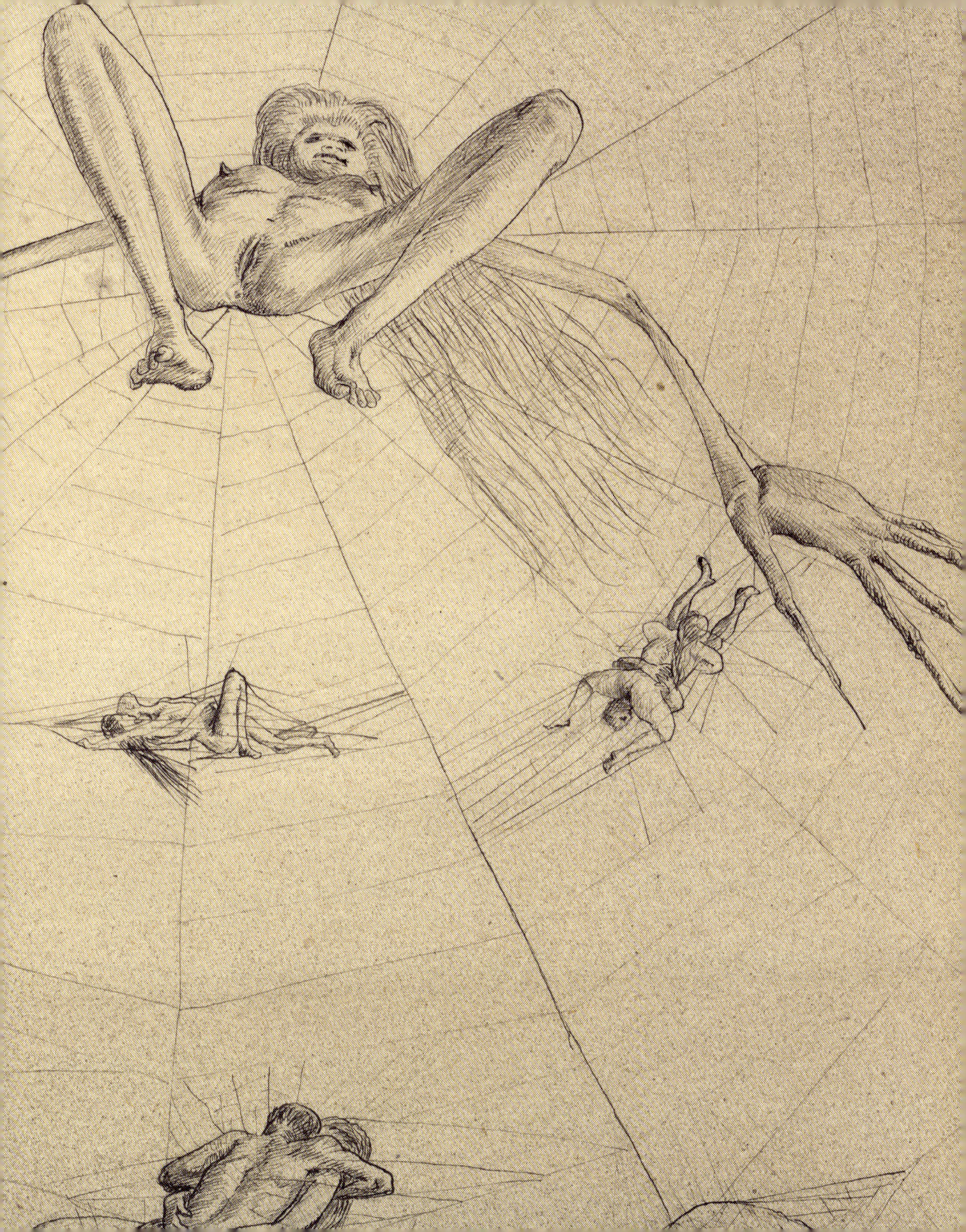

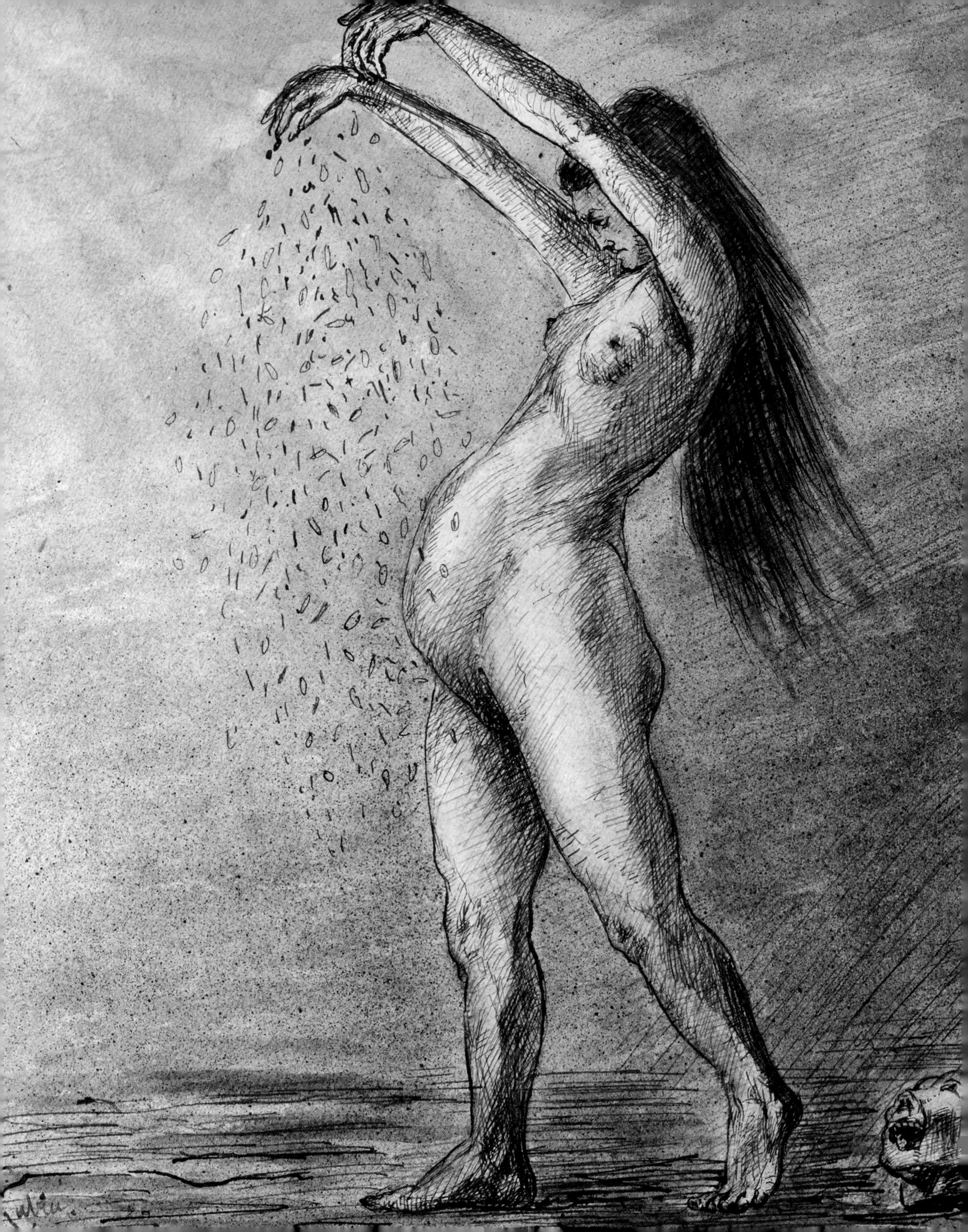

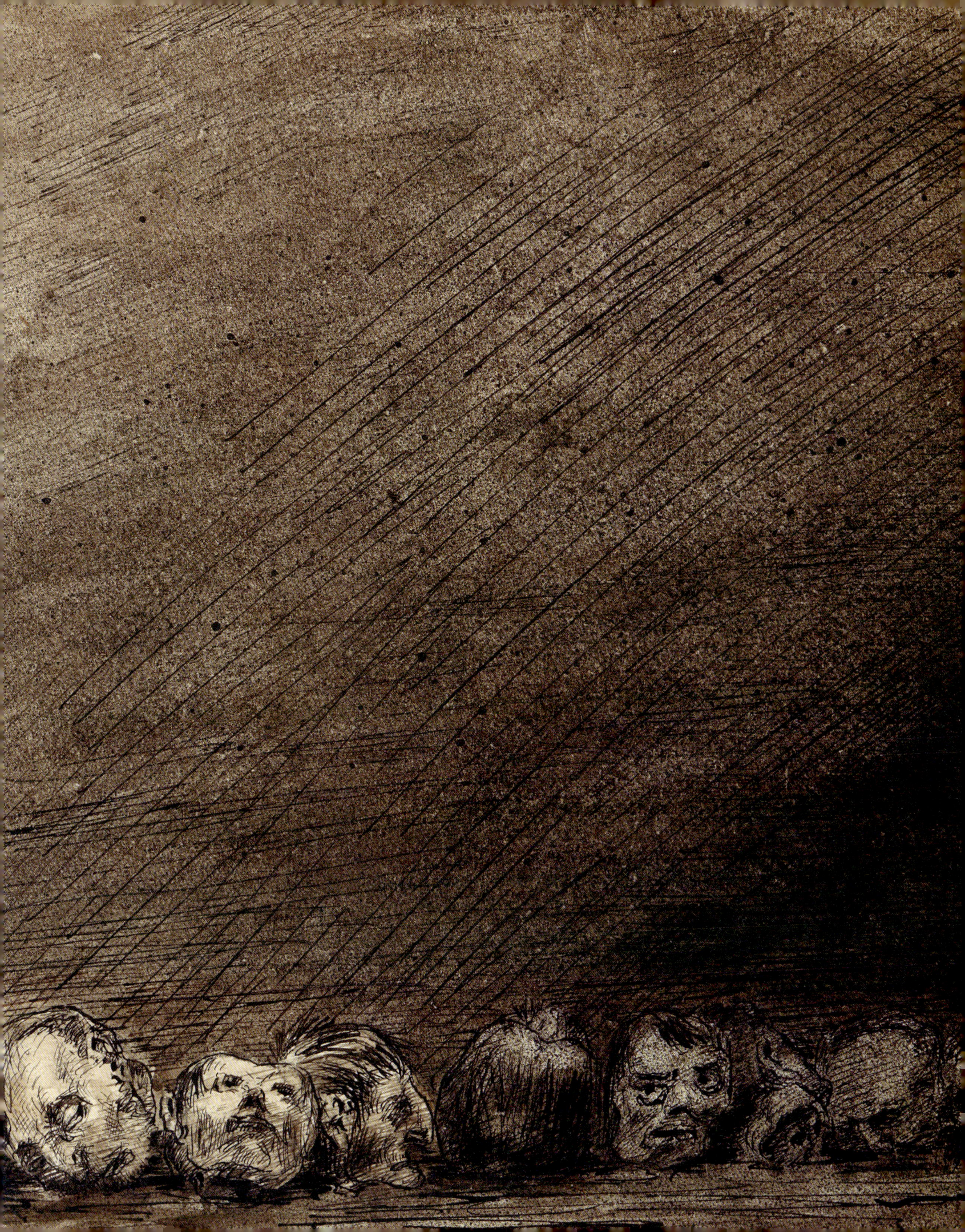

CONTENT

PREFACE AND ACKNOWLEDGE-MENTS

Hans-Peter Wipplinger

The art of Alfred Kubin, the great artist, illustrator, and author of the novel *The Other Side,* seems more topical than ever today—not least in view of current geopolitical conflict and military confrontation: violence, war destruction, epidemics, natural disasters, manipulation of the masses, and other abysses of the human condition all informed his strongly narrative-oriented works. The oeuvre of this fantastic creator confronts us with pessimistic visions that—in the spirit of Schopenhauer, whom Kubin greatly revered—lay out *the worst of all possible worlds.*

Kubin's childhood and youth were marred by failure and depression: being expelled from high school, dropping out of an apprenticeship as a photographer, early loss of his mother, an attempted suicide by her grave, a nervous crisis after a short period in the military, and other blows of fate characterize his traumatic coming-of-age. Kubin's way out was moving to Munich in 1898, where he began to study art. His first visit to the Alte Pinakothek left him "ravished with bliss and amazement." He described viewing Max Klinger's etchings as a "torrent of visions of black-and white-images." As he related in his autobiographical notes, he subsequently became "acquainted with the entire graphic work of Klinger, Goya, de Groux, Rops, Munch, Ensor, Redon, and similar artists." From this variety of impressions and artistic positions, but above all from his own worlds of experience and sensation and an abounding imagination, Kubin created an incomparable, mysteriously fantastic oeuvre.

The exhibition at the Leopold Museum is a first-time attempt to get a grasp of the art of Kubin's dream worlds, which all too often moves far out into nightmarish and gloomy spheres, also in its relation to the unconscious, to the deep dimensions of the psychic. Kubin's works are placed in a dialogue with works by artists of the 19th century and classical modernism, who served as sources of inspiration for his own work. Kubin's dystopian visualizations, which take up and continue symbolism and the fantastic art of the 19th century, are composed of real and imaginary realities: a synthesis in which the uncanniness of pessimistic world constructions is also more than on once infused with humor, irony, and hyperbole.

The realization of an exhibition always is the result of cooperation partnerships with numerous institutions and individuals. A very special thanks goes to university professor Dr. August Ruhs. As psychoanalyst and psychiatrist, he devotes his essay to the psychological disposition of the fantastic draftsman and the influence of Kubin's drastic life experiences on his artistic oeuvre. I would like to thank Dr. Annegret Hoberg, the veteran Kubin scholar and long-time director of the Kubin Archive at the Munich Lenbachhaus, very much for her insightful image analyses, which have informed this catalog.

My deepest sympathy and mournful compassion is due to the family of philosopher Dr. Burghart Schmidt, who passed away, in his 80th year, just a few weeks before this catalog went to press. Last active as a professor of language and aesthetics at the University of Offenbach, the philosopher had very close ties to Vienna through his approximately 20 years of teaching here, e.g., as a professor at the University of Applied Arts and the Academy of Fine Arts. As of 2018, he was also a member of the Leopold Museum's "Vienna 1900" scholarly advisory board. Over the years, he generously let the Leopold Museum partake of his almost inexhaustible interdisciplinary knowledge and verbal brilliance in various discursive event formats as well as essays. His last text, on Kubin's abysmal phantasmagoria, only reached us shortly before his death. He leaves a great gap, both on a personal and a professional level. With his profound writings, this great thinker will remain in our memory.

Great thanks go to the many lenders from Austria and abroad who generously made artworks from their possession available for the exhibition. Without the support of the museums and private collections named below, this project, the preparations for which were hampered by several lockdowns, could not have been realized on such a scale: Albertina, Vienna; Archiv Attersee; Belvedere, Vienna; Katharina Büttiker Gallery , Zurich; Lentos Kunstmuseum Linz; *LETTER Stiftung, Cologne;* Museum Georg Schäfer, Schweinfurt; Museum Ortner, Vienna; Museum voor Schone Kunsten, Gent (Belgium); OÖ Landes-Kultur GmbH, State of Upper Austria; Altnöder Collection, Salzburg; Klewan Collection, Munich; Staatliche Museen zu Berlin, National Gallery, Scharf-Gerstenberg Collection; Städtische Galerie im Lenbachhaus und Kunstbau München; The Daulton Collection, Los Altos Hills, California, as well as private lenders, who do not want to be named.

On behalf of the Leopold Museum, I want to extend my thanks to the Board of Directors, represented by its chairman Dr. Josef Ostermayer, and to Dr. Elisabeth Leopold who passionately supported this Kubin project. In addition, my thanks go to Managing Director Moritz Stipsicz and the entire Leopold Museum team, whose great commitment made the realization of the exhibition and the catalog possible in the first place.

In connection with this exhibition catalog, my cordial thanks go to Lena Scholz—both as author of the Kubin biography and as managing catalog editor. Cordial thanks are also in order to the restoration team with Sandra Maria Dzialek, Stephanie Strachwitz, Monika Sadek-Rosshap, and Beatrix Zeugswetter, as well as to Nicola Mayr and Johannes Semotan for their mindful exhibition management. My special thanks go to Dominik Papst for his curatorial assistance and perspicacious project coordination. I would also like to thank the entire museological team who were given particularly active support by Milena Telsnig and Marjana Uhde. And I want to thank Veronika Werkner and Klaus Pokorny for their press and public relations work, Julia Kemetner for all marketing activities, and Michael Terler for his handling of technical matters.

Last but not least, the Leopold Museum wishes to thank all public funders and sponsors of the museum, particularly the project sponsor of this exhibition, the Auktionshaus im Kinsky and its two managing directors Michael Kovacek and Ernst Ploil. To them all who contributed to the success of this exhibition with their commitment, idealistic or financial, we wish to express our sincere gratitude.

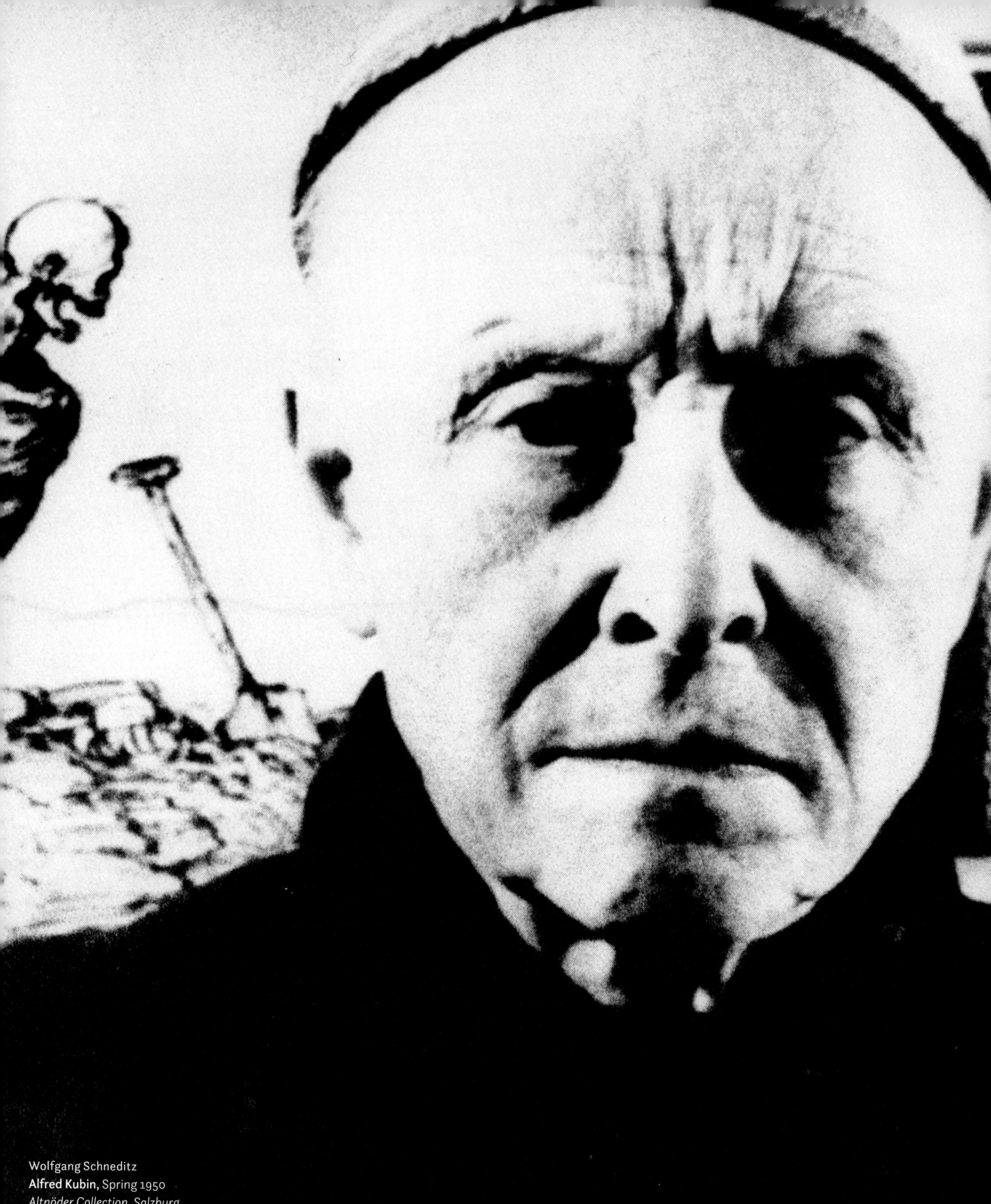

Wolfgang Schneditz
Alfred Kubin, Spring 1950
Altnöder Collection, Salzburg

I am the organizer of the uncertain, hermaphrodite, crepuscular, dreamlike. My aspiration is inhabit that mysterious realm, deeply rooted in my humanity, and cast it in solid artistic forms.*

Alfred Kubin

* Alfred Kubin about himself, 09.01.1908, quoted in Fritz von Herzmanovsky-Orlando, *Sämtliche Werke, Band VII. Der Briefwechsel mit Alfred Kubin 1903 bis 1952*, ed. Michael Klein (Salzburg/Vienna, 1983), p. 10.

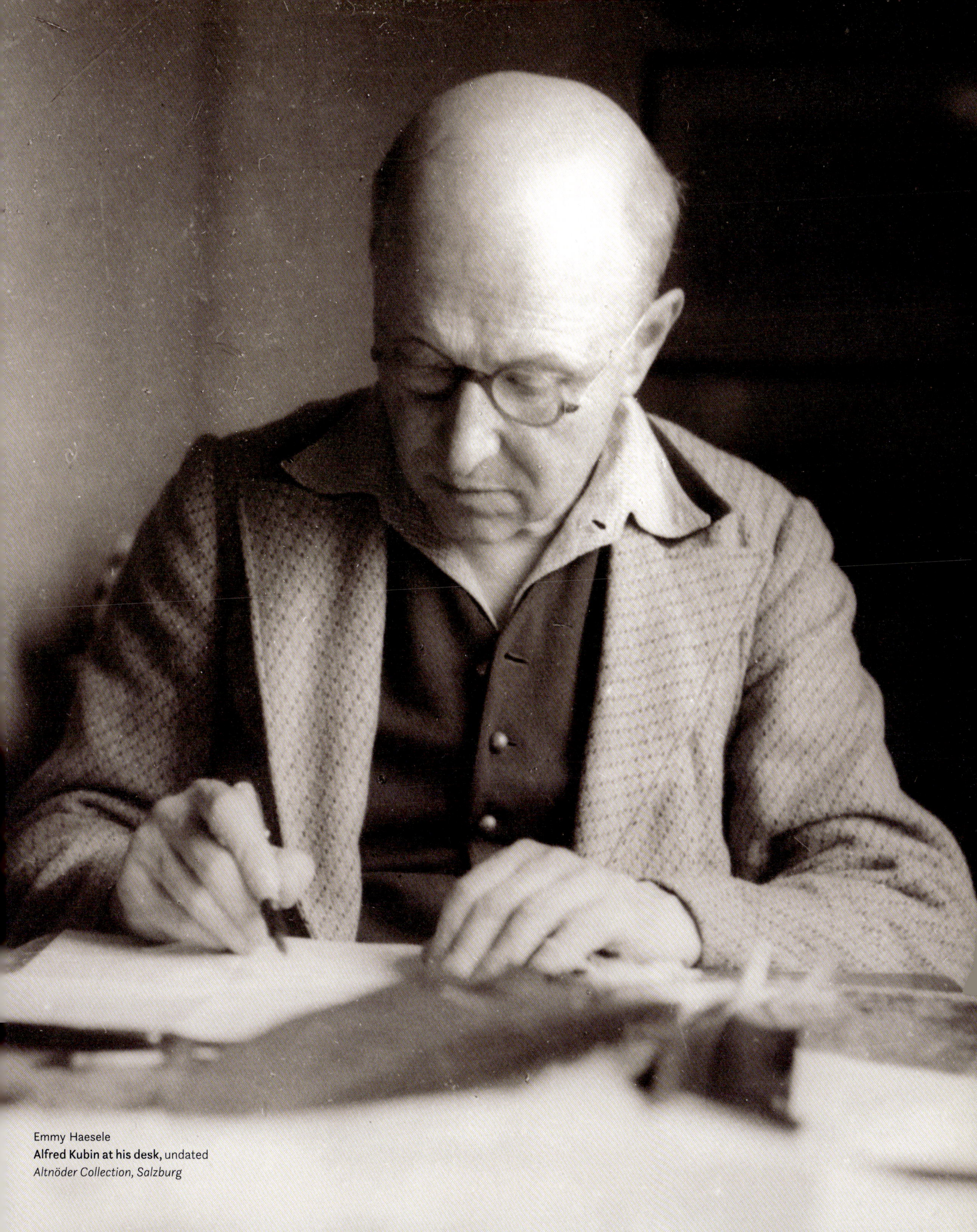

Emmy Haesele
Alfred Kubin at his desk, undated
Altnöder Collection, Salzburg

ALFRED KUBIN. TRAVELING THE LABYRINTH OF THE SOUL

Hans-Peter Wipplinger

This essay focuses on the insular central themes of our exhibition, which places the work of Alfred Kubin in context with precursors from art-history, his contemporaries and sources of inspiration: Following his works means taking a journey into the world of the artist's innermost feelings, a journey into the labyrinth of Kubin's soul, guided by the powers of his profuse imagination. It also means immersing oneself in cultural-historical and social phenomena that were constitutive for the spiritual and intellectual climate of the declining Habsburg empire and essentially informed both Kubin's character and art. An early reviewer of his work came to realize that Kubin's drawings were the "most poignant, venomous epigrams on the current affairs of state and church, on love and death, on glory and honor"[1], and that this was due to his sensitive, aware-of-his-environment character, about which the artist himself once said that "I am, next to an artist, a muser, seer."[2] After approximately sixty years, Kubin left behind a very comprehensive oeuvre if with some variation in quality. An oeuvre that also saw major stylistic changes but nevertheless maintained its continuity in the dominant motifs and themes that shaped his worldview and in the visions that haunted him.

THE POWER OF DREAMS AND THE IMAGINATION

The worldview of the era around 1900 oscillated between bourgeois-positivistic faith in science and reason and irrational, anti-utilitarian fatalism. Angst-ridden as he was, Kubin can unquestionably be counted among the second group—the dream as the central element of his pictorial motifs interlaces with real-life reality in his works. By no means, though, can dreams in Kubin be thought of as a mere escape from reality, as is put in a nutshell in a diary entry about the situation he suffered under over decades: "Perhaps this is precisely what life is: A dream and an anxiety."[3] To relate the sources of Kubin's pictorial worlds merely to "inner" images of his daydreams and nightmares would fall short. There are far too many art-historical as well as literary points of reference—which Kubin also expounded on—that characterize his motivic and formal aesthetic vocabulary. Francisco José de Goya y Lucientes (1746–1828), Félicien Rops (1833–1898), James Ensor (1860–1949), Max Klinger (1857–1920), Odilon Redon (1840–1916), and Edvard Munch (1863–1944) are just a few of the most important artists to be named here, the latter three of whom he would later also meet in person. E. T. A. Hoffmann (1776–1822), Edgar Allan Poe (1809–1849), Gérard de Nerval (1808–1855), August Strindberg (1849–1912), Gustav Meyrink (1868–1932) and others, whose works he illustrated numerous times,[4] can also be mentioned as kindred spirits in fantastic literature.

It was Max Klinger who, with his *Handschuh* cycle of drawings, which Kubin saw in late 1899 at the

Munich Kupferstichkabinett (today: State Graphic Art Collection), caused a "torrent of visions" in him. Kubin describes this awakening experience and the subsequent bout of hallucinatory sensations that occurred during a variety theater show: "There something very strange to the soul and crucial for me happened, which I still do not fully understand today although I have thought a great deal about it. As the small orchestra was beginning to play, my entire surroundings all of a sudden appeared clearer and sharper to me as if in a different light. In the faces of the people sitting around me, I suddenly saw something strangely animal-human; all sounds were oddly alien. [...] I got sad, although a strangely pleasurable feeling was flickering through me, and I thought of the Klinger drawings once again, musing how I would now work. And there I was, overcome all of a sudden by a whole torrent of visions of black-and-white images—the thousandfold richness that my imagination made me see is beyond description. I quickly left the theater, because the music and the many lights were now disturbing to me, and aimlessly wandered around the dark streets, all the time overwhelmed, virtually raped by some dark force that magically put strange animals, houses, landscapes, grotesque and fearful situations before my mind."[5] Directly following this experience was an extended creative frenzy full of fantastic visions, and it brought forth an exceptional early work (1899–1902), which elicited both indignation and admiration in 1901/02 at his first major exhibition shown at the Berlin gallery of Paul Cassirer. The art critic Fritz Stahl, for example, felt prompted by the show to write of Kubin reveling "in sickly fantasies"[6], whereas the poet Richard Schaukal enthusiastically praised him as a "a draughtsman of boundless imagination, an inexhaustible wealth of ideas, and the most idiosyncratic creativeness."[7]

Whether these grotesque-fantastic imaginative powers were fed by nocturnal dreams or, as in the case of the Klinger drawings, by daydreams is of secondary importance for Kubin's work, since for him as the "organizer of the uncertain, hermaphrodite, crepuscular, dreamlike"[8], it was first and foremost about explorations of the human abyss in the twilight zone of existence, no matter whether awake or in sleep. For, as Kubin wrote to Fritz von Herzmanovsky-Orlando, "sometimes I feel as if the pain of the soul were actually necessary to make those most deeply rooted feelings in me become an image."[9] These dreamlike moods, however, do not entail any direct, immediately impulsive transposition onto paper: "Dedicated as a viewer, active as a draftsman, I dissect the vision and build it up anew, trying, as it were, to shape a rarefied dream image." In that same passage, he also indicates "two components that come to artistic expression: I. rhythm, II. the clear premeditated idea of form: construction"[10] The contents of dreams are thus captured not least through formal criteria "after an extremely pliable control by consciousness"[11]—or, to describe this transformation process in the words of the draftsman: "Let us consider the dream as a picture; just like the dream composes, so I wanted to draw, knowingly, as an artist."[12] In Kubins novel *The Other Side,* published 1909, he similarly describes that neither day nor night exists in the fictitious city of Perle but that "reality" is only perceived in permanent twilight by the somnambulistic protagonists.

In 1911, Kubin wrote to Herzmanovsky-Orlando that he had "done a whole course of study on dreams and what is known about them—I think I am the first one to have actually drawn and used dreams—or rather, scraps of dreams."[13] If Kubin follows "the traces of old eerie things"[14] and, in his drawing *Unter Hyänen (Among Hyenas)* (01), a bent male figure is shown threatened from all sides by snarling wild animals, this is reminiscent of

01
ALFRED KUBIN
Study for India ink drawing
Among Hyenas, c. 1934
OÖ Landes-Kultur GmbH, Land Oberösterreich, Graphic Collection, Günter Rombold Collection, Ha II 15877

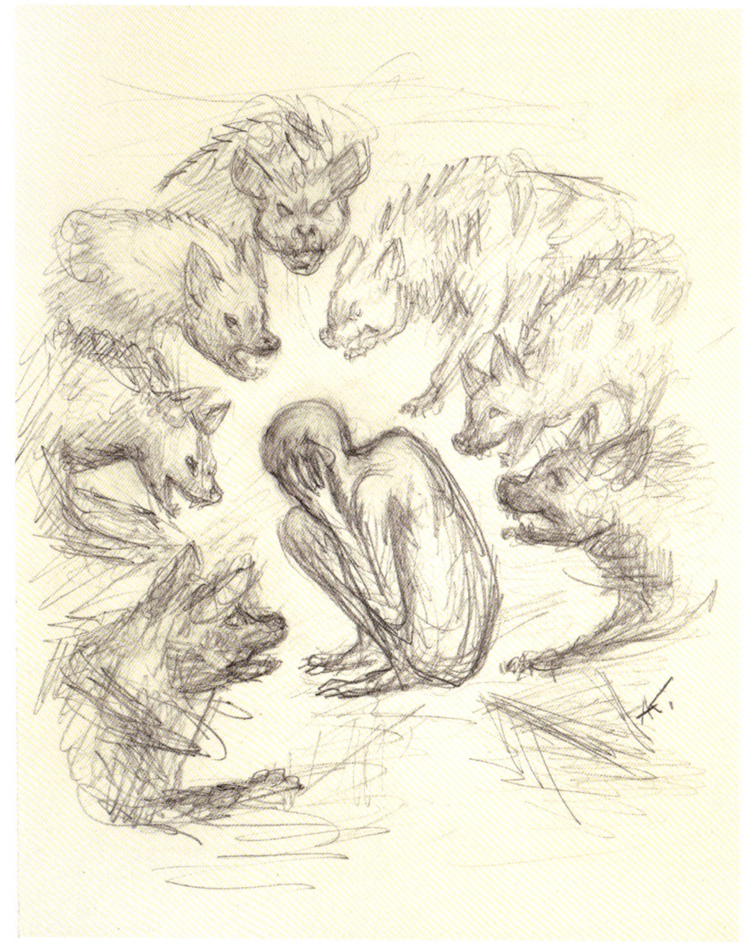

Goya's dream scenario in his aquatint *The Sleep of Reason Produces Monsters* (p.63)[15], whose protagonist is likewise tormented by grimaces, faces, and animals in his sleep.

GROTESQUE MASQUERADES AND BIZARRE HYBRID CREATURES

In Kubin's oeuvre, depictions of grotesque and carnivalesque iconographies keep reappearing again and again, reminiscent, not without reason, of James Ensor whose work Kubin greatly revered. Like in Goya, in Ensor's *Demons Tormenting Me* (p. 66), it is inner states that make his life a torment. He immortalizes himself in this self-portrait as a character filled with fear, beleaguered—probably as a symbol of the threat of insanity —by all sorts of apocalyptic monsters and hermaphroditic creatures. While in this etching, there still is a gravestone standing behind him as a symbol of death with his name and the year 1885 inscribed in it, her replaced it in the colored lithograph (p. 67) with a crowing rooster that can be read as a symbol of resurrection.

Ensor, the master of masked human crowds, saw this grotesque and horrific pandemonium as a possibility of depicting characters and exposing them through the very masquerade: "In this way, I was able to philosophically contemplate the sanctimonious, hypocritical, calculating, and deceitful face of the cowards that were destroyed by my contemptuous transformations."[16] It is, however, not only the instrument of character uncovering that Kubin was obviously interested in but also those numerous unreal creatures, demons, and figments of the imagination that, bizarre and macabre, populate Ensor's stage space: "In the night, I composed or explored my dreams"[17], Ensor writes. From these nocturnal sessions, his pandemonium of strange frogs, krakens, or spiders with extremely distorted human grimaces emerged that bear numerous analogies to Kubin's own repertoire of figures as well as to their shared forebears Hieronymus Bosch (1450–1516) und Pieter Brueghel (d. 1569). Unlike in the scenarios of hell and horror of Bosch, Goya, or Brueghel, it is worth noting that in Kubin the depiction of the grotesque oftentimes has humoristic and satirical traits to it, as if the unbearable graveness that the demoniac holds would thereby dispel the fear and the uncanny. And the way he deals with self-made human projections in the almost child-like drawing *Der liebe Gott (The Good Lord)* (p. 77) does not leave anything to be desired in terms of mordant mockery. Kubin shows the pilgrims worshipping an oversized god-like scarecrow. What speaks from this scenery is the spirit of Friedrich Nietzsche that God is dead or has abandoned humankind.

In Richard Schaukal's description of Kubin's work, however, this aspect is pushed to the background: "These [...] drawings are a world of the strangest, wildest, ghastliest, most uncanny, most gripping visions. [...] Feverish fantasies, allegories, wild-eyed allegories, cruel pamphlets and gruesome fairy tales are captured by this reckless, wondrous pen in tender and grandiose, lyrical and heroic lines."[18]

In many of Kubin's depictions, a synthesis of realistic sceneries with fantastic, unreal pictorial motifs takes place. Monstrous forces or grotesque animal-human metamorphoses as in Goya (p. 229) or Franz von Stuck's *Lucifer* (p. 237) ideally lend themselves, with their imputed animal character traits, to symbolic visualizations of mythological tales or nightmarish experiences.

APOCALYPSE AND THE INFERNO OF WAR

In his *Last Days of Mankind,* Karl Kraus gave a dire warning of Austria being an "experimental station of the end of the world." As is well known, his cautionary pamphlets, intended as an alert against imminent apocalypse, went unheard. Although Kubin lived in Munich between 1898 and 1906 before returning to the hermitage of his native region, his work in the main took place in the cultural area of Kakania and hence against the backdrop of political and social upheaval and a "permanent twilight state", pierced by the "driving forces of the instincts"[19]. Kubin's drawings of around 1900 showing war sceneries full of agony, torture, chaos, and murder were an anticipation of the pandemonic events of the two world wars. The outbreak of the First World War and the atrocities it brought did not stop the demise of Kakania, which Robert Musil had described, looming as it had been for some time, although this was the hope cherished by many.

Kubin himself was spared from active military service in the First World War because of his feeble health. Constant fretting about being drafted for duty and fear of dying in the war much exhausted him, as his brother-in-law Oscar A. H. Schmitz noted. And he was hit hard by the wounding or even death of fellow artists and friends like August Macke (1877–1914) or Franz Marc (1880–1916), with whom he had exhibited together as a member of the Blaue Reiter group. At the end of the war, he created a work entitled *Die Anarchie (Anarchy)* (p. 99), which shows an androgynous figure, obviously a personification of wartime chaos, that causes the collapse of the world.

Similarly out of proportion, a warrior, naked but armed with shield, helmet, and axe, marches, fearlessly and recklessly, over an onrushing army in Kubin's *Der Krieg (The War)* (p. 95). While, here, it is male omnipotence as a metaphor for the brute force of war, a motivically similar subject is found in Rops's *Les Sataniques* (p. 183), even though the adversary here is Satan, walking across town in long strides and strewing female bodies—"the brood of witches"—like a sower. What, in Rops, may still be read as entertaining satire—as dramatic as the scenery appears—however, is dire reality, an existential threat, in Kubin's *Der Krieg*.

Kubin lived through the great human catastrophe of the Second World War secluded on his country estate but was keenly aware of the anti-humanistic threat posed by the Nazis, who had classified his work as "degenerate". He stayed cautiously reserved in dealing with the regime and represented in his drawings in enciphered form the megalomania and race obsession of the Nazi dictatorship.[20]

MYTH AND ALLEGORY: FEMALE IMAGES OF DÉCADENCE

At all times but especially in the epoch of the fin de siècle, artists created pictures and sculptural works that—born out of wishful dreams or nightmares—portrayed the feminine as monstrous and demonic on the one hand, and on the other—quite in line with Christian religious teachings—represented woman as the "good" mother and saint.[21]

In Alfred Kubin's drawn enactments resultant from his projections onto the feminine, the kind woman, or the idea of an ideal mother image, is all but nonexistent, which may have to do with the traumatic experiences of his childhood and youth. A neutral portrayal of the woman, in which neither fear nor horror burden the relationship of the sexes also occurs only as an exception. Instead, it is man-eating sirens and various types of femme fatale that are omnipresent in his (male) imagination. Here, Kubin—driven by fears and urges—is probably the most ruthless and most direct of all. In his oeuvre, there are various different articulations of female archetypes to be found, in which one of the seven deadly sins, lust (Lat. luxuria), plays the central role, embedded in allegories of fate, power, ruin and destruction.

The male view of women in the late 19th and early 20th centuries may seem wildly absurd, even ludicrous to observers today but at the time had—not least because of the literary and philosophical tenets of the worldview of Décadence—a major influence on the role of women in society and the female image in general. In the following remarks, different typologies of Kubinian women figures will be discussed that are considered well-established types in art history and literature. Whether Salome or Judith, whether sirens or sphinxes, they all belong—particularly so in symbolist art—to the typical cast of female characters in mythical allegories. All too often, they are grotesquely overdrawn into epitomes of the "cruel" woman. The feature that these female representations with their oversexualized habitus have in common is the alliance of Thanatos and Eros, of lust and death.

DREAM AND TRAUMA

Kubin's image of women was essentially informed by his early traumatic experiences with the female sex. The loss of his mother who died after long suffering from pulmonary tuberculosis when he was ten and the memory image of his father running desperately around the apartment with her dead body on his arms had a formative artistic repercussion in his drawings. And finally—as Kubin himself writes in his autobiography[22]—there was an incident of sexual molestation by a nude pregnant woman that he had to experience as an eleven-year-old and that was not without

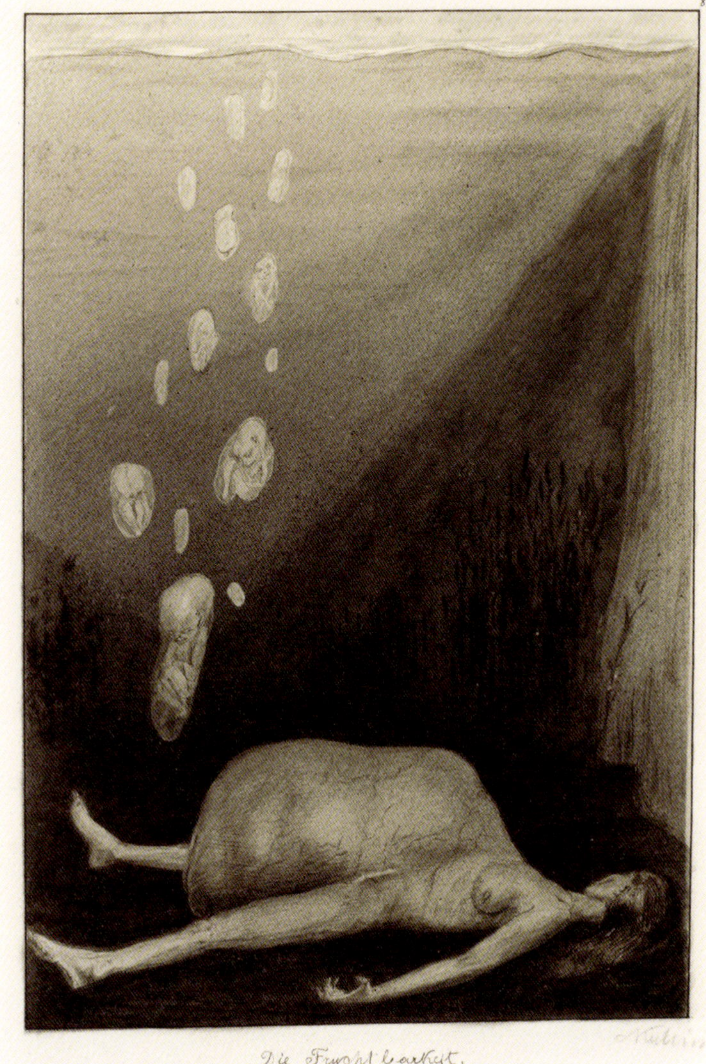

02
ALFRED KUBIN
Fertility (1st Version), c. 1901/02
Leopold Museum, Vienna

traumatic impact. It was particularly in numerous depictions of pregnant women that this image of the woman as a threatening force came to expression: "I was just eleven and a half when I was involved in sexual games by an older woman, which upset me beyond measure and cast a shadow well into my manhood years."[23] In Kubin, the male protagonist is either shown as a ridiculously weak puppet or—in complete reversal—as an extreme violator. These roles of victim and victimizer that Kubin assigned to the man are the consequences of repression mechanisms rooted in feelings of anxiety.

Yet another traumatic experience to be mentioned here is the tragic death, on December 1, 1903, of his first great love, Emmy Bayer, who he had met toward the end of his time in Munich (1898–1906). Kubin himself speaks in his writings of "that marvelous time", in which he came to "know a young compatriot with whom I soon got engaged, and now my earthly bliss had reached its zenith. Everything that had previously come to me under the name of 'love' now completely paled next to the deep and real passion that had now taken hold on me. […] But everything turned out different than I thought back then. My bride fell ill when she once came to visit me in Munich, and died after ten days in hospital. As I was standing by her dead body, it hit me like a blow that the greatest happiness was gone for me forever."[24] In the year of that event, which threw him into deep depression, Otto Weininger's book *Sex and Character* came out, the misogynist treatise that Kubin read as a 25-year-old and to whose ideas he was quite susceptible after what he had experienced. If Weininger in his hatred of women utterly reduces them to their sexuality and even talks of their permanent coital readiness, Kubin's *Die Fruchtbarkeit (Fertility)* (02) can be read as a visualization in drawing of that grotesque proposition. For the pregnant woman makes new life possible and thus creates the precondition for new death, which Weininger interpreted as inextricably interrelated and a crime.

Another informant that analyzed the alleged cruelty of woman in his novella *Venus in Furs* was found by Kubin in Leopold von Sacher-Masoch (1836–1895) who contended "that woman, as nature has created her and as man is at present educating her, is his enemy: She can be only be his slave or his despot, but never his companion."[25] In this story, the character of 16-year-old Severin slavishly submits himself to the wealthy widow Wanda von Dunajew. He accepts her as his despotic mistress, lets himself be tormented by her but at times also receives tokens of loving attention from her. In the male fantasies of Décadence, it seemed better in any case "to let oneself be ruined by a beautiful demonic woman than be bored your entire life, and bogged down mentally, with a so-called woman of virtue."[26] It takes a long time for Severin to break away from Wanda and be finally able to start a new life, which, however, makes him show himself as a ruler and subjugator of femininity, relegating the very idea of gender equality to the realm of fantasy. Kubin's female-male cast of characters is reminiscent of this narrative and not least a reflection of the battle of the sexes and male fear of women's emerging self-consciousness and the female emancipation movements of the era. Nike Wagner aptly describes that battle of the sexes in the context of the eroticism of Viennese modernism: "The estrangement between the sexes, in which the cultural refinement of around 1900 had as much a share as did restrictive bourgeois sexual morals, had become impossible to overlook. Rising up from the abyss of alienation that the rift in creation had deepened into were images of fear of which the Austrian painter Alfred Kubin has the most dreadful and most accurate expression."[27] Christoph Settele rightly pointed out that also "Kubin, like many of his contemporaries, contributed to 19th-century conservatism, which they purported to be actually fighting against."[28] Kubin's mythically charged female characters thus keep oscillating between being helpless slaves and murderous despots.

WOMAN AS THE GODDESS OF FATE

Allegorizations of woman in which Kubin mostly reduces the feminine to being libidinous and bound by its nature, are numerous. Central to them is the figure of woman as the executor of Fate (p. 259), which for Kubin always ends fatally. In *Unser aller Mutter Erde (Our All Mother Earth)* (p. 257), too, the woman is the fateful figure striding naked across an inhospitable landscape with her arms held up high. She sows seeds that promise fertility in front of her, and her bulging pregnant body also symbolizes nascent life, with a trail of guillotined male heads behind her. Creation and decay are impressively epitomized in this female ruler over life and death. The nudity of Kubin's women protagonists is, with few exceptions, exemplary as in the Salome reception and speaks to the association of Eros and Thanatos—a theme that is omnipresent in Kubin's oeuvre and finds an apt motivic rendering in *Jede Nacht besucht uns ein Traum (Every Night A Dream Visits Us)* (03).

Borrowed for art history from the Old Testament narrative, the motif of altruistic Judith, who selflessly surrenders herself to cut off the head of the tyrant Holofernes and save her people, sees in Kubin a complete inversion of the original iconographic tradition, which again aligns with a specific fin-de-siècle image of women. Judith is shown in *Schlachtfest (Slaughterfest)* (p. 156) not as the overcomer of evil but as a bloodthirsty and cruel annihilator about to deliver the final blow to the phallically impaled torso. It is a depiction strikingly reminiscent of Goya's plate 237 from *Los desastres de la guerra*, entitled *Esto es peor (This is worse)* or of Jacques Callot's (1592–1635) *La pendaison (The Hanging)*, even if the political context

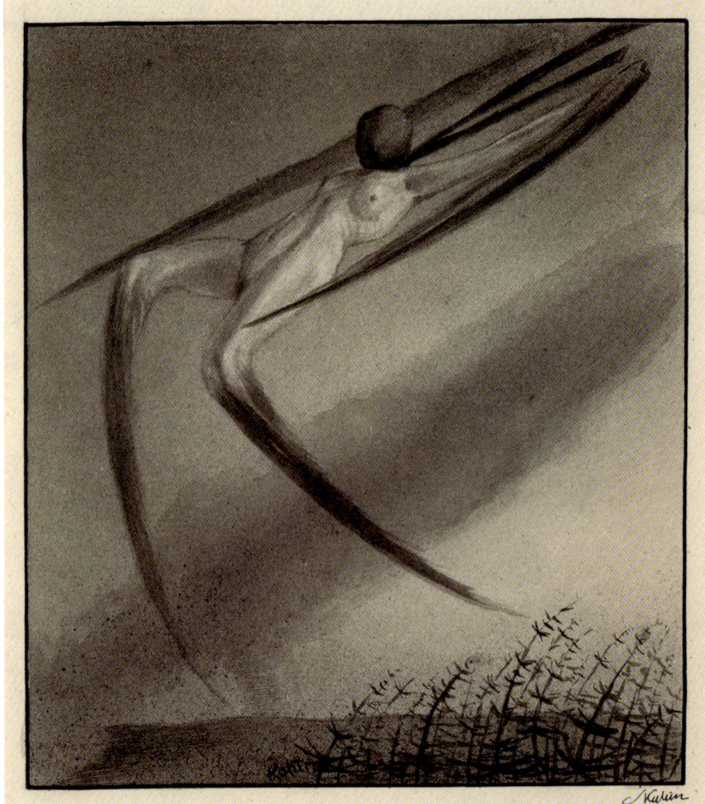

03
ALFRED KUBIN
Every Night a Dream Visits Us, c. 1902/03
Albertina, Vienna

and hence the real horrors of war are missing with Kubin, and it is solely the battle of the sexes that is in the center of the narration. These pictures bring to mind Werner Hofmann's characterization of this stoically sadistic type of woman of the late 19th century: "The characters of the great paramours almost always have an air of night and death about them, they are shrouded in inscrutable serenity, their unmovedness bordering on the masklike, on the lifelessness of an idol, their cruelty that runs through all limbs is like that of a sleek predator stalking its prey."[29]

A prime example of another very unperturbed Kubinian victimizer—a modern Judith, so to speak, who no longer needs a sword–appears in his work *Untergang (Downfall)* (p. 138). Motionless and coolly looking over her shoulder, she watches a drowning figure of whom only the hands, begging for rescue, are reaching out of the pond. Also the rigorously corseted, crop-holding *Dame auf dem Pferd (Lady On The Horse)* (p. 157), not by chance reminiscent of Empress Elisabeth in the saddle, can be said to belong to the circle of motifs of Judith and Salome,[30] although it is no longer a single figure that is made to be the victim[31] here: Under the hooves of the animal, or under the cradle knife on the sharp blades of which it stands, men are butchered indiscriminately and with utter indifference. Like her iconographic models, she is an embodiment of the femme fatale. But carnal ecstasy and erotic expose move to the background in favor of a societal discourse that addresses the intellectual potency, strengthened self-consciousness, and new self-perception of women. Christoph Settele conjectures that the lady on horseback might be "a representative of the women's movement, which definitely gained in significance in the age of the bourgeois revolution [...] So what comes to expression in this work is the social menace of the emancipated woman as a traumatic anxiety fantasy."[32]

The type of the hetaeric harlot, as was common around the turn of the century as the antithesis of the childbearing mother type, was especially popular with the exponents of Décadence as a philosophy of life. Kubin, who most certainly was one of them during his dandyish years in Munich, knew the ambivalent prostitution narrative from his own observation: on the one hand, the proponents of the melancholic doomsday mood adored the high potential of sadism, which often went along with masochism; on the other, they yearned, in their overwrought nervous condition, for an unleashing of libidinous instincts, which all too often led to thoughts of self-destruction in the end. In the wild hetaerae, they believed to have found the personification of this fulfilling idea, whose characteristics can be summed up as follows: "refinement of desires, sensations, taste, luxury, amusements, neurosis, hysteria, hypnotism, morphine addiction, scientific charlatanism, effusive veneration of Schopenhauer's philosophy are the harbingers of social decay."[33]

From these few examples it becomes apparent that while Kubin drew on models from art history for orientation and inspiration and also borrowed formal aspects, if fragmentarily, he nevertheless developed pictorial concepts from his specific biographical experience and original form vocabulary.

PROJECTIONS OF MALE OMNIPOTENCE

As a motivic counterpart of the supernatural female power that finds representation in the female perpetrator and seductress, woman also plays a role in numerous works as a victim of male desire. This demonization and debasement in the depiction of women may—as already intimated—be an echo of the loss of patriarchal power structures at that time. Strikingly, what can be seen in the exclusively male artistic projections is an enormous potential of almost animalic aggressiveness that could not be any more obvious. This shows exemplarily in the violation scene in the drawing *Notzucht an einer mährischen Bäuerin (Rape of a Moravian Peasant Woman)* (p. 180). This (self-) destructive phenomenon is also pointed out by Peter Gorsen: "The male fantasy producer, the artist or art viewer, slips into the powerless sexist role of the woman, enjoying his aggression under a passive-masochistic aspect, in the fantasized role of the female object. Almost needless to say that this self-victimizing ritual leads to no identification with the real social role of femininity but remains caught up in freely associating and picturing the opposite-sex feminine part of the male psyche."[34] Kubin's washed and sprayed pen-and-ink drawing *Heidnisches Opfer (Pagan Sacrifice)* (p.185) also shows this brutality with a strong erotic connotation. A martial-looking man offers the will-less or already dead woman to the six-eyed idol as a sacrifice.

As a reader of *Zarathustra*; Kubin was likely familiar with the lines: "And thus spoke the little old woman: 'You go to women? Don't forget the whip.'"[35] Nietzsche, the classical philologist, puts the statement not in Zarathustra's mouth but—as the quotation shows—in the little old woman's. But even so, Nietzsche's reputation as a philosophical misogynist was out in the world. Kubin's depictions, however, do not stop at the chastising whip. The horrors of the human abyss are shown in motifs of torture, rape, or murder. One possible reading of the visualized fantasies in Kubin's representations of both male and female victims may be the repression of male sexual fears, like castration anxiety.

Libidinal urges and the accompanying male cruelty are often transferred onto symbolic animal figures, as in *Geier mit Schwert und nackte Kauernde (Vulture Holding a Sword and Cowering Nude)* (p. 167). The vulture, whose sword has something phallic to it, is the merciless executioner here. It remains open whether what is going to happen is the execution of a death sentence or a sodomizing rape.

I IS ANOTHER—ESTRANGEMENT FROM THE SELF

The individual was put through scrutiny and revaluation in many different areas of knowledge in Vienna around 1900, which eventually also had reverberations in art. In 1903, the writer Hermann Bahr published an article entitled *Das unrettbare Ich (The Unsavable Self)* in which he described the crisis of the modern subject around the turn of the century, invoking the theories of physicist and philosopher Ernst Mach who had postulated an instability of the subject already in 1886. At last, Sigmund Freud created in psychoanalysis a complex structural model of the psyche, which gave special consideration to parapraxes and dreams as revealing unconscious facets of the personality. In particular, Freuds analyses of repressed or childhood desires are reflected in his theory of dreams, published 1899 in his seminal *The Interpretation of Dreams.*

With his specific character traits, Kubin would have made an ideal client for Freud: highly gifted, melancholic, highly sensitive, and nervously overwrought. Kubin kept being haunted by terrible visions from his childhood and adolescence, accompanied by anxieties, guilty feelings, and inferiority complexes that made him weary of life and even drove him to a suicide attempt. Allegories of madness, as in depictions of infernal lunatic asylums or prisons—always with the idea in mind that the mad and the seers are heralds of the unheard-of—are motivic reflections of this.[36] For him, drawing was both a liberation and a relief from his frightful visions.

It is only logical therefore that these conflicts are reflected, consciously or unconsciously, not only in Kubin's drawings but also in his literary work *The Other Side.* This publication, Wieland Schmied noted, is "a self-presentation of Kubin's state of mind"[37], even if, as Annegret Hoberg has pointed out, the artist was skeptical about Freud's psychoanalysis and only read *The Interpretation of Dreams* years later. Instead, he had a pronounced interest in Carl Gustav Jung's concept of archetypes. Whether coming from the depths of a collective unconscious or being the "legacy of a monstrous personal past"[38]—questions of birth, life and death keep recurring with Kubin and are summarily represented in the drawing *Das Ei (The Egg)* (p. 171). The drawings *Fruchtbarkeit (Fertility)* (p. 169),[39] *Die Stunde der Geburt (The Hour of Birth)* (p. 199), and *Aus meinem Reich (From My Realm)* (p. 195) can be seen as a pictorial sequence about the development of fateful human life.
The emerging fetuses rising to the surface from the monstrous belly of an incessantly birthing pregnant woman in *Fruchtbarkeit* are shown being pulled out of the water by some primordial crustacean animal with a shell that is an oversized skull in the drawing *Die Stunde der Geburt* and—quite in the sense of Heidegger's "thrownness"—discharged into the world on their own. In *Aus meinem Reich,* the embryonic-looking hybrid creature is seen toddling off into an uncertain future. At this point, a reference to Kubin's father complex is permissible if one follows his brother-in-law O. A. H. Schmitz, who relates the Kubin was extremely distraught as a small child by the return of his father after a two-year absence in Dalmatia: "Boundless jealousy had seized him because he suddenly had to share his everything, his mother, with that foreign man."[40] What added to the situation was that his father punished him for his failures in school not only with beatings but also with a withdrawal of love. Quite a few drawings show, in indirect self-portraits, meek figures exposed to often giant outside forces that are indicative of what Kubin himself called "the superexistence of the father." Not least does the motif of the formally elegant Jugendstil piece

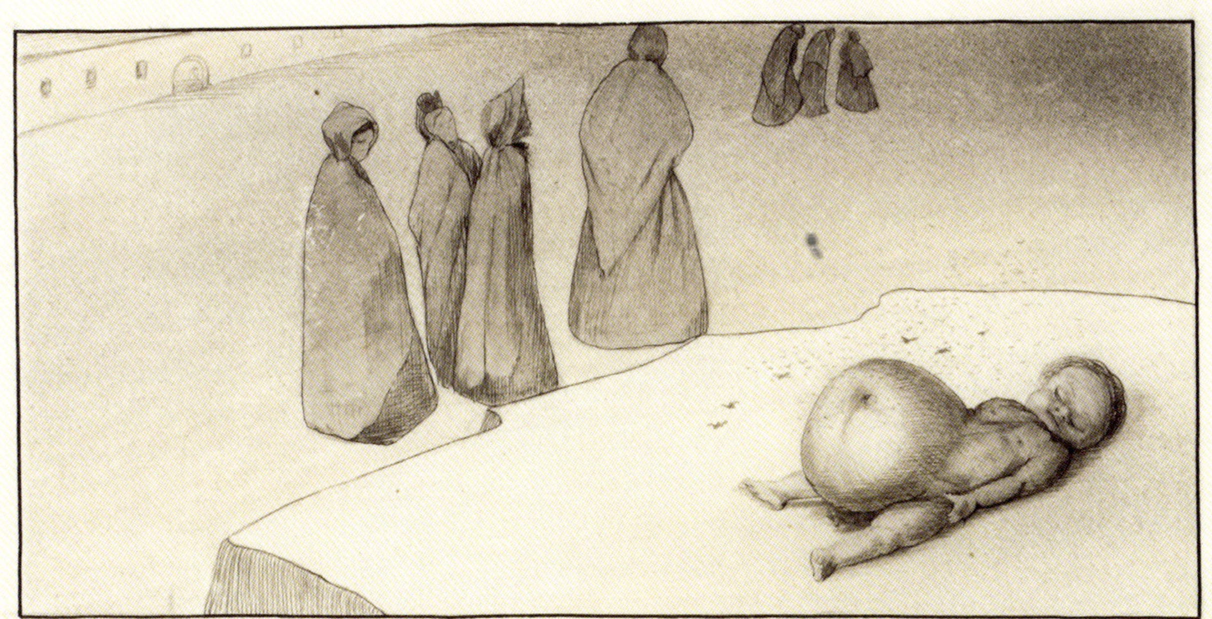

04
ALFRED KUBIN
The Swellbelly, 1902/03
Leopold Museum, Vienna

Der Bamsen (The Swellbelly) (04), which cannot deny the influence of Aubrey Beardsley (1872–1898), speak to an autobiographical inspiration. It shows an abandoned child, sick or perhaps already dead, with a procession of women indifferently walking by. The depiction of the unattended and deserted child harks back at the early death of his beloved mother.

Snakes also occupy a prominent place in Kubin's work, where they make their appearance as ambiguous key symbols, whether as a metaphor, or mediator, between this world and the next, as a symbol of power and fate, or as a signal of seduction. Not least is the association of woman and snake interpreted in a sexual context in psycho analysis, as a symbol of the phallus and hence of male libido. In Stuck's *Die Sinnlichkeit (Sensuality)* (p. 129), the serpent winding around the female body is unmistakable as a phallic symbol. The snake takes on a similar meaning in Kubin's *Sauger (Suckers)* (p. 215), which was not without reason given the second title *Der Onanist (The Onanist)*. Moreover, in Kubin's diary notes, there is talk, again and again, of the "devilish worm that every now and then comes up to me, flat-headed, flickering its tongue."[41] Generally, he showed himself disgusted by his helplessness against his sexual urges: "The worm will someday be dead, no, completely annihilated, having never been, and I will be free!"[42] As possibilities of freeing himself from this "sexual demon", he named in his notes from the years 1921, 1922 and 1930 "purity", "Indian calm," "mind and spirit", and "Dionysian creative indifferentism."[43]

In fact, Kubin had a quite dialectical relationship to his own sexuality and practical instinctual life. During his time in Munich, he recklessly indulged in all sorts of dissipation, "such as women, eating, boozing, traveling, carousals" until he was gripped by "disgusted horror" at it all."[44] However, in his married life with Hedwig, lived by bourgeois moral standards, he had to "rein in my sexuality,"[45] and yet, infidelities were recurrent events: "Instinct now always wins over any ethos," he noted in his diary on July 14, 1924. The explanation given by Gorsen in his *Sexualästhetik* may provide a key to an understanding not of Kubin alone, but of the time around 1900 at large: "Cultural suppression of sexuality, a lack of sexual self-realization, provokes an exaggerated recurrence of what was suppressed, an excess of sexuality."[46] Torn in himself, he wrote in his diary on October 12, 1931, that "actually only with Hedwig everything [is] full and pure—connected in chastity in a truly motherly bond."[47] This antipodal attitude toward sexuality—between asceticism and excess—would be a dominant not only in his private life but also in his entire oeuvre of drawing.

POWERLESS BACK INTO NOTHINGNESS

"Death, nothingness is the fate of the world, and hence of what is in it, the individual forces that together constitute the world. Each and every one runs down a predestined path, unconditionally, like a machine,"[48] the only 27-year-old declared during his Munich time. It is peculiar, uncanny landscapes in which Kubin stages life as a world theater. Isolation, loneliness, and exposure characterize these sceneries, from which there is no escape, no way out, because there is no getting away from the deadly tragedy. The fateful inevitability manifests itself exemplarily in *Der Mensch (Man)* (p. 265) when the figure, fixed on wheels and tracks, unstoppably rushes at a hellish speed from this world into the beyond and thus into an unknown void. Kubin's pessimistic ideation of the world also becomes evident in *Das Grausen (The Horror)* (p. 267) when, in a stormy sea, an oversized skull with one eyeball bulging out announces their end to the ship's crew before they are pulled under by the maelstrom into the unfathomable depth. Kubin seems to have felt at once pleasure and disgust at these scenarios of existential threat: "More profoundly, I behold the wonder that the horror is magnificent, that the abyss is eternally alluring."[49]

And yet, the feeling of angst is omnipresent in these drawings, particularly so when animal figures or animal-human hybrid creature step into the role of the fateful figure, as is also the case in the pictures of sphinxes, sirens, nymphs, or vampires by Franz von Stuck (pp. 129, 132, 174, 176/177), Fernand Khnopff (1858–1921) (p. 117), or Max Klinger (pp. 110, 126, 152) even though with them the erotic-sensual aspect is prevalent while, by contrast, Kubin foregrounds the predatory evil and destructive. This is also true of his work *Das letzte Abenteuer (The Last Adventure)* (p. 143) in which a large snake—a symbol of temptation and sin—with a woman's head and long hair lies in wait for her next male victim, and it is obvious that this will be his end. Aside from this clear indication of sexual fears toward the female sex, Kubin's hybrid creatures are also influenced by his studies of Indian philosophy and mythology where animal-human metamorphoses are not uncommon.[50]

Aside from symbolically charged hybrids like the mentioned snake-woman, the Kubinian cast of horrors also includes pure animal figures. In the work *Macht (Power)* (p. 222), a giant seal sits enthroned on a pile of human bones. In disproportionately large *Seegespenst (Sea Monster)* (p. 223), it is clear at a glance that the humans in their ship do not stand a chance against the monstrous beast. In Kubin's drawing *Die Spinne (The Spider)* (p. 141), it is equally clear and predictable where the narrative is headed: An anthropomorphized spider lies naked—surrounded by copulating couples—with legs spread wide in the middle of its web. As this is the case in reality with various spider species, namely, that the female spider kills and

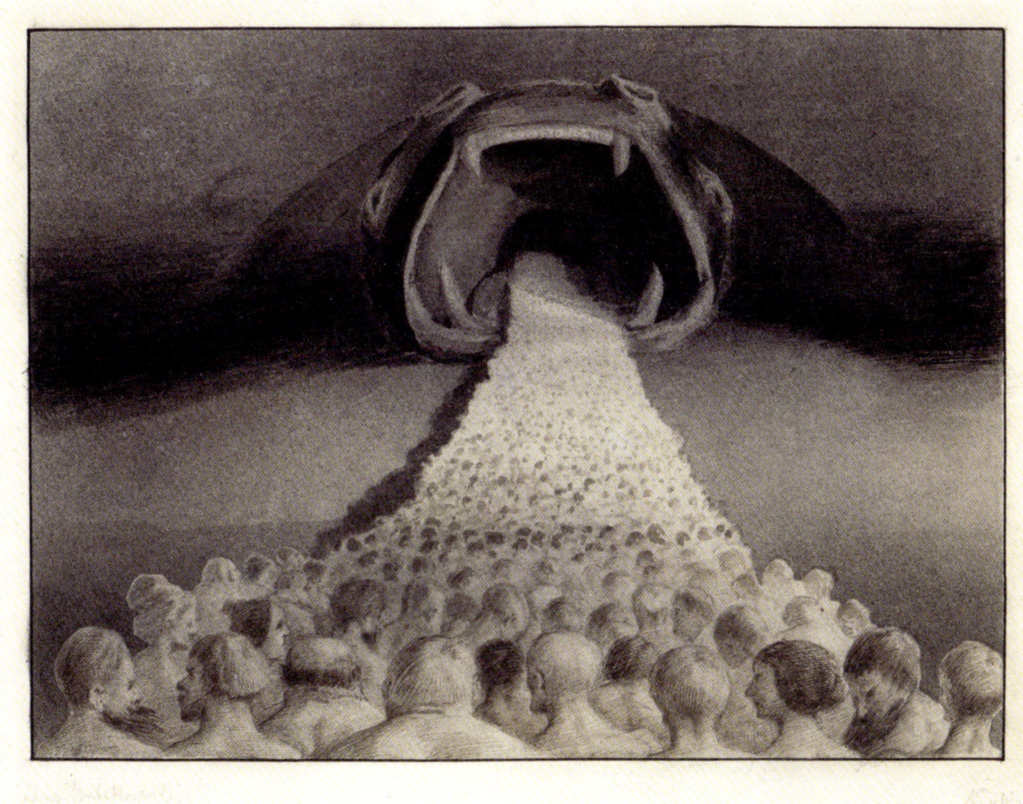

05
ALFRED KUBIN
Into the Unknown,
1900/01
Leopold Museum, Vienna

eats the male after mating, this is precisely the outcome that the drawing suggests. The recurrent idea of helpless exposure to a fatal higher power is once again related to the menace of femininity as exemplified in Kubin's works *Ins Unbekannte (Into the Unknown)* (05) or in *Das große Maul (The Big Mouth)*. What comes into play in both cases is the phenomenon of the "vagina dentata," the vagina with teeth, which appears in Indian, Japanese as well as South-African mythology and was reflected not least in Freudian psychoanalysis around 1900 as emblematizing male castration anxiety. This aspect is also referred to Kubin's novel *The Other Side:* "And, like the onset of a storm, the sexes fell upon each other. [...] I saw that a yellow-haired prostitute had castrated a drunken man with her teeth."[51]

COSMIC PRINCIPLE

In many of Kubin's depictions, woman is represented—as already indicated above— as a birth-giving force in lush primeval nature. This world-creation mythology, derived from Johann Jakob Bachofen's theories about the mother as a life-giving goddess in a setting of a swamp vegetation, fed into fin-de-siècle notions of matriarchy, prompting a discourse about the battle of the sexes, which was not without influence on Kubin who was familiar with Bachofen's writings.
Over decades, this association of woman with swampy nature, the "primordial soup", if you will,

is evident with Kubin, and inherent in his representation of the Great Mother is a desire for a reconciliation of opposites: of self and world, of the human and nature. This paradisiacal primordial fantasy is found in many artworks of the time; just two mentionable examples are Klimt's *Silver Fish* or his drawing *Blood of Fish* published in the 1898 volume of *Ver Sacrum*.

These places of primordial creation are not only the sites of birth from water—as, for example, in the *Fruchtbarkeit* drawings—but also of narratives of destruction in which women who were violated and murdered return to the harmonious unity of nature. This dualistic view of the female nature is once again found in Bachofen: "The generative power is at the same time the power of destruction. He who awakens life works for death. In tellurian creation coming into being and passing away run side by side."[52] Consider in this context also the previously discussed piece *Unser aller Mutter Erde*. Of aesthetic relevance are, outside such protohistoric and mythical-cosmic conceptions, also water corpses, surfaced from Kubin's childhood memories: "I had a burning interest for—corpses, for example. Often enough, the fisherman Hölzl, my mentor, gravedigger and genius of all trades, pulled a decayed body out of the lake [...] This is where my pronounced interest for such gruesome scenes comes from."[53]

The interest for deep see creatures was something that Kubin shared with his French colleague Odilon Redon: In 1905, Kubin visited him in Paris and presumably also saw his series, created the year before, of dream-like oceanic creatures and colorful fantasy landscapes. Kubin began to occupy himself with analyzing under the microscope structures invisible to the naked eye. From the exploration of these microscopic worlds, numerous animal fantasies emerged around 1906, richly experimental in shapes and colors.[54] (pp. 272–279)

EERIE PLACES

When the fog fell high above Inn river as early as September, not to dissipate again until late spring, the region around Kubin's manor in Zwickledt appeared, similarly to his literary dream realm Perle, like behind a dusky gray-brown filter for almost half a year—a meteorological facet that may have played into Kubin's fantasies and somberly dark worlds of thought: "My relationships to night, twilight, forest, swamp, animals, corpses will be entirely different from those of a philosopher, collector, farmer, day laborer, a prayerful old woman or a young harlot. There would likely be no end to examples; everybody finds what they are in for, their birth, their bliss, their misfortune, and their death. The more peculiar, imaginative a man is, the more pronounced it will all play out for him. In short, fate is everything. That's why I am a fatalist."

The places of the dreaming pessimist Kubin show themselves with signs of grotesquerie, distortion and decay in his visual dream realm. As if fallen out of time, crumbling or collapsing walls and houses mostly lie in ominous twilight. Rivers bursting their banks or trees violently shaken by a storm are forebodings of imminent doom or appear like the result of a natural disaster. In *Das Rattenhaus (The Rat House)* (p. 269), Kubin visualizes the centuries-old fear of the muroid rodents considered to be harmful carriers of parasites and in medieval Europe responsible in part for the deaths of millions of plague victims. Nearly two decades after the creation of this drawing, the Spanish Flue would be ravaging the world, eventually taking a larger toll of human life than the entire First World War. [55]

Even as his refuge in Upper Austria, which he lovingly called his "ark," became his home for decades, it continued to be an eerie place for him—like, presumably, any other place in the world. Compared to his younger years, Kubin's anxieties were alleviated with age but not resolved. Schopenhauer's dictum of *The World as Will and Representation* may have given him the detachment necessary to endure his existence—not least through his artistic work—and thereby diminish, or sublimate, his fears: "all this is due to the fact that [...] the in-itself of life, the will, existence itself, is a constant suffering, partly miserable, partly horrible; on the other hand, the same thing as representation alone, purely intuited, or repeated in art, free from pain, affords a meaningful spectacle."[56] Receiving treatment on his deathbed in 1959, Kubin spoke the much-quoted sentence that was significant for both his life and his artistic work: "Don't take my fear away from me, it is my only capital." [57]

Notes

1 Hans Holzschuher, 1904, quoted in *Alfred Kubin—Das zeichnerische Frühwerk bis 1904*, ed. Hans Albert Peters, (Baden-Baden, 1977), p. 35 (exh. cat.Staatliche Kunsthalle Baden-Baden, 01.04.–30.05.1977; Bayerische Akademie der Schönen Künste München, 06.06.–06.08.1977; Graphic Collection Albertina Vienna, 06.10.–11.12.1977).

2 Alfred Kubin, quoted in Wieland Schmied, *Der Zeichner Alfred Kubin* (Salzburg, 1967), p. 13.

3 Alfred Kubin in his diary, 28.10.1939.

4 According to Germanist Johann Lachinger, the work of illustrations is comprised of more than 2,360 pictures, see *Alfred Kubin (1877–1959)*, ed. Peter Assmann (Cologne, 1996), p. 24 (exh. cat. Musée d´Ixelles, Brussels, 21.11.1996–26.01.1997).

5 Alfred Kubin, "Aus meinem Leben" (1911), in Wolfgang K. Müller-Thalheim (ed.), *Erotik und Dämonie im Werk Alfred Kubins. Eine psychopathologische Studie* (Munich, 1970), pp. 26ff.

6 Fritz Stahl, "Im Salon Cassirer", *Berliner Tagblatt,* 21.01.1902, p. 2.

7 Richard Schaukal, "Ein österreichischer Goya: (Alfred Kubin)", *Wiener Abendpost. Beilage zur Wiener Zeitung,* 03.01.1903, p. 7.

8 Alfred Kubin about himself, quoted in Fritz von Herzmanovsky-Orlando: *Sämtliche Werke: Band VII. Der Briefwechsel mit Alfred Kubin 1903 bis 1952*, ed. Michael Klein (Salzburg/Vienna, 1983), p. 10.

9 Ibid.

10 Alfred Kubin, *Aus meiner Werkstatt. Gesammelte Prosa mit 71 Abbildungen,* ed.Ulrich Riemerschmidt, (Munich, 1973), pp. 60f.

11 Ibid., p. 46.

12 Ibid., p. 7.

13 Alfred Kubin in a letter to Fritz von Herzmanovsky-Orlando, 27.09.1911, in: Herzmanovsky-Orlando 1983 (see n. 8), p. 65.

14 Alfred Kubin in a letter to Fritz von Herzmanovsky-Orlando, 31.12.1907, in ibid., p. 9.

15 "Sueño" means both sleep and dream in Spanish although dream, which evokes the haunting visions, seems the more apt translation here.

16 James Ensor in a letter to Edgar Picard, 08.02.1906, in James Ensor: *Lettres*, ed. Xavier Tricot (Brussels, 1999), p. 271.

17 James Ensor, 21.06.1934, in *James Ensor. Sterben für die Unsterblichkeit. Meisterwerke der Grafik,* ed. Meinrad Maria Grewenig (Heidelberg, 2011), p. 15 (exh. cat. Saarlandmuseum Saarbrücken, 16.12.2011–15.04.2012).

18 Schaukal 1903 (see n. 7), p. 7.

19 Werner Hofmann, "Über einige Motive des Romans 'Die andere Seite'" (1909), in *Alfred Kubin 1877–1959*, ed. Annegret Hoberg (Munich, 1990), p. 103 (exh. cat. Galerie im Lenbachhaus München, 03.10.–02.12.1990).

20 E.g. in depictions of Napoleon or in drawings where he addresses the Nazi racist ideology.

21 Cf. C. G. Jung, *"Psychological Aspects of the Mother Archetype", in Jung, Four Archetypes, trans. R.F.C. Hull (Princeton, New Jersey, 1970)* as well as Werner Hofmann, *Das irdische Paradies: Kunst im 19. Jahrhundert*, (Munich, 1960), pp. 310ff.

22 The very many extant self-expressions in letters and diaries afford a more authentic insight into the author's personality than his autobiography, first published 1911, which he kept working, presumably with some glossing over, throughout his lifetime.

23 Alfred Kubin, *Dämonen und Nachtgesichte* (Dresden, 1926), p. 8.

24 Kubin 1911 (see n. 5), p. 77.

25 Leopold von Sacher-Masoch, *Venus in Furs,* trans. Fernanda Savage (New York, 2004) p. 122.

26 Leopold von Sacher-Masoch, *Meine Lebensbeichte* (Berlin/Leipzig, 1906), pp. 43f.

27 Nike Wagner, *Geist und Geschlecht. Karl Kraus und die Erotik der Wiener Moderne* (Frankfurt am Main, 1982), p. 149.

28 Christoph Settele, *Zum Mythos Frau im Frühwerk Alfred Kubins* (Lucerne, 1992), p. 117.

29 Hofmann 1960 (see n. 21), p. 315.

30 Already in Klimt's painting *Judith II*, Salome is named in parentheses and thus used as a synonym for this type of woman.

31 In Max Klinger's *Die Neue Salome,* the protagonist is no longer content with a single killing; instead, two decapitated heads are presented.

32 Settele 1992 (see n. 28), p. 68.

33 In: *Le Décadent,* 10.04.1886, quoted in Mario Praz, *Liebe, Tod und Teufel: Die schwarze Romantik* (Munich, 1963), p. 275.

34 Peter Gorsen, *Sexualästhetik: Zur bürgerlichen Rezeption von Obszönität und Pornographie* (Reinbek bei Hamburg, 1972), p. 172.

35 Friedrich Nietzsche, *Thus Spoke Zarathustra,* trans. Adrian Del Caro (Cambridge, 2006), p. 50.

36 About this see also Alfred Kubin, "Die Kunst der Irren", *Das Kunstblatt,* ed. Paul Westheim, no. 5 (May 1922), pp. 185ff.

37 Schmied 1967 (see n. 2), p. 22.

38 Alfred Kubin, "Zur Eröffnung einer Kubinausstellung", in Kubin 1973 (see n. 10), p. 26.

39 As regards the concept of the germination of life from water, or from "tellurian waters" (Bachofen), Kubin seems to have been influenced by Odilon Redon, specifically by the latter's series *Les Origines* (1883) as well as the lithograph *Germination* (1879).

40 O. A. H. Schmitz, *Brevier für Einsame. Fingerzeige zu neuem Leben* (Munich, 1923).

41 Alfred Kubin in his diary, 03.02.1931.

42 Alfred Kubin in his diary, 14.09.1921.

43 Quoted in Settele 1992 (see n. 28), p. 103.

44 Alfred Kubin in a letter to Hermann Hinterhuber, 08.05.1902, quoted in Peters 1977 (see n. 1), p. 17.

45 Alfred Kubin in his diary, 23.02.1922.

46 Gorsen 1972 (see n. 34), p. 371.

47 Alfred Kubin in his diary, 12.10.1931.

48 Alfred Kubin in a letter to his sister Maria Kubin-Bruckmüller, 22.02.1904, quoted in Peters 1977 (see n. 1), p. 19.

49 Alfred Kubin in a letter to E. W. Bredt, 1912, in: E. W. Bredt, *Alfred Kubin* (Munich, 1922), p. 72.

50 Indian and Buddhist literature was part the holdings of Kubin's library.

51 Alfred Kubin, *The Other Side: A Fantastic Novel,* trans. Denver Lindley (New York, 1967), pp. 209 f.

52 Johann Jakob Bachofen, *Myth, Religion, and Mother Right: Selected Writings of J. J. Bachofen,* trans. Ralph Manheim (New York, 1967), p. 126.

53 Kubin 1973 (see n. 10), p. 13.

54 It must be mentioned here that the distemper technique, which Kubin learnt from Koloman Moser in 1905, was part of the reason for his new, if short-lived, color experiments.

55 Alfred Kubin, quoted in Schmied 1967 (see n. 2), p. 16.

56 Arthur Schopenhauer, *The World as Will and Representation,* trans. Judith Norman, Alistair Welchman, Christopher Janaway, vol. I, (Cambridge, 2010), § 52, p. 295.

57 Alfred Kubin, quoted in Otto Breicha, *Alfred Kubin: Das zeichnerische Frühwerk bis 1904* (Salzburg, 1977), p. 200.

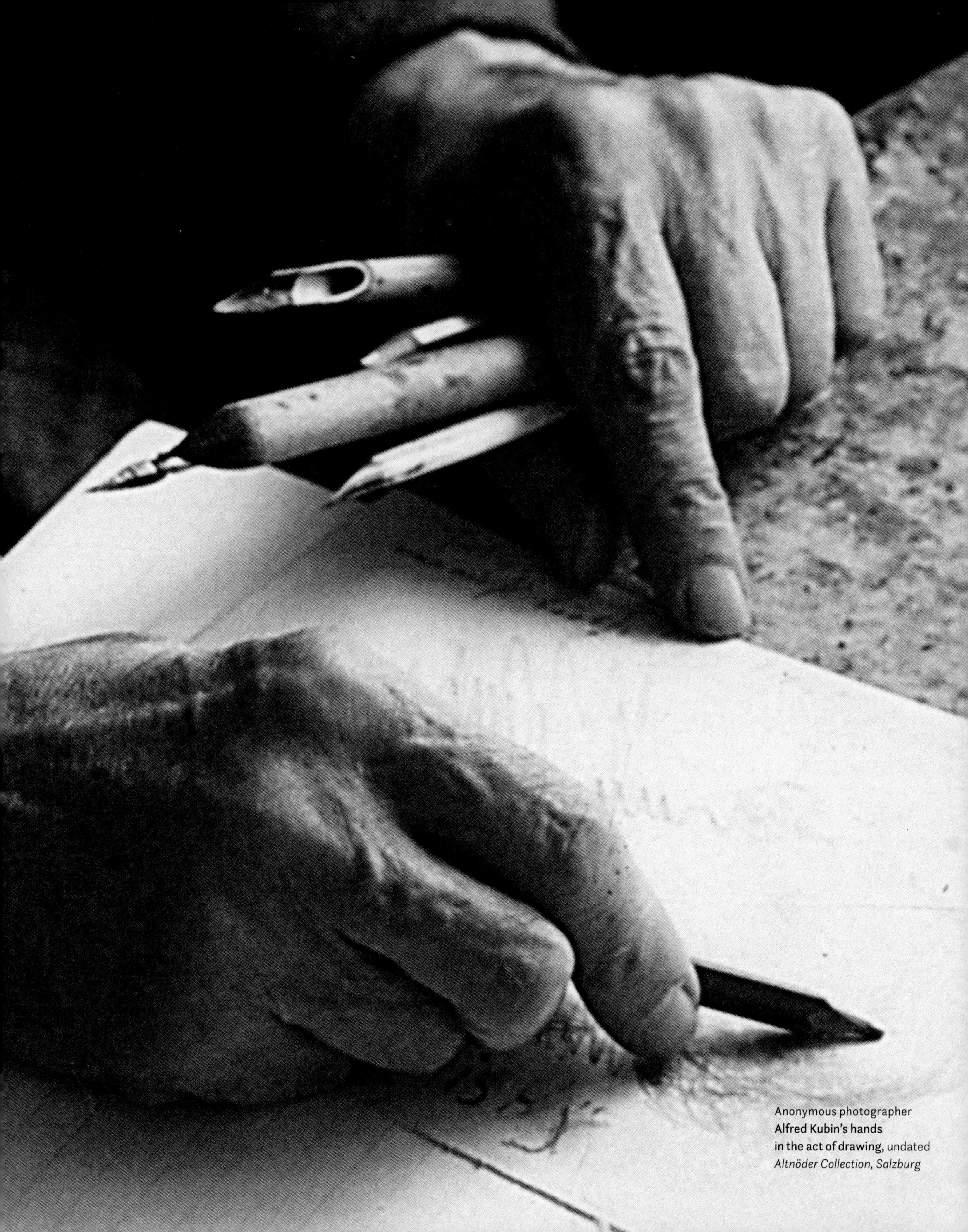

Anonymous photographer
Alfred Kubin's hands in the act of drawing, undated
Altnöder Collection, Salzburg

The pen has been my favorite tool for many years [...]. With its elastic pliancy, it secures for us direct transmission not only of the imagination but also of the accompanying excitement, unspeakably more intimate.*

Alfred Kubin

* Alfred Kubin, "Der Zeichner", in: *Aus meiner Werkstatt. Gesammelte Prosa,* ed. Ulrich Riemerschmidt (Munich, 1973), p. 57.

THE TAMING OF THE PHANTASM INSIDE THE PHANTOM

August Ruhs

At the bottom of things,
everything is imagination.[1]
Alfred Kubin

In Alfred Kubin, we encounter an artist whose grievous biography and more than comprehensive oeuvre are separable from one another only to a degree, all the more so considering that he himself always made a point of them being interwoven and interlocked. This is evidenced above all by his "Selbstdarstellung" (Self-Representation) which he published in 1926 under the title of *Dämonen und Nachtgesichte (Demons and Nocturnal Visions)*. If reference books cite Kubin not only as a graphic artist and writer but also as a book illustrator, the main portion of his visual work may in fact, from this aspect, be viewed as an illustrated life-story.

Categorizing him with the, for the most part, formally and technically informed styles of his artistic contemporaries therefore seems mistaken, despite the real-life closeness he had with them. One might think that the zeitgeist of the era was a far lesser impulsive factor for him than his individual psychological state, imbued as it was with the eeriness of re-actualized memories and illusive visitations, which for one thing were aching for projective externalization and, for another, mobilized intellectual powers to tame them, discursively and rationally, and to keep them at bay. In both cases in which cathartic and calming measures at once counteract the high-strung agitation, Kubin's pronounced literary talent, dedicated in essence to the narrative, came in useful. For the most part, it would find expression in an almost inestimable wealth of visual narrations or illustrations of narrations but proved its worth with respect to literariness. In this view, his novel *Die andere Seite (The Other Side)*, which gave Kubin a second identity as a poet, was not only the manifestation of a second aspect of his capacity of expression, not only the description of an eventually doomed dream realm on the far side of the world; it was not only inspired by the unfulfillable wish for a different story and an alternative life beyond a reality that was felt to be mostly cruel but it also points to that other side of the personality of the author which, like in any other personality, is the counterpart, and in fact also the basis, of conscious waking life with its various perceptions, ideas, and sensations. This area of the soul, metaphorically often described in terms of an abyss or depth, though not always aptly so, emerged from the dogged struggle of the *id* as a cauldron full of seething passions with the drive-taming agents of the *superego,* unknown, unconscious, and unseen in its nature, enigmatic, perturbing, and frightening in its manifestations, holds in itself both the documents of the early history of the subject and the residues and traces of its everyday repressions. Unless they remain absolutely inaccessible for failure to inscribe themselves in the psyche or bring themselves to memory—doing so, however, mostly jumbled like in dreams, parapraxes, or symptoms—the intended traceability of the origins is a given. The explicit encouragement to explore them, the core endeavor of the psychanalytic process, formulated by Freud as "Where id was there shall ego be", and rephrased by Lacan as "Where it was, there must I come to be", is programmatic in that the appropriative act of making aware of motivations outside the ego affords a freedom of disposal over them which includes the ability of disposal of them.

In Kubin's permanent self-analysis which, on the one hand, was along the lines of his urge for knowledge and creativity and, on the other, was meant to ward off the ever-repeating threats to his mental stability, remembrance was at work in its characteristic manifestations: as a mental process of recollection and as largely unconscious repetitions, which then also found expression in his artistic and poetic works.

Kubin had a strong proclivity for reminiscing. It is astonishing, though, to see him astonished at the fact that he had absolutely no memory of the first two years of his childhood. In any case, he allegedly was a crybaby.

And then, as his earliest memory, "the slender pale face of my mother."[2] Soon after his birth on April 10, 1877, in Leitmeritz (Litoměřice) in Bohemia (today: Czech Republic), where he was baptized with the name Alfred Leopold Isidor, his mother moved to Salzburg with him where his first encounter with his father would imprint itself on his memory. A former Imperial and Royal Army officer and later a land surveyor in public service, he had spent two years on duty in Dalmatia before being transferred to a post in Salzburg.

It was not the best of memories. Later, it was described as meeting a "disagreeable man" whose presence gave the little boy cause for violent jealousy. Alfred spent the main portion of his childhood from his fifth year in Zell am See where the family had moved after his father had once again been transferred. A "wild child"[3] that resolutely resisted pressure, he also hated school, which in its recalcitrance helped him develop cunning and smarts but also drove him to seek aggression release, among other things, in the torturing of small animals. Eventually, he could not help but capitulate. "Church and school" had put "unbreakable reins on the beast-child"[4], and under their restraint, his life became outwardly calmer. He could enjoy playing with his mates and reading fairytale books and transform his sadism into milder forms like bird catching and fishing. This was the time when he made his first drawings, done with a "penchant for exaggeration and fantasy"[5], full of the strangest shapes and scenes, "the whole later Kubin was already there, in embryo"[6] While previously a guilty conscience had had an impulse-controlling and sublimating effect on him, now the first spiritual stirrings were making themselves felt: the old parish church of Zell had become a place of refuge and of "mystical elevation and true contemplation."[7]

What may have contributed to this was the painful relationship he had with his tuberculous mother. When she, apparently a sensitive-to-nervous woman whose musical disposition had formerly led her to become a pianist, died in 1877, Alfred was only ten years old. Even though he, per his own words, experienced her death as a release from her agonizing suffering and although at the time he would not and, given his age, really could not accept the finality of her passing as a fact, the event subsequently turned into a trauma. In an obviously lifelong work of mourning, the primal image of the mother with her slender pale face was invariably associated with a different memory, that of a lifeless countenance, which from then on, spreading also all over his later artistic work, preserved in a myriad of figures and shapes the memory of "the first human being I saw die."[8] The way his mother lived on in him also became manifest in his repetitive mental breakdowns whose symptoms included instances of imaginary identification.

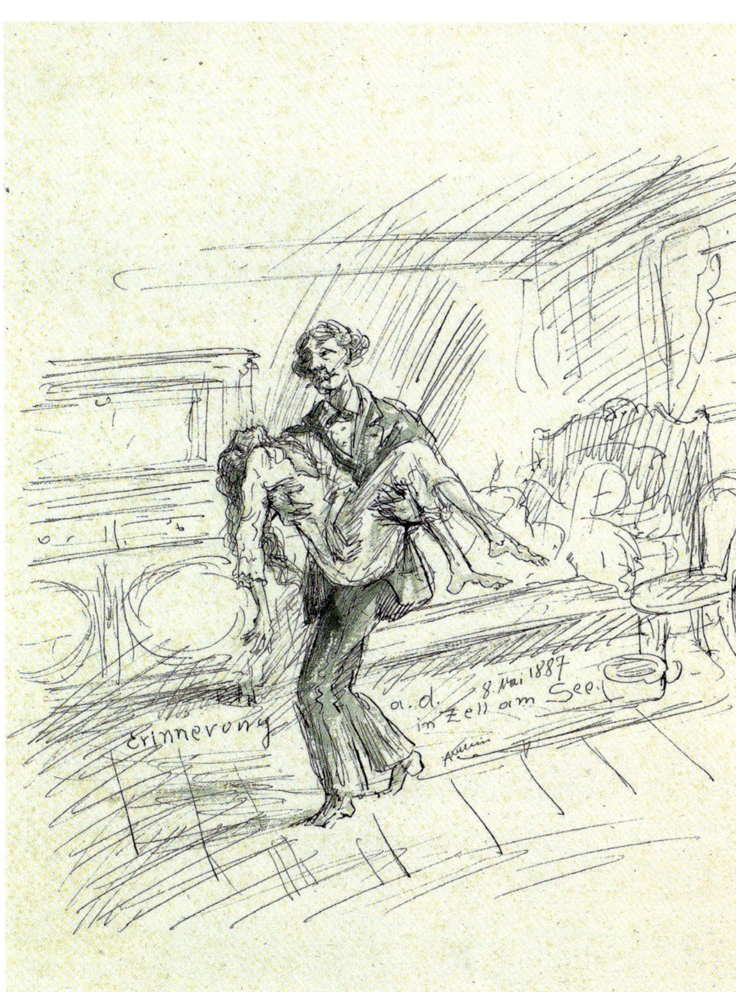

01
ALFRED KUBIN
Dying Mother, 1930
Courtesy of Ketterer Kunst GmbH und Co. KG

From the "Selbstdarstellung", we learn that the boy remembered his father's reaction to the tragic loss as even more disconcerting than the loss itself. In his utter despair, his father had "lifted the emaciated woman's long dead body up from the bed, carrying her around in the entire apartment, weeping and as if crying for help."[9]

While, following the initial stark rejection of the father as an intruder in the affectionate relationship with his mother, the boy's attitude toward him changed so that he was able to see in him an identification figure as an "epitome of male strength and beauty"[10], the father's previous "measured fondness"[11] was eclipsed by the sight of this frightening horrified behavior that stood in the way of any further idealization.

This was all the more the case as his father remarried one year later. However, what made the new family situation even more precarious was that his now stepmother was his own mother's sister. Having her close in the context of a new oedipal constellation appears to have been particularly challenging for the boy's libidinal state, particularly as the conflict-fraught relationship with his father had become worse. An admission from Kubin that he, at the age of eleven and a half, was seduced into "sexual plays"[12] by an older woman in any case justifies such an assumption. The inordinate upsetment about this had left deep traces and hampered the development of his own love life well "into the early manhood years." [13]

Two years later, another death. Alfred was already in grammar school in Salzburg, when his stepmother died in childbed. Expelled from school for lack of success and returning to the recently broken family situation, he went through a "period of real hell"[14] that fomented hatred and murderous thoughts in him. As a failure and "disgrace to the family"[15] he was to stay out of sight of his "hapless and torn"[16] father, who nevertheless meted out draconian and brutal punishments. He endured the many canings with his head drawn in, like petrified; the rivalry with his little sisters and his madness at her mean and negligent nurse did the rest.

But as an unbearable situation had once before, by way of reaction formation, mobilized his creative and intellectual powers, so he now was again

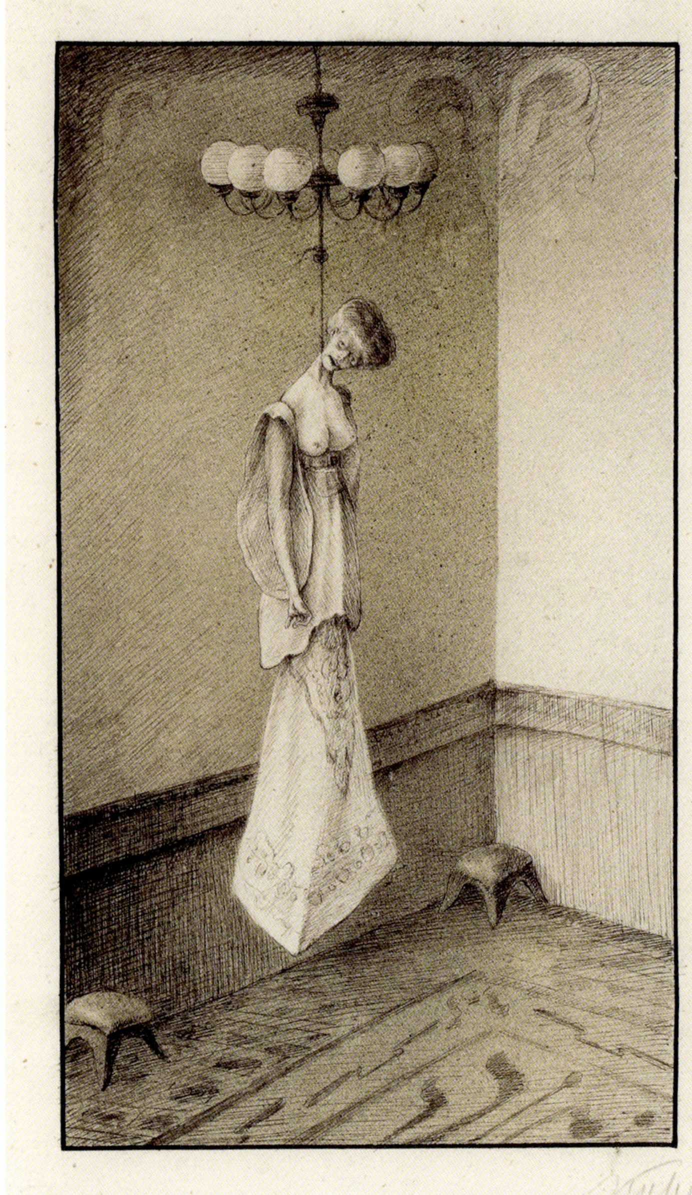

02
ALFRED KUBIN
Madame (also: Modern Chandelier Decoration), 1900/01
Leopold Museum, Vienna

able to wrest a compensatory gain from a bad lot: “This time of utter desolation, however, turned out immensely enlivening for my imagination. Reveling in fantasies of primeval outbursts of force and catastrophes had always given me a palpable sense of happiness, like a rush accompanied by a tingling sensation down my spine. Watching a thunderstorm, a fire, a torrential flooding was one of my highest pleasures; I could be regularly found at brawls, at arrests, at cattle markets as an onlooker.”[17] And just as much as he was fascinated by everything related to army life and war heroism, dead and decayed bodies, the languishing sick, and the disgusting businesses of the butcher and the knacker all were objects of his burning curiosity.

Under irate threats from his father, he eventually gave in to the paternal dictate and enrolled at the arts-and-crafts school in Salzburg. Although he now was receiving good and even excellent grades in subjects he used to hate, he was assessed as being the “weakest in freehand drawing”[18] and left school with no qualifications.

In the meantime, his father had married his third wife and thereby entered into a family relationship with a brother-in-law who ran a photographic studio in Klagenfurt; so he decided to send Alfred to this new uncle as an apprentice. As it turned out, this attempt to prepare for a satisfactory and gainful working life as a landscape photographer, was also doomed to fail. The uncle, whom, being a “surrogate father”[19], he met with highly mixed feelings, often was away on business-related travels but kept constantly sending photographic material from all parts of the world to Klagenfurt for development and processing. Such ancillary assignments strengthened his sense for landscape but were not enough to really learn the photographic profession. Disillusioned and bothered by his undefined status between apprentice and nephew, he buried himself in books, which grew into a true reading fever.

This retreat into resignation came to an end when he, aged seventeen, was promoted to photographic assistant on a regular salary. The gain in freedom led him to indulge in a now "dissolute life"[20]. While, except for an erotic interest in "well-preserved mature women between thirty and forty years of age"[21], he had mainly had disdain for the fair gender before, there now were amorous feelings making themselves felt "which regularly went unrequited and then petered out in sexual dreams."[22] Let us leave open the question of how far the phantasmagorias of these dreams were also populated by those binary-sexually connoted "snakes and all kinds of vermin"[23], which Kubin was then keeping as bizarre house pets.

But although he went easy on the booze in the drinking parties at the studio that his uncle's many absences gave occasion to his excessive lifestyle turned out to be quite consequential. Increasingly high-strung, confused, and irascible as he was, even resorting to literature and philosophy again, where the pessimistic writings of Schopenhauer held a special place, could not remedy his confusion nor prevent his outbursts of rage. Experiments with hypnosis, which were the result of a chance visit to a variety show and initially were fascinating for him, were even more detrimental to his mental state.

Following a heated argument with some colleague, he fled Klagenfurt head over heels, weighed down by the darkest thoughts, intent on taking his own life with a cheap old revolver by his mother's grave at the place of his childhood in Zell am See. Later, matured, Kubin would look back on this "romantic youthful crisis"[24] with a wistful smile: "When I got to my mother's grave, I prayed to the good Lord, just in case; likewise, in my mind, I asked my mother to send me the necessary firmness of resolve and prevent me from being a coward. Then I kept waiting till the next toll of the bell, hoping for help to come from somewhere—but nothing came, and the idea of quickly walking over to my father's, of being sent back to Klagenfurt and having to ask everyone for forgiveness was far too shameful to be even considered, simply impossible. With the muzzle to my right temple where I had made a scratch mark using an anatomical picture in order not to miss the brain I pressed the trigger. But the rusty old firearm failed, and I lacked the mental strength to pull the trigger a second time—I got miserably sick. After lying down in bed in a nearby inn for a couple of hours, I went to my parents' house and was sent back to Klagenfurt right away by my father—incidentally, without further reproach."[25]

03
ALFRED KUBIN
Death (As a Woman) Comes for the Draftsman (Self-Portrait), 1930
Leopold Museum, Vienna

Now his uncle was no longer willing to keep his nephew in the house. He gave him an apprenticeship certificate and threw him out.

In this awkward situation, entry into military service seemed to Kubin to be the last way out. But after only a few weeks with a regiment in Laibach (Ljubljana) he was overcome with increasing nervousness, which soon escalated into behavioral problems with frantic hyperactivity and eventually led to a psychotic, delirious-looking breakdown. Delusional ideas—e.g. of being a Bourbon prince with a residence in Borneo—and convulsive fits, as, according to his later memory, he had frequently witnessed in his sick mother, necessitated his admission to the garrison hospital in Graz. When his father picked him up four months later, he was able to leave the institution in apparently satisfactory remission.

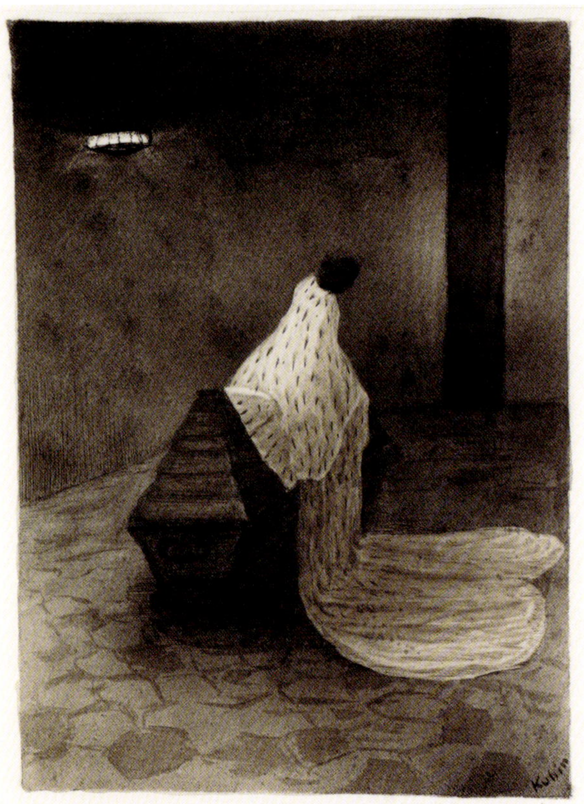

Returning to the parental home went along a certain reconciliation with his now apparently more considerate and almost spoiling father. Following a year-long recuperation phase that the meanwhile twenty-year-old spent busying himself with drawing, he let himself be persuaded to attend, on the advice of a friend of his father's, a private art school in Munich. His first years in the big city with its major galleries, with "rooms like heaven itself"[26], with the "overwhelming overall impression"[27] of the Alte Pinakothek indeed came to be young Kubin's most pleasant memories, except perhaps for the enjoyment of his now completely free life in the bohemian world and the circle of his artist friends.

Once again heeding a suggestion from his father, he enrolled in the Munich Academy of Arts but soon grew unhappy with the prevailing atmosphere there and the modern models he found himself presented with because they were not at all in line with the ideals he had come to know and appreciate about the Old Masters. Such devaluing tendencies on the one hand and idealizations on the other, although both were also directed at himself, reveal Kubin's fundamental narcissistically informed psychic structure, in which a grandiose inflated sense of self had to permanently assert itself against internalized accusations and recurrent feelings of guilt and inferiority. It is not surprising to learn that these disappointing Munich experiences, connected as they were with an unconscious resistance against the renewed paternal influence on his life, which, however, he knew not how to counter with anything of his own, did not leave his mind and spirit unshaken.

04
ALFRED KUBIN
Memorial Work for My Bride Who Died in 1903, 1903
Leopold Museum, Vienna

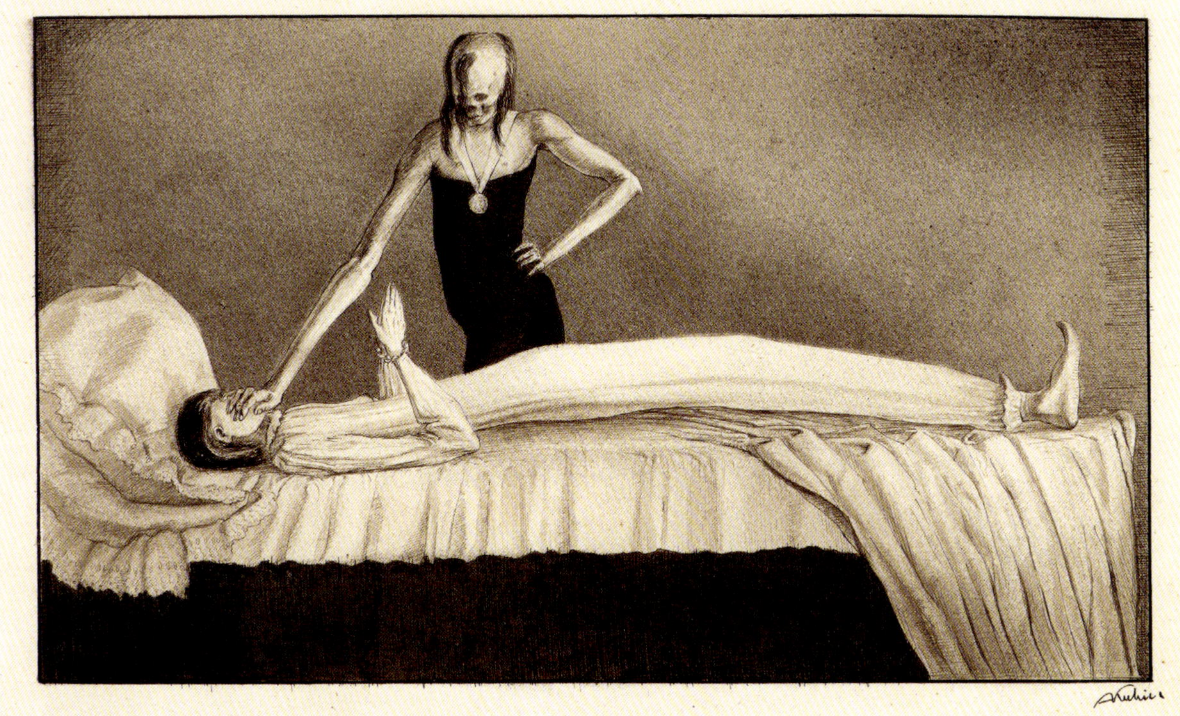

05
ALFRED KUBIN
The Best Physician, c. 1901
Leopold Museum, Vienna

Here, like before, the confrontation with authoritarian power and external constraints showed signs of repudiation, which means a defense that, being more energetic than symptom-forming repression, gives appearance to the inacceptable in real constructions as a delirious metaphor, a sinthome in the sense of Lacan. In any case, this helps better understand that "strange cosmogony" of the "son as a wanderer of worlds"[28] which Kubin now developed in "feverish haste"[29]. In notebooks written full and many drawings of "spooky ideas and caricatures"[30], he imagined that a per se extratemporal, eternal principle, called "the Father", had, for some unfathomable cause, created a self-consciousness—"the Son"—together with a world that was inseparable from him. "In this scheme I myself was, of course, the Son, who deceives himself, torments and persecutes himself as long as this is well pleasing to his true and gigantic Father, who spontaneously created him as a sort of mirror image. Such a Son can therefore disappear at any instant along with his world and be assimilated into the superexistence of the Father. There is only one Son, and from his recognizing viewpoint, one could, speaking relatively allegorically, say that this whole mimicking and agonizing world process only happens for the Father to become aware and gauge from this confusion his own omnipotent clarity and endlessness." [31]

And even if Kubin believed to have found his footing again in the calm symbolist "feeling worlds" of a Max Klinger, he was not spared from "ghostly" derealization phenomena as he had experienced during his time of military service. The emerging of grotesque and horrifying fantasies that he desperately tried to rid himself of in a series of ink drawings resisted any attempt of artistic self-healing and forced another stay in a clinic, albeit a brief one.

The subsequent dropping out of the academy and the cutting of ties with the artist friends associated in the "Sturmfackel" group, however, was not just another failure. Rather, twenty-four-year-old Kubin received, much to his joy and satisfaction, his first-ever invitation to take part in an exhibition. And even though his works were not an all-out success and scathingly criticized in some reviews, he could rely on the appreciative judgement of prominent mentors and the admiration of supportive friends who provided a benevolent counterpoise to the conflict-charged father imago. A stormy infatuation, which very soon led to an engagement, was the crowing point of this, all in all, rather happy period, in which Kubin's financial worries also diminished.

Once again, fate struck brutally. His fiancée fell ill, when she came to visit him in Munich, and ten days later, she died. Although his reaction to this was not quite as excessive as his father's had been at the death of his mother, his despair was "infinite"[32], and he lost "all will to live"[33], squandering his savings, withdrawing from all friends and acquaintances, and being haunted by hurtful memories of the "blossoming young creature"[34] .

Not unlike his father in such matters, however, he was soon able to open up for a new relationship. In Hedwig Gründler, a widow and mother of a son, he happened to meet a woman who was understanding of his situation and "instilled trust and love"[35] in him. In 1904, in his twenty-seventh year, he finally married her.

The couple went on travels to France and Italy before settling down in Zwickledt, Upper Austria, where Kubin purchased a small country estate with a small manor house in 1906. Incidentally, it was not far from where his father had taken residence in a small town in the region.

Staying abroad, particularly in Paris, had led Kubin, who at times well enjoyed experimenting, to give more room to painting in his artistic work, which, however, did not necessarily mean progress for him but rather caused a new creative crisis, intensified by a protracted intestinal illness accompanied by hypochondriacal anxieties.

In 1907, his father died. It was a loss that Kubin, per his own words, could never really overcome. Generally speaking, this is also indicative of the failing of the work of mourning particularly in those cases in which love and hate have, over the person's lifetime, become an irreconcilable dichotomy. In these circumstance, death seemed to Kubin to be "a meaningless worldly contrariety that only through truly artistic and mystic contemplation can have grandeur and profound significance."[36]

Depressive and jaded and under the impression of having lost certain emotions forever, he took to reading ancient mystics, dealing with the many animals in his household, roaming the rural areas, and made the resolution to rigorously return to drawing. Colors were obviously no longer conducive to expressing his mental state of resignation.

But when his drawing capability also failed him, he was able to fall back on the devices of language to work through his oppressive and painful thoughts and redirect them toward the dream of a saving utopia. Completed in a matter of twelve weeks, his novel *The Other Side,* published 1909, not only marked the transition from "absurdly combinative fantasies" to the confrontation with "life in general that weaves so mysteriously in humans, animals and plants"[37], not only explored the boundaries and mutual incursions of dreams and reality, but also was an attempt to come to terms with his father's death. As easy as it is to extricate the figure of the father from the demiurgic central character, Claus Patera,[38] so it is only logical to read the impressive narrative as an epic and graphic elaboration of his cosmogony, however abstruse, of the "son as a wanderer of worlds" from the early years of his time in Munich. While there the issue was the involvement, framed as a primal myth, of a son with his all-powerful father in whom he eventually disappears through identification with him, in order to demonstrate to him his grandiosity but also the limits of his power, here, at the end of the novel, it is about performing a symbolic castration on the great creator of worlds, Patera, who in a reckless battle with his adversary not only must live to see the destruction of his dream realm but also the loss of his very existence. From becoming one with his opponent, he can only emerge as a hermaphroditic creature.

Satisfied with the result of his literary ambitions and also with the success of his book, Kubin took up his work of drawing again, which continued to explore the subject of dreams and thereby acknowledged their psychic reality as a reality of their own. Although he had, through his brother-in-law, the poet Oscar A. H. Schmitz, who knew Freud and C. G. Jung, some vicarious knowledge of the basics of the psychoanalytic theory of dreams and its interest in the latent wishfulness of the oneiric, he stayed with representing the luxuriant imagery of manifest dream contents in his large series of dream pictures. Aside from doing numerous book illustrations, he took part in projects and exhibitions of the Blaue Reiter group but to protect his individuality and personal style was careful not to get involved too much in this artist collective. Being relatively closest to what later would emerge as Surrealism, he did not much care for Impressionism and Cubism nor for Expressionism and Abstract Art.

The terrors and hardships of World War I, which drove him and his family in financial dire straits, weighed down heavily on Kubin with persistent states of grief and dejection. They did, however, not impair his artistic work in any lasting way, even though they had an influence on its mood and subject matter, like in the *Totentanz* series or in his many book illustrations.

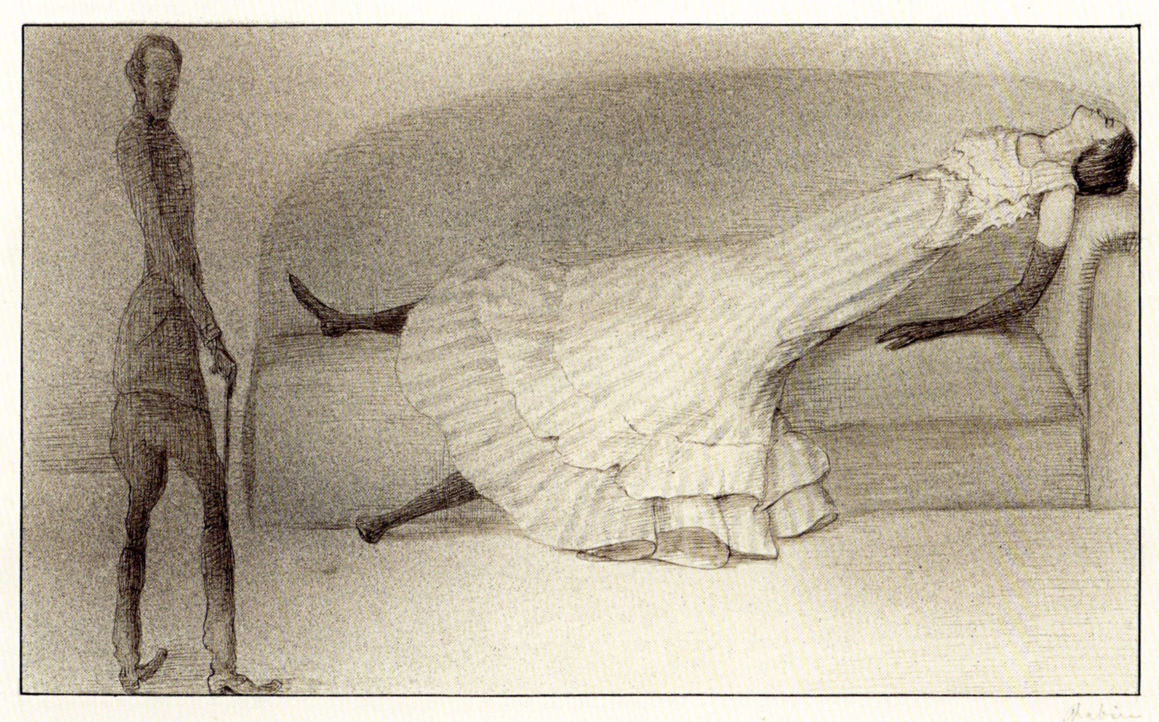

06
ALFRED KUBIN
Hysteria, c. 1901
Leopold Museum, Vienna

While he had already turned away from pessimistic philosophies some time ago, his then new "demure skepticism"[39] also included a fascination with Nietzsche whose writings, though, he did not receive without some critical objection. An additional turn to Buddhism was only very short-lived, thwarted by his lack of observance of the entailed orthopractic rules.

When in 1926 Kubin, almost fifty years old, concluded his "Selbstdarstellung", he complained of several years of "bodily signs of old age" and "hypochondriacally imagined restrictions"[40], which, however, did not prevent him from having a brief amorous episode with a young female artist. It soon came to an end with his remorseful and loving return to his wife.

Despite ever-present thoughts of mortality, intensified still by the loss of many friends and, above all, his marital partner, who died in1948, he lived out the rest of his life with almost undiminished creativity and in relative peace of mind before he crossed over in 1959, in his 82nd year, to the completely other side of life. As reports have it, he was calm, unafraid, and in no agony.

Notes

1 Alfred Kubin: „Bekenntnis", in Kubin: *Aus meiner Werkstatt. Gesammelte Prosa,* ed. Ulrich Riemerschmidt (Munich, 1973), p. 18.
2 Alfred Kubin: *Dämonen und Nachtgesichte. Mit einer Selbstdarstellung des Künstlers und 130 Bilddaten,* (Dresden, 1926), p. 5.
3 Ibid.
4 Ibid., p. 7.
5 Ibid.
6 Ibid.
7 Ibid., p. 6.
8 Ibid., p. 7.
9 Ibid.
10 Ibid.
11 Ibid., p. 8.
12 Ibid.
13 Ibid.
14 Ibid.
15 Ibid., p. 9.
16 Ibid., p. 8.
17 Ibid., p. 9.
18 Ibid., p. 10.
19 Ibid.
20 Ibid., p. 12.
21 Ibid.
22 Ibid.
23 Ibid.
24 Ibid., p. 13.
25 Ibid., p. 13f.
26 Ibid., p. 17.
27 Ibid.
28 Ibid., p. 20.
29 Ibid.
30 Ibid.
31 Ibid., p. 19f.
32 Ibid., p. 24.
33 Ibid.
34 Ibid.
35 Ibid., p. 25.
36 Ibid., p. 30.
37 Ibid., p. 31f.
38 This is also pointed out by Jane Kallir in her essay "Visions from the Other Side" (New York, 1983).
39 Kubin 1926 (see n. 2), p. 40.
40 Ibid., p. 53.

I’ve always found our world to be ghostly through and through.*

Alfred Kubin

* Alfred Kubin: “Die Befreiung vom Joch”, in: *Aus meiner Werkstatt. Gesammelte Prosa*, ed. Ulrich Riemerschmidt (Munich, 1973), p. 18.

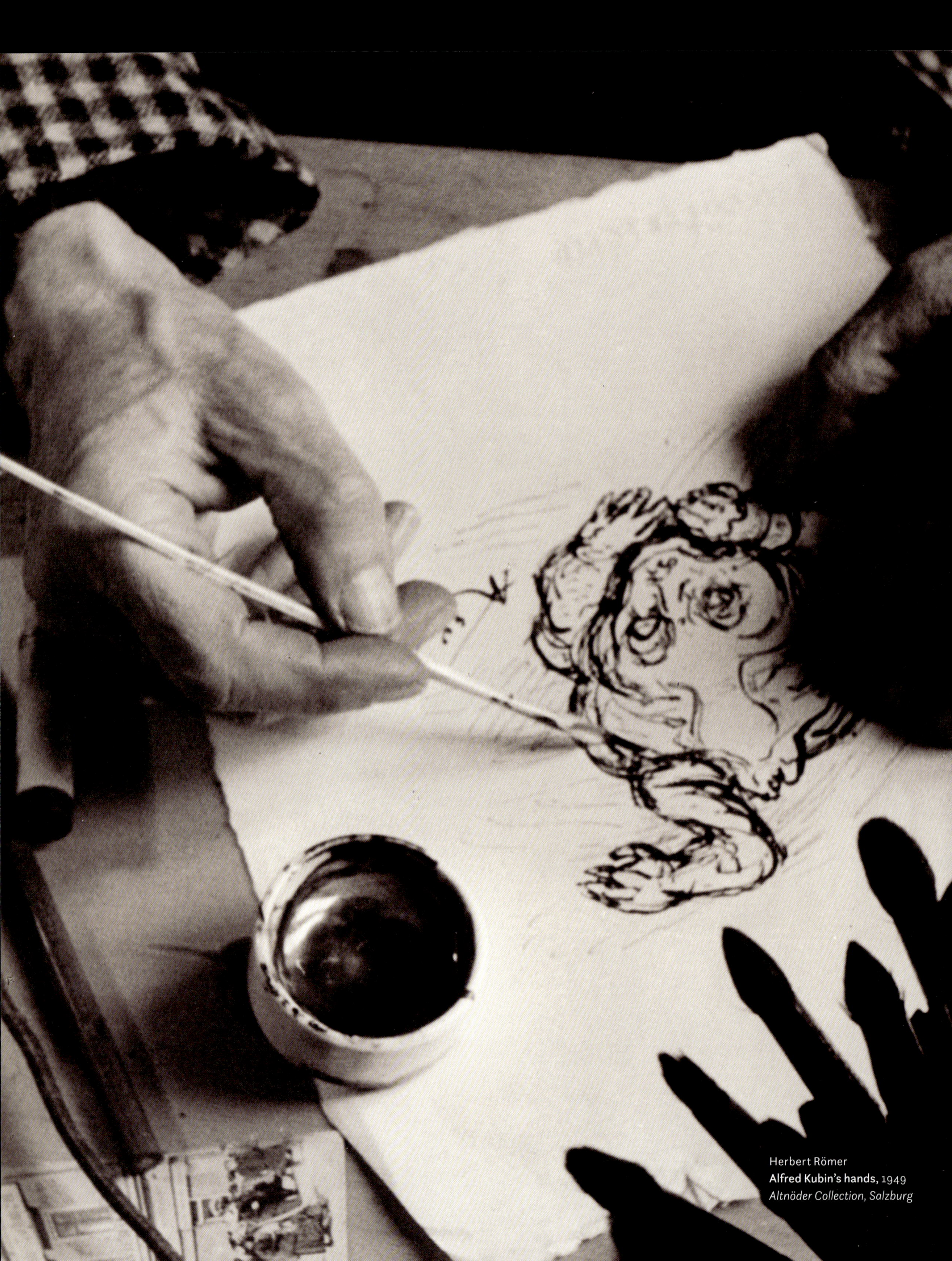

Herbert Römer
Alfred Kubin's hands, 1949
Altnöder Collection, Salzburg

Known until recently only among his circle of friends, the artist, a draughtsman of boundless imagination, an inexhaustible wealth of ideas, and the most idiosyncratic creativeness, is a young man of 27 years, little, pale, with a mighty forehead and accentuated features. His demeanor is unfree, his voice without expression. He is hasty and faltering, excitable and self-conscious, wayward and curious. *

Richard Schaukal

* Richard Schaukal: "Ein österreichischer Goya: (Alfred Kubin)", *Wiener Abendpost. Beilage zur Wiener Zeitung,* 03.01.1903, p. 7.

KUBIN AND THE HISTORY OF WAR AND BLISS OF THE PHANTASMAGORIC

Burghart Schmidt

Wherever there is talk of art, it is the imagination that is said to be at work in it, as if art were the most important purpose of the productive power of imagining. In fact, the imagination may as well bring other consequences, namely, scientific or technical inventions. So there is a bifurcation here. The imagination does not at all come to the surface but keeps on weaving inside the mine of the soul, as Hegel puts it in his *Lectures on Aesthetics*. To which Ernst Bloch responds in *The Spirit of Utopia* that nothing being turned outside and everything remaining inside must not stay that way. Turning the inward out and thereby bringing the outward inside is, he says, a central task of philosophizing when it interacts with art.

Such interaction has made itself felt since the era of Romanticism, and also earlier, in Mannerism and along its lines of descent from the late Gothic period. Let us stay with the branch of the fantastic and imaginative; after all, the other one was striving for a philosophy of nature from which the fantastic was to be ushered out—soberness instead of exuberance. This is where we find the counterpart of the imagination, the act of being on the side of the real world, instead of wildly roaming fancy informed only by its own imaginative working.

Nevertheless, it remains clear that the naturalistic, once brought to representation, i. e., not staying inside the mine, also requires much imagination in terms of materials, tools, motives, etc. Imagination thus works in both ways, toward the natural and toward the fantastic. This can be clearly seen in the Gothic cathedral of Notre Dame in Paris. On the Western façade, above the portal, the gallery of realistically and individually sculptured kings can be admired. The gargoyles, however, show the fantastic world of demons, reminiscent of the demonology of the pillars and column capitals of the Romanesque period. This demonology did not recede from the realm of imagination with the advent of the Gothic period.

And now, with the fantastic, yet another division into two branches emerges, partly directed against one another and set to collide. What is meant here is the separation between, and opposition of, the eerie fantastic and the blissful fantastic. Just think of the late Middle Ages in the work of Hieronymus Bosch with the *Garden of Earthly Delights* in confrontation with the pictures of Hell. This separation and opposition of the blissful and the eerie fantastic returns again in Mannerism and then in Romanticism. In the case of the latter, there even is a special term for it: Black Romanticism. But there also are, e.g. in Caspar David Friedrich's painting *The Abbey in the Oakwood* (01), instances of coincidence of the blissfully uplifting with the eerie fantastic.

But let us once again return briefly to the separation-opposition relationship in Mannerism. Here, too, we find leanings toward the natural and toward the fantastic combined in the visual-art works. These works produce an extremely heightened naturalism through descriptive geometry

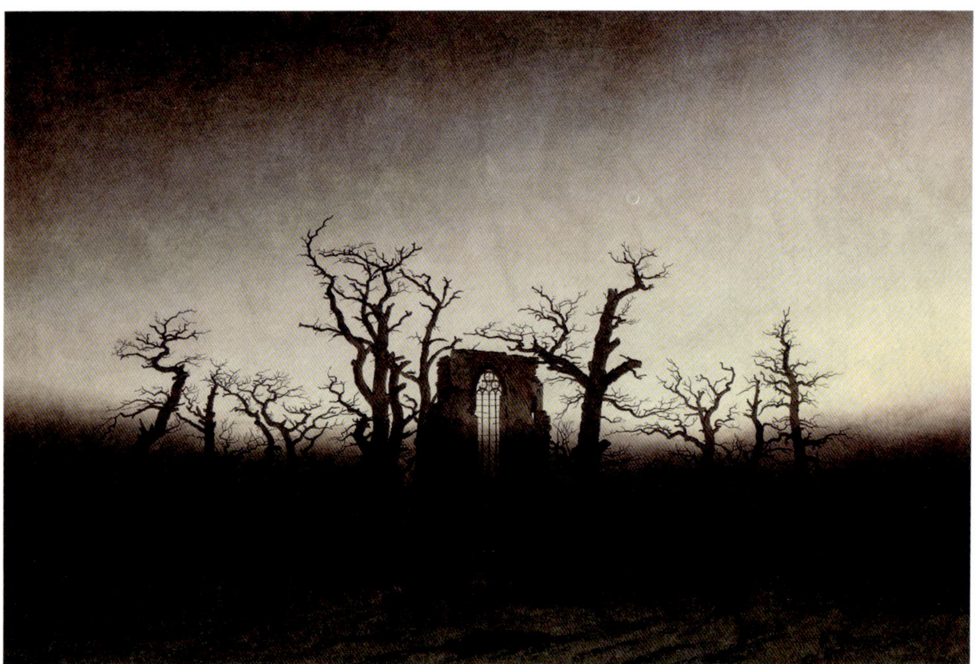

01
CASPAR DAVID FRIEDRICH
The Abbey in the Oakwood,
1809/10
Nationalgalerie, Staatliche Museen zu Berlin

but also, and in the same way, phantasms beyond compare.

The eerie-demoniac fantastic in particular is usually preceded by societal catastrophes, as the late Gothic period was by wars involving large numbers of mercenaries, the lansquenets. Mannerism again was preceded—or rather accompanied—by the Thirty-Years' War with its monstrous atrocities. Romanticism emerged at the time of the Napoleonic wars or the wars against the French Revolution.

As a remark on the side, in the case of Mannerism, there is yet another central condition that applies: the development of optical technology—a prerequisite for the representation of extreme naturalisms.

And there is yet another note to be made before we can return to the main strand of the argument. It refers to the entire process of aesthetic development throughout the Romantic period up until late Romanticism. Among other things, the process undercuts the absolute claim of positivist-oriented naturalism, according to which only that exists which is somehow accessible to our faculty of visual perception. Against this, Romanticism contends that what our realm of imagination, our fantasies, produce does exist as well. Romanticism therefore does not repudiate the naturalism of science with its waking consciousness, it only resists making it absolute. And it does so with the hypothesis of the actual existence of our dreams, be they fearful, nightmarish, or happy, whose parts and elements are taken from the waking conscious perception of a scientific mentality after all. Romanticism wants to bring both together, the waking world and the world of dreams. Related and similar processes take place against the background of the horrors of the First World War, which, being a battle of material, had turned out entirely different from any of the wars before. Yes, the chances of winning were assessed by the firepower of the artilleries, and no longer by the number of troops.

From the entirely different character of that war, Walter Benjamin inferred a different mode of experience and reaction for the human who, running back and forth between his apparatuses, was still needed to switch buttons on and off to open or

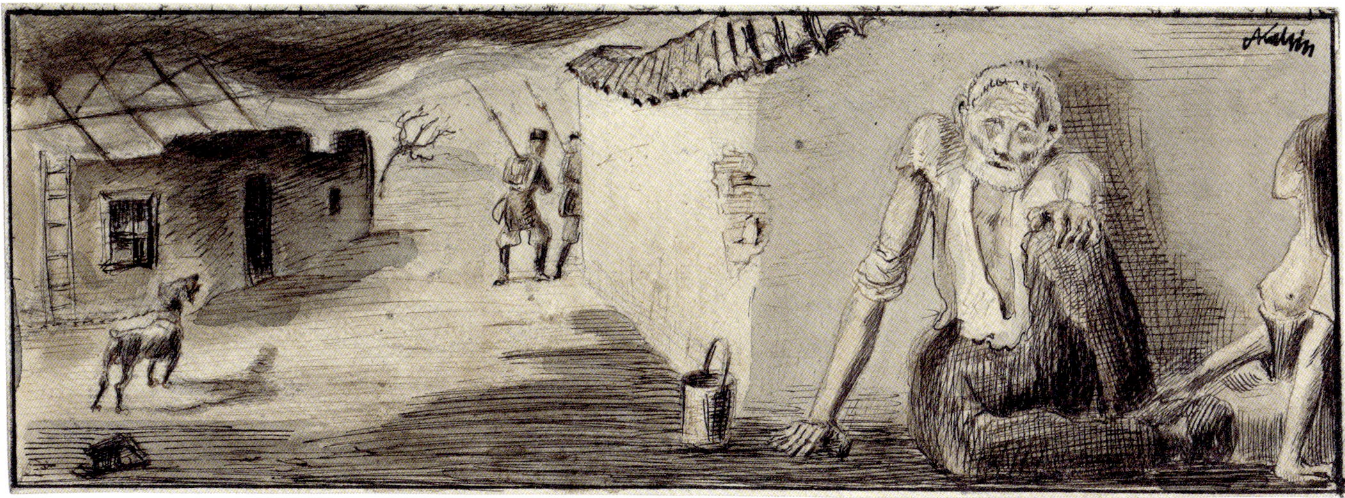

cease fire: immediate reactions without much consideration, without much engagement of the intellect, at the split of a second. Benjamin calls this the experiential and action modes of the destructive.

The processes indicated before as being related to this of the Romantic period developed from metaphysical and then Magic Realism through Surrealism all the way to Fantastic Realism, which sought to revitalize, and give topicality, to the Surreal after World War II.

What was there for Austria to pick up on when its artists were having so many difficulties, for example, with Concrete Art in the Bauhaus spirit? Eventually, though, with the turn from the concrete to the informal, Art informel, the concrete came to appeal to the anarchic sense of the Austrian spirit after all. It brought on the non-committal and brought out an entertaining and happy side. One must not forget that sudden reversals into happiness are inherent in everything mournful and melancholic. This is most strongly felt in the beginnings of modern-era music, e. g. in Claudio Monteverdi's madrigals. This is a strain, though, that continues to run through melancholic fantasies, musical and visual, from Gustav Mahler and Concrete Art up until Marc Chagall. Both the melancholic and the horrific can probably not be represented without it. It is something that crime writers know, particularly Edgar Allan Poe, but let's not forget Conan Doyle, Georges Simenon, and Agatha Christie either.

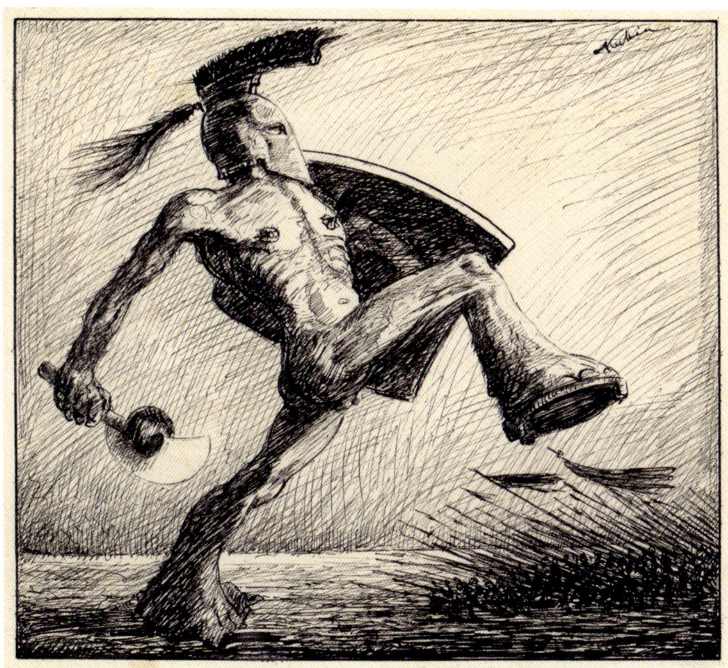

02
ALFRED KUBIN
War Scene, c. 1900
Private Collection, Austria

03
ALFRED KUBIN
The War, 1907
Städtische Galerie im Lenbachhaus und Kunstbau München

Everything said here on the subject of the historical structures of phantasms and the fantastic becomes particularly manifest in the work of Alfred Kubin, more so than with other Surrealists, and before them, Mannerists and Romanticists. Those others had all probably been more focused on one structure of the fantastic or another, while with Kubin everything occurs next to, and inside of, one another. This may have to do with the fact that Kubin was an illustrator. In illustrations, as if they were texts, so much more can—beyond language—be "laid out" and interwoven. And also, Kubin's fantastic work is evocative of the factor of the historicity of those phantasms, above all the context of the horrific wars. With Kubin, it even is the nexus with that heinous new type of war (as explained above) which cast its dark shadows not only years ahead, but also back in time. After all, it was a time when an arms race was going on between the major European powers, which manifested itself in threatening gestures of parading displays of new arms. This suggested that what was coming was a war totally different from any previous one. But already the Thirty Years' War had brought horrifying innovation with huge armies of mercenaries instead of small battle forces of highly specialized knights.

It is not only the conditions of insane innovation in warfare that make Kubin's work comparable to the whole history of the phantasmagoric. Above all, it is the insistence on a structural efficacy of fantasizing beyond the natural. What does that mean? The work of this creative imagination consists in bringing forth the real from potentiality. For there is that "objectively real possibility" that Ernst Bloch always insisted on. The fantastic therefore is not at all about some never-never land but about steering efficacies within the real and the possible. From the bottomlessness, it puts in bottoms and

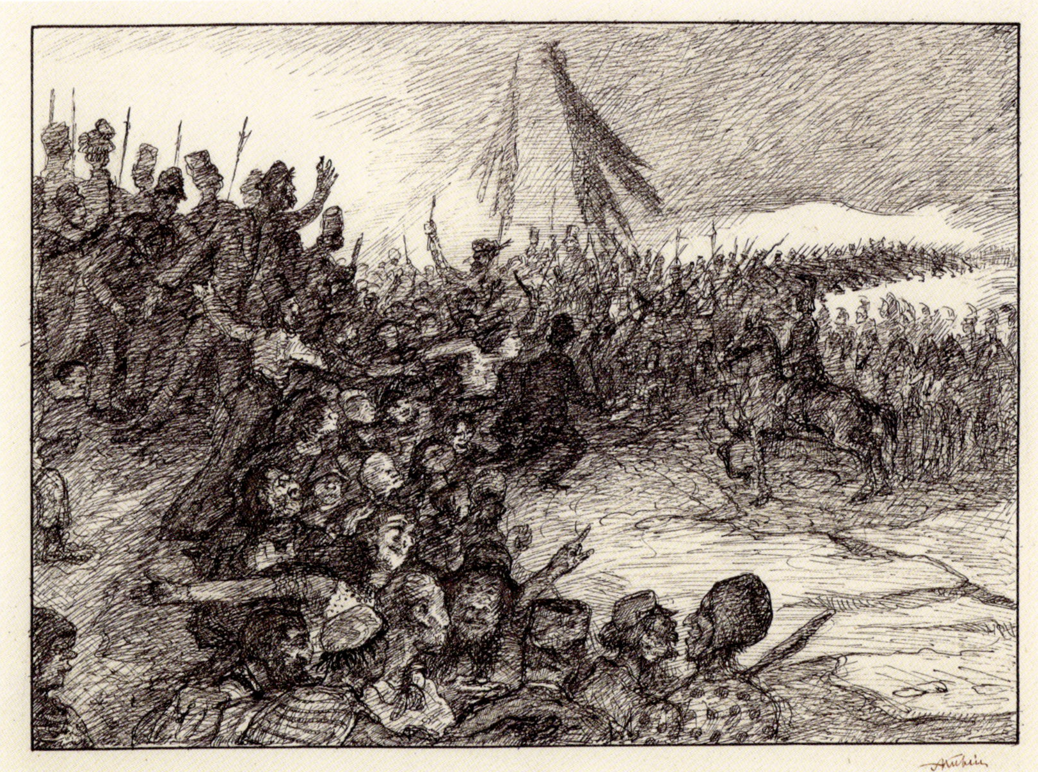

04
ALFRED KUBIN
Uprising, from the *Sansara* portfolio, 1909/10
Leopold Museum, Vienna

puts up ladders. Of course, Sigmund Freud's depth psychology has a say in this, too. Yet another point of comparison with the phenomenological and historical emergence of the fantastic in all of those times is found in Kubin's depictions of black apocalypse (04 & 05).

It so happens that from their horrors and dark views jubilant sounds of exaltation keep making themselves heard—successful moments, moments of visio beatifica. The confluence of visualness and musicalness also applies to the work of Kubin. His pictures convey to people with a synesthetic sense musical sounds (which is different from program music, which supplies acoustic picture contents). So it becomes necessary for music to have pictures added to it, whether it is done by the imagination of the listener, or by visual art, that is, through illustrations. This is also what art does for texts, namely, pictorializing them. Texts, of course, have contents, and reading them, these come visibly before one's eyes. It is something that every reader's imagination is capable of; nevertheless, there is much enthusiasm for graphic ornamentation, for illustrations by a foreign hand. Here, an interest for greater memorability through engagement of several perceptual senses comes in, considering the various translations in the act of reading. There is, first, visual registration, then combination into words and sentence structures, and then visualization through the imagination. If illustrations are compared, they are compared to the pictures of others who also engaged in this work.

And there is still another aspect not yet discussed about the subject, not even mentioned. It is the fact that, compared to the natural, which at least appears to be what meets the eye, phantasms—even if their individual parts were taken from the natural—appear alien. And to those who see it as alien, the alien seems exotic. Exoticism, however,

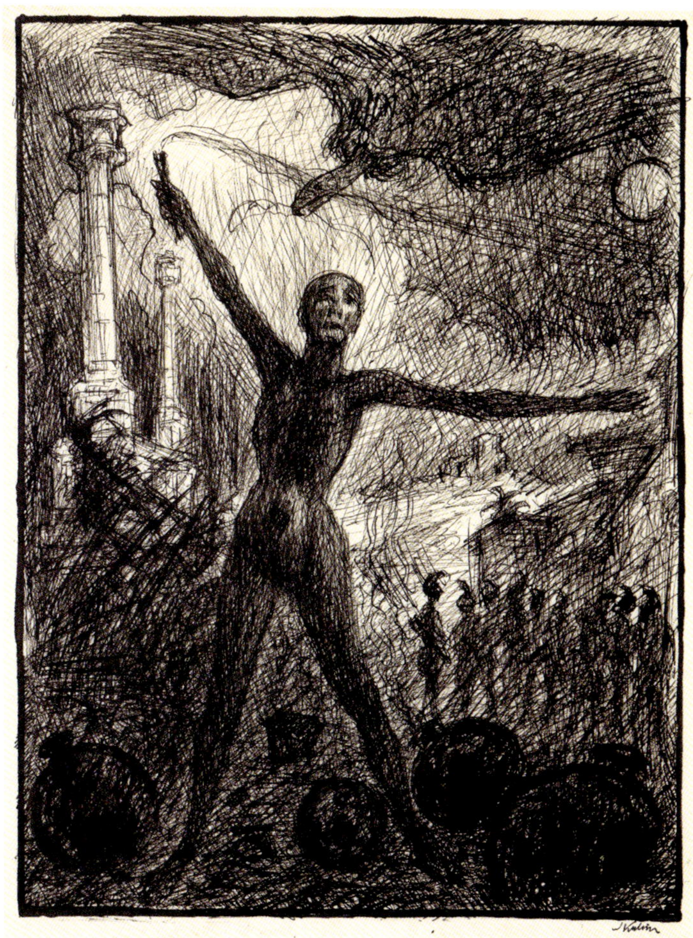

05
ALFRED KUBIN
Anarchy, c. 1918
Private Collection, Austria

is defined by double-facedness. What is exotic for others is not at all exotic to itself.

So, this brings us back to the many-facedness of Kubin's oeuvre whose pictorializations mostly run like a film, continually pushing each another, interchanging, complementing each other, or cutting each other short. What lies before the eye, the natural, then increasingly turns into the exotic, and to the dreamwalkers, the waking world appears exotic and alien. Let us now leave the text here, and with it, the diversions and digressions that we have gone through. And let the viewers of Kubin's works immerse themselves in their own mind games that engage them on walking though the exhibition, looking.

DREAM WORLDS

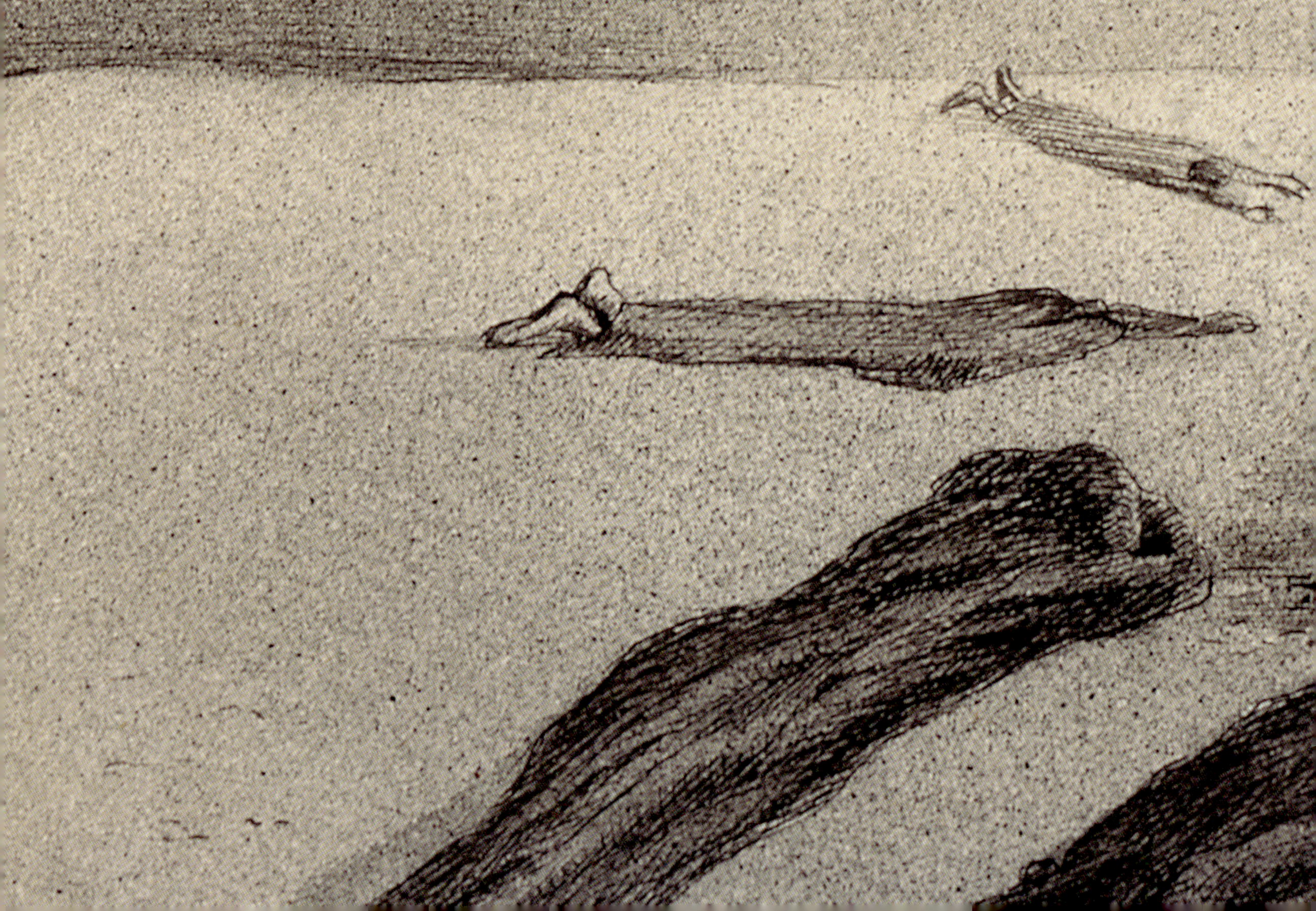

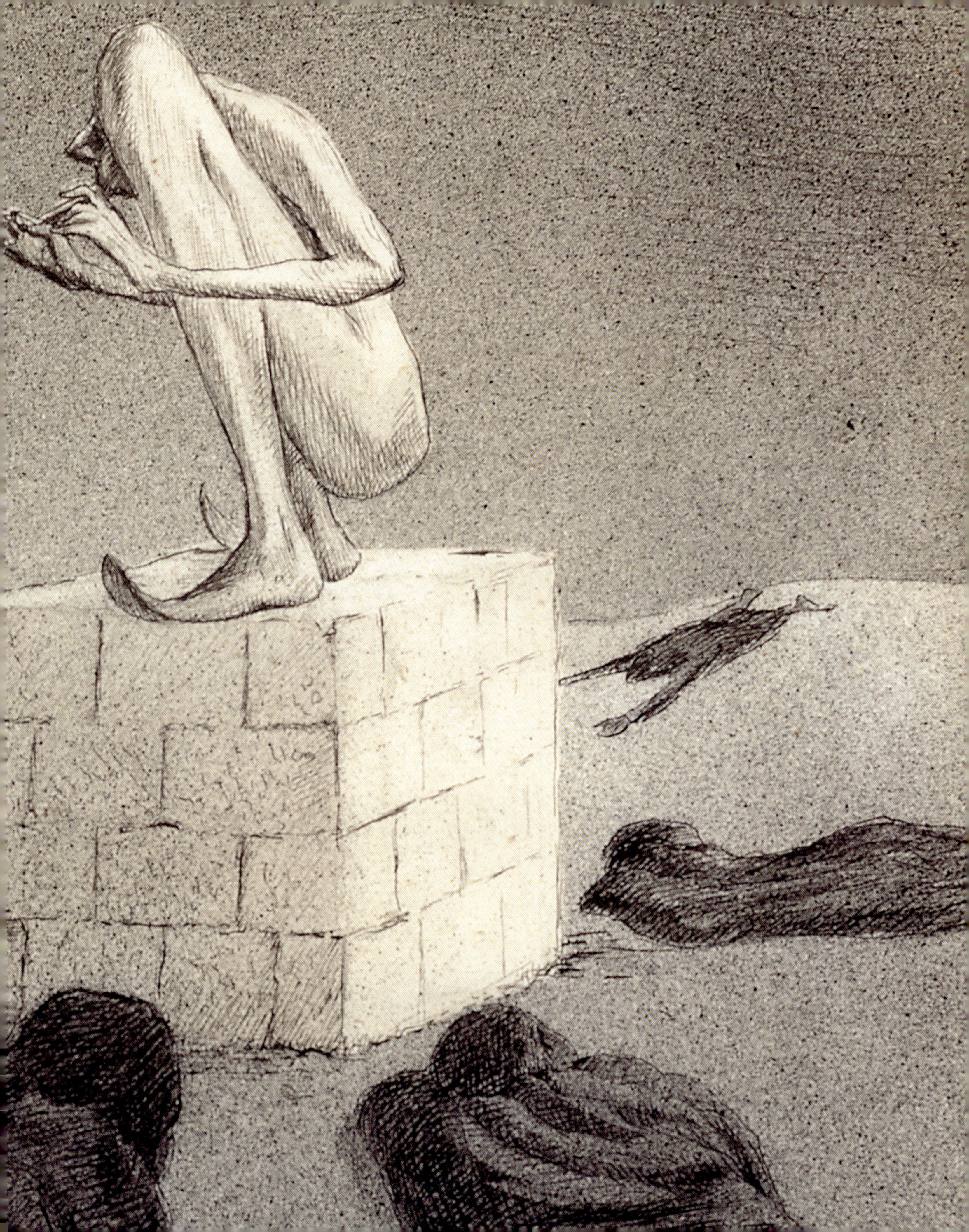

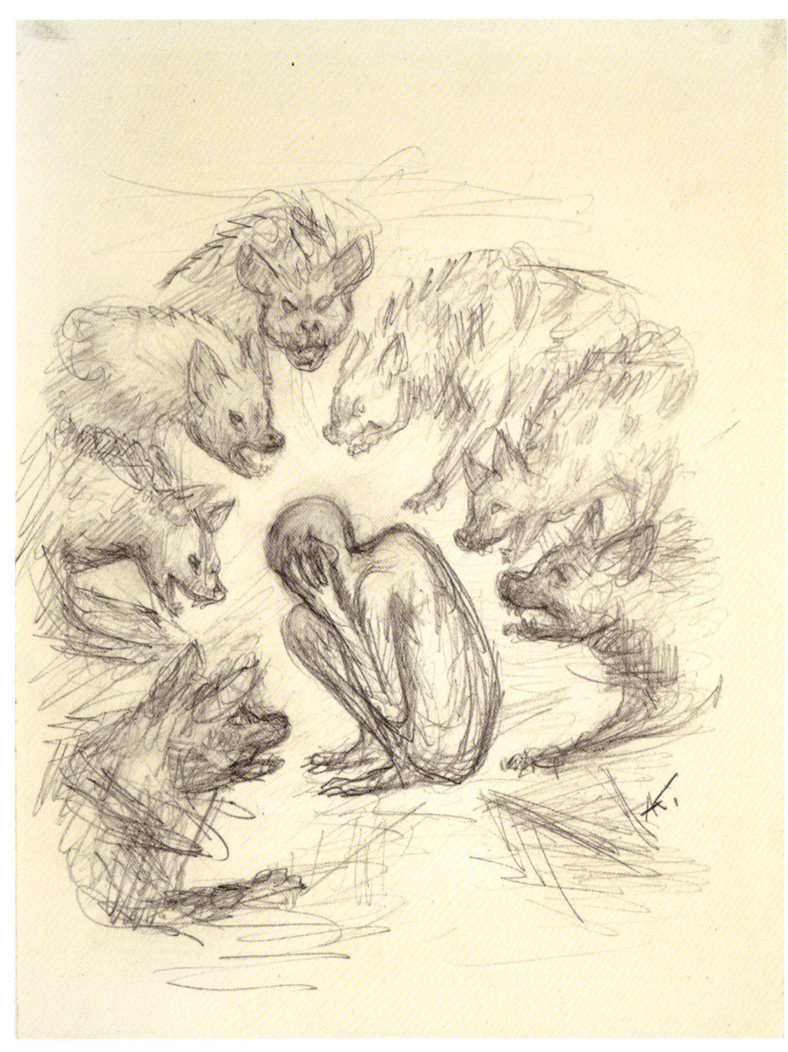

ALFRED KUBIN
Study for India ink drawing *Among Hyenas,* c. 1934
OÖ Landes-Kultur GmbH, Land Oberösterreich,
Graphic Collection, Günter Rombold Collection, Ha II 15877

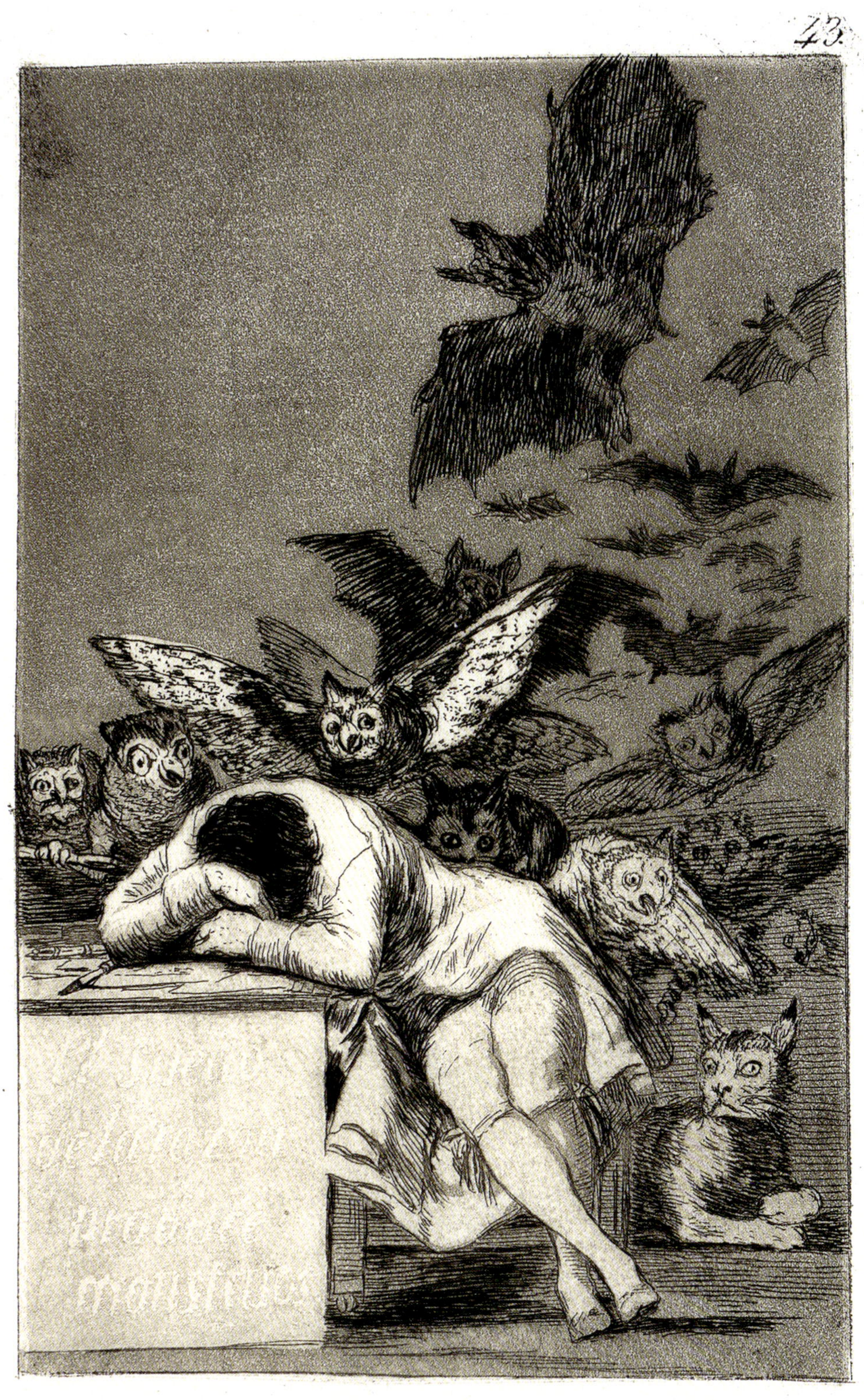

FRANCISCO JOSÉ DE GOYA Y LUCIENTES
The Sleep of Reason Produces Monsters, from the series *Los Caprichos*, c. 1799
OÖ Landes-Kultur GmbH, Land Oberösterreich, Graphic Collection, Ka II 634

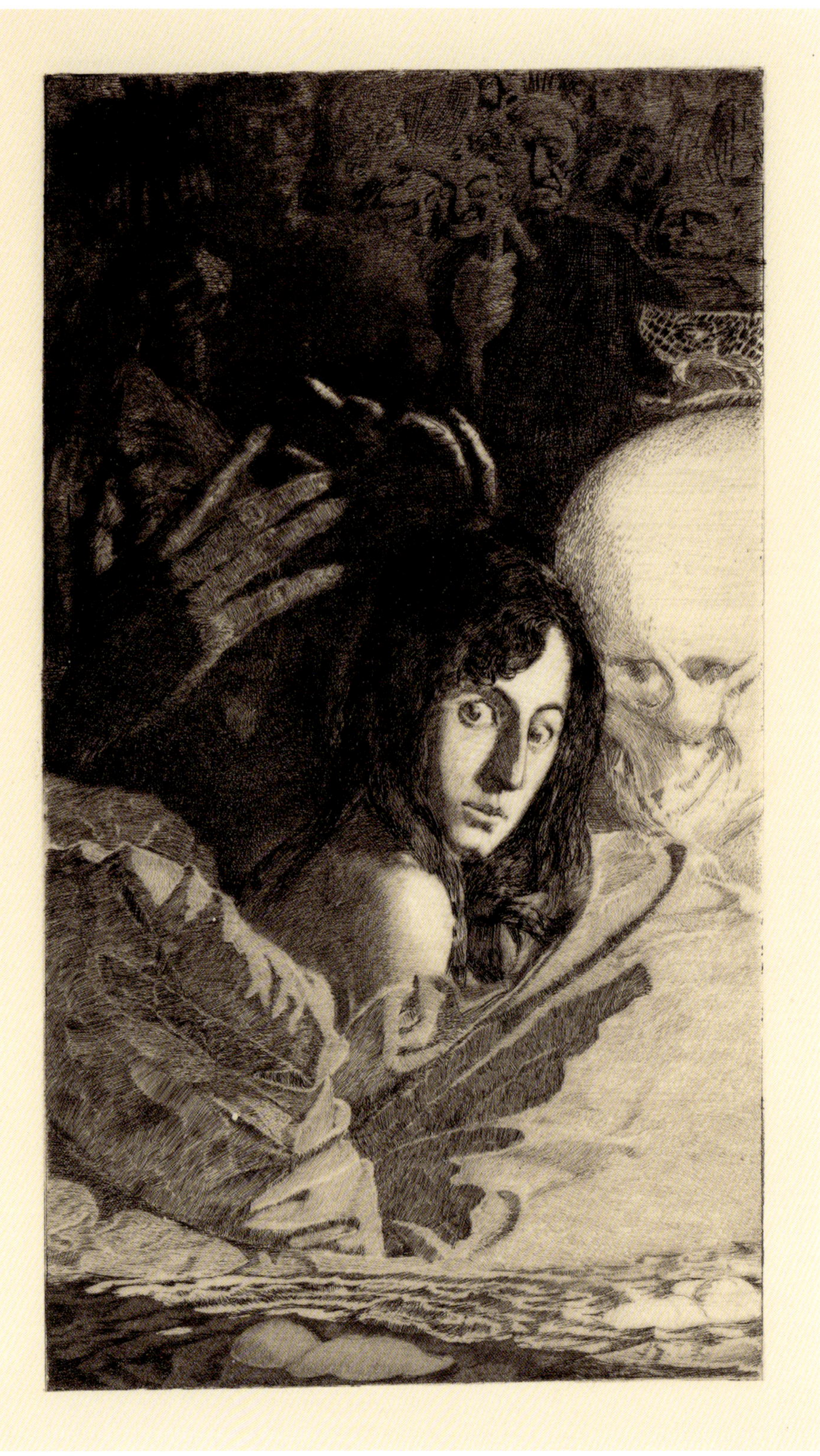

AUGUST BRÖMSE
The Dream, c. 1901
The Daulton Collection, Los Altos Hills, California

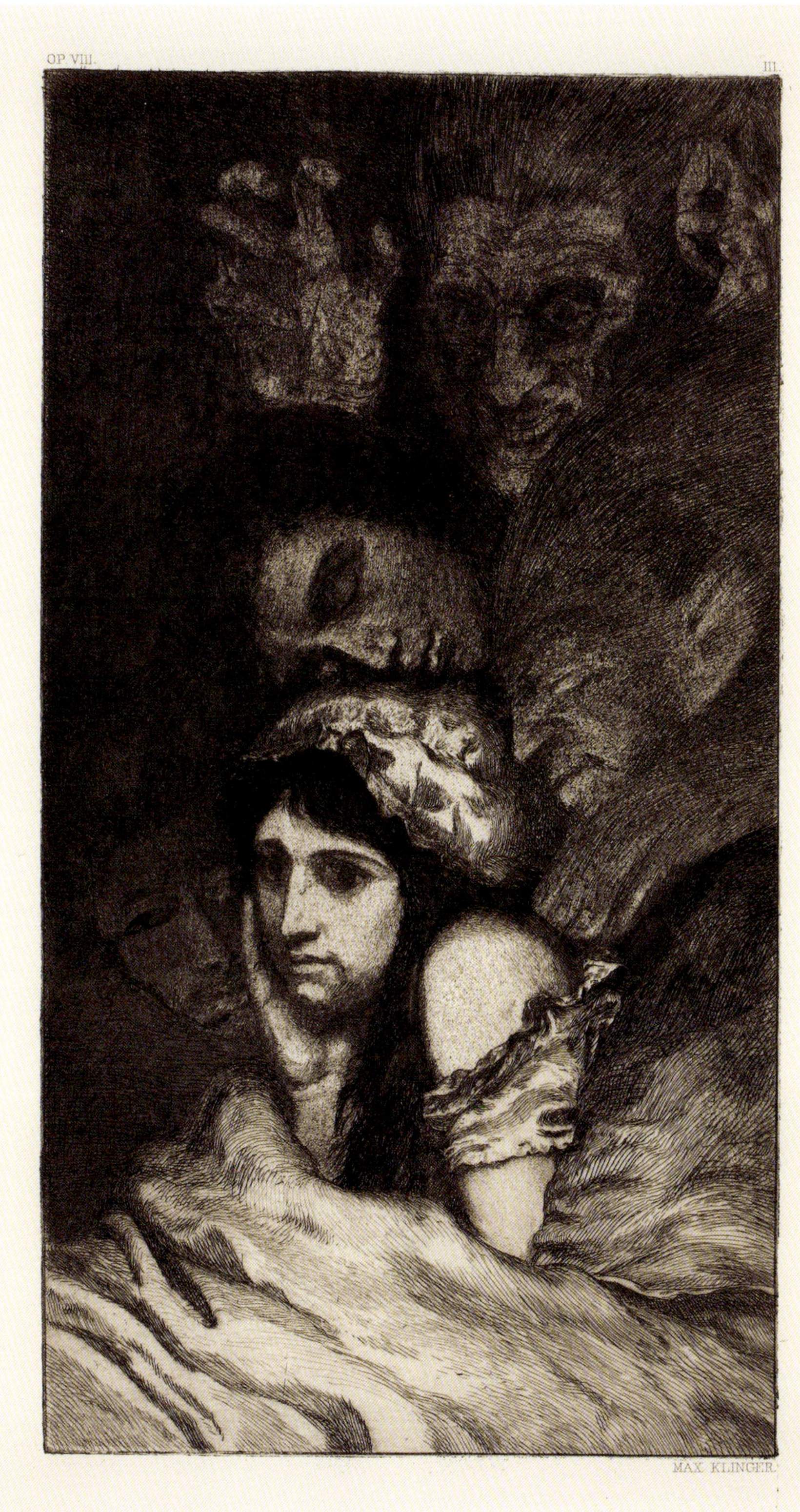

MAX KLINGER
Dreams, print 3 of portfolio *A Life*, between 1880 and 1884
LETTER Foundation, Cologne

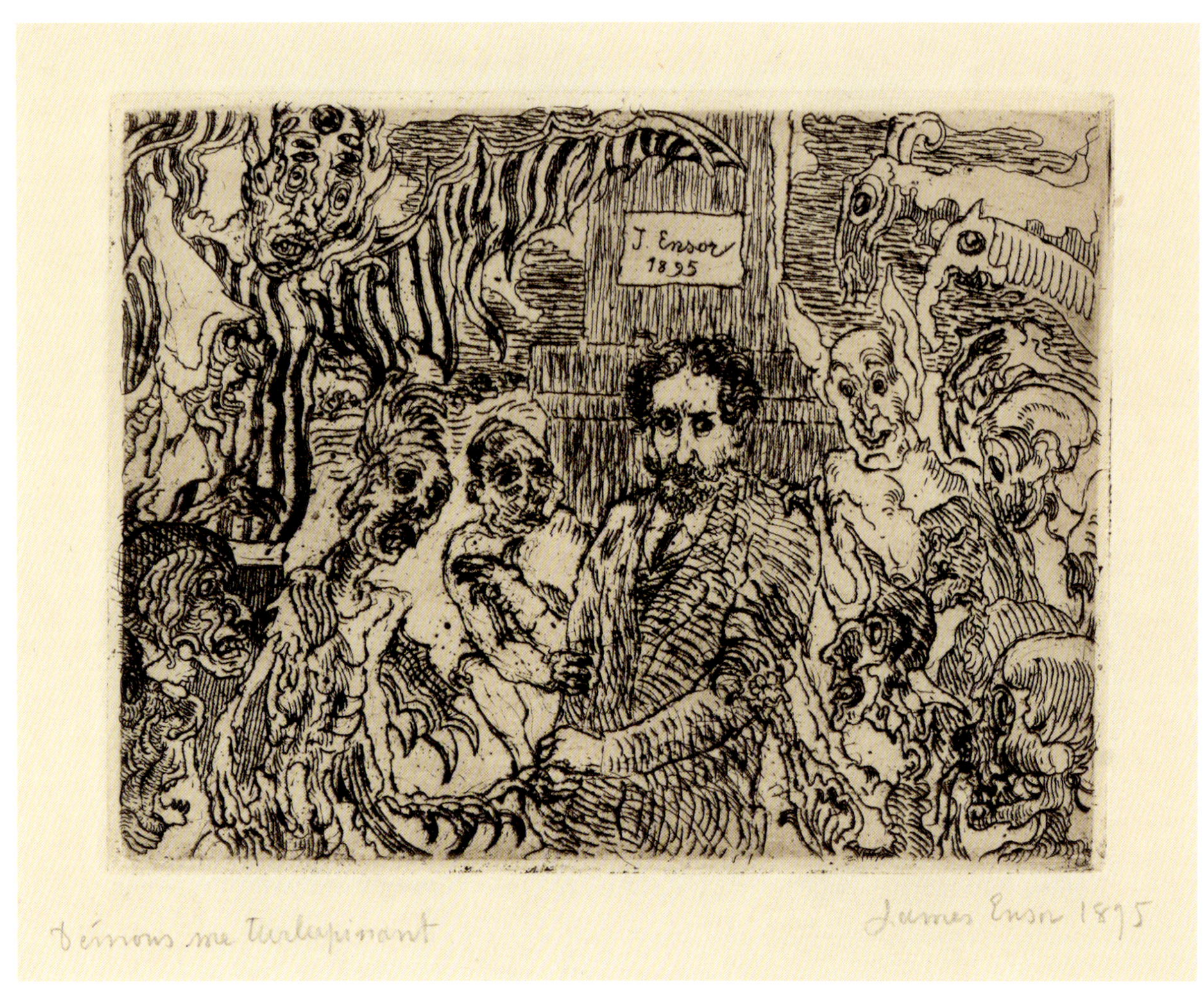

JAMES ENSOR
Demons Tormenting Me, 1895
Leopold, Private Collection

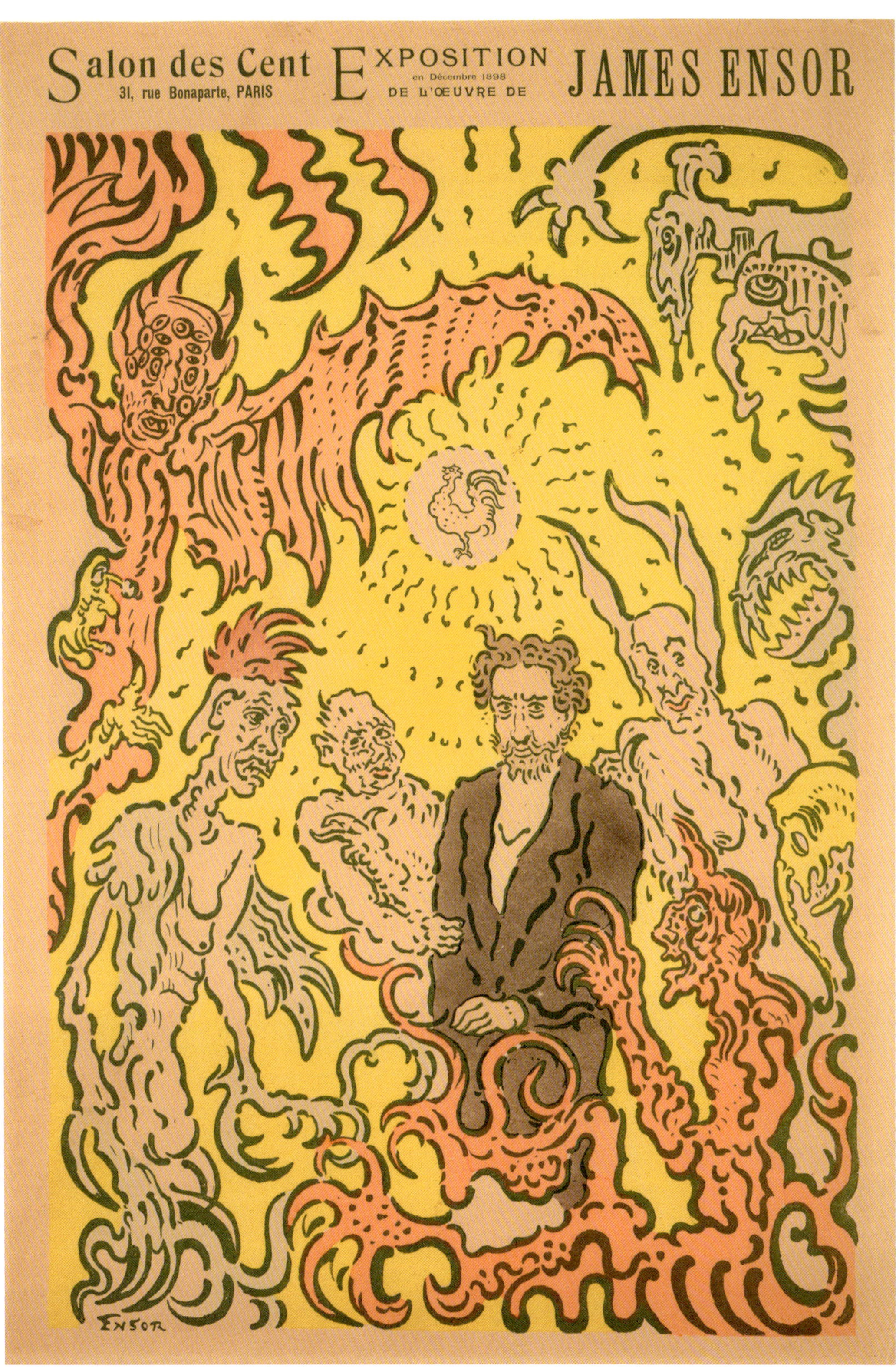

JAMES ENSOR
Self-Portrait, 1898
Klewan Collection, Munich

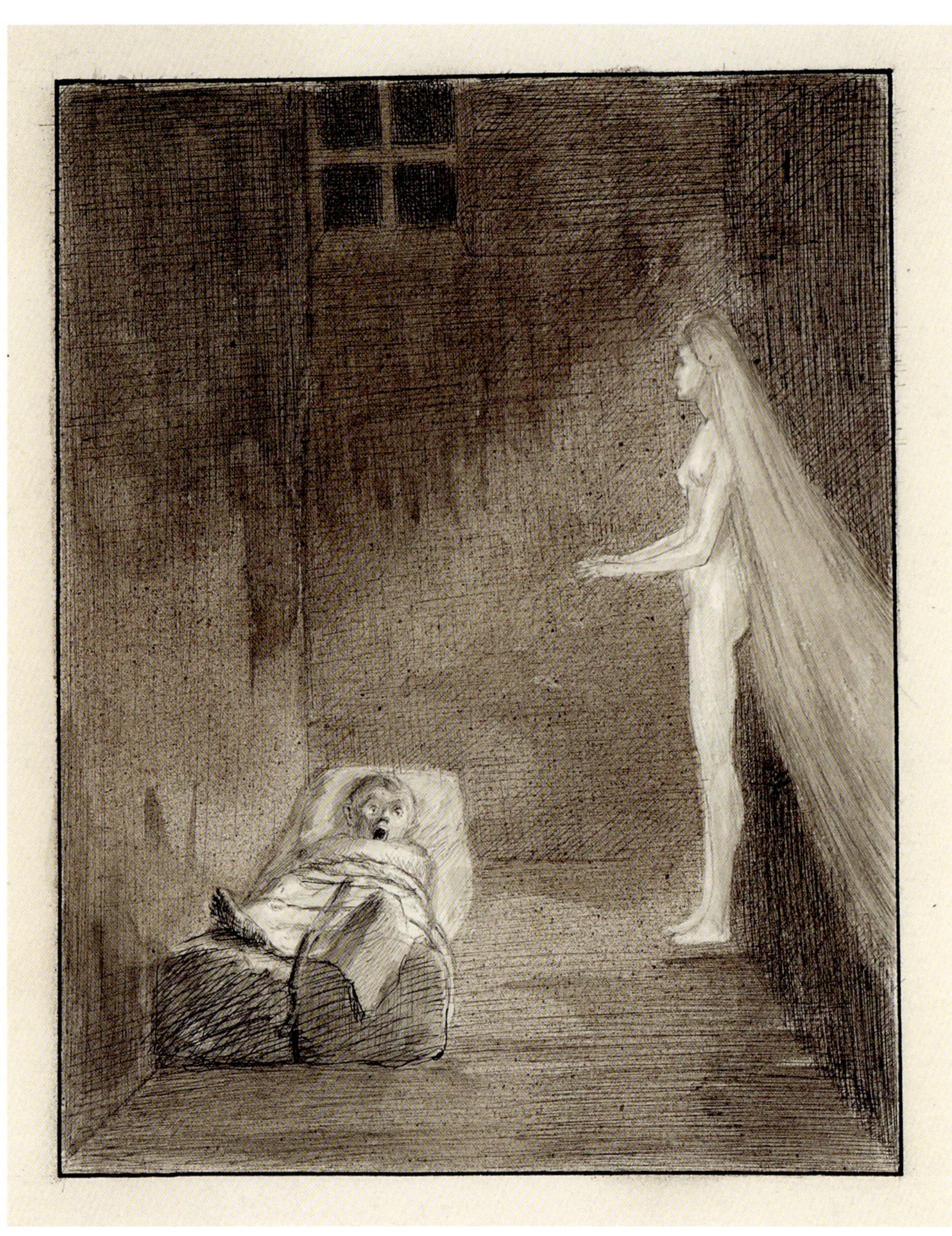

ALFRED KUBIN

The Prisoner's Dream, 1899

Städtische Galerie im Lenbachhaus und Kunstbau München

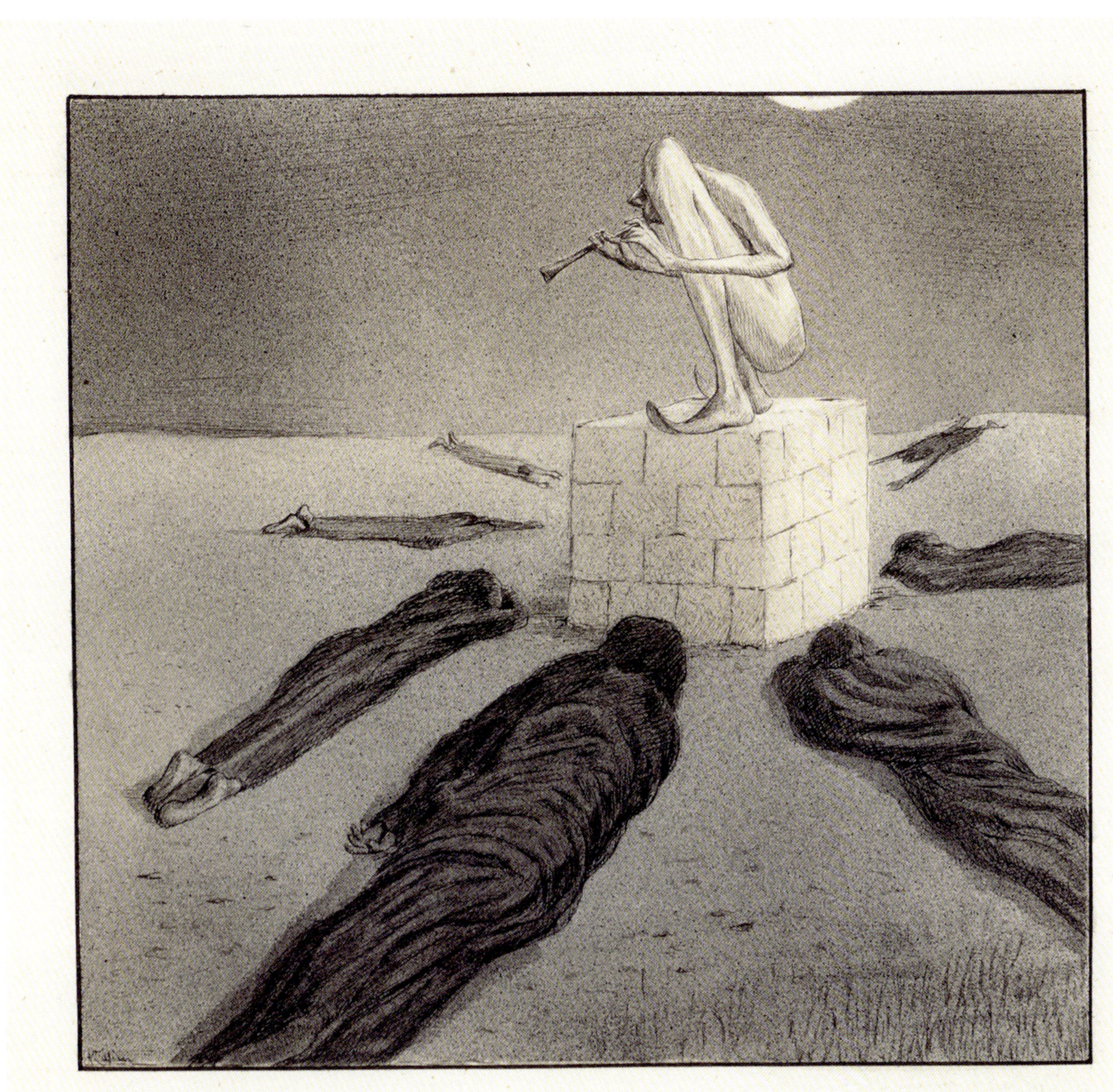

ALFRED KUBIN
Sleep, 1901/02
Leopold Museum, Vienna

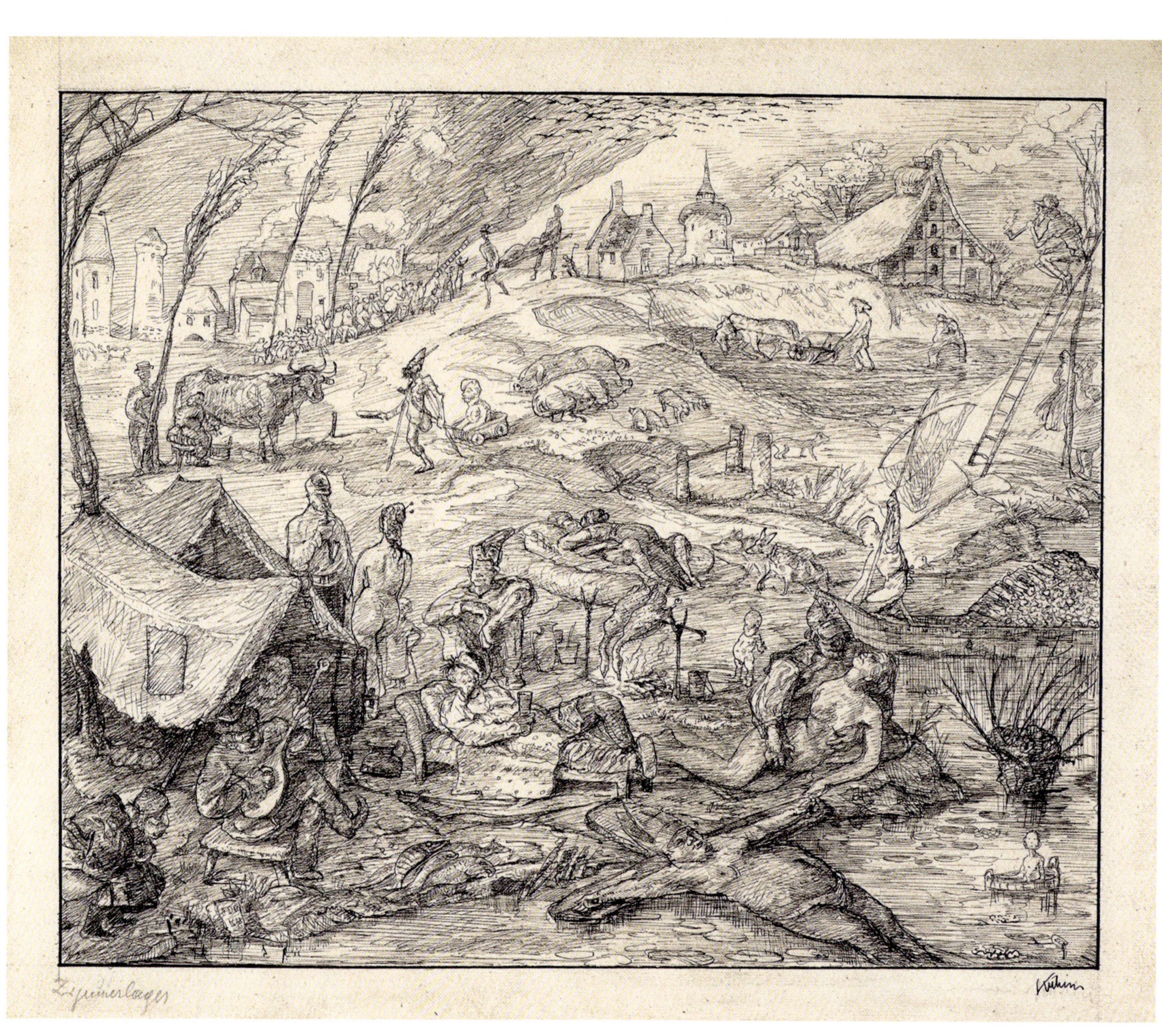

ALFRED KUBIN
Gypsy Encampment, 1909/10
Leopold Museum, Vienna

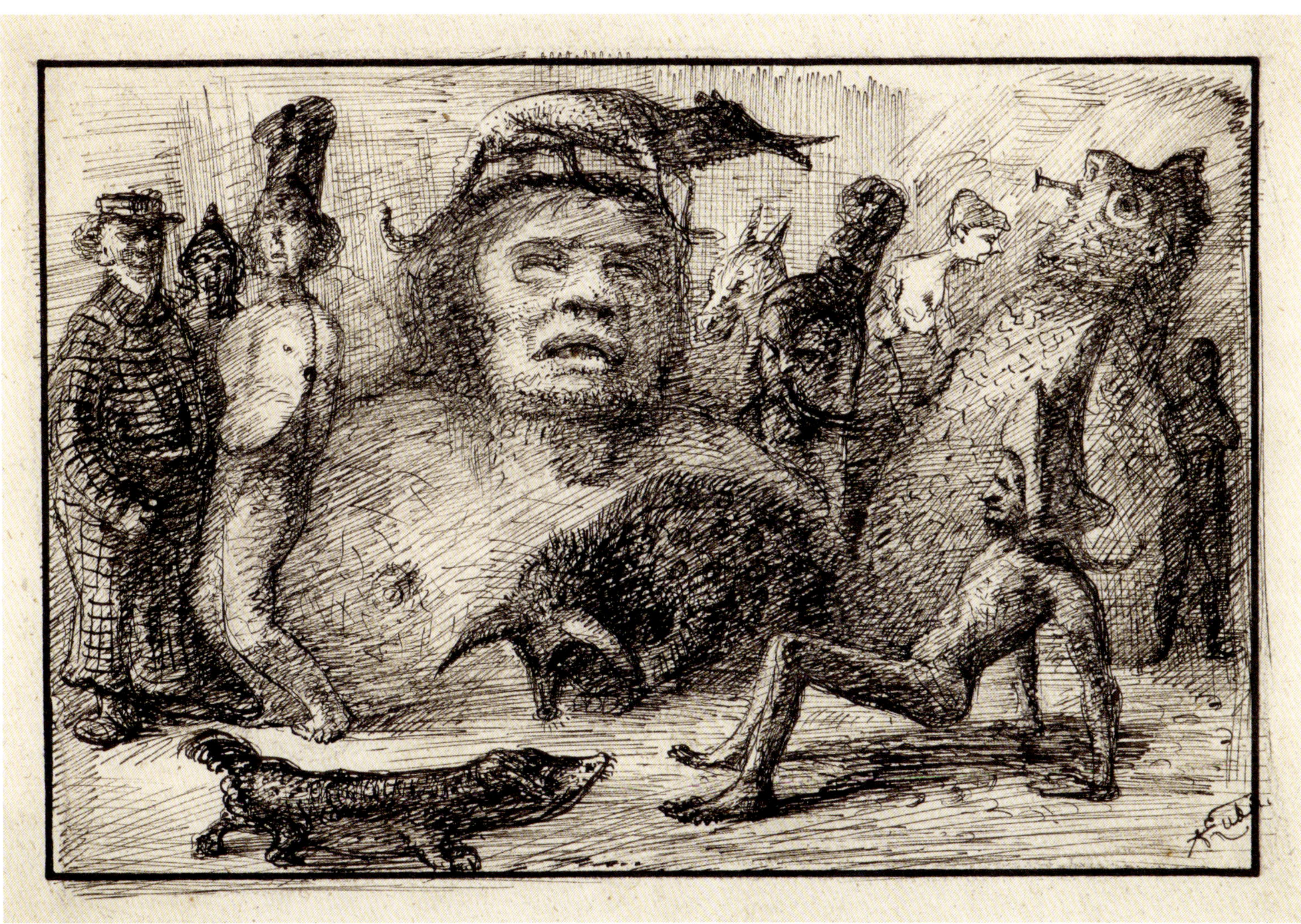

ALFRED KUBIN
Nightmare, 1899/1900
Leopold Museum, Vienna

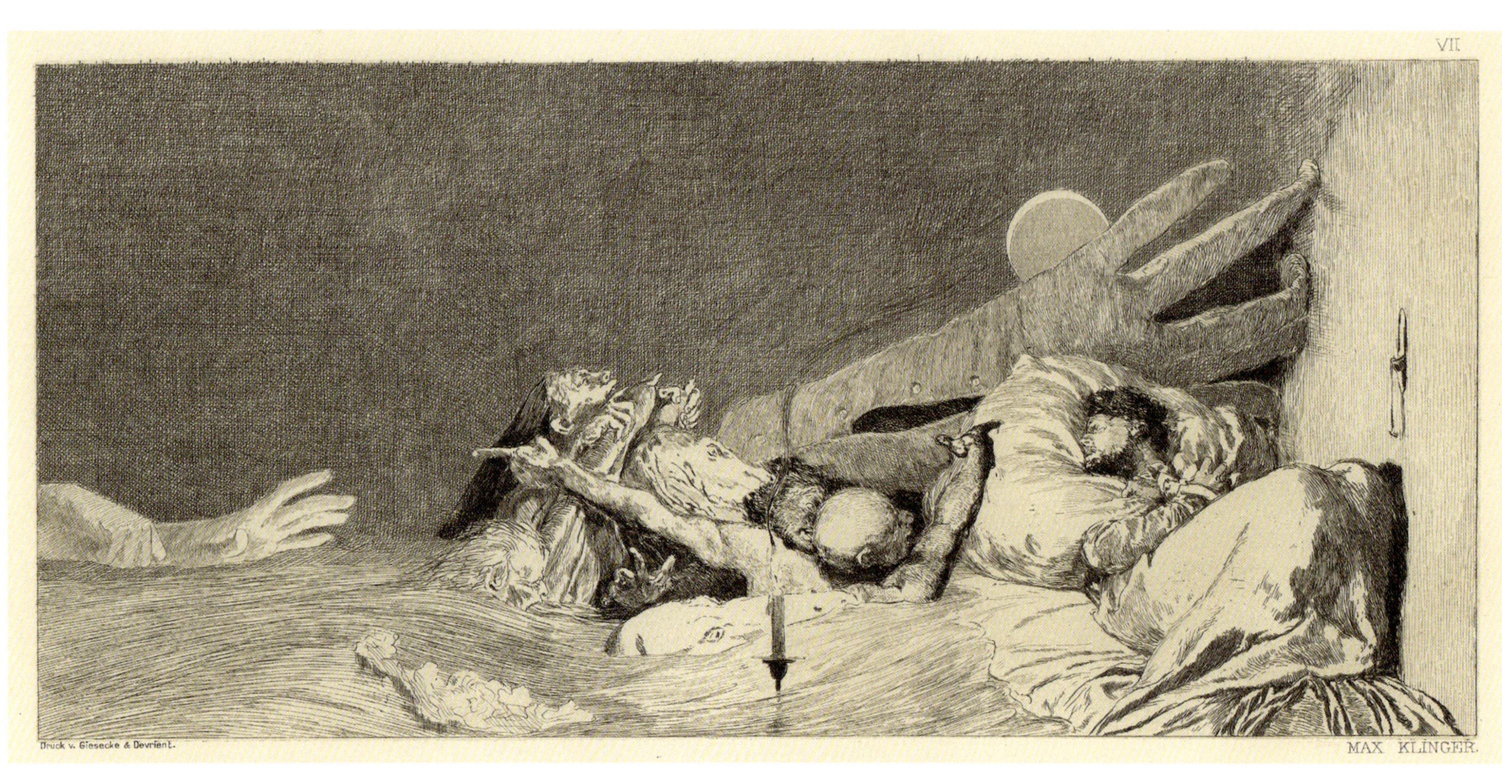

MAX KLINGER
Anxieties, print 7 of series *Paraphrase on the Finding of a Glove,* 1880 or 1881
LETTER Foundation, Cologne

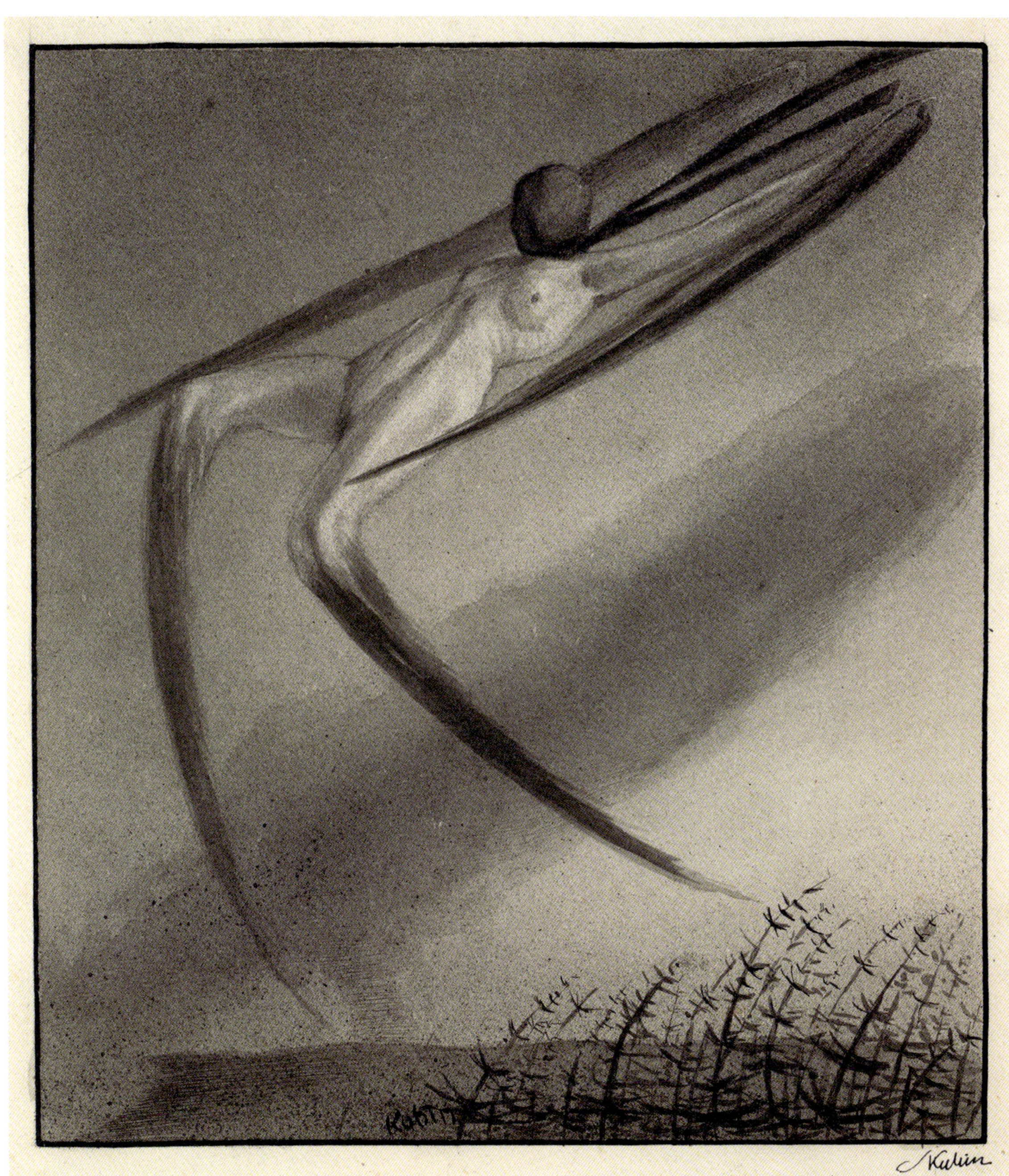

ALFRED KUBIN
Every Night a Dream Visits Us, c. 1902/03
Albertina, Vienna

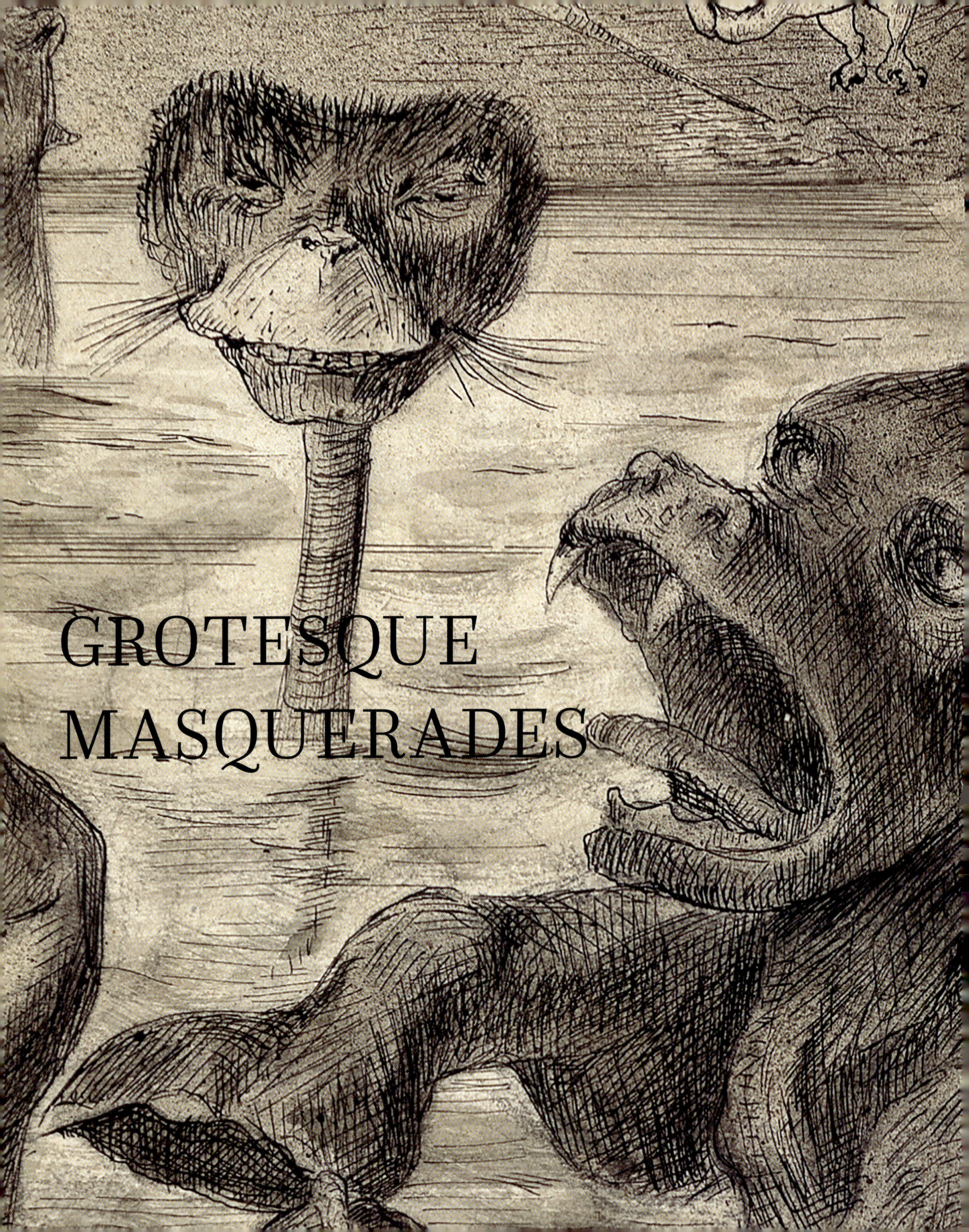

GROTESQUE MASQUERADES

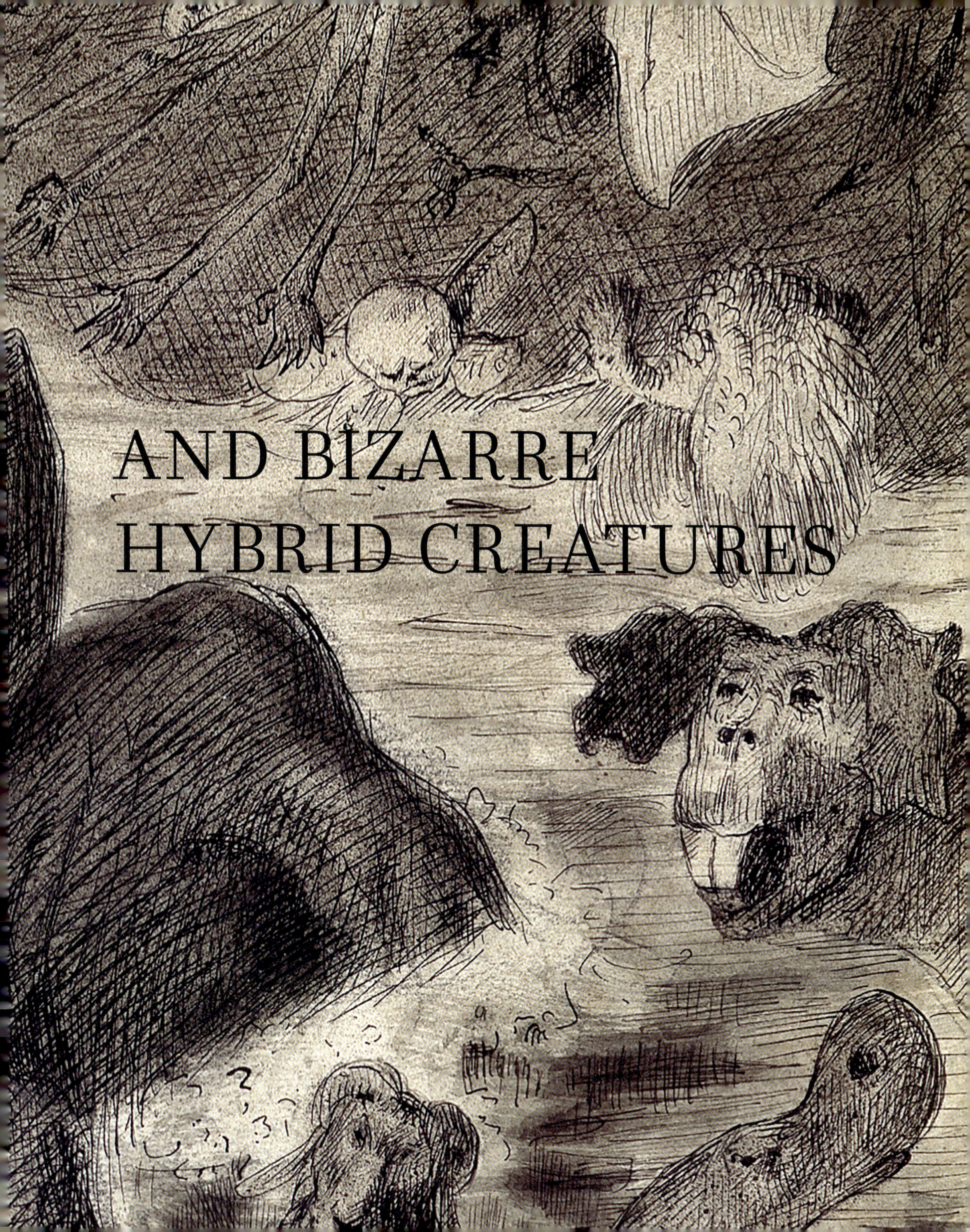

AND BIZARRE HYBRID CREATURES

THE GOOD LORD

The mocking—or at least the metaphorical and exposing ciphering—of prevalent societal forces, such as religion, capital, labor and state, is the theme of a series of works on paper from Kubin's early oeuvre. Here, it is God who is sitting enthroned over a landscape in the guise of an enormous scarecrow and is thus taken apart as a fetish. However, the monumental size of the figure, with processions of tiny people flocking towards it as in a pilgrimage, illustrates superior power—something which Kubin kept paying homage to in an ambivalent manner in his fantasies of impotence and power. The artist employed the caricature-like drawing of his early period as a deliberate stylistic device in these works on paper, while at the same time revealing his imagination's Biedermeier character and obsession with the past.

Annegret Hoberg

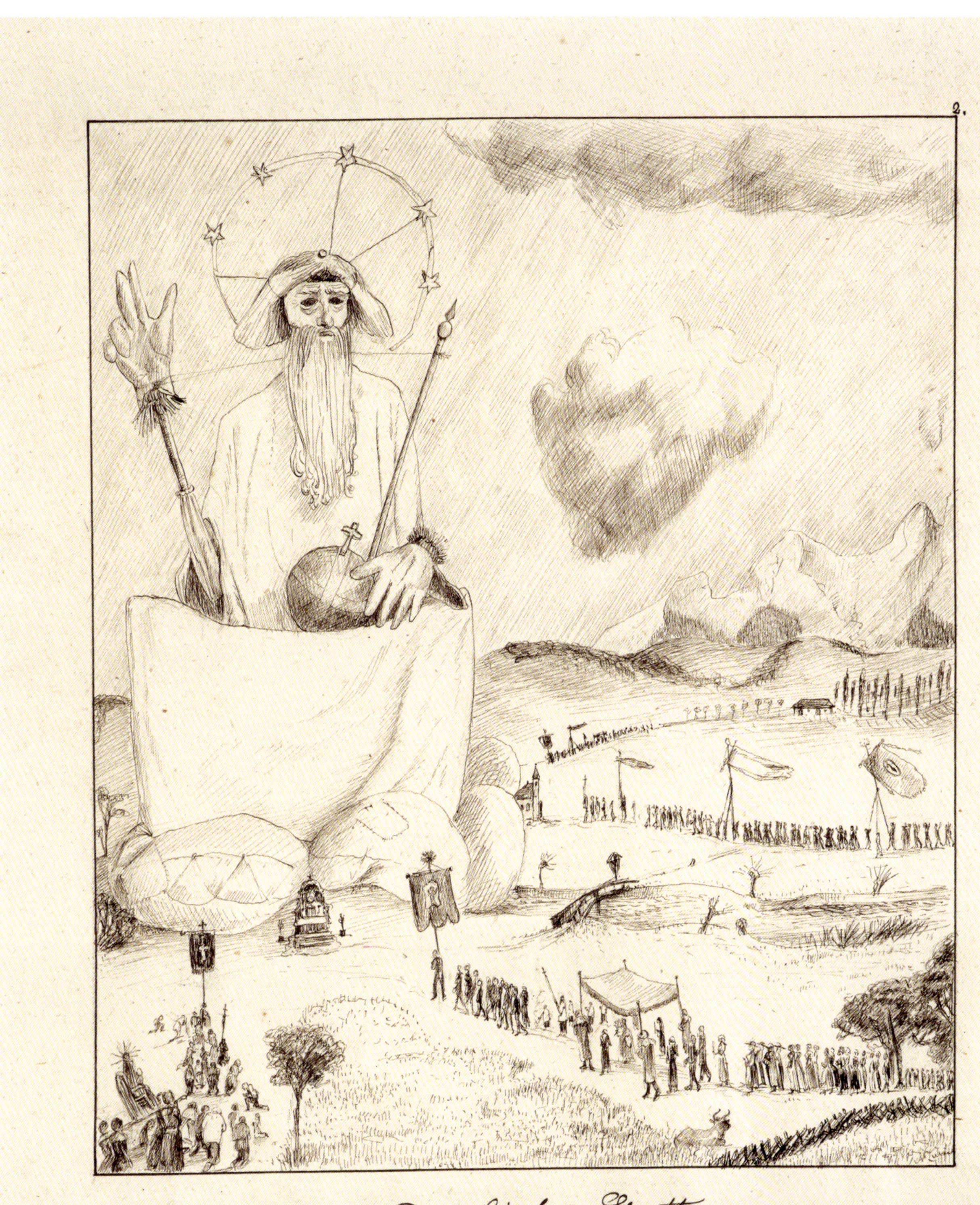

ALFRED KUBIN
The Good Lord, c. 1900
Leopold Museum, Vienna

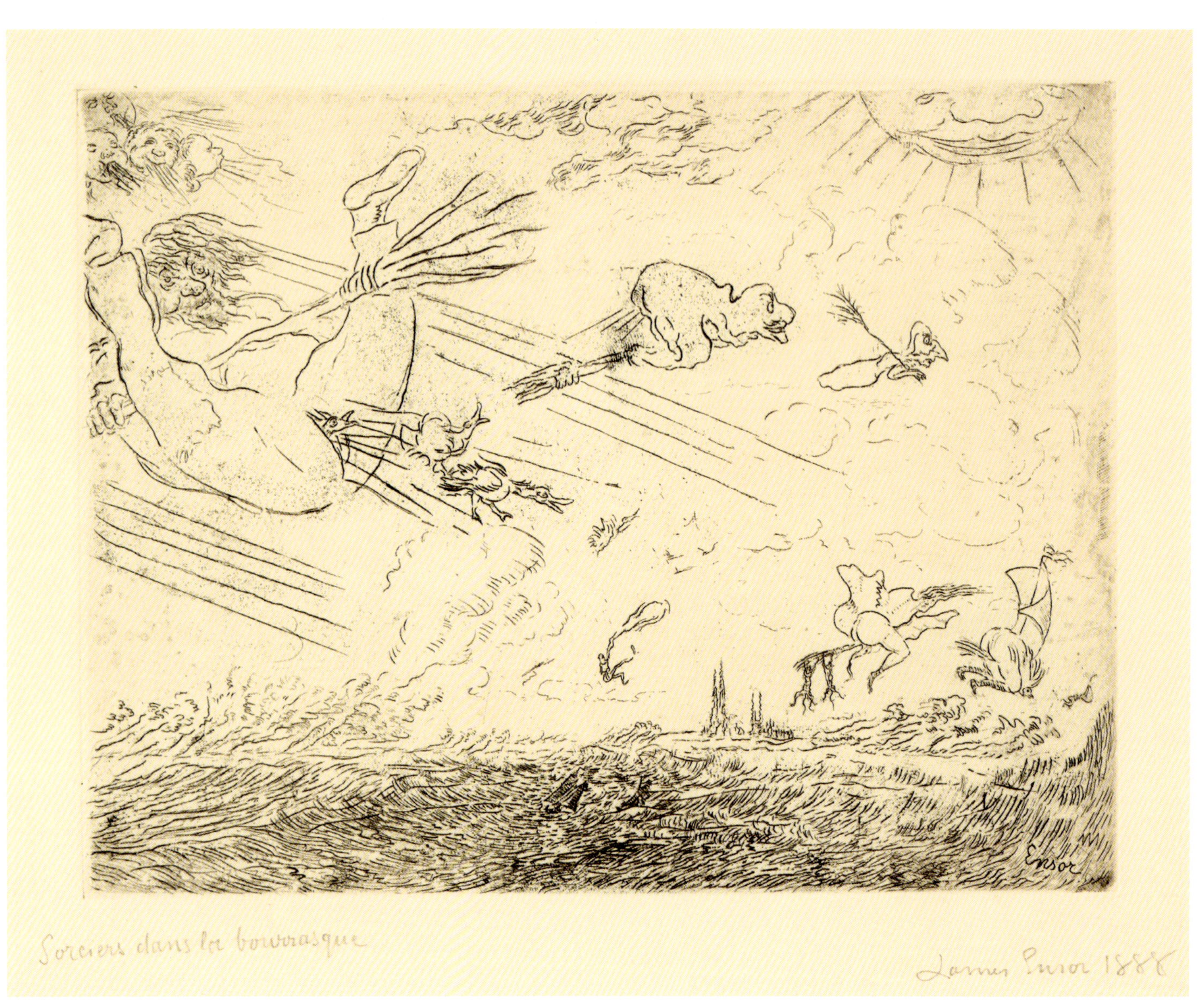

JAMES ENSOR
Wizards in the Wind, 1888
Leopold, Private Collection

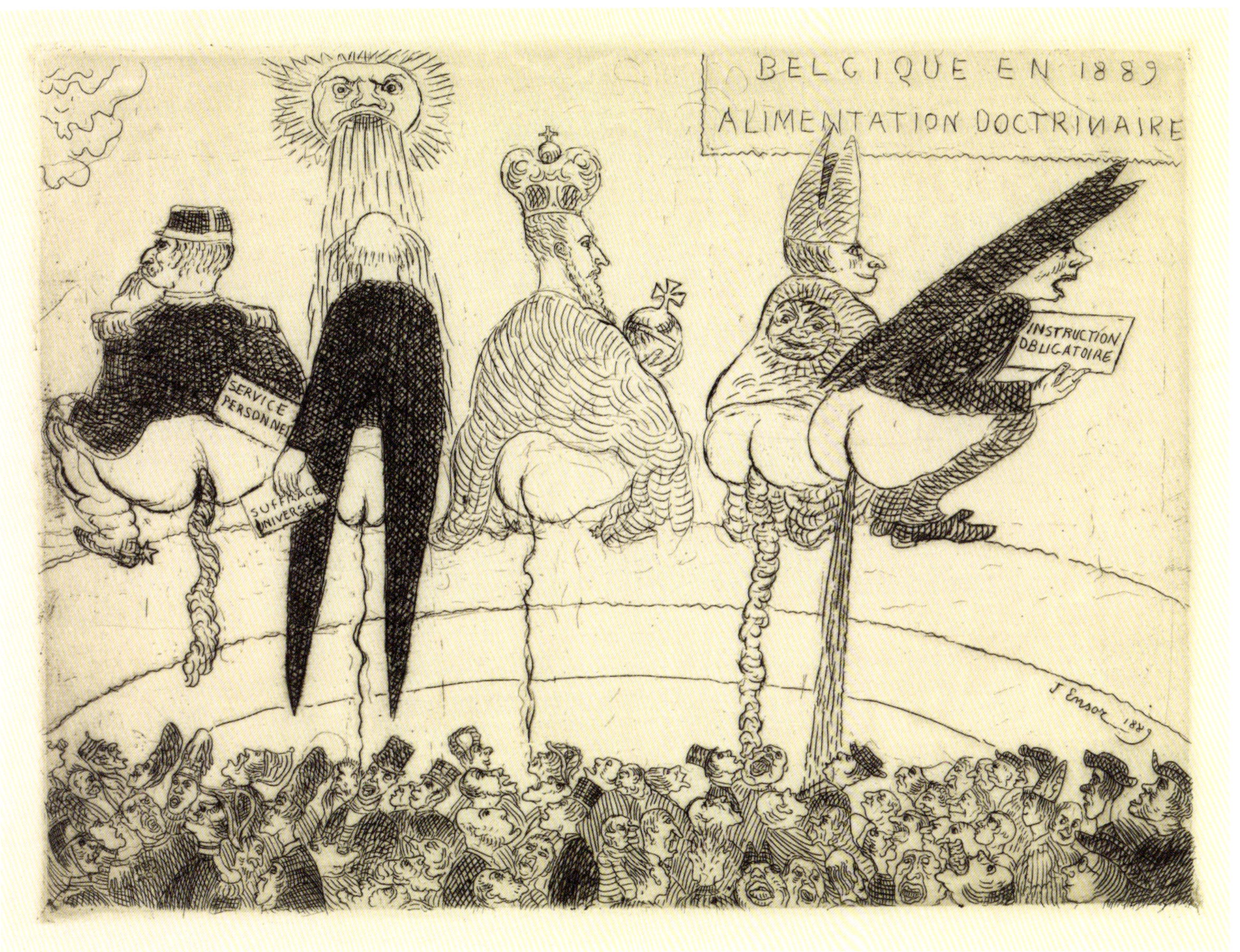

JAMES ENSOR

Doctrine Feeding, 1889

Museum voor Schone Kunsten, Gent (Belgium)

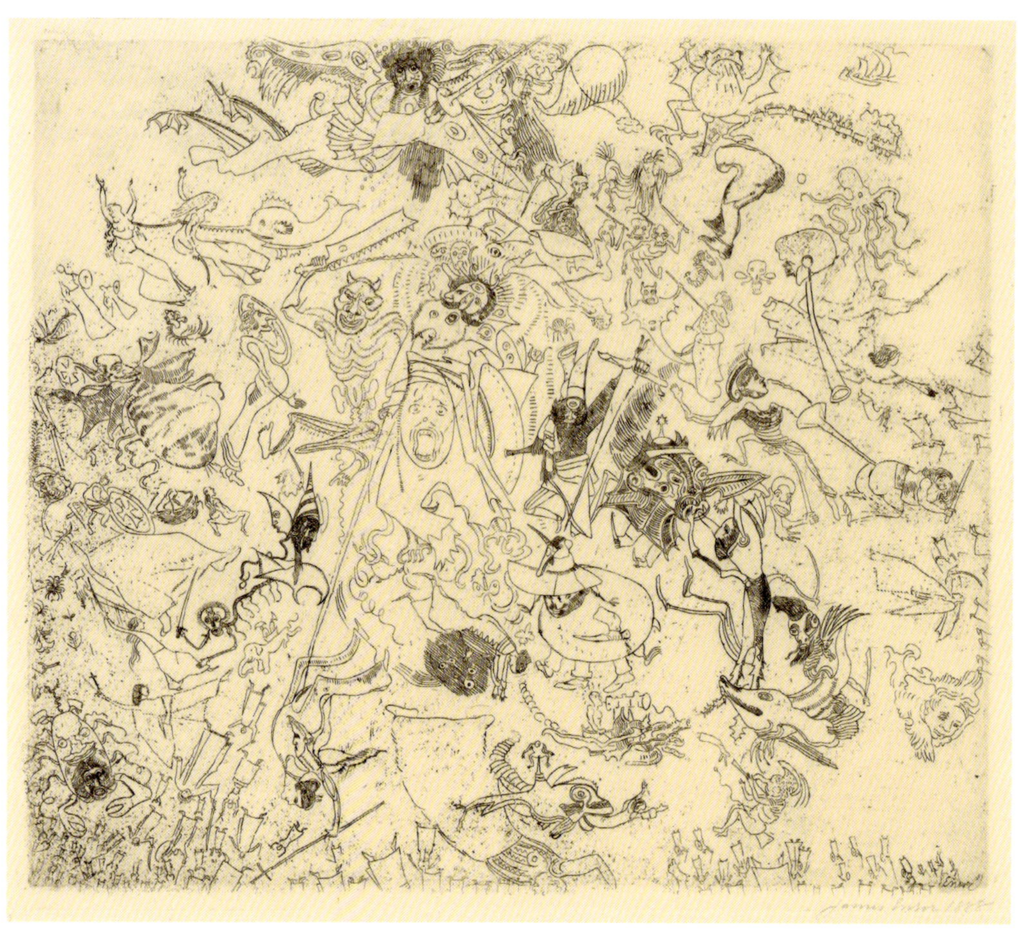

JAMES ENSOR
The Battle of the Demons, 1888
Albertina, Vienna

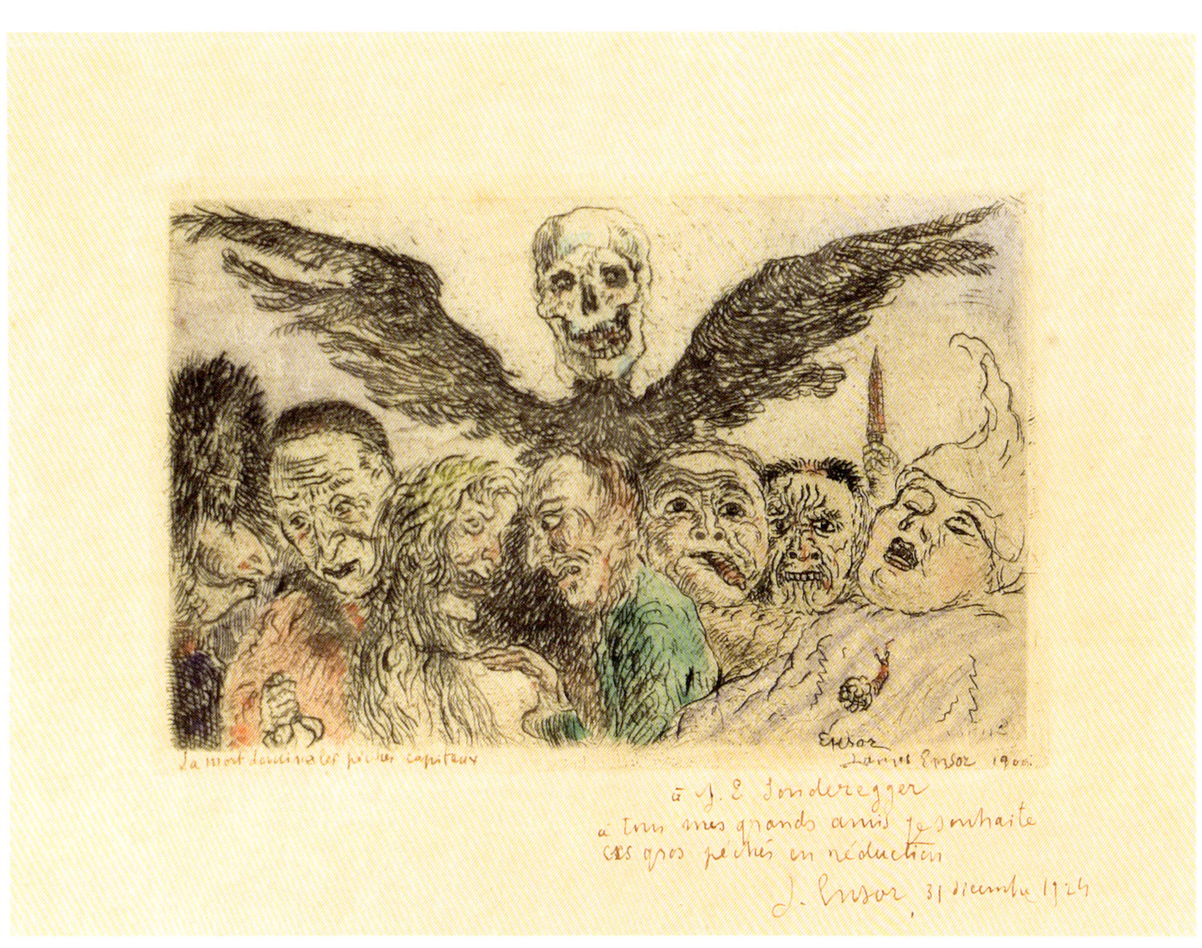

JAMES ENSOR
The Deadly Sins Dominated by Death, 1904
Leopold, Private Collection

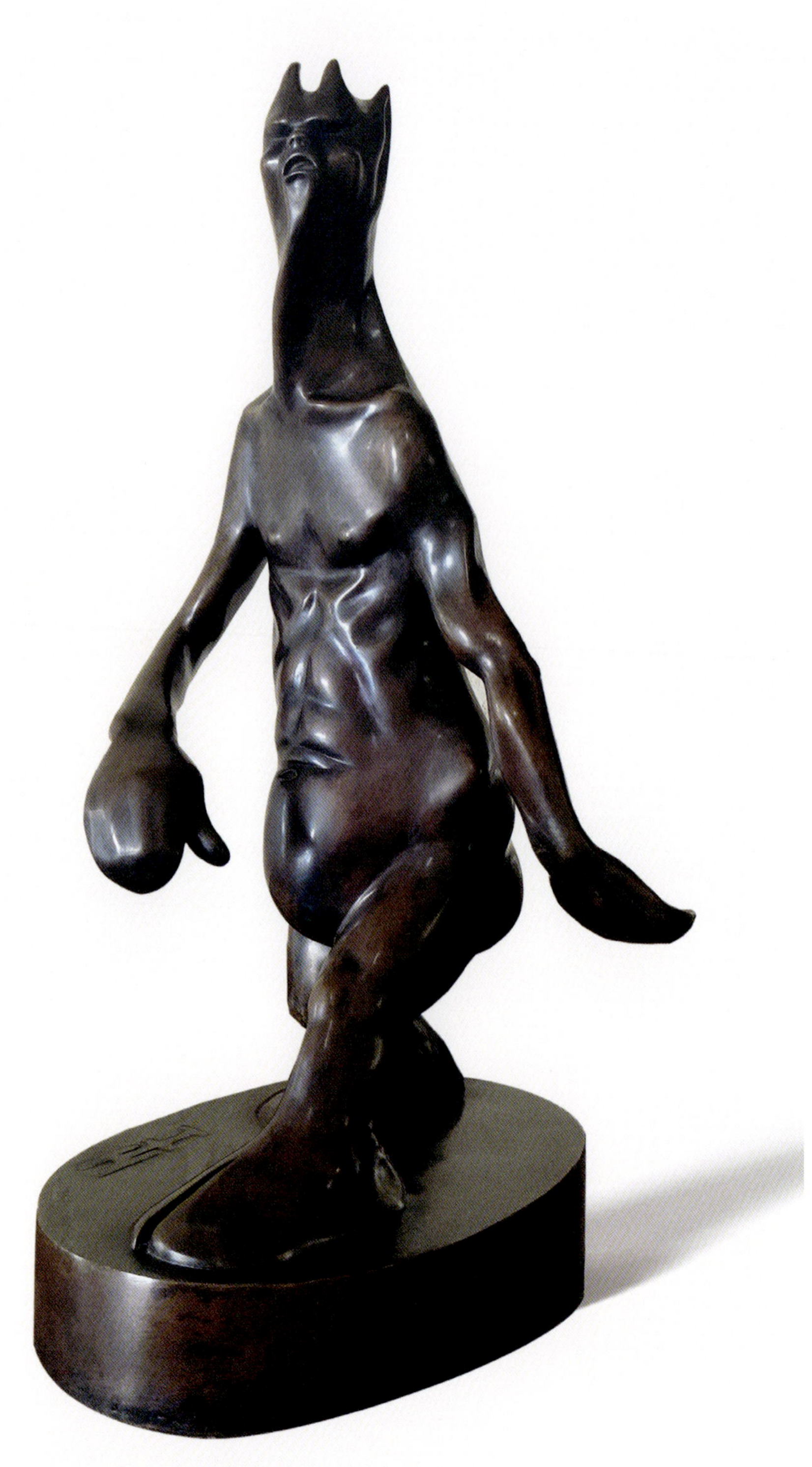

THOMAS THEODOR HEINE
Devil, 1904
Private Collection

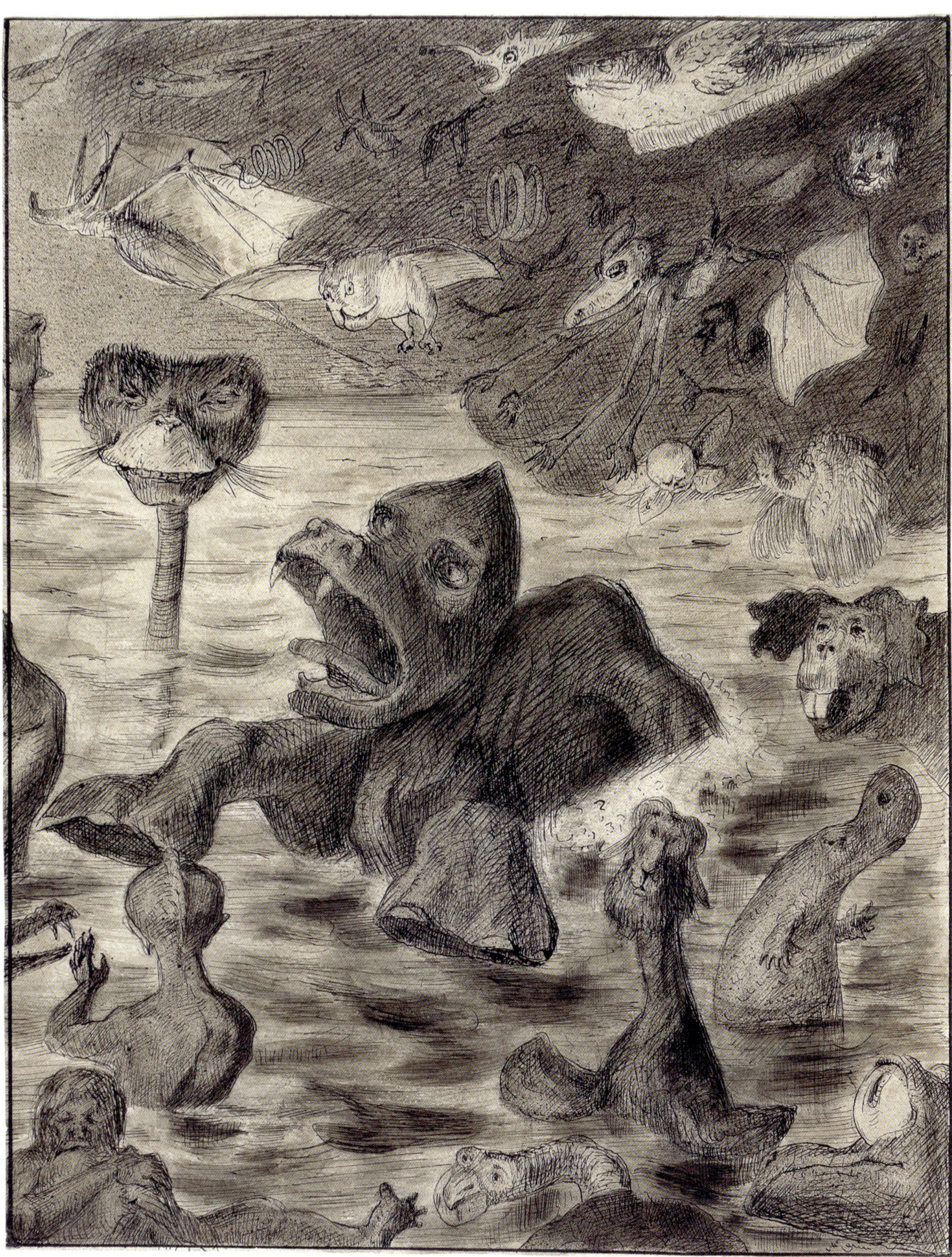

ALFRED KUBIN
Grotesque Animal World, c. 1898
OÖ Landes-Kultur GmbH, Land Oberösterreich, Graphic Collection, Ha II 7361

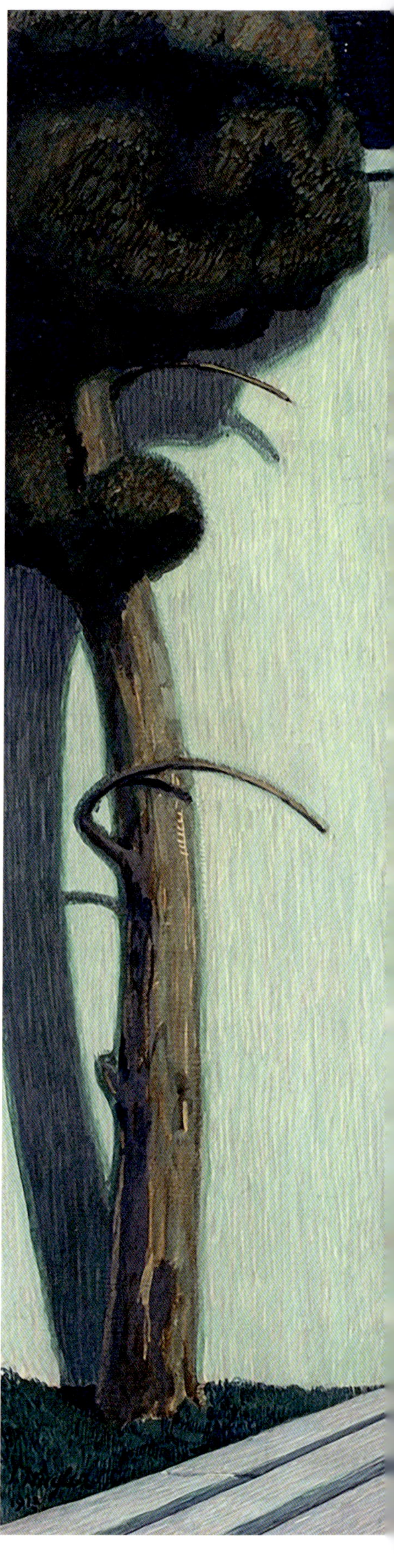

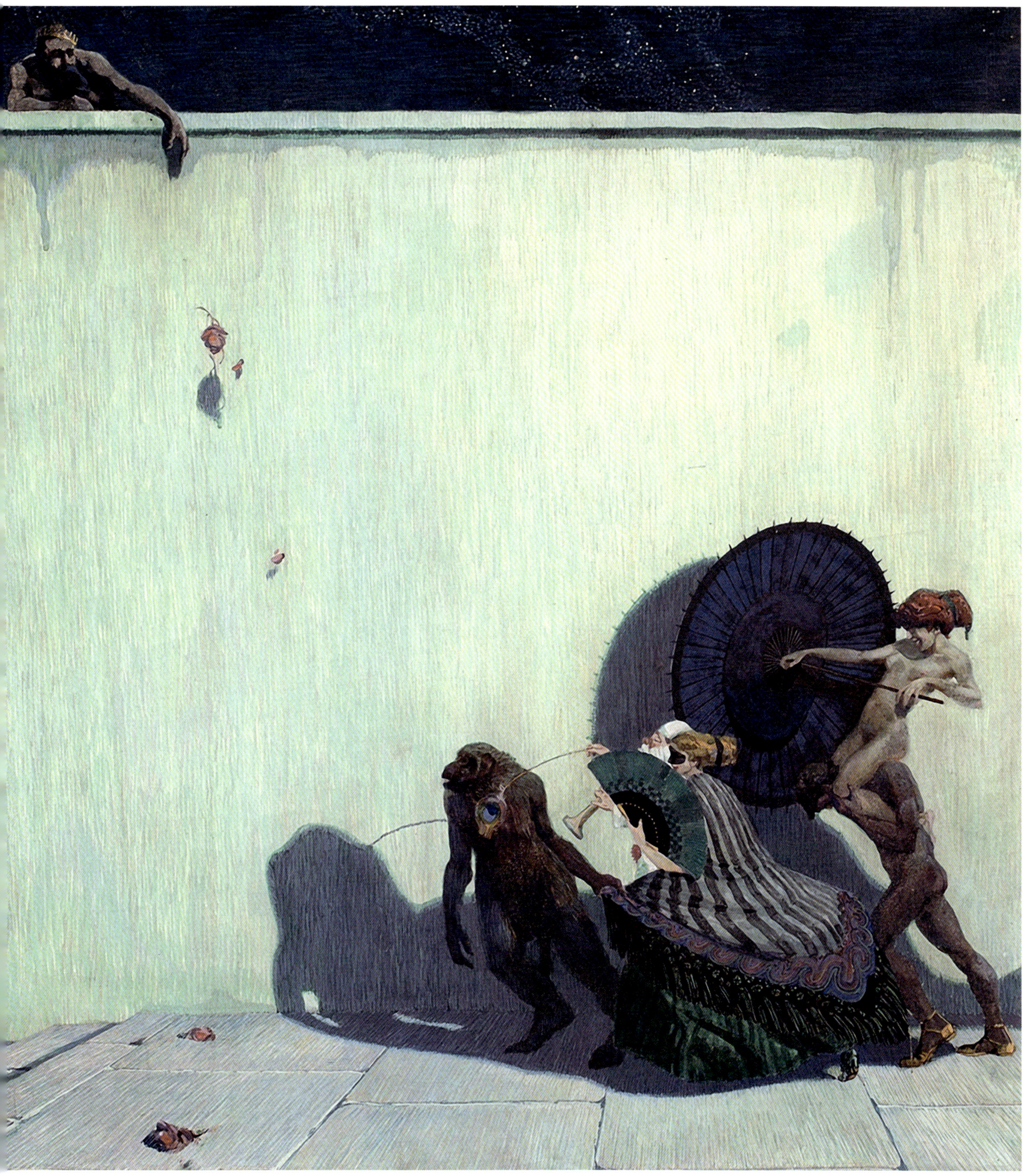

JOSEF KUGLER
Capriccio, 1913
Private Collection

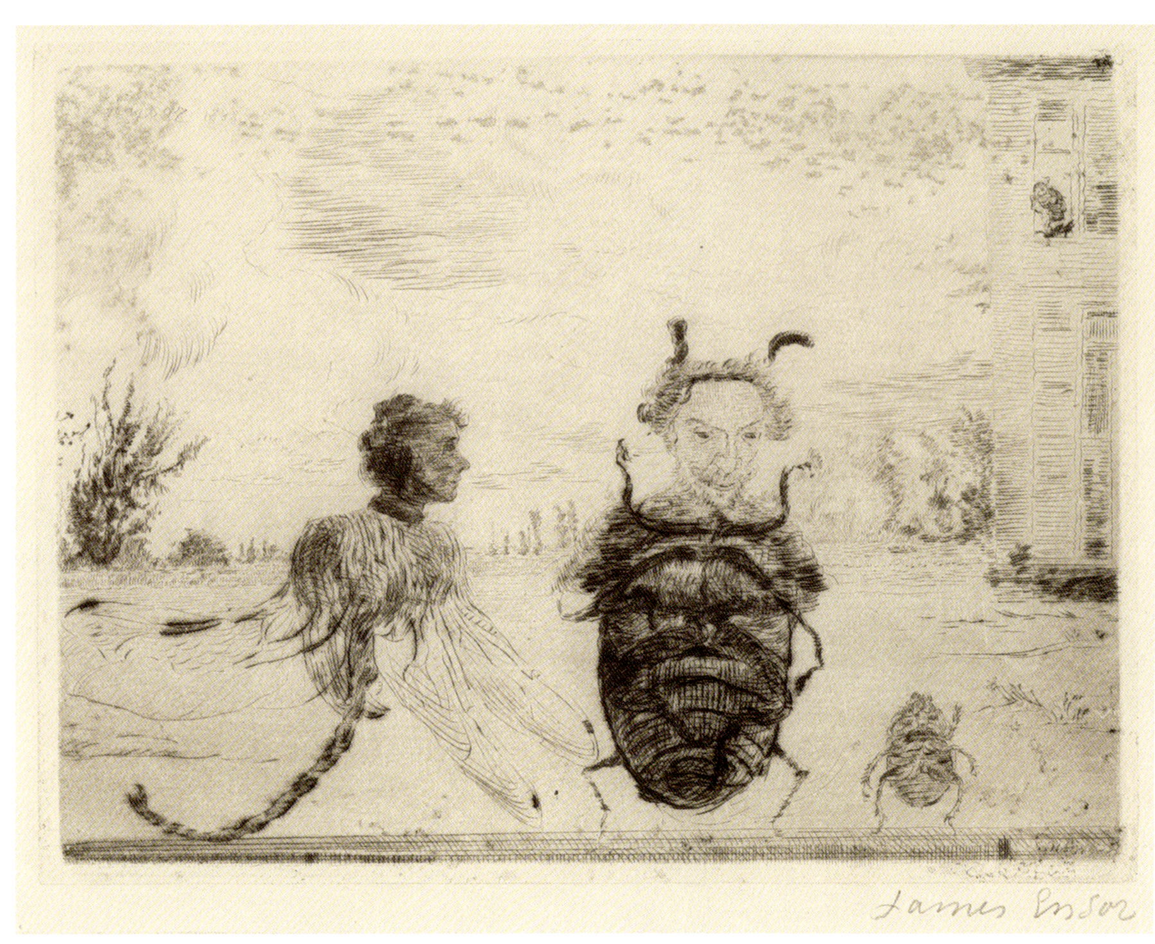

JAMES ENSOR
Peculiar Insects, 1888
OÖ Landes-Kultur GmbH, Land Oberösterreich,
Graphic Collection, KS II 844

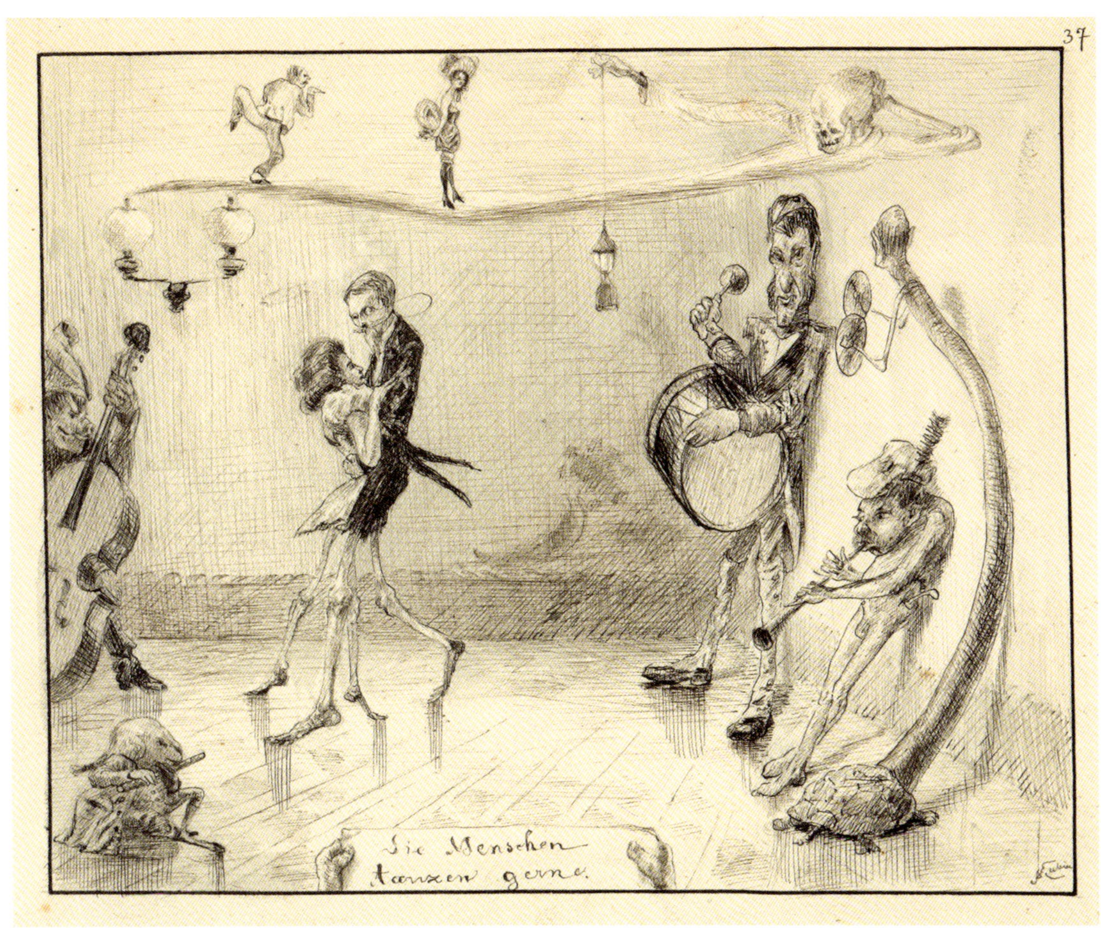

ALFRED KUBIN
People Love to Dance
Leopold, Private Collection

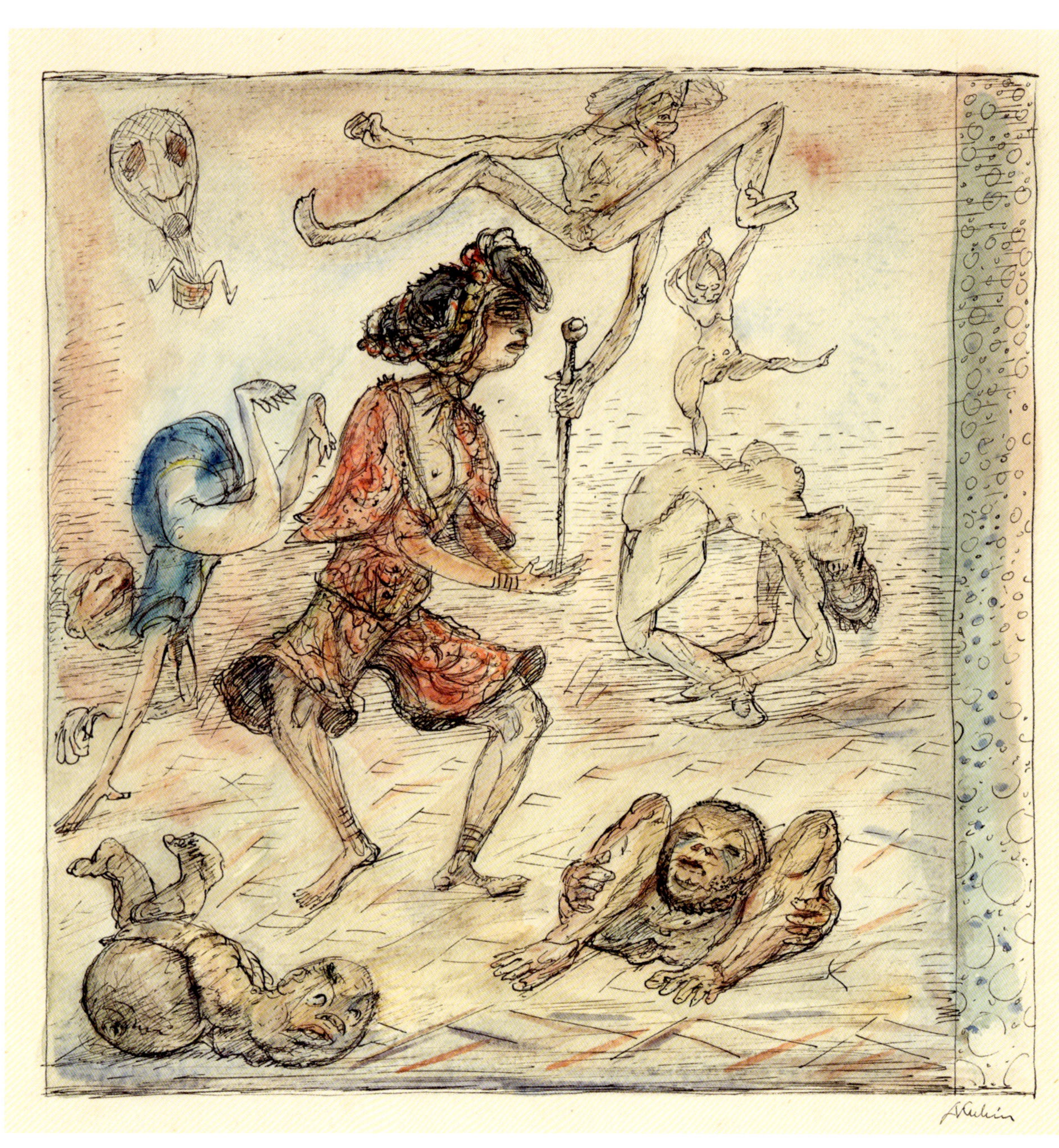

ALFRED KUBIN
The Malaysian Variety Show, c. 1915
Private Collection, Austria

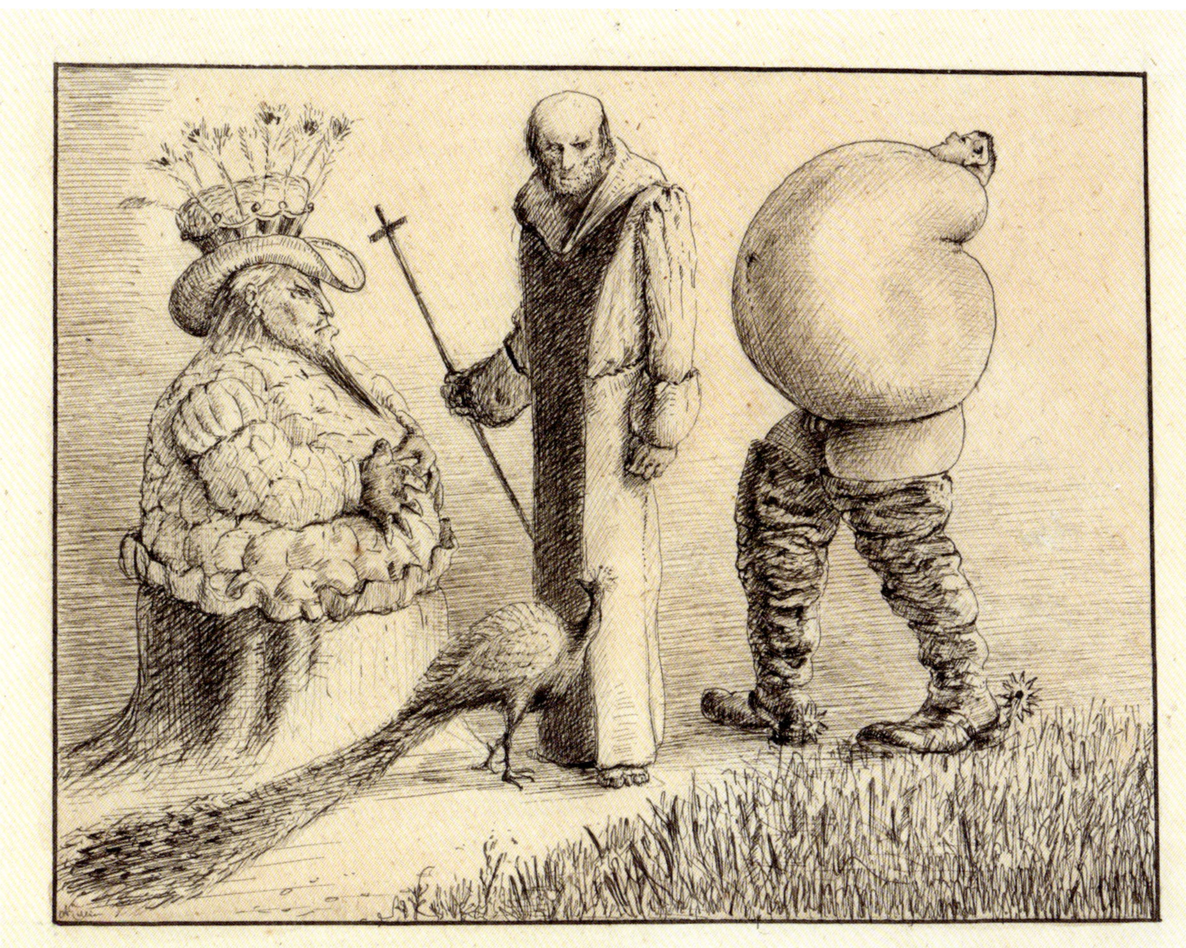

ALFRED KUBIN

Voracity and Self-Denial in Satan

Leopold, Private Collection

Alfred Kubin about Odilon Redon, James Ensor and Edvard Munch

Up until the present day, we can often find ghostly subjects addressed by artists otherwise aloof from any superstition. Thus in the drawings and lithographs of Odilon Redon, a Frenchman who passed in 1917, in many works on paper and paintings by the Belgian James Ensor as well as in the early graphic works of the Norwegian Edvard Munch. So much is certain: no artist would ever choose those recondite subjects unless he felt compelled to do so. In some corner of his soul, the painter believes in the impulses of his imagination. It is the experience of the supernatural that we encounter here on artistic ground, and there are many people who must probably have a finer sense of this still insufficiently recognized and described area, for otherwise such works could not be of general interest.*

* Alfred Kubin, "Malerei des Übersinnlichen", in: *Aus meiner Werkstatt. Gesammelte Prosa*, ed. Ulrich Riemerschmidt (Munich, 1973), p. 43.

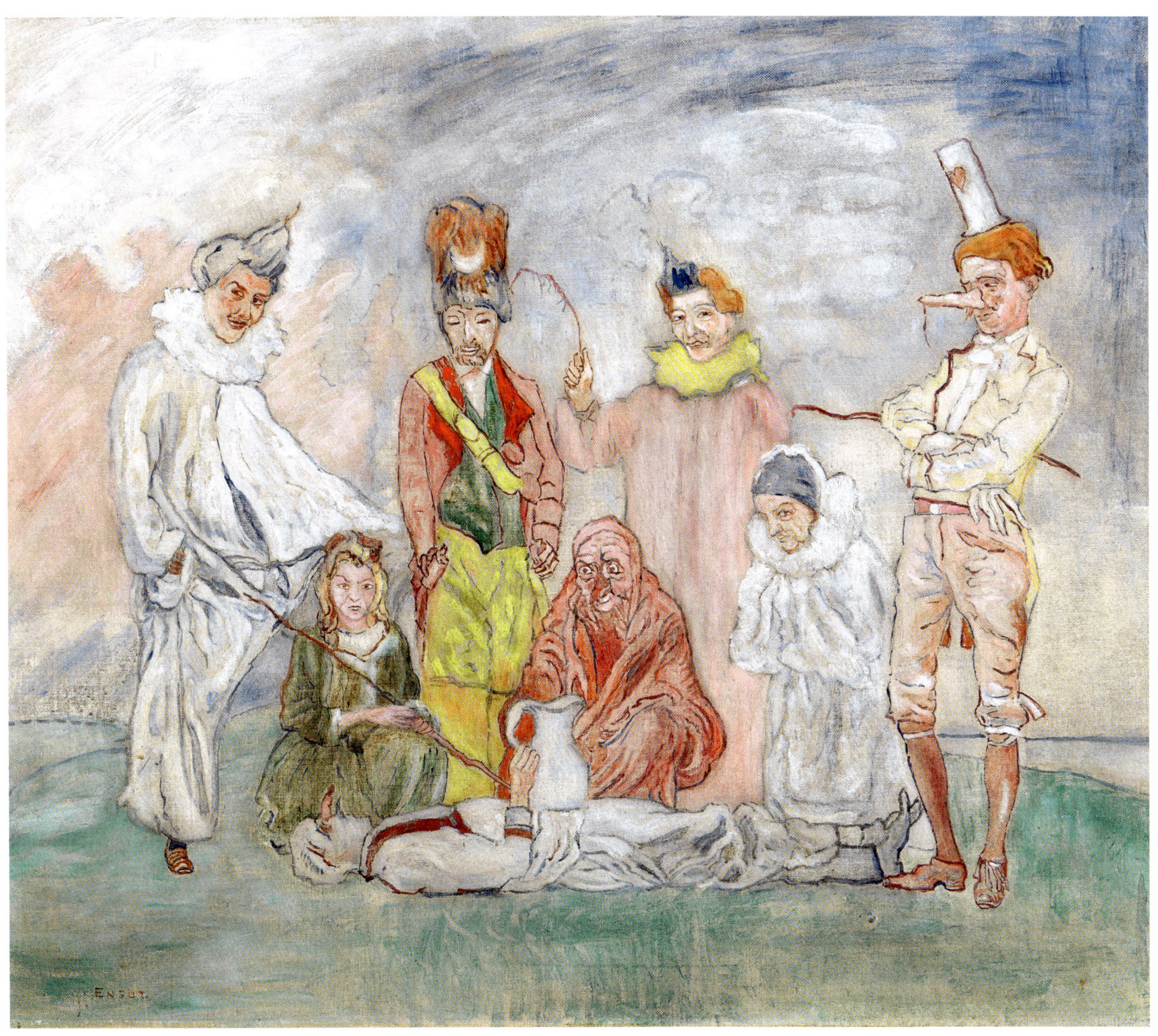

JAMES ENSOR
Baptism of Masks, 1925–1930
Private Collection

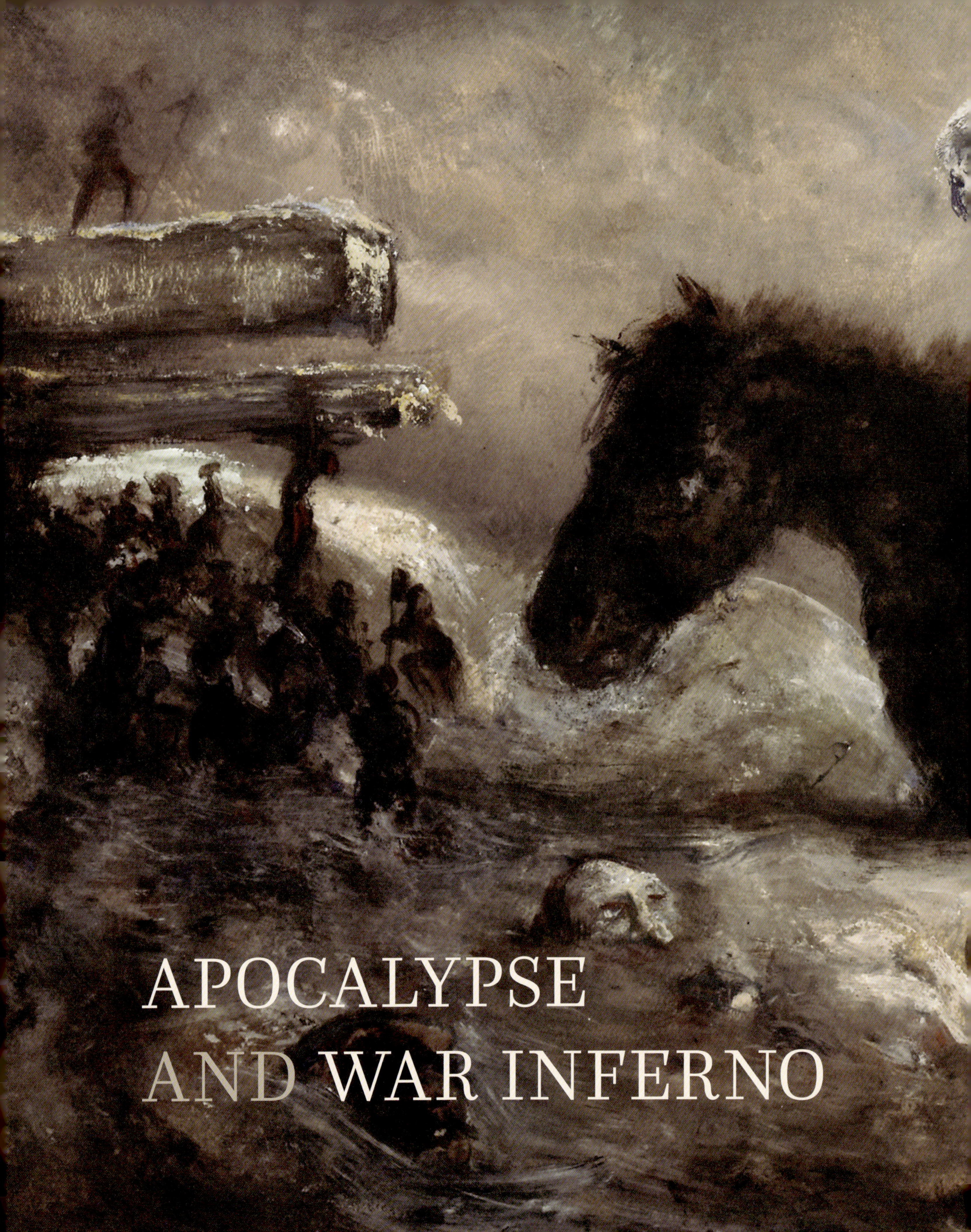
APOCALYPSE
AND WAR INFERNO

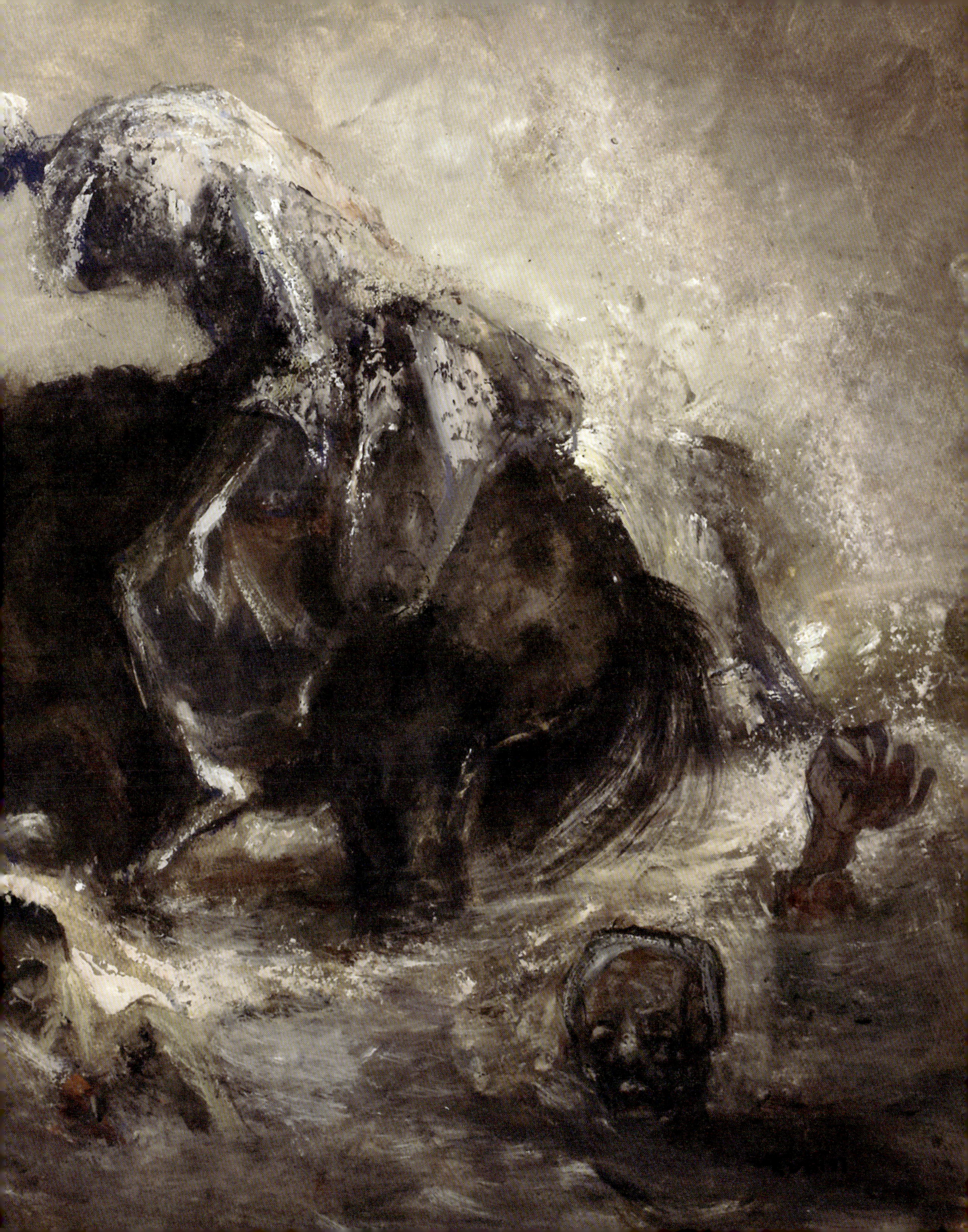

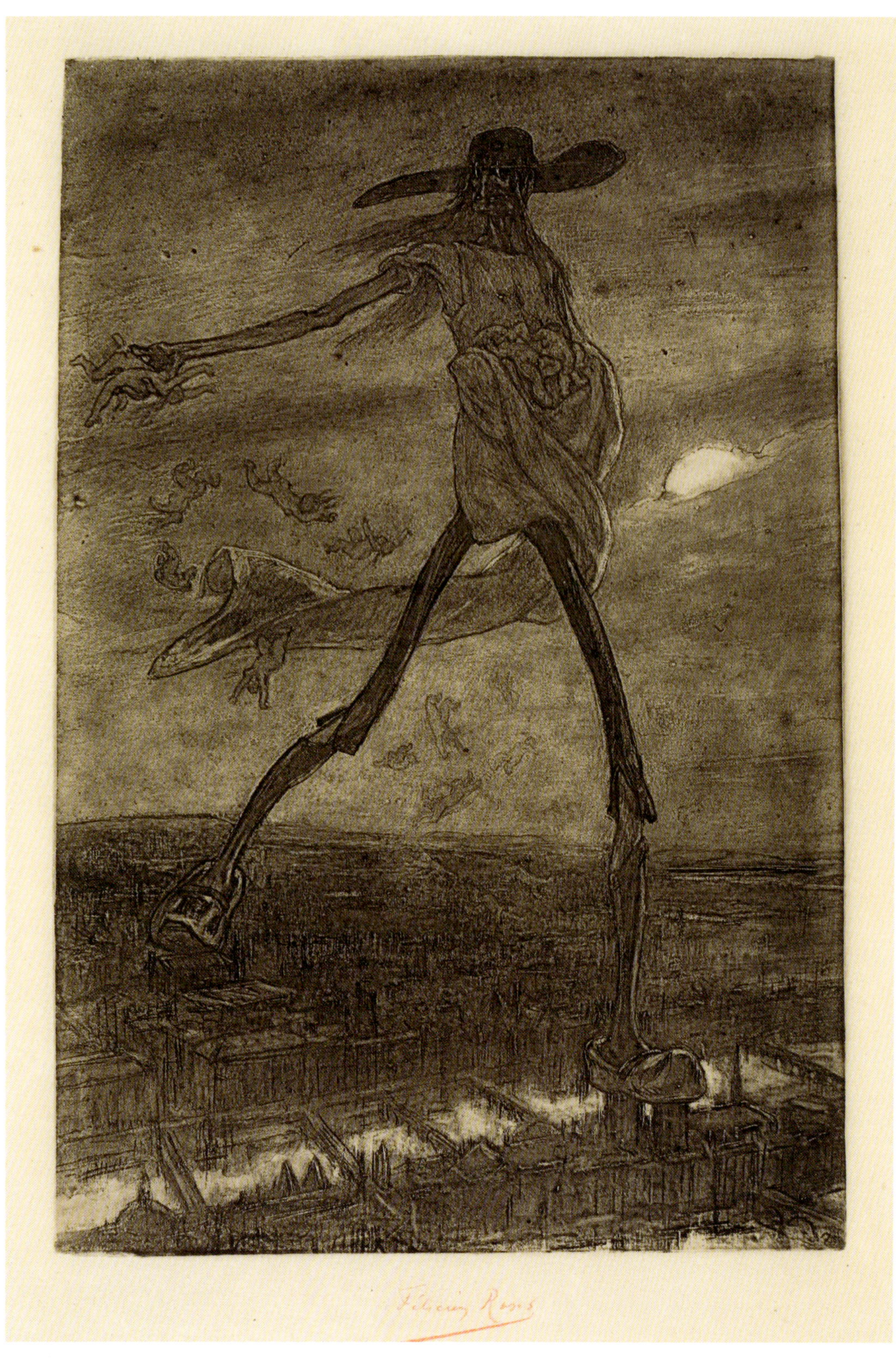

FÉLICIEN ROPS
Satan Sowing Tares, from the series *Les Sataniques,* 1878–1882
Museum voor Schone Kunsten, Gent (Belgium)

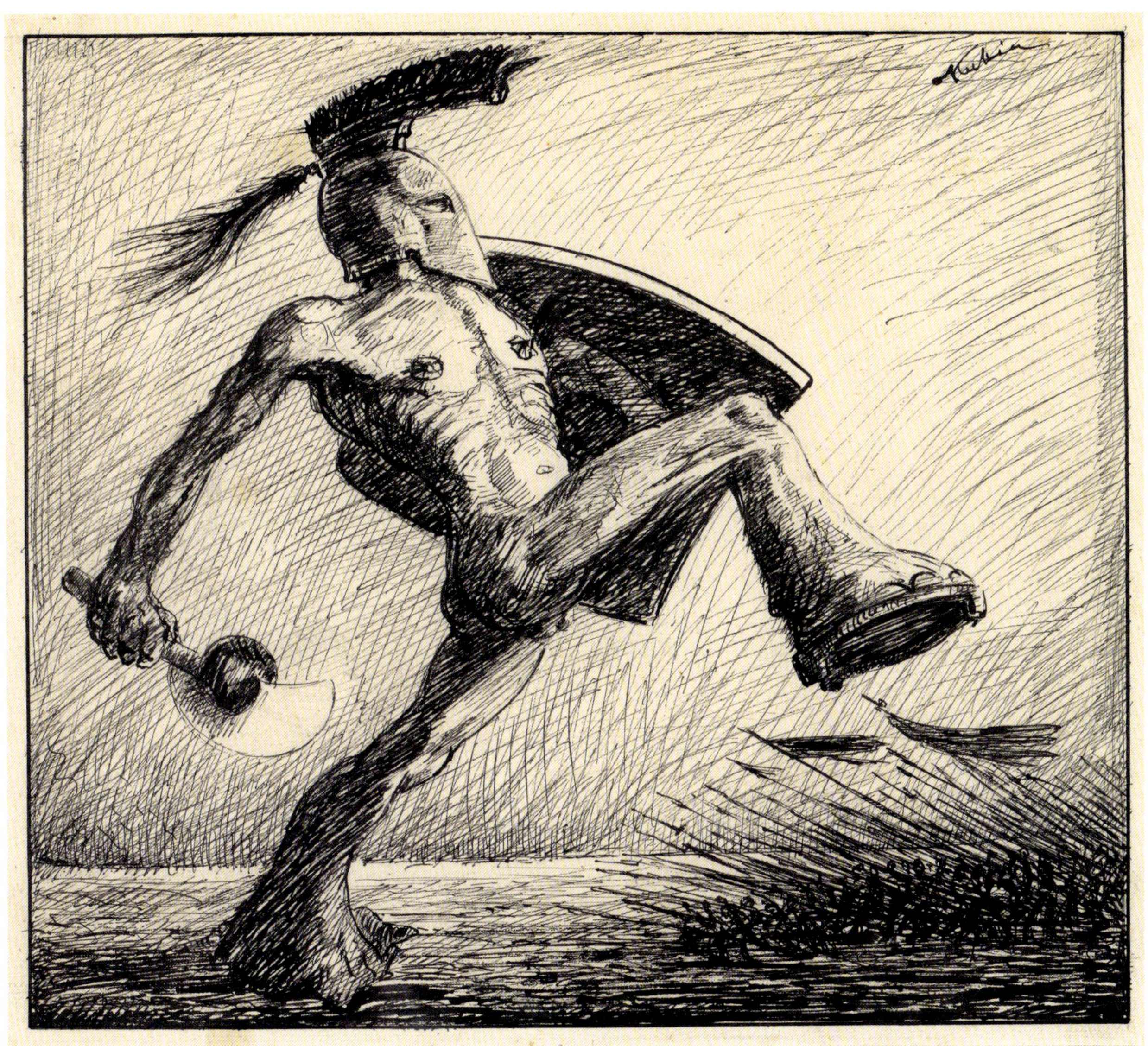

ALFRED KUBIN
The War, 1907
Städtische Galerie im Lenbachhaus und Kunstbau München

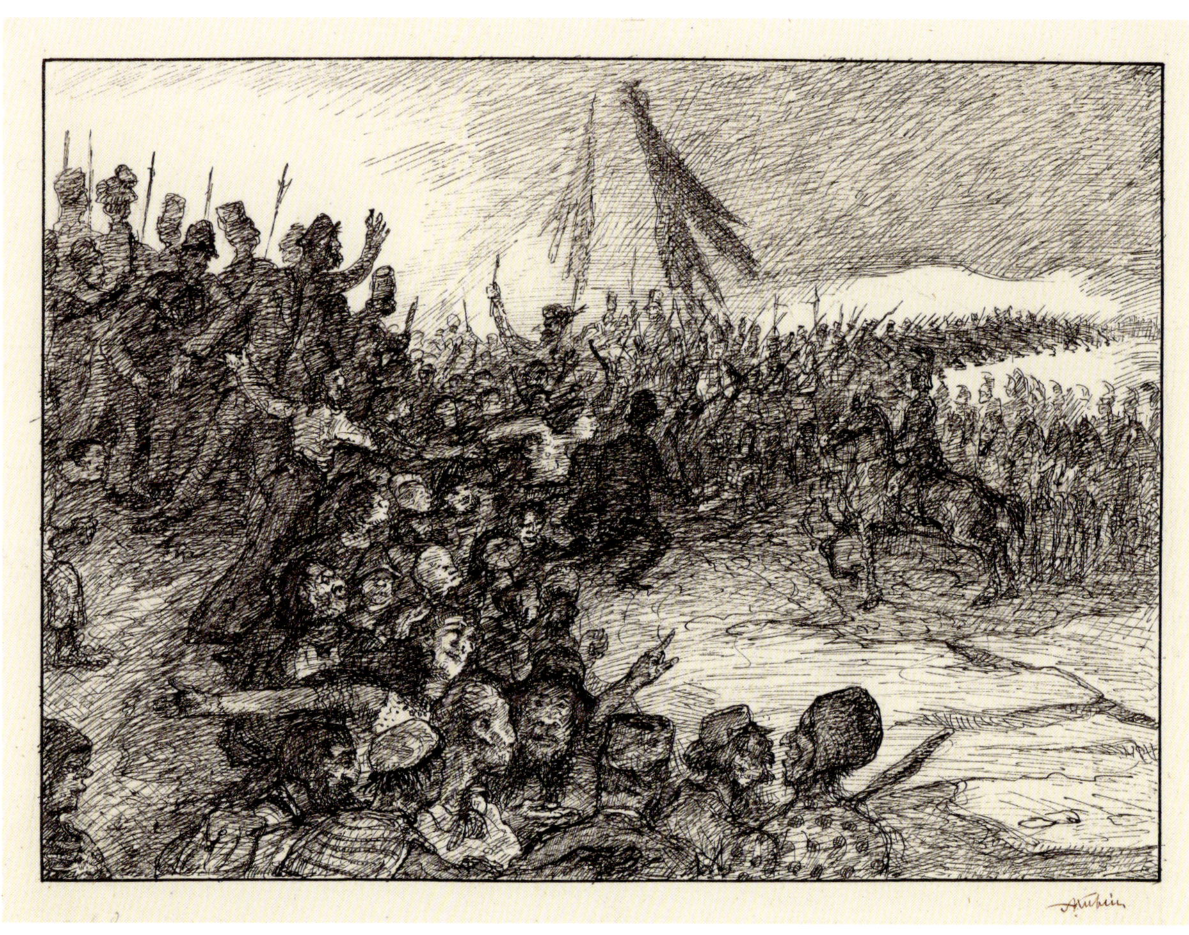

ALFRED KUBIN
Uprising, from the *Sansara* portfolio, 1909/10
Leopold Museum, Vienna

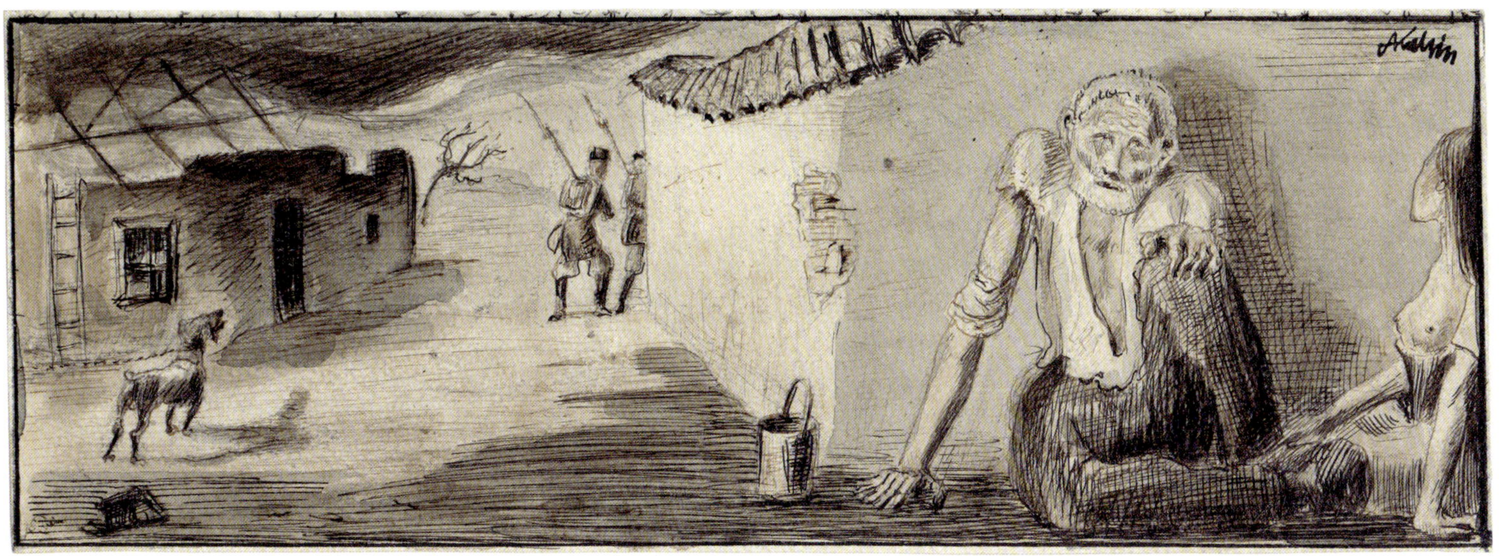

ALFRED KUBIN
War Scene, c. 1900
Private Collection, Austria

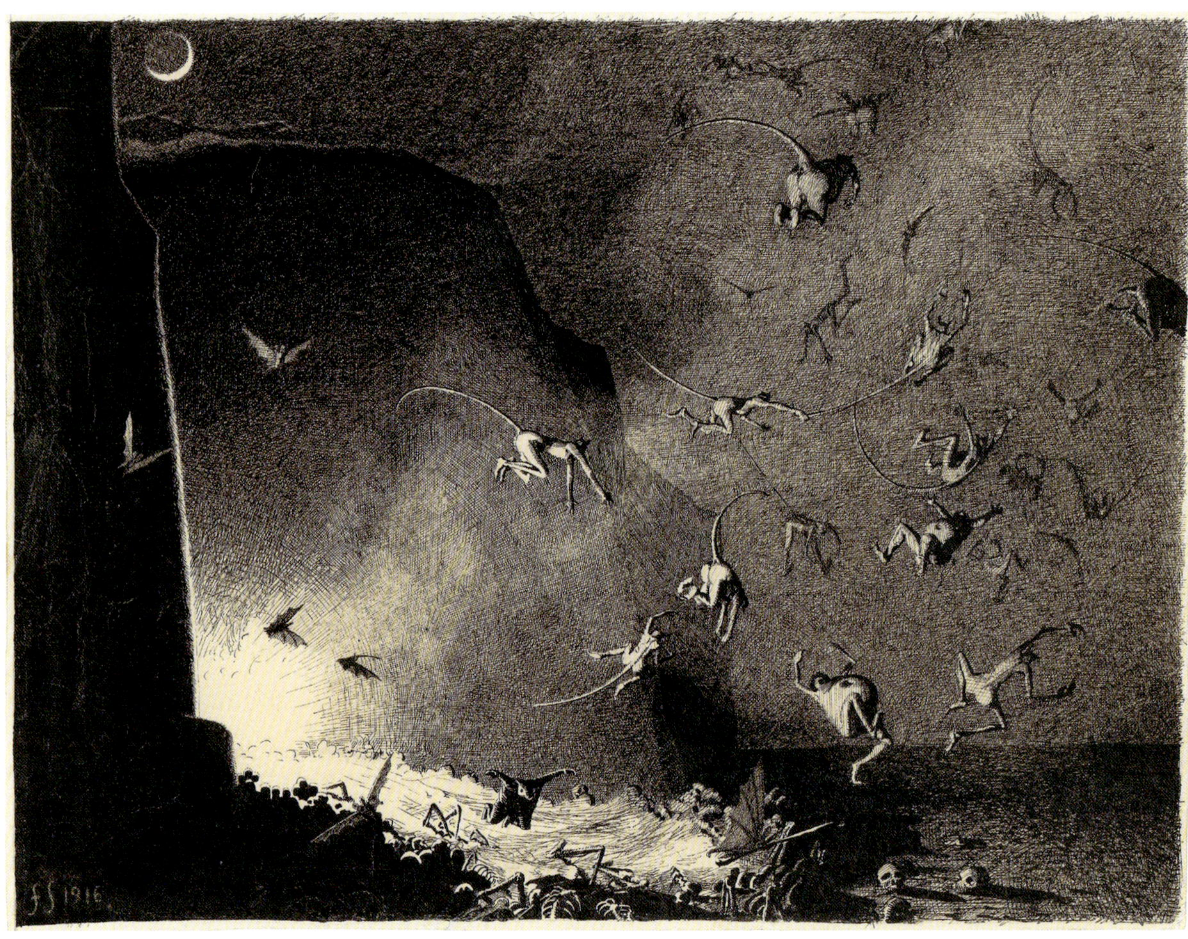

FRANZ SEDLACEK
Gate of Hell, 1916
Museum Ortner, Vienna

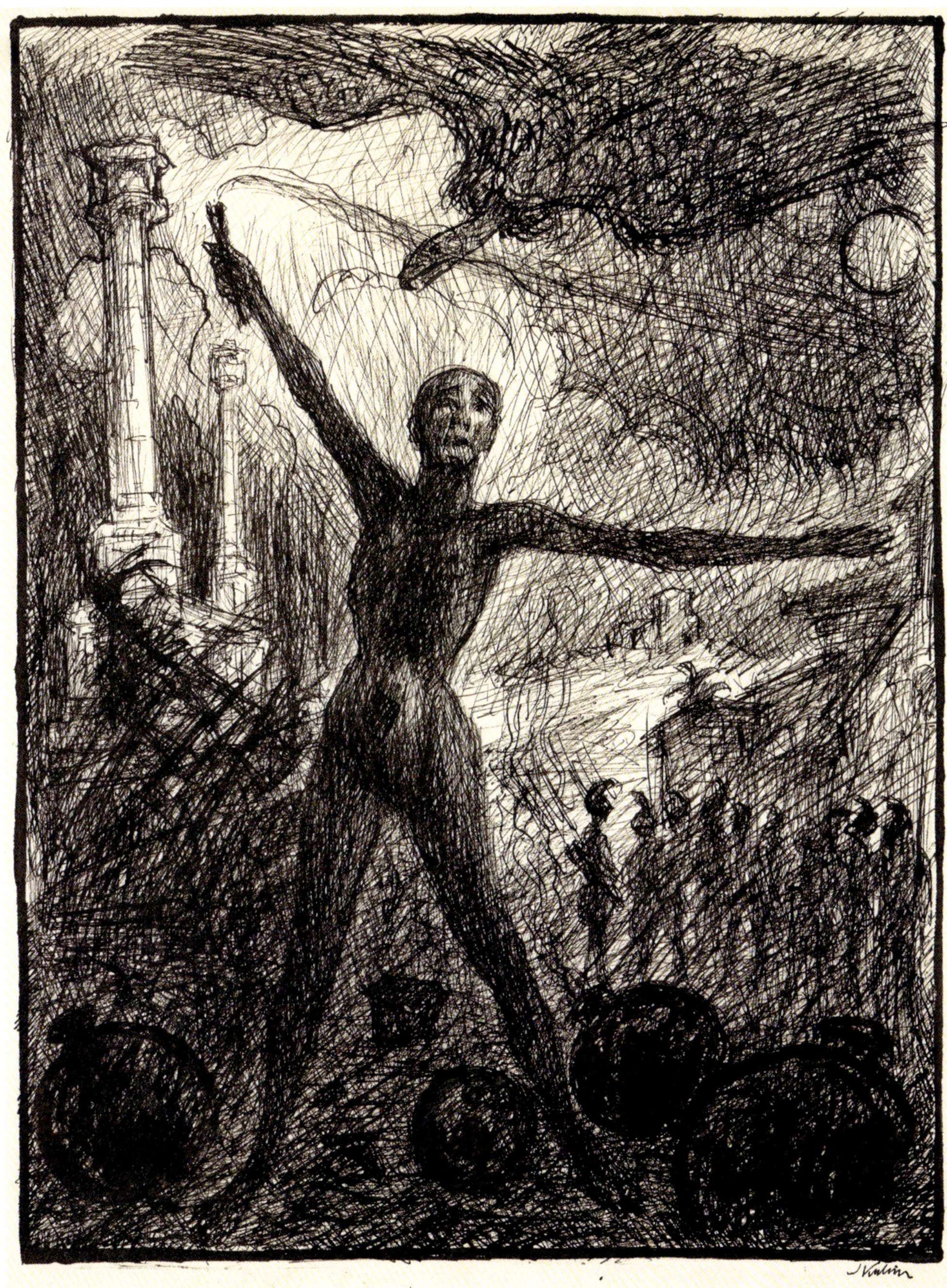

ALFRED KUBIN
Anarchy, c. 1918
Private Collection, Austria

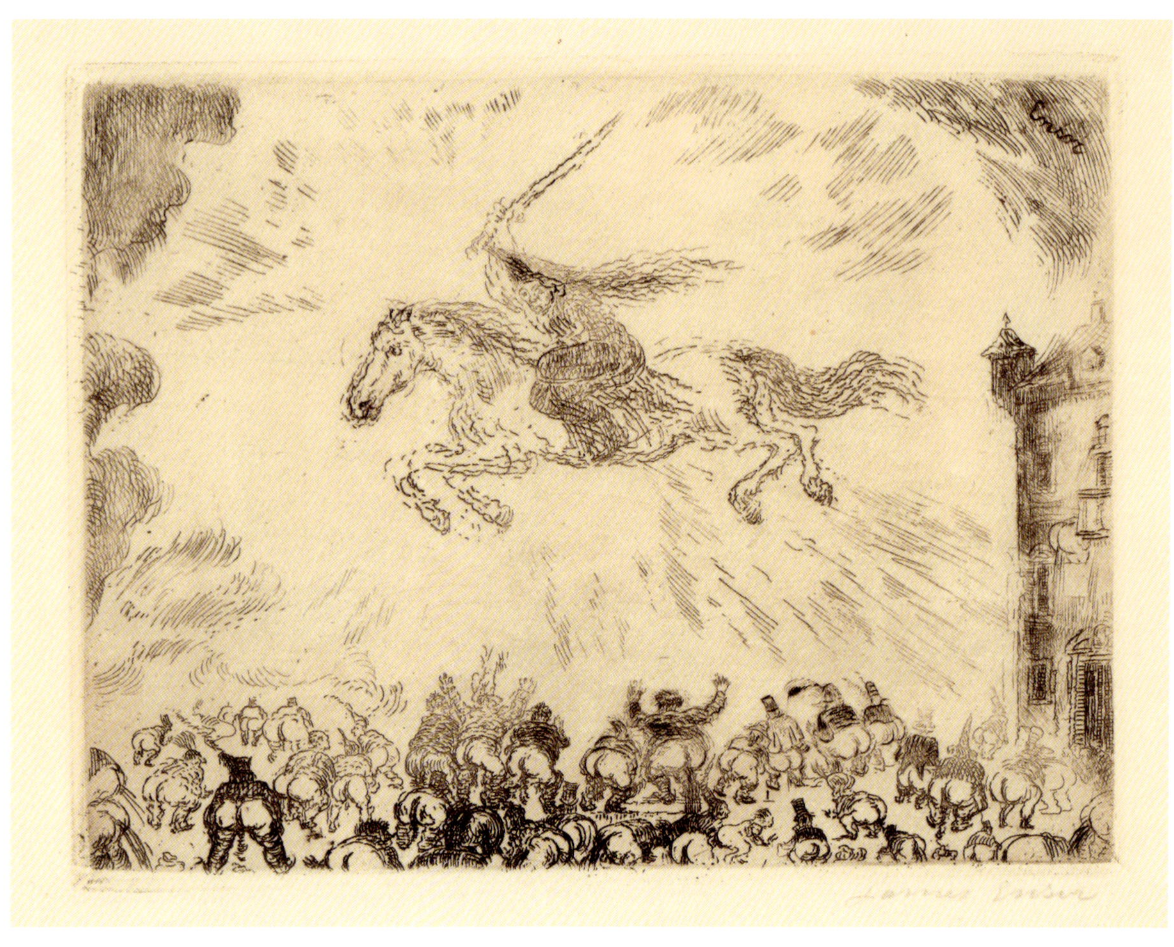

JAMES ENSOR
The Destroying Angel, 1889
Leopold, Private Collection

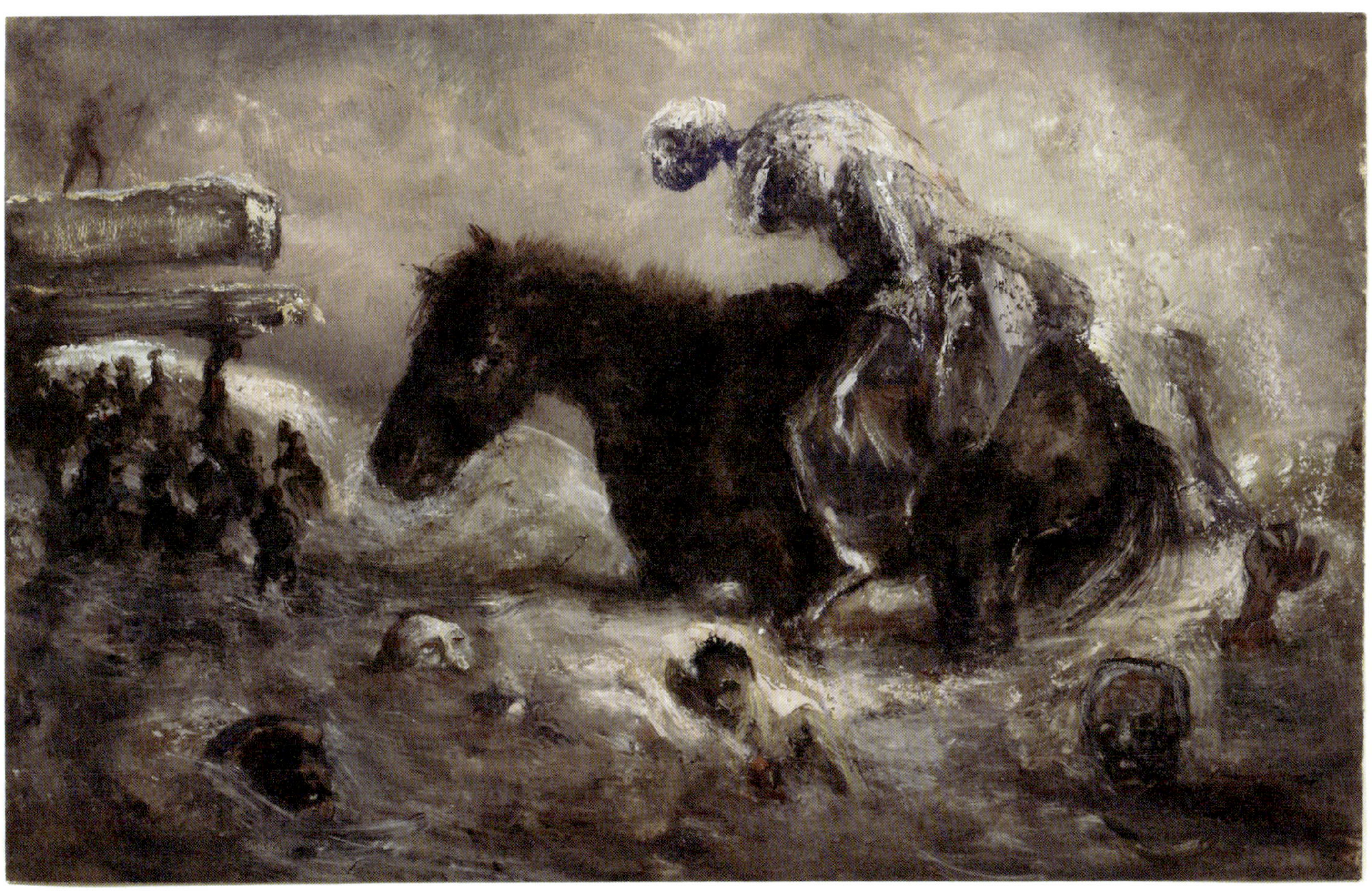

ALFRED KUBIN
Death as a Horseman, 1906
Leopold Museum, Vienna

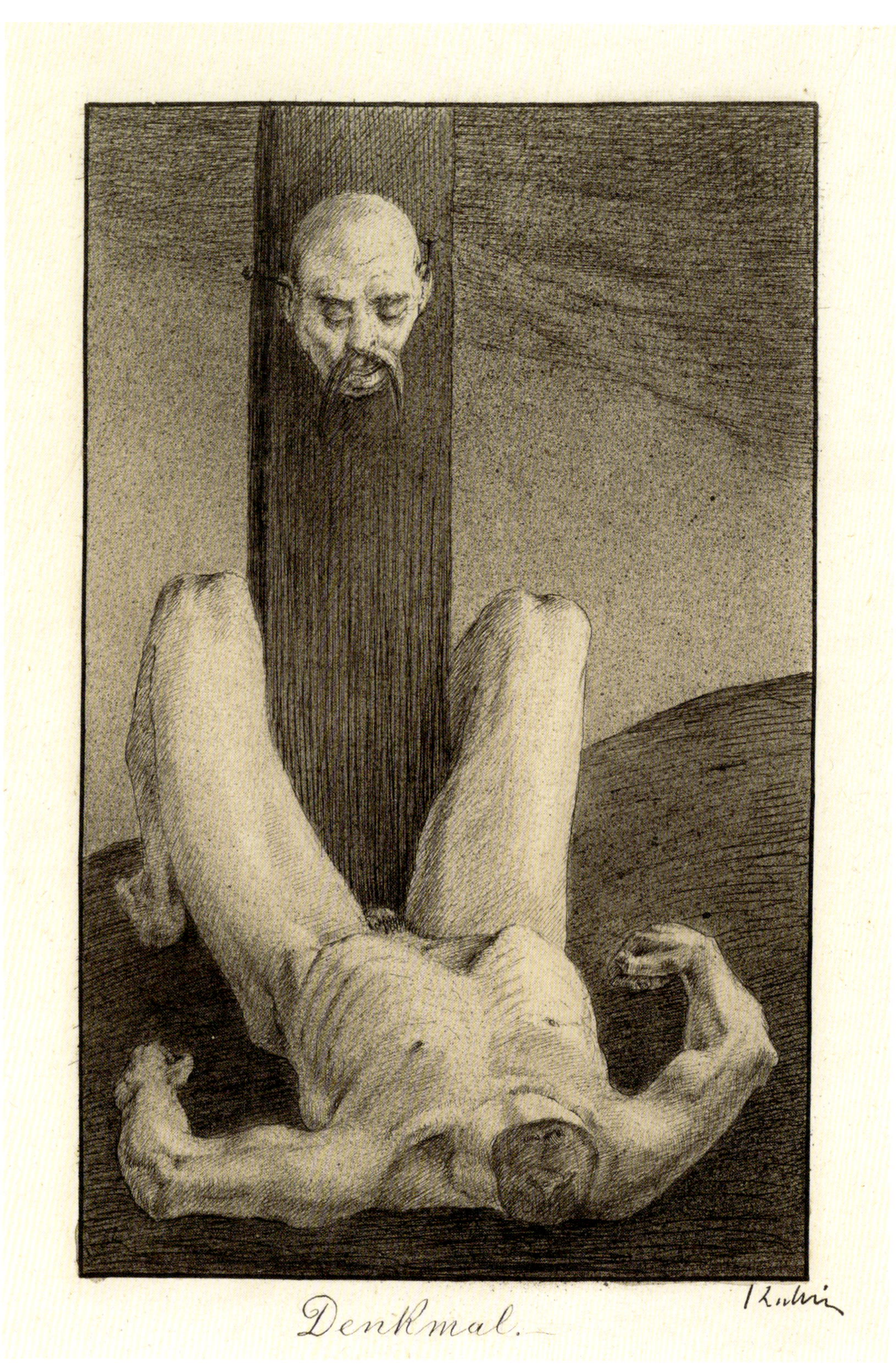

ALFRED KUBIN
Monument, c. 1900/01
OÖ Landes-Kultur GmbH, Land Oberösterreich, Graphic Collection, Ha II 3177

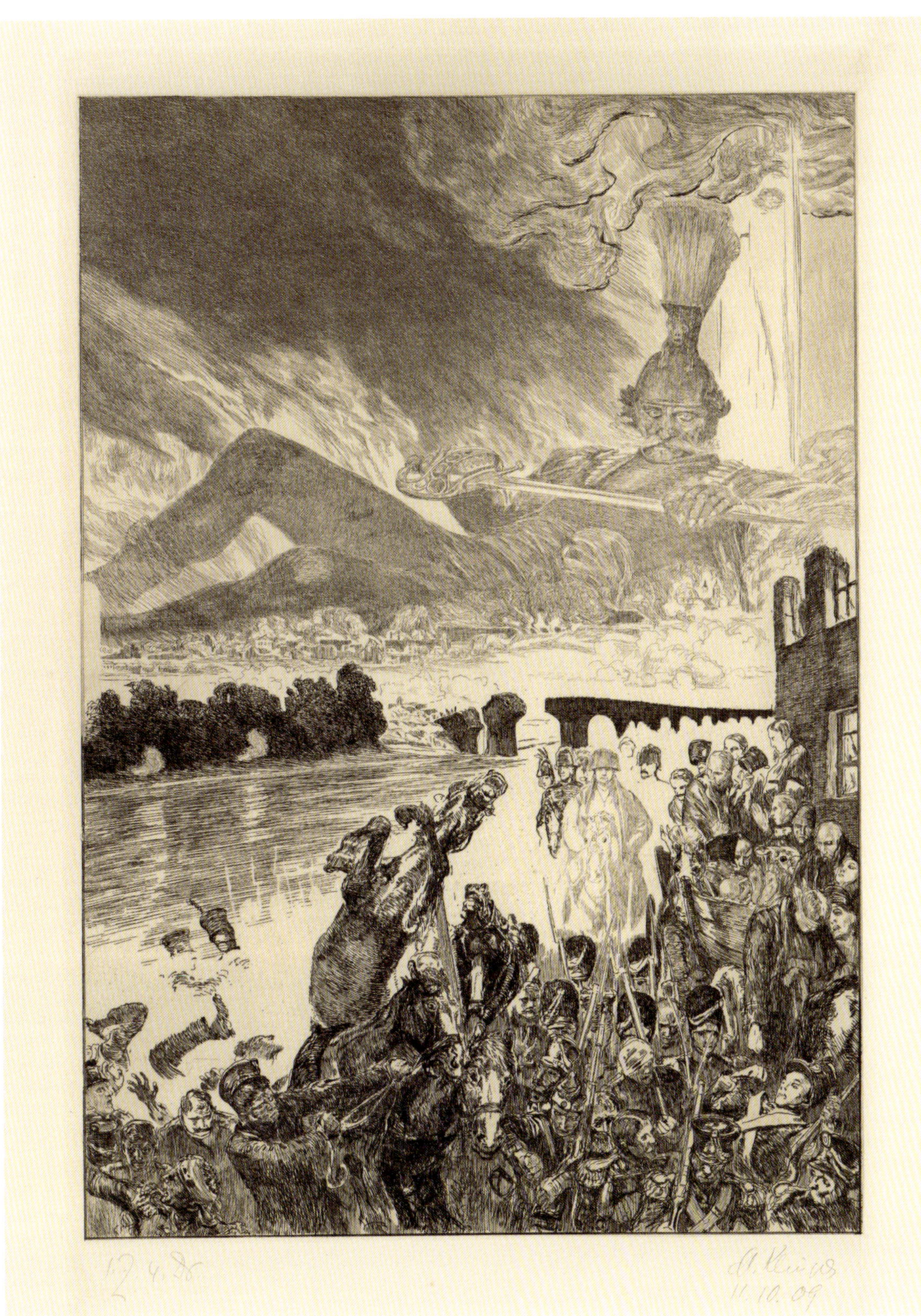

MAX KLINGER
War, from the portfolio *On Death, Part 2*, 1909
The Daulton Collection, Los Altos Hills, California

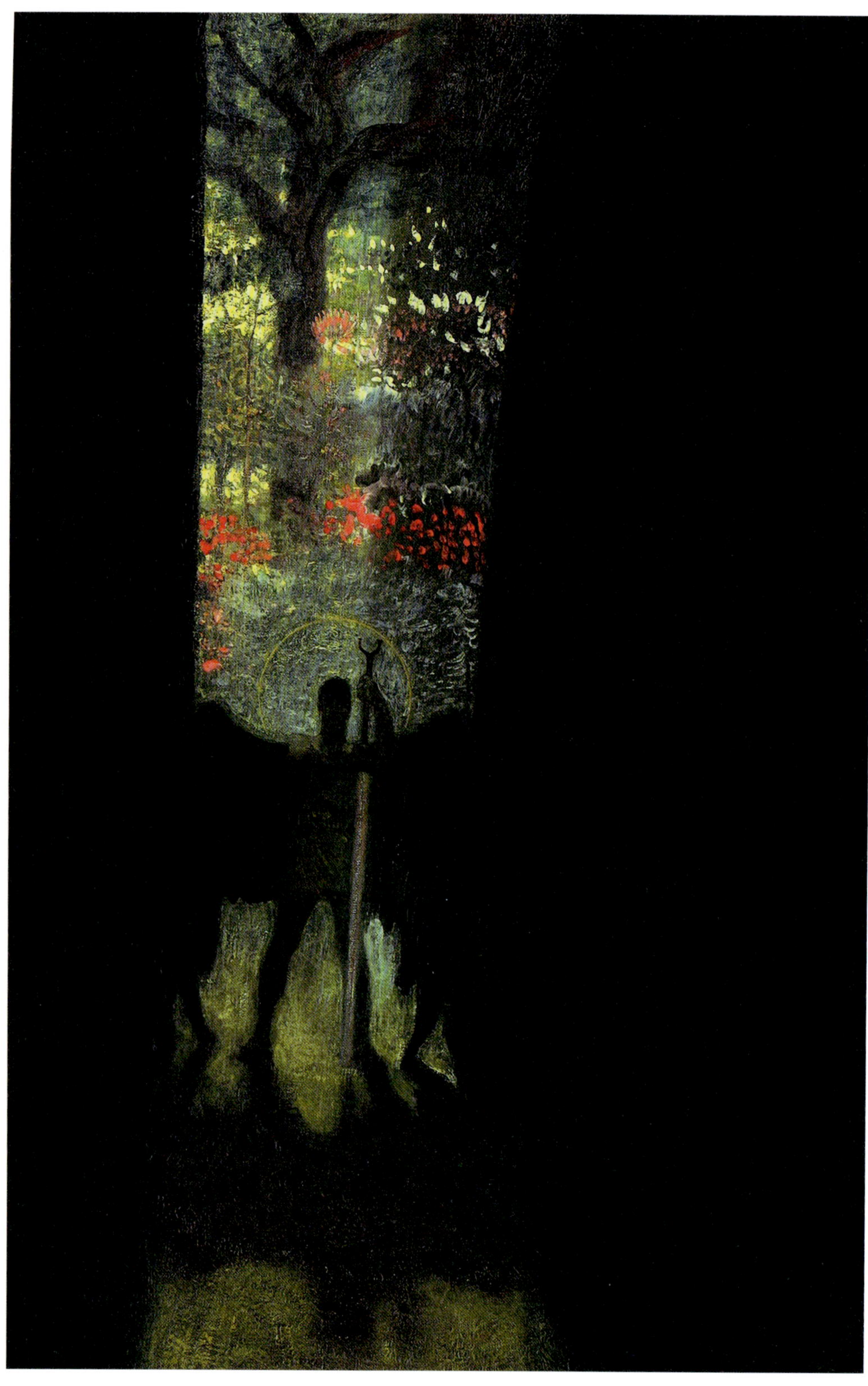

FRANZ VON STUCK
Paradise Lost, c. 1890
Private Collection

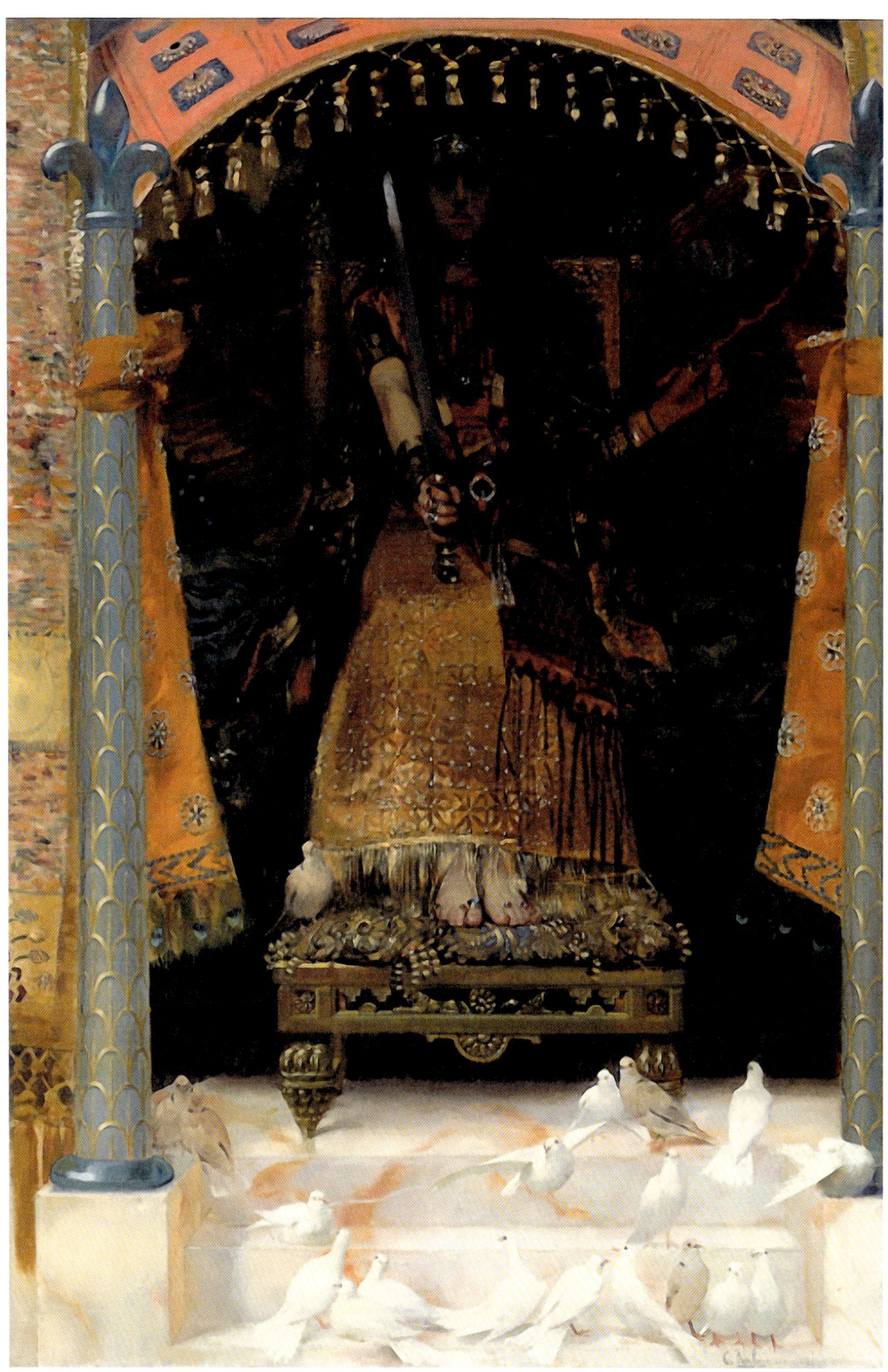

GEORGES ANTOINE ROCHEGROSSE
War and Peace, 1886
Private Collection

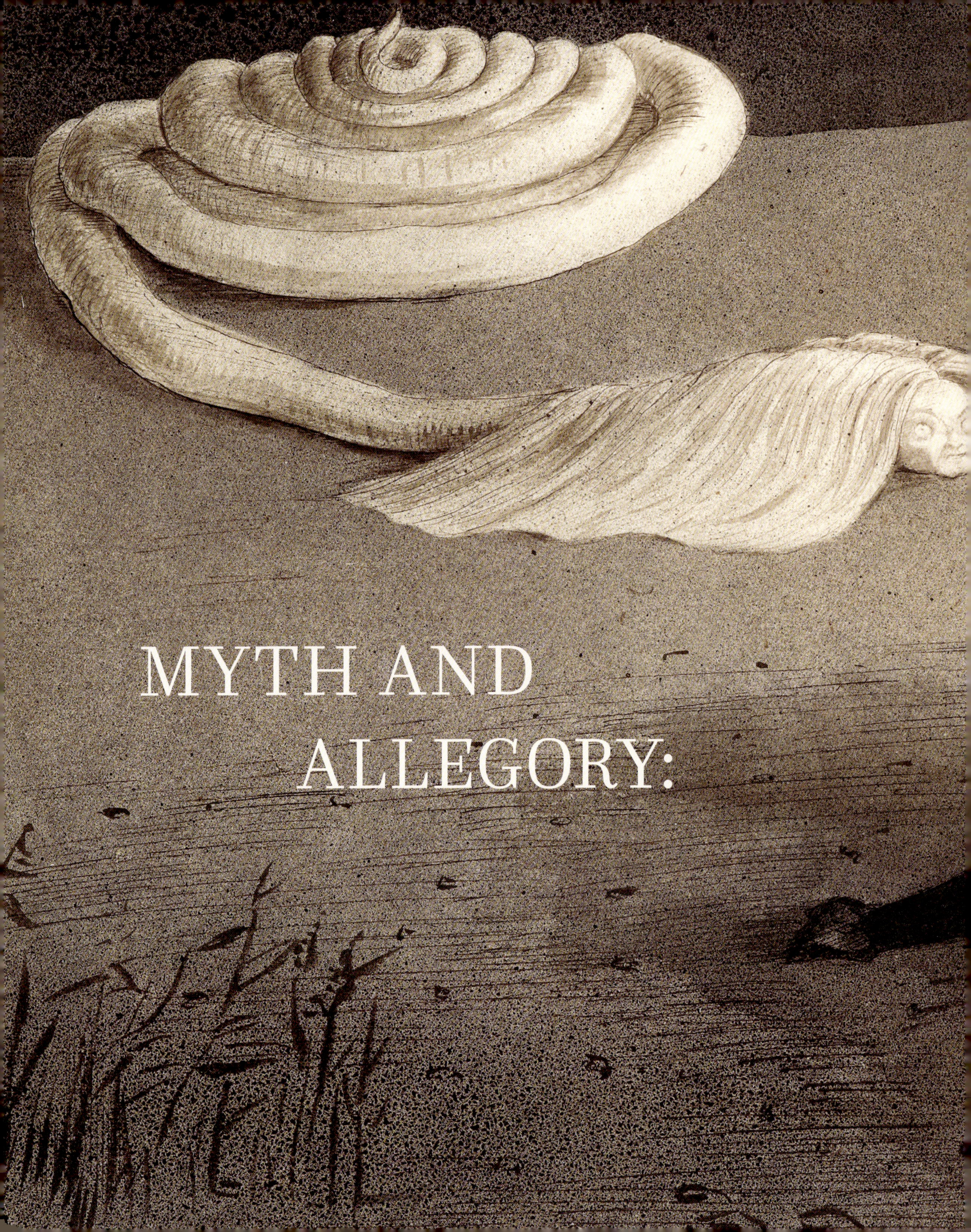

MYTH AND ALLEGORY:

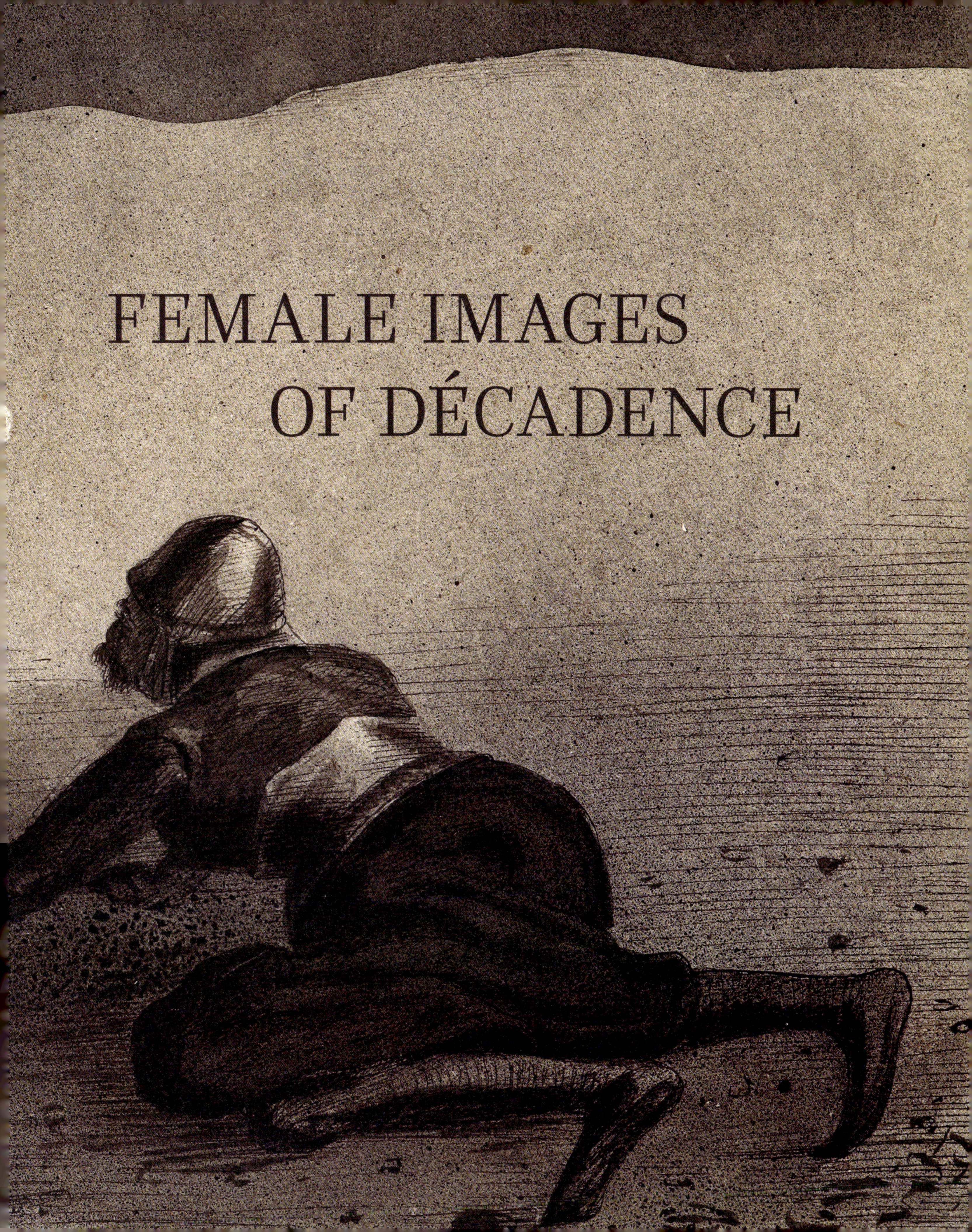

FEMALE IMAGES OF DÉCADENCE

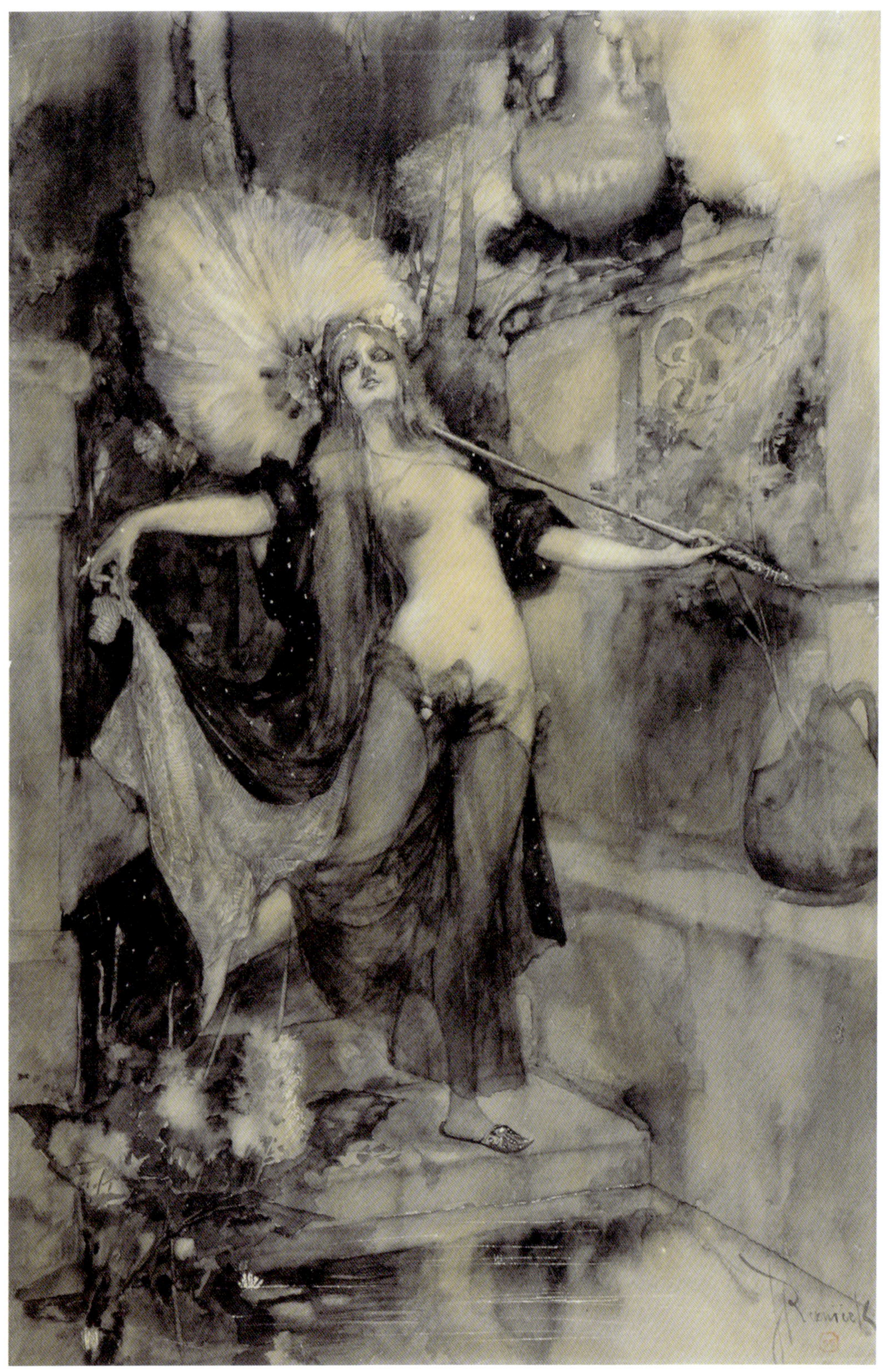

FERDINAND FREIHERR VON REZNIČEK
Salome
Museum Georg Schäfer, Schweinfurt

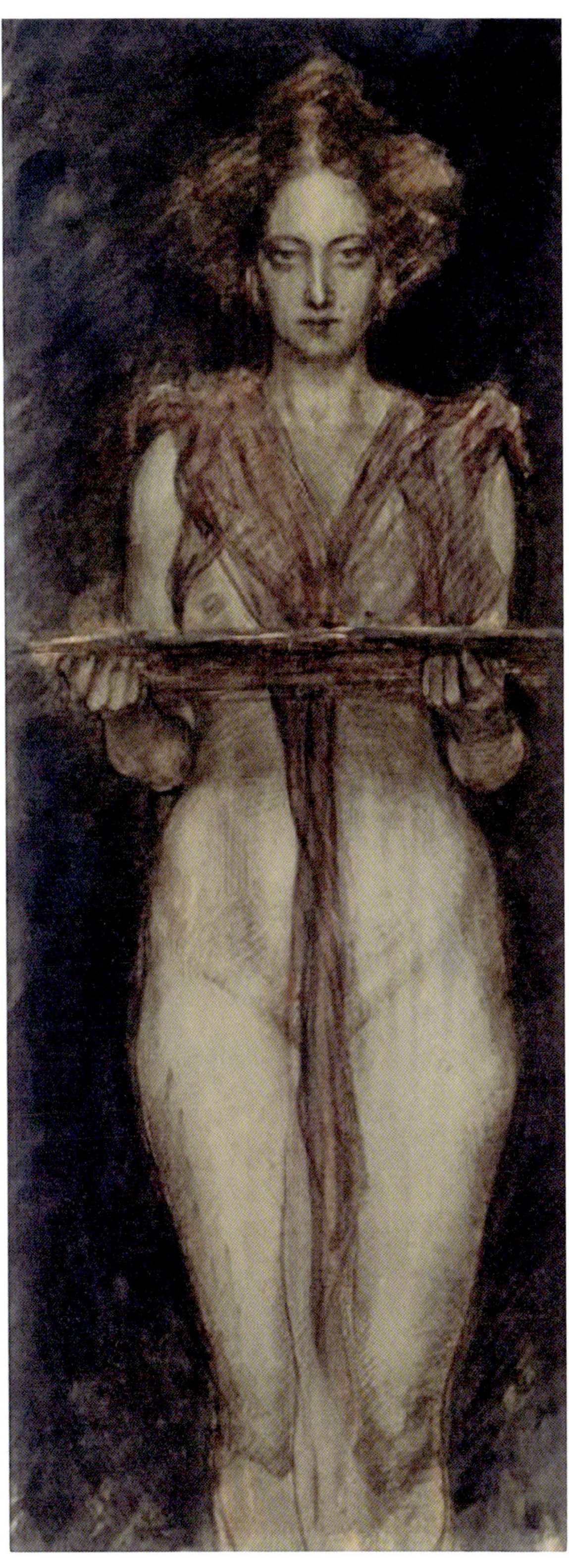

JOSEF ENGELHART
Salome, 1900
Private Collection

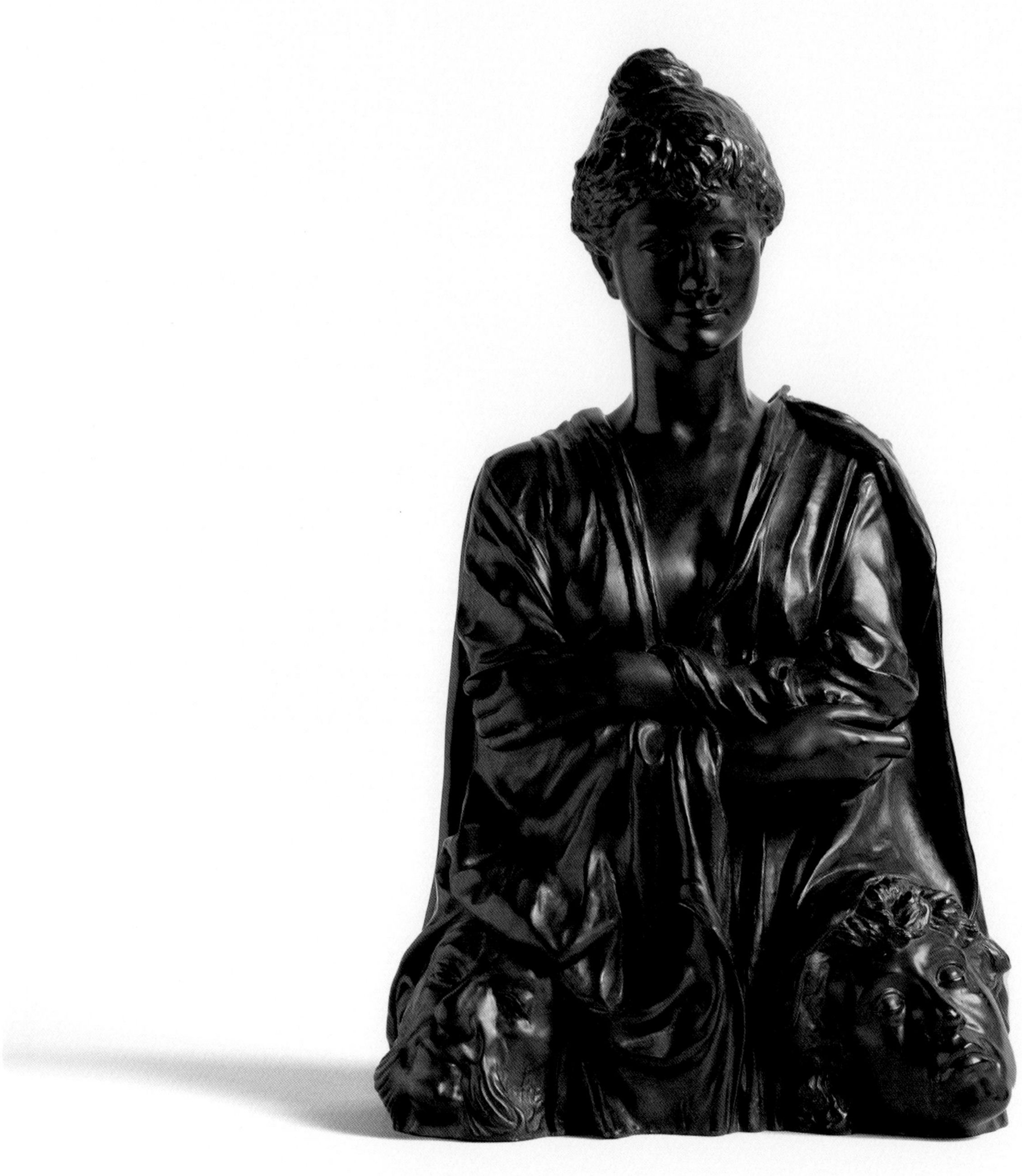

MAX KLINGER
The New Salome, c. 1903
Leopold Museum, Vienna

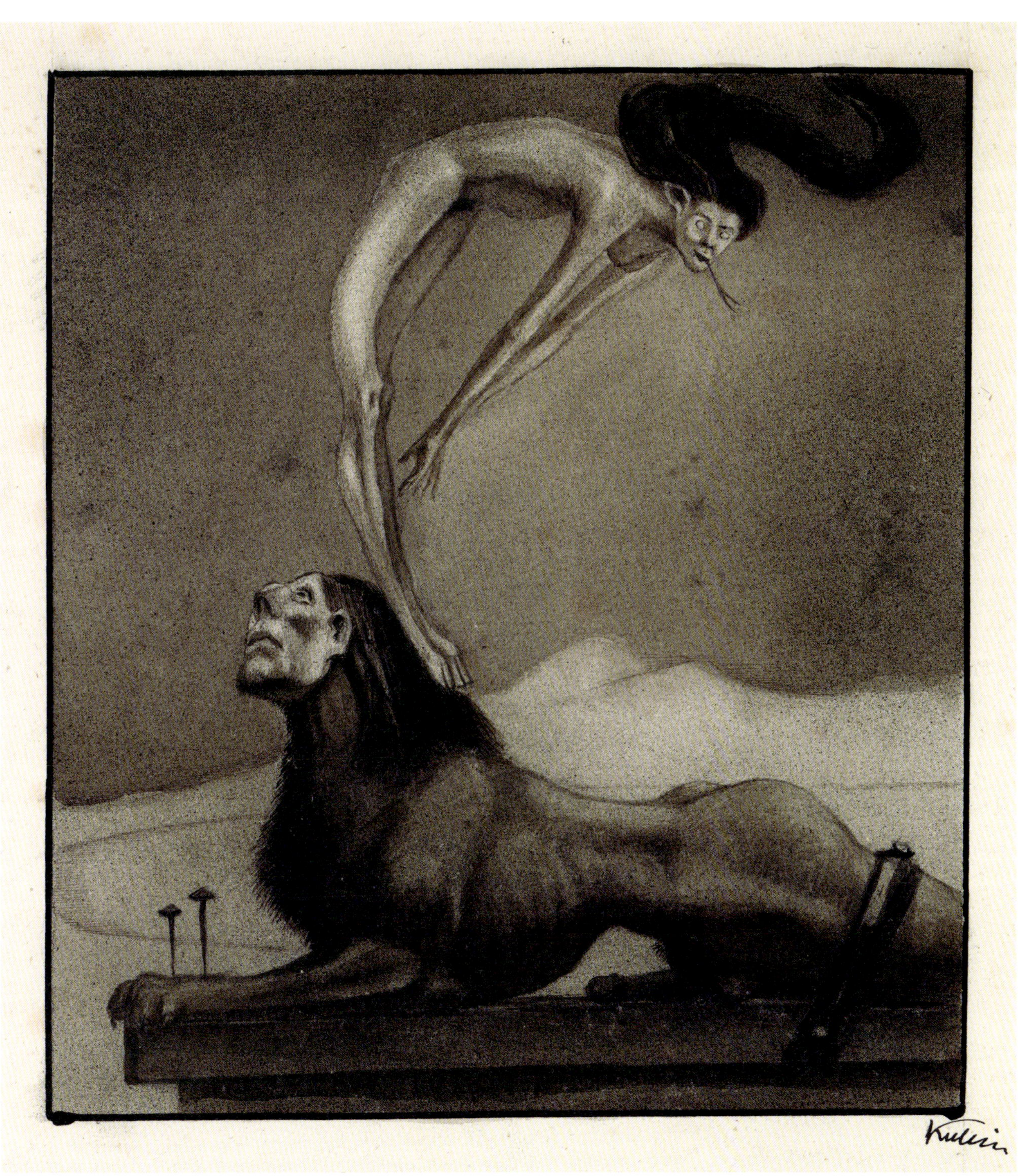

ALFRED KUBIN

The Male Sphinx, 1903

Städtische Galerie im Lenbachhaus und Kunstbau München

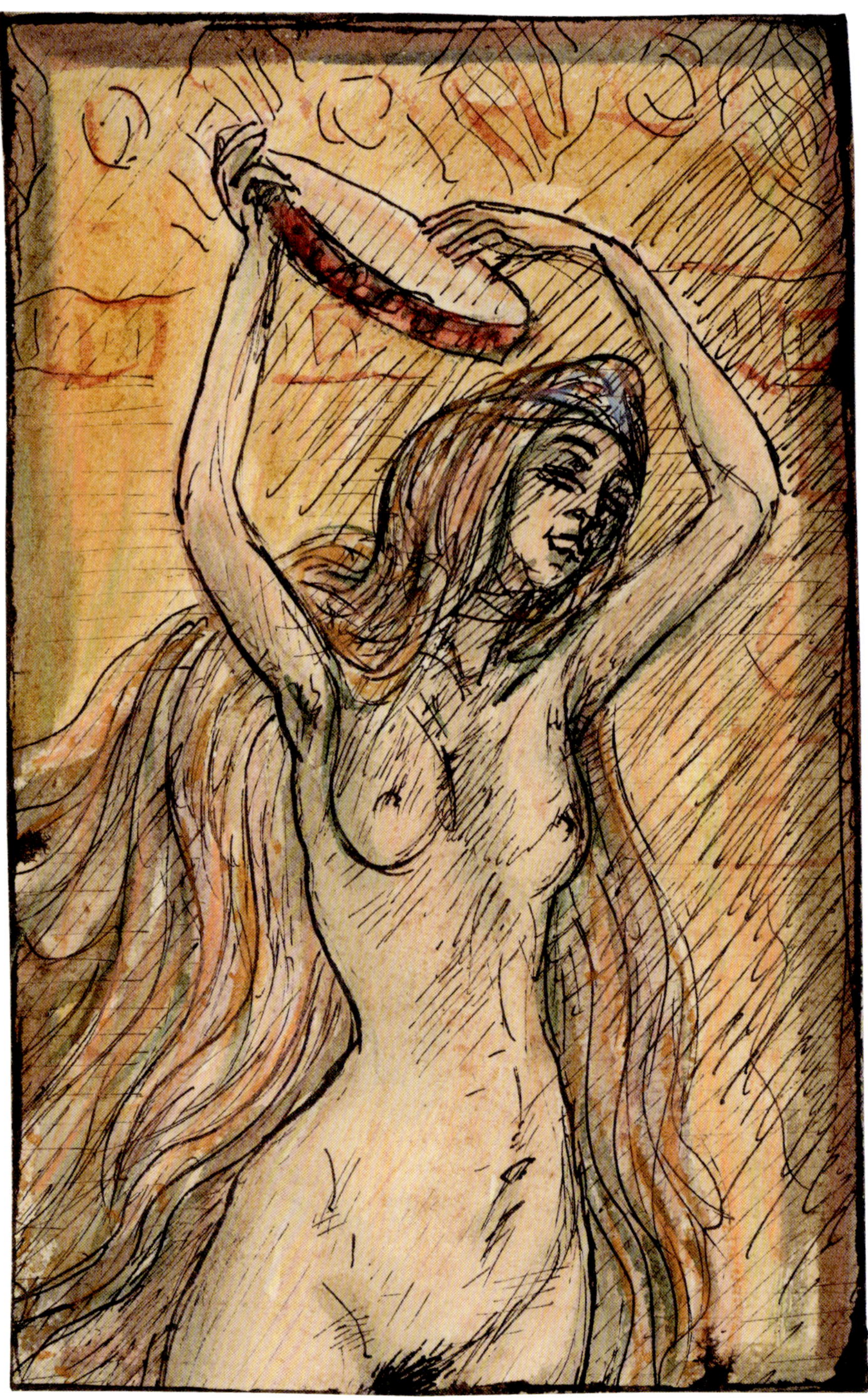

ALFRED KUBIN
The Dancing Salome with Tambourine, c. 1910
Klewan Collection, Munich

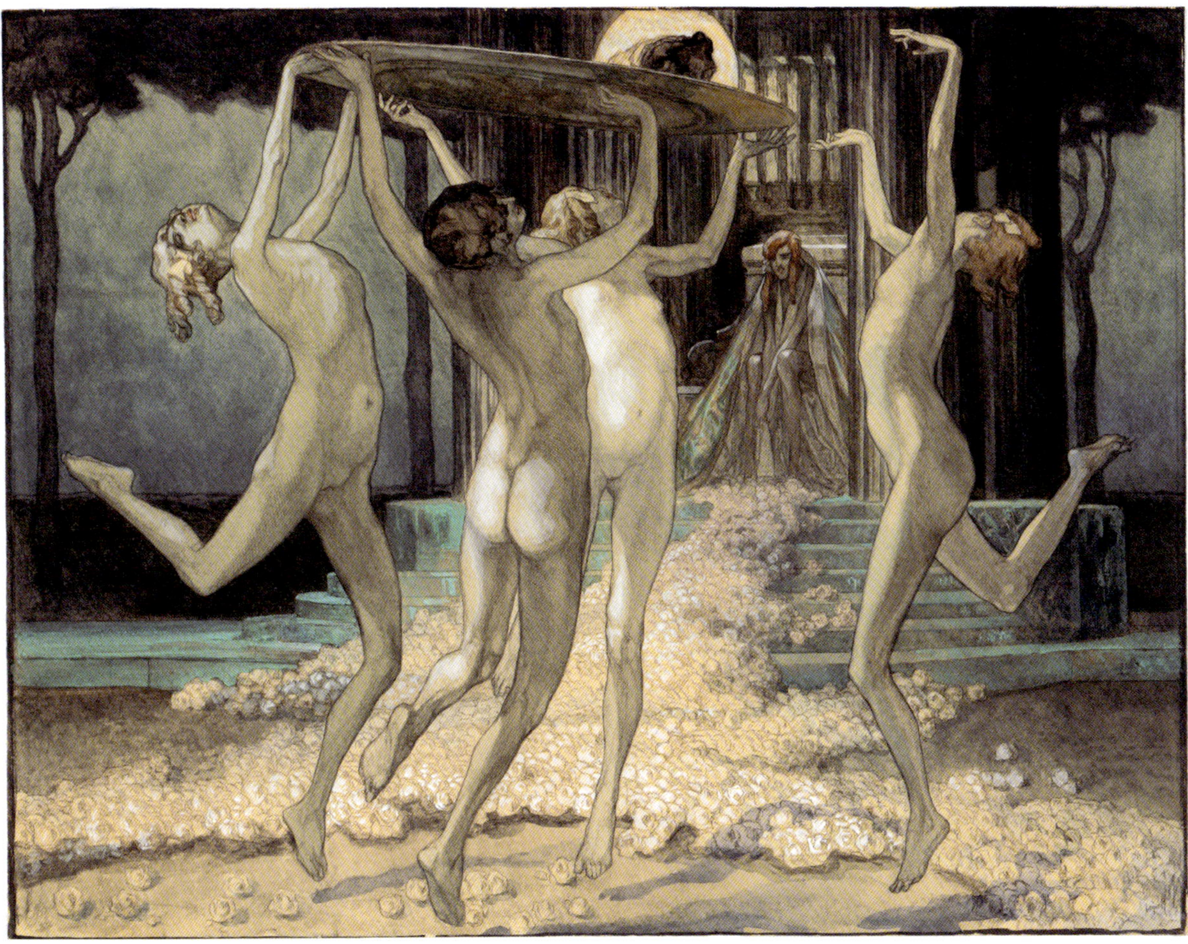

FRANZ VON BAYROS
Sisters of Salome, probably before 1920
The Daulton Collection, Los Altos Hills, California

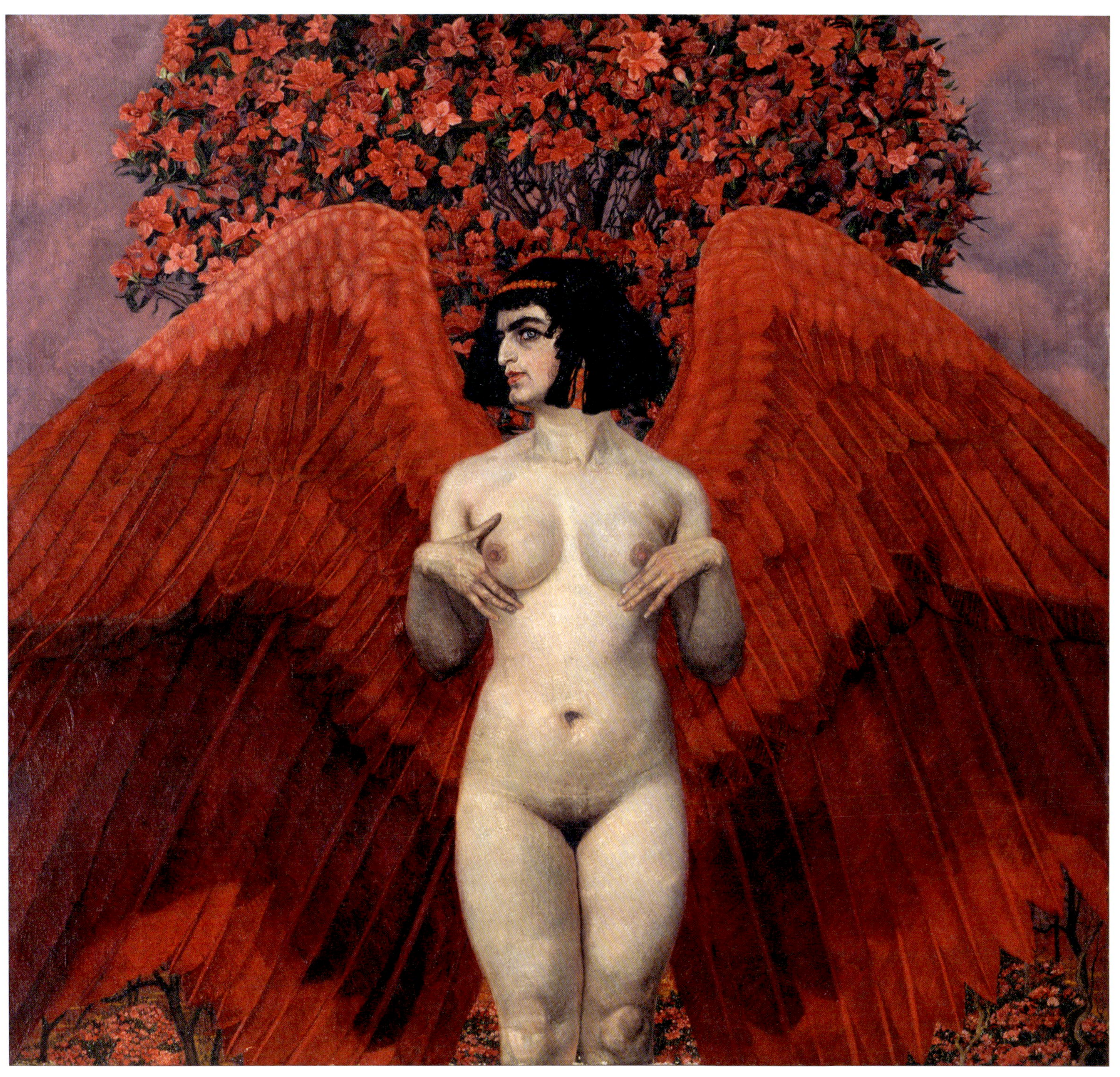

KARL MEDIZ
Red Angel, 1902
Archive Attersee

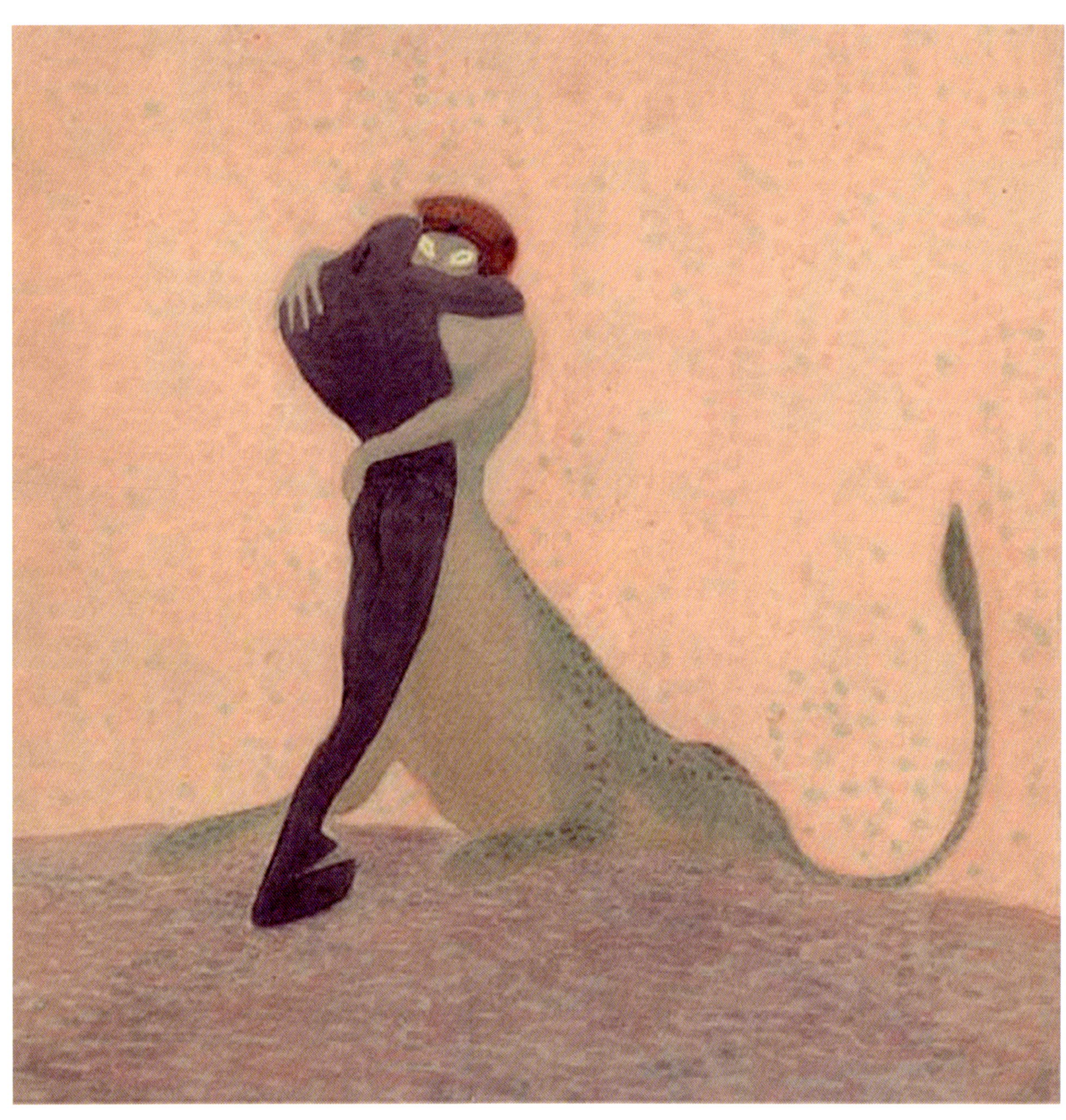

BERTRAM HARTMAN
The Embrace, 1912
Private Collection

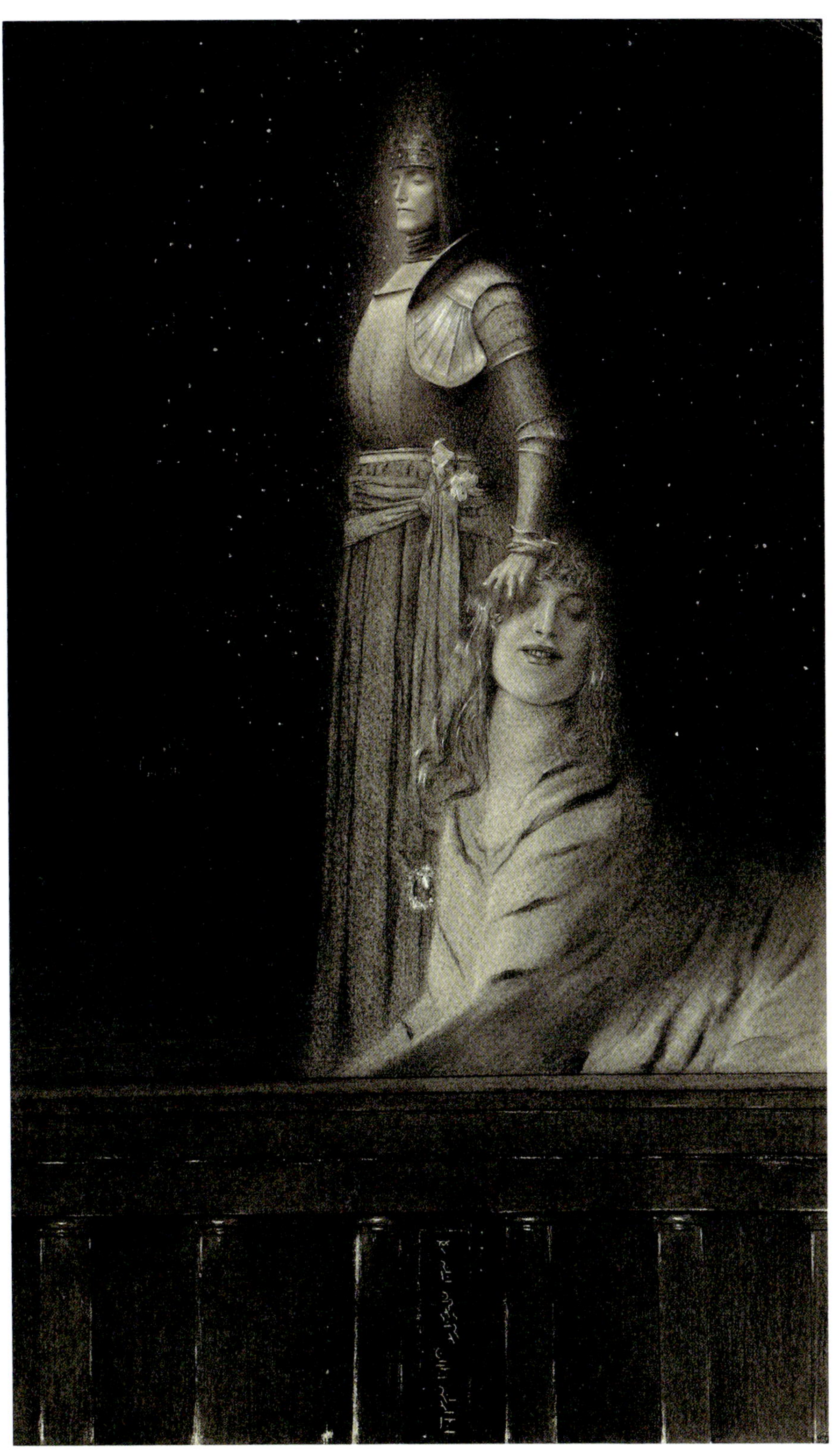

FERNAND KHNOPFF
With Verhaeren. An Angel, 1889
Private Collection

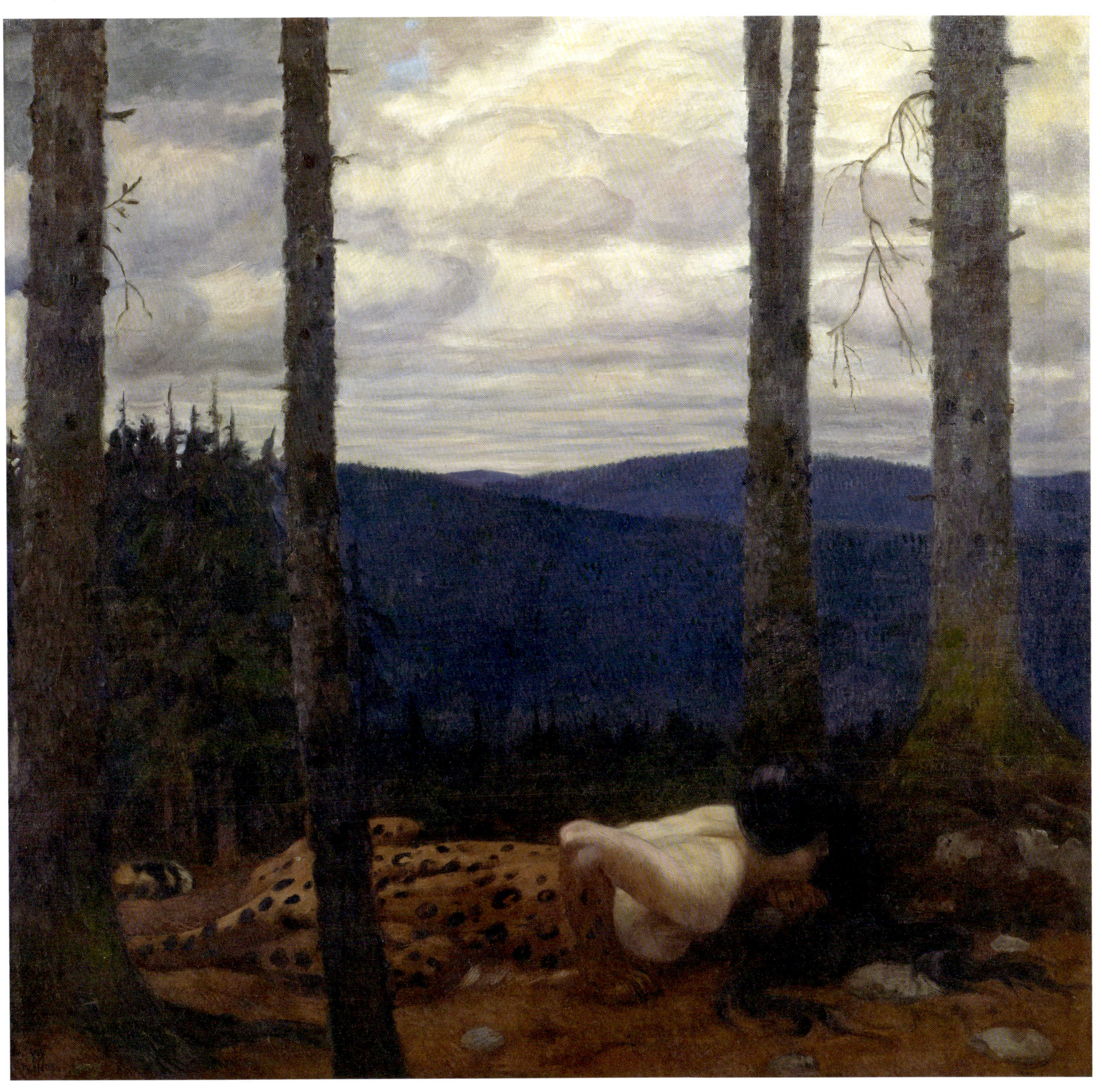

VIKTOR MÜLLER
Sphinx, 1906
Belvedere, Vienna

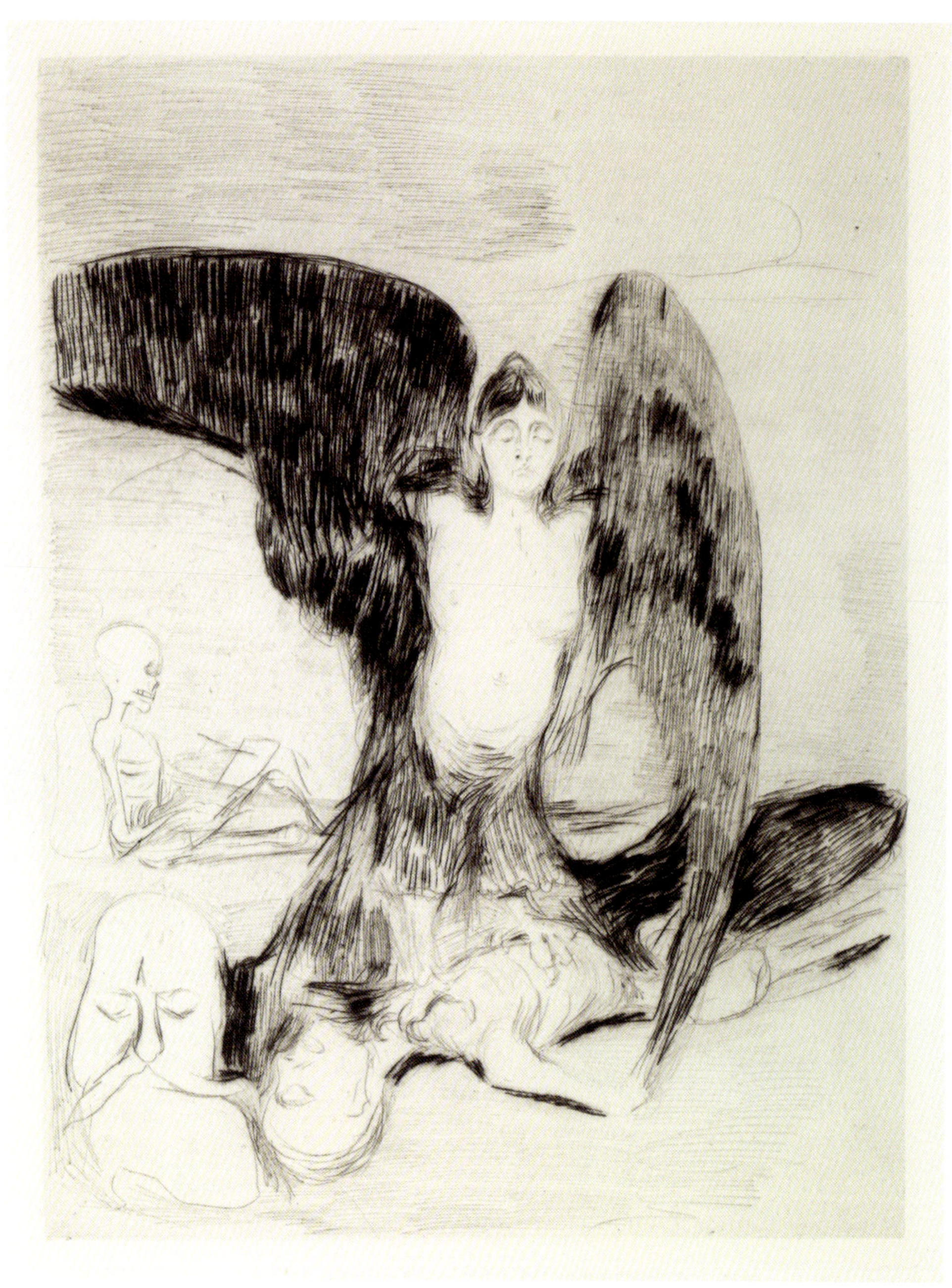

EDVARD MUNCH
Vampire, 1894
Staatliche Museen zu Berlin, Nationalgalerie,
Scharf-Gerstenberg Collection

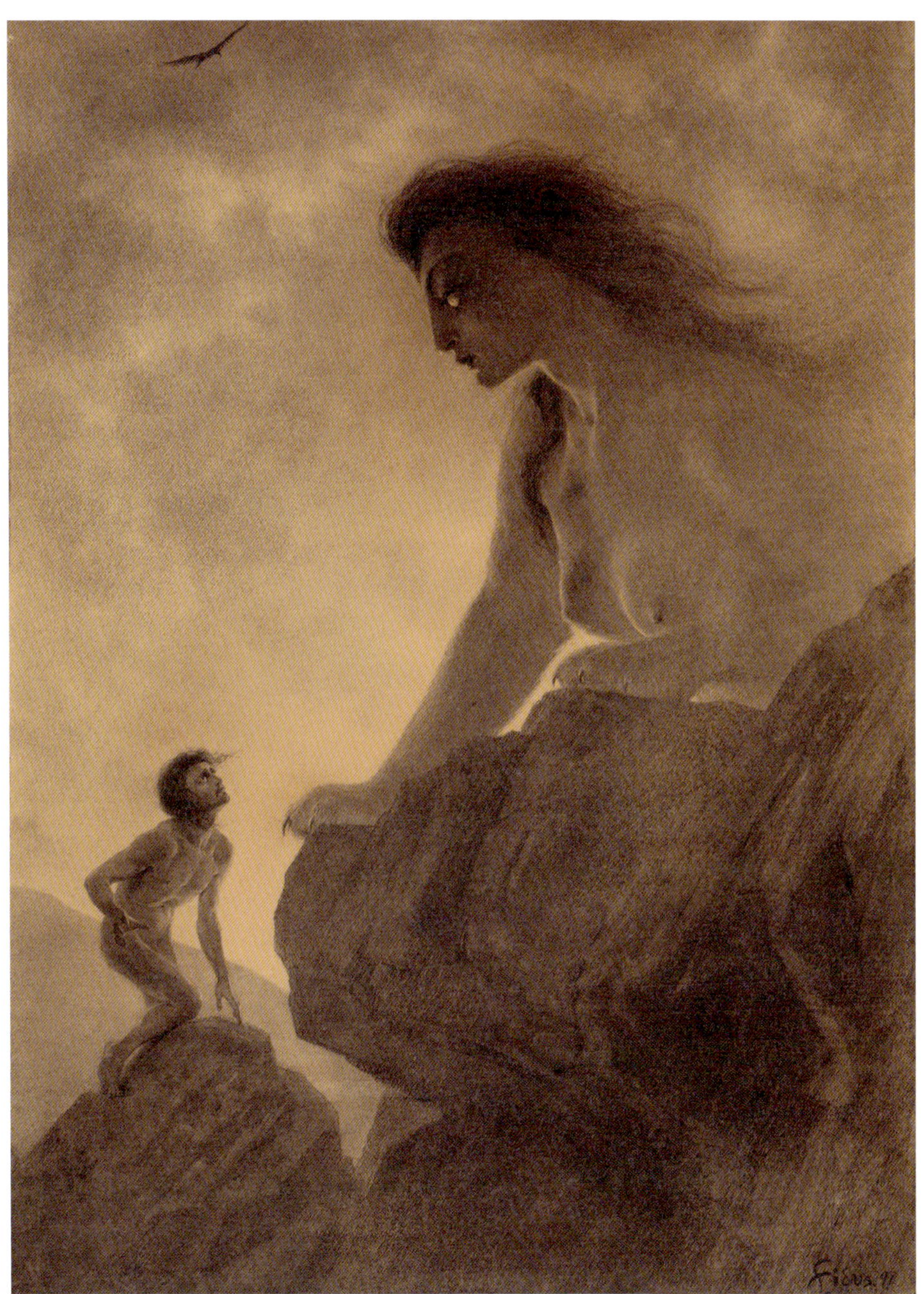

HUGO HÖPPENER (FIDUS)
Sphinx of Life, 1891
The Daulton Collection, Los Altos Hills, California

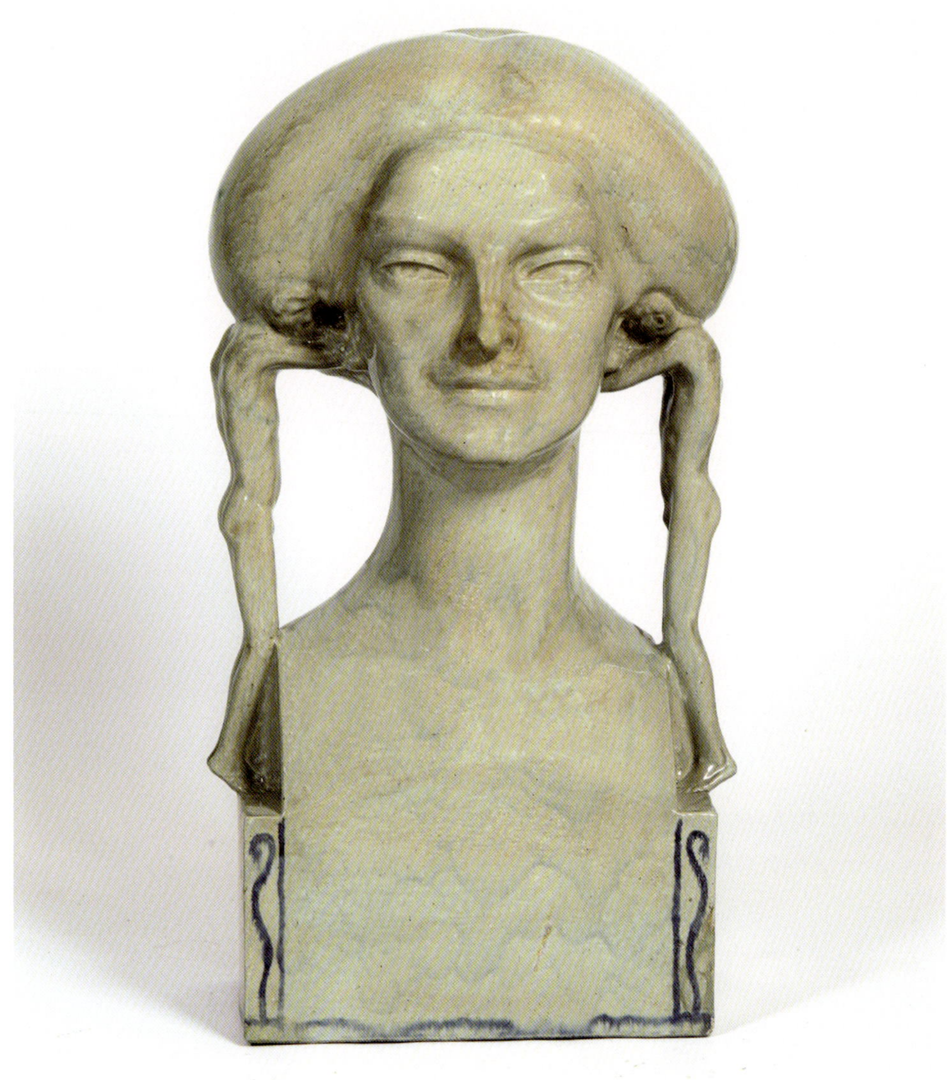

RICHARD LUKSCH
The Insinuation, 1902/03
Leopold Museum, Vienna

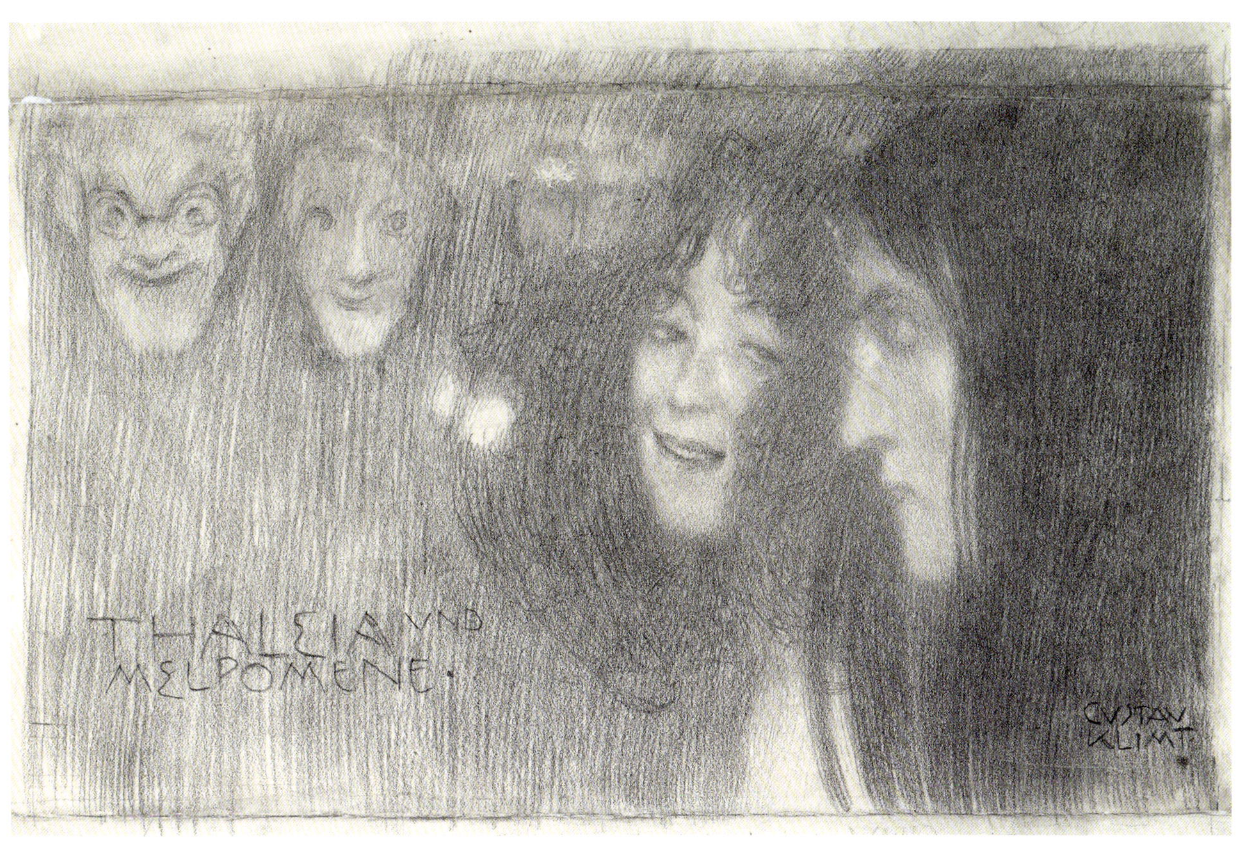

GUSTAV KLIMT
Thaleia and Melpomene, 1898
Albertina, Vienna

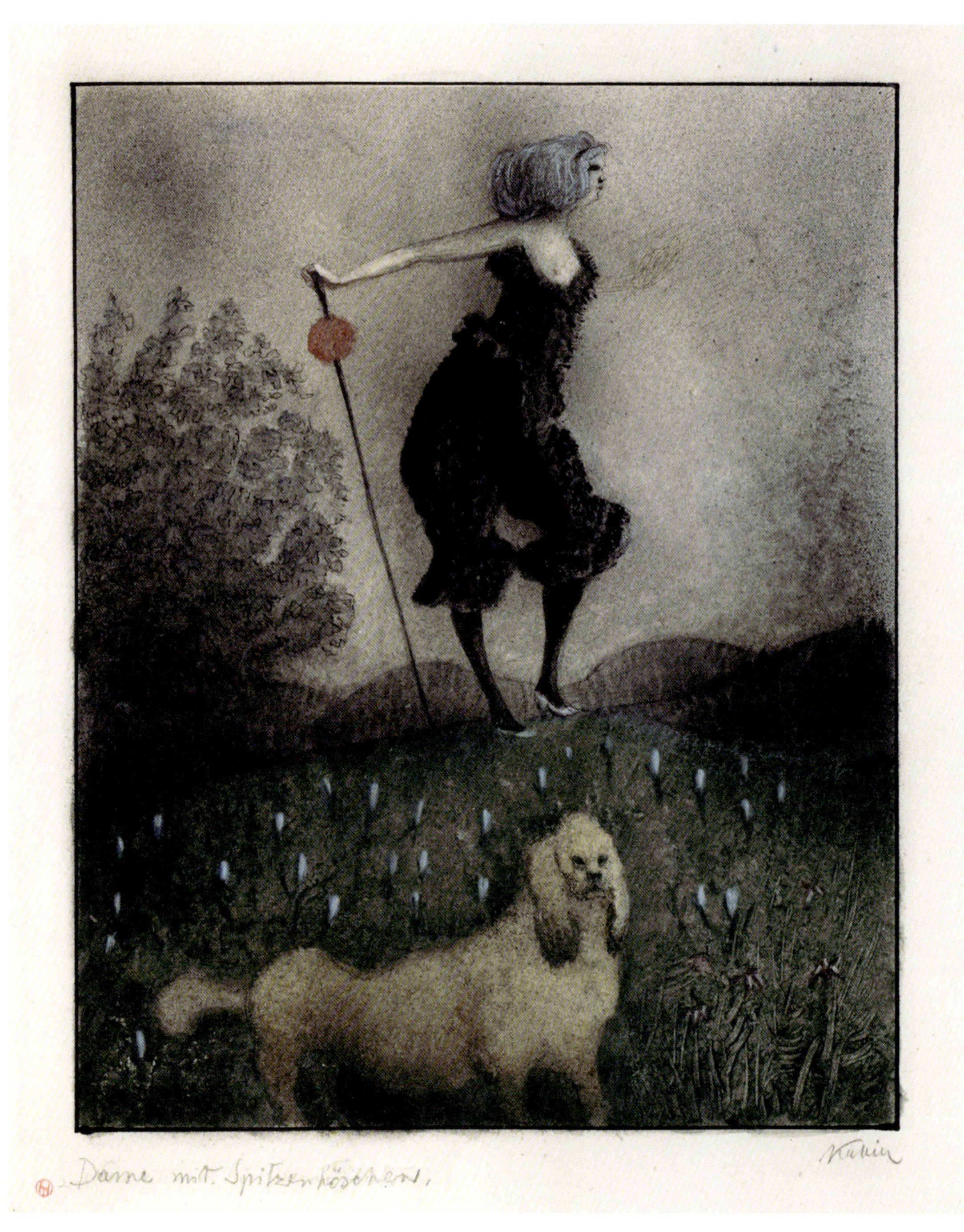

ALFRED KUBIN

Lady with Lace Panties, 1903/06

Leopold Museum, Vienna

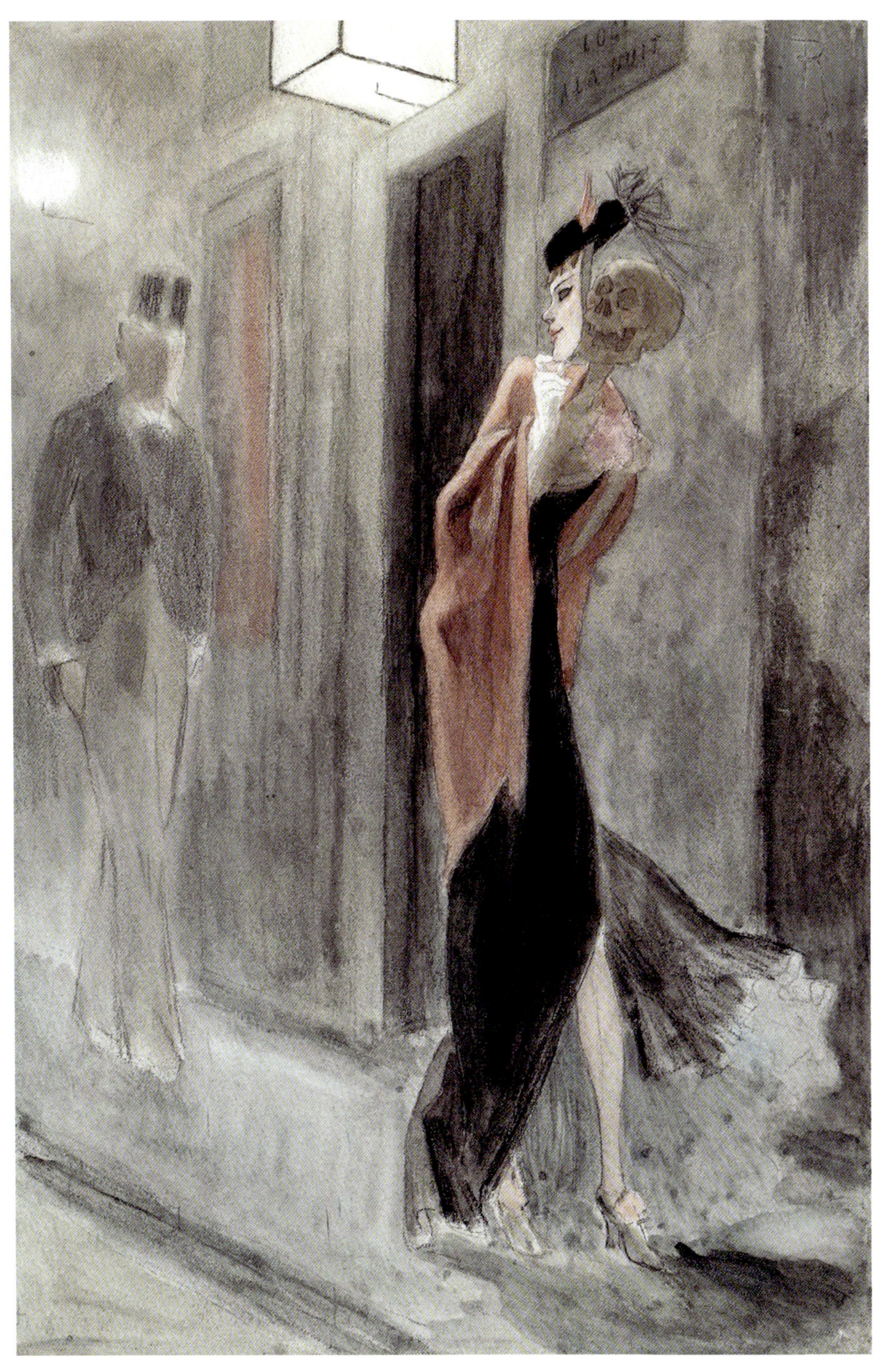

FÉLICIEN ROPS
Street Corner, Four O'Clock in the Morning (Human Parody), 1878–1881
Private Collection

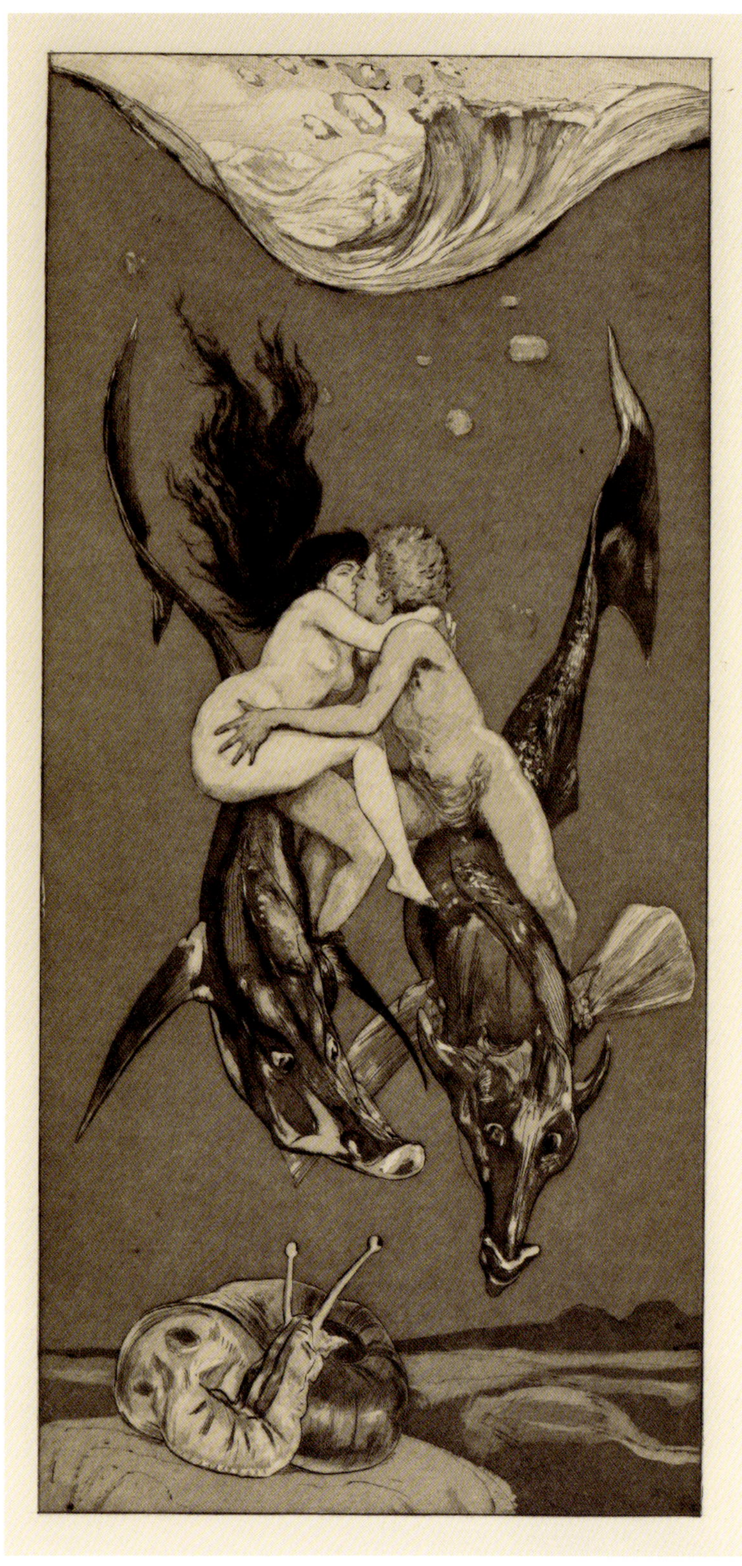

MAX KLINGER
Temptation, from the cycle *A Life,* 1884
The Daulton Collection, Los Altos Hills, California

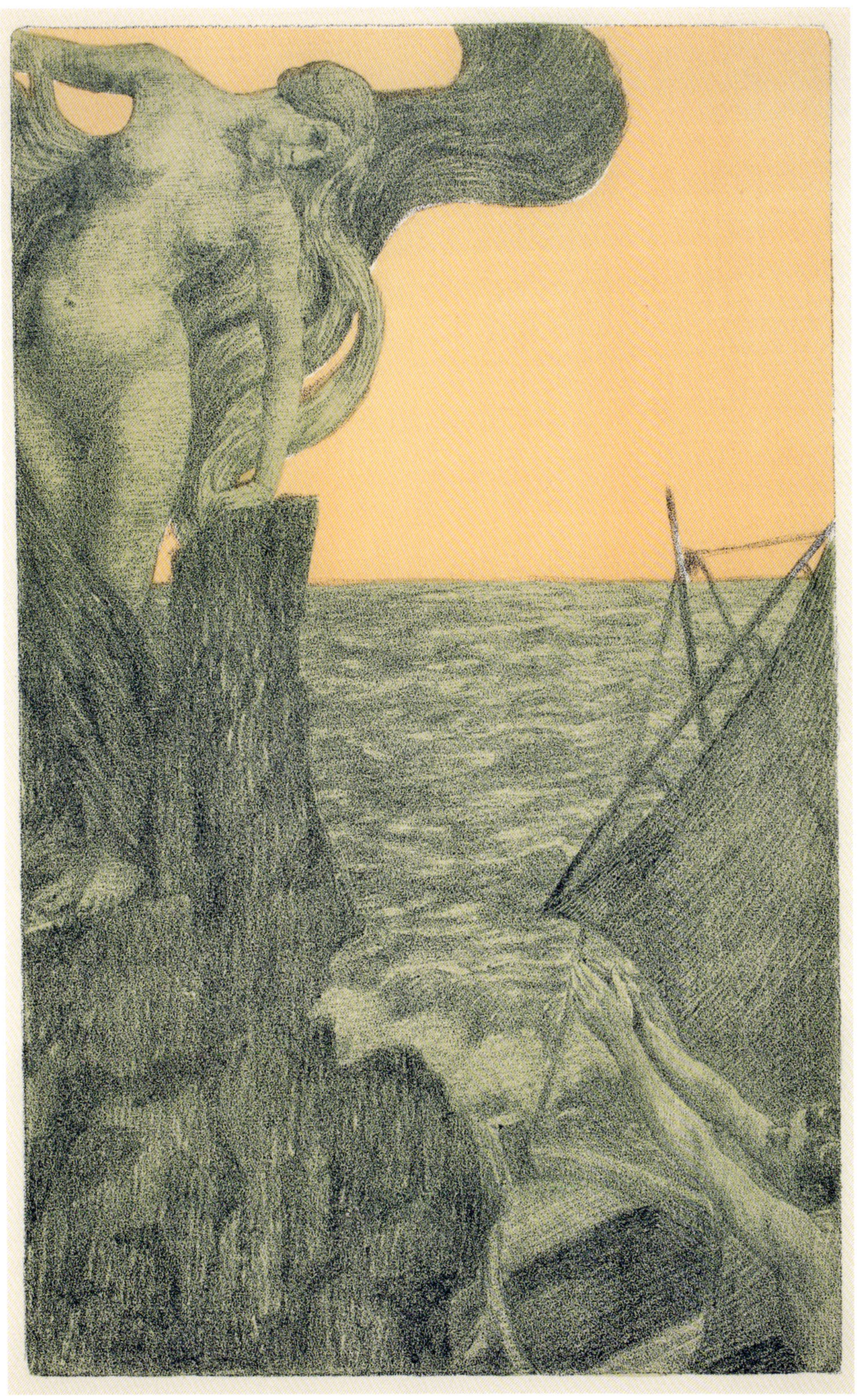

WILHELM LIST
The Siren, print 9 of portfolio *Lithographs of Viennese Artists*, c. 1900
LETTER Foundation, Cologne

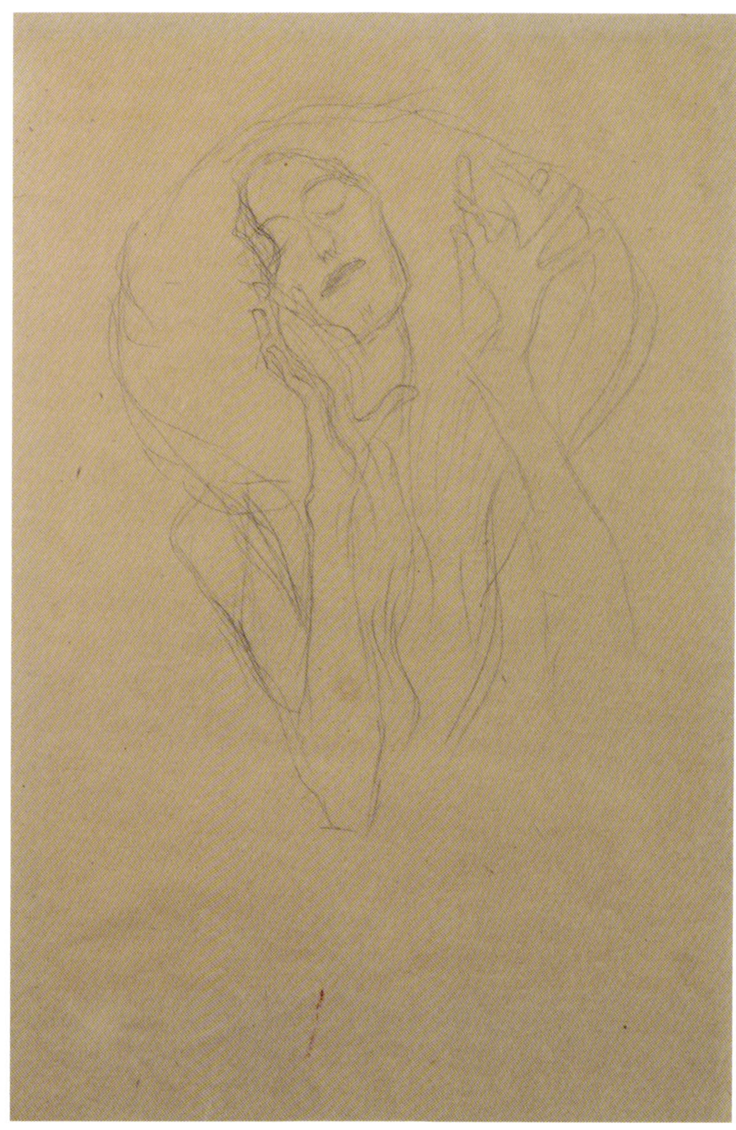

GUSTAV KLIMT
Bust Picture of a Woman With Her Hands in Her Hair, c. 1905
Museum Georg Schäfer, Schweinfurt

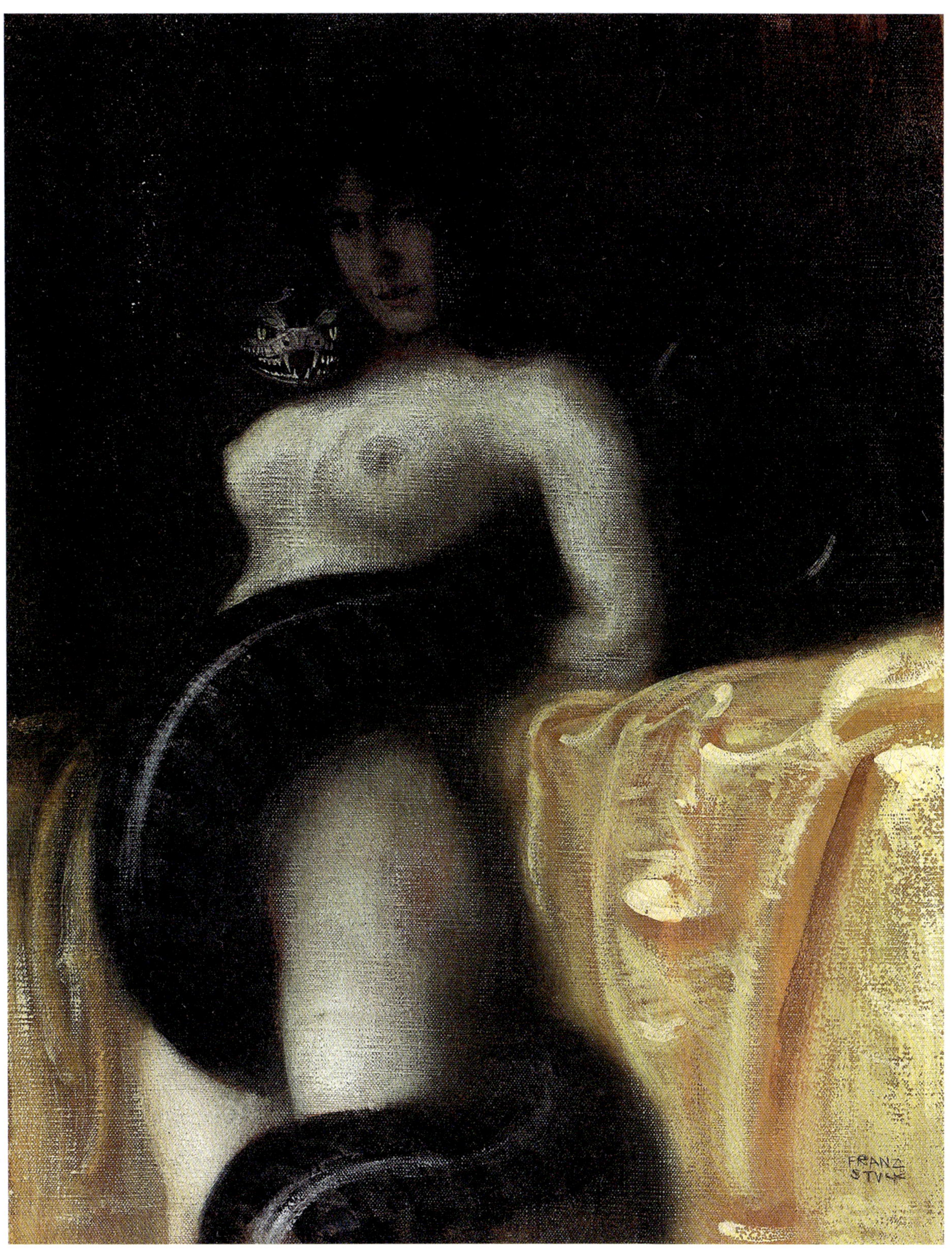

FRANZ VON STUCK
Sensuality, c. 1891
Katharina Büttiker Gallery, Zurich

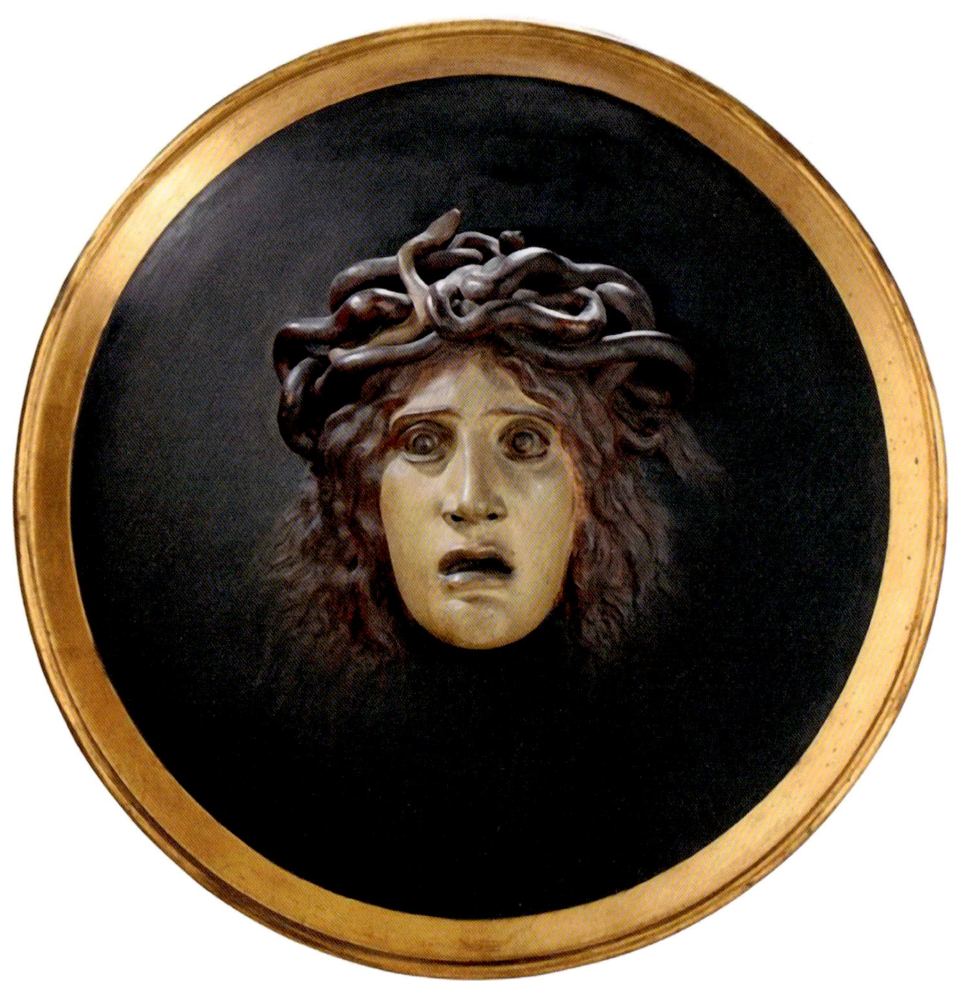

ARNOLD BÖCKLIN/PETER BRUCKMANN
Shield with the Head of Medusa, 1887
Private Collection

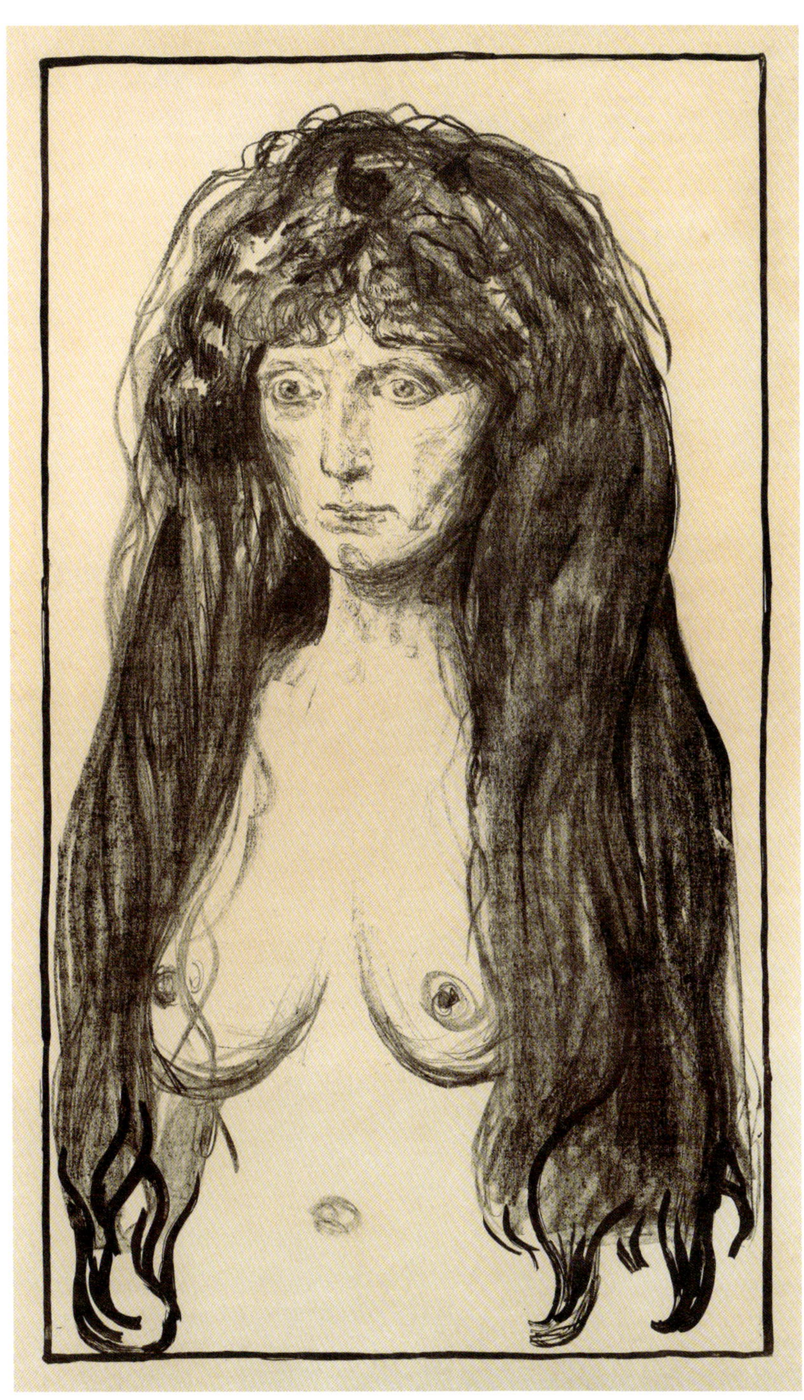

EDVARD MUNCH
The Sin, 1902
Leopold Museum, Vienna

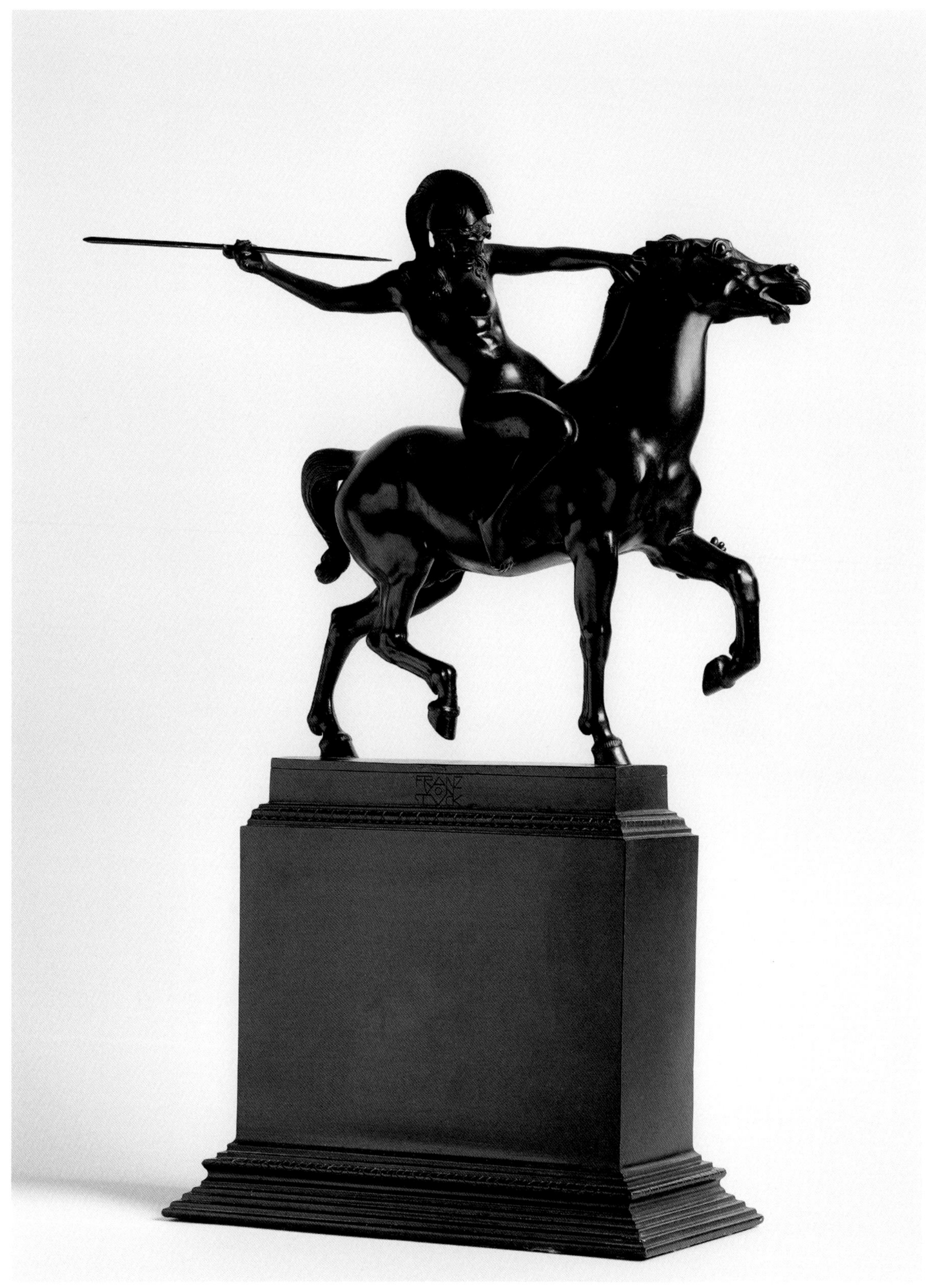

FRANZ VON STUCK
Amazon, 1897–1905
Leopold Museum, Vienna

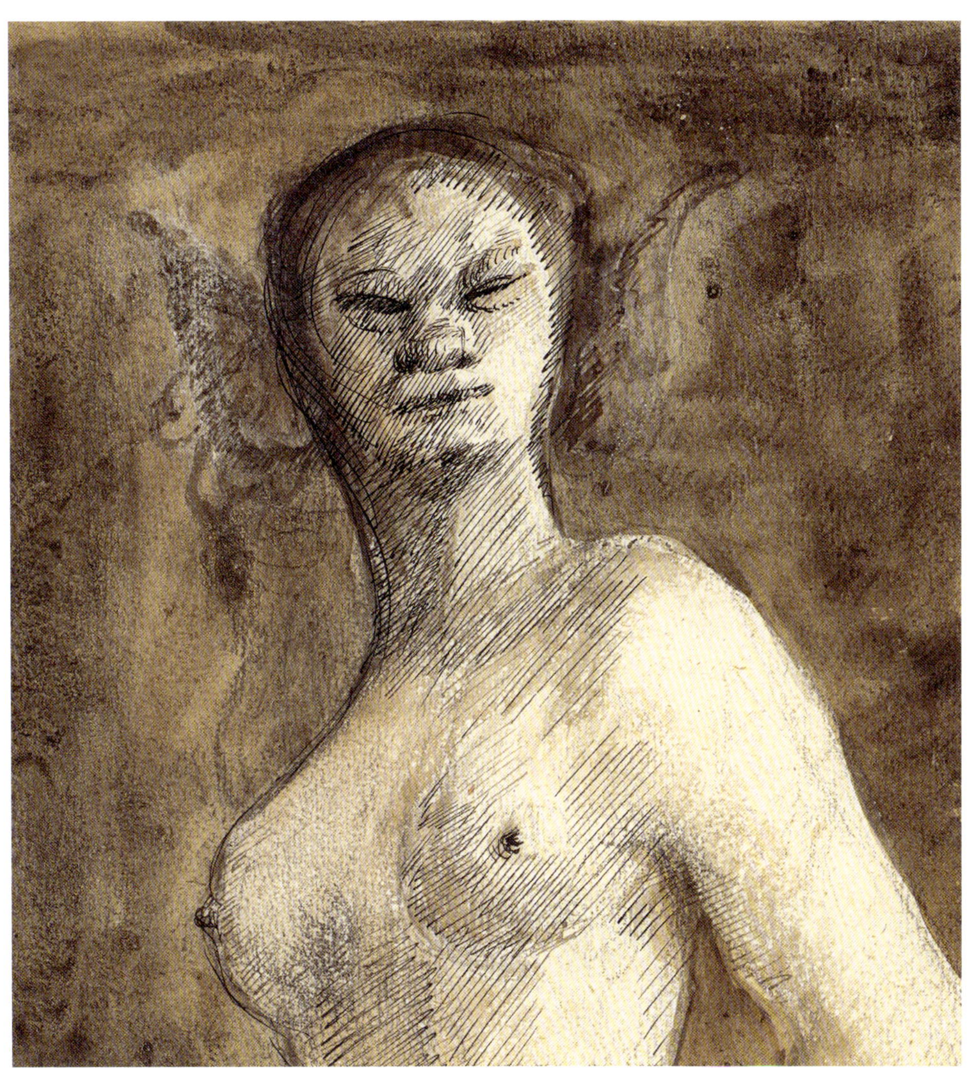

ALFRED KUBIN
Semi-Nude (Catwoman), c. 1910
Leopold, Private Collection

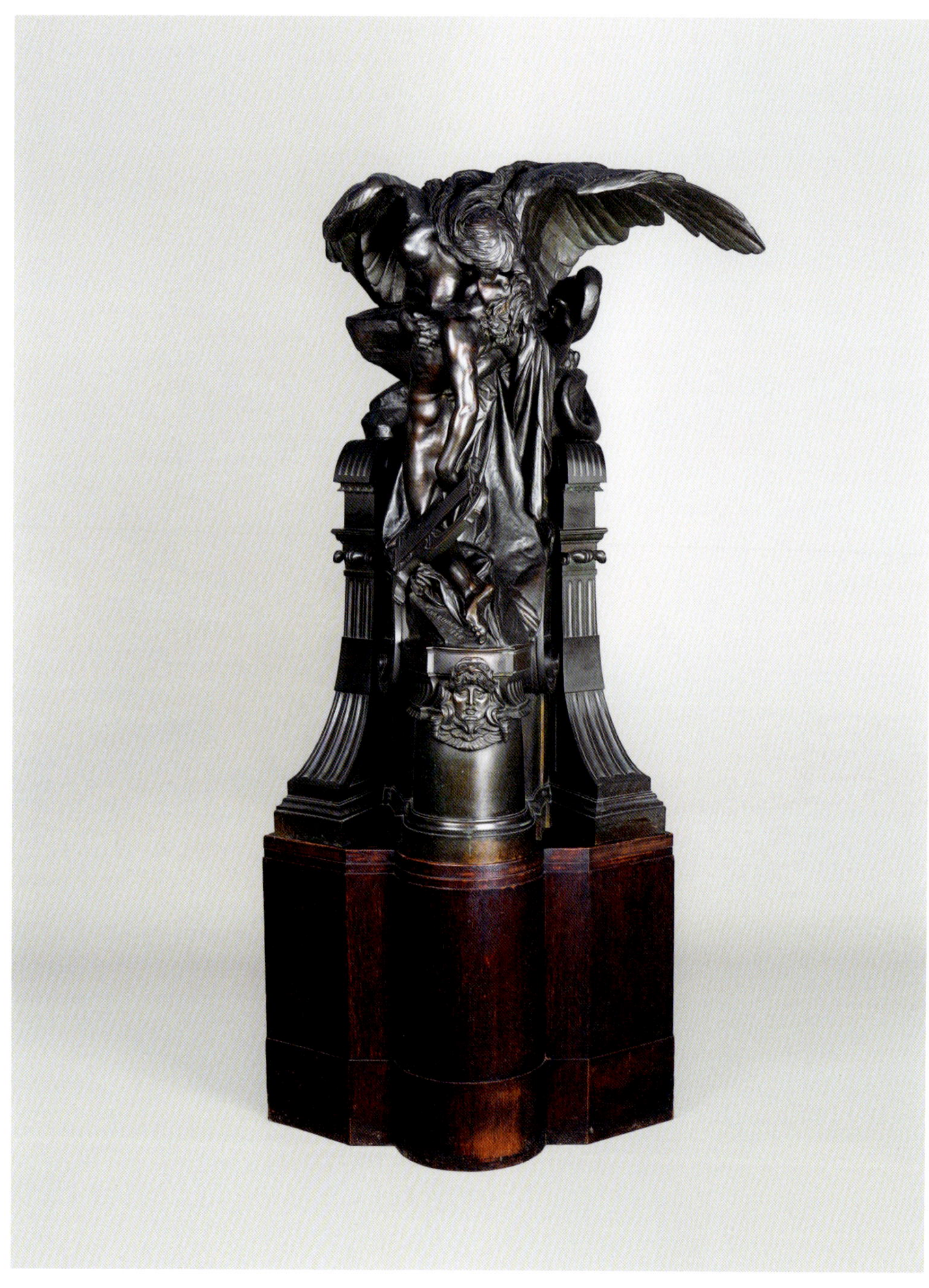

CHRISTIAN BEHRENS
Sphinx, 1880 (model)/1894 (casting)
Belvedere, Vienna, Permanent loan LETTER Foundation, Cologne

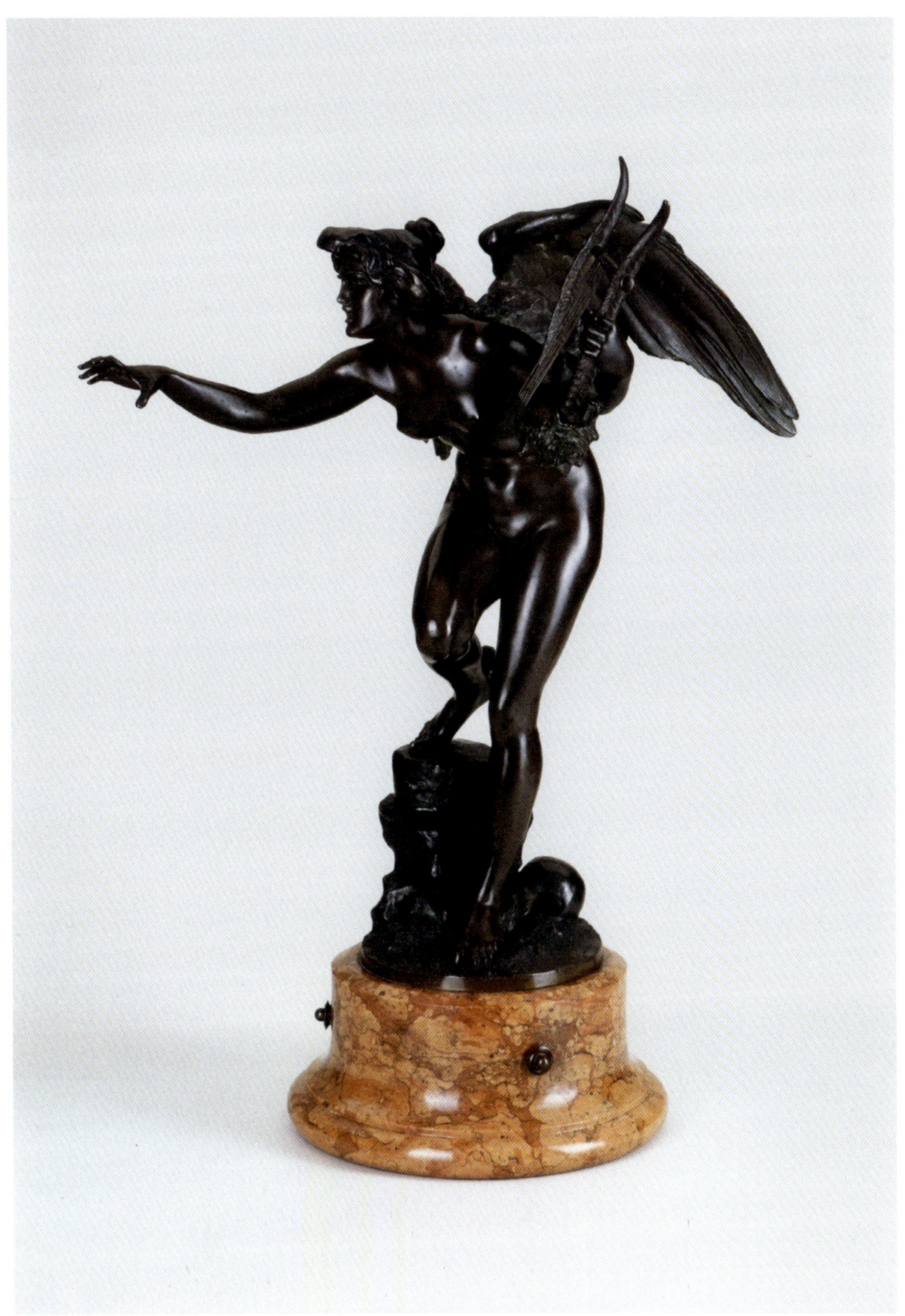

RUDOLPH HÖLBE
Siren, 1885
LETTER Foundation, Cologne

Alfred Kubin about Edvard Munch

Neither did I much care for the paintings, meant to be impressionist, that newly emerged in Germany around 1900. I understand the compulsion for new ways that conveys itself to many modern creators, and I readily admit that, lifted from the depth of the soul in this way, a surprising source of inspiring beauty comes to light. What seems most important to me is the syntheses. The Norwegian Edvard Munch who invited me to visit him I first met in Berlin in 1903. The syntheses that Edvard Munch created however, ease our fundamental feeling where analytic experiments can hardly intrigue any longer.*

* Alfred Kubin, "Feststellungen 1949", in Abraham Horodisch: *Alfred Kubin als Buchillustrator* (Amsterdam, 1949), p. 42ff.

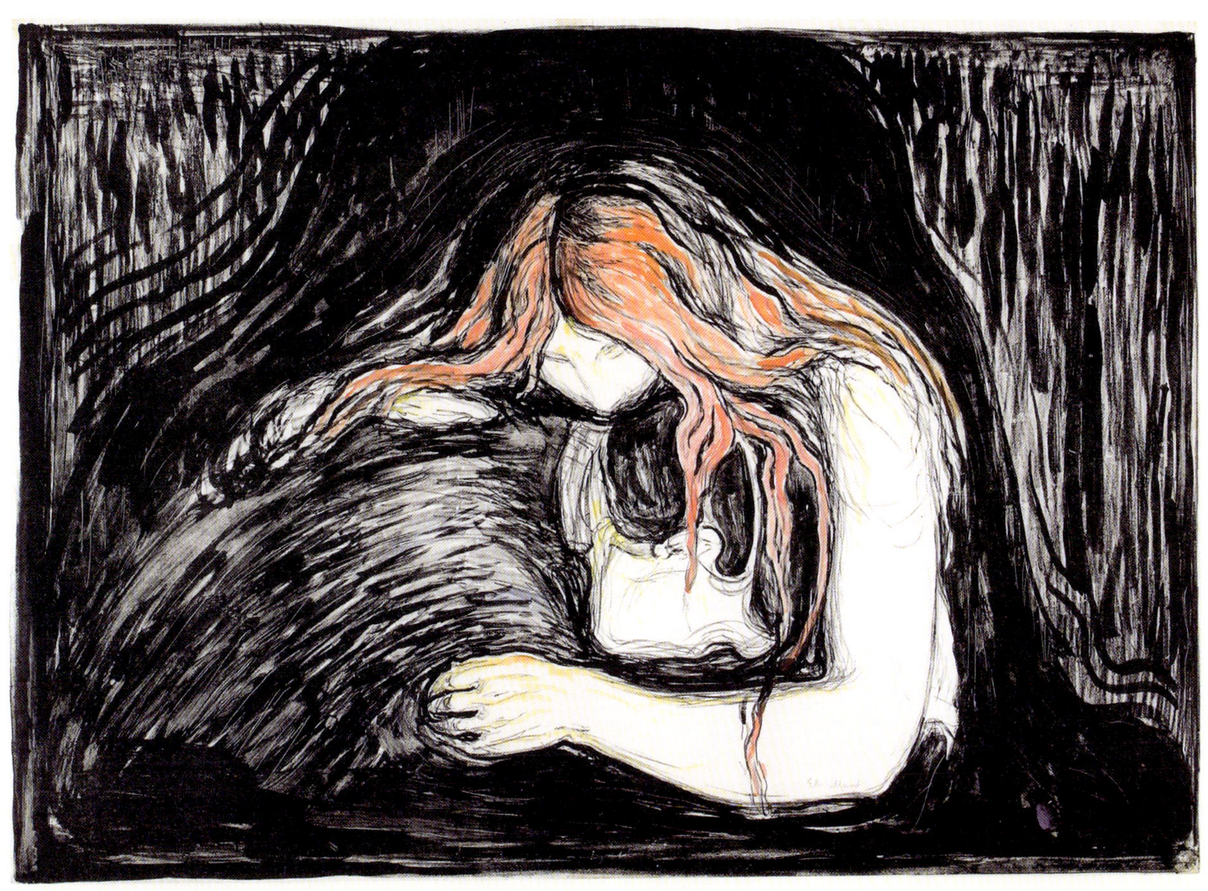

EDVARD MUNCH
Vampire II, 1895–1902
Private Collection Vienna

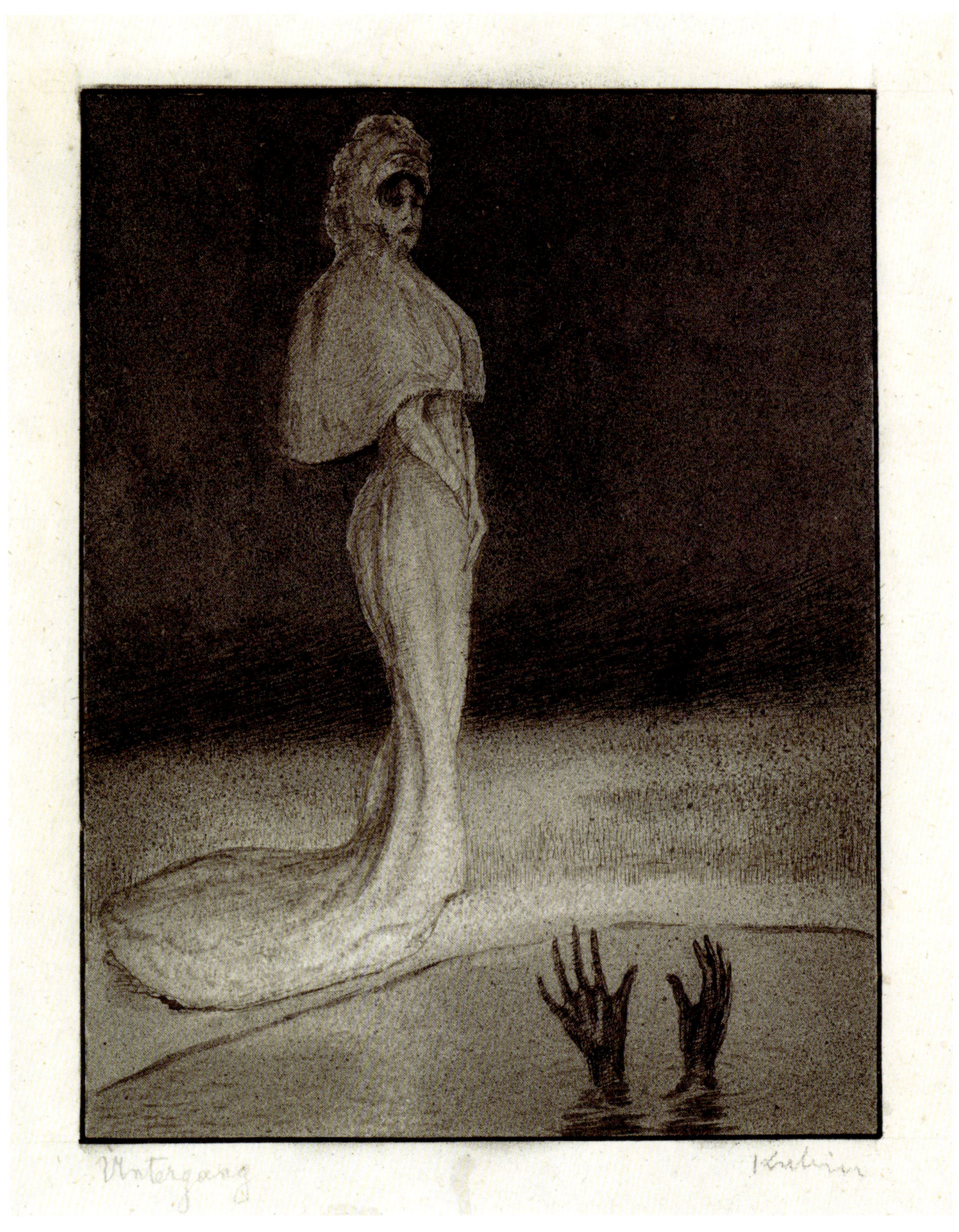

ALFRED KUBIN
Downfall, 1903
Staatliche Museen zu Berlin, Nationalgalerie,
Scharf-Gerstenberg Collection

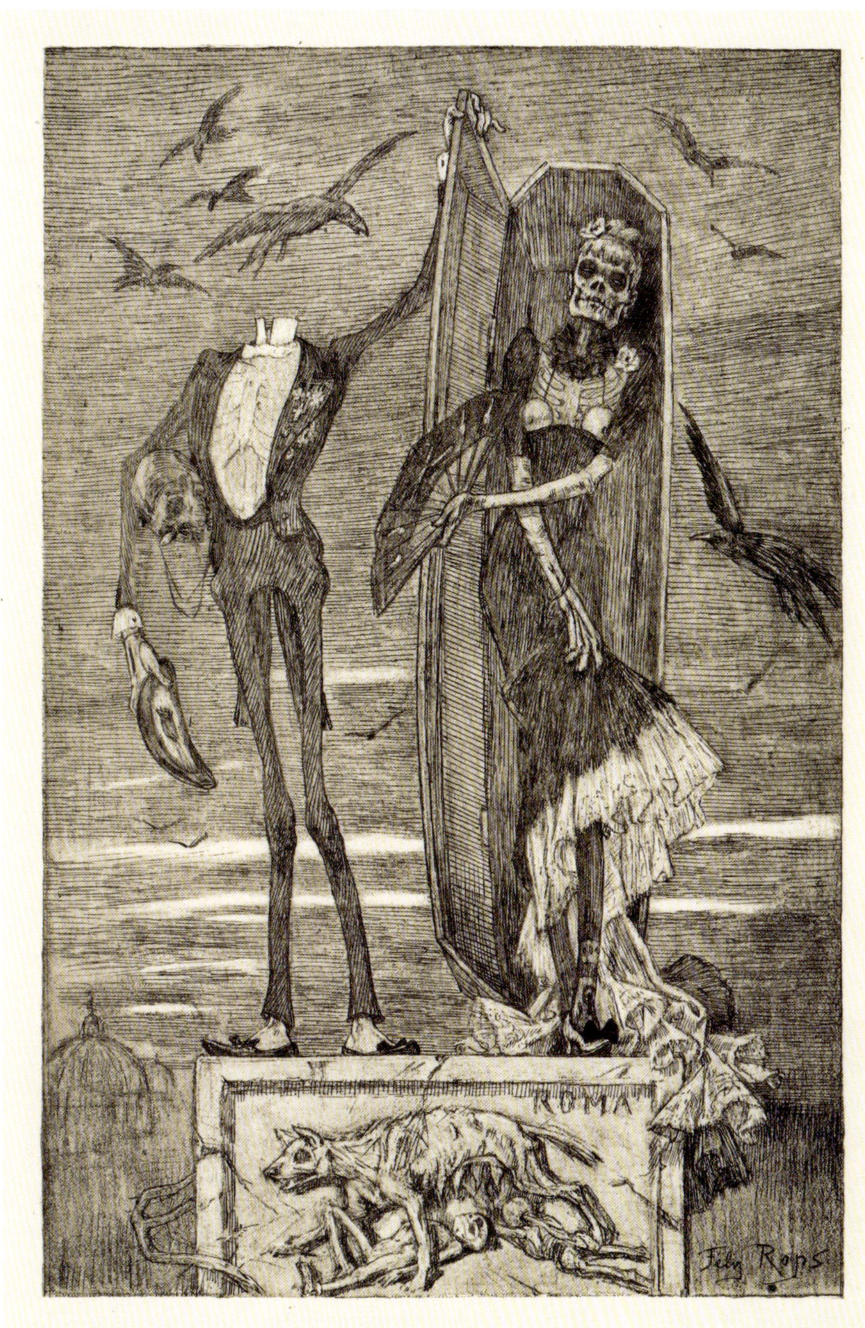

FÉLICIEN ROPS
Frontispiece for *Le vice suprême* by Joséphin Péladan, 1884
Museum voor Schone Kunsten, Gent (Belgium)

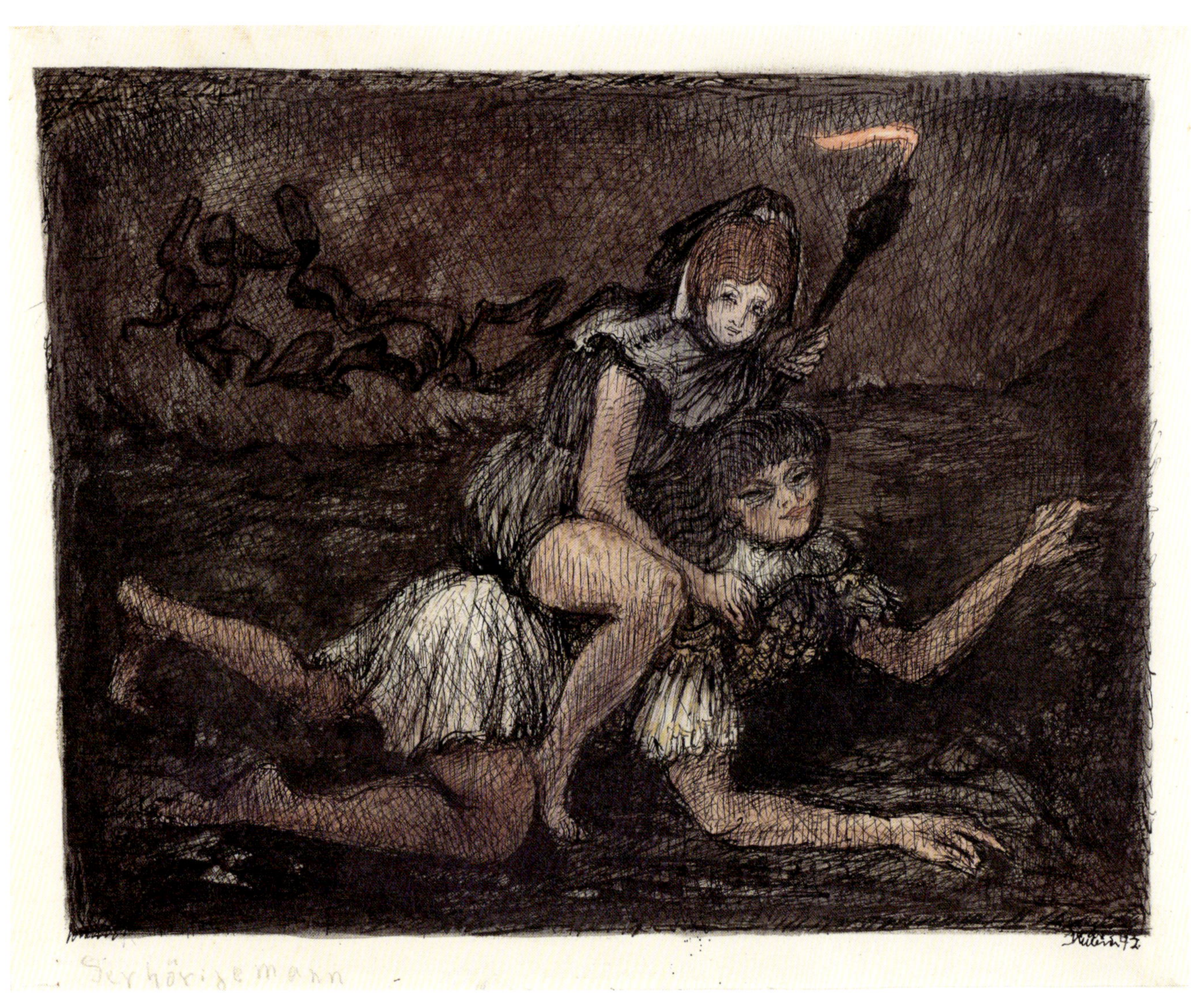

ALFRED KUBIN
The Obedient Man, 1942
Lentos Kunstmuseum Linz

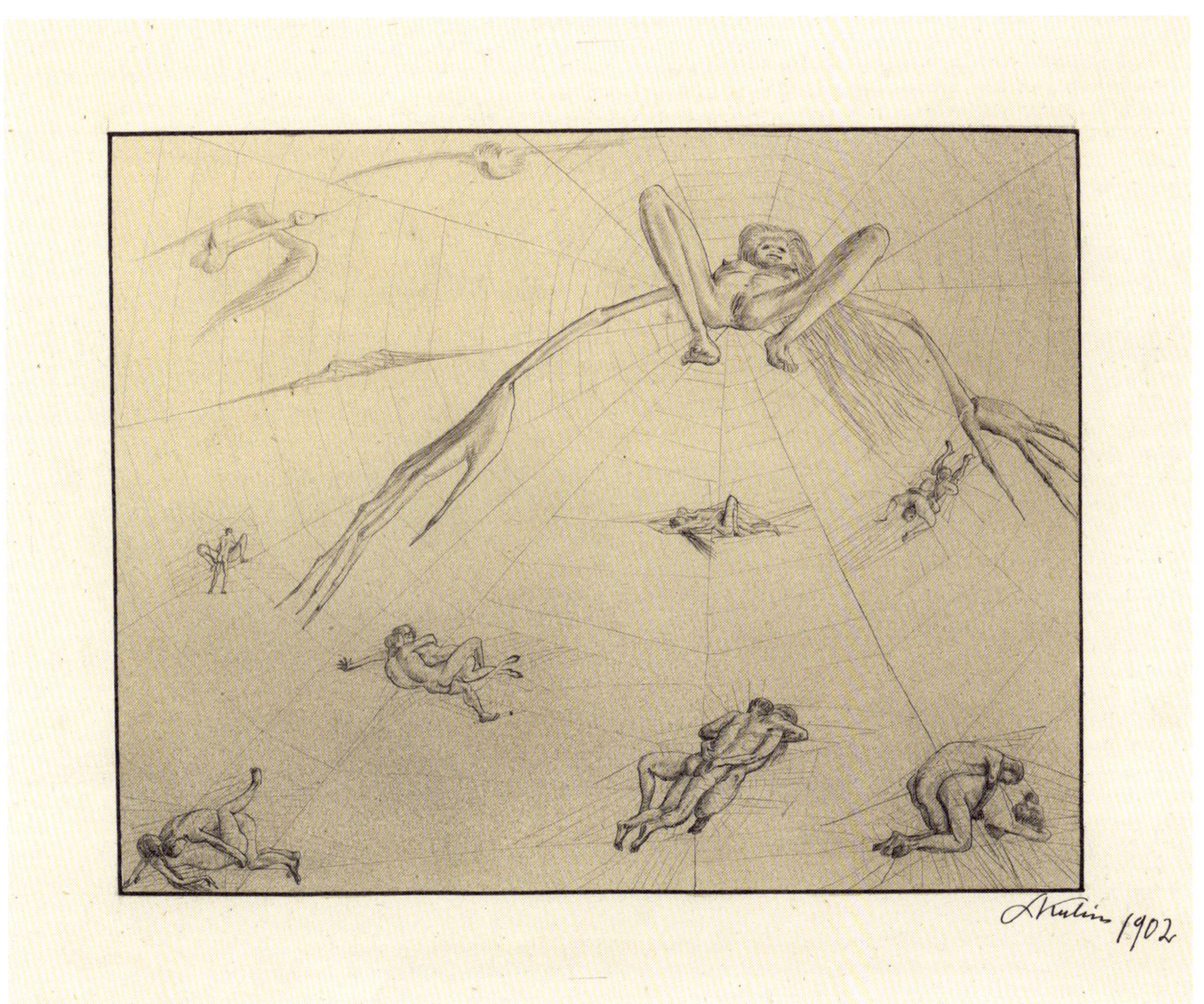

ALFRED KUBIN
The Spider, c. 1901/02
Albertina, Vienna

THE LAST ADVENTURE

The work *The Last Adventure,* which shows the encounter between a woman—coiled up like a snake, her head with its deadly, burning eyes thrust forward under a broad, flowing mane of hair—and a helmeted warrior in a dark desert landscape. It was described in an emphatic manner by Christoph Brockhaus: "The sexes brutishly creeping towards each other, literally and metaphorically, the man becomes hesitant, insecure and fearful."* Furthermore, it is the disgust—the nameless paralysis triggered by the reptile-like apparition—that perverts the spellbinding fascination of the feminine. This blend of horror and disgust, which Kubin explored in many of his works, was referred to already in 1911 by Wilhelm Michel: "Disgust appears like a mask of horror, or rather, as its companion. For disgust is the strongest sensation of the untoward, it is nearly no longer an emotion but rather a blind instinctual protection against the repugnant that the body cannot bear; a shaking off of dirt and vermin too deplorable to fight; the disgust, the panicked dread of the meek and dull body, a sensation which represents a degradation of the mind in and of itself.**

Annegret Hoberg

* Christoph Brockhaus, in: *Alfred Kubin. Das zeichnerische Frühwerk bis 1904*, ed. by Hans Albert Peters (Baden-Baden, 1977), p. 158 (exh. cat. Kunsthalle Baden-Baden, 01.04.–30.05.1977)

** Wilhelm Michel: *Das Teuflische und Groteske in der Kunst* (Munich, 1911), p. 67

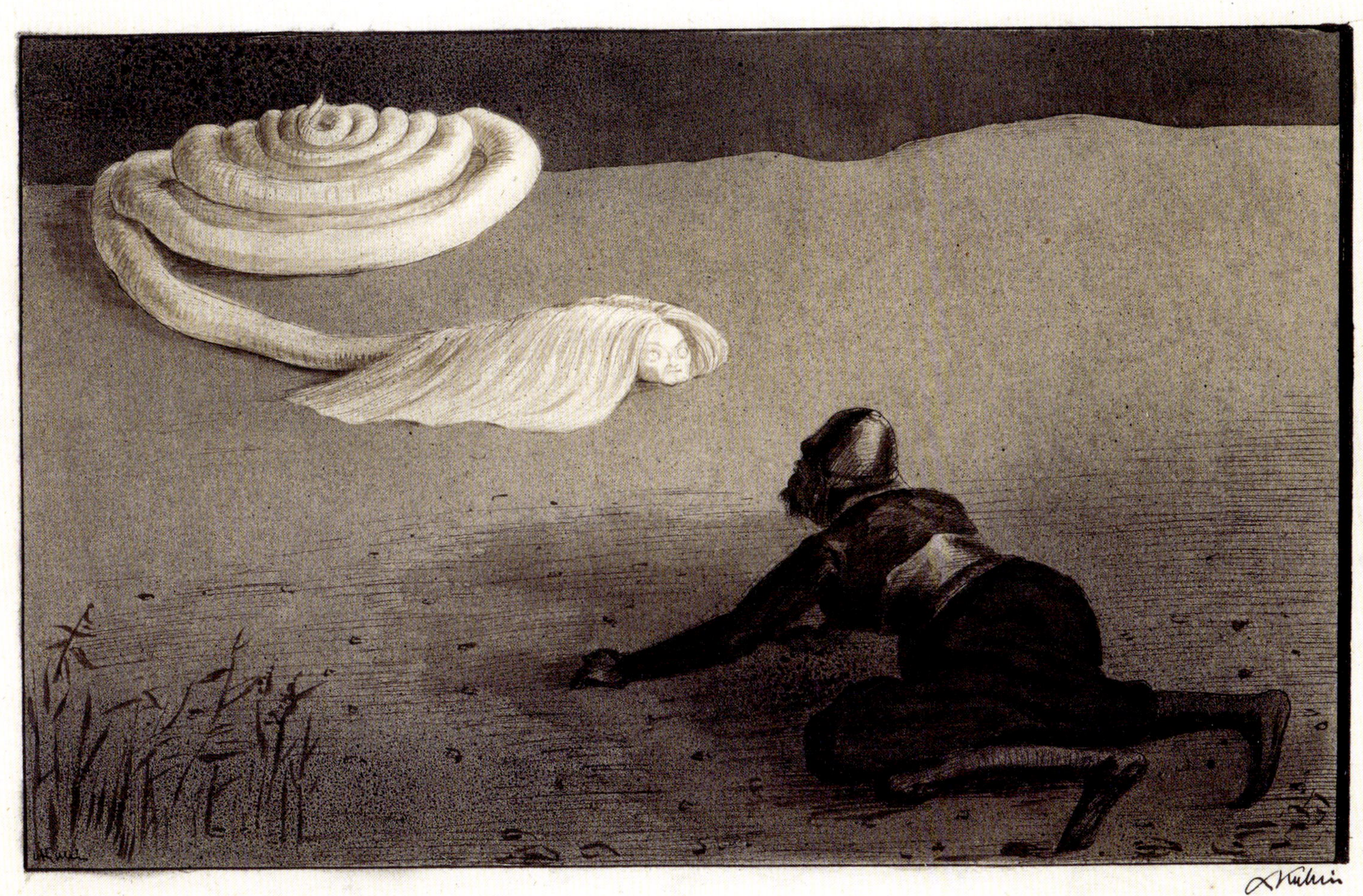

ALFRED KUBIN
The Last Adventure, c. 1901
Leopold Museum, Vienna

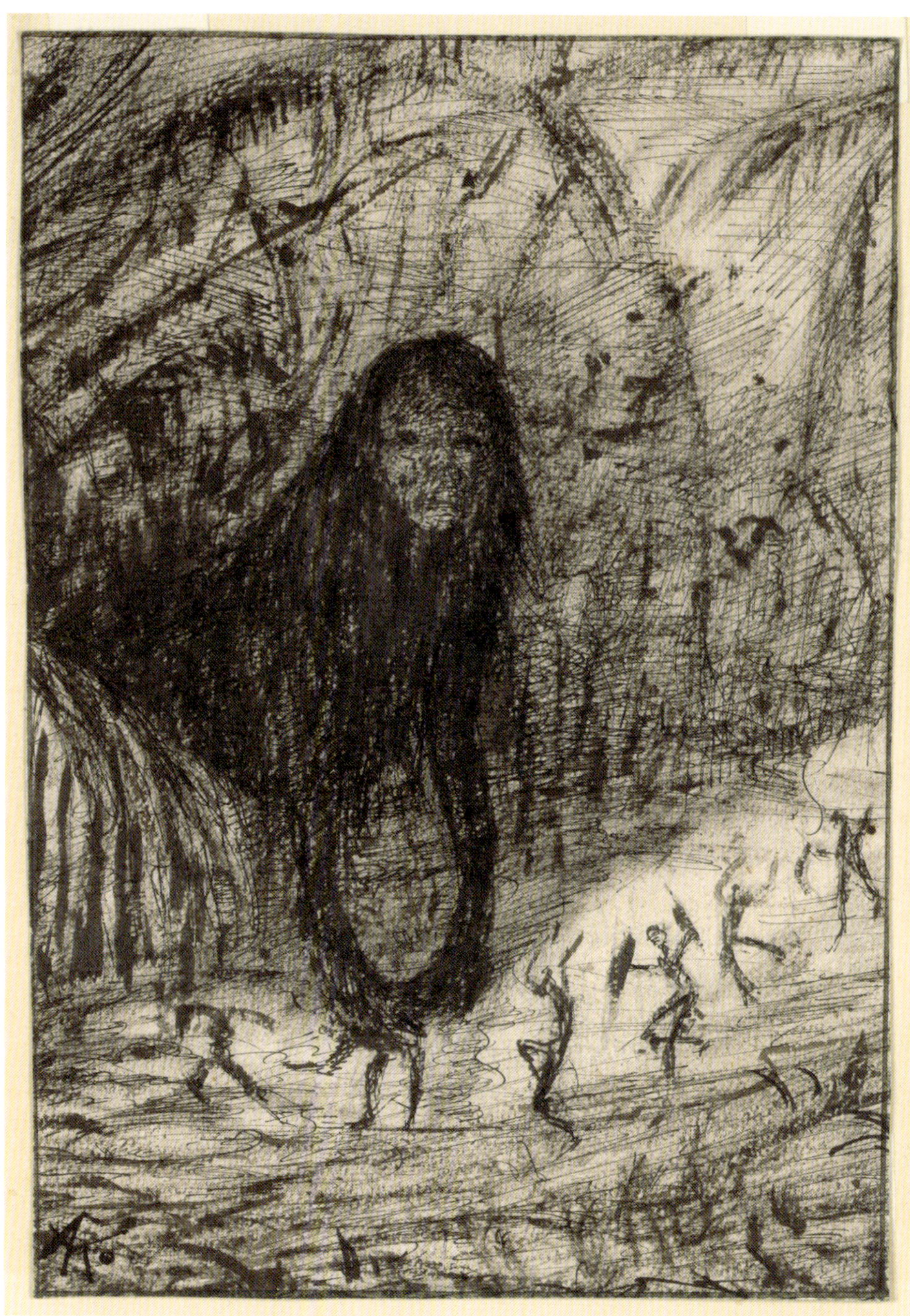

ALFRED KUBIN
Goddess of Fate, c. 1910
OÖ Landes-Kultur GmbH, Land Oberösterreich, Graphic Collection, Günter Rombold Collection, Ha I 15584

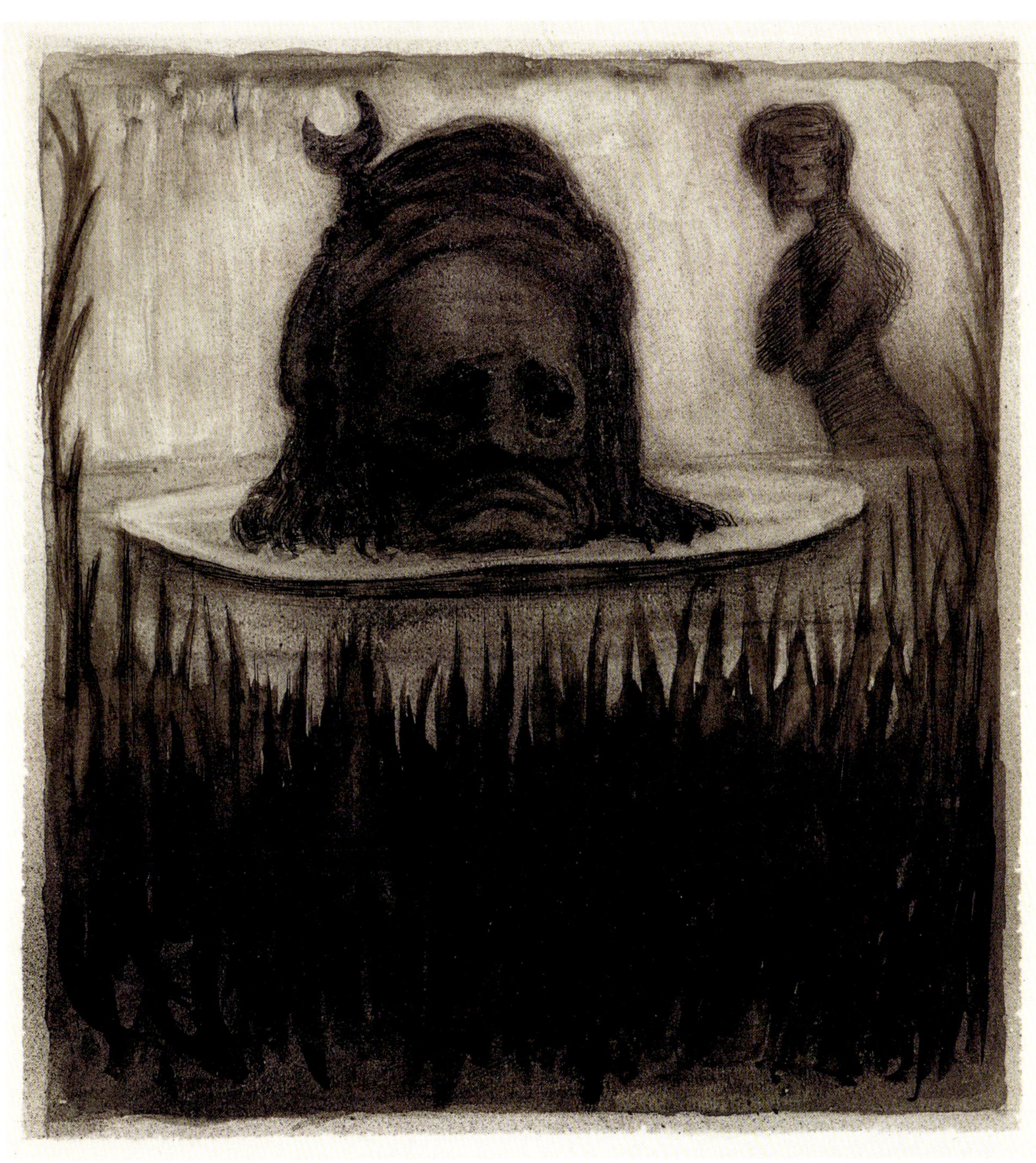

ALFRED KUBIN
Black Flowers (also: Salome), c. 1904
Leopold Museum, Vienna

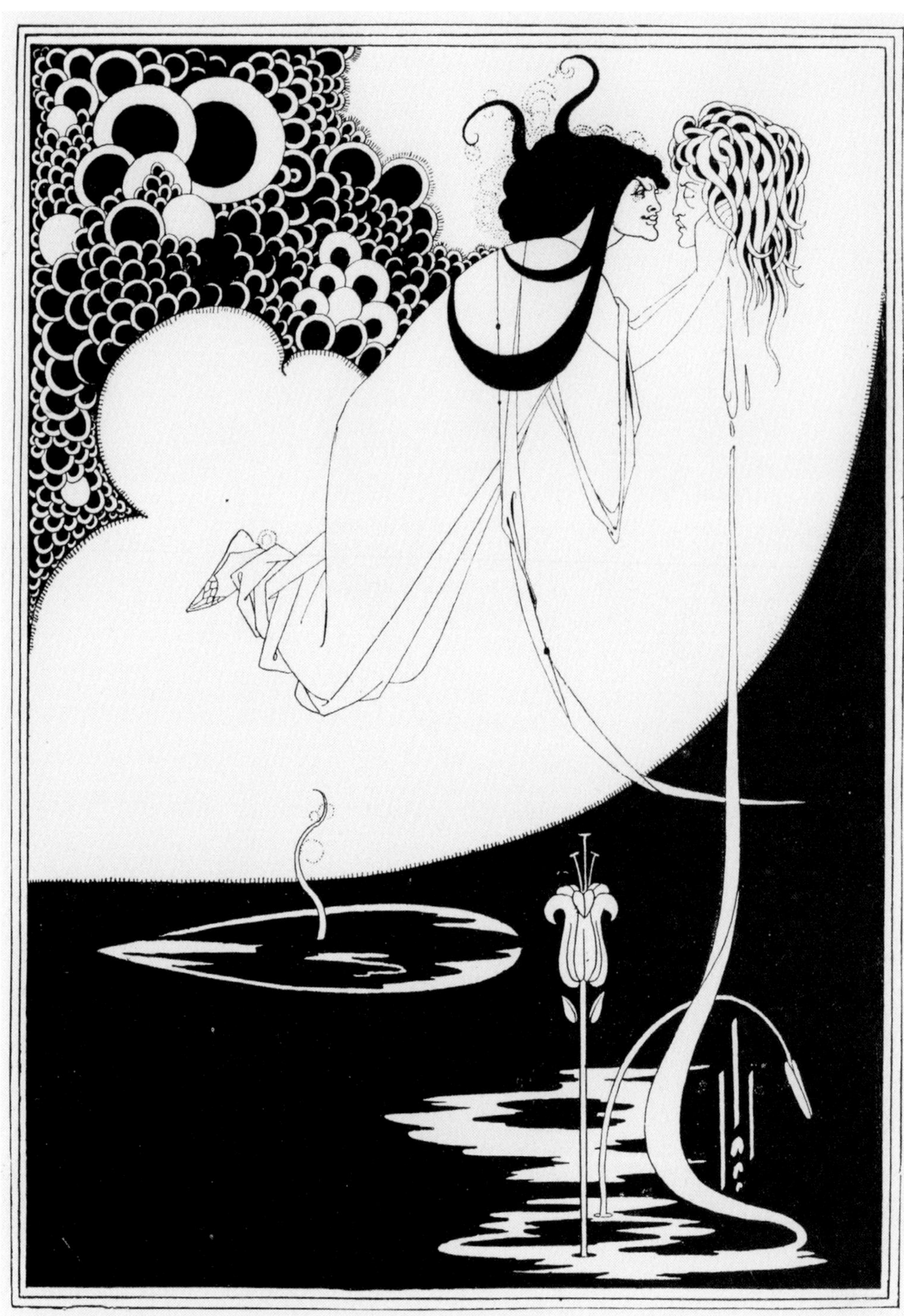

AUBREY BEARDSLEY
Apotheosis, illustration for Oscar Wilde's *Salome,*
published in: ***The Studio***, vol.1, no. 1, 1893
Private Collection

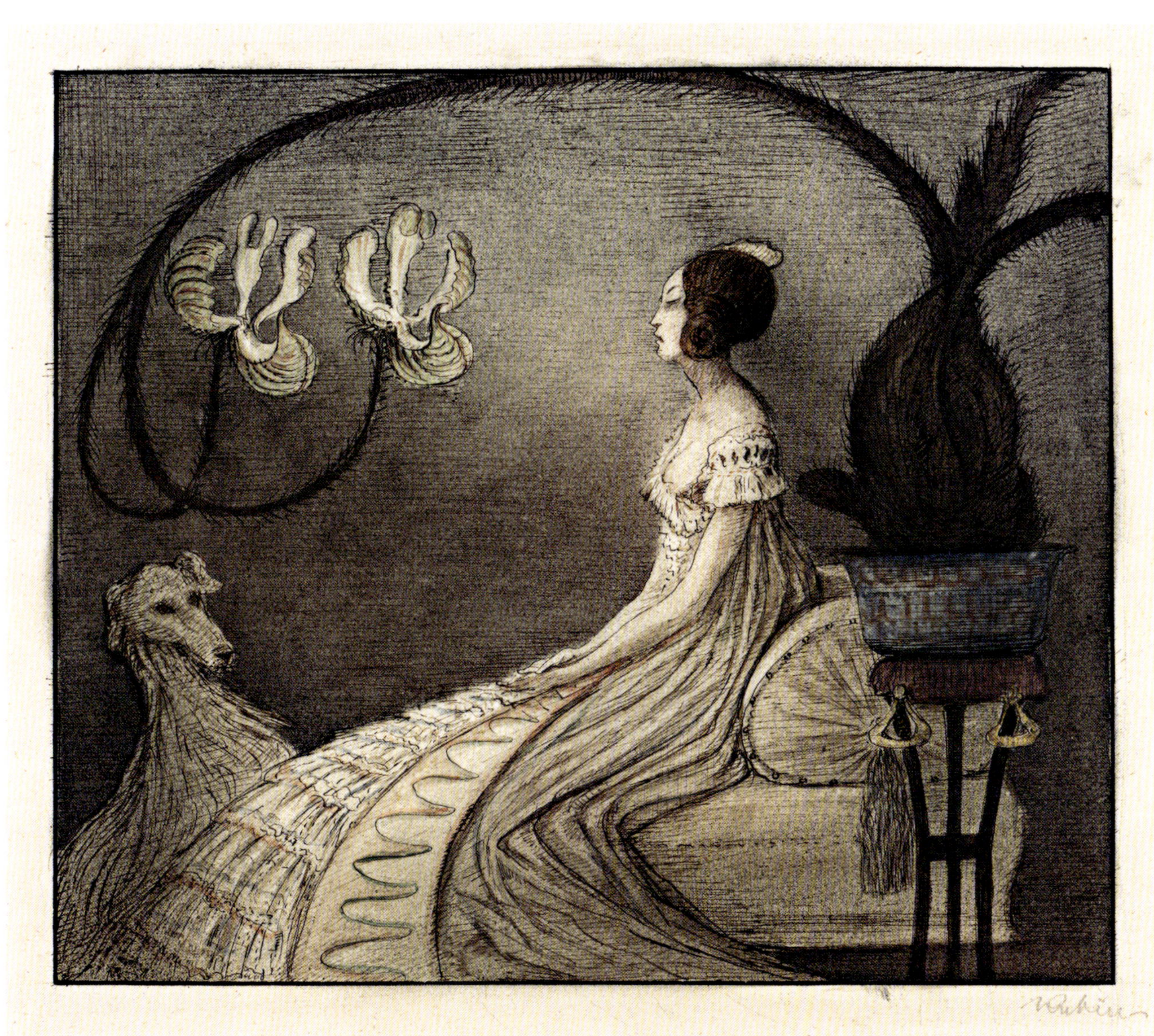

ALFRED KUBIN
The Orchid, 1902/03
Leopold Museum, Vienna

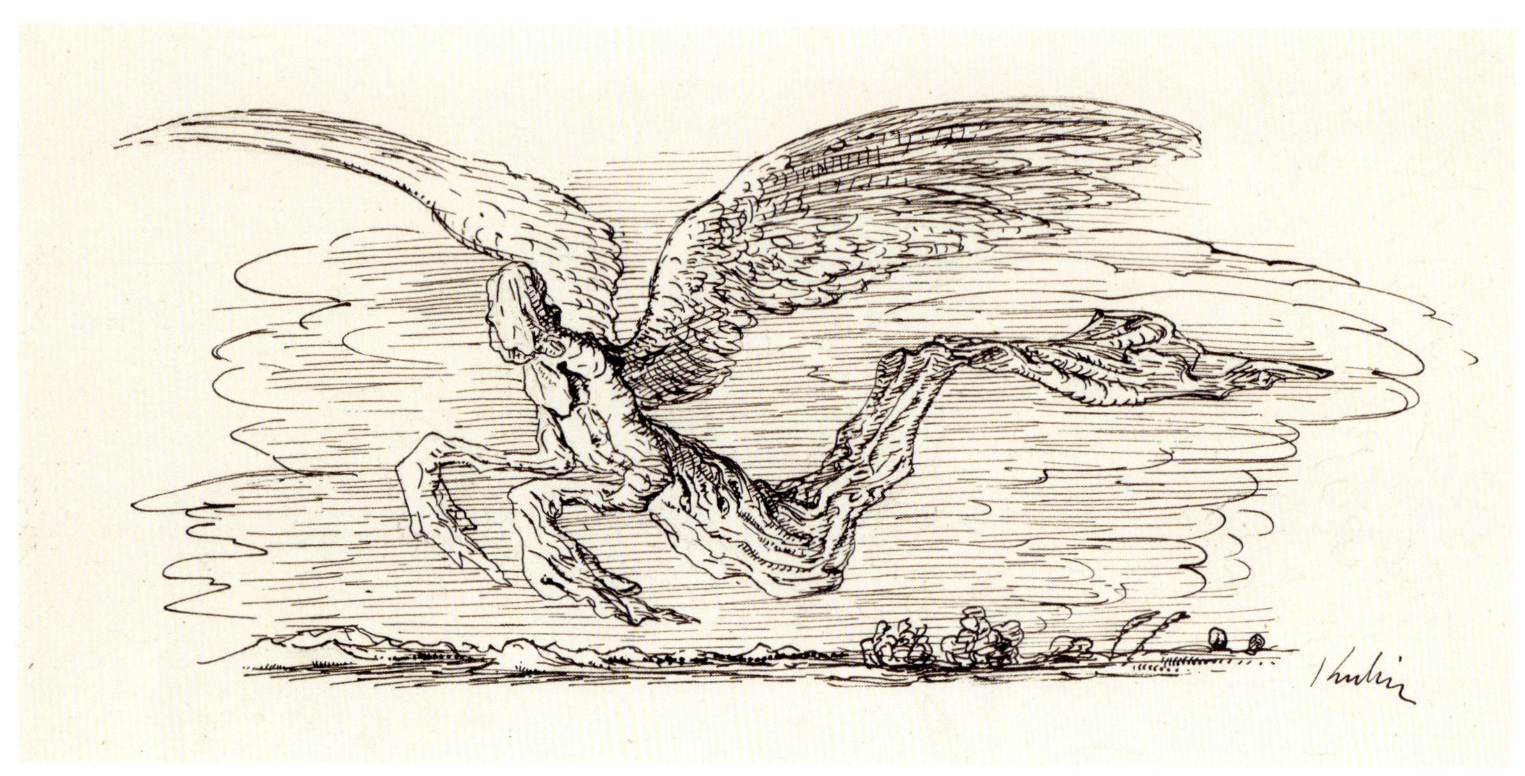

ALFRED KUBIN
The Angel of Death, 1910
Leopold Museum, Vienna

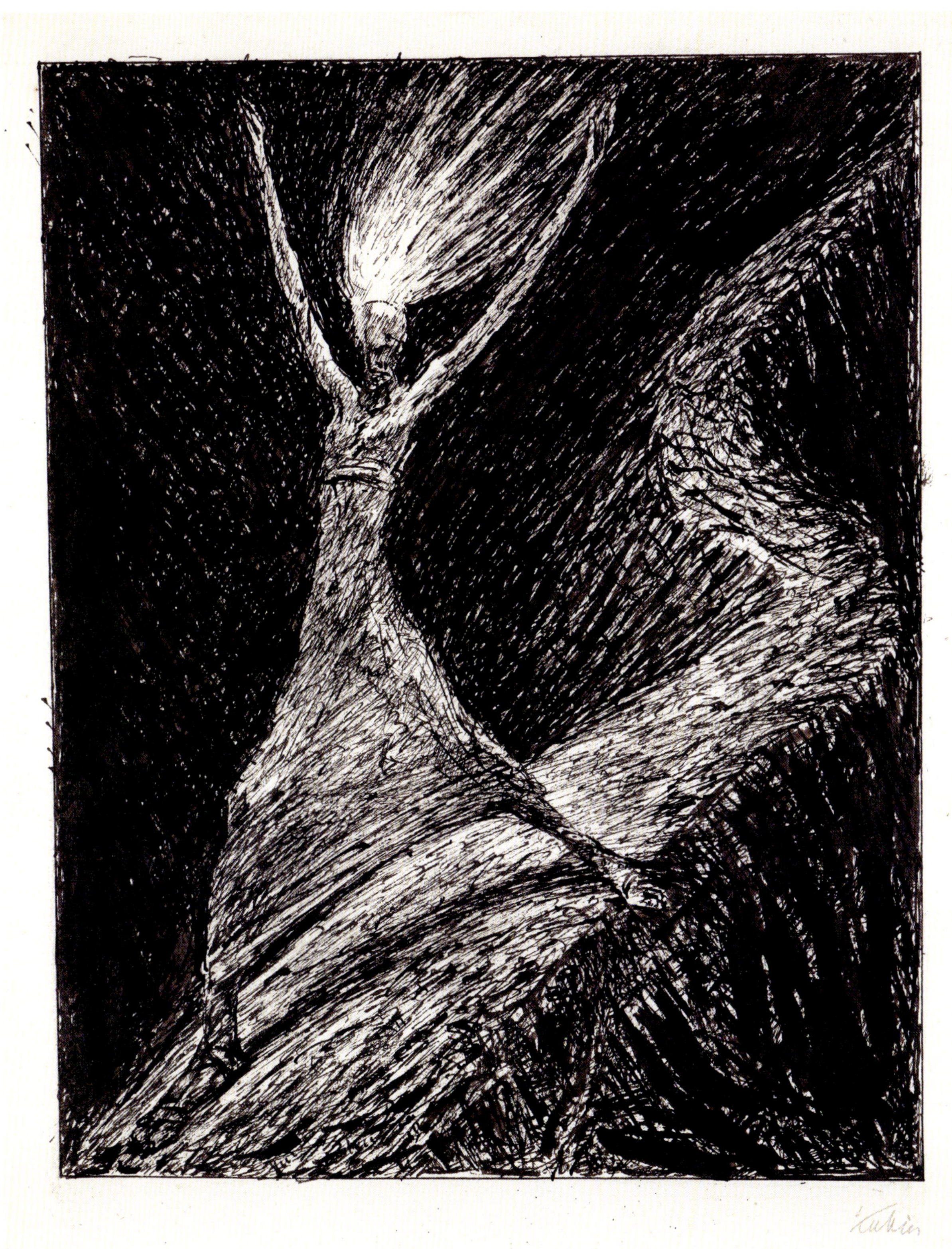

ALFRED KUBIN
God of Light, c. 1911
Leopold Museum, Vienna

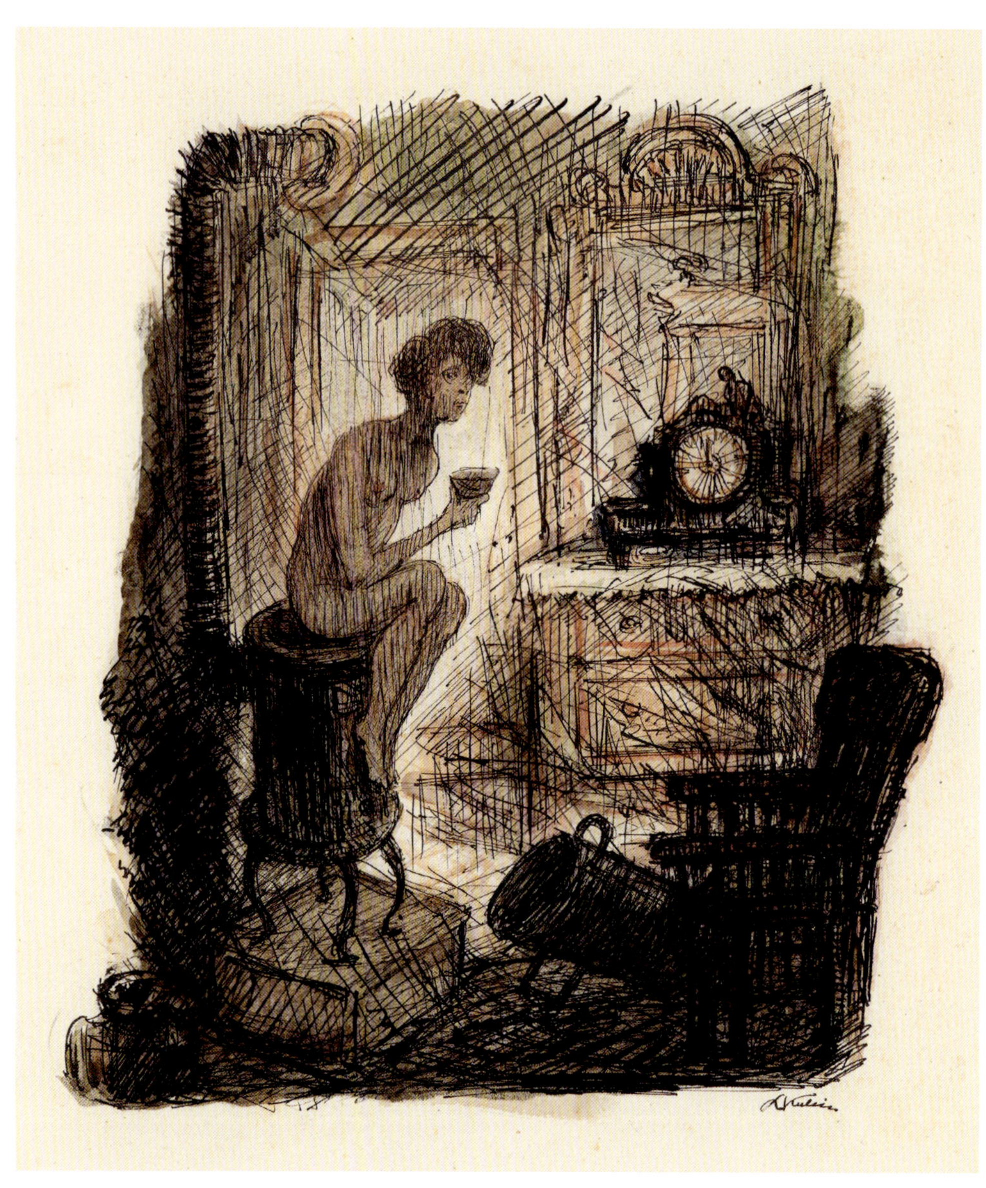

ALFRED KUBIN
Witch's Apartment, c. 1932
Klewan Collection, Munich

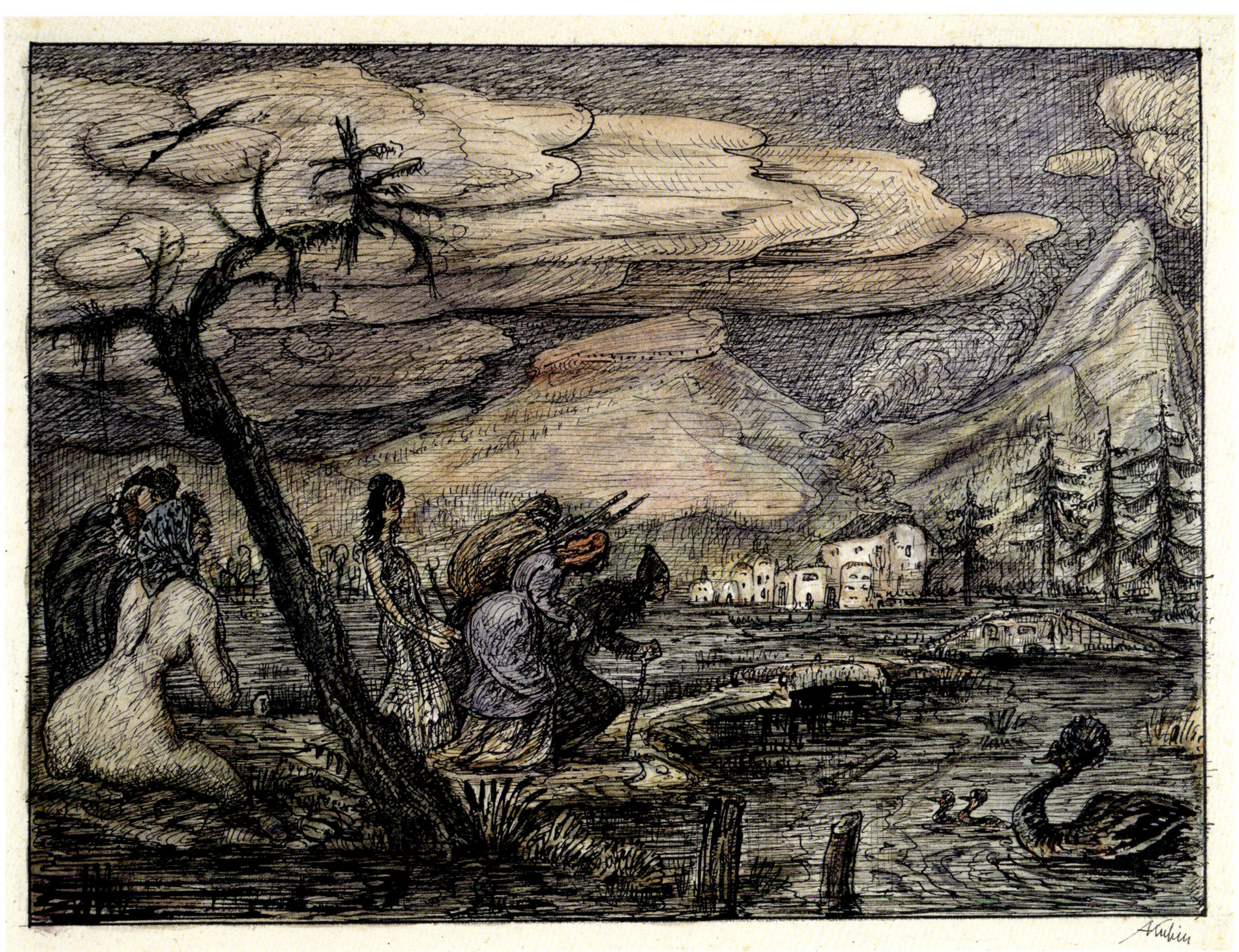

ALFRED KUBIN
Walpurgis Night III, 1920
OÖ Landes-Kultur GmbH, Land Oberösterreich, Graphic Collection, Günter Rombold Collection, Ha II 13187

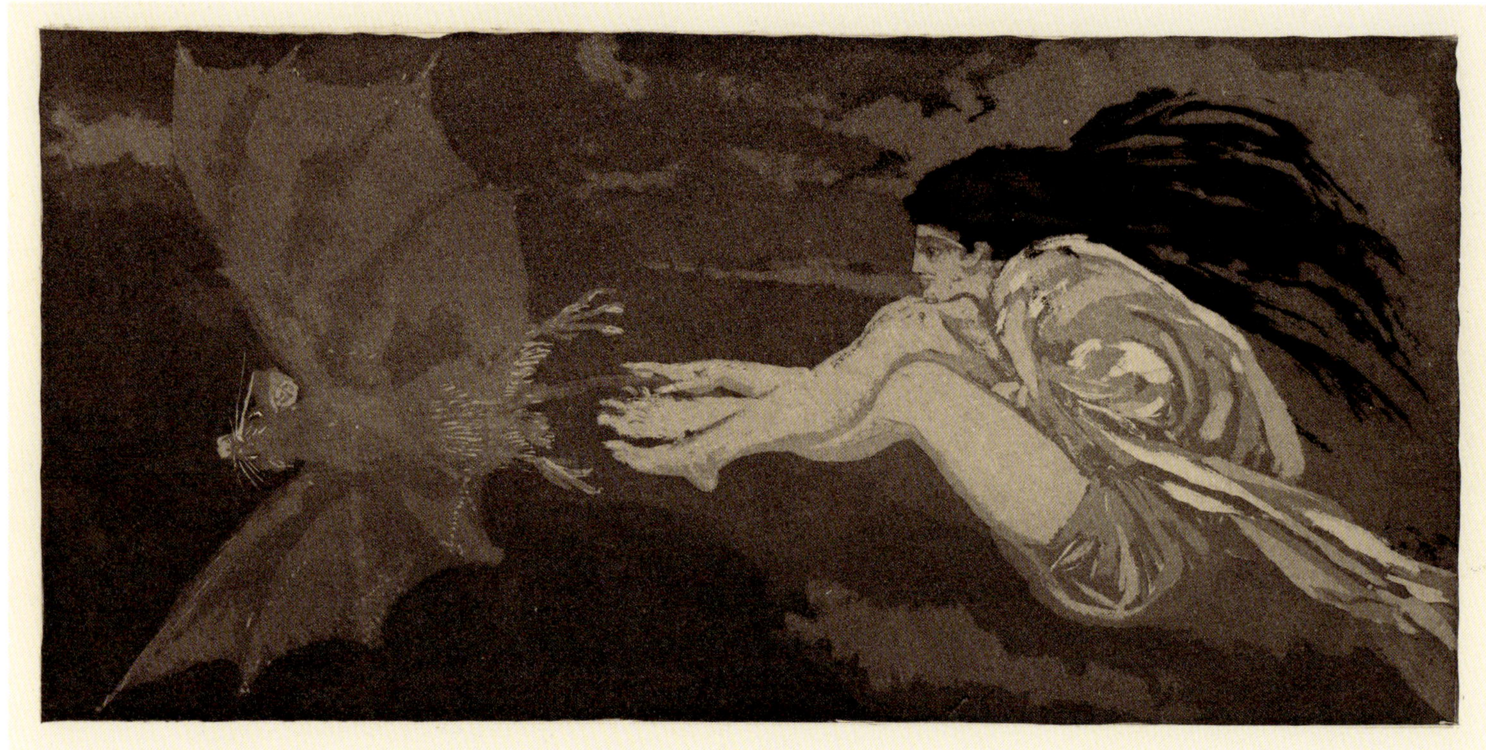

MAX KLINGER
Witch and Bat, 1880
The Daulton Collection, Los Altos Hills, California

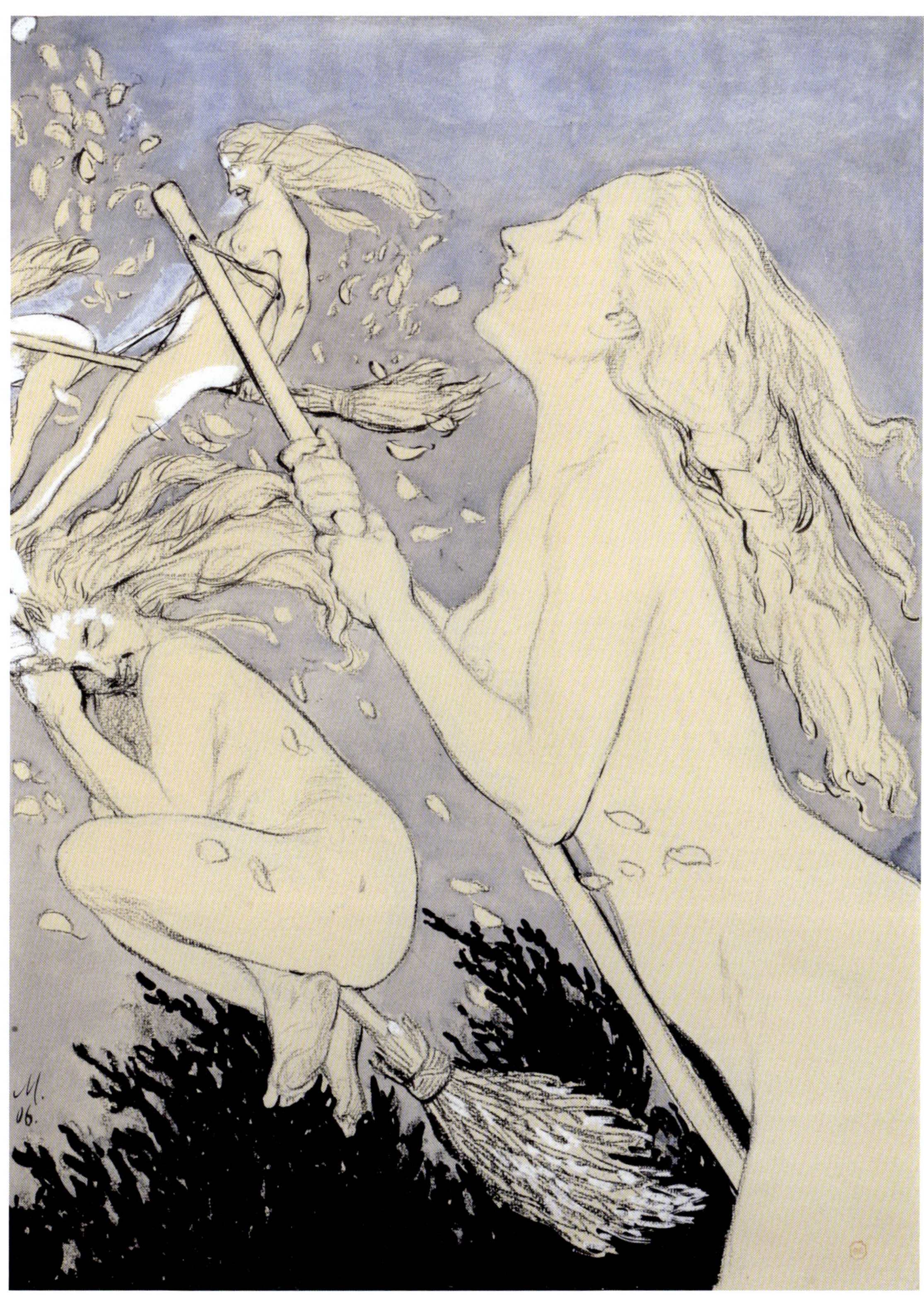

ADOLF MÜNZER
Witch Riding, 1906
Museum Georg Schäfer, Schweinfurt

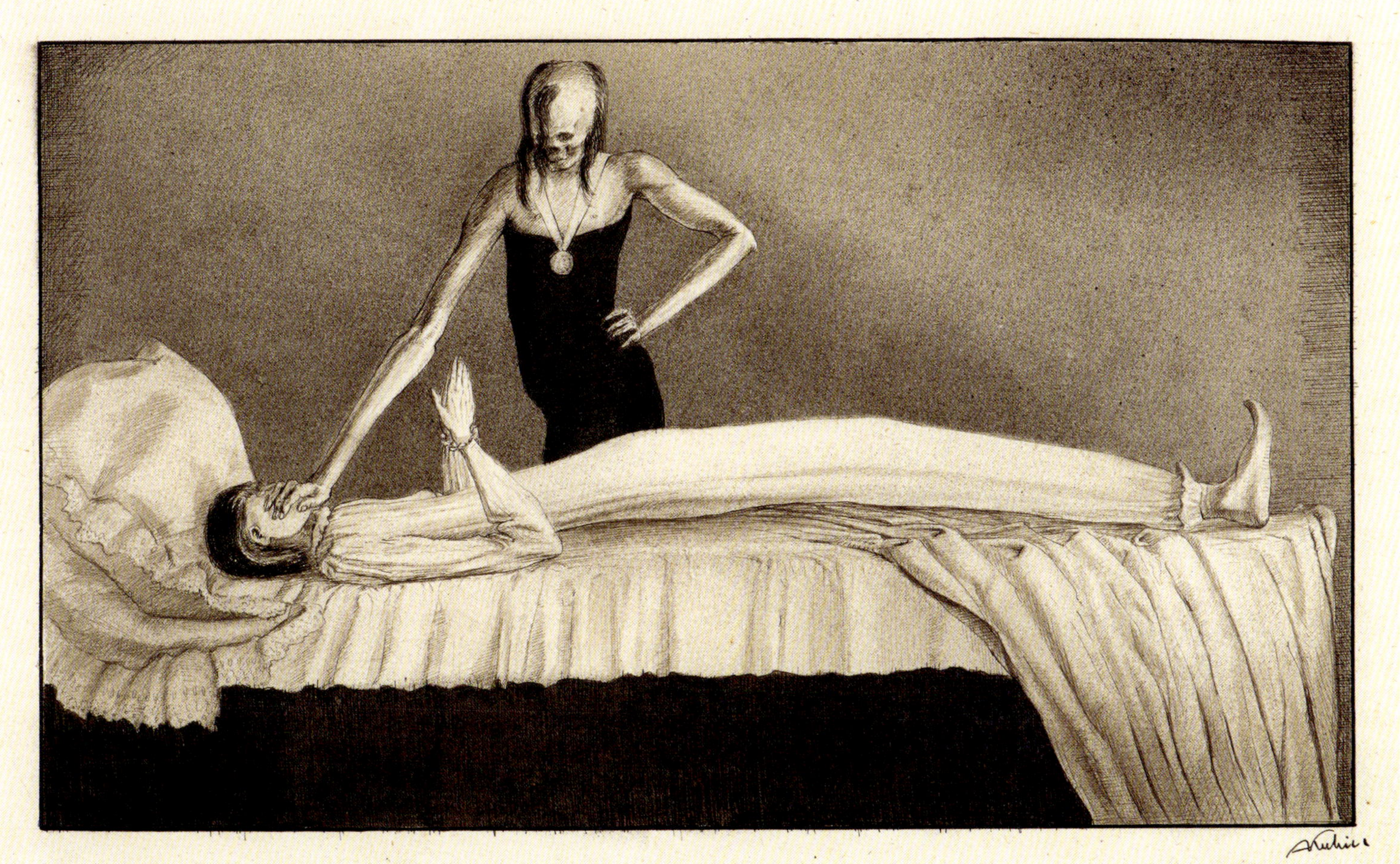

ALFRED KUBIN
The Best Physician, c. 1901
Leopold Museum, Vienna

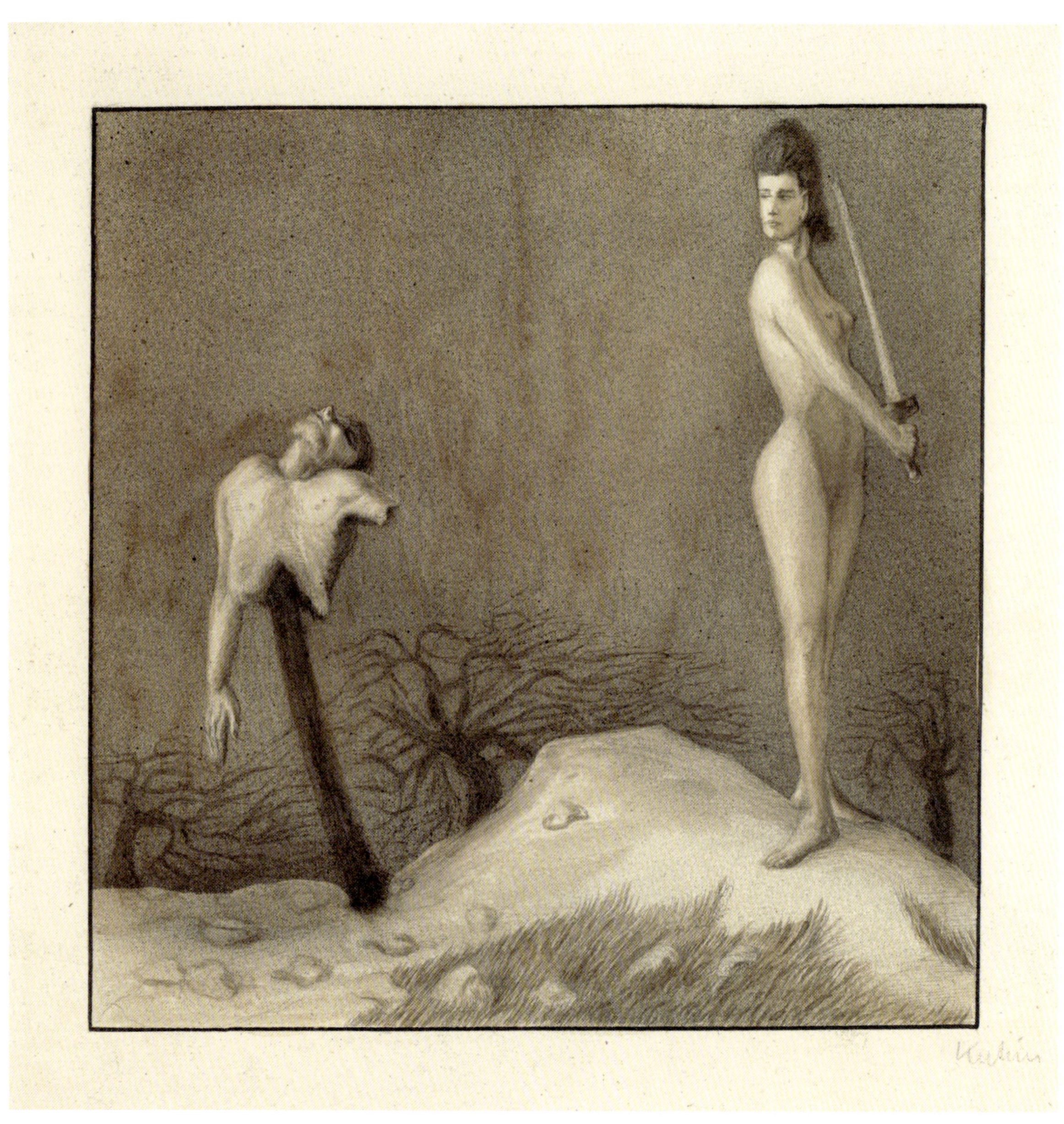

ALFRED KUBIN
Slaughterfest, c. 1900
Albertina, Vienna

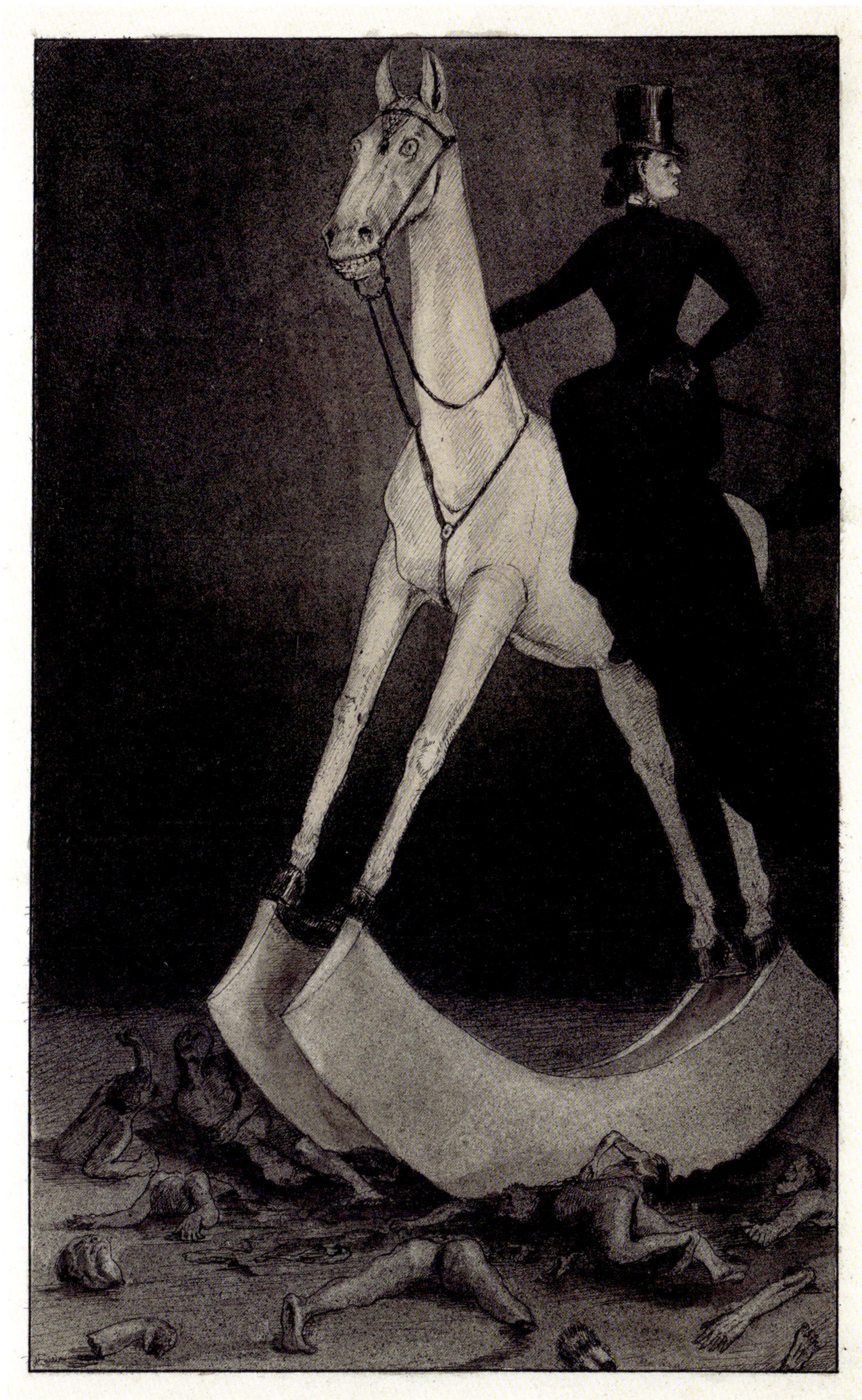

ALFRED KUBIN
The Lady on the Horse, c. 1900/01
Städtische Galerie im Lenbachhaus und Kunstbau München

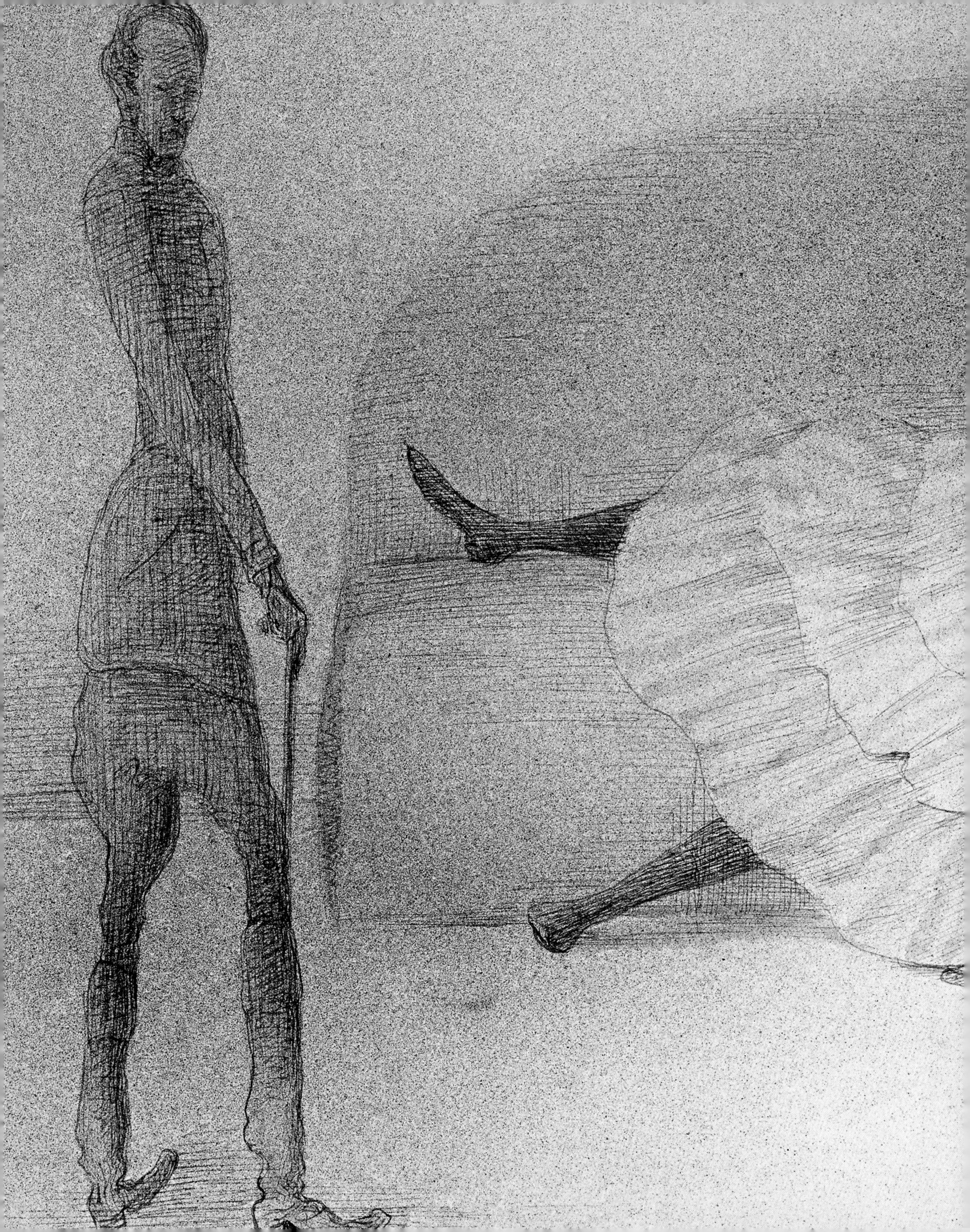

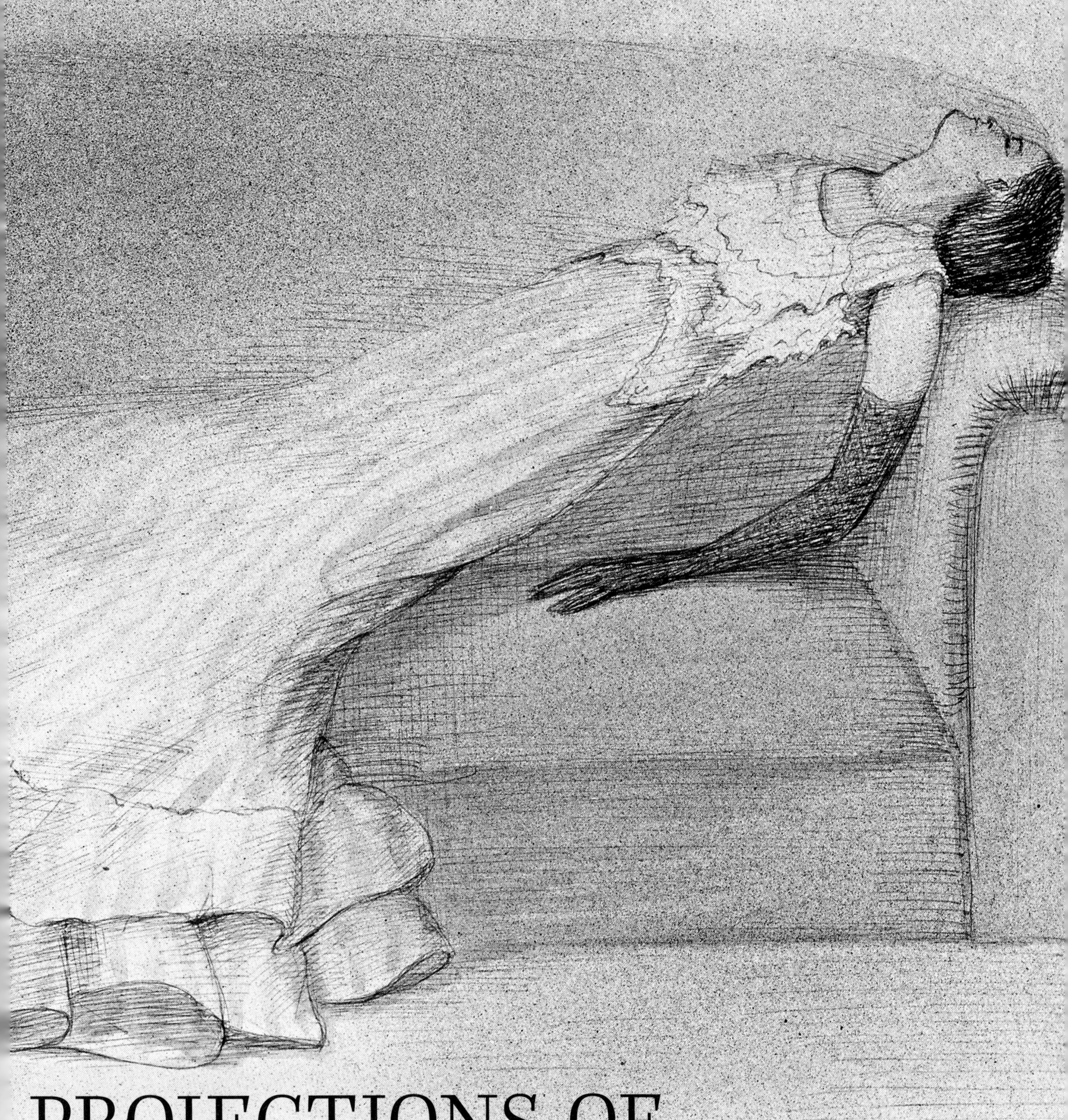

PROJECTIONS OF MALE OMNIPOTENCE

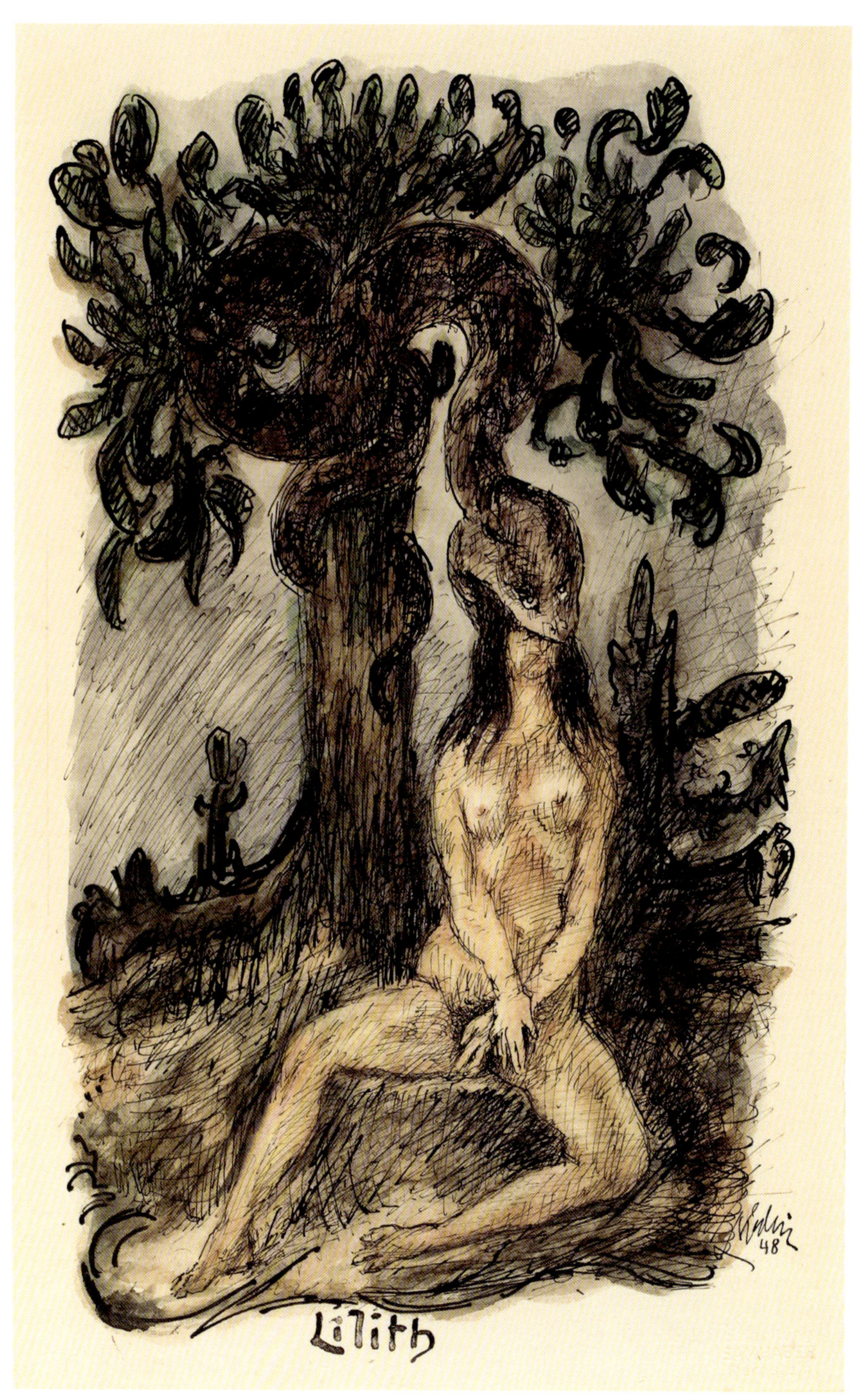

ALFRED KUBIN
Lilith, 1948
Leopold Museum, Vienna

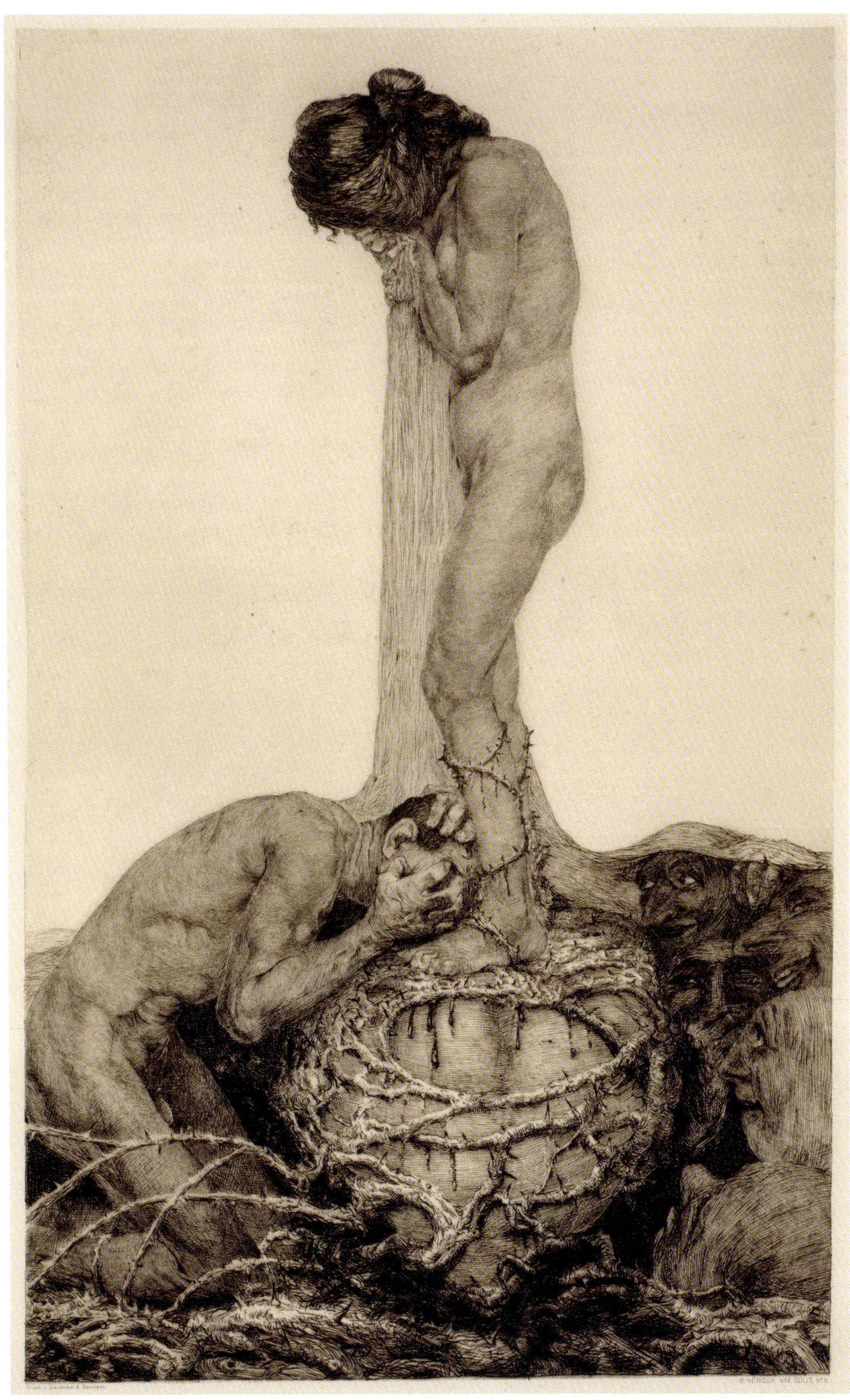

LOUIS CARL BRUNO HÉROUX
Pain, print 5 of portfolio *Vae Solis*, between 1909 and 1914
LETTER Foundation, Cologne

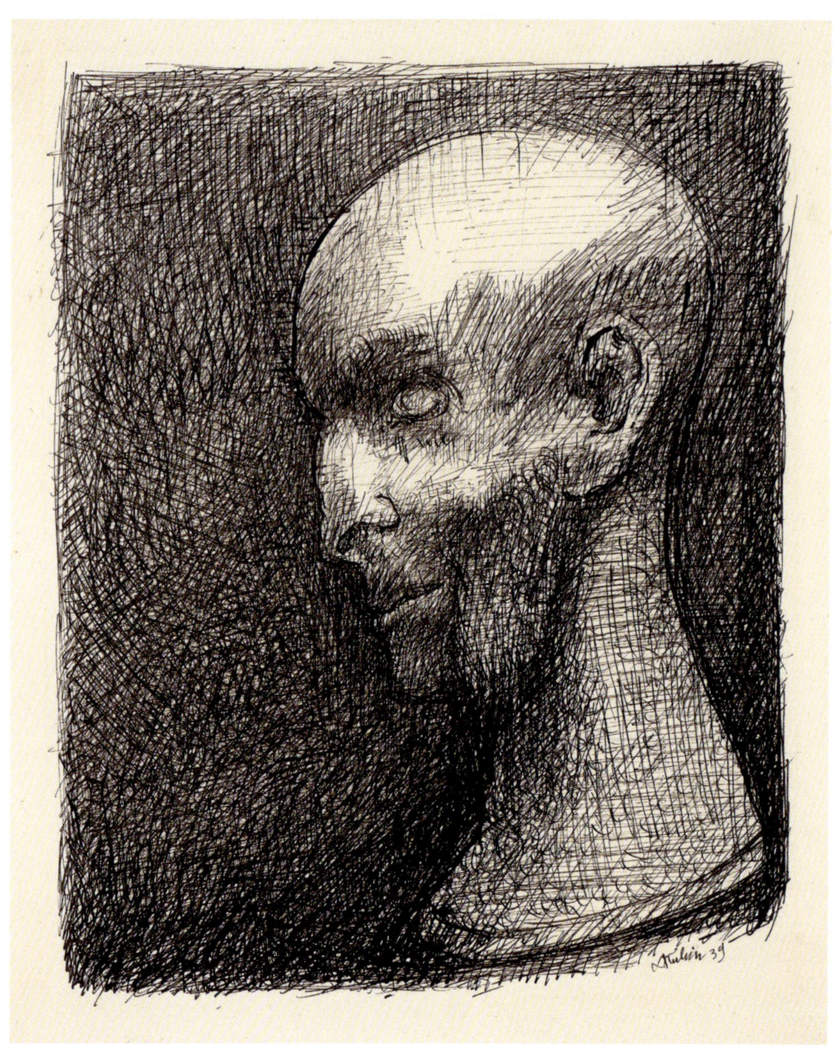

ALFRED KUBIN
Lord Devil, c. 1920
Leopold, Private Collection

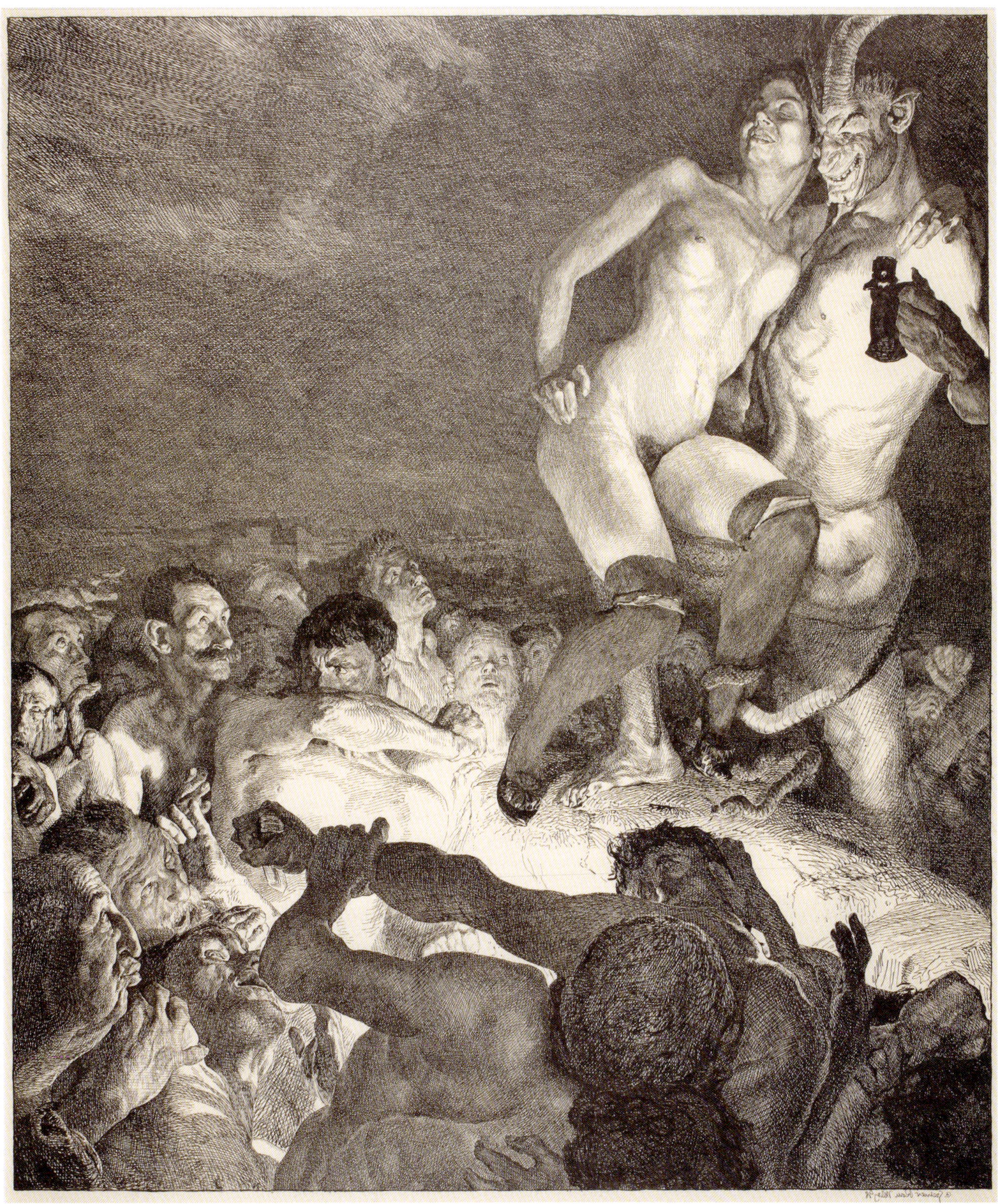

OTTO GREINER
The Devil Presenting Woman to the Folk, print 3 of series *Of Woman*, 1898
LETTER Foundation, Cologne

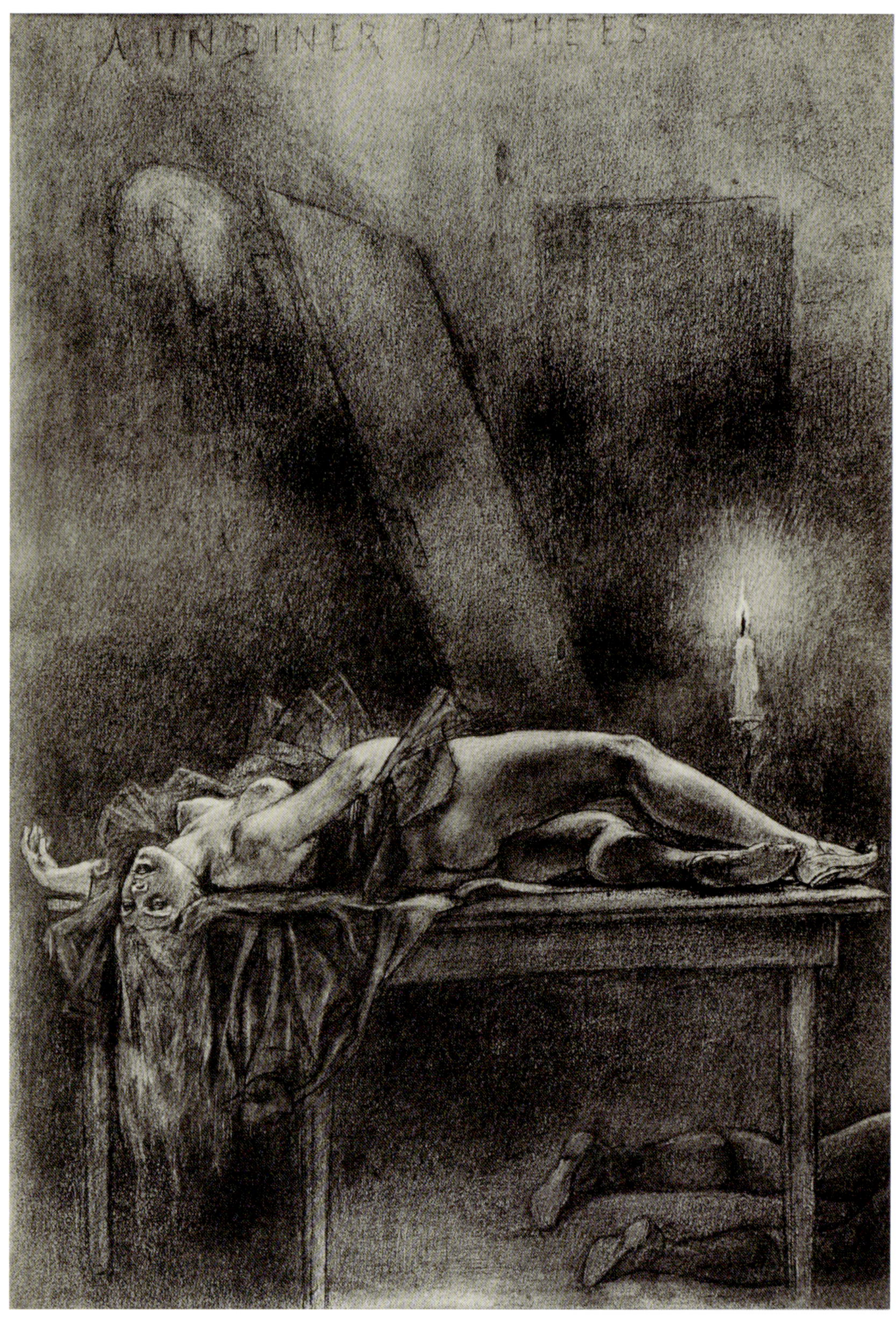

FÉLICIEN ROPS

The Atheists' Dinner, illustration for Les Diaboliques by Jules Barbey d'Aurevilly, 1882

Museum Georg Schäfer, Schweinfurt

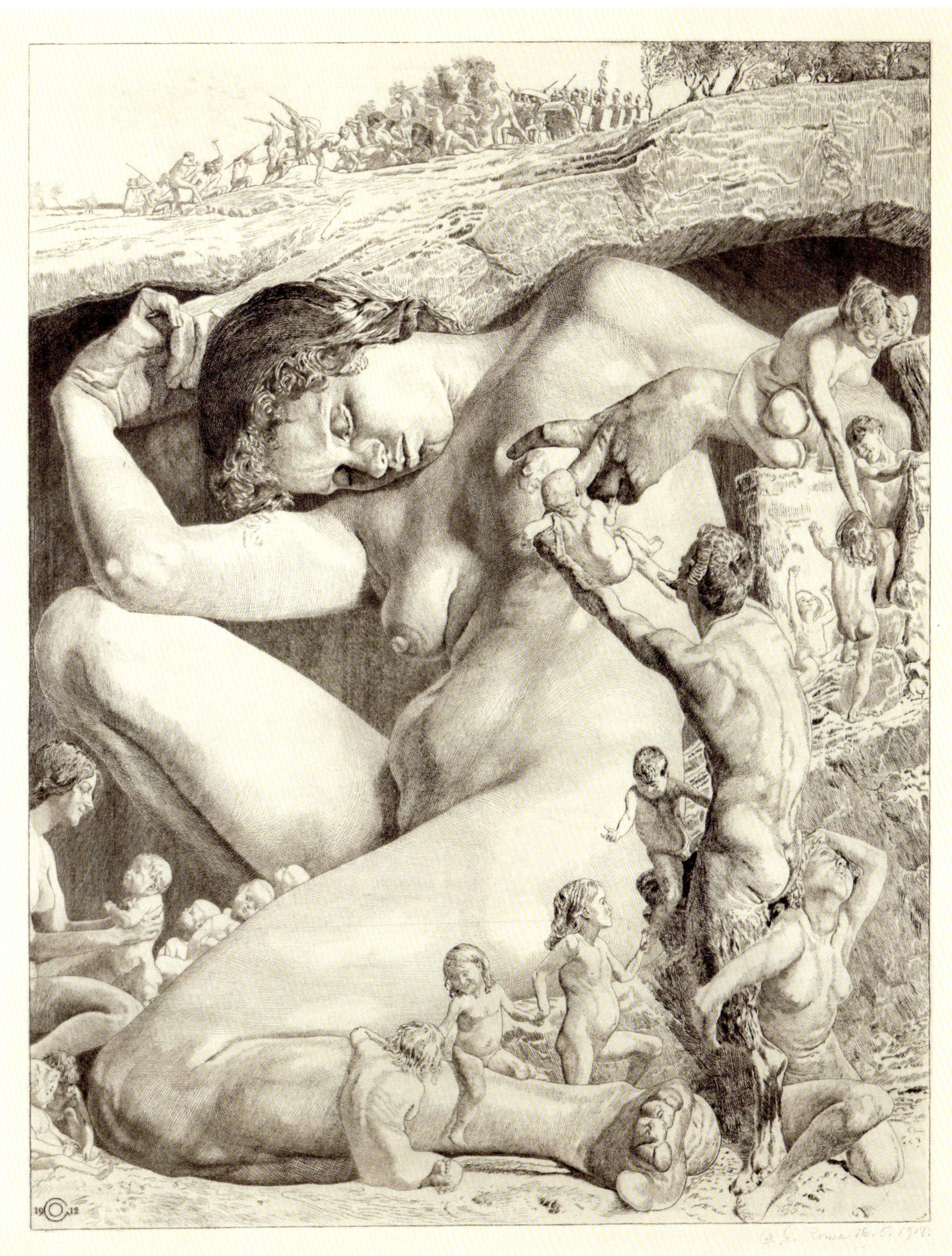

OTTO GREINER
Gaia, 1912
Leopold Museum, Vienna

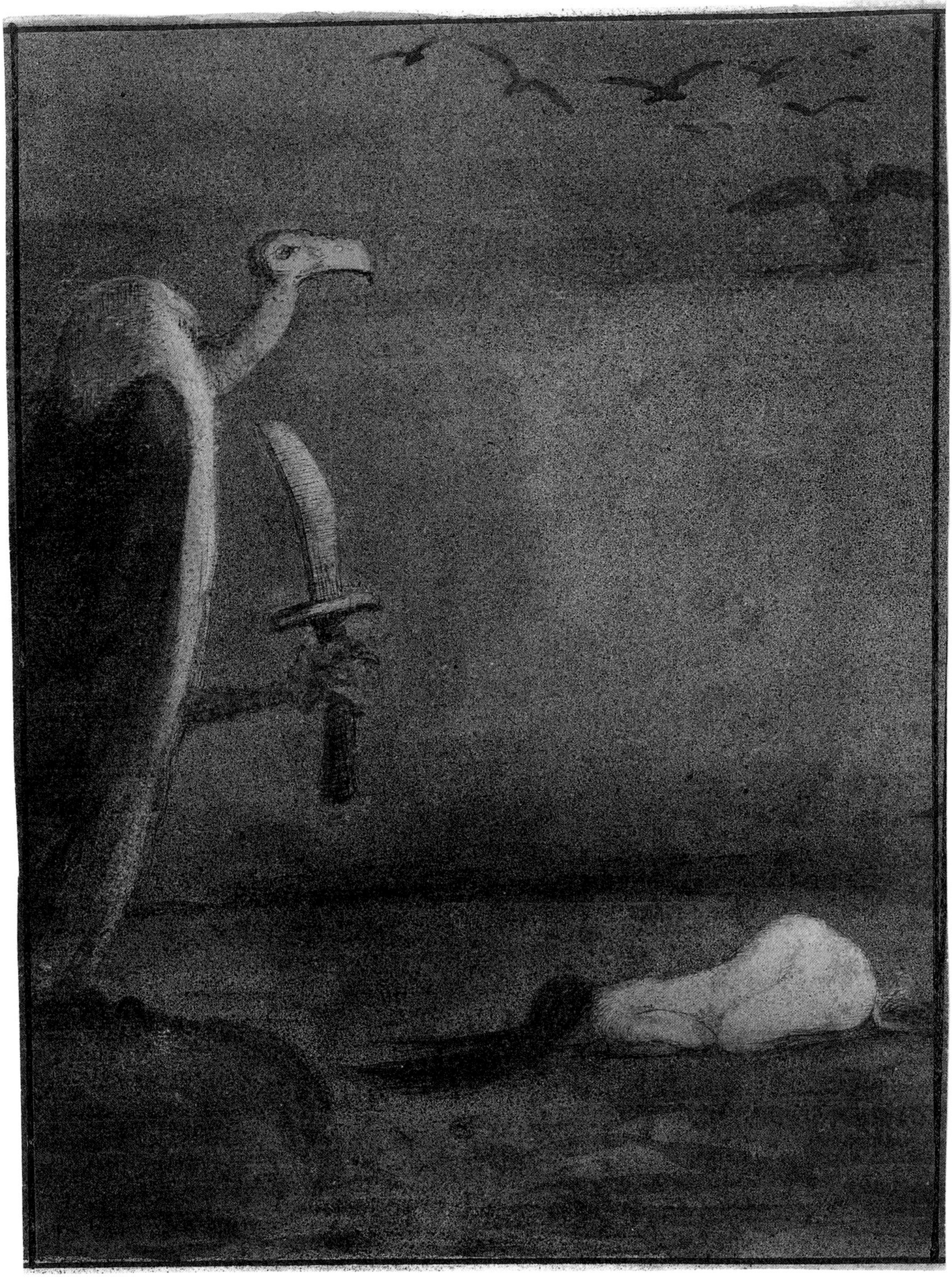

ALFRED KUBIN
Untitled (Vulture Holding a Sword and Cowering Nude), 1902
Private Collection, Austria

FERTILITY

The work *Fertility* presents woman's ability to give birth as a curse, as a gruesome and deadly deformation of the body condemned to unremittingly bring forth nonviable fetuses at the bottom of a swampy pond. Even today's beholders involuntarily associate the work with the notion, prevalent around 1900, that life was created from the swamp and with the affiliation of the maternal line with the original swamp. Klaus Albrecht Schröder commented on the work by citing a line from Otto Weininger's work *Sex and Character*: "All that is born of woman must die. Conception, birth and death are inseparably linked."* This highlights the concept of women as shackled to creatureliness, something which Kubin illustrated in this depiction with rare brutality. For what smacks of cultural recrimination with Weininger takes on the dimensions of existential distress and subjection with Kubin. The emaciated pregnant woman has her legs spread apart by her enormously bloated, veined belly in a similar manner to those of the small figure of a man undergoing agonizing torture in Kubin's early work on paper *Scenes from Hell*, created in 1900.

Annegret Hoberg

* Klaus Albrecht Schröder: *Alfred Kubin. Leben. Ein Abgrund*, ed. by Österreichische Länderbank/ Oberösterreichisches Landesmuseum (Munich, 1985), ill. 62.

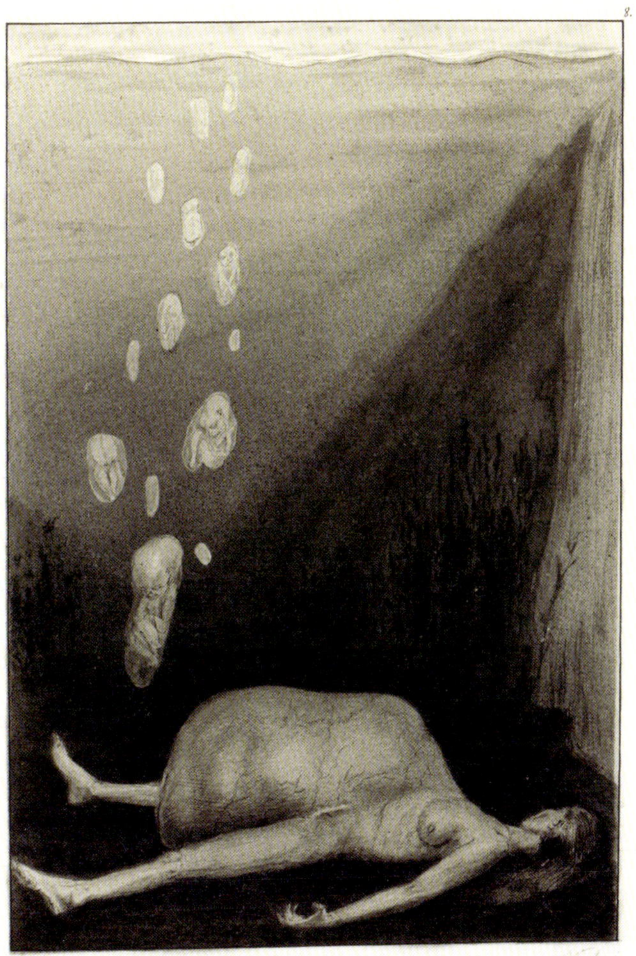

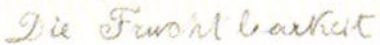

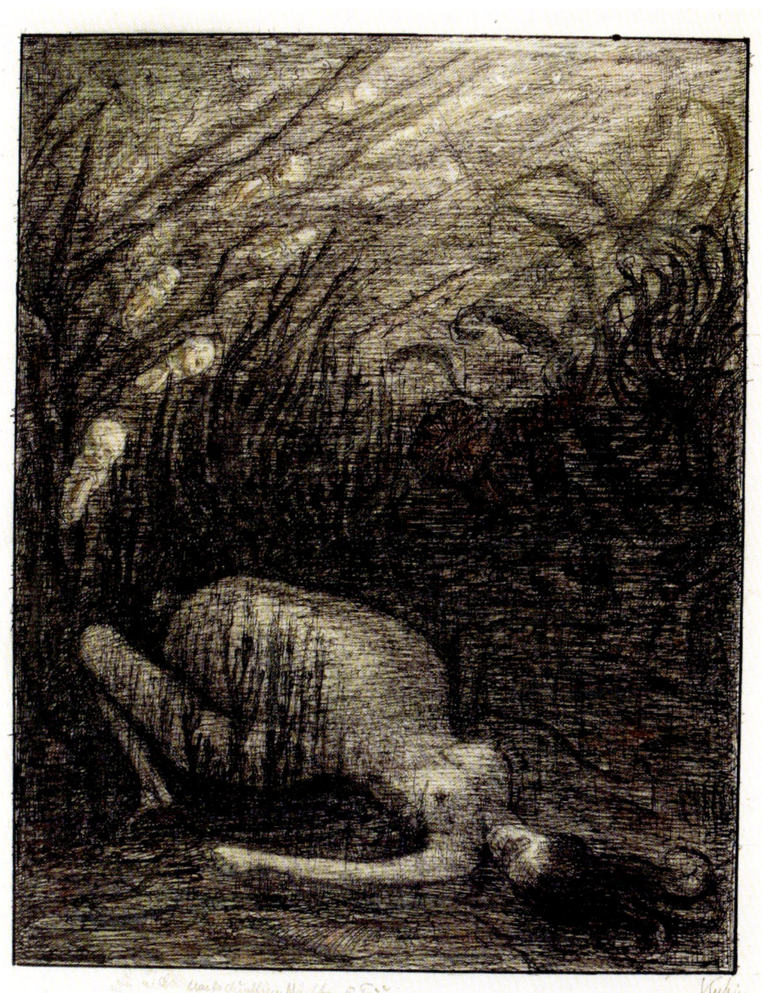

ALFRED KUBIN
Fertility (1st Version), 1901/02
Leopold Museum, Vienna

ALFRED KUBIN
Fertility (2nd Version), 1909/10
Leopold Museum, Vienna

THE EGG

Christoph Brockhaus explored the ingenious rendering *The Egg*, which plunges mystical depths, in a profound analysis. The work depicts a half-skeletonized woman in a dark, time- and placeless space. Her pregnant body, distended into the shape of an egg, emits an inner shine that radiates far into the darkness. "An idol, only discernible in its outlines, appears in her shadow on the same horizontal line on which the egg 'comes to rest'. The diagonal connection between the woman and the idol is accompanied by an open well symbolizing a grave. This makes for an antithetical image of the two notions, going hand in hand, of coming into being and passing away, of life and death, which are invested with a mystical quality through the egg shape and with a mythical one through the idol." The associations with the "far-away, pre-historic past" and the conviction that "from time immemorial, unborn life is already doomed to die" point to the basic ideas expressed by Johann Jakob Bachofen in his investigation of the symbolism of ancient tombs, *Versuch über die Gräbersymbolik der Alten* (1859), which met with enthusiastic approval at the time by the exponents of the Munich Cosmic Circle surrounding Ludwig Klages, Alfred Schuler and Karl Wolfskehl.* Kubin showed *The Egg* at the *9th Phalanx Exhibition* in 1904, the first major presentation of his works in Munich.

Annegret Hoberg

* Christoph Brockhaus, in: *Alfred Kubin. Das zeichnerische Frühwerk bis 1904*, ed. by Hans Albert Peters (Baden-Baden, 1977), p. 176ff (exh. cat. Kunsthalle Baden-Baden, 01.04.–30.05.1977)

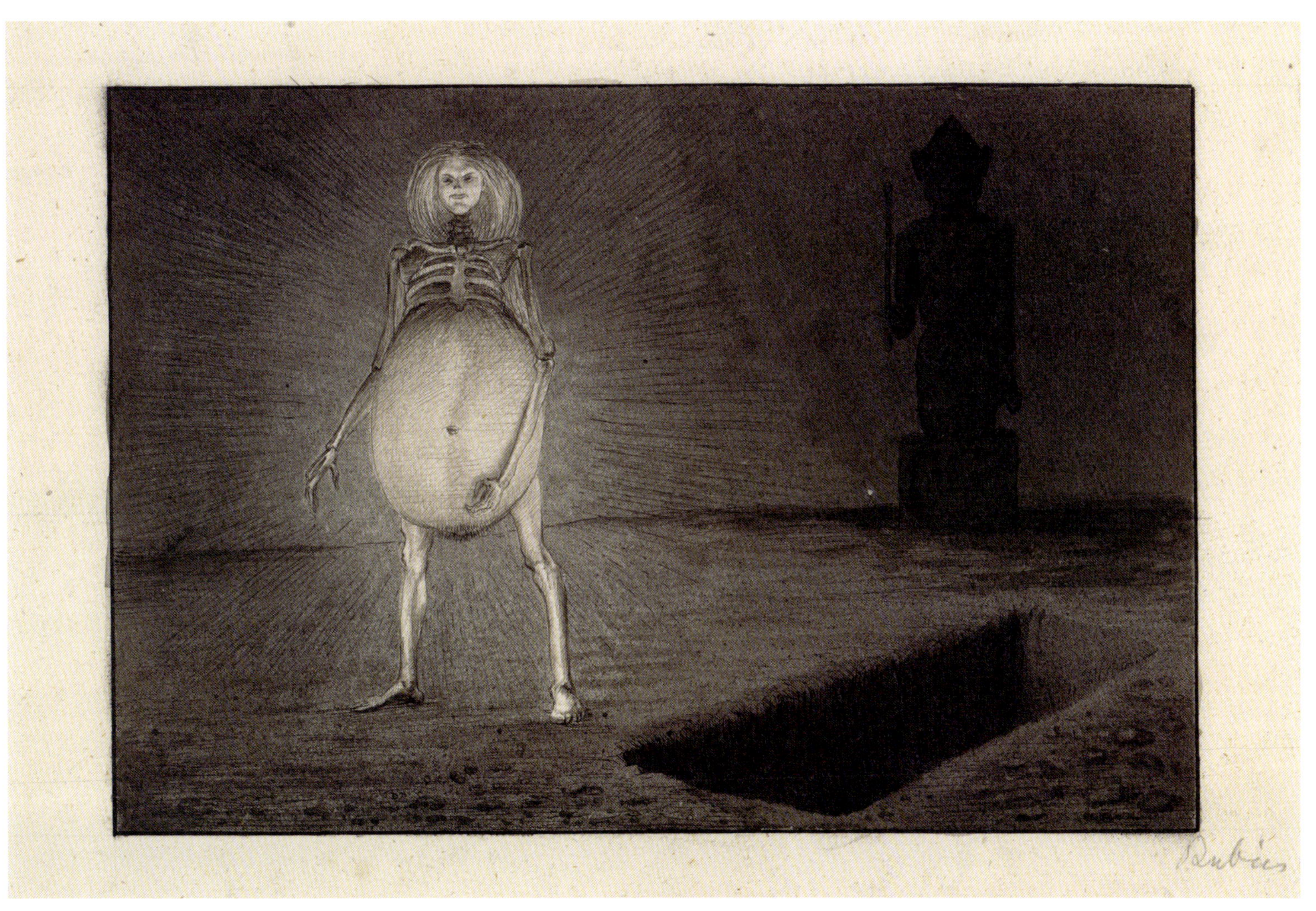

ALFRED KUBIN
The Egg, c. 1901/02
Albertina, Vienna

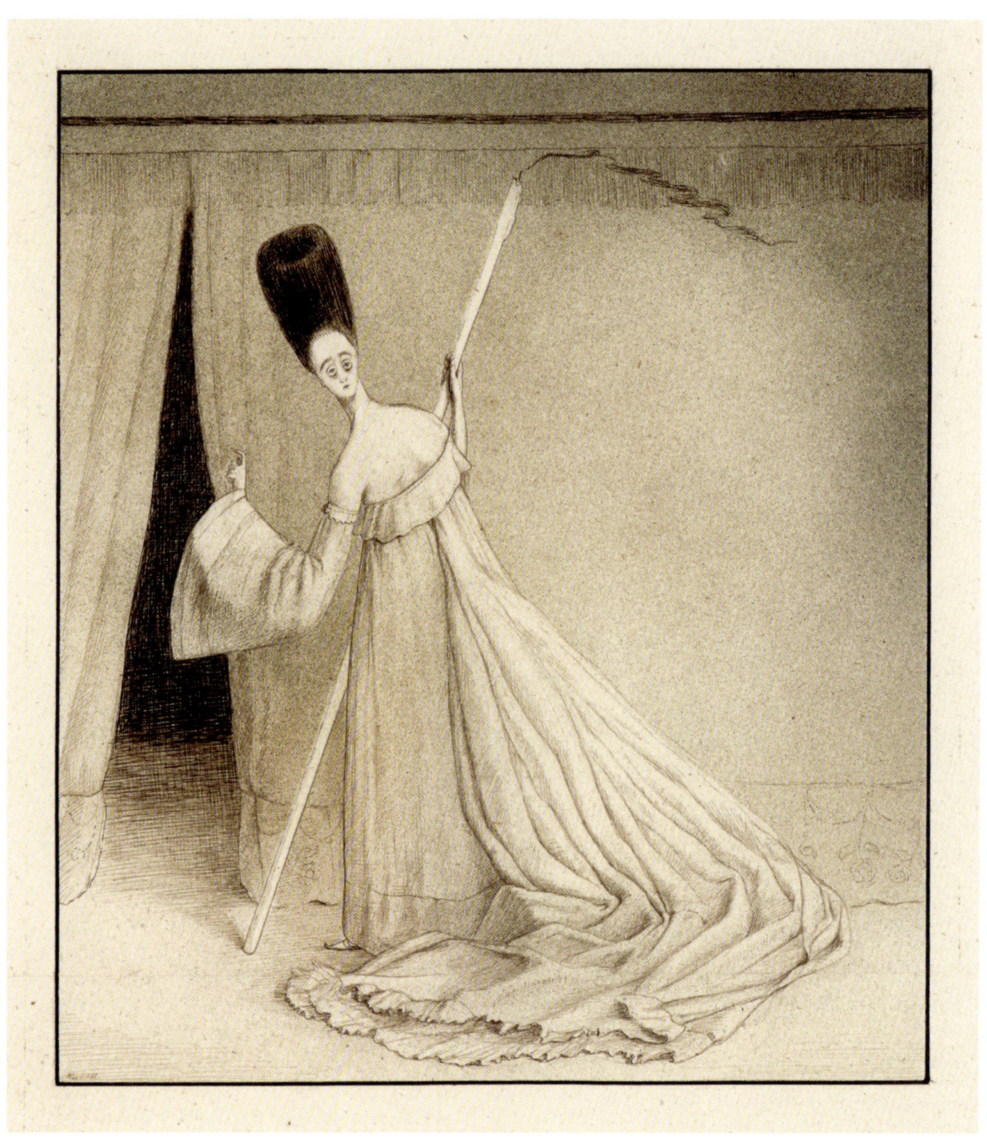

ALFRED KUBIN
Masturbation, 1900/01
Leopold Museum, Vienna

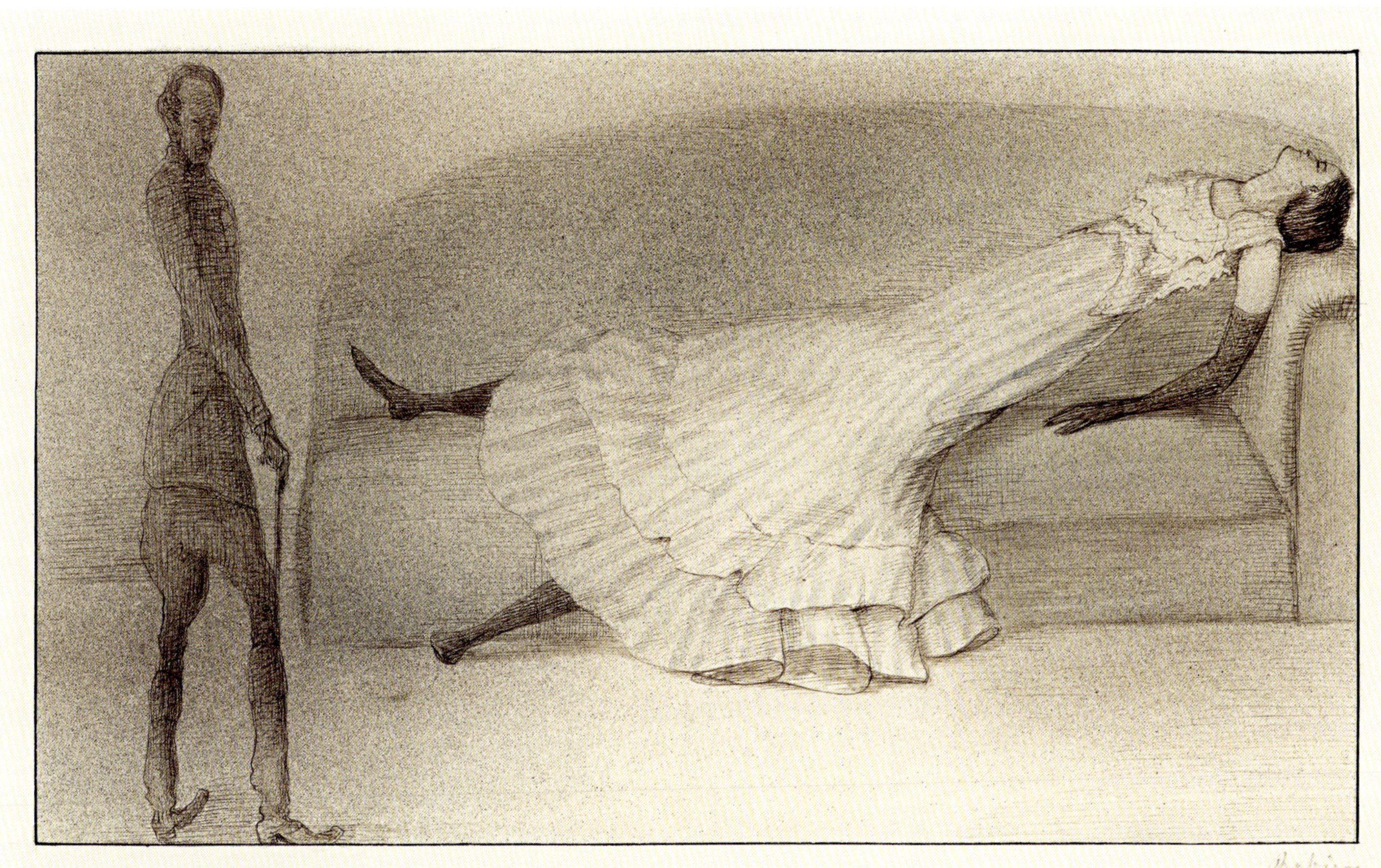

ALFRED KUBIN
Hysteria, c. 1901
Leopold Museum, Vienna

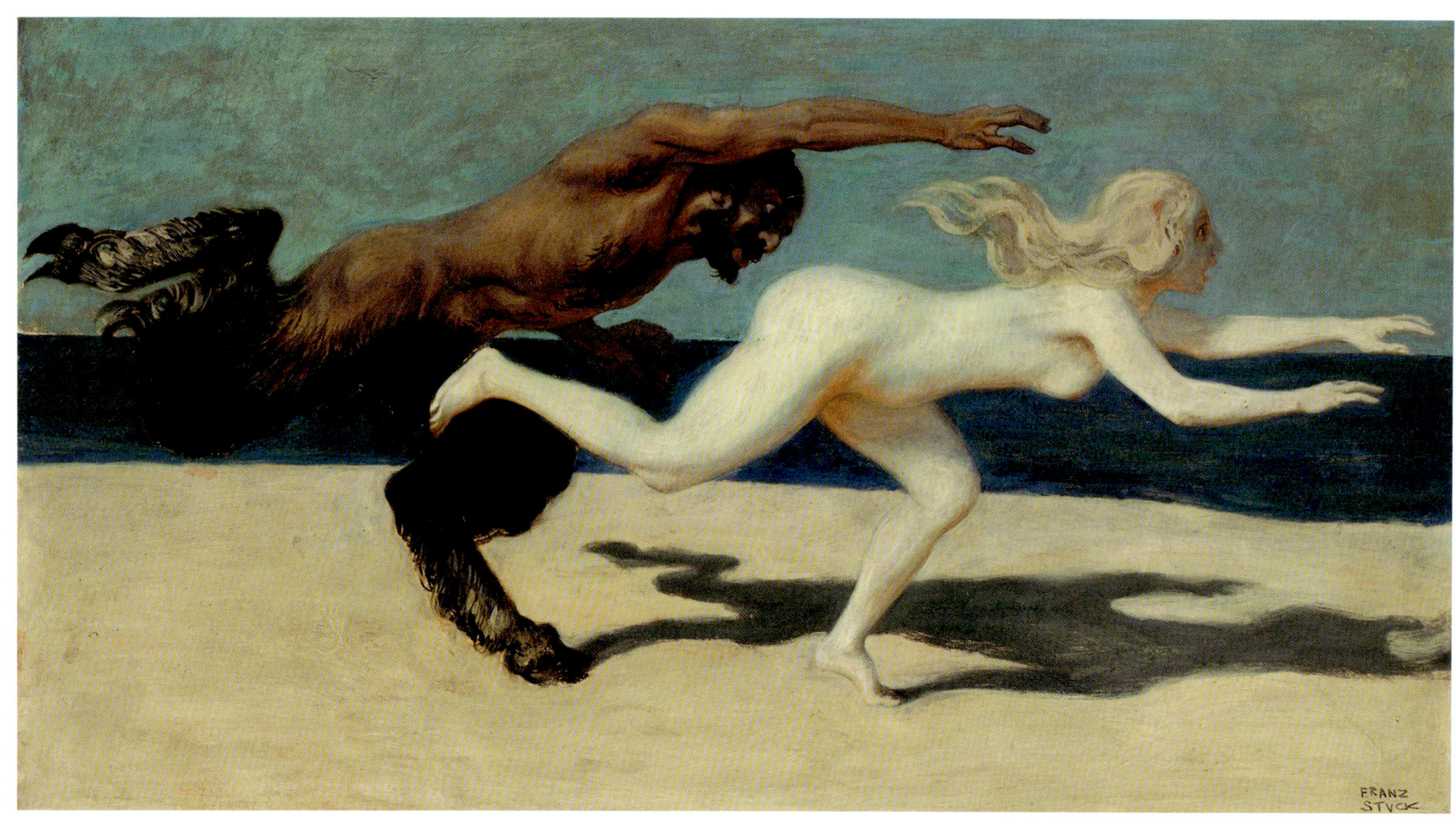

FRANZ VON STUCK
Faun and Nymph, c. 1892
Private Collection

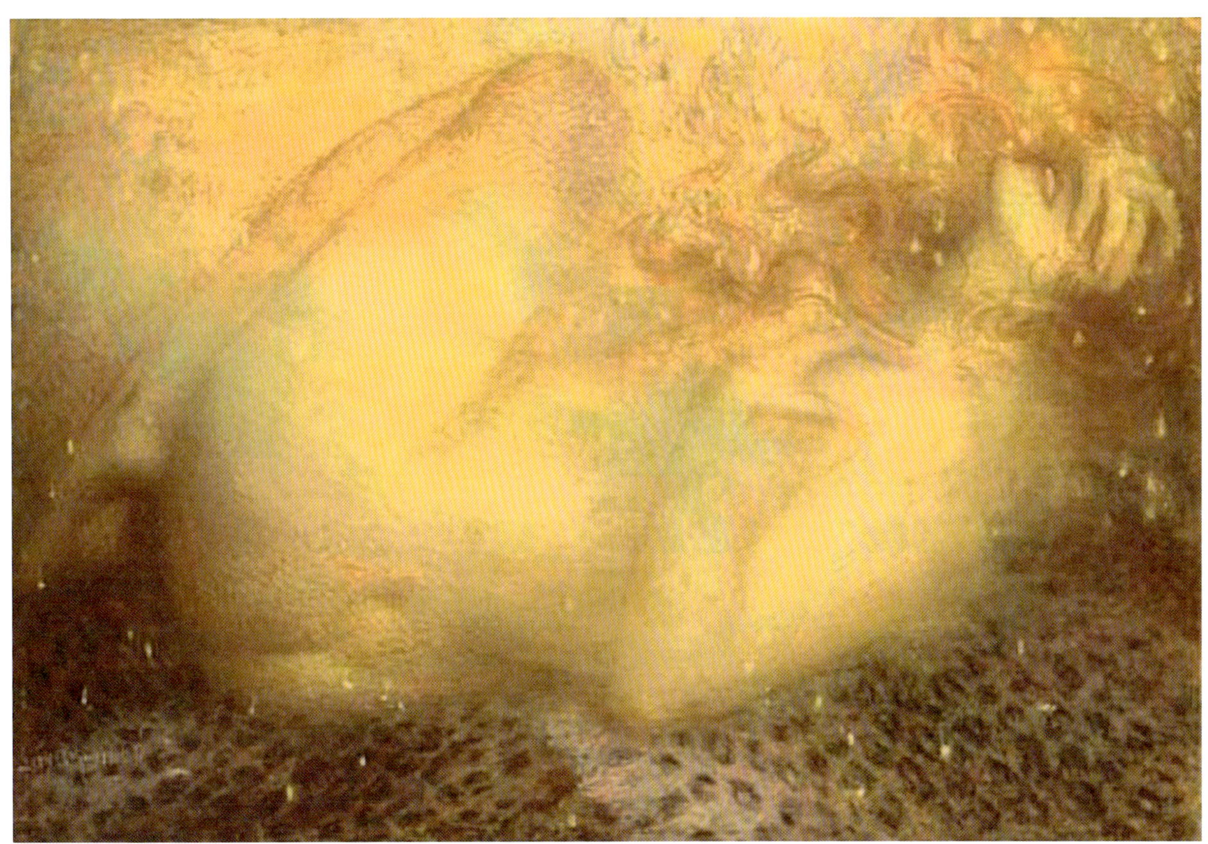

LUCIEN LÉVY-DHURMER
Danaë, c. 1900
Private Collection

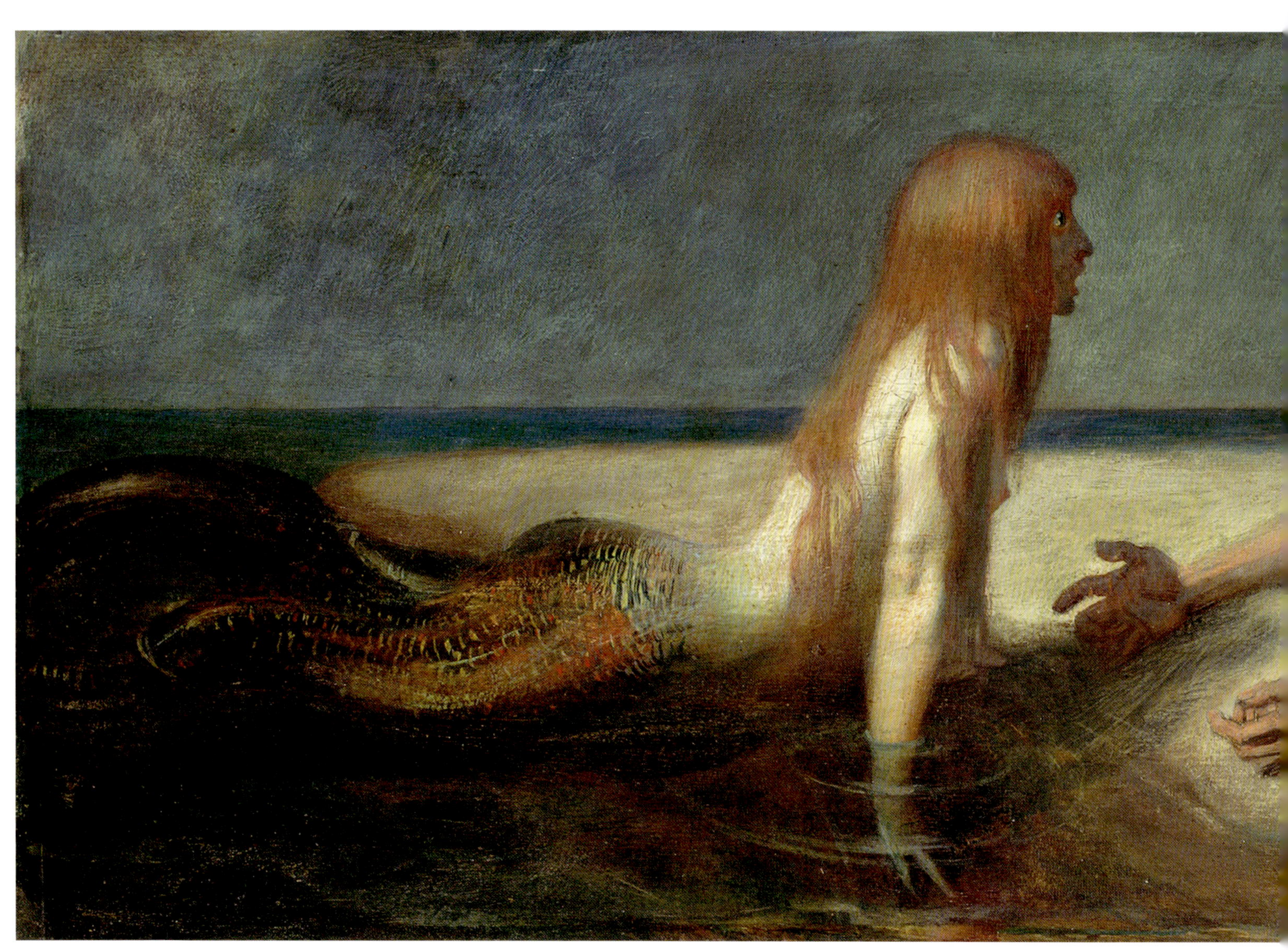

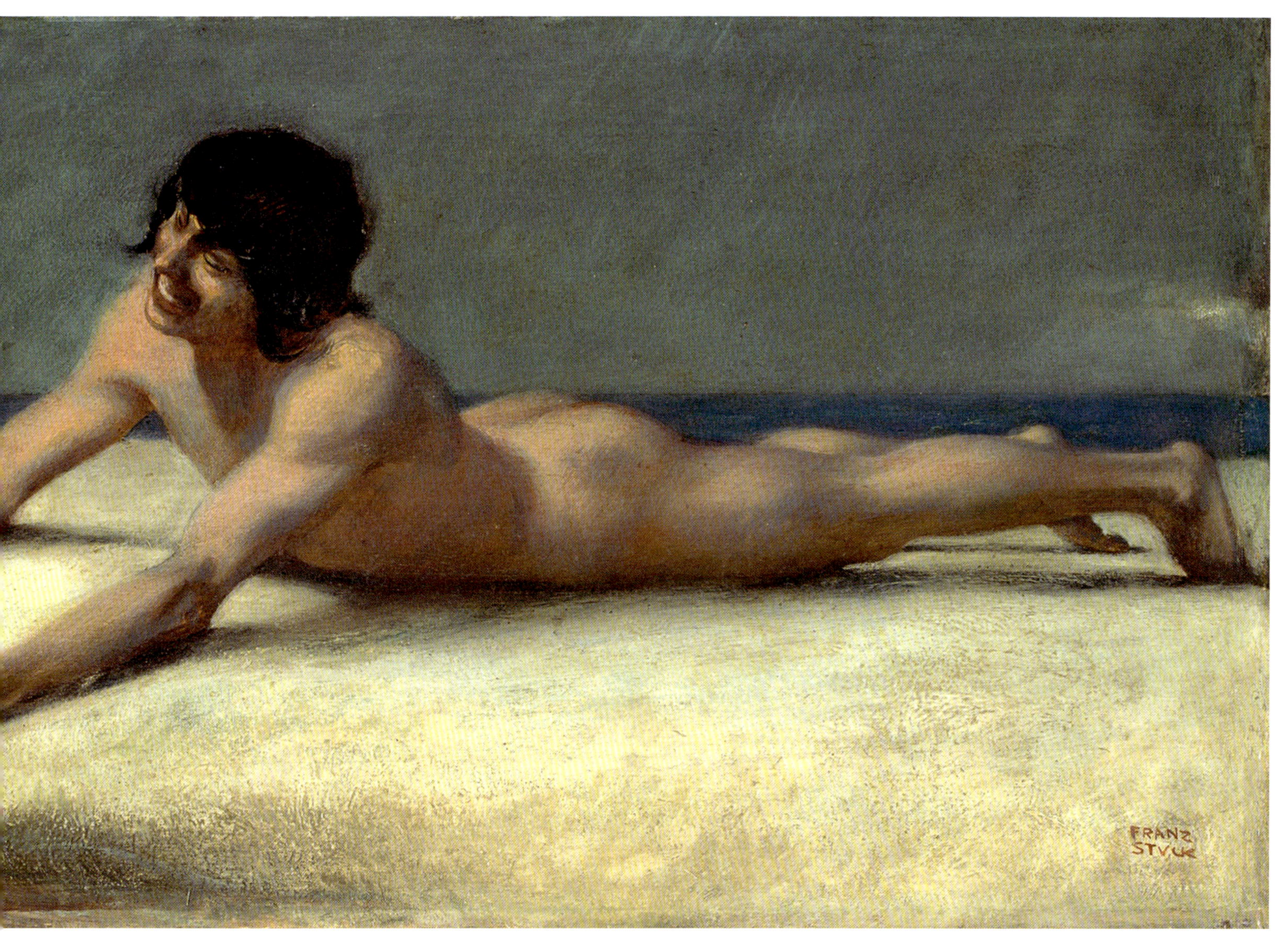

FRANZ VON STUCK
Mermaid, 1891
Private Collection

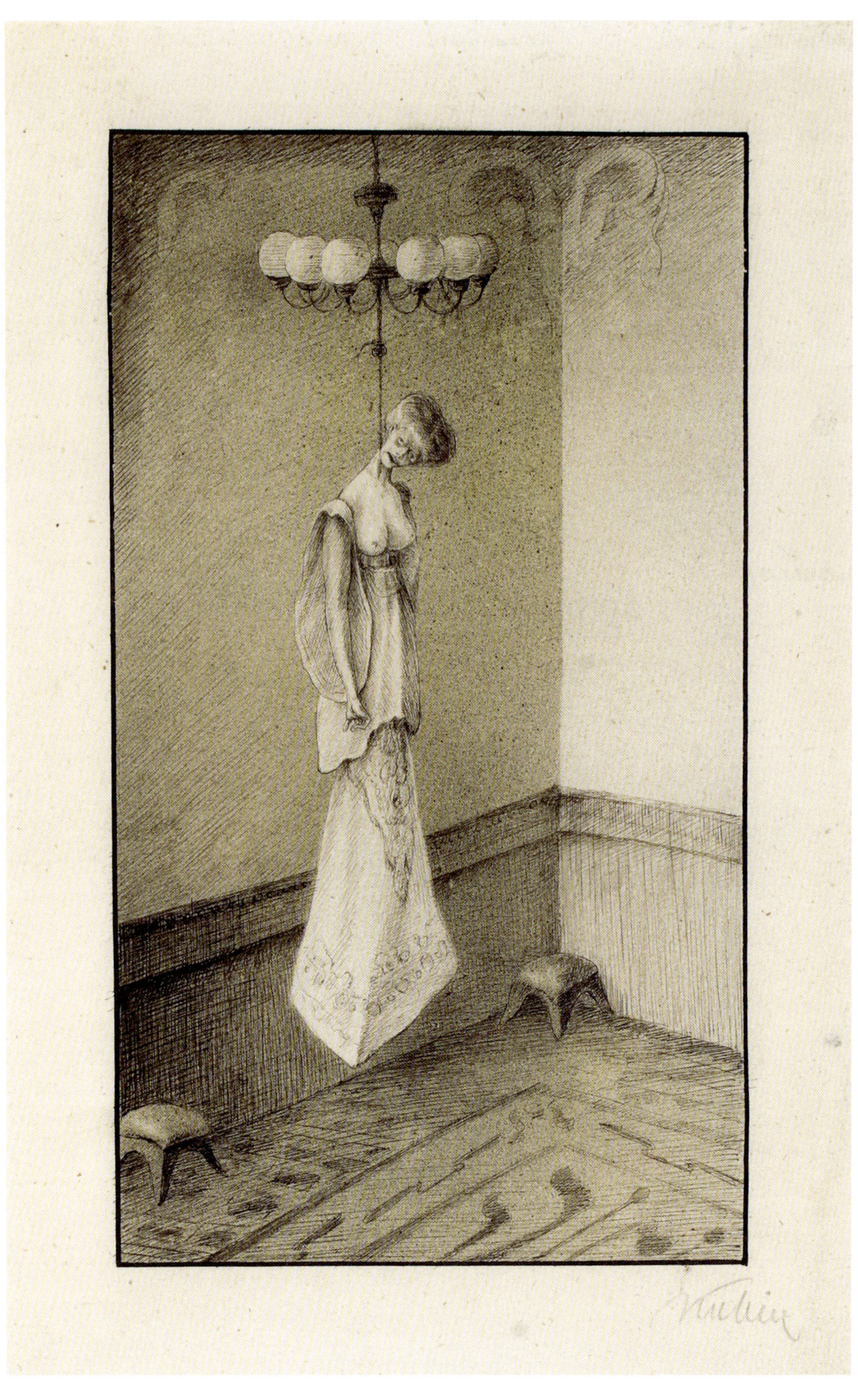

ALFRED KUBIN
Madame (also: Modern Chandelier Decor), 1900/01
Leopold Museum, Vienna

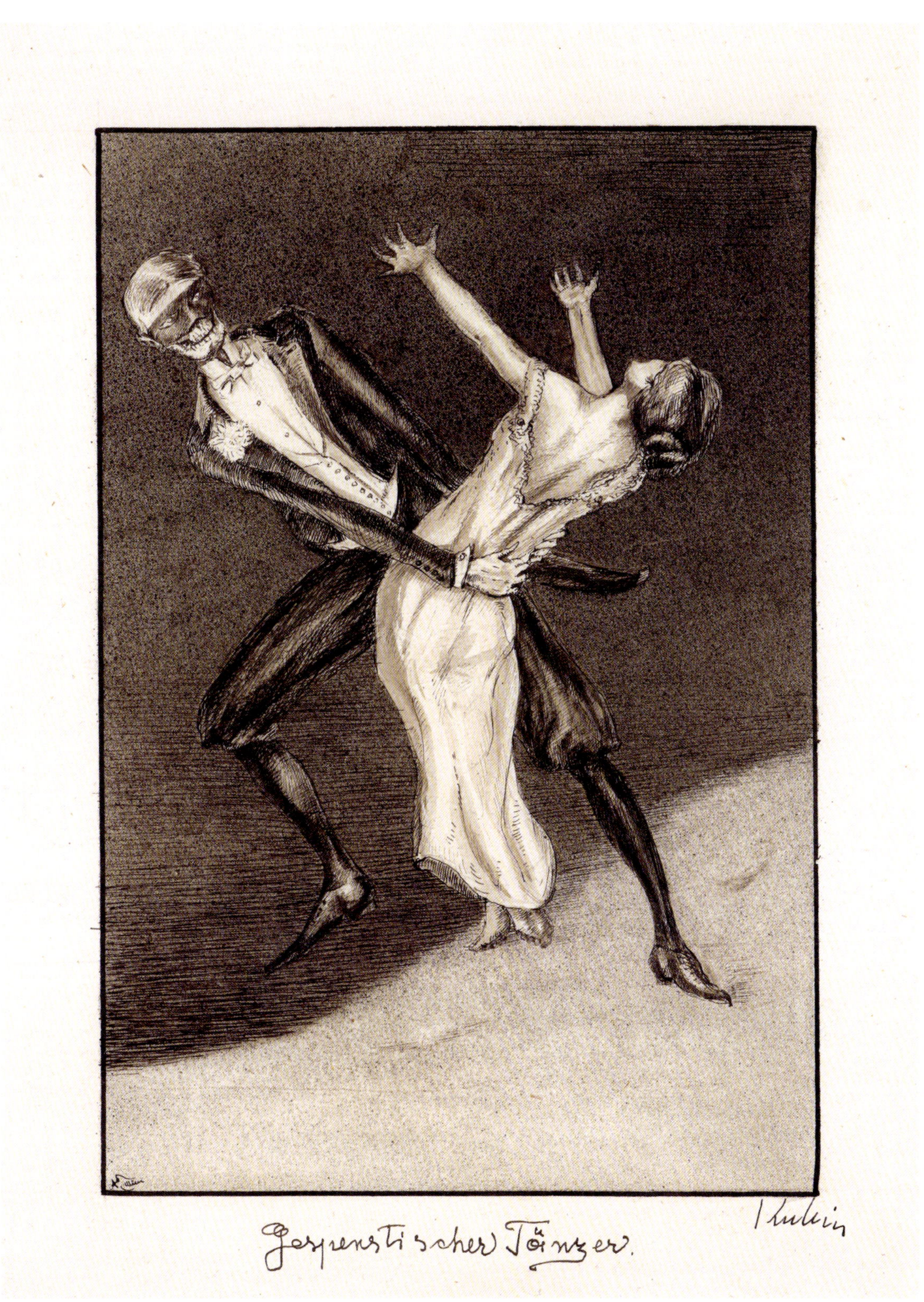

ALFRED KUBIN
Ghostly Dancer, 1899/1900
Leopold Museum, Vienna

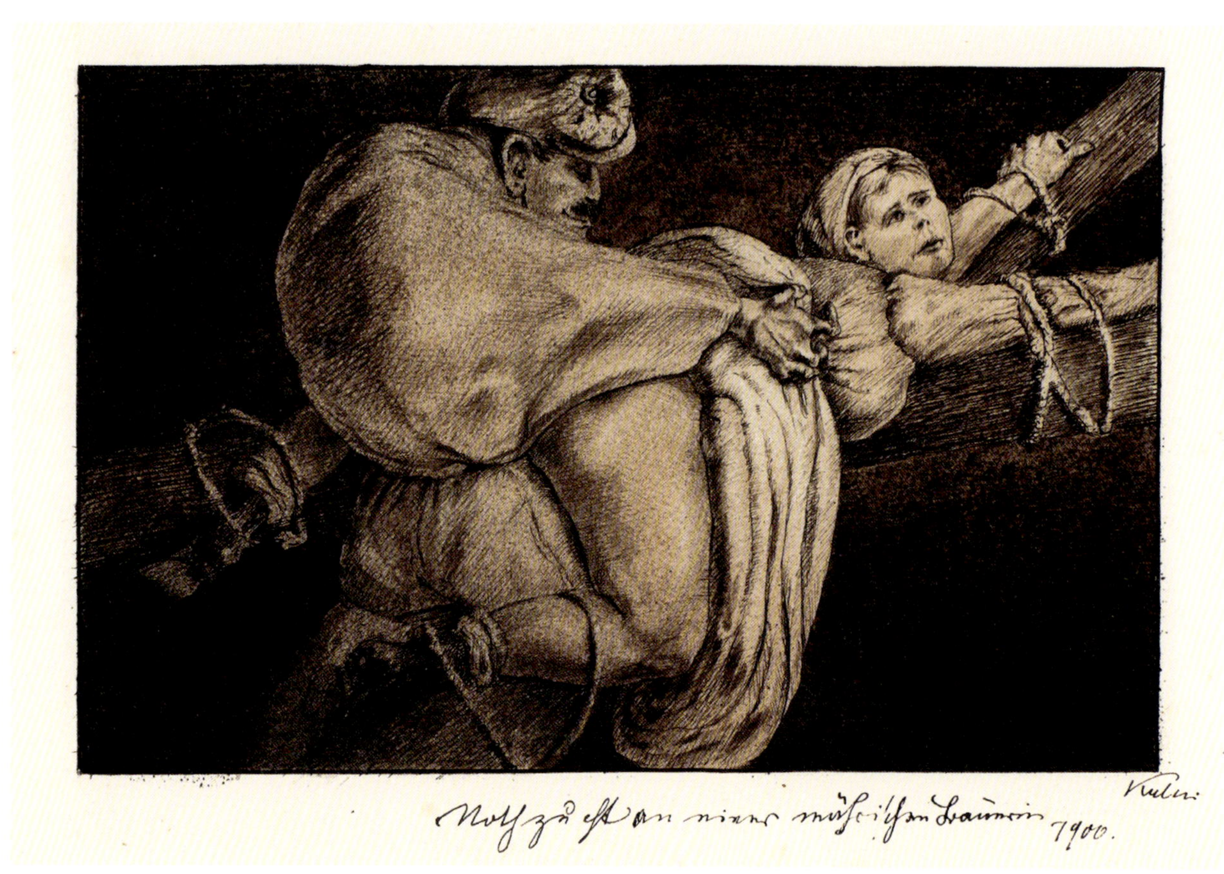

ALFRED KUBIN
Rape of a Moravian Peasant Woman, 1900
Private Collection

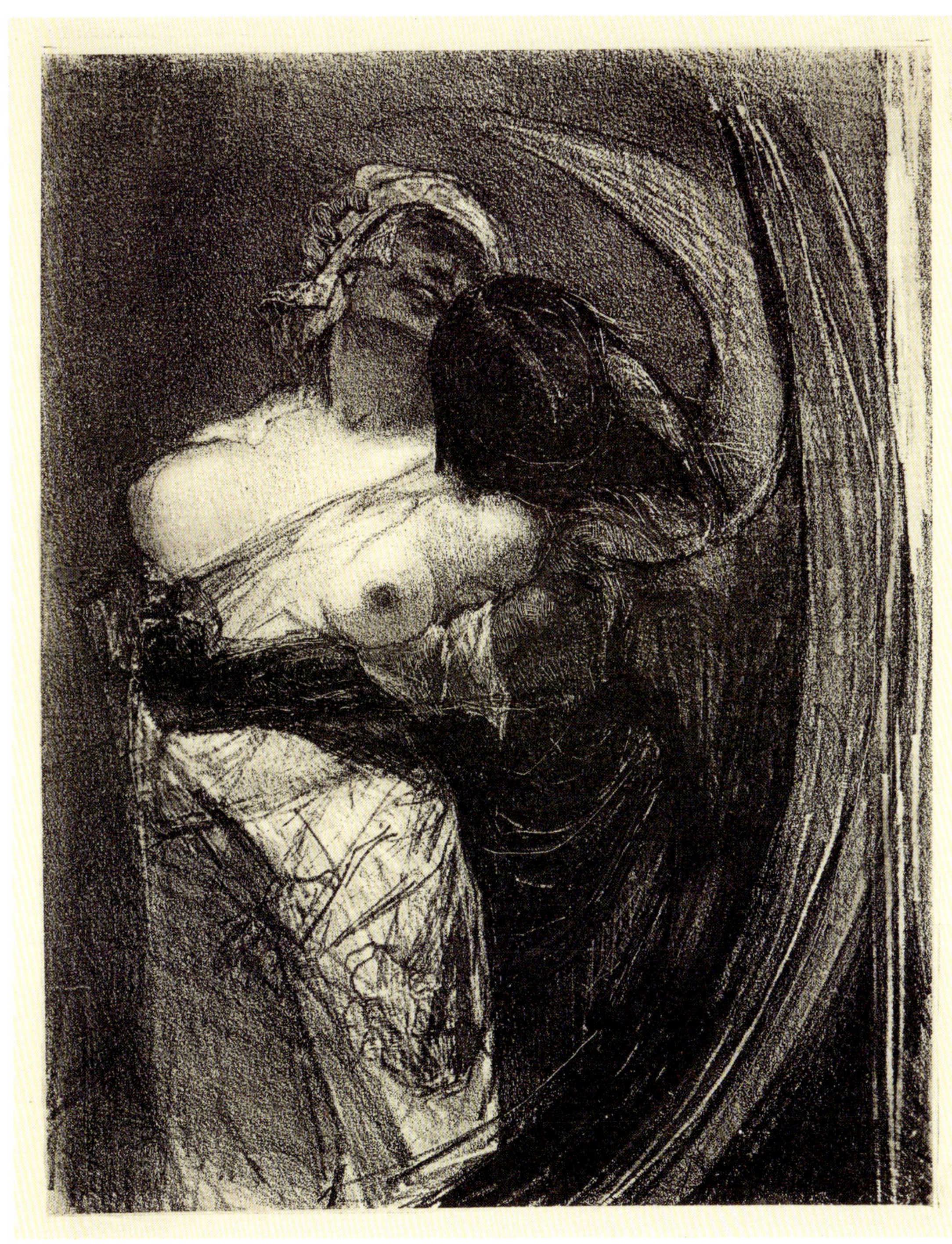

FÉLICIEN ROPS
The Cold Devils, 1905
Leopold Museum, Vienna

Alfred Kubin about Félicien Rops

I am still under the impression of the Rops drawings.—These great pieces are without doubt the most significant, from Rops. I still feel fear, thinking of that gargantuan lust that is reflected in these works.*

* Alfred Kubin in a letter to Hans von Weber, 1902.

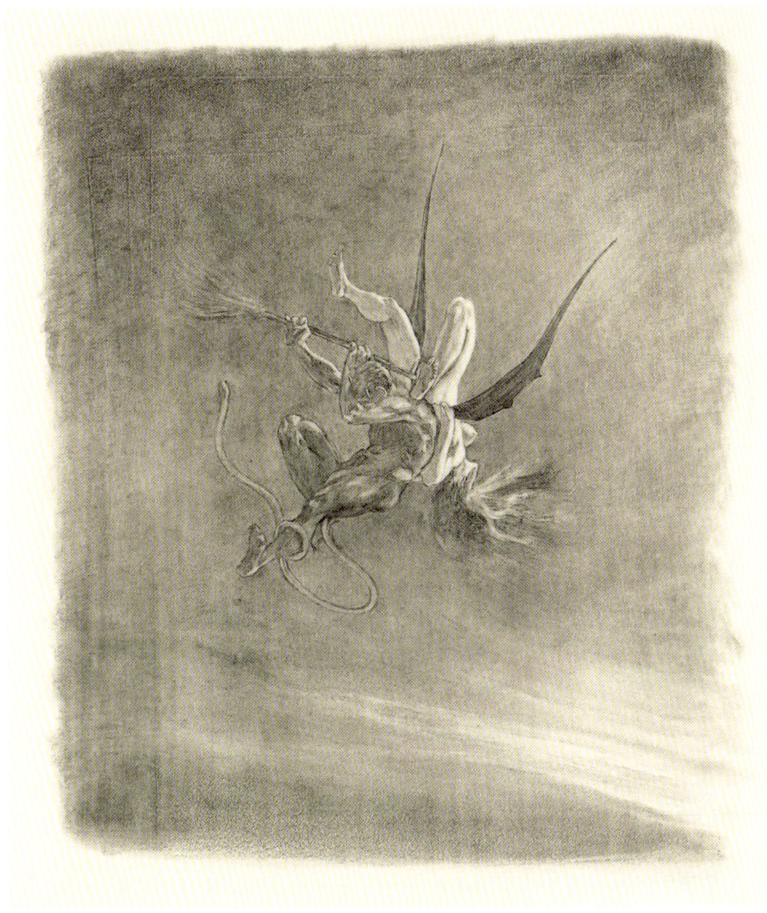

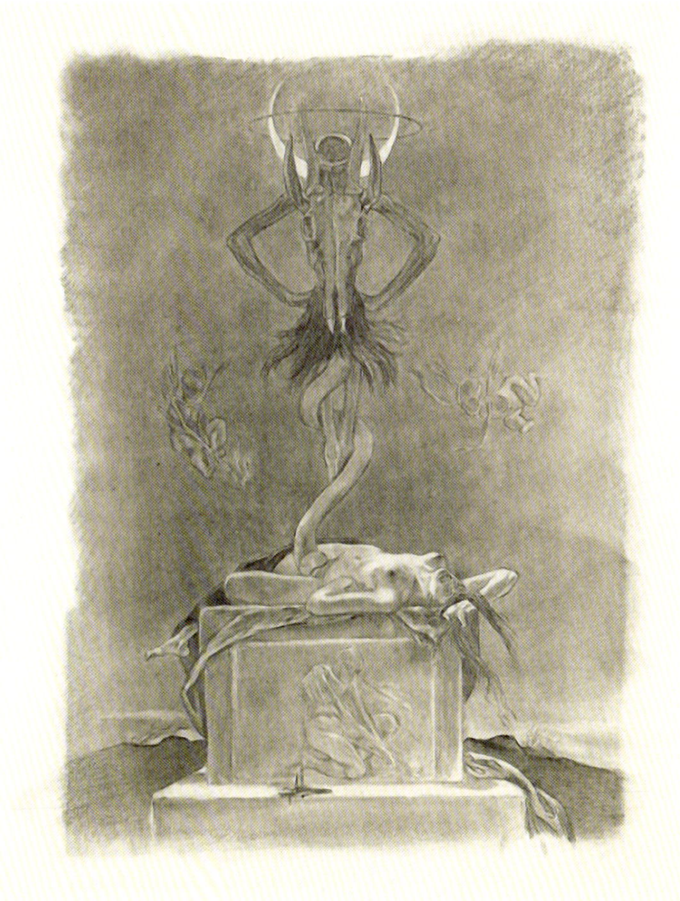

FÉLICIEN ROPS
The Abduction, from the series *Les Sataniques,* 1878–1882
Private Collection

FÉLICIEN ROPS
The Sacrifice, from the series *Les Sataniques,* 1878–1882
Private Collection

PAGAN SACRIFICE

The depiction *Pagan Sacrifice* is part of a series of early works on paper by Kubin, in which the themes of sexuality and cult are condensed into impressive pictorial symbols despite the artist's almost pubescent imagination and rather clumsy strokes. Comparable renderings are the slightly later works *The Idol* which shows a naked woman with long, flowing hair—a sign of erotic power—kneeling voluptuously before a giant rhinoceros elevated to a cultic figure, and *Adoration* which sees a nude woman holding a censer and bowing to a hermaphroditic idol. While these later works show devotion through adoration, the present work sees the victim of the sacrifice itself performing the act of worship. An executioner in medieval dress, the type we know from Kubin's torture scenes inspired by Goya, is carrying a nude and exposed young woman towards a fantastical, six-eyed idol. Despite such irrational and contrived cult figures, Kubin's contemporaries understood such drawings as the expression of an authentic myth, among them Arthur Holitscher who wanted to exclude Kubin from the art development of his time also on account of his crudely shaped idols incarnating the "religious horror" of aboriginal peoples.*

Annegret Hoberg

* Arthur Holitscher: "Kubin", in: *Die Kunst für Alle*, vol. 18, no. 7, 1903, p. 163.

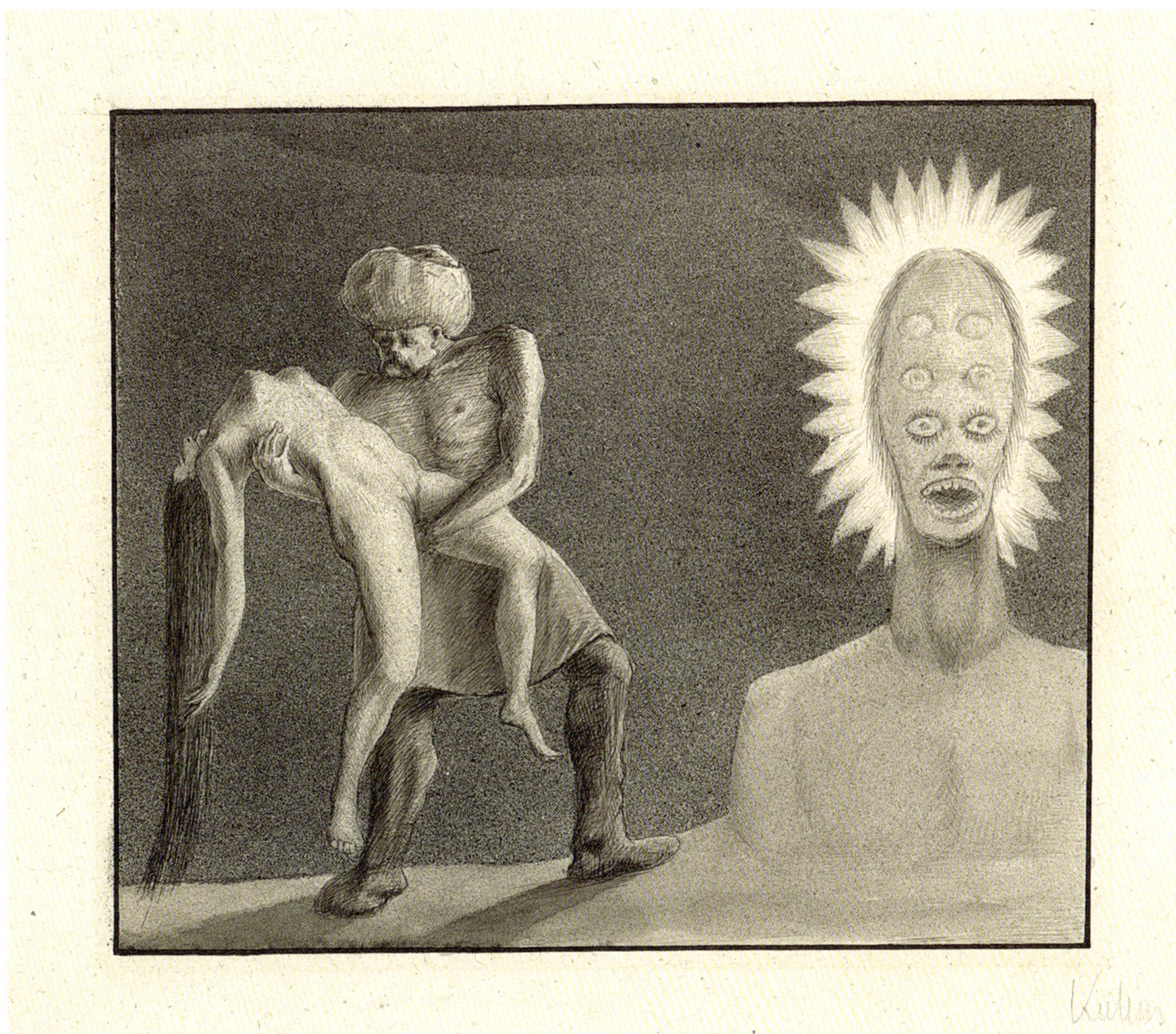

ALFRED KUBIN
Pagan Sacrifice, c. 1900/01
OÖ Landes-Kultur GmbH, Land Oberösterreich, Graphic Collection, Ha II 3180

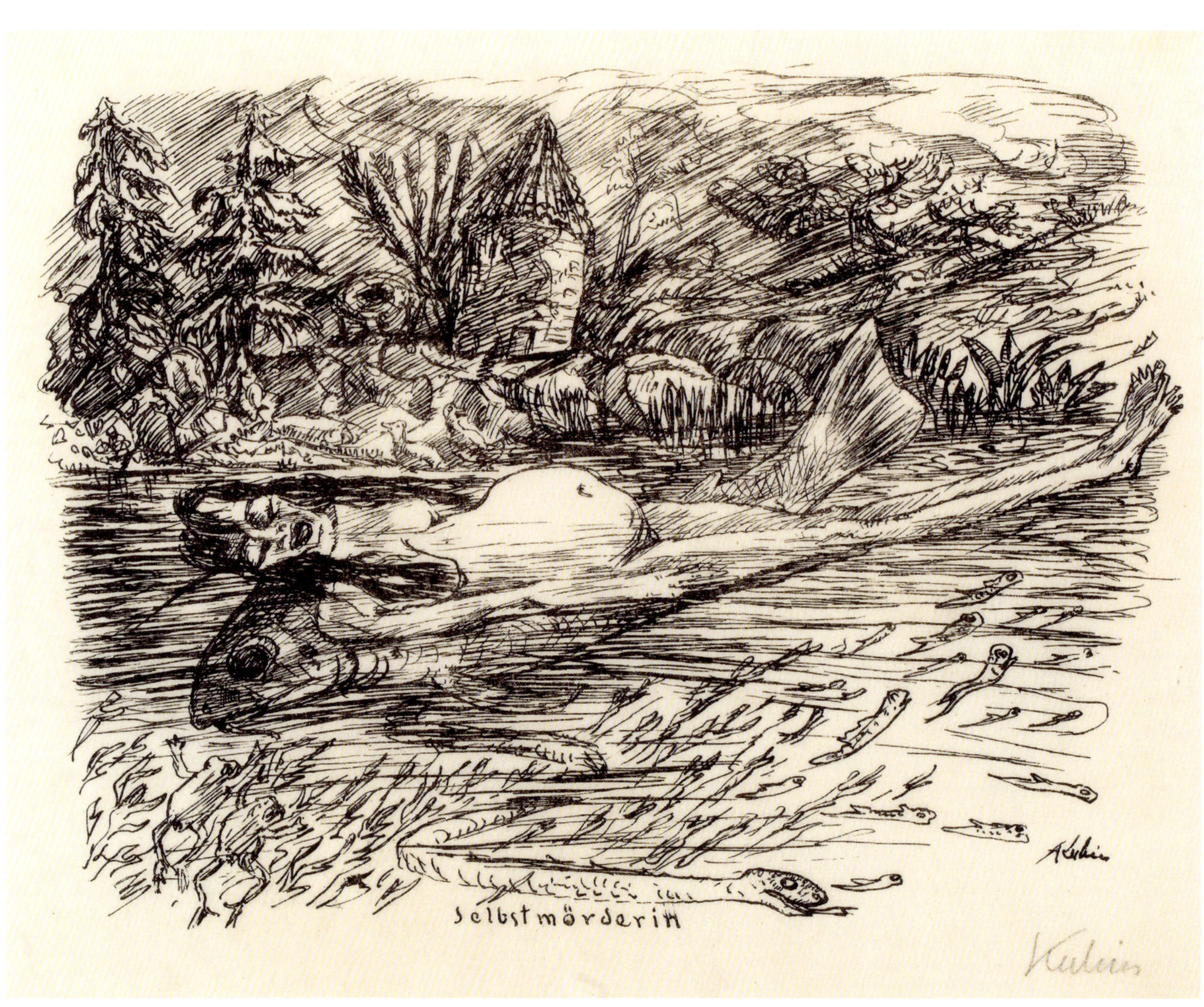

ALFRED KUBIN

The Suicide (Dreamland I and II), 1922

Leopold Museum, Vienna

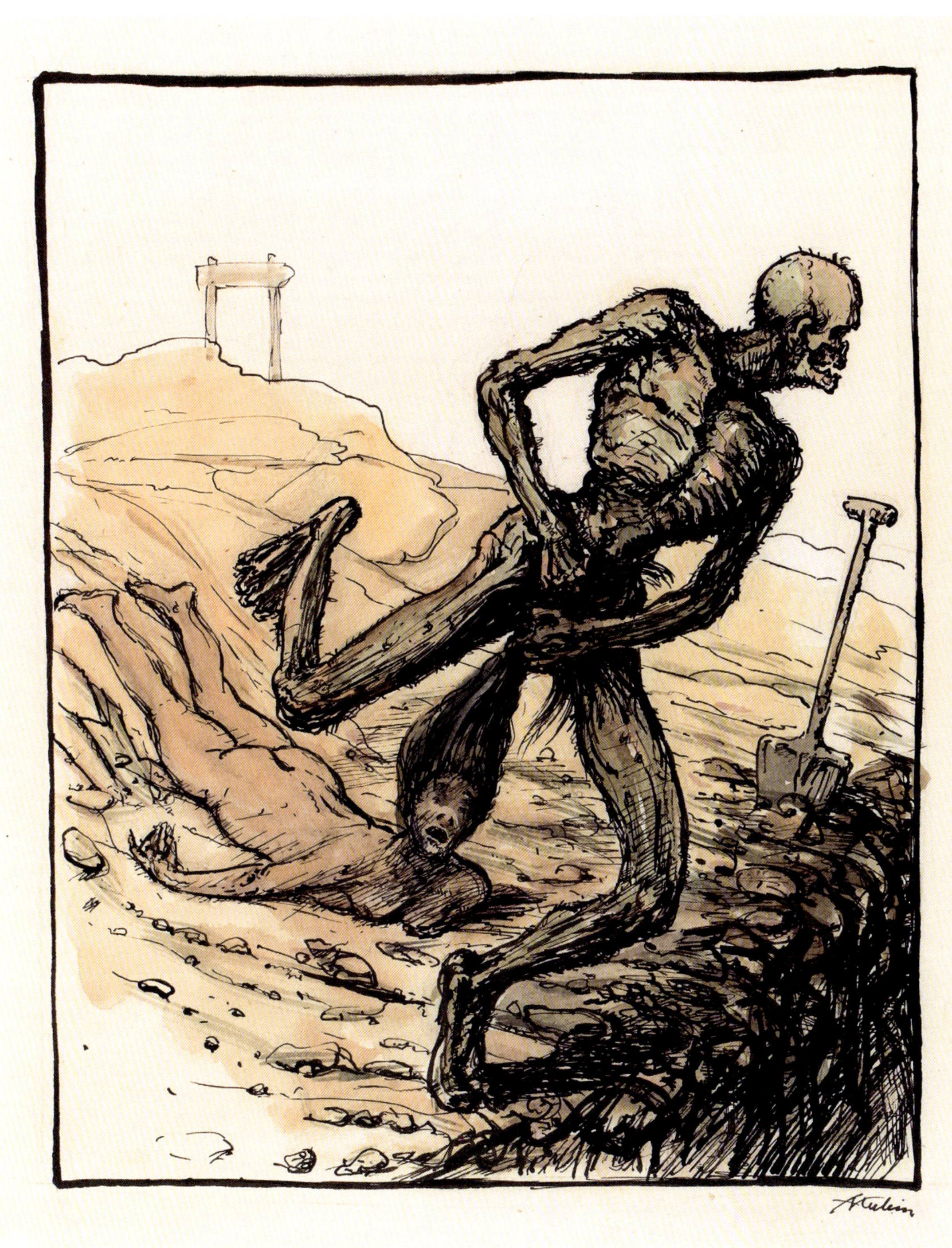

ALFRED KUBIN
Death at Work, c. 1923
Leopold Museum, Vienna

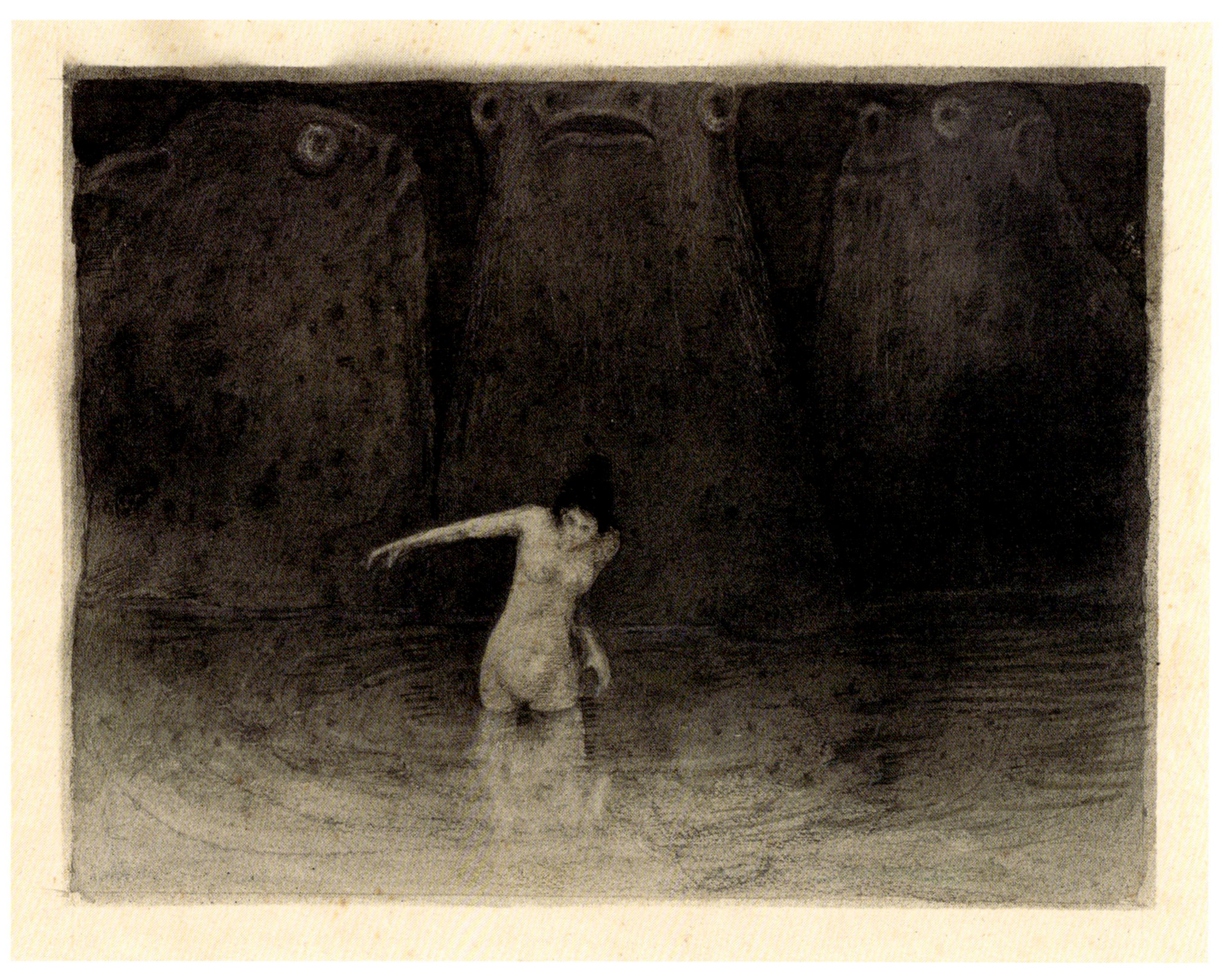

ALFRED KUBIN
The Swamp, c. 1903–1905
Lentos Kunstmuseum Linz

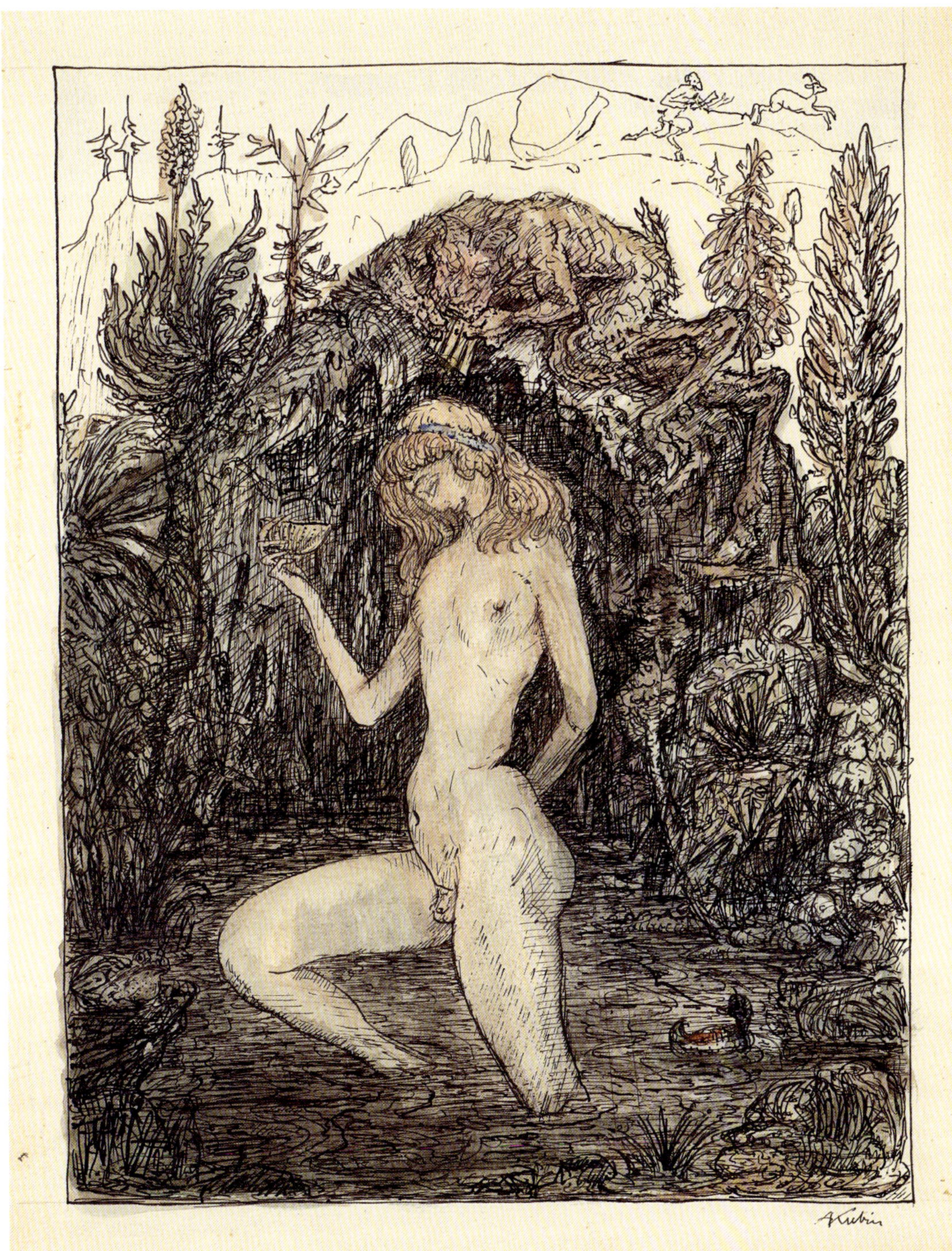

ALFRED KUBIN
Narcissism, c. 1930
Leopold, Private Collection

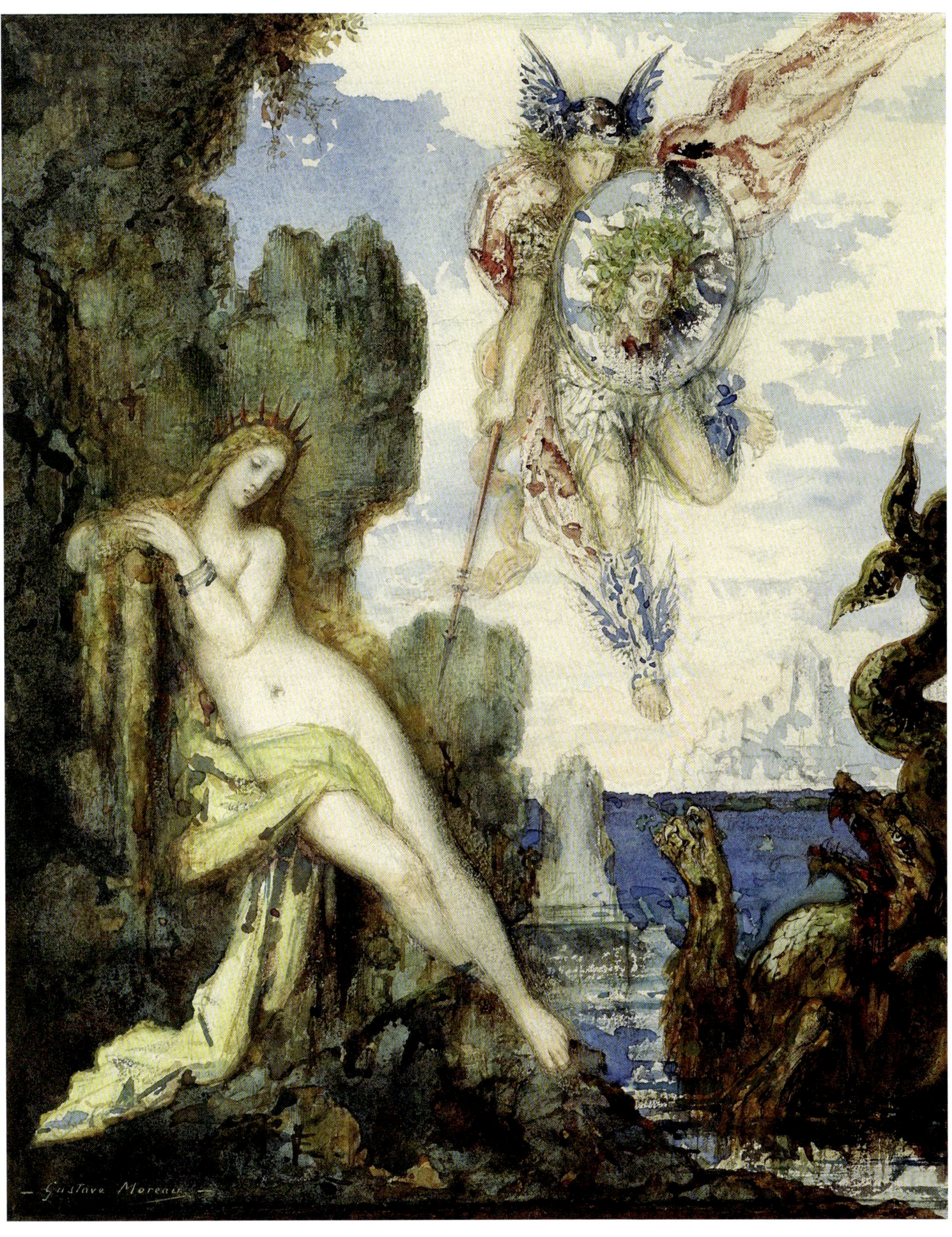

GUSTAVE MOREAU
Perseus and Andromeda, 1882
Private Collection

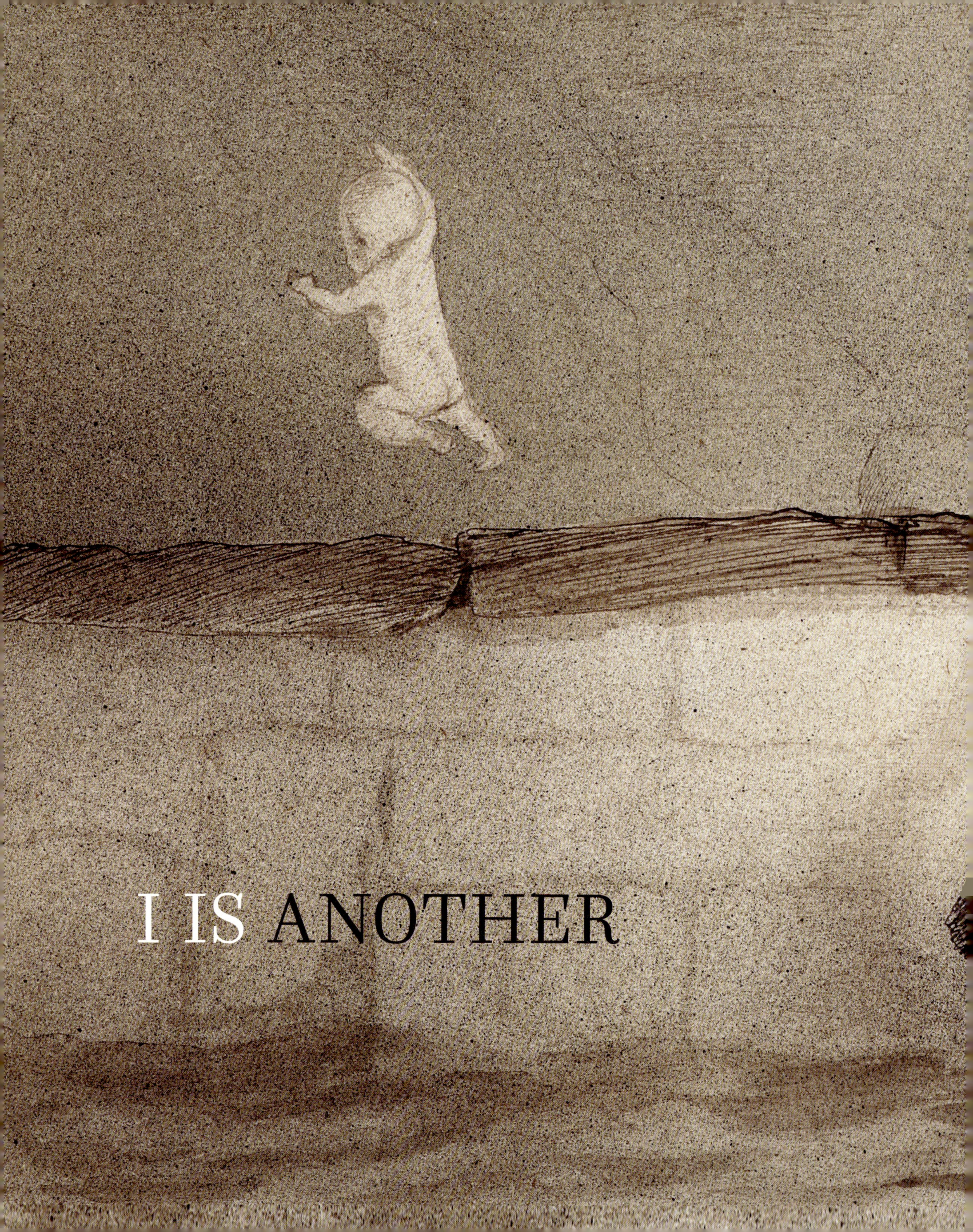
I IS ANOTHER

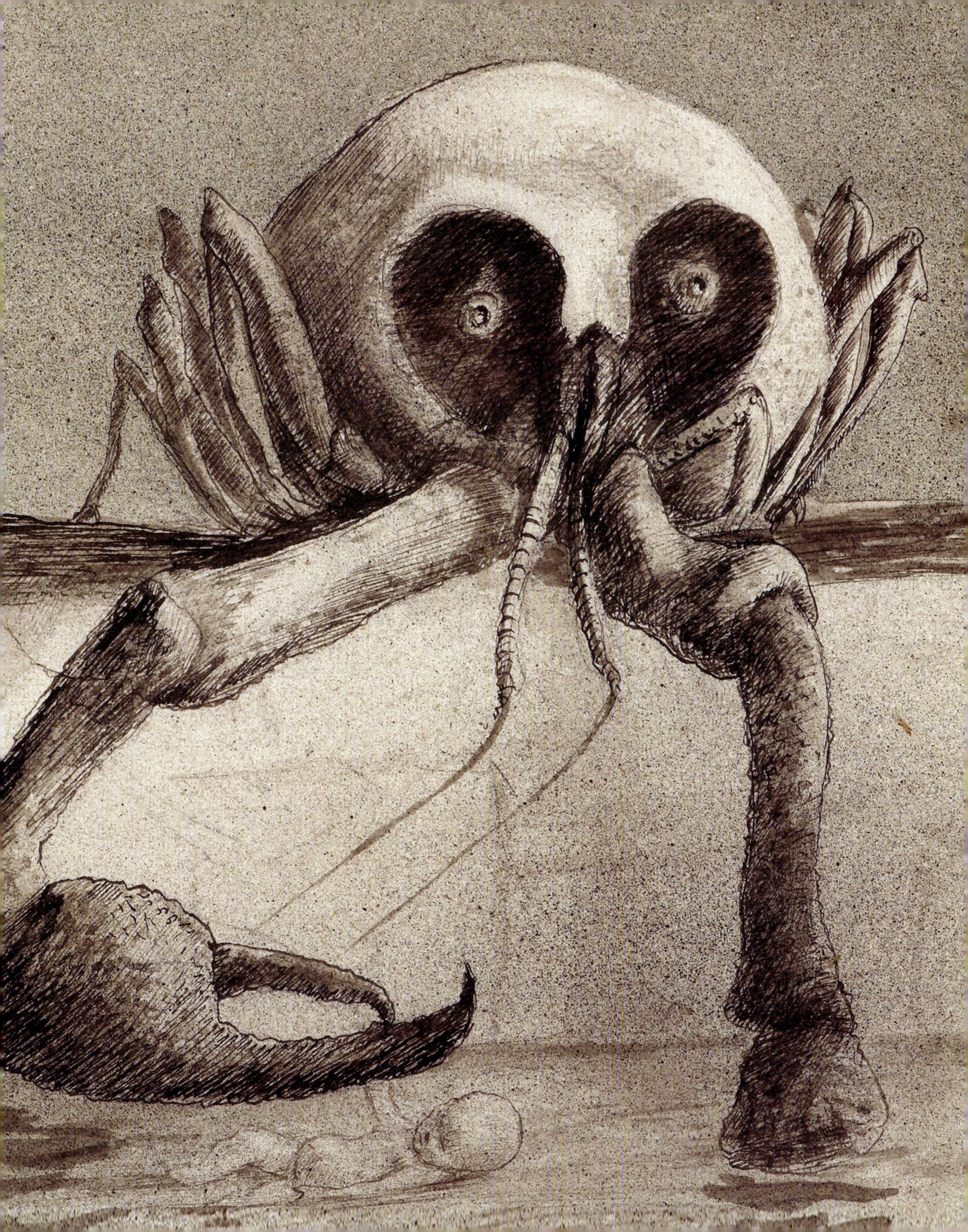

FROM MY REALM

The mysterious picture complex *From My Realm* was explored by Christoph Brockhaus in a thorough analysis. Kubin translated the far-reaching father complex into a downright Freudian psychoanalytic flip-flop image whose contemporary character is strangely reinforced by the two observers in the foreground clad in modern, urban dress. During his early years in Munich, Kubin verifiably worked on a philosophical fragment whose "peculiar basic idea" he outlined in his autobiography: "My conception was that an external, extratemporal principle—I called it the Father—for some unfathomable reason created Self-consciousness—the Son—together with the world, which was inseparable from him. In this scheme I myself was, of course, the Son, who deceives himself, torments and persecutes himself as long as this is well pleasing to his true and gigantic Father, who spontaneously created him as a sort of mirror image. Such a Son can therefore disappear at any instant along with his world and be assimilated into the superexistence of the Father."*
In the work, "the Father" appears as a giant, inflated and indifferent phantom floating in the background, while his creature, "the Son", is rendered as a senile embryo, indissolubly shackled to the world with suction feet, enveloped by the "almighty" figure of his creator and doomed by the impossibility of his own development.**

Annegret Hoberg

* Alfred Kubin: *Dämonen und Nachtgesichte. Mit einer Selbstdarstellung des Künstlers und 130 Bilddaten* (Dresden, 1926), pp. 19f.

** Christoph Brockhaus, in: *Alfred Kubin. Das zeichnerische Frühwerk bis 1904*, ed. by Hans Albert Peters (Baden-Baden, 1977), no. 7 (exh. cat. Kunsthalle Baden-Baden, 01.04.–30.05.1977).

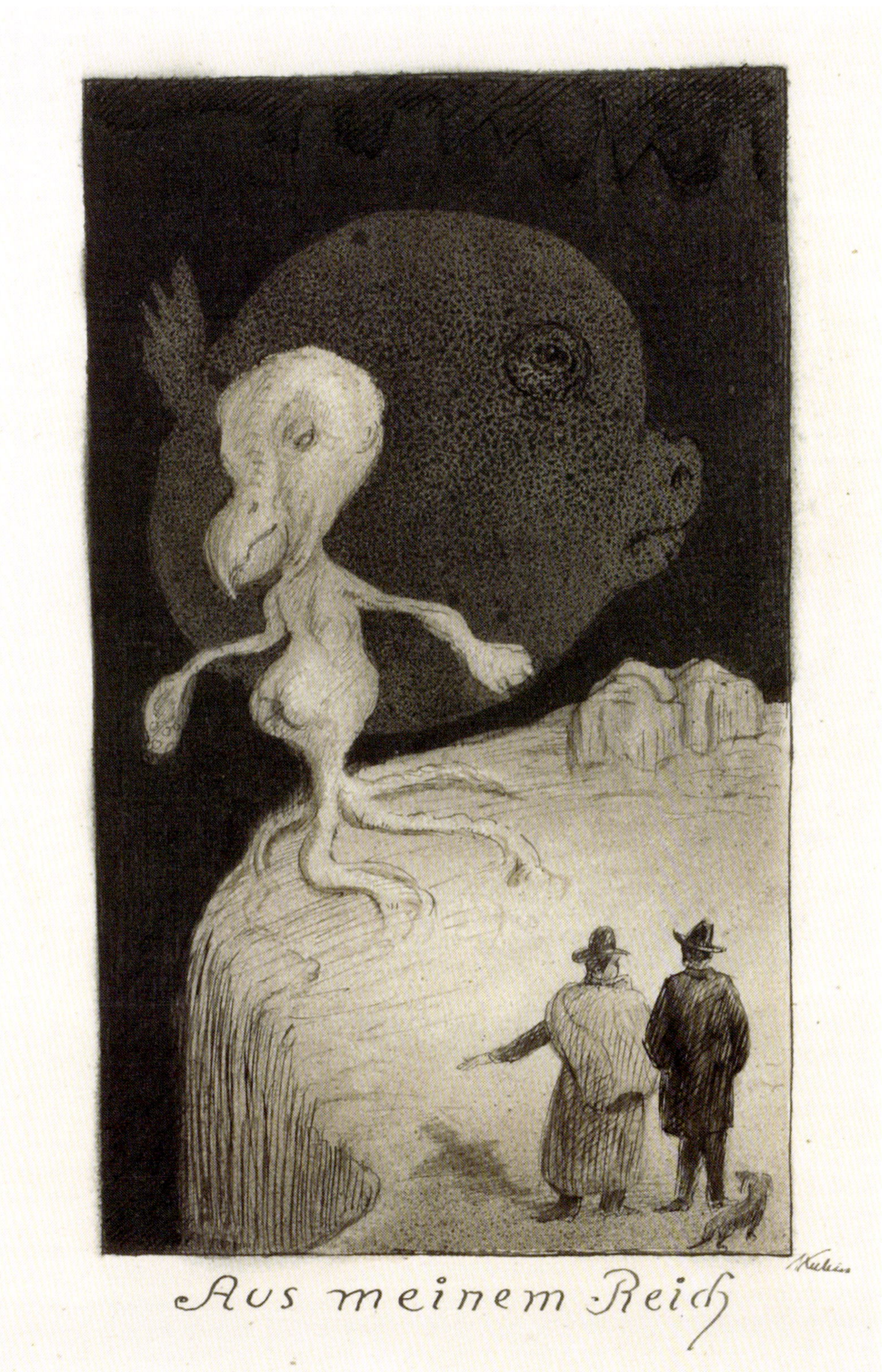

ALFRED KUBIN
From My Realm, 1900
Leopold Museum, Vienna

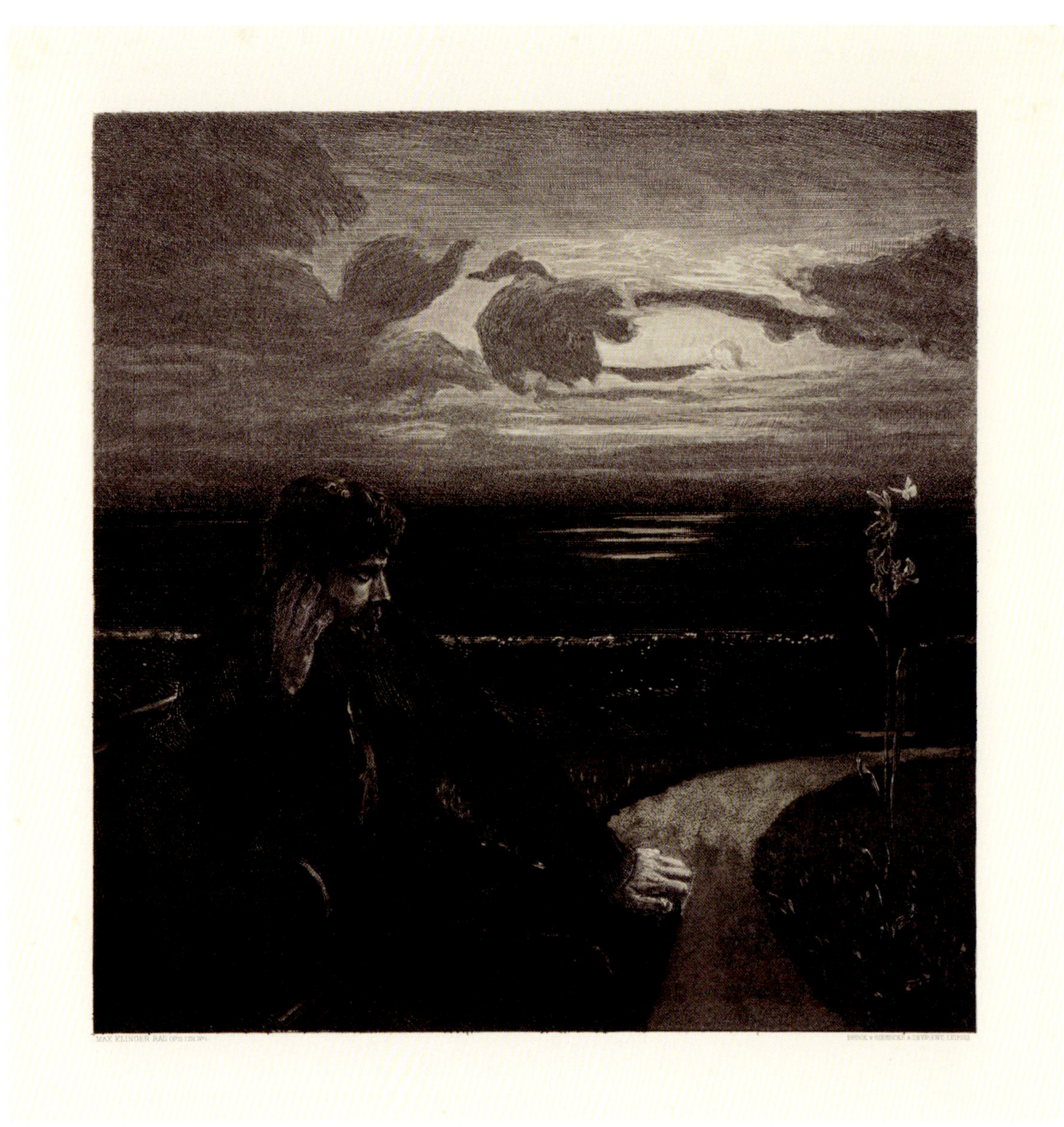

MAX KLINGER
Night, from the cycle *On Death. Part 1,* 1897
Leopold Museum, Vienna

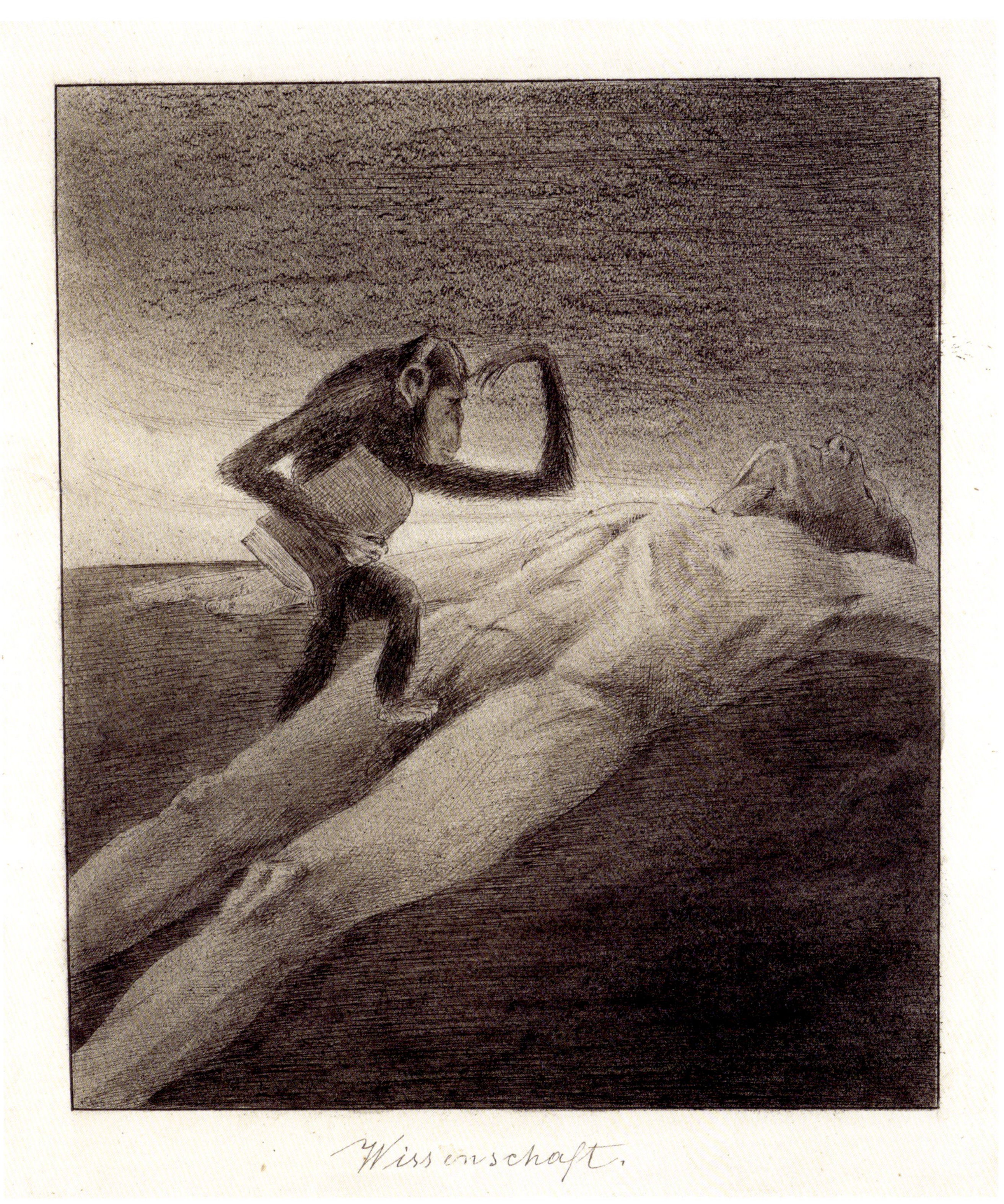

ALFRED KUBIN
Science, c. 1902
Leopold Museum, Vienna

THE HOUR OF BIRTH

In his 1903 review of the portfolio *Weber-Mappe* for the magazine *Die Gegenwart,* J. Norden reasoned as follows: "From 'the hour of birth', when a giant crustacean with horrible claws hurls the little children into the gray nothingness, to the last breath, when death, as the 'best physician' (p. 155) appears at the sickbed, the deliverer from the torments which, in the artist's opinion, make up life, it is one and the same mood that pervades every work." And while he called Kubin a lonely martyr of his own world-view, Norden conceded that this outlook was also "rooted in the pessimism of our time". As Christoph Brockhaus stated, Kubin's contemporaries were not only interested in the nihilism of being thrown into nothingness without hope or protection but also in the beginnings of mankind and its purported origins in the water.*

No other work by Kubin comes closer to his role model Max Klinger than *The Hour of Birth*, the similarities even extending to the treatment of forms: Klinger's 1879 etching *Siesta I* shows two lobsters placed on a band of rocks in a comparable parallel manner. One of them reaches down with its sharp claw into the water to grab the tail of a fish. Kubin "denaturalized" the vague, dull sense of threat that pervades Klinger's work and heightened its individual elements to convey his own message.

Annegret Hoberg

* Christoph Brockhaus: *Alfred Kubin. Das zeichnerische Frühwerk bis 1904*, ed. by Hans Albert Peters (Baden-Baden, 1977), no. 48 (exh. cat. Kunsthalle Baden-Baden, 01.04.–30.05.1977)

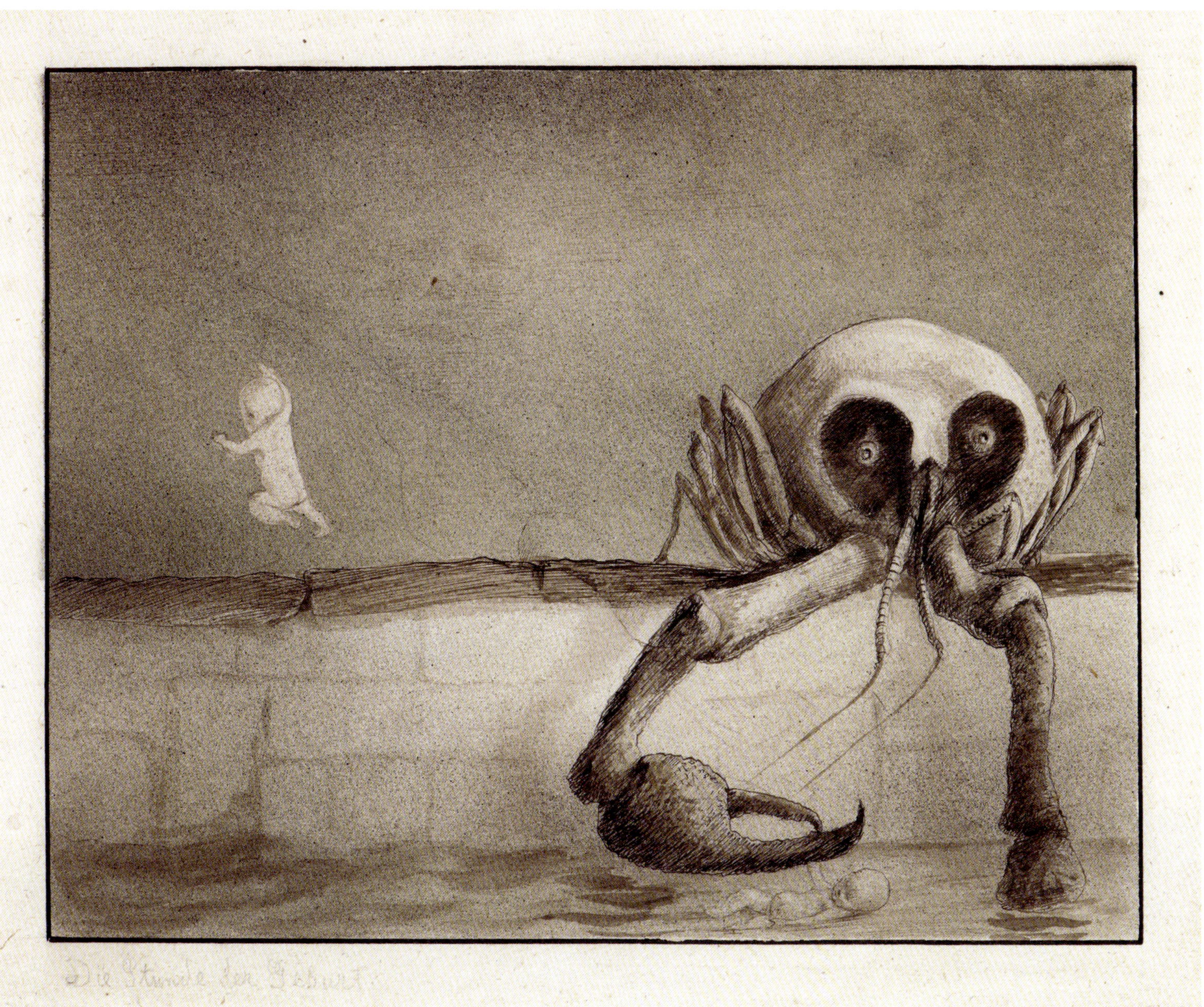

ALFRED KUBIN
The Hour of Birth, 1901/02
Leopold Museum, Vienna

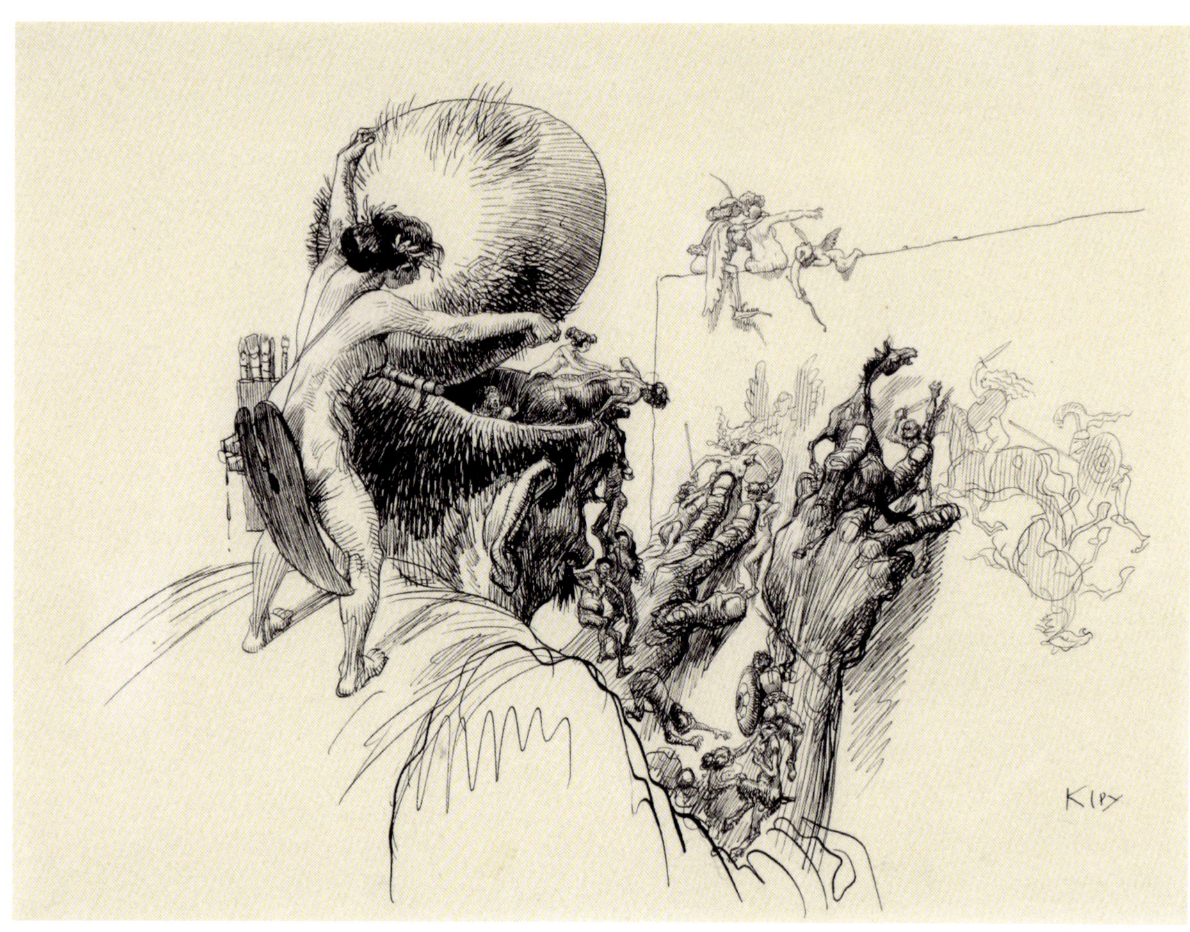

HEINRICH KLEY
Inspiration (Self-Portrait), 1912
Museum Georg Schäfer, Schweinfurt

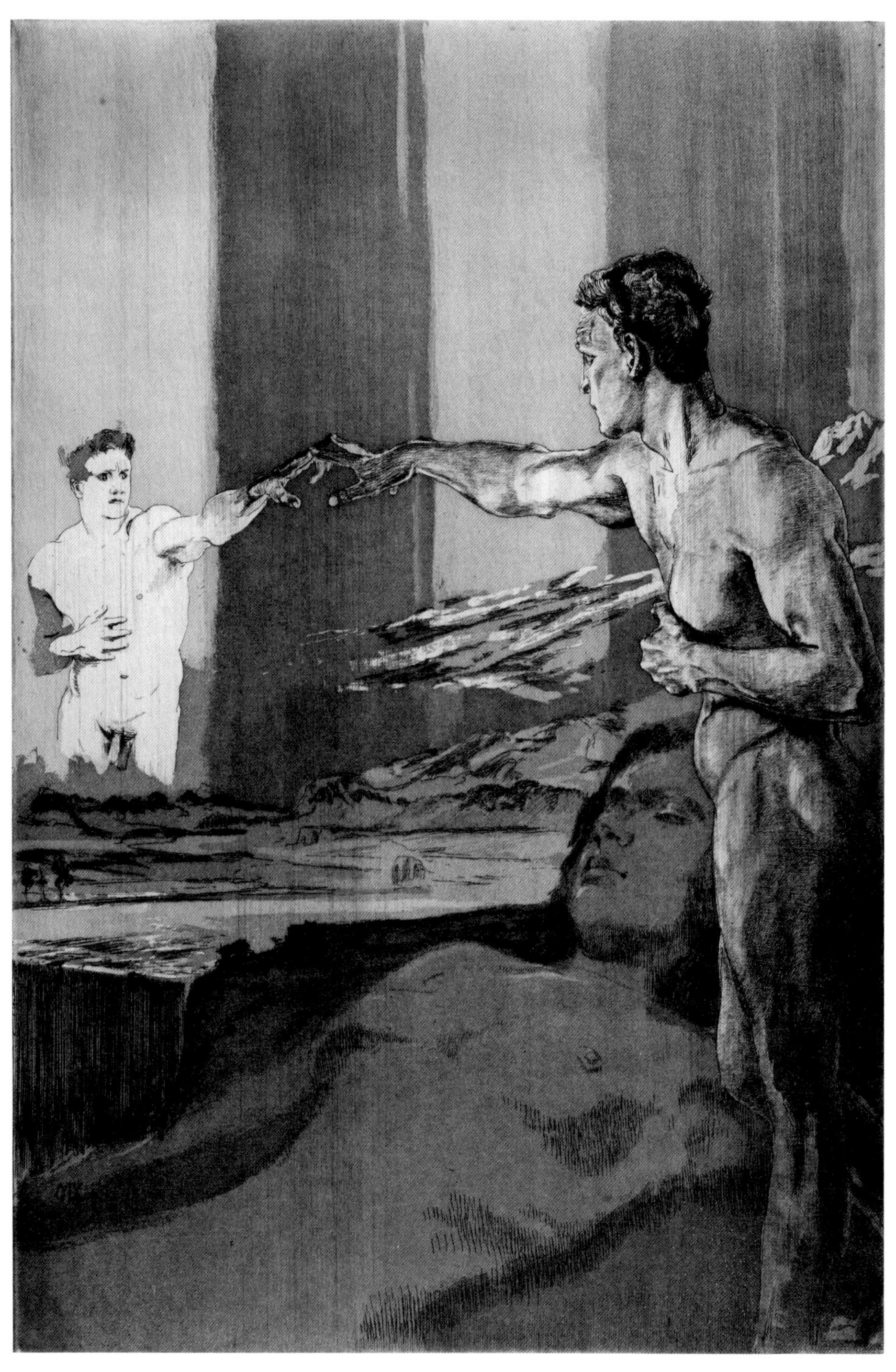

MAX KLINGER
Philosopher, print 3 of portfolio
On Death. Part II, 1910
LETTER Foundation, Cologne

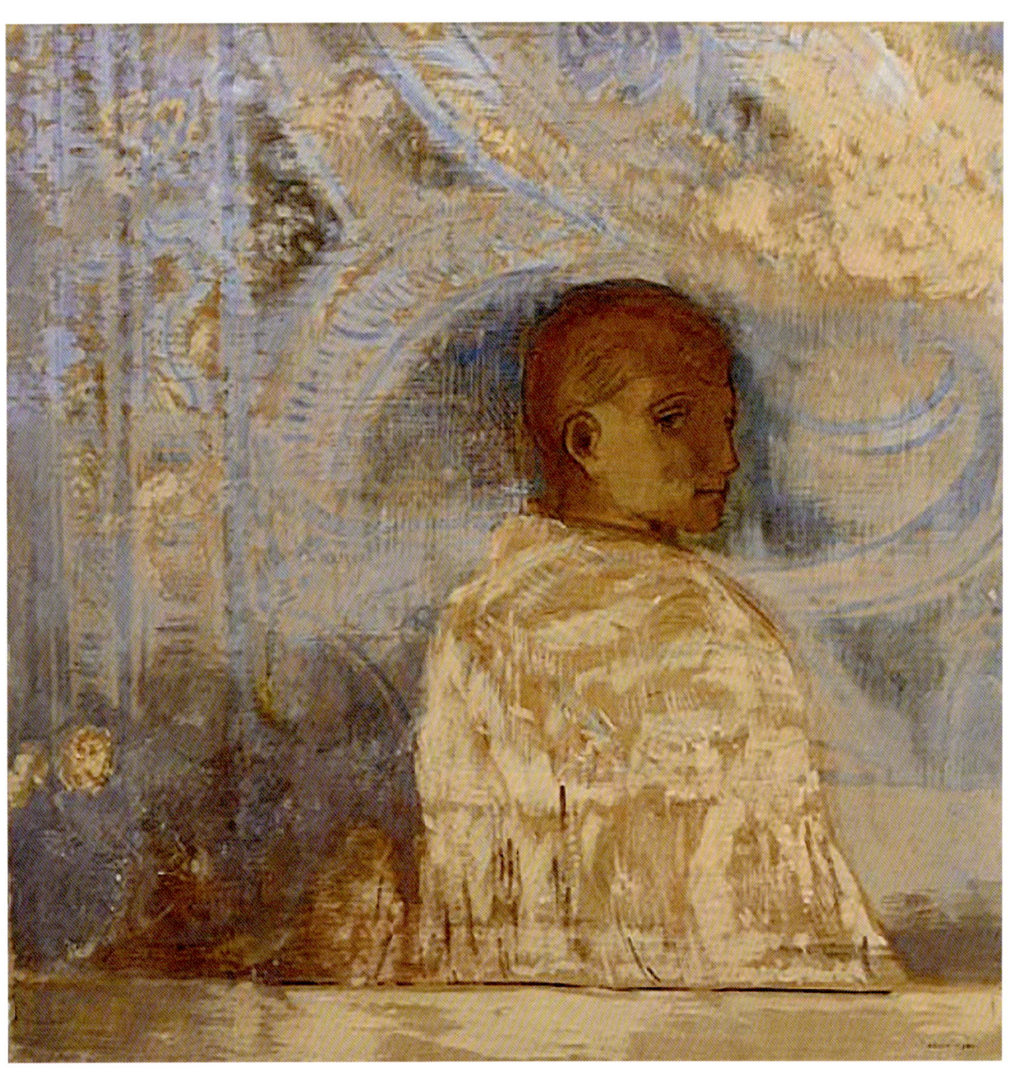

ODILON REDON
The Gaze, 1910
Private Collection

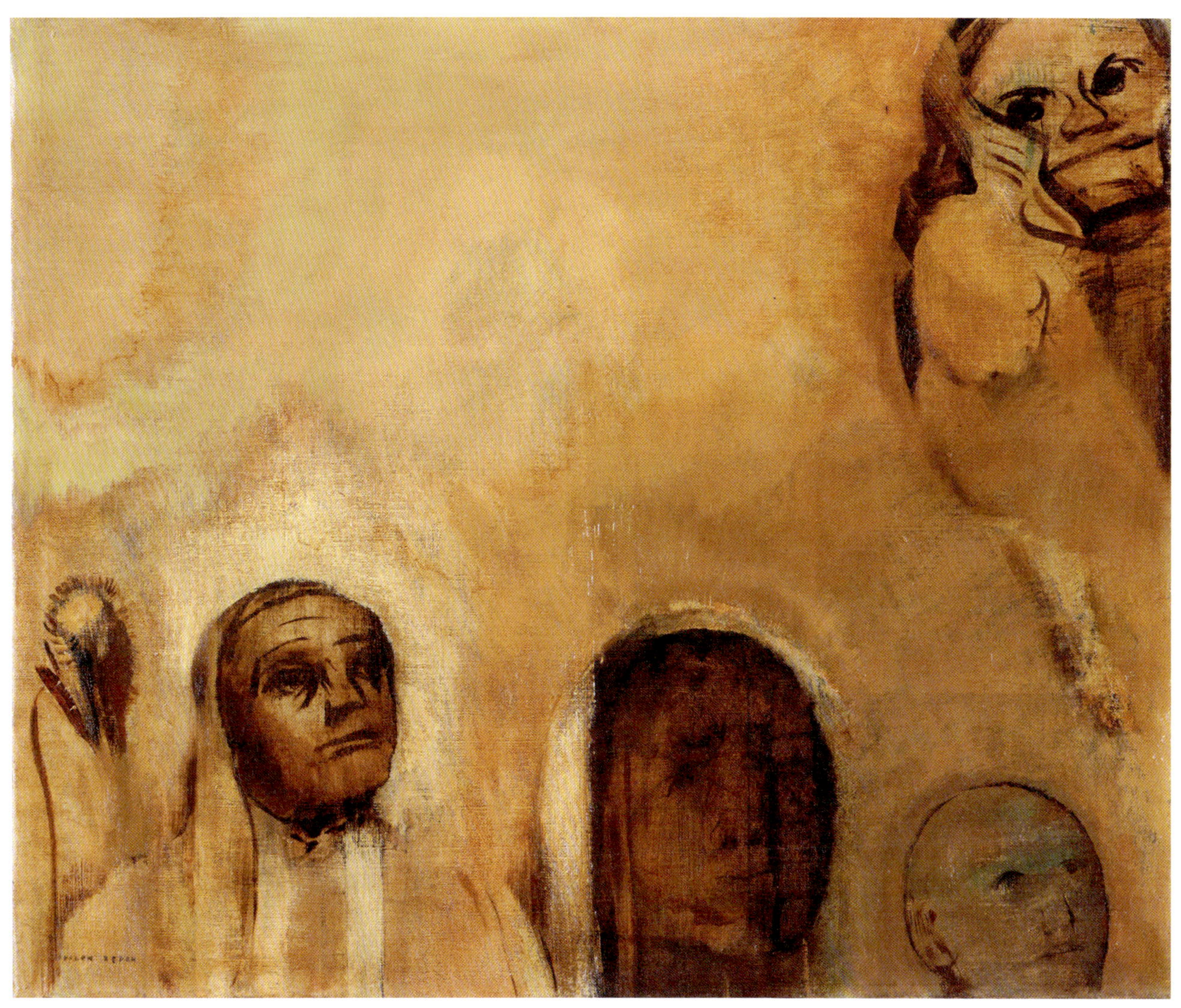

ODILON REDON
Ecstatic Figures, 1910/11
Klewan Collection, Munich

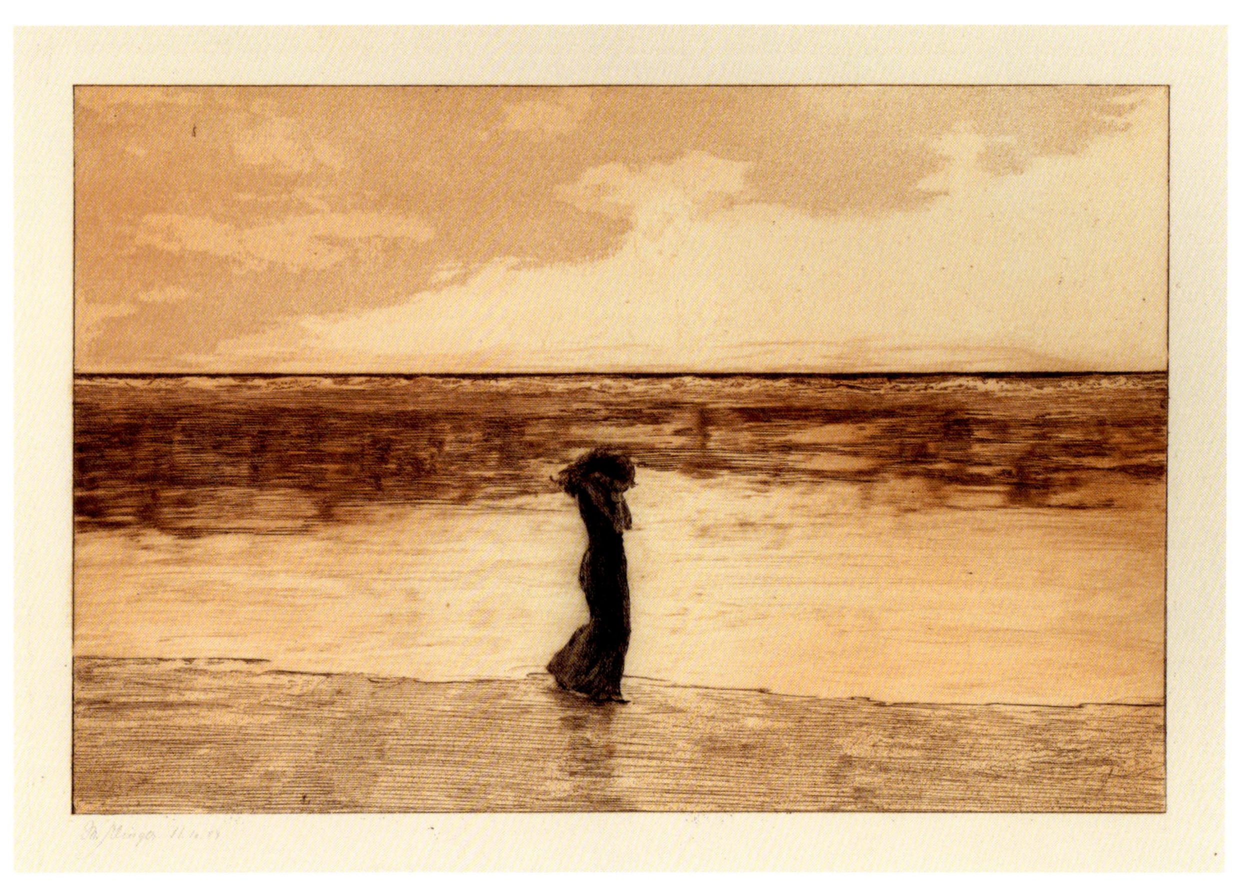

MAX KLINGER
Abandoned, from the cycle *A Life*, 1884
The Daulton Collection, Los Altos Hills, California

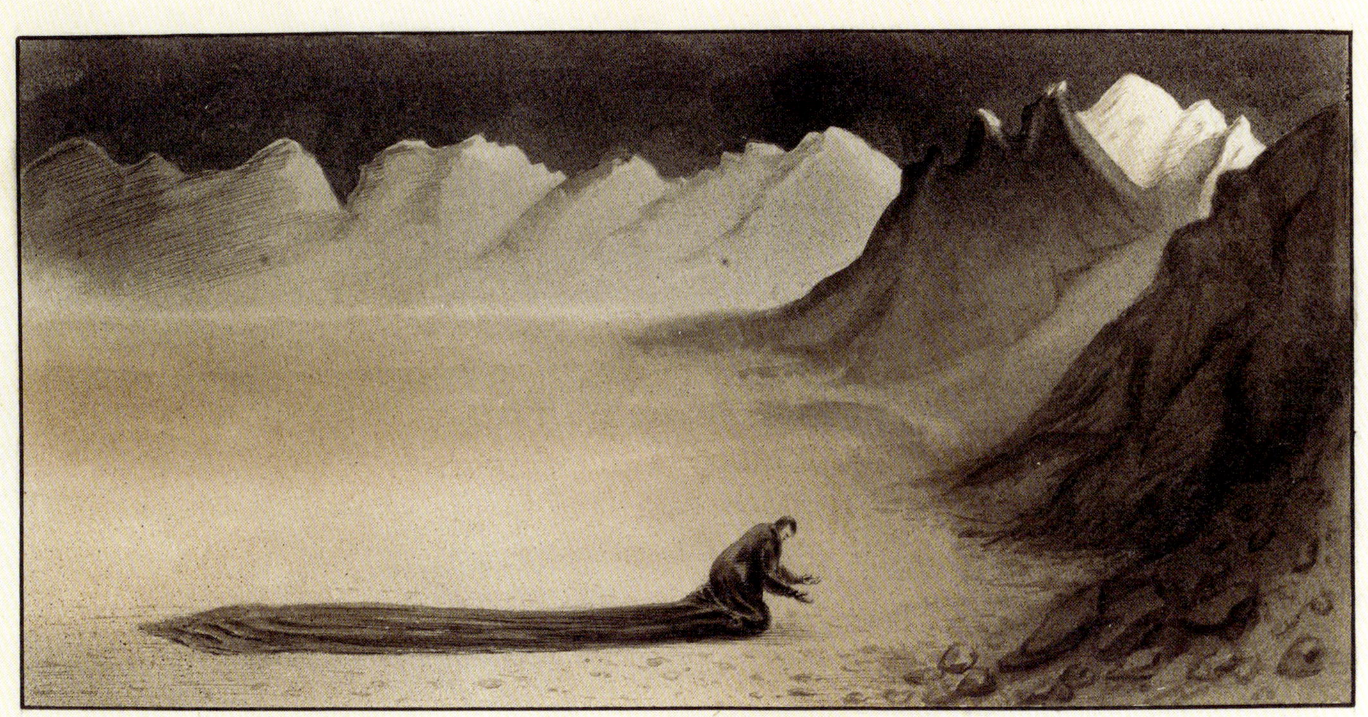

ALFRED KUBIN
Solitude, c. 1905
Leopold, Private Collection

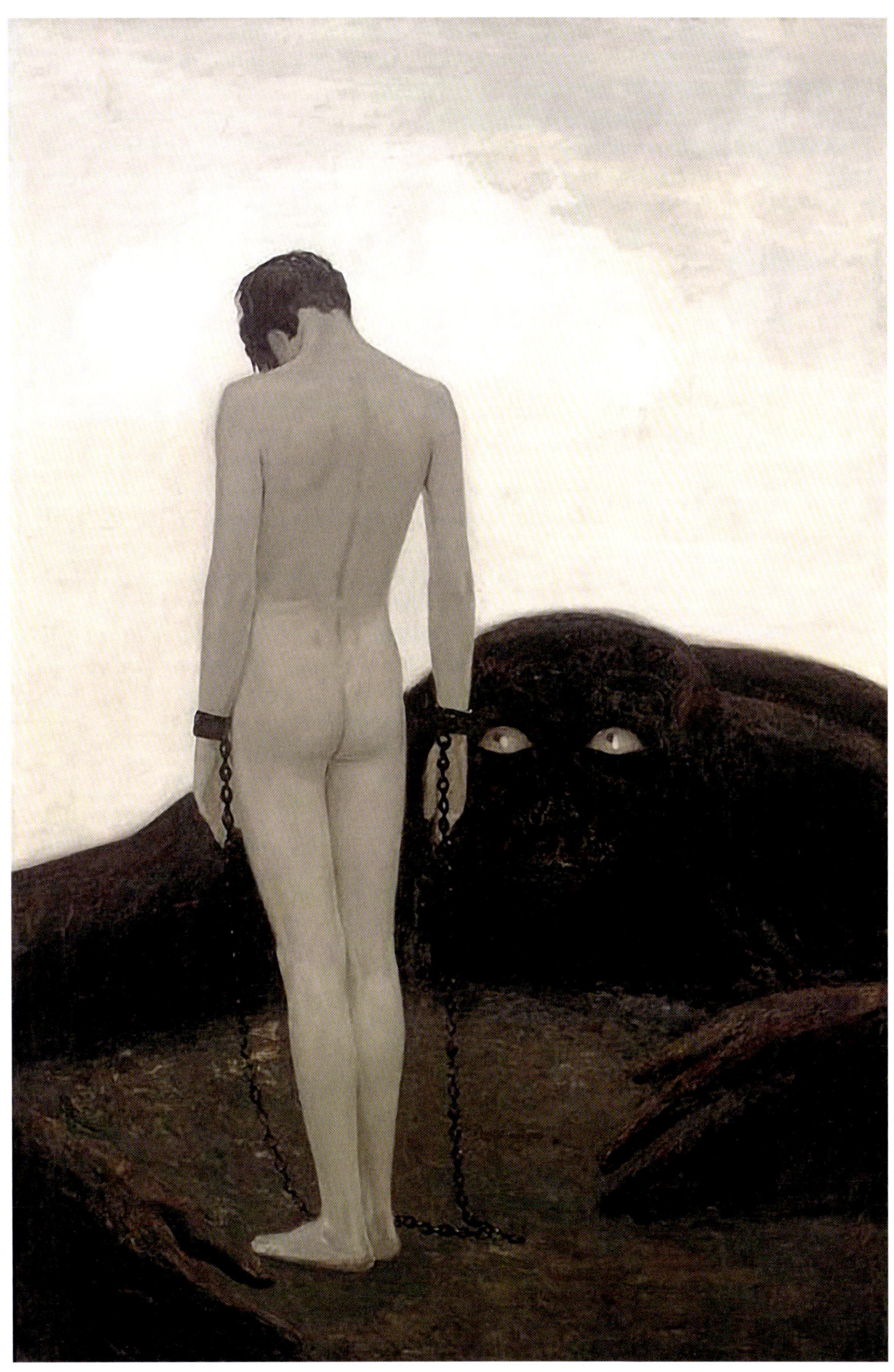

SASCHA SCHNEIDER
Feeling of Dependence, c. 1893
Private Collection

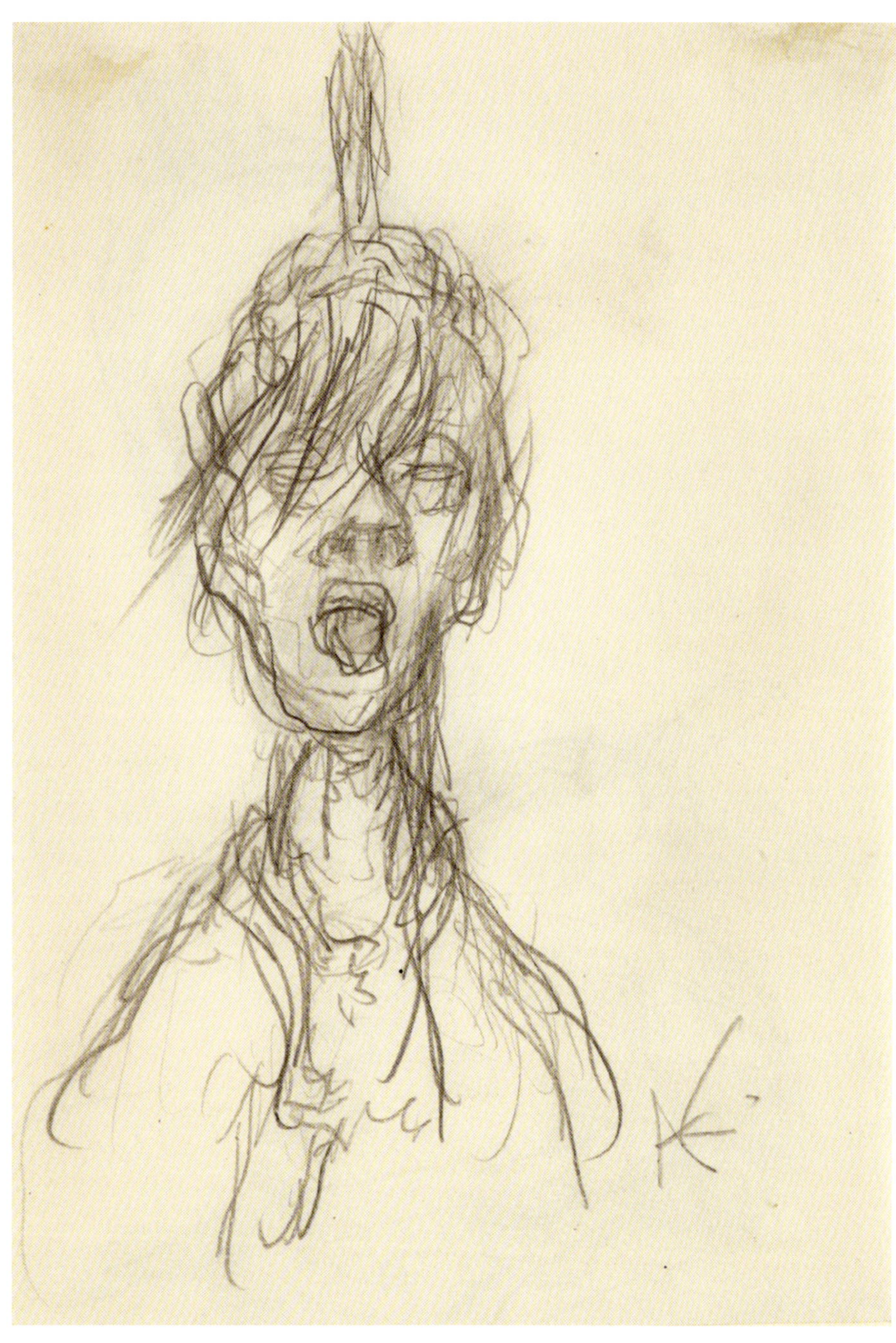

ALFRED KUBIN
The Hanged Man (Study), 1920/25
Leopold Museum, Vienna

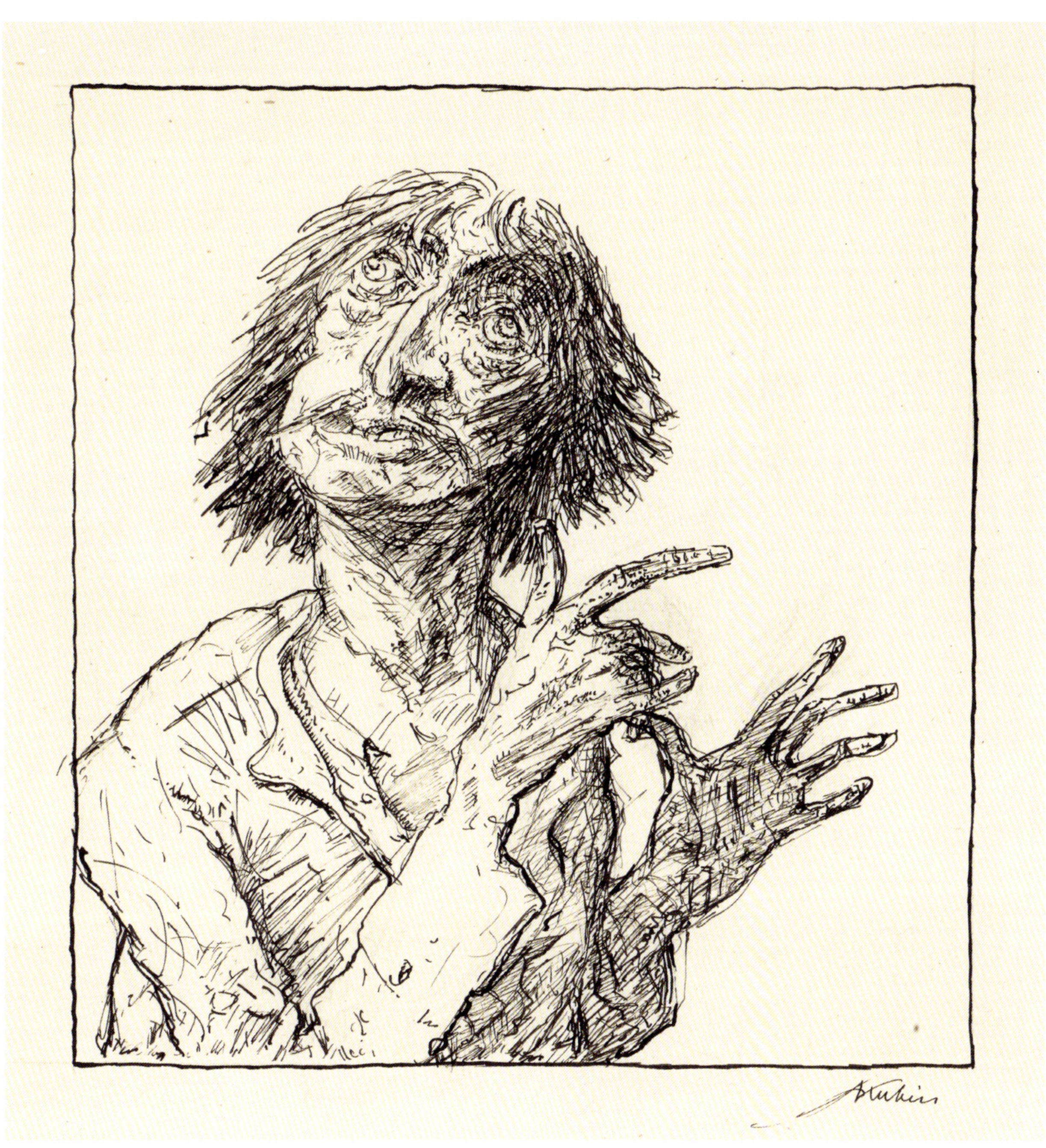

ALFRED KUBIN
The Fool, 1918/19
Leopold Museum, Vienna

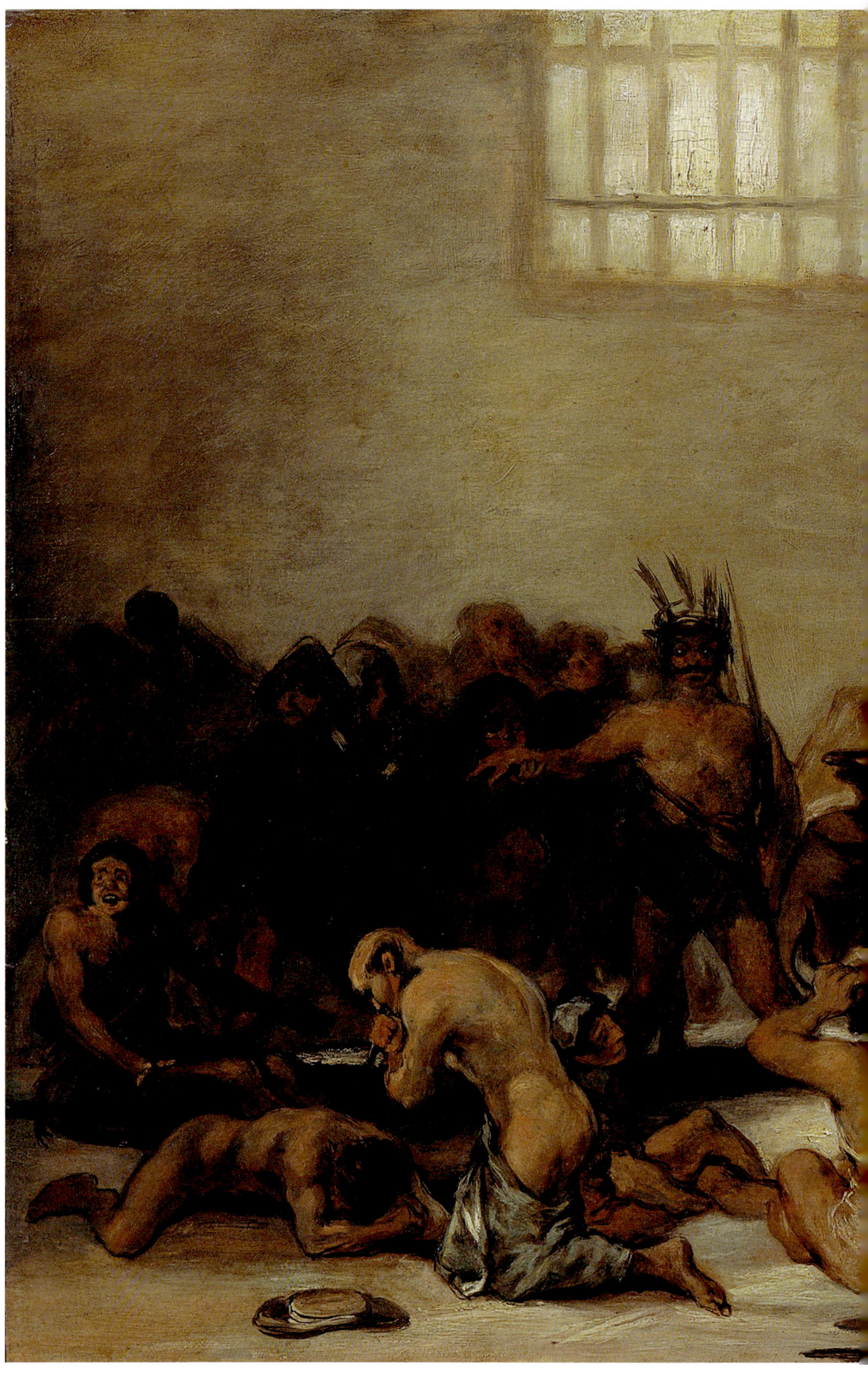

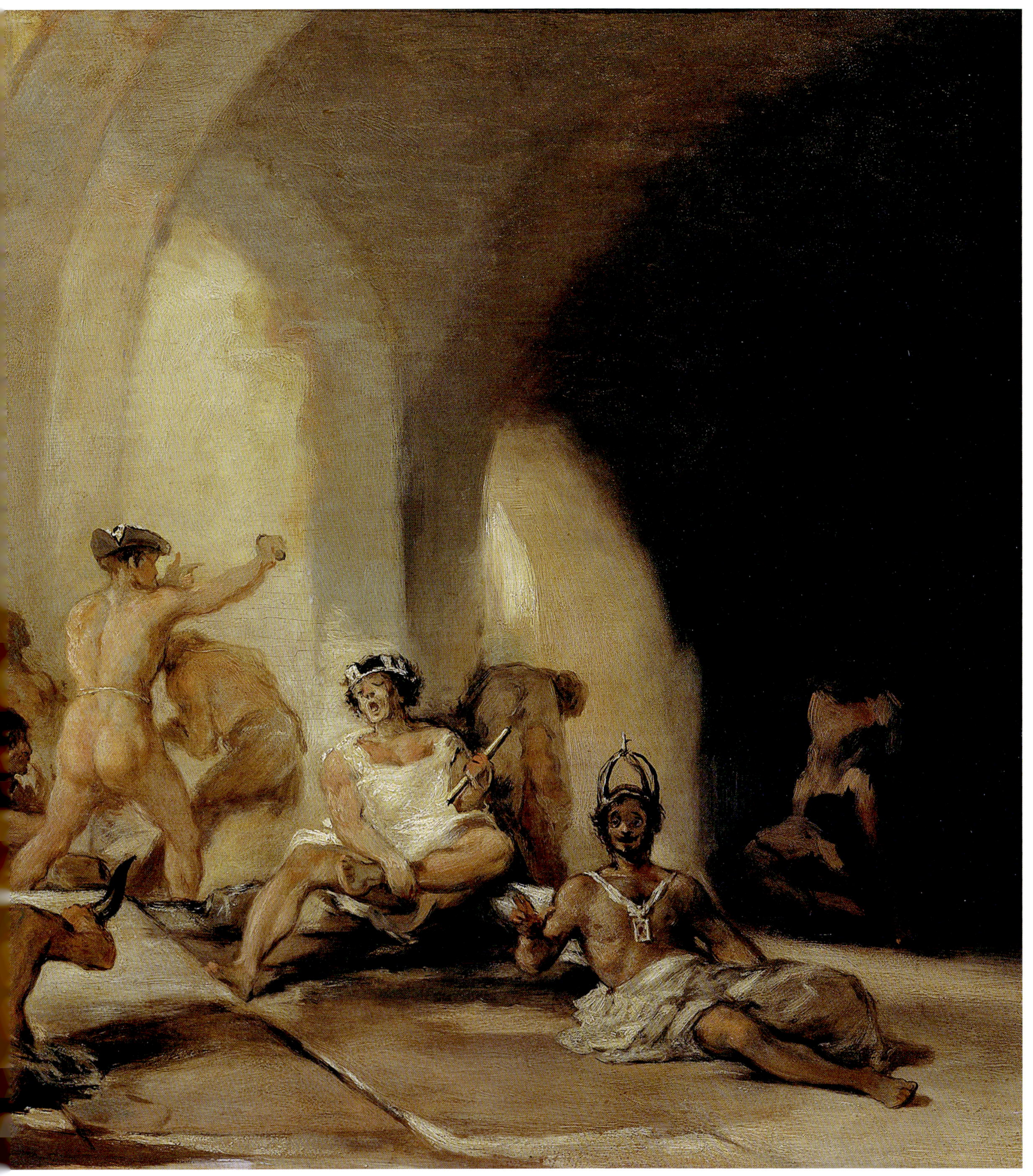

FRANCISCO JOSÉ DE GOYA Y LUCIENTES (attributed to)
Madhouse, after 1794
Belvedere, Vienna

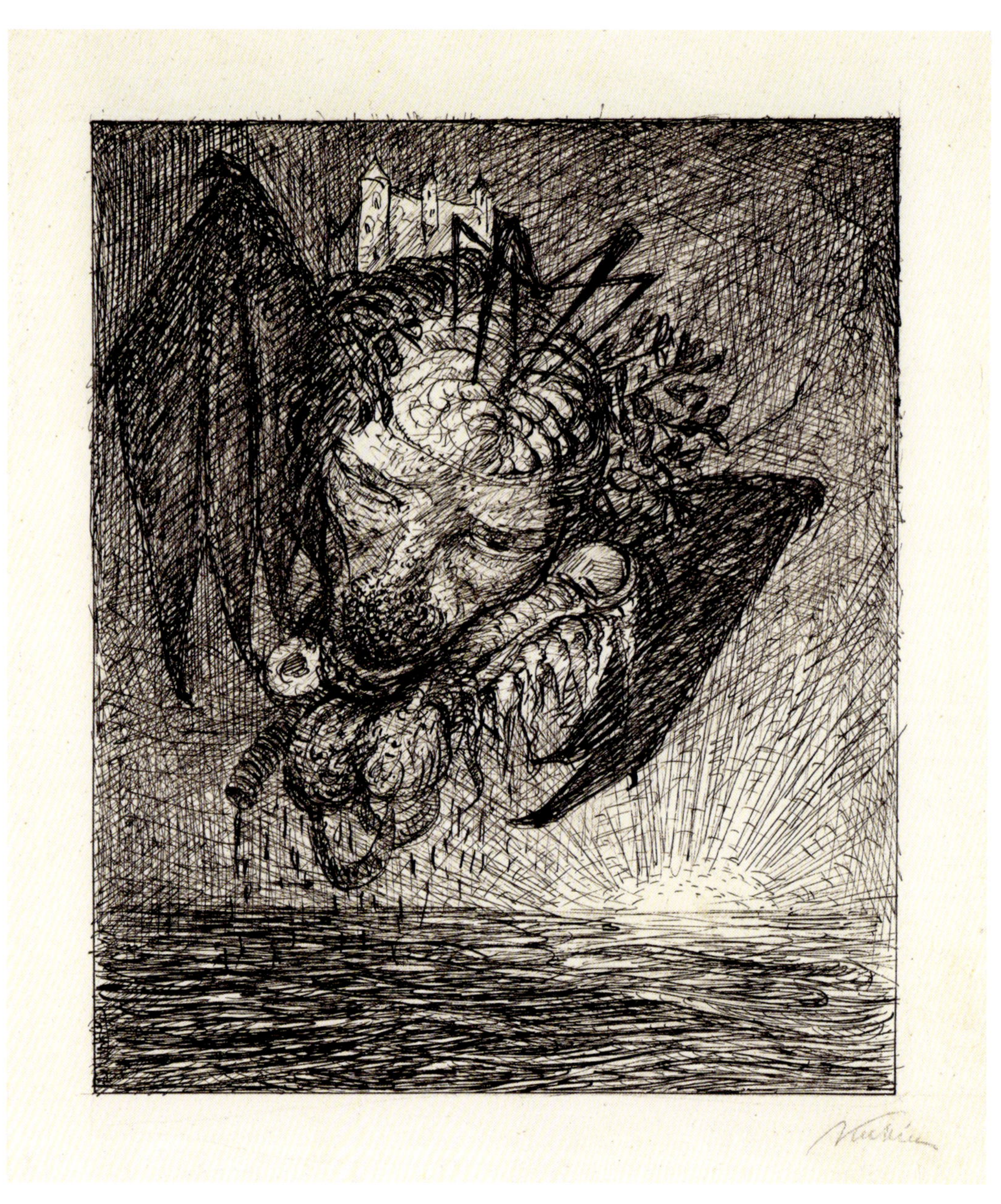

ALFRED KUBIN
The World's Fool, c. 1910
Leopold Museum, Vienna

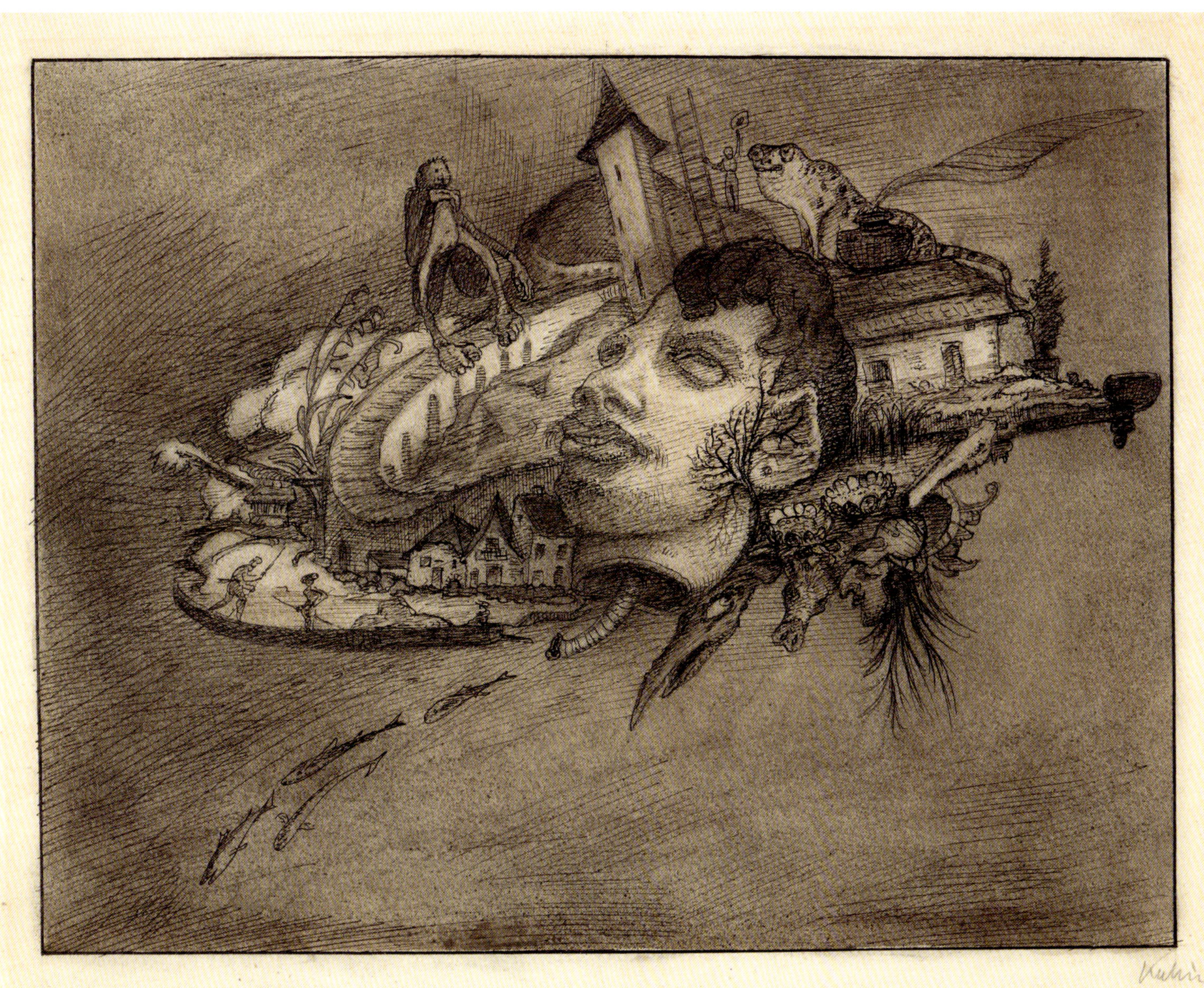

ALFRED KUBIN
Memories of a Friend, 1904
Leopold, Private Collection

SUCKERS

This work shows tentacles, squirmy worms and other creatures attacking a standing naked man whose body is already covered in sucking marks. Kubin depicted this motif several times; mostly showing women whose erogenous zones are sucked by leeches, polyps and the like, as if these were trying to eat them alive with obsessive desire. In the case of the man, the tentacles represent the autoerotic act. A later drawing from 1920, showing a man with tentacles from the front before a wall—which appears to have been prefigured in the earlier depiction by a projection on a wall representing a place of secrecy—, carries the unambiguous title *The Sin of Onan*. The present work featured in Müller-Thalheim's 1970 book with the title *The Onanist.*[*]

Annegret Hoberg

[*] Wolfgang K. Müller-Thalheim: *Erotik und Dämonie im Werk Alfred Kubins. Eine psychopathologische Studie* (Munich, 1970), p. 33.

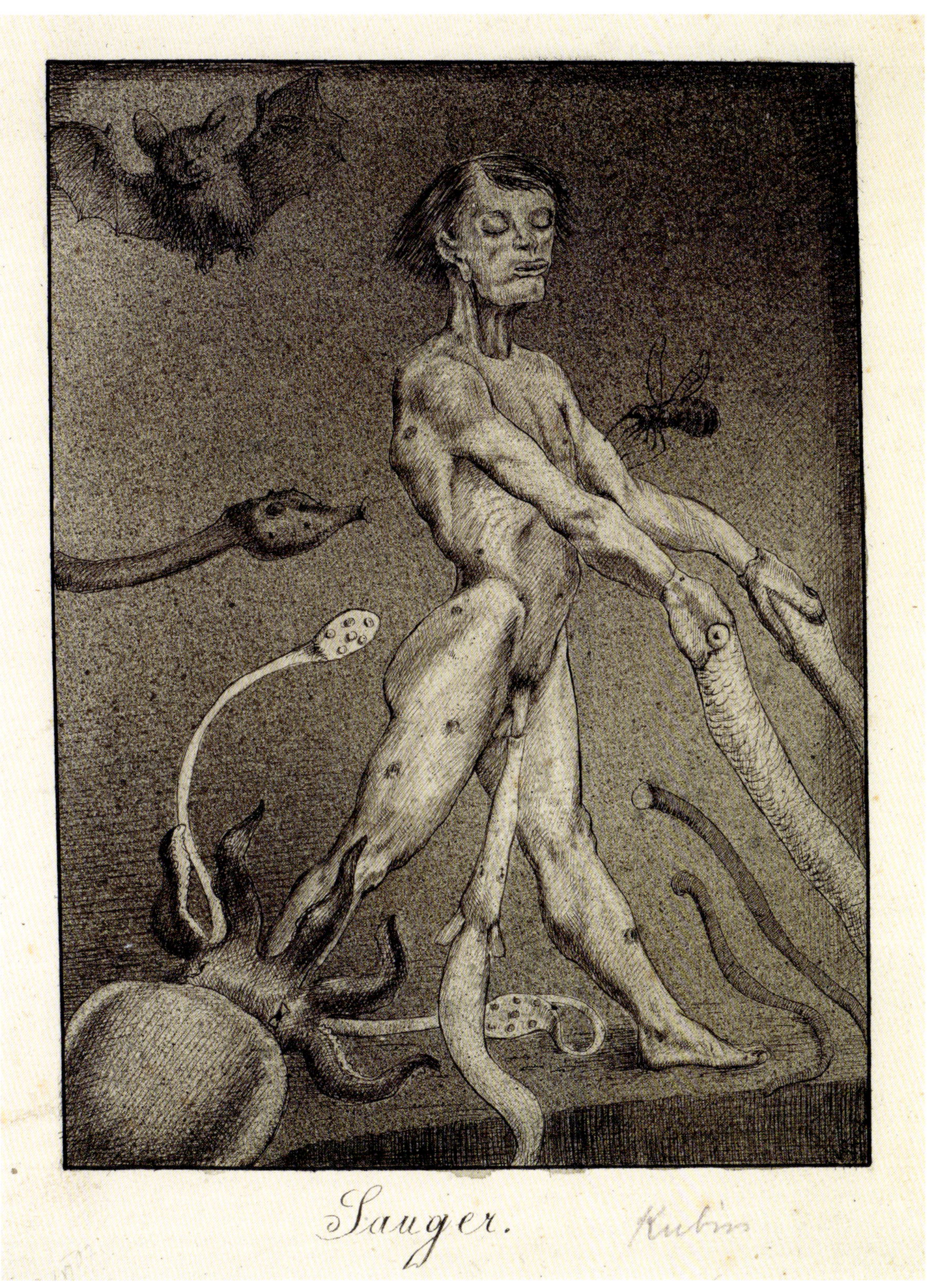

ALFRED KUBIN

Suckers, c. 1901

Städtische Galerie im Lenbachhaus und Kunstbau München

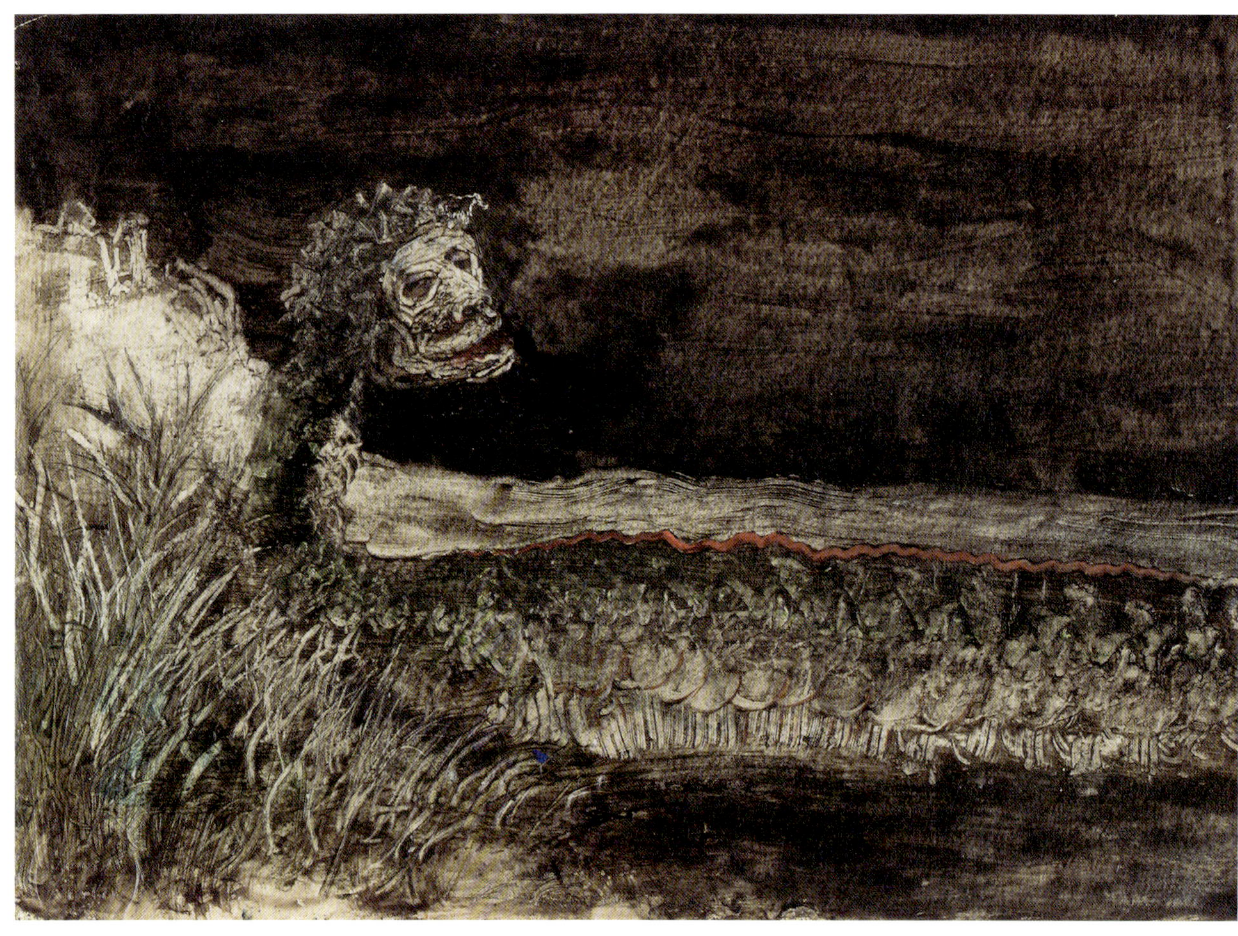

ALFRED KUBIN
Vision of Death, c. 1914
Leopold, Private Collection

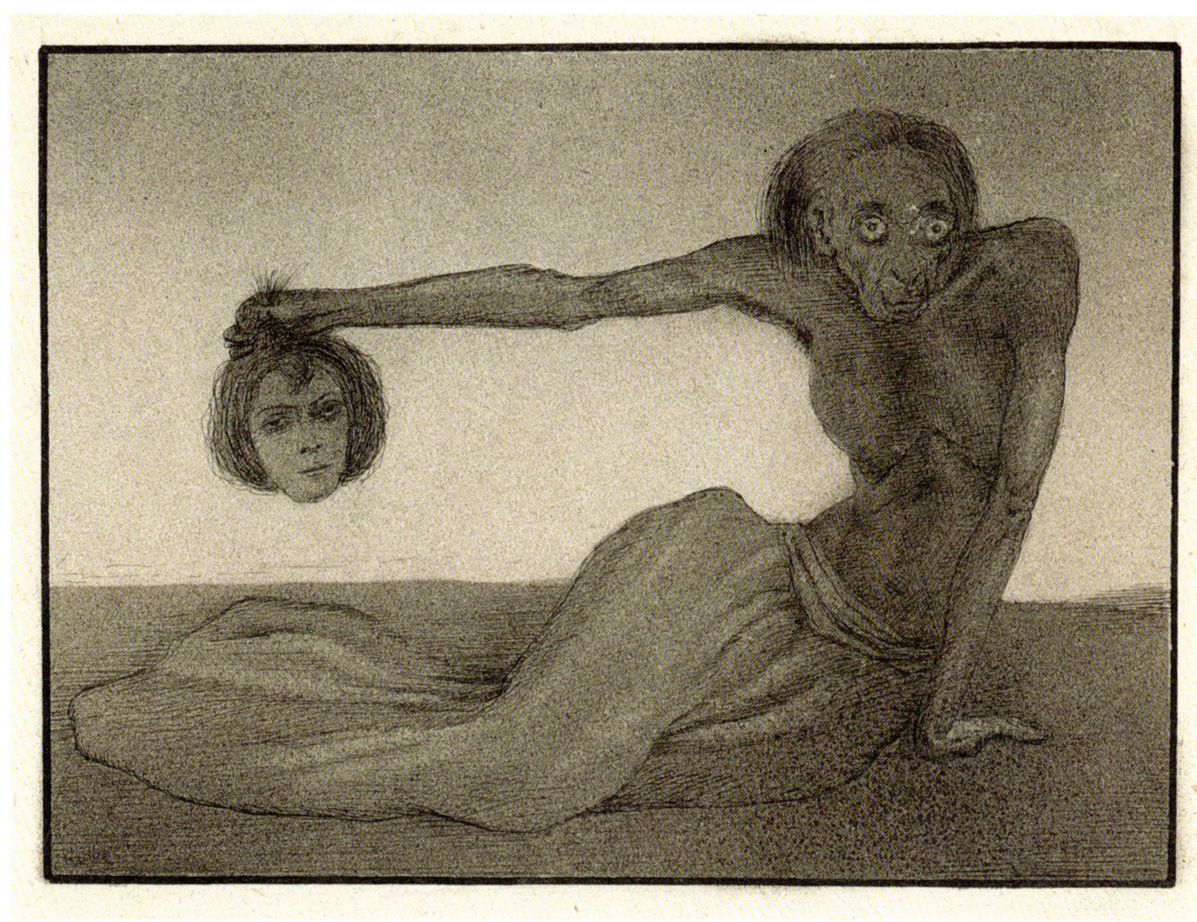

ALFRED KUBIN
Unmasked, 1903
OÖ Landes-Kultur GmbH, Land Oberösterreich, Graphic Collection, Günter Rombold Collection, Ha II 13182

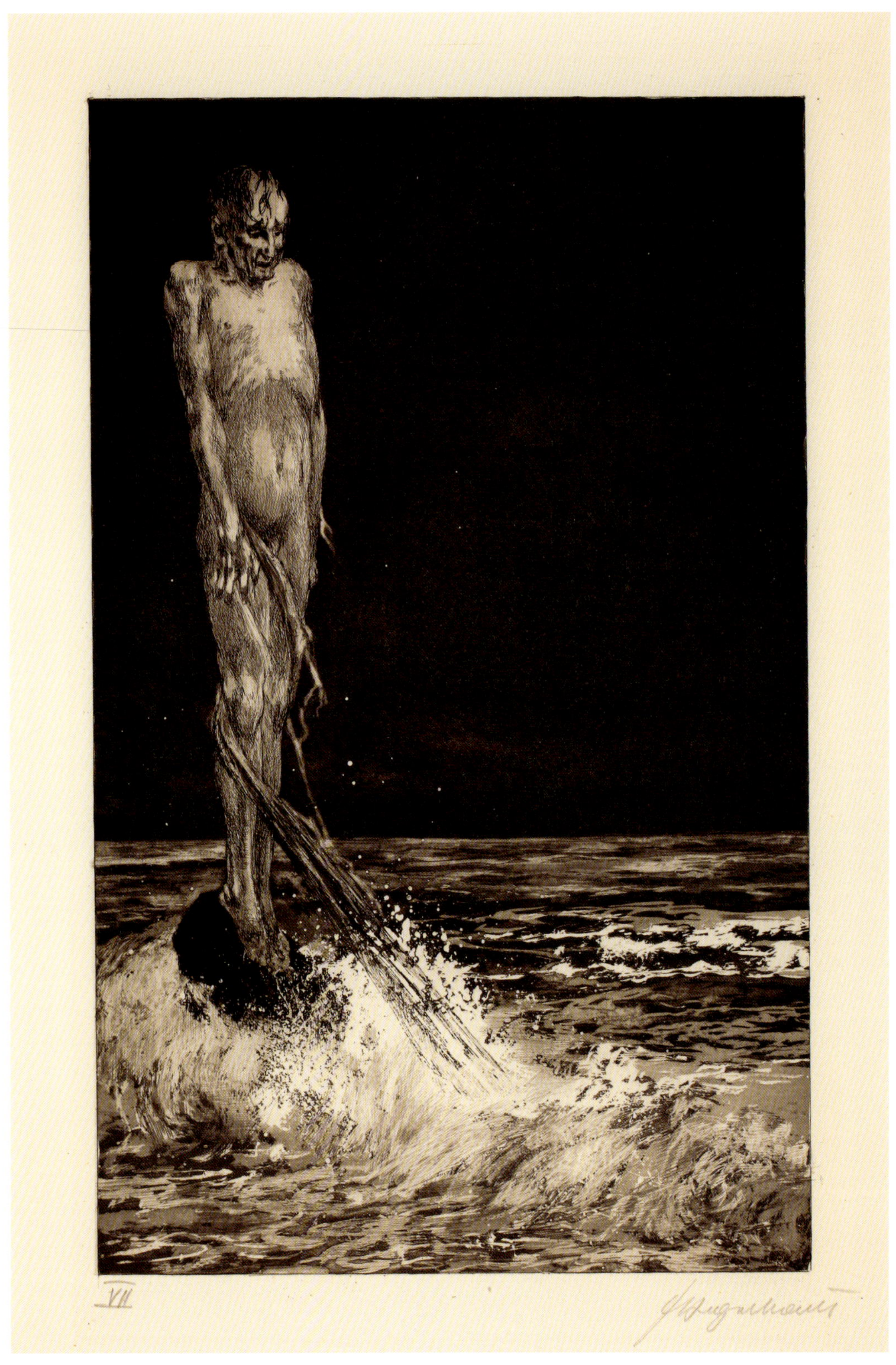

FRITZ HEGENBART
The Plight, print 7 of portfolio *A Canon of Life,* c. 1910
LETTER Foundation, Cologne

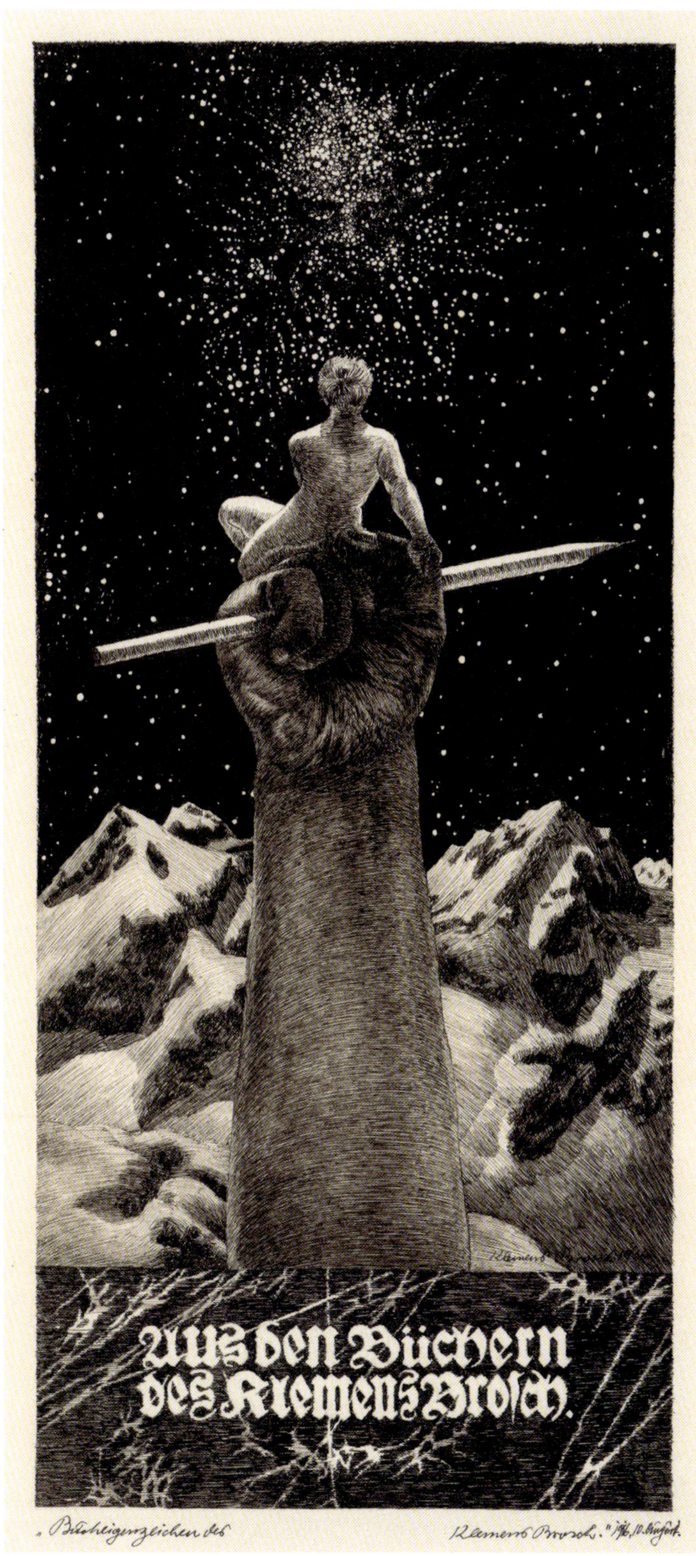

KLEMENS BROSCH
The Artist's Bookplate, 1916
OÖ Landes-Kultur GmbH, Land Oberösterreich,
Graphic Collection, Ha II 1422

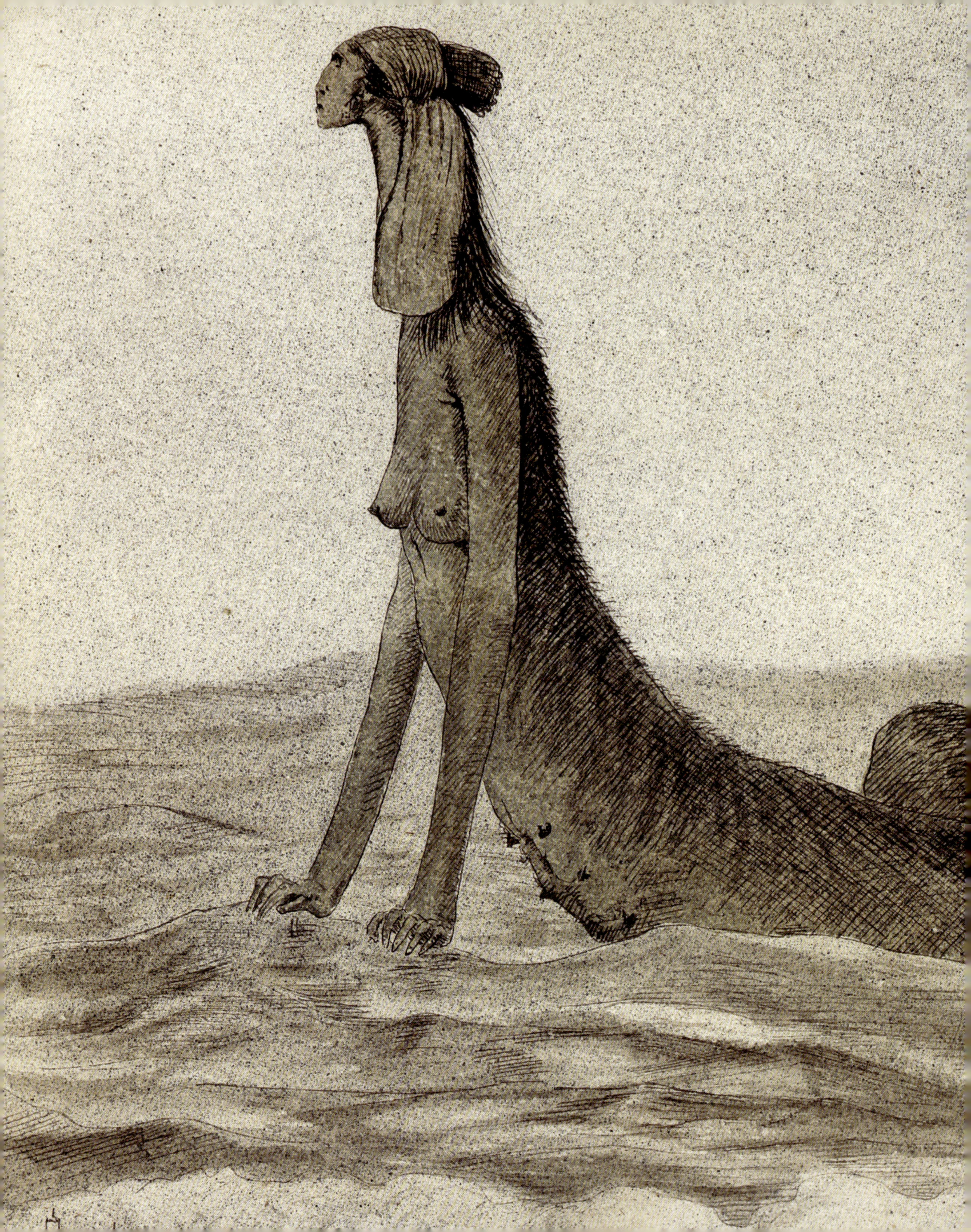

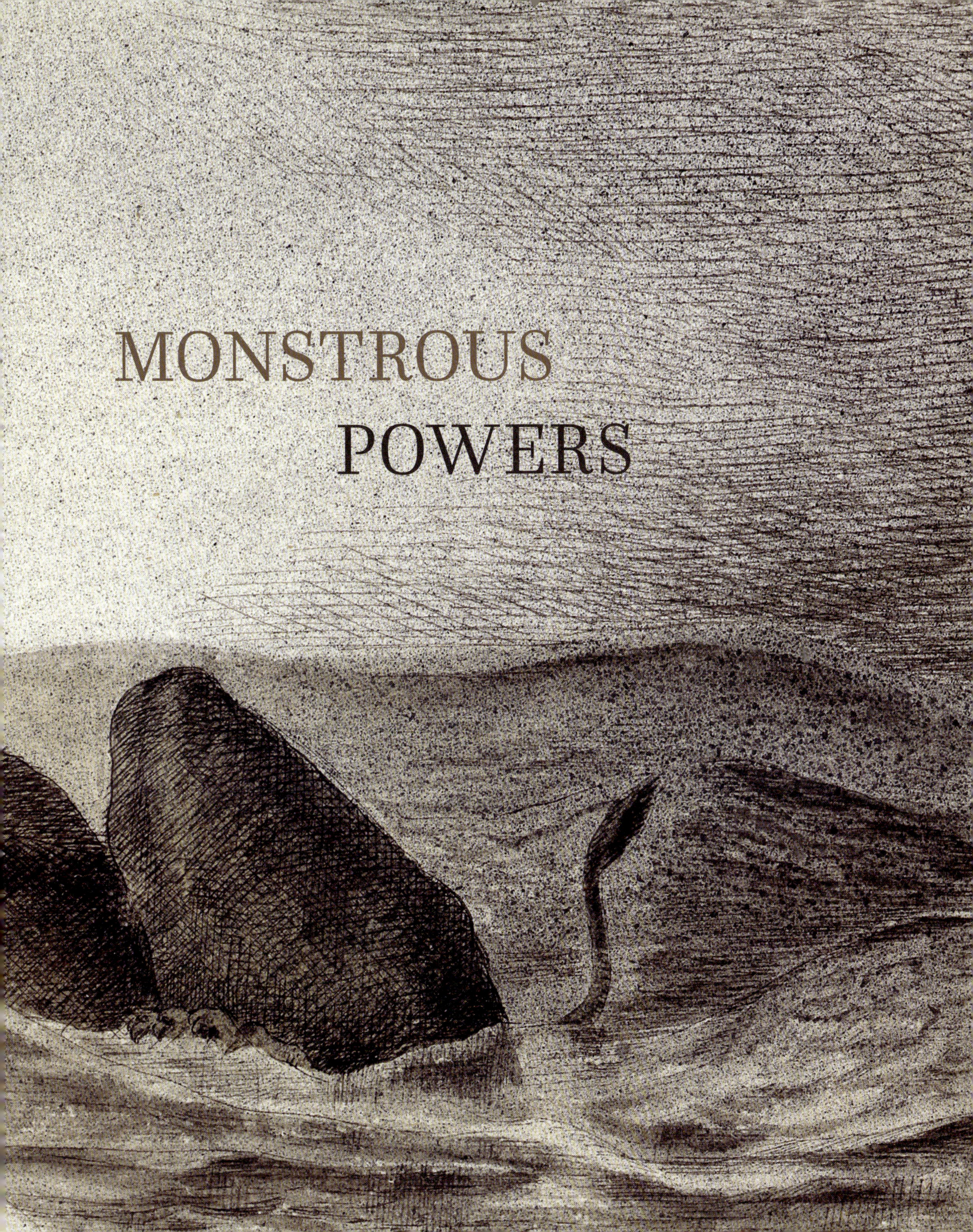
MONSTROUS
POWERS

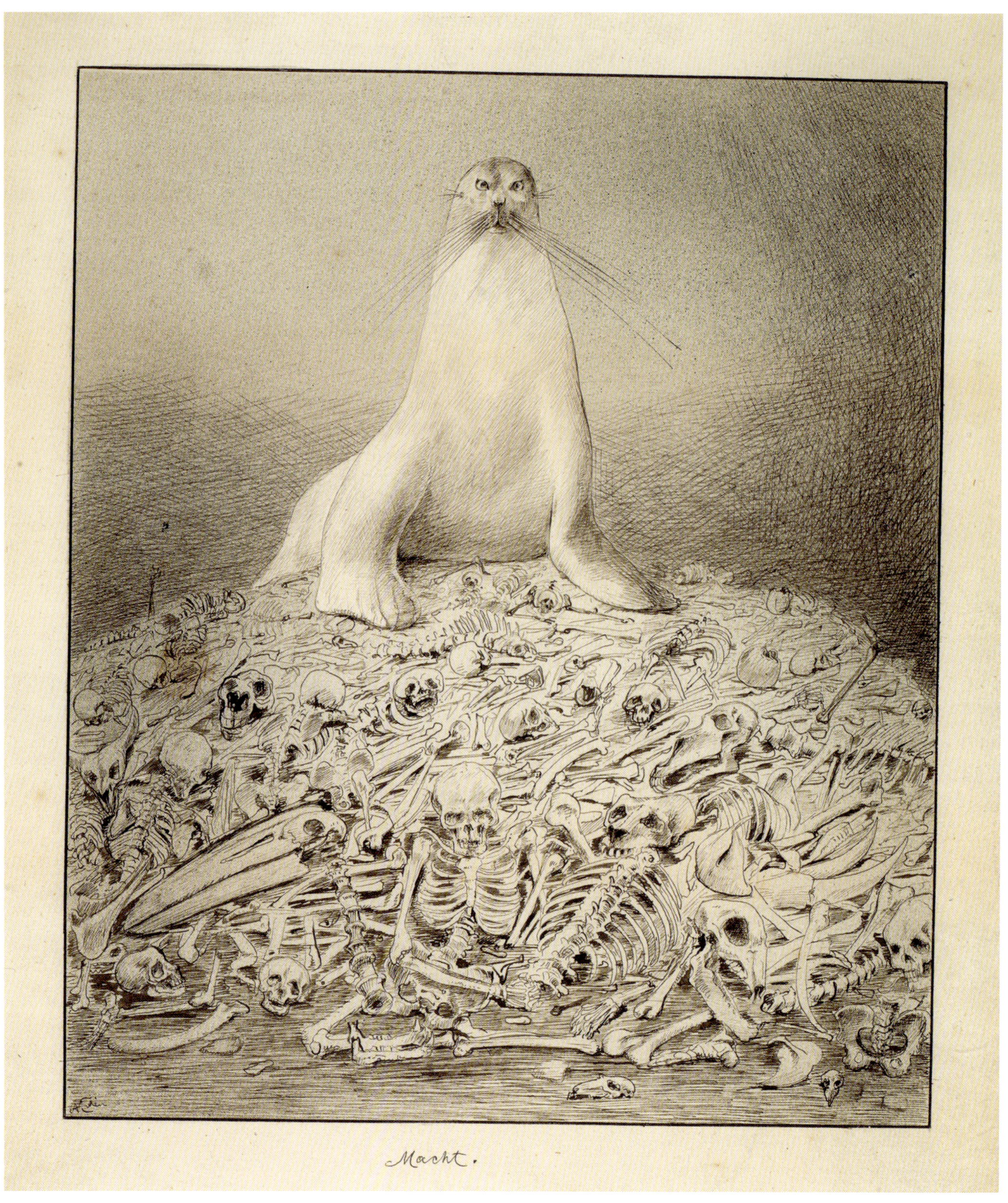

ALFRED KUBIN
Power, c. 1903
Städtische Galerie im Lenbachhaus und Kunstbau München

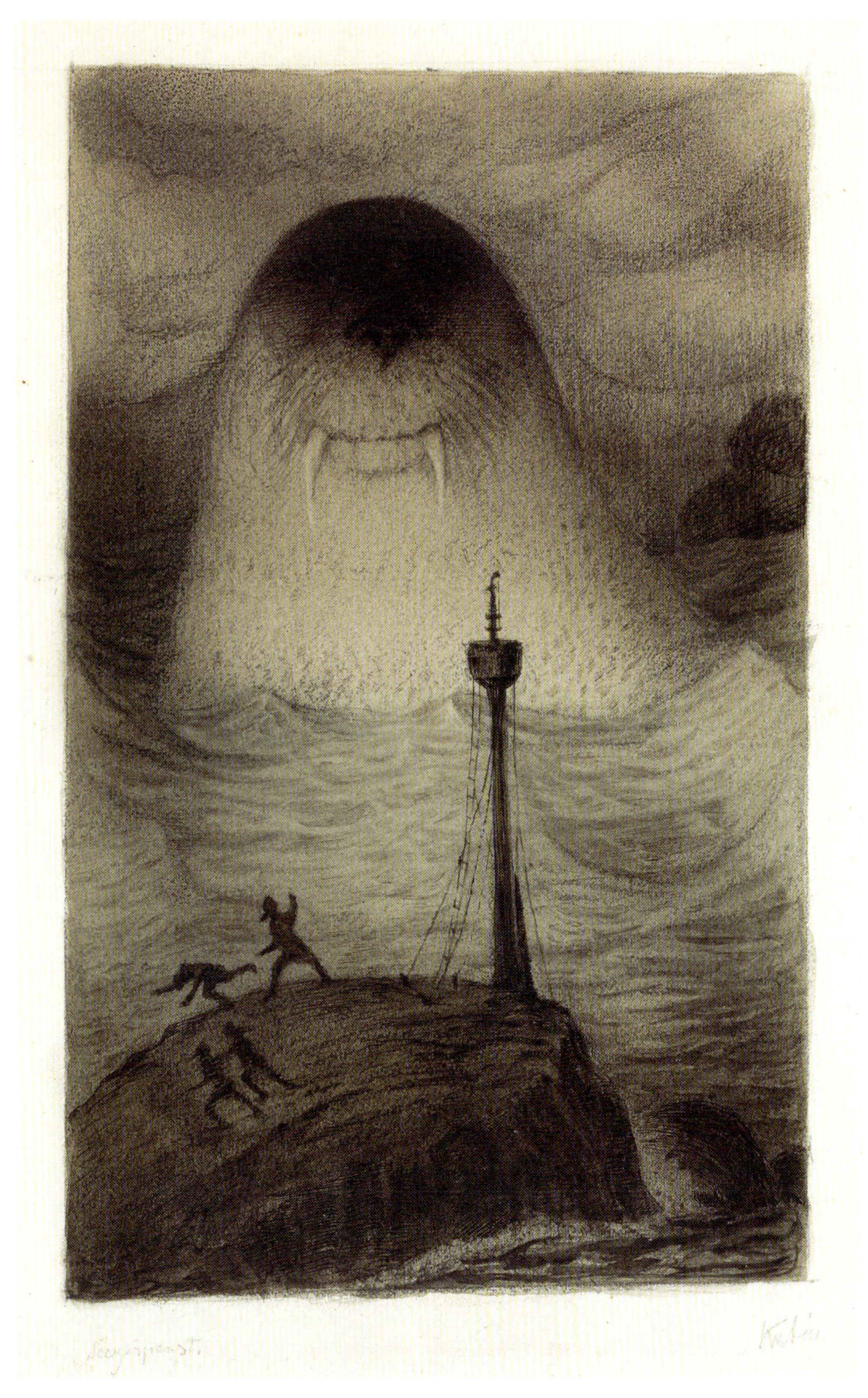

ALFRED KUBIN
Sea Monster, 1901/02
Leopold, Private Collection

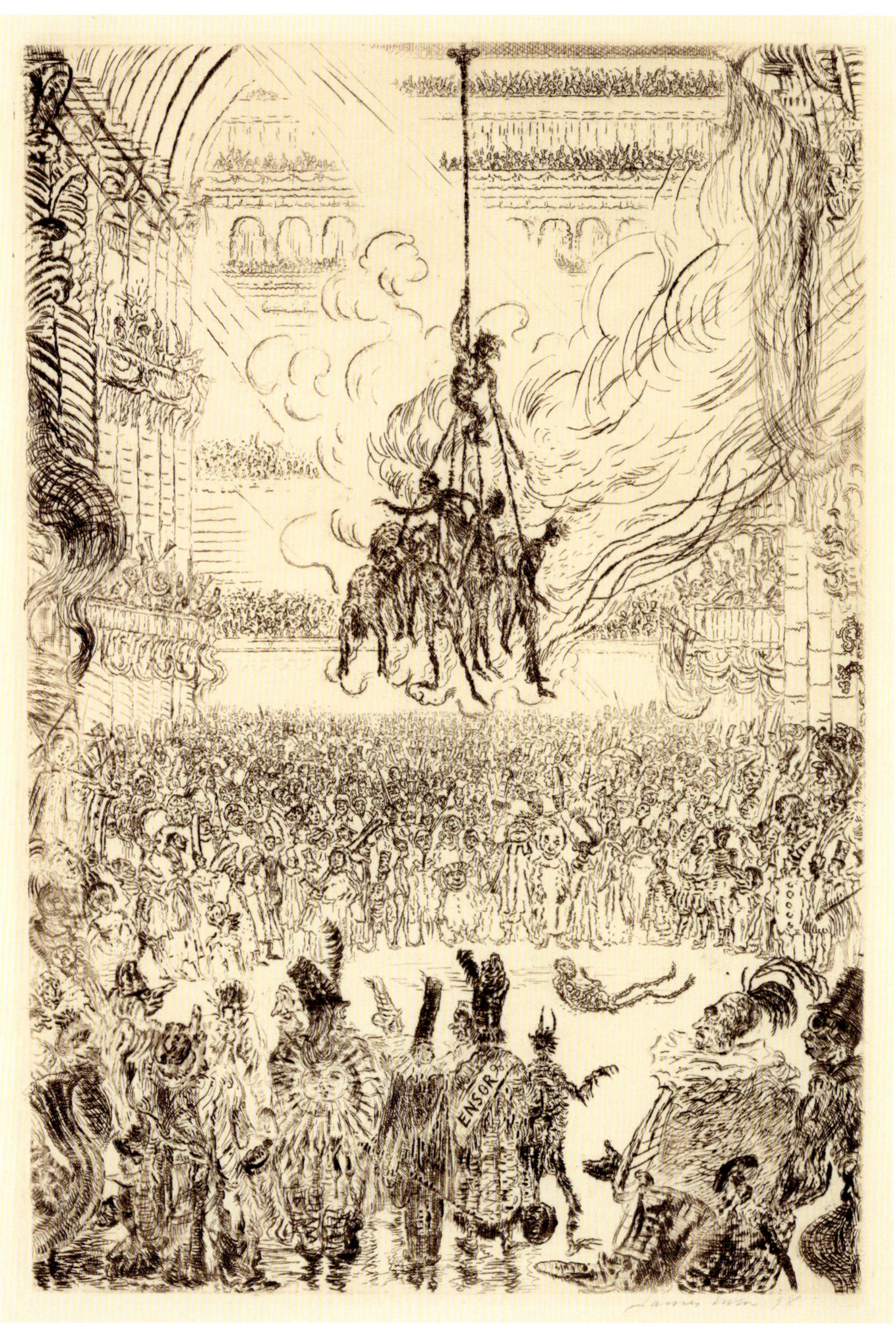

JAMES ENSOR
Hop-Frog's Revenge, 1898
Leopold, Private Collection

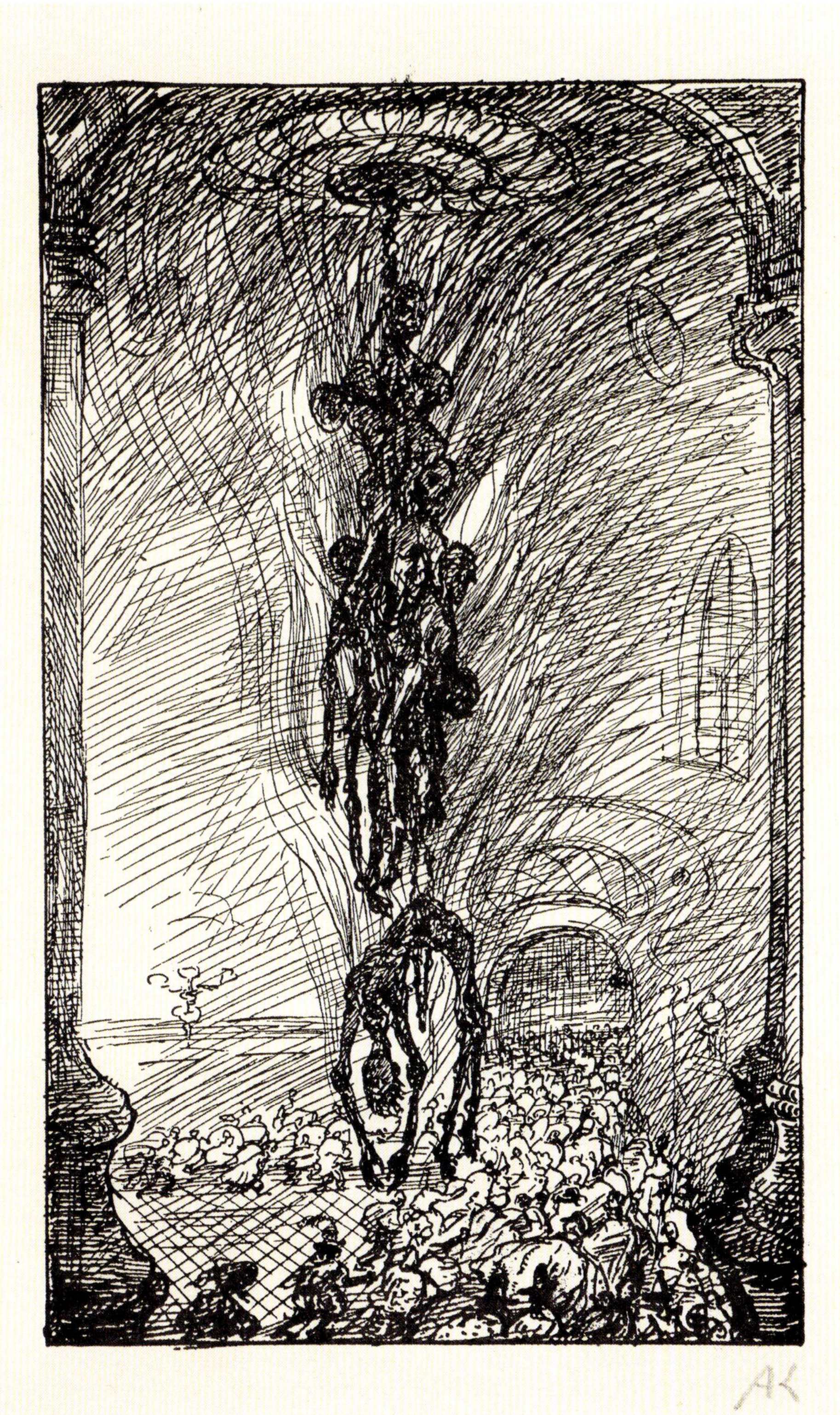

ALFRED KUBIN
Illustration of *Hop-Frog*, for Edgar Allan Poe's
The Tell-Tale Heart and Other Tales, 1909
Lentos Kunstmuseum Linz

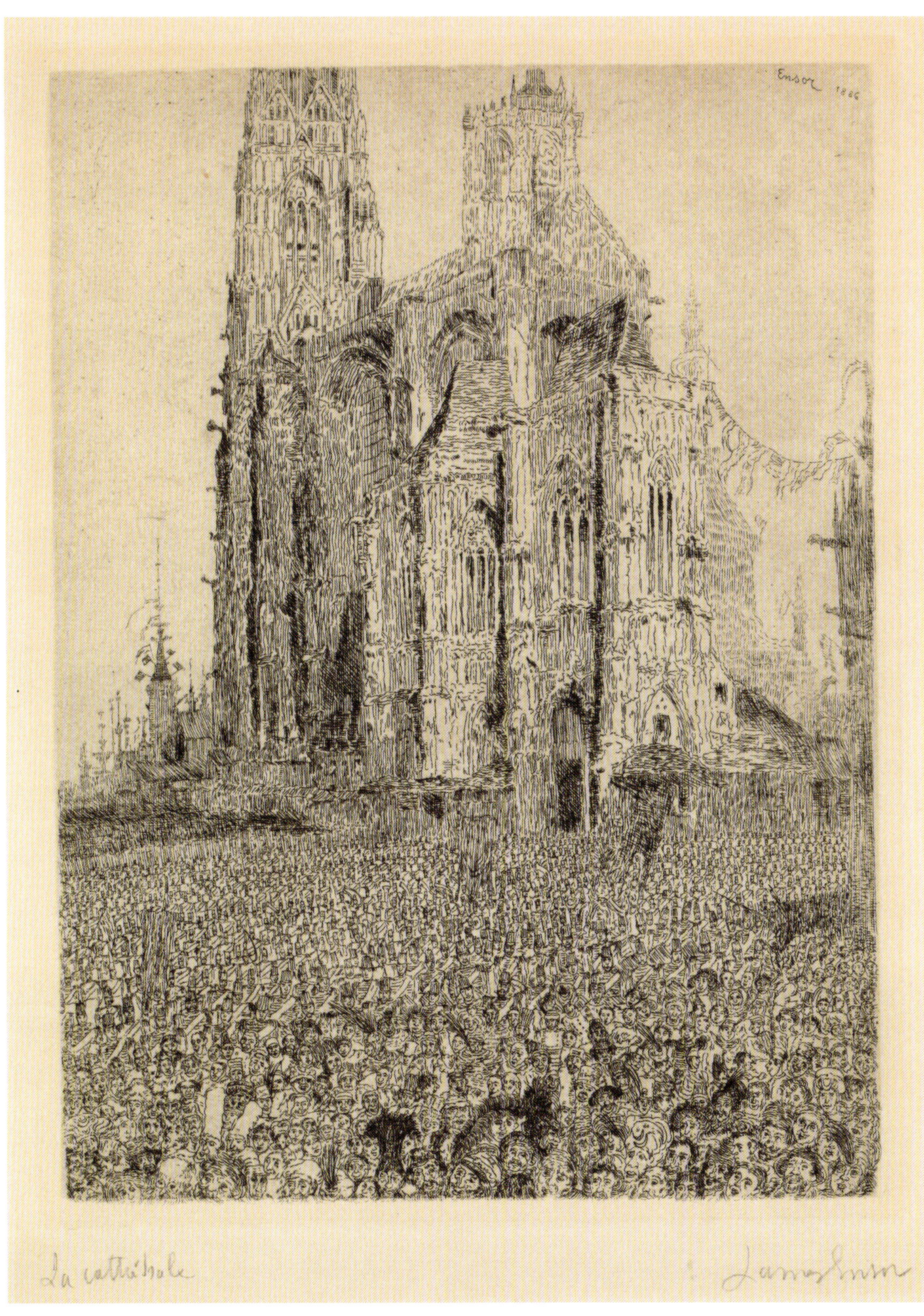

JAMES ENSOR
The Cathedral, 1886
Leopold, Private Collection

Alfred Kubin about Francisco José de Goya y Lucientes

Ghosts play large role in Old Painting influenced by religious ideas. Let me remind of the many so-called 'Temptations' of saintly hermits that are full of strange fantastic creatures, of dying scenes surrounded by evil and good spirits, of healings of the possessed with the Devil or toads popping out of their mouths, and similar representations. Even in the later period of Enlightenment, in which belief in demons had really become quite questionable, there are, again and again, very important individual artists to be found whose works give broad room to never-seen-before phantoms. I am thinking here of the consequences of etchings with the fabulous witches and monsters by the Spanish painter Goya, but also of the ghastly 'Nightmare' of the Swiss Füßli and many others.*

* Alfred Kubin, "Malerei des Übersinnlichen", in: *Aus meiner Werkstatt. Gesammelte Prosa,* ed. Ulrich Riemerschmidt (Munich, 1973), p. 43.

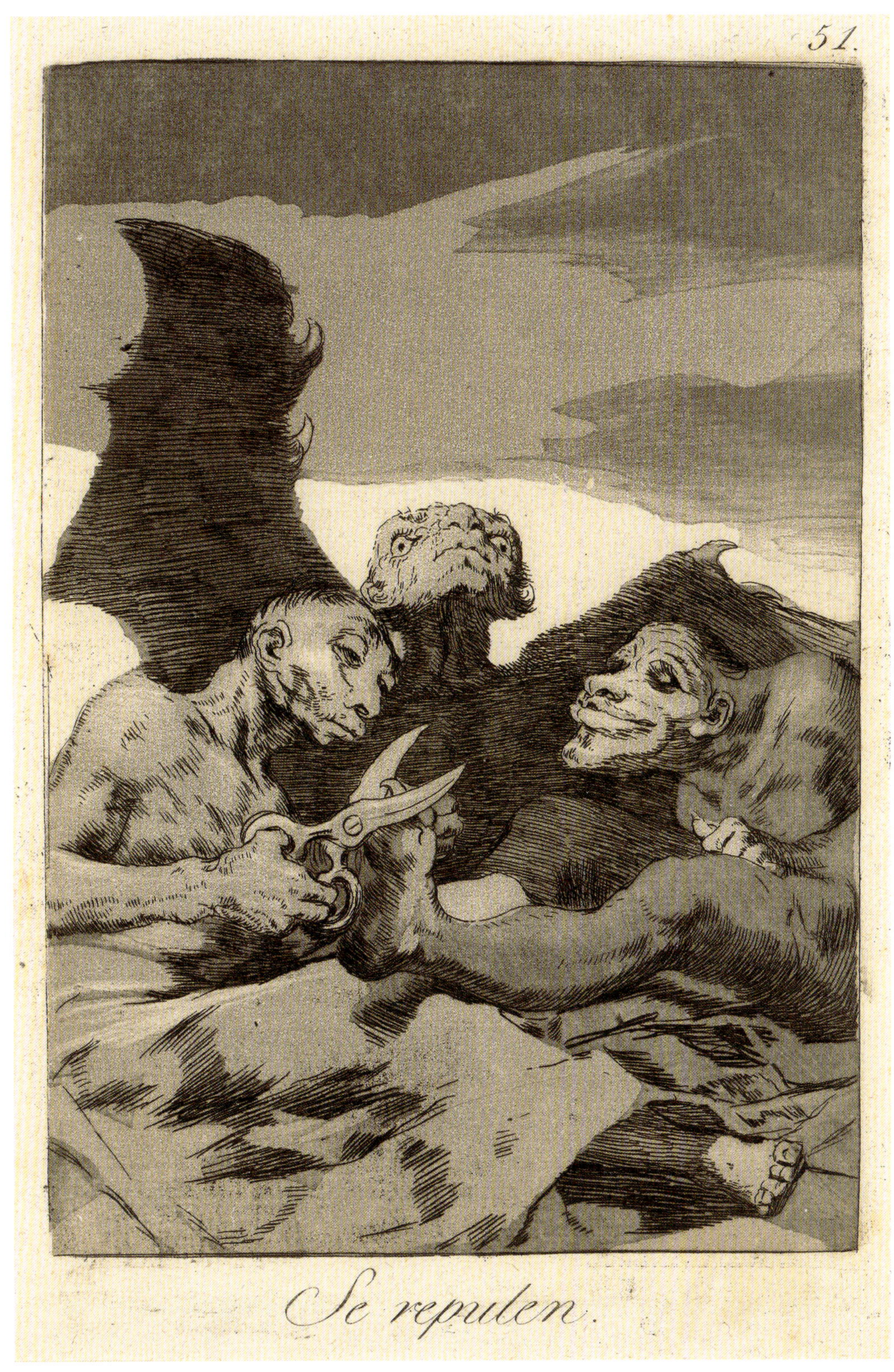

FRANCISCO JOSÉ DE GOYA Y LUCIENTES
Sprucing Themselves Up, from the series *Los Caprichos*, 1799
Albertina, Vienna

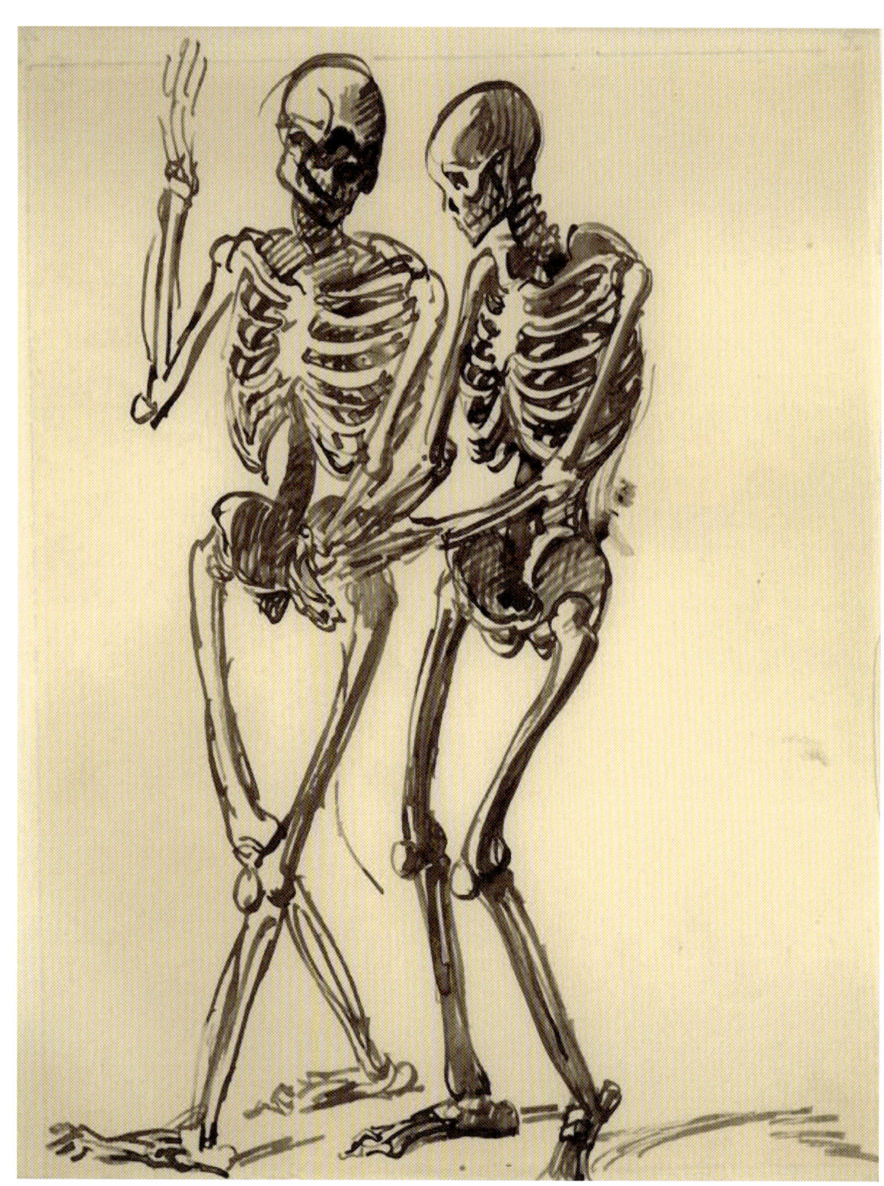

THÉOPHILE ALEXANDRE STEINLEN
Dance of Death, c. 1900
Private Collection

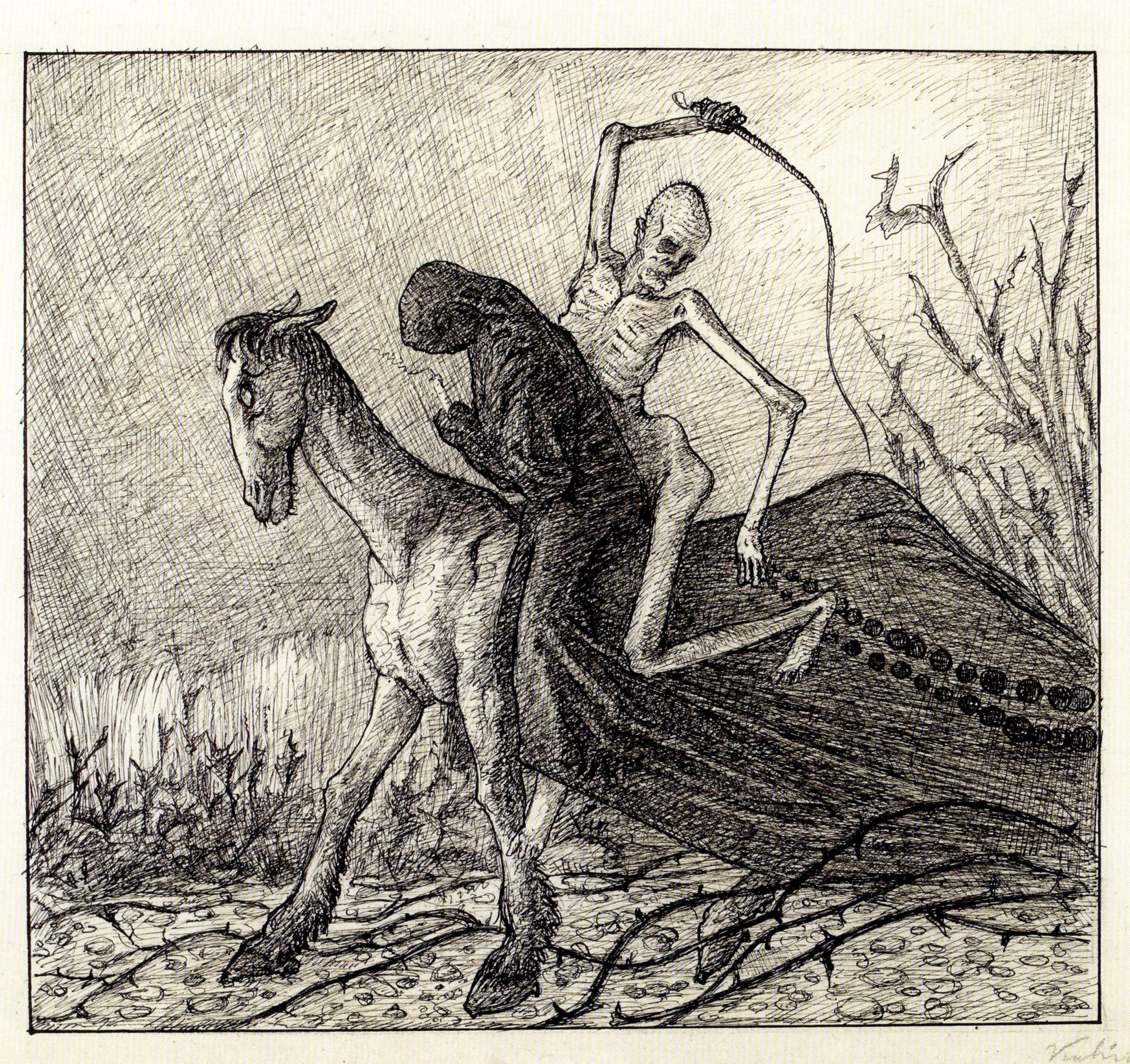

ALFRED KUBIN

Melancholy, c. 1910

Leopold Museum, Vienna

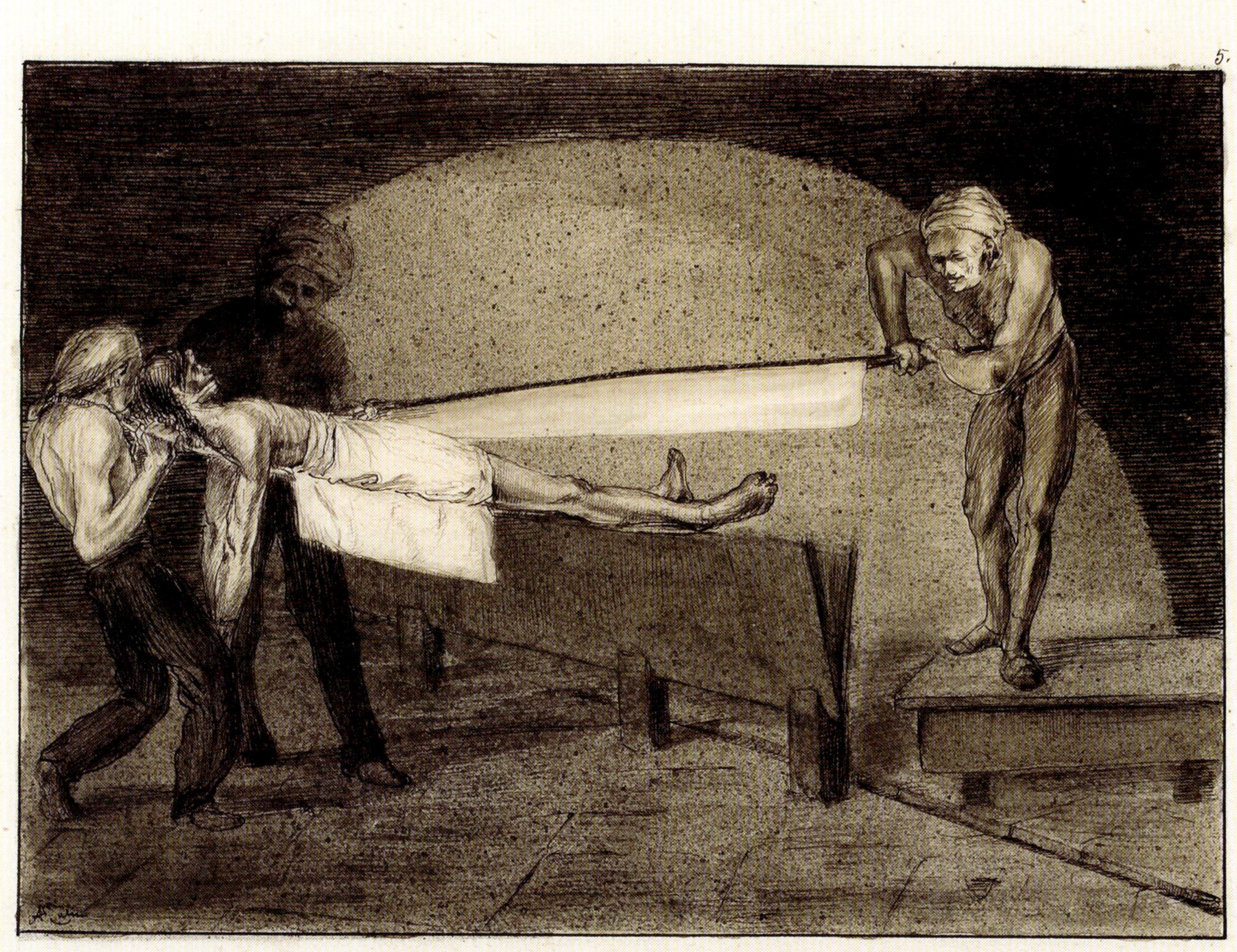

ALFRED KUBIN
My God, My God, What Are You Doing?, 1899/1900
Leopold Museum, Vienna

STARVATION

“On an infinitely wide, barren plane, delineated on the horizon by dead mountains, a headless, ghostly rider is speeding along on a panting racer whose front half is still a startled horse but whose back half is nothing more than a mere skeleton. The rider, with his plump legs, is pushing the spurs deeply into the horse’s sides, his ragged coat fluttering in the icy wind, while the thrust-out long lance carries the wild rider’s ghastly head, furrowed by the voracious traits of hunger and the unfettered dumb beast—the thought of hunger hurrying ahead of the racing rider. Every stroke in this rendering speaks of hunger and need.” This was the assessment of Hanns Holzschuher, who wrote the preface to the portfolio *Weber-Mappe*, of this drawing from the portfolio in a later article. Klaus Albrecht Schröder has rightly pointed out that even this highly fantastical pictorial vision of Kubin’s is permeated by the spirit of a historical time, more specifically of the 18th century, something which is further indicated by the visible half of the rider’s uniform.* The fine, almost pretentious drawing of the horse and lance bearer, too, seems to have been modeled on “classical” French role models from this time.

Annegret Hoberg

* Klaus Albrecht Schröder: *Alfred Kubin. Leben. Ein Abgrund*, ed. by Österreichische Länderbank/ Oberösterreichisches Landesmuseum (Munich, 1985), p. 10.

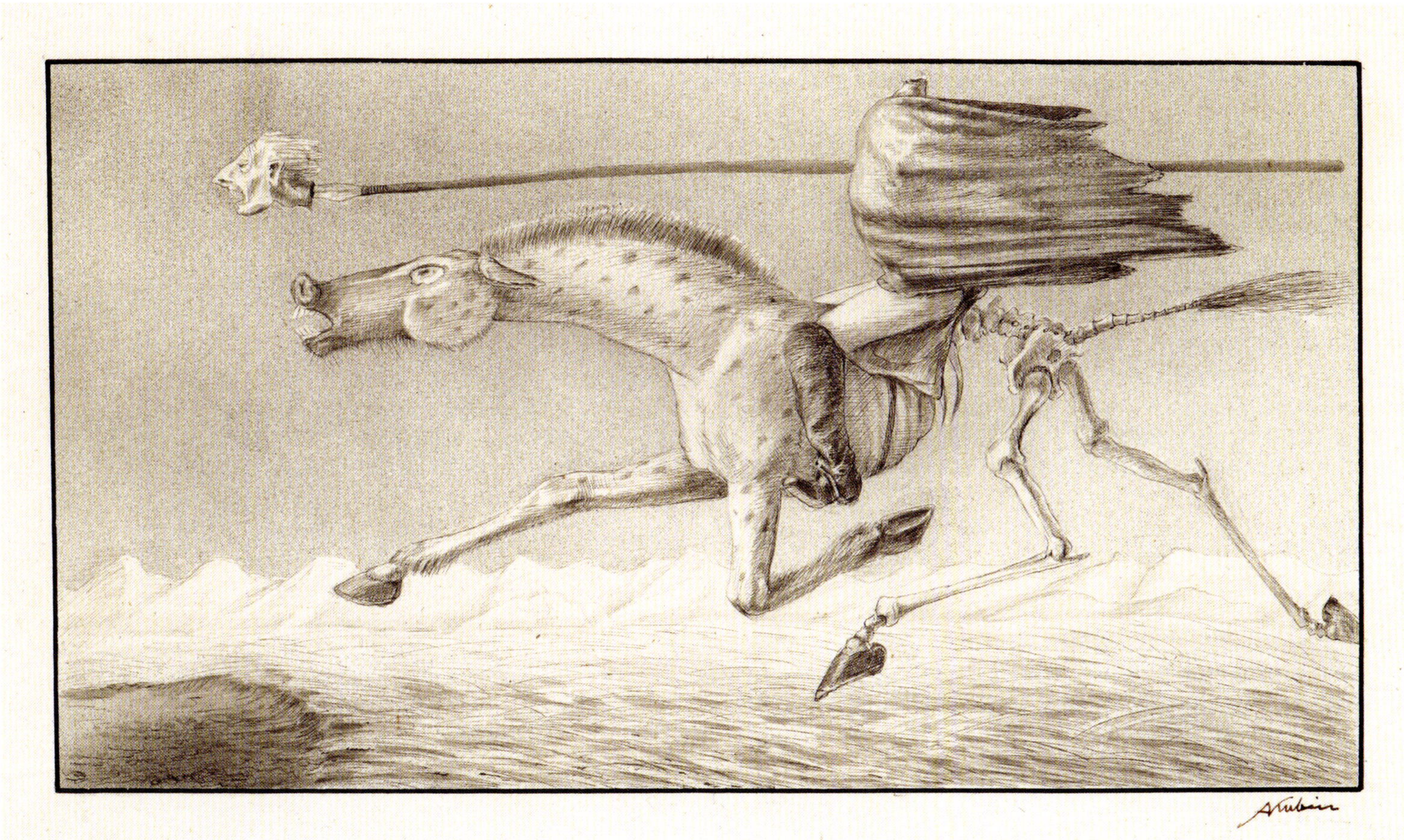

ALFRED KUBIN
Starvation, c. 1901
Leopold Museum, Vienna

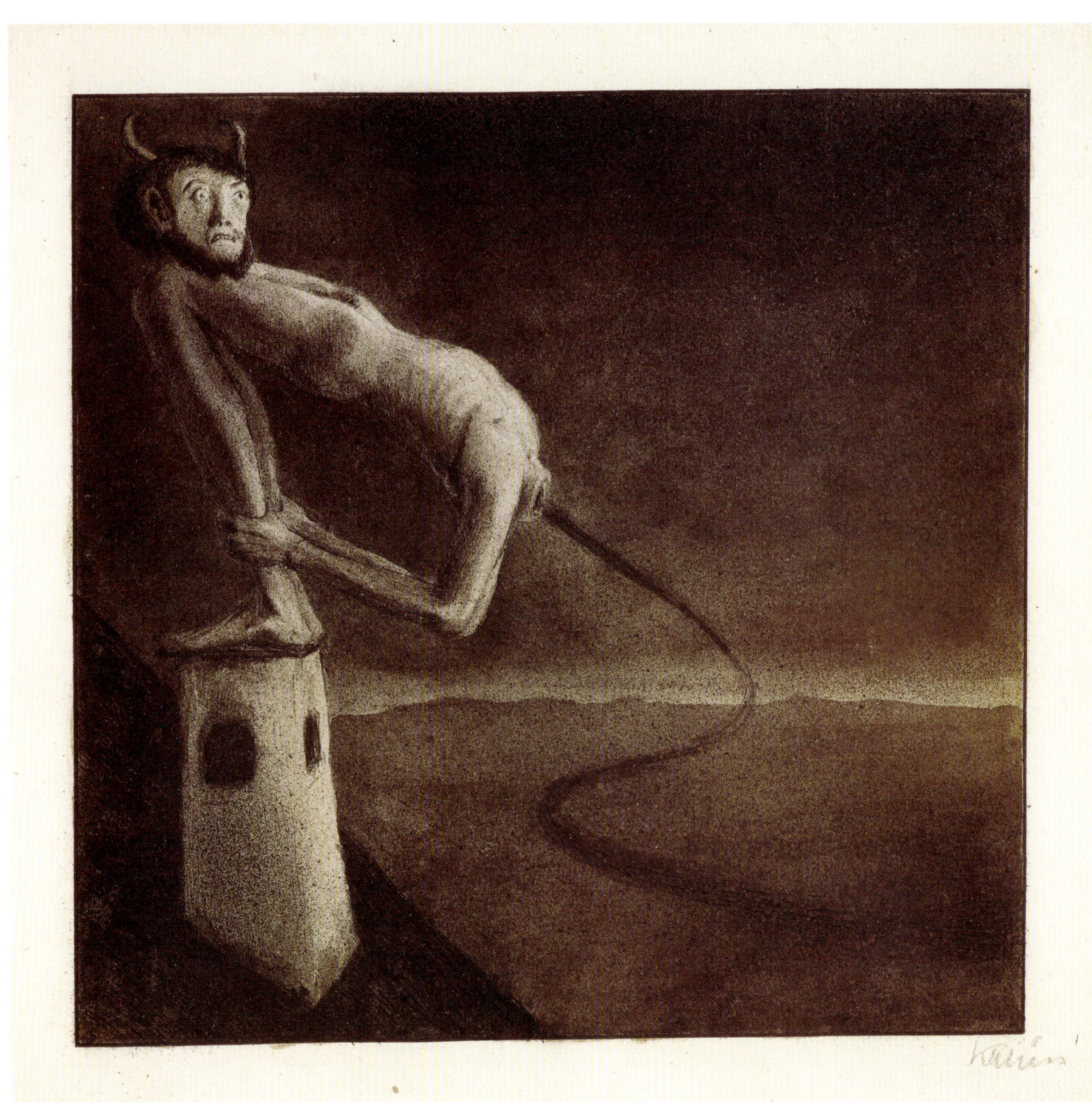

ALFRED KUBIN
The Devil on the Chimney, c. 1902
Leopold Museum, Vienna

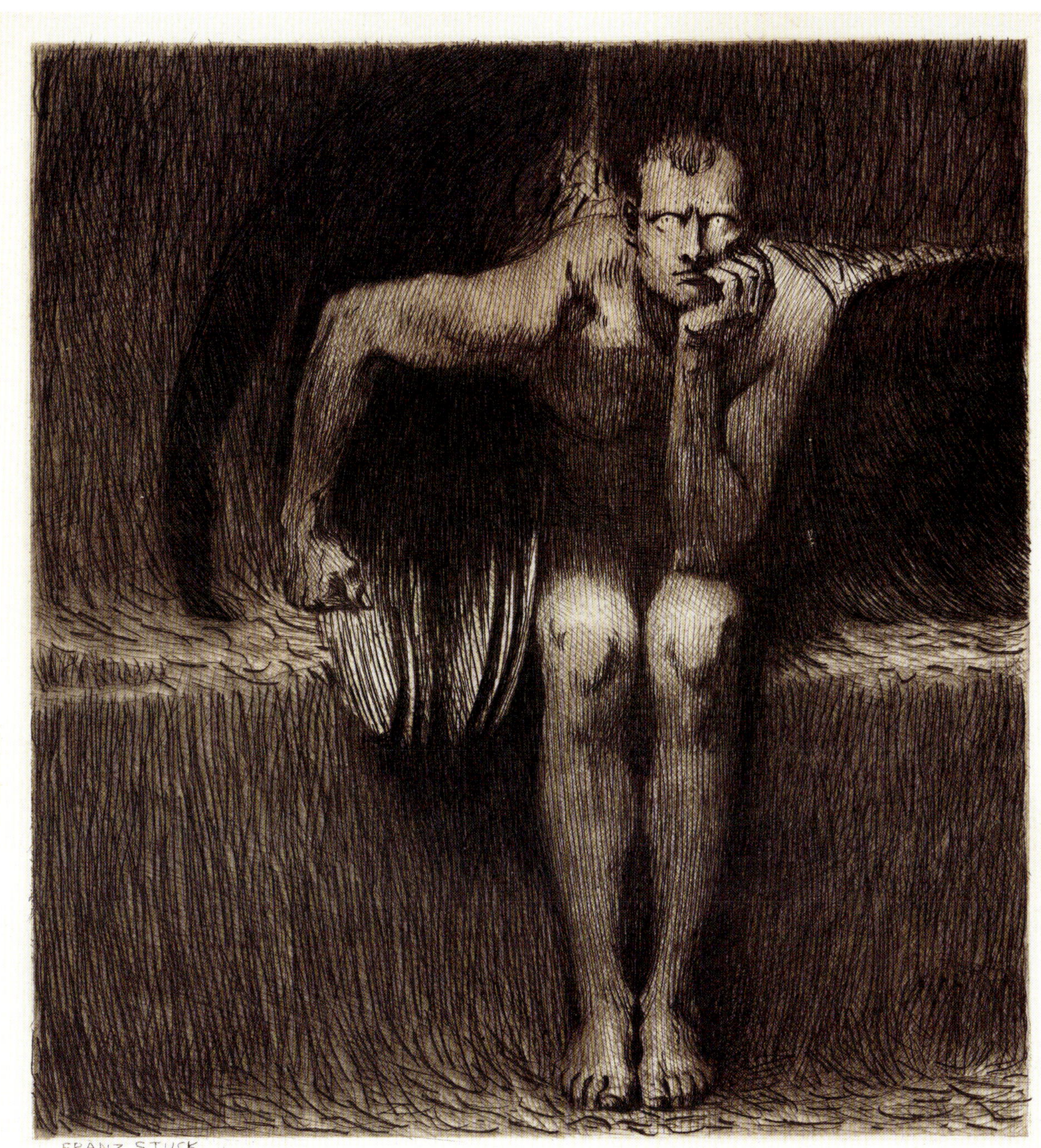

FRANZ VON STUCK
Lucifer
Leopold Museum, Vienna

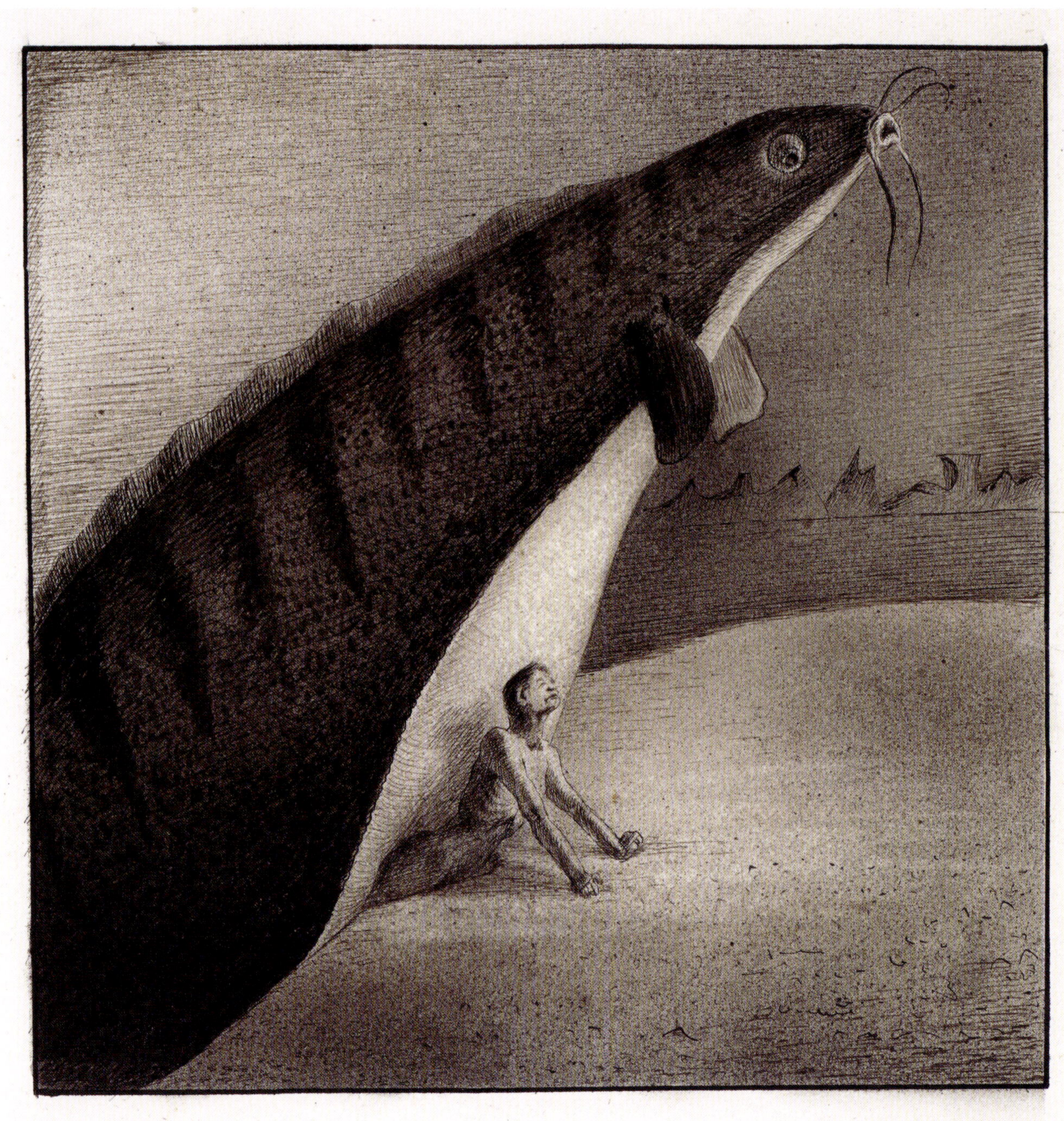

ALFRED KUBIN
The Oppressive, 1900/01
Leopold Museum, Vienna

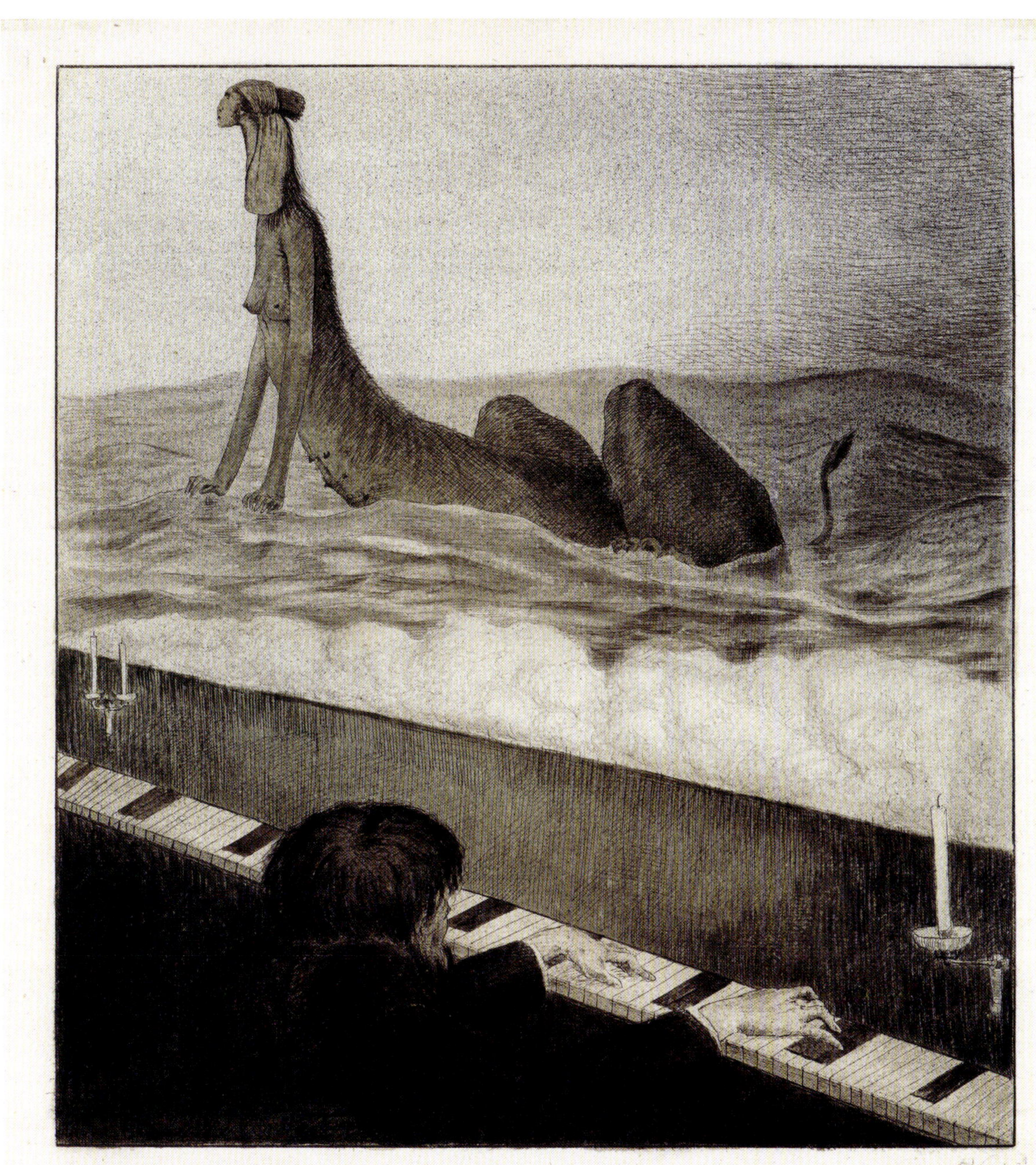

ALFRED KUBIN
The Symphony, 1901/02
Leopold Museum, Vienna

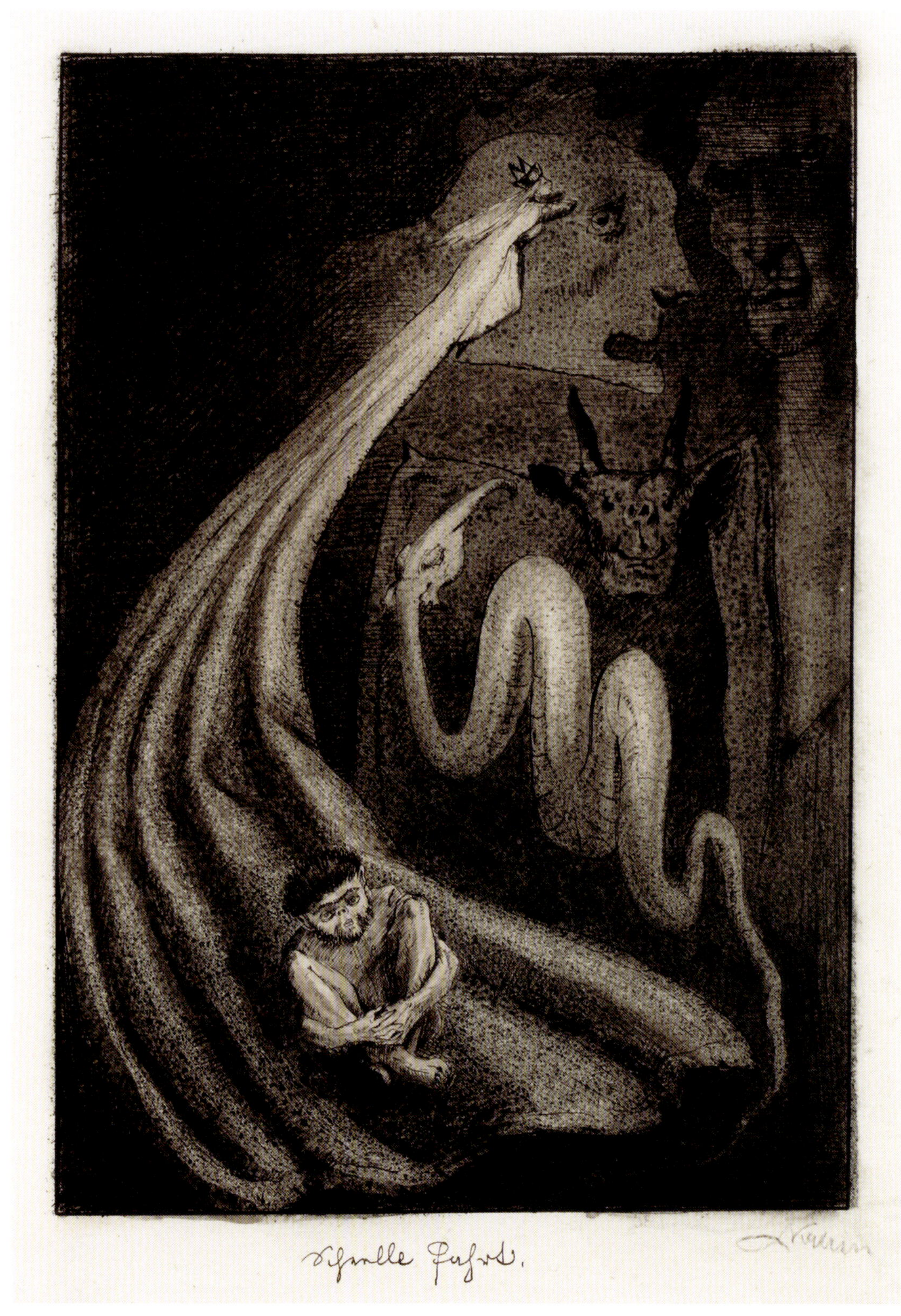

ALFRED KUBIN
Swift Ride, 1902/03
Leopold Museum, Vienna

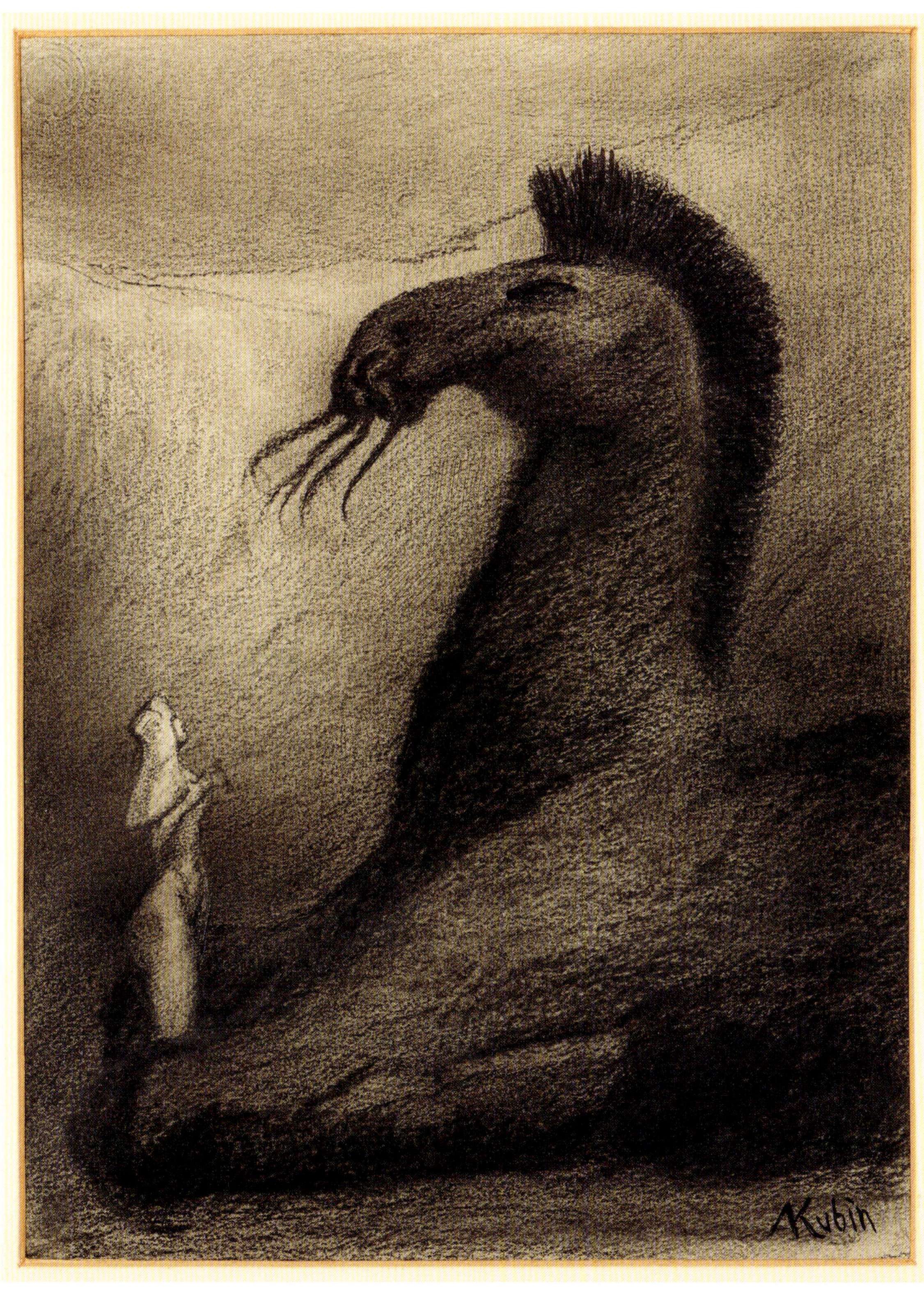

ALFRED KUBIN
The Trojan Horse, 1905
Leopold, Private Collection

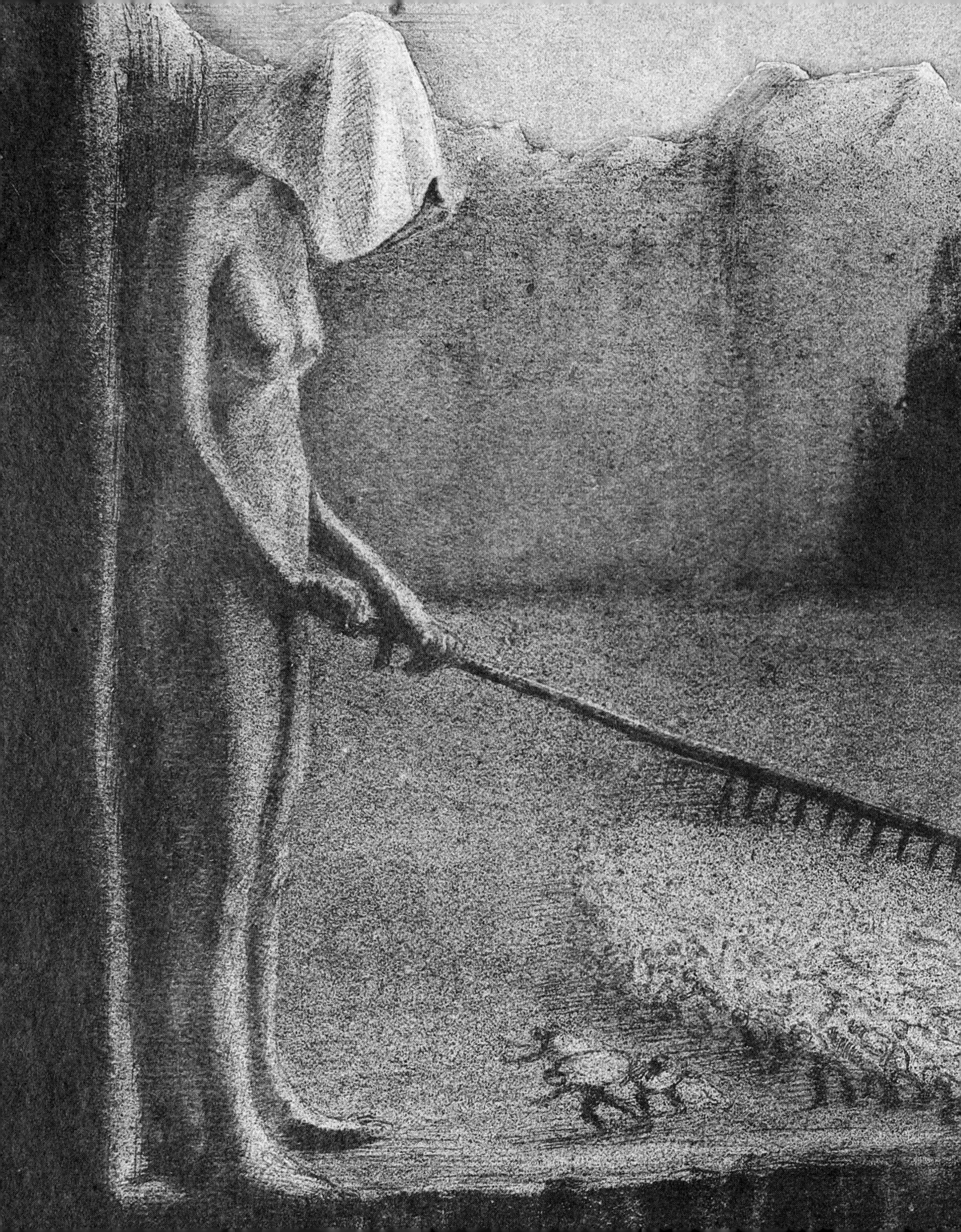

HELPLESS RETURN TO NOTHINGNESS

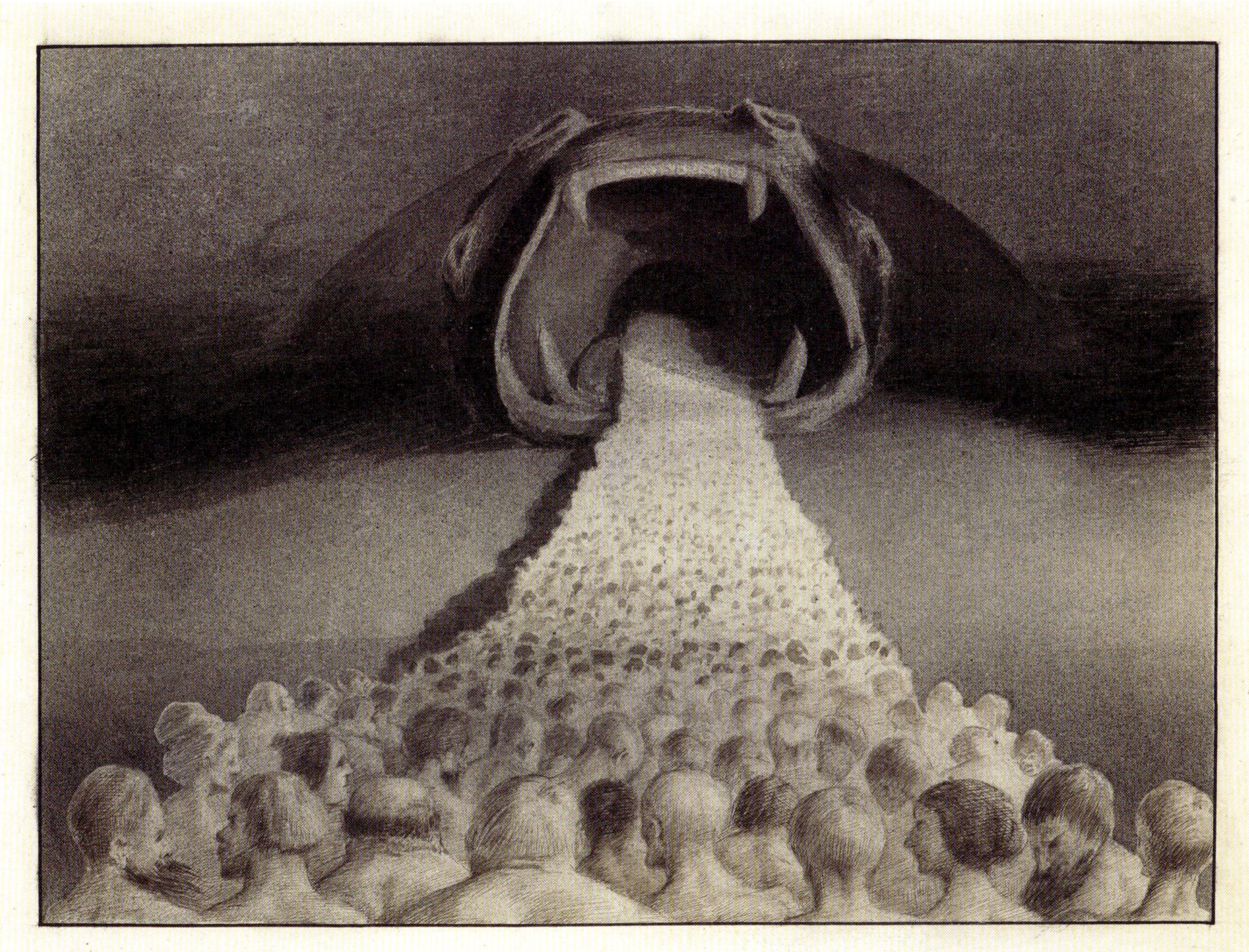

ALFRED KUBIN
Into the Unknown, 1900/01
Leopold Museum, Vienna

AFTER THE BATTLE

Among the prints of the *Weber* portfolio, *After the Battle* is, formally, one of the most ambitious ones: In an anthropomorphous landscape allegory, which references Klinger's etching *Night* from his *Brahms Fantasy* series of 1894 in motif, and in form his often almost surrealistically empty wide picture horizons, human destruction and decay are heightened into cosmic significance. In his critique of the portfolio, Edgar Alfred Regener remarked: "Especially his drawing *After the Battle* appears like a rigid and powerful ballad. In the foreground a dead lake... the background ends in a strange mountain range. We can clearly discern the outlines of a decaying human body, down to the arm with the clenched fist, which stretches long and lifeless into the plane." A long swarm of vultures flies towards it from the foreground: "A lifeless gray in the air, a loud pain in the flapping of the birds' wings, a mute, harrowing, almost cruel image in the interplay of its effects."* However, like Avenarius, Regener criticized an exaggeration of the effect and the overly emphasized, "sober" distortion of the giant arm which, he found, exposed Kubin as a novice compared to Klinger. In the same year, Kubin's friend Alexander von Bernus dedicated the verses *Before the Battle* from his first book of poems *Aus Rauch und Raum [Of Smoke and Space]* to Kubin. The lines transpose the pictorial metaphor into poetry.

Annegret Hoberg

* Edgar Alfred Regener: „Die Kunst unserer Tage. VI. Alfred Kubin", in: *Deutsche Zeitschrift,* vol. 5, no. 11, 1903.

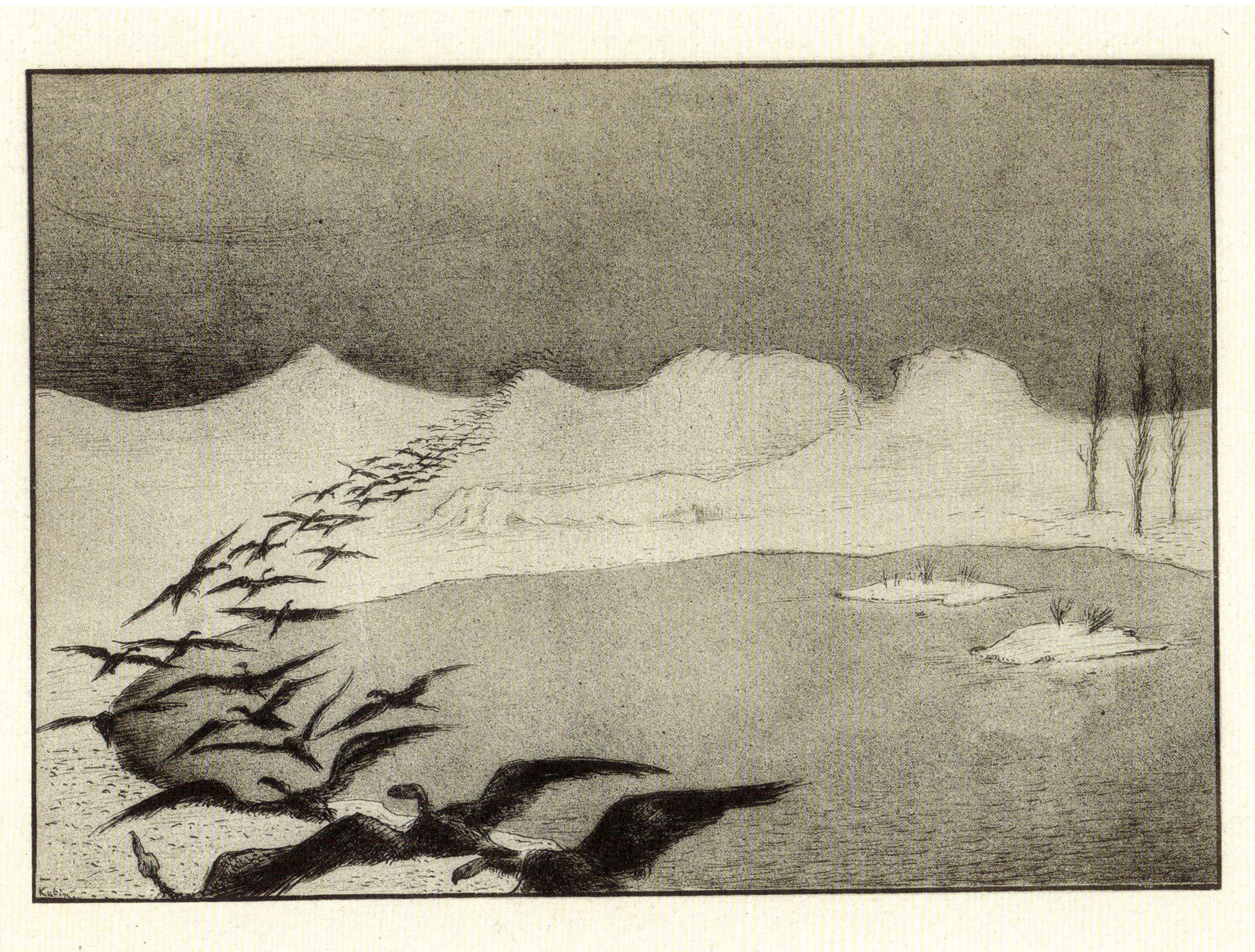

ALFRED KUBIN
After the Battle, 1901
Museum Ortner, Vienna

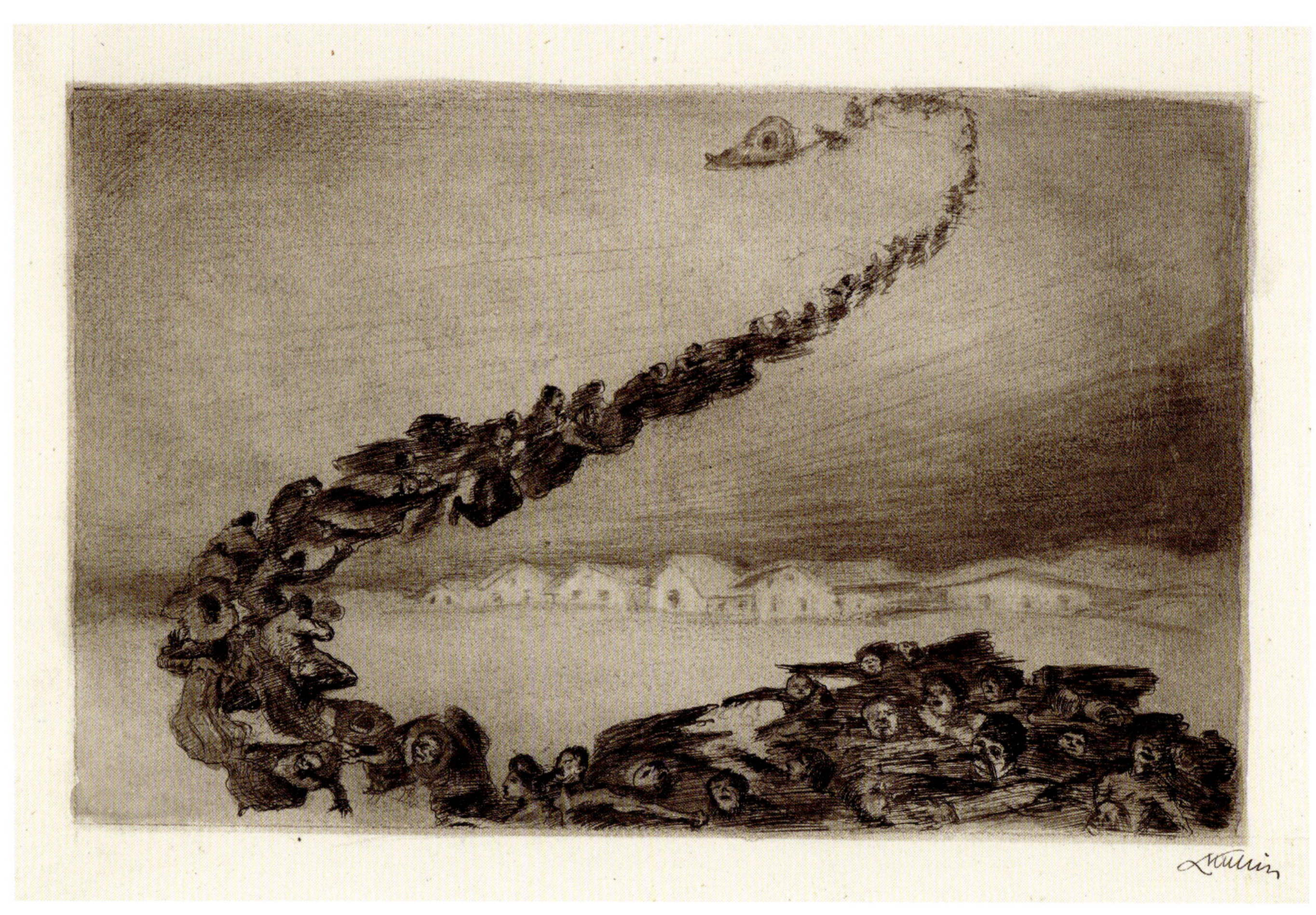

ALFRED KUBIN
Swarming Spirits, c. 1904
Leopold Museum, Vienna

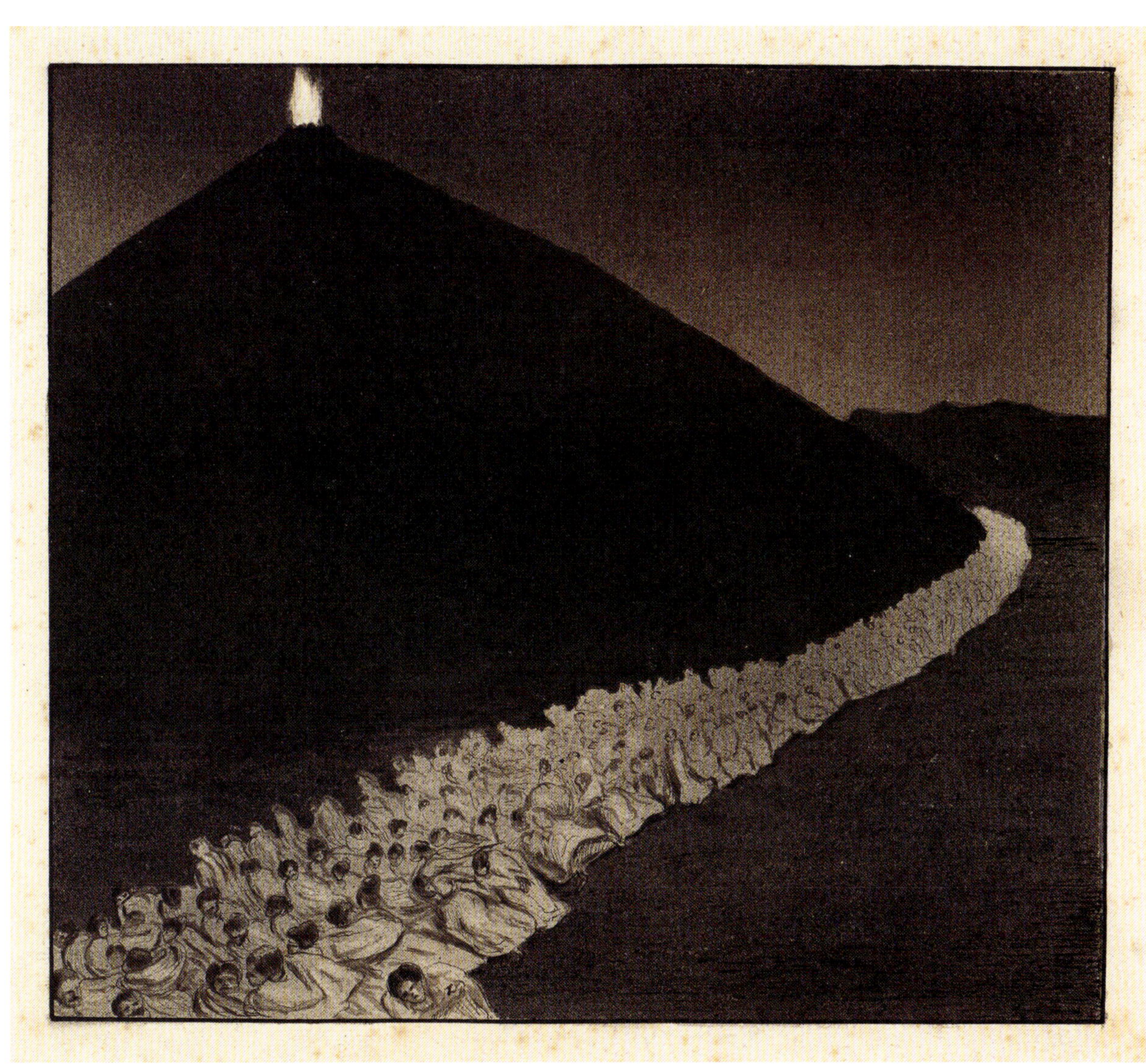

ALFRED KUBIN
The Sign, 1902
Lentos Kunstmuseum Linz

Alfred Kubin about Max Klinger

And there I was, overcome all of a sudden by a whole torrent of visions of black-and-white images—the thousandfold richness that my imagination made me see is beyond description. I quickly left the theater, because the music and the many lights were now disturbing to me, and aimlessly wandered around the dark streets, all the time overwhelmed, virtually raped by some dark force that magically put strange animals, houses, landscapes, grotesque and fearful situations before my mind.*

* Alfred Kubin, "Aus meinem Leben" (1911), quoted in Wolfgang K. Müller-Thalheim: *Erotik und Dämonie im Werk Alfred Kubins. Eine psychopathologische Studie,* (Munich, 1970), p. 75.

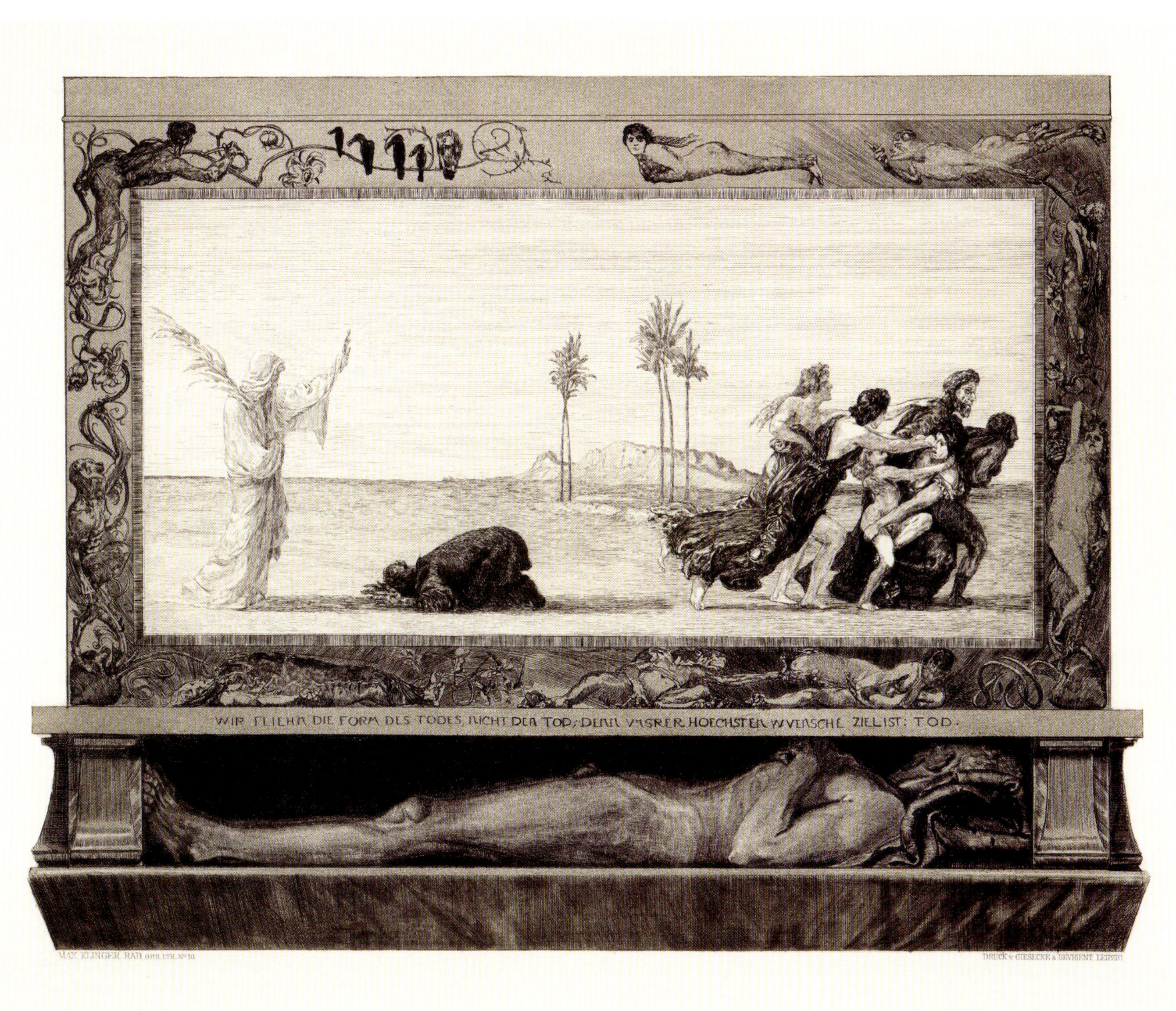

MAX KLINGER
Death as Saviour, from the cycle *On Death. Part 1,* 1897
Leopold Museum, Vienna

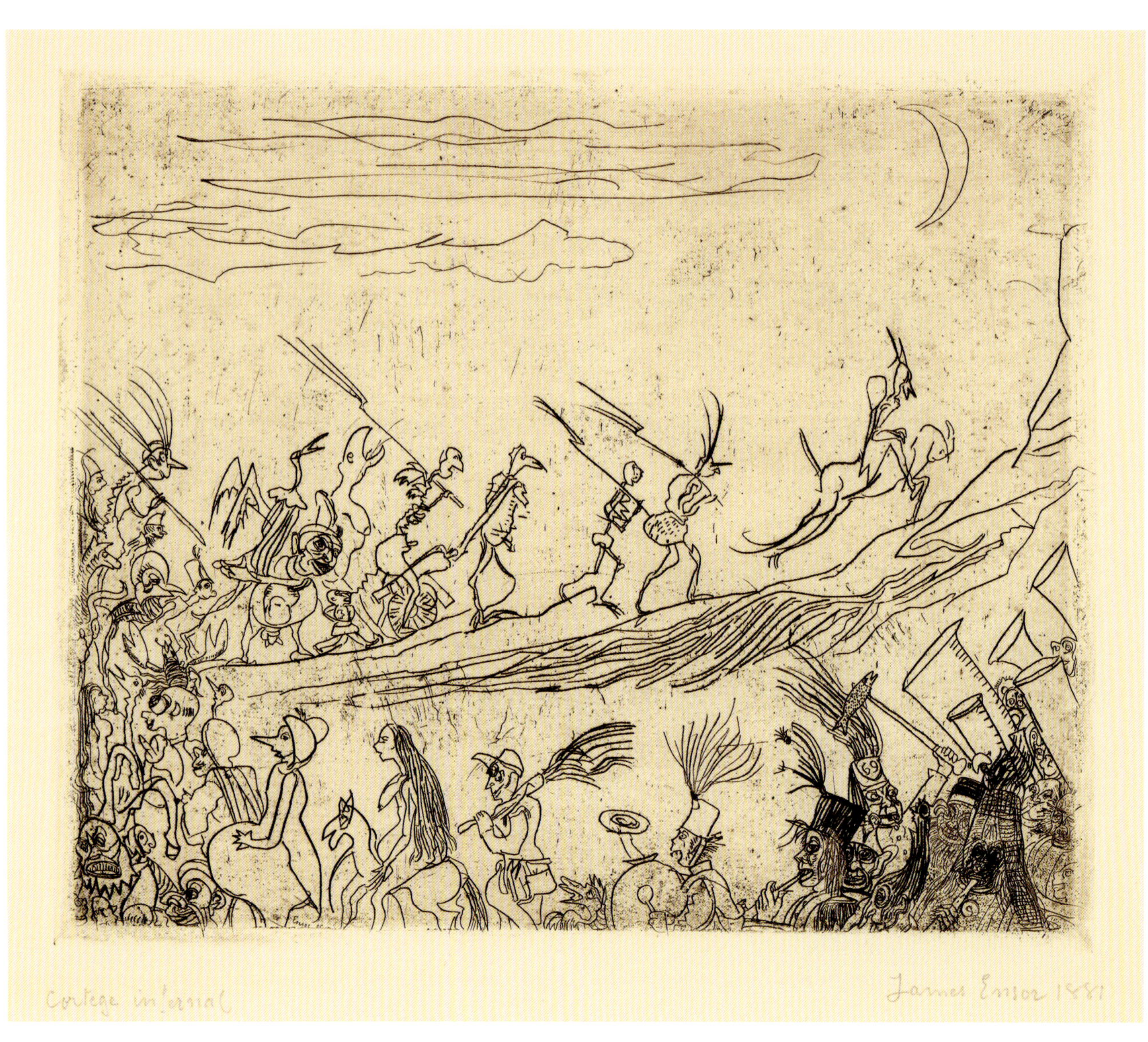

JAMES ENSOR
The Infernal Procession, 1887
Leopold, Private Collection

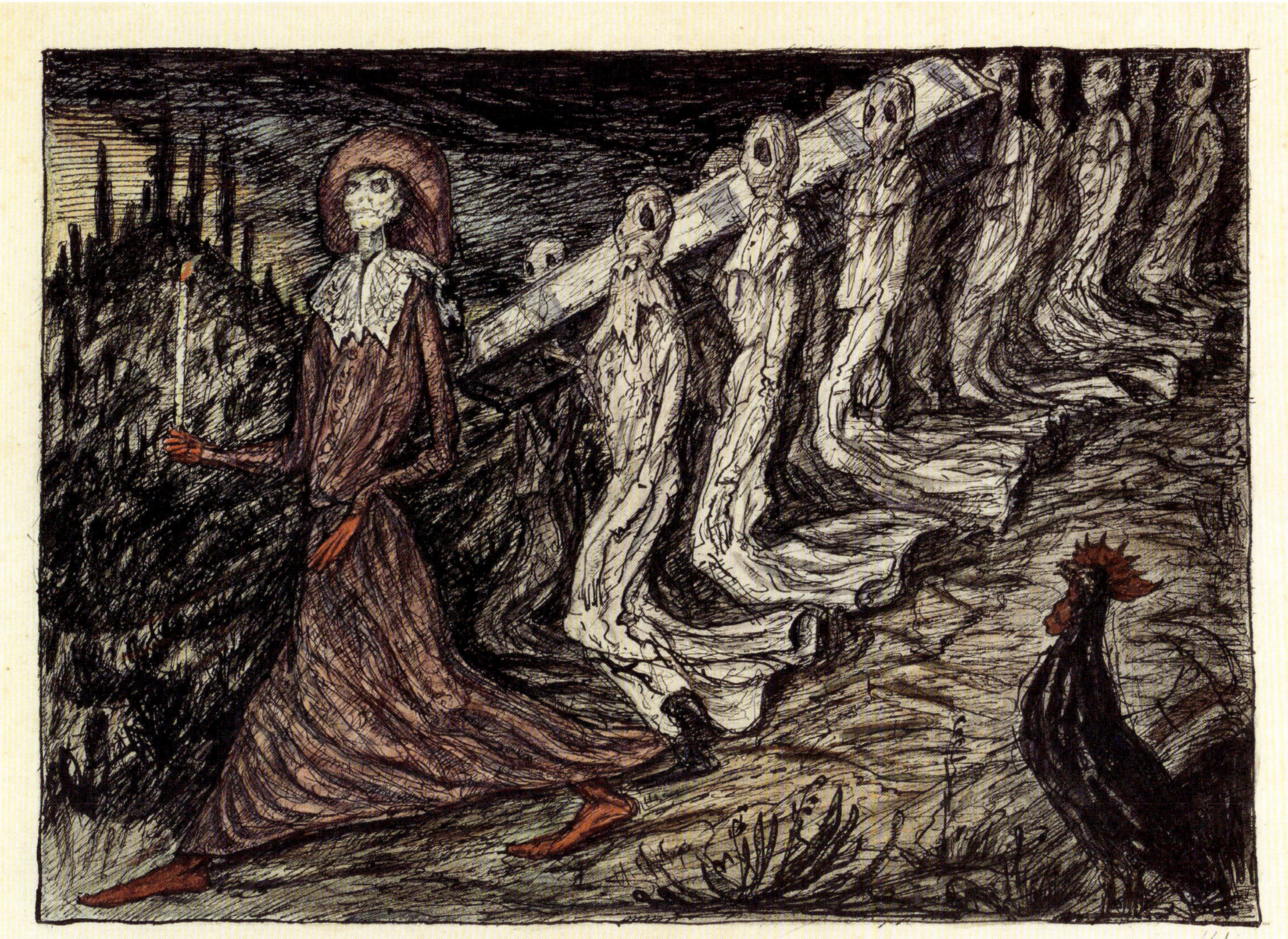

ALFRED KUBIN
Funeral March, c. 1910
Leopold, Private Collection

THE HOUR OF DEATH

"The Hour of Death: On a high tower rising up into the night, the clock hand, shaped like a saber and idly sliding, cuts off the horror-stricken human heads on the dial." This was how Richard Schaukal described the dreadful scene, which was incorporated the same year into the portfolio *Hans von Weber-Mappe*, in his article on Kubin first published in January 1903 in the newspaper *Wiener Abendpost*. It is indeed the dial of a tower clock that has been converted with relish and in the manner of Edgar Allan Poe into an execution device. At the top of every hour, the dial, sharp as a saber, inevitably cuts off a human head which, bleeding profusely, falls into a net below. Christoph Brockhaus commented on the "tragic allegory" of man's subjection and subjugation by citing comparable nihilistic ideas expressed in Arthur Schopenhauer's philosophy.*

Annegret Hoberg

* Christoph Brockhaus: *Alfred Kubin. Das zeichnerische Frühwerk bis 1904*, ed. by Hans Albert Peters (Baden-Baden, 1977), no. 27 (exh. cat. Kunsthalle Baden-Baden, 01.04.–30.05.1977)

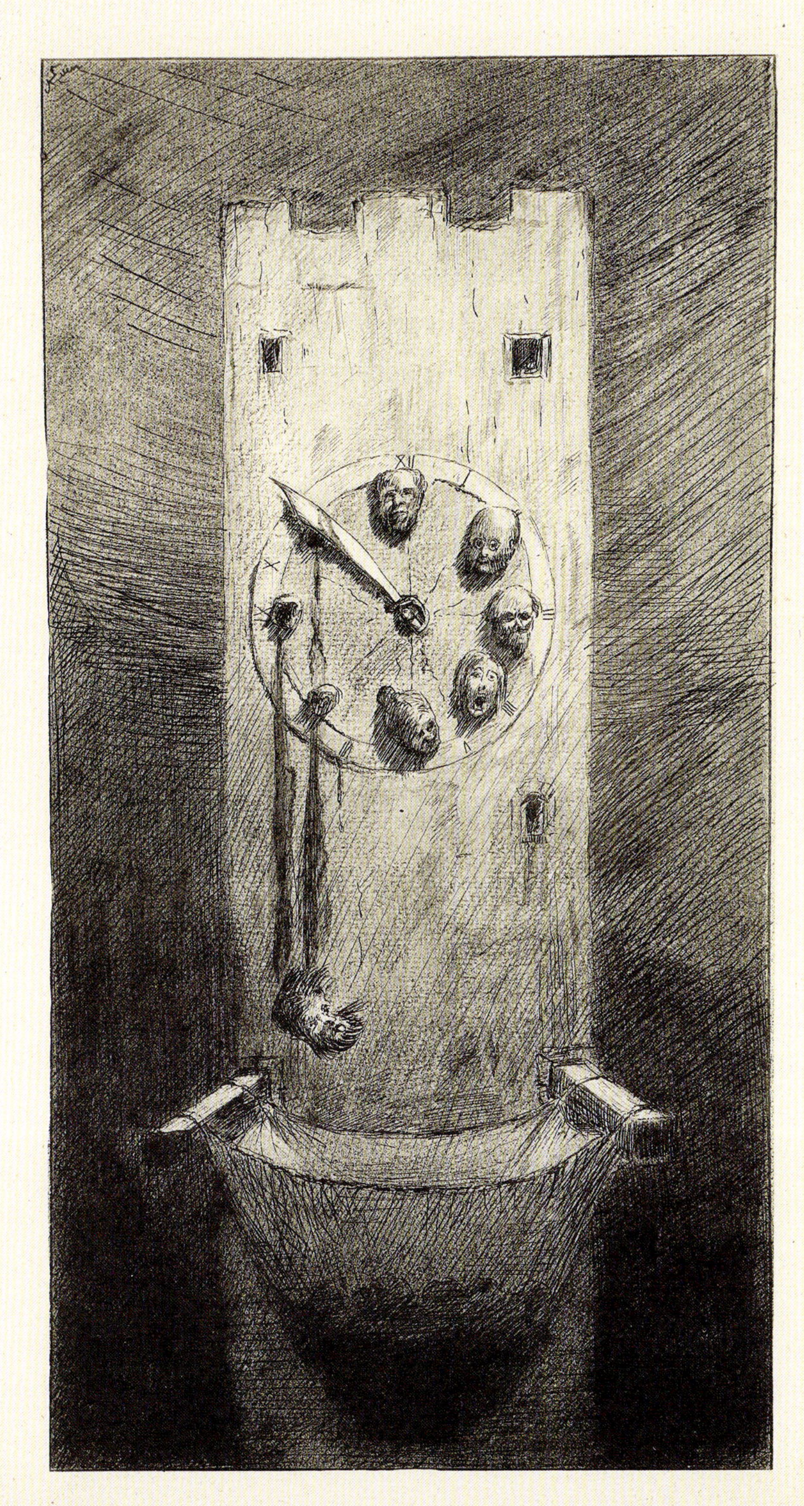

ALFRED KUBIN
The Hour of Death, print 14 from the *Hans von Weber*-portfolio, 1903
Leopold, Private Collection

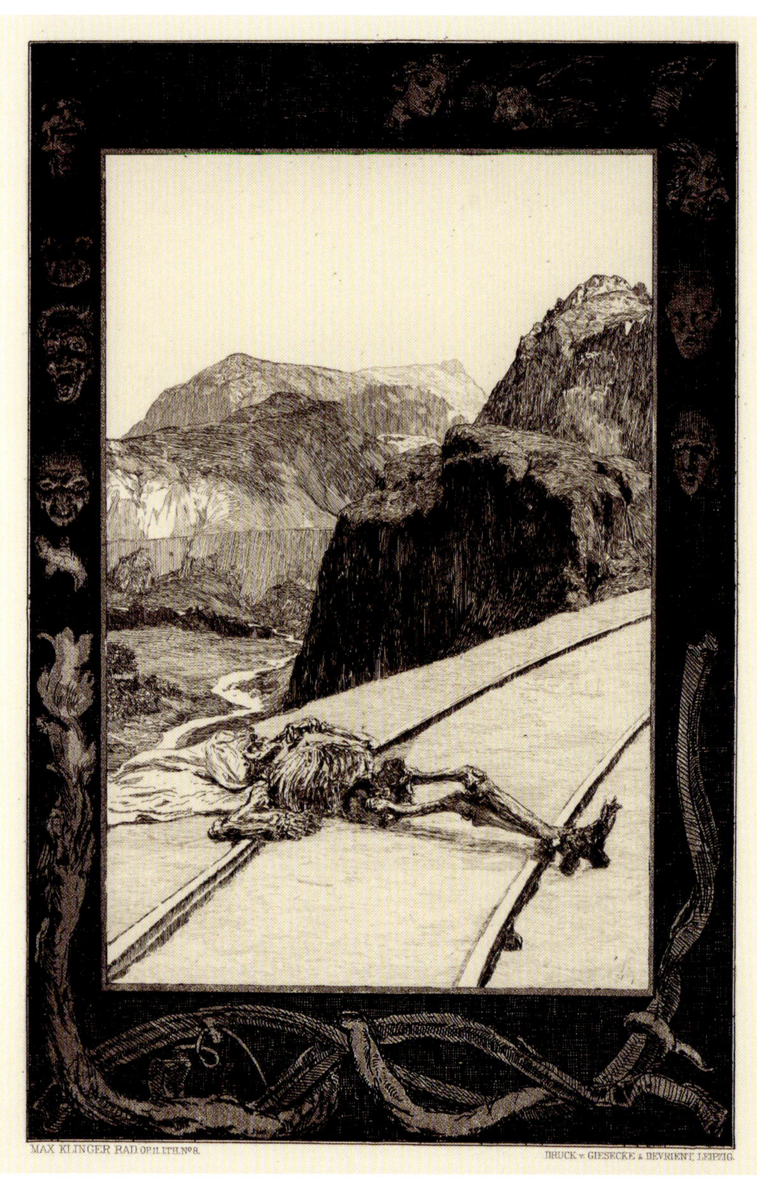

MAX KLINGER
On the Rails, from the cycle *On Death. Part 1,* 1897
Leopold Museum, Vienna

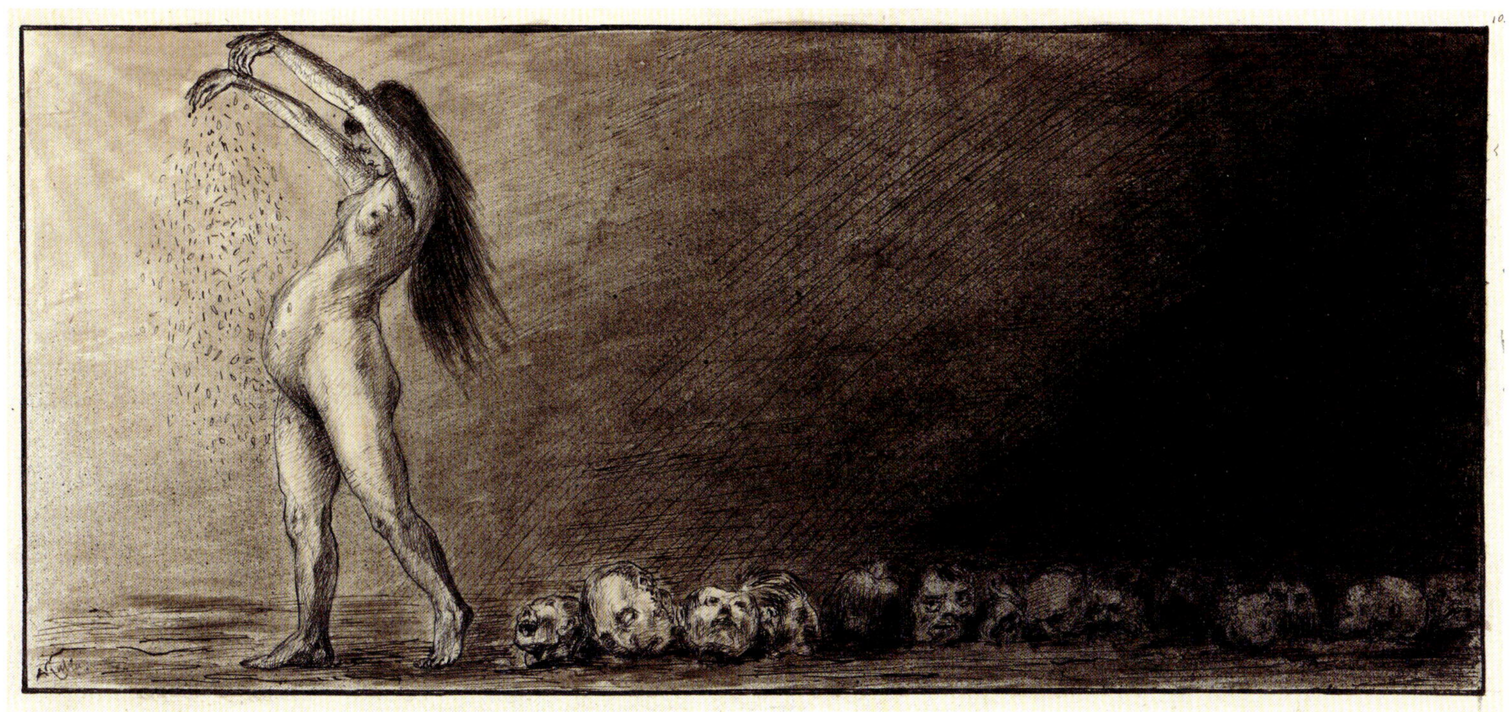

ALFRED KUBIN
Our All Mother Earth, 1902
Leopold, Private Collection

THE FATE OF MANKIND

Along with the now lost work *War*, the rendering *The Fate of Mankind* rightly is among the most highly praised works from the portfolio *Weber-Mappe*. The whereabouts of the original version of this work, too, are unknown, the present one being a slightly later version that Kubin created in 1903 for his young friend and collector Felix Grafe. It later found its way via Max Morgenstern—who made the drawing available on Kubin's request for the large-scale retrospective of the artist's work held at the Albertina in 1937—into the collection of Kurt Otte. The motif captivates through its superior, clearly structured composition: Above a dark precipice—running parallel to the bottom edge of the picture and opening abruptly both to viewers and the teeming ant-like crowd of humans—appears a rectangular space created by the mountains of a valley closed in from three sides. While this valley offers no possibility for escape, the towering figure of a young, naked woman with a veiled head stands on the left, sweeping the crowd of people with a large rake and a dispassionate gesture towards the abyss. "Her head cloaked by a cloth, the figure continues the tradition of the fateful allegories of *Night* which, with different contentual emphases and references, lead us from Carstens, Goya and Blake all the way to Hodler."[*] It is especially the natural nonchalance with which the embodiment of fate consigns the frantic activities of man to doom—a fact that was emphasized already by one of the first reviewers of the portfolio *Weber-Mappe*, Edgar Alfred Regener—that makes fate's absolute inescapability a certainty.

Annegret Hoberg

* Christoph Brockhaus: *Alfred Kubin. Das zeichnerische Frühwerk bis 1904*, ed. by Hans Albert Peters (Baden-Baden, 1977), p. 232 (exh. cat. Kunsthalle Baden-Baden, 01.04.–30.05.1977)

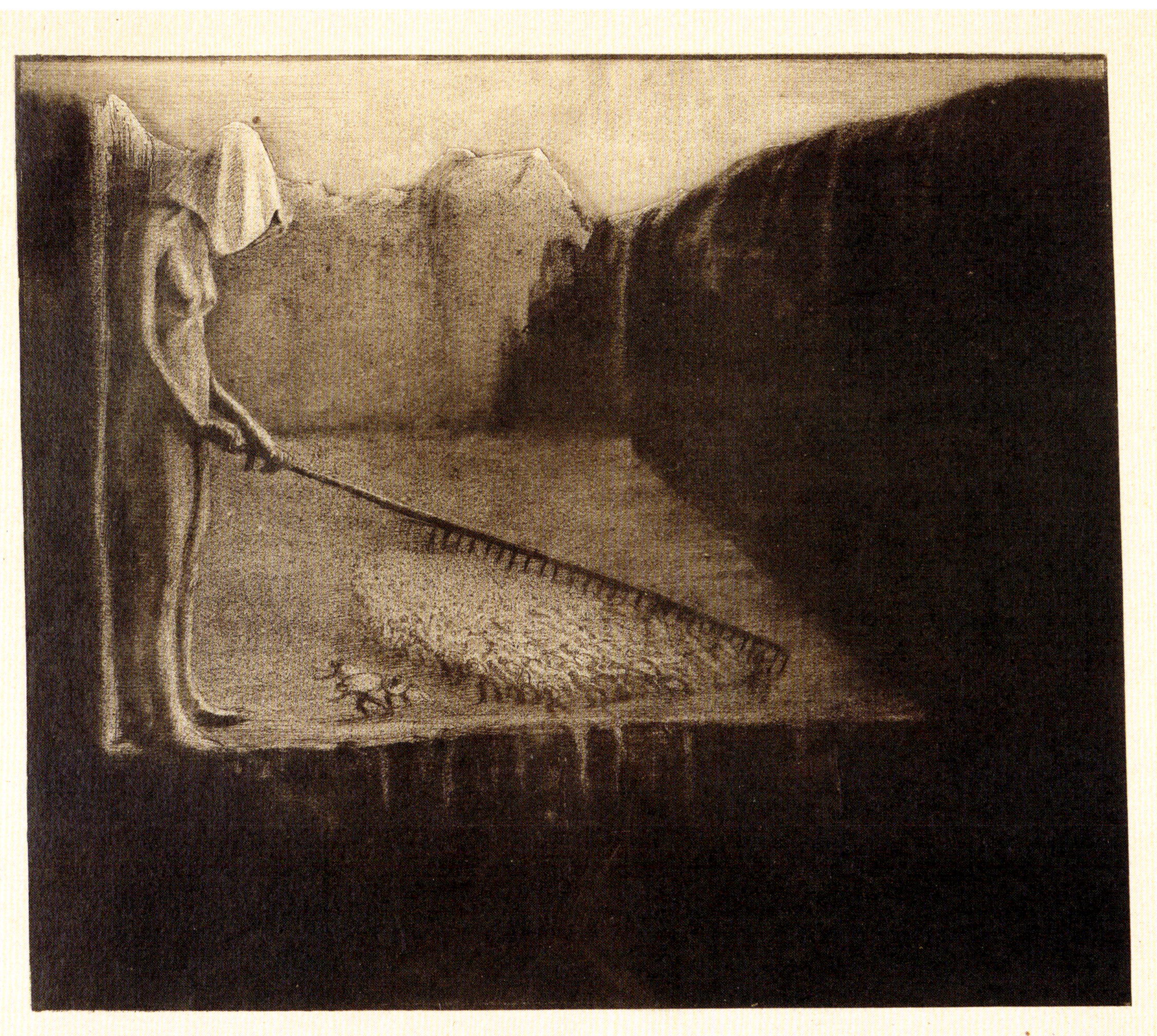

ALFRED KUBIN
The Fate of Mankind, print 1 from the *Hans von Weber*-portfolio, 1903
Leopold, Private Collection

THE PAST (FORGOTTEN—SUNKEN)

On 16th March 1903 the magazine *Kunstchronik* published a review of the portfolio *Weber-Mappe* with the heading *Münchner Brief [Munich letter]* by the art historian and writer Franz Düllberg whom Kubin would befriend shortly afterwards through the Munich Cosmic Circle around Karl Wolfskehl and Countess Reventlow. Like almost all the critics at the time, Düllberg, too, mentioned the technical "inaptitude" of the young Kubin and closed with the observation: "The last piece of the series, *Forgotten-Sunken,* makes up for a lot. It shows a massive, lithic creature sitting in the dead of night on a low block of stone, the hands resting on the knees, like one of the Colossi of Memnon. The arms and legs are angular like granite, while the chest is arched in a hard round line. The crop-like neck ends in a bird's head with a mighty beak and a small, barely visible eye. The deity throws its head back with the arrogance of eternity. 'Egypt', one might say, but what is five-thousand years old is presented here in a new guise."

Annegret Hoberg

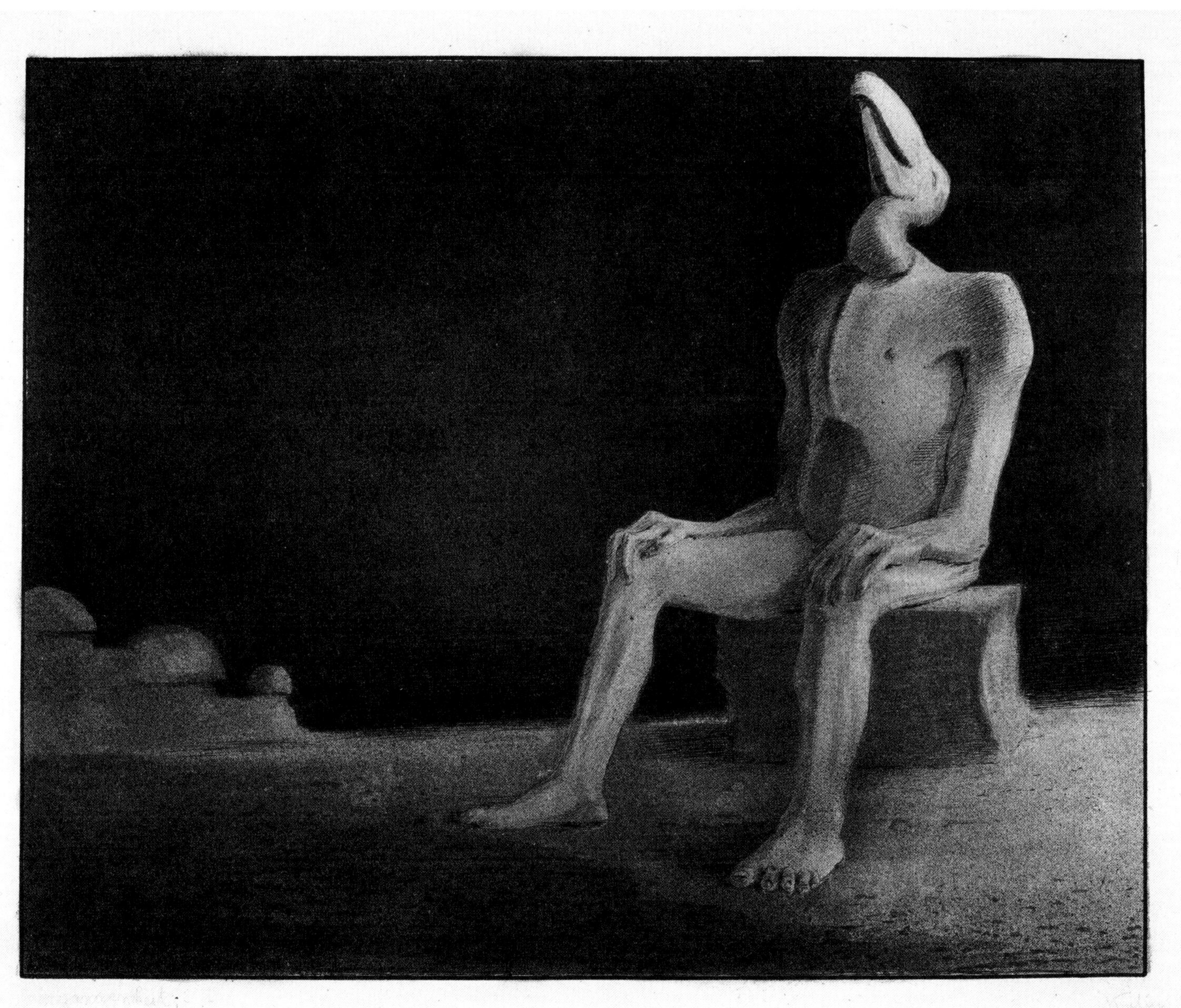

ALFRED KUBIN
The Past (Forgotten—Sunken), 1901
Leopold Museum, Vienna

DANGER

The impressive work *Danger* featured in Kubin's first solo exhibition at Galerie Paul Cassirer in Berlin in the winter of 1901/02 along with numerous other drawings, and was given a special mention in almost all press reviews. The reviewer of the newspaper *Magdeburger Zeitung* appeared undecided about the "many philosophical bon mots and sarcastic jokes of a highly peculiar, often grotesque and gruesome character", for instance, "when danger is epitomized by an enormous hand on a long arm, and when this hand belongs to a body sprawled out over a rock plateau; the hand groping for ships in the storm-tossed sea, with a snake-shaped neck, protruding from the body and topped with a small head, towering over the sea in a tremendous curve." The motif of the "strong hand" was also highlighted by Ferdinand Avenarius as the predominant impression in his critique of the work. Two years later, he would write a distinctly positive appraisal of the immediate and absorbing character of Kubin's depictions, describing his as a dream-like style of creation: "This is even more true of the work *Danger*, showing gigantic hands approaching the beholder—every one of us has dreamed something similar a hundred times, but how few have tried to depict it!"*

Annegret Hoberg

* Ferdinand Avenarius: "Traum-Bildnerei", in: *Kunstwart*, vol. 16, no. 11, 1903, pp. 595ff.

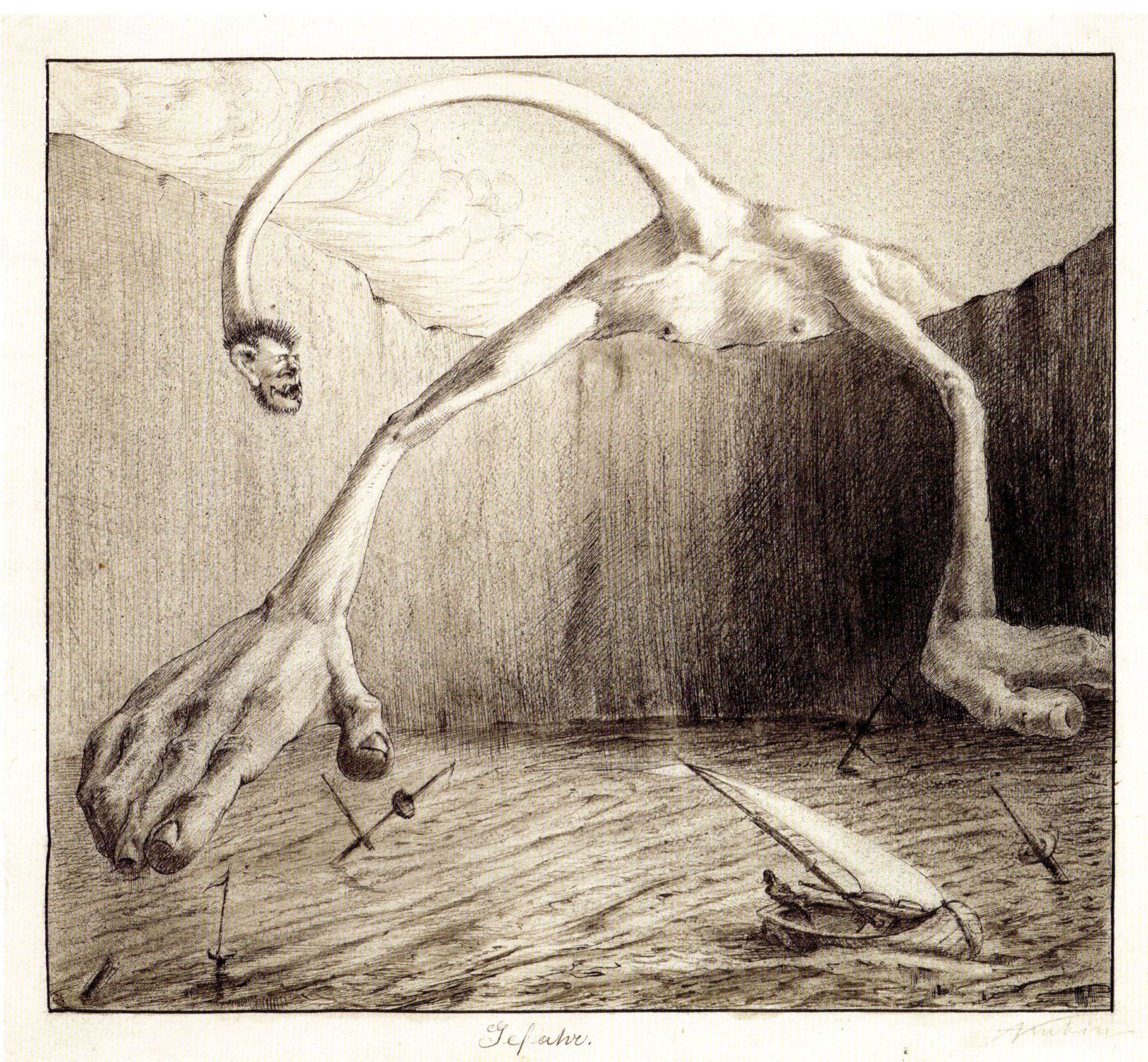

ALFRED KUBIN
Danger, c. 1901
Leopold Museum, Vienna

MAN

Kubin's drawing of a naked man with flowing hair, his arms tied to the body and his feet wedged between wheels, racing into nothingness on a precipitous rail, can be understood as an existential formula of that era. Reproduced several times in the first twenty years after its creation, this was clearly also how the work was seen by Ernst Jünger who addressed it in a letter to Kubin dated 10th February 1929: "You will hardly remember me: Years ago, I sent you a short poem on your work *Man*."* Since it was published by Raabe, the poem has been quoted numerous times, its first lines reading: "Dream, glowing, becomes vision, crystal / Archetypal question as being turns to insanity, cataract: / Upright man; cast into the universe, / In his hair a tempest, pale, alone, naked."

With his symbol of the inescapable thrownness of man into cosmic emptiness, Kubin expressed his own fundamental conviction, which he put into words in his famous "suicide letter" addressed to his sister Marie and dated 22nd February 1904: "Death, nothingness, is the fate of the world, [and all] those individual forces which together constitute the world. Each and every one runs down a predestined path, unconditionally, like a machine."**

Annegret Hoberg

* In: *Ernst Jünger – Alfred Kubin. Eine Begegnung* (Frankfurt am Main, 1975), p. 14.

** Cf. Paul Raabe: *Alfred Kubin. Leben. Werk. Wirkung*, (Hamburg, 1957), p. 26.

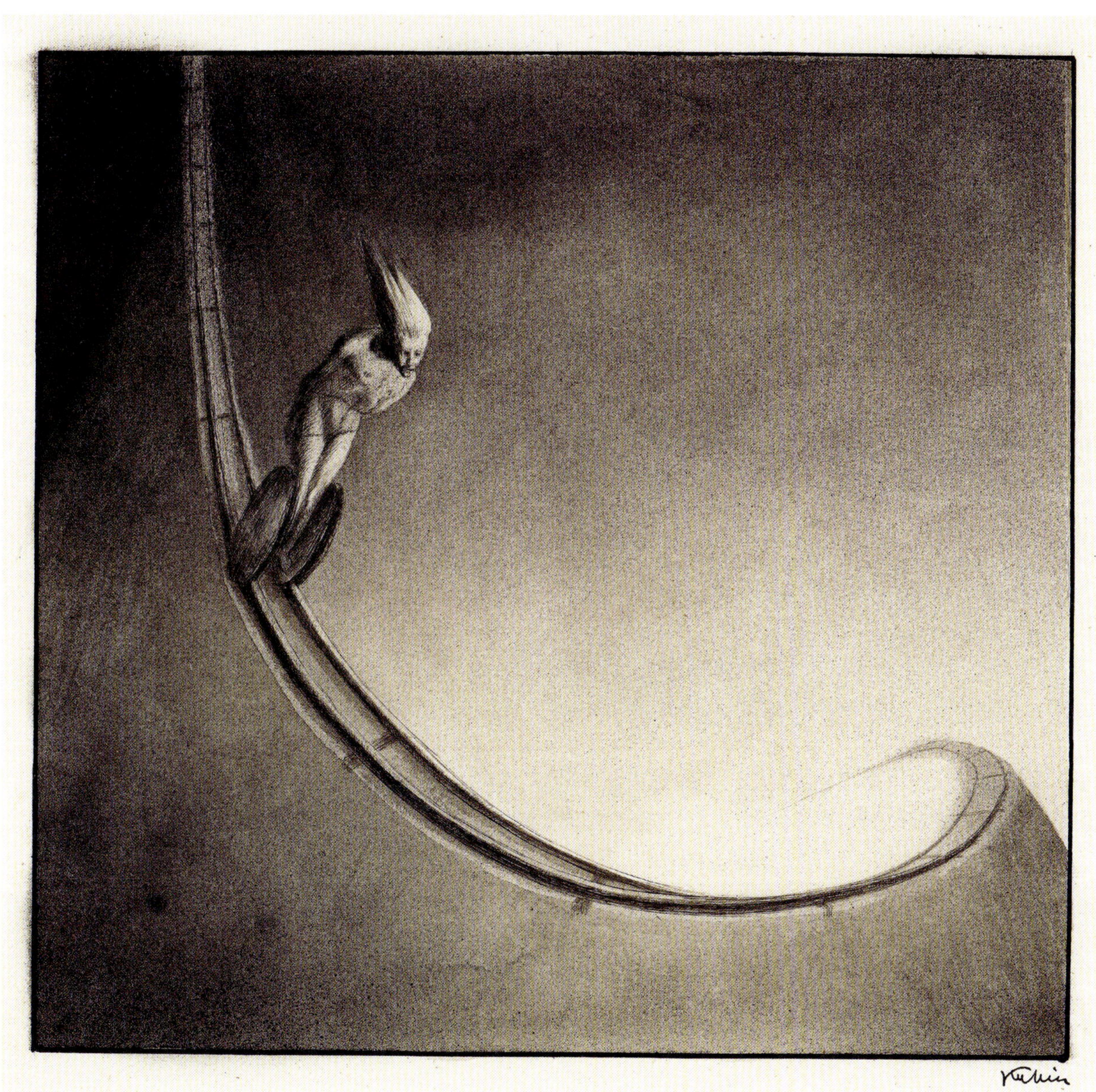

ALFRED KUBIN
Man, c. 1902
Leopold Museum, Vienna

THE HORROR

The depiction *The Horror*, which was included in the portfolio *Weber-Mappe* published in 1903, caused quite a stir when it was exhibited in 1901/02 at Galerie Cassirer. To quote the reviewer of the newspaper *Rheinisch-Westfälische Zeitung*, Hans Bethge: “Let us look at the excellent work he calls *The Horror*. It is fascinating in its way. It shows a small, wrecked ship with a broken mast floating on the stormy sea, while the trembling people it carries realize that they can no longer elude death. Just then, the horror emerges from a mighty wave before them, a grinning skull with hideous teeth on a long neck, and while one eye lies in a deep cavity, the other bulges out like a baleful plague-spot that dominates the entire face. It is terrifying to even imagine encountering such a hideous face in real life. One would die of dread.” A similar version of this motif of a bulging, mercilessly gaping eye features in a picture from *Hyaku monogatari [One Hundred Ghost Stories]* by the Japanese artist Hokusai, created in 1830, in which the ghost of a murdered woman appears above her killer. The fact that Kubin’s rendering was further inspired down to the smallest details by Edgar Allan Poe’s tale *A Descent into the Maelström*, as Christoph Brockhaus has been able to prove, — as was, in fact, the work *Danger* (p. 263) whose “rock plateau” must be read as the colossal wall of a vortex — does nothing to disparage Kubin’s ingenious pictorial invention, who added the motif of the all-dominating head of his own accord.

Annegret Hoberg

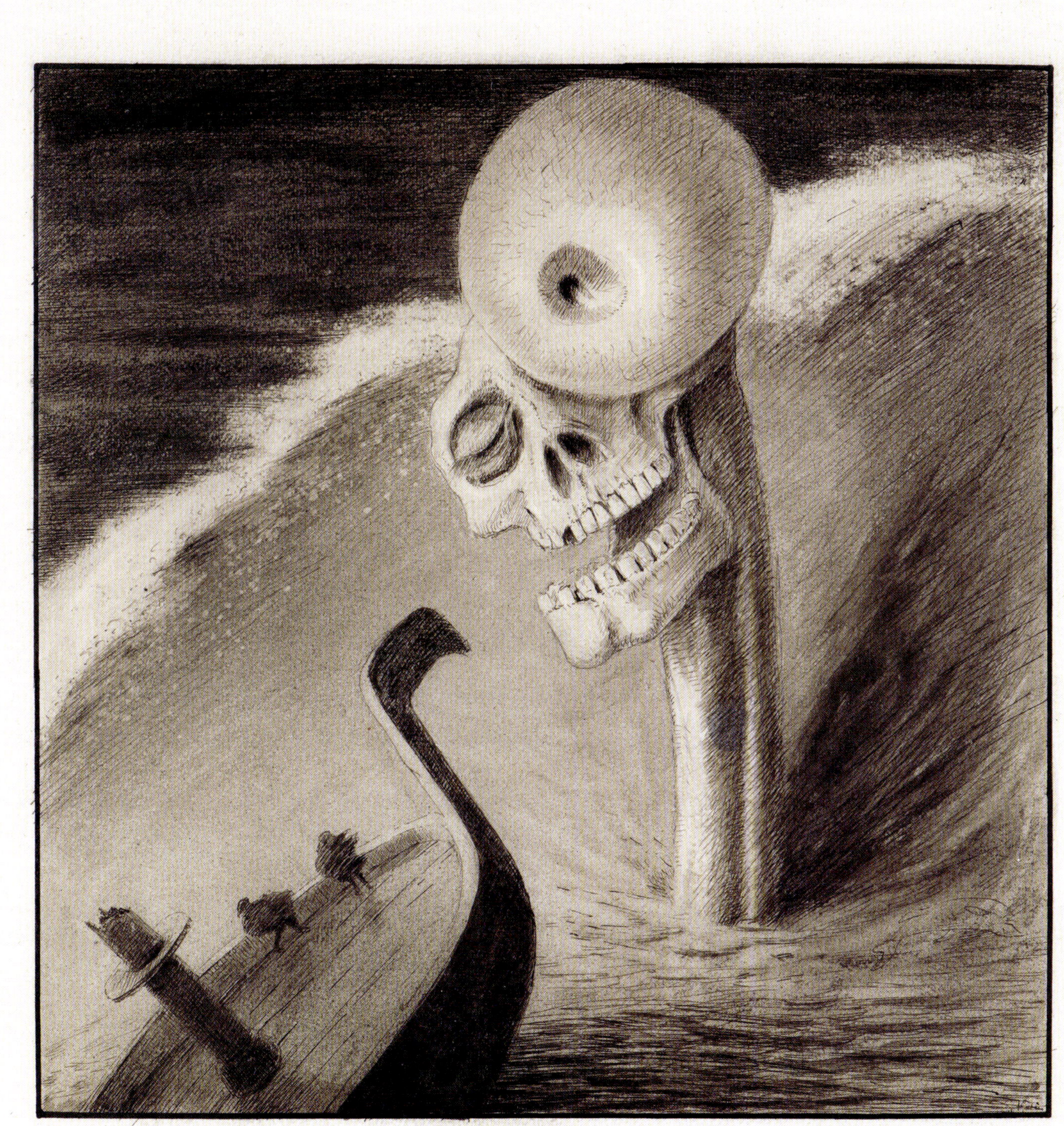

ALFRED KUBIN
The Horror, c. 1902
Leopold Museum, Vienna

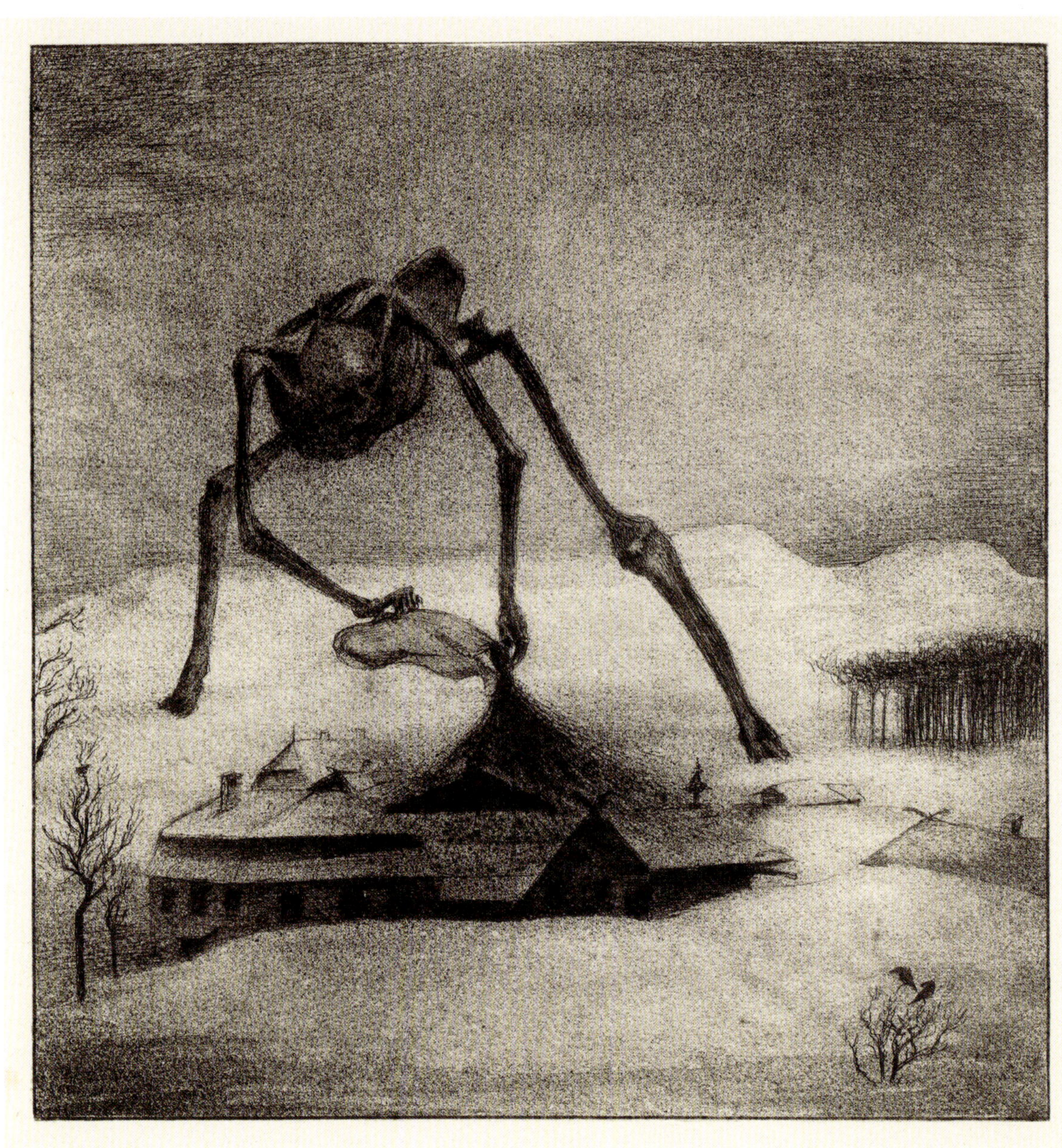

ALFRED KUBIN
Epidemic, print 7 from the *Hans von Weber*-portfolio, 1903
Leopold, Private Collection

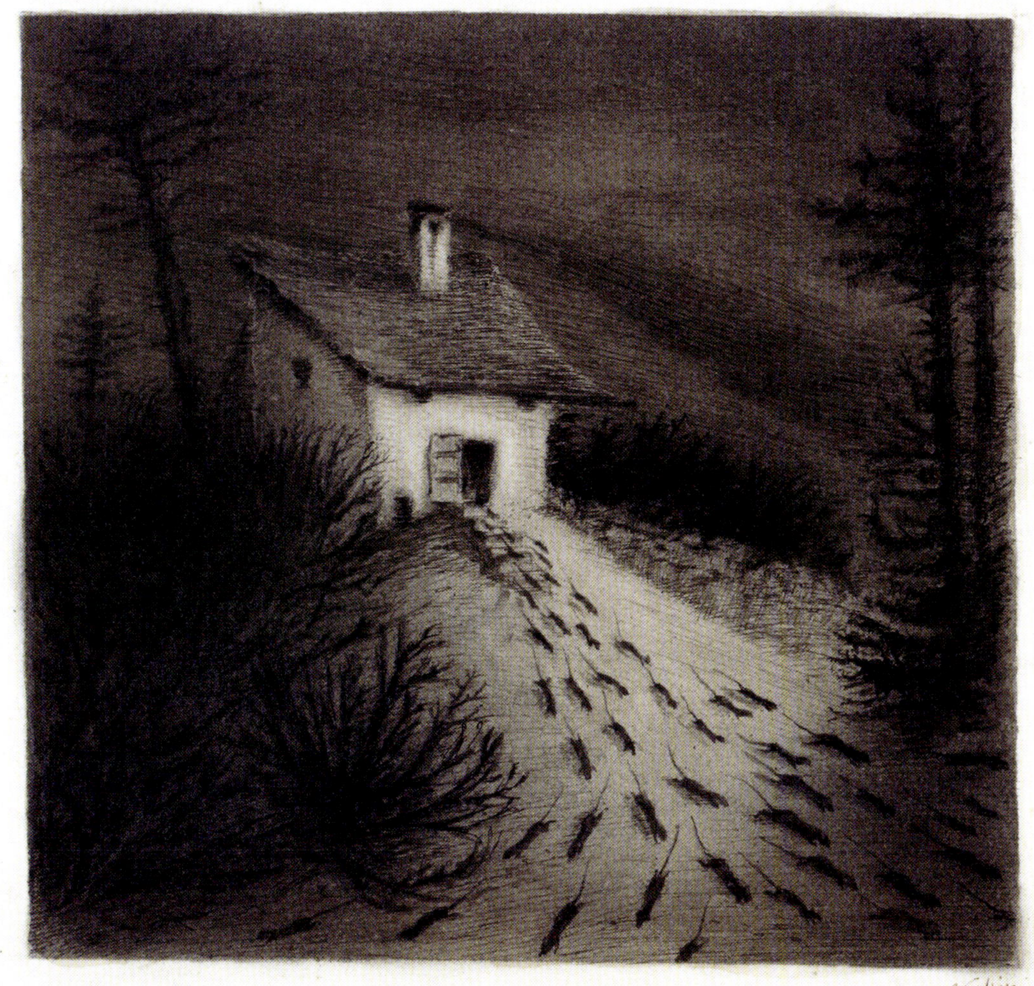

ALFRED KUBIN
The Rat House, 1902
Leopold Museum, Vienna

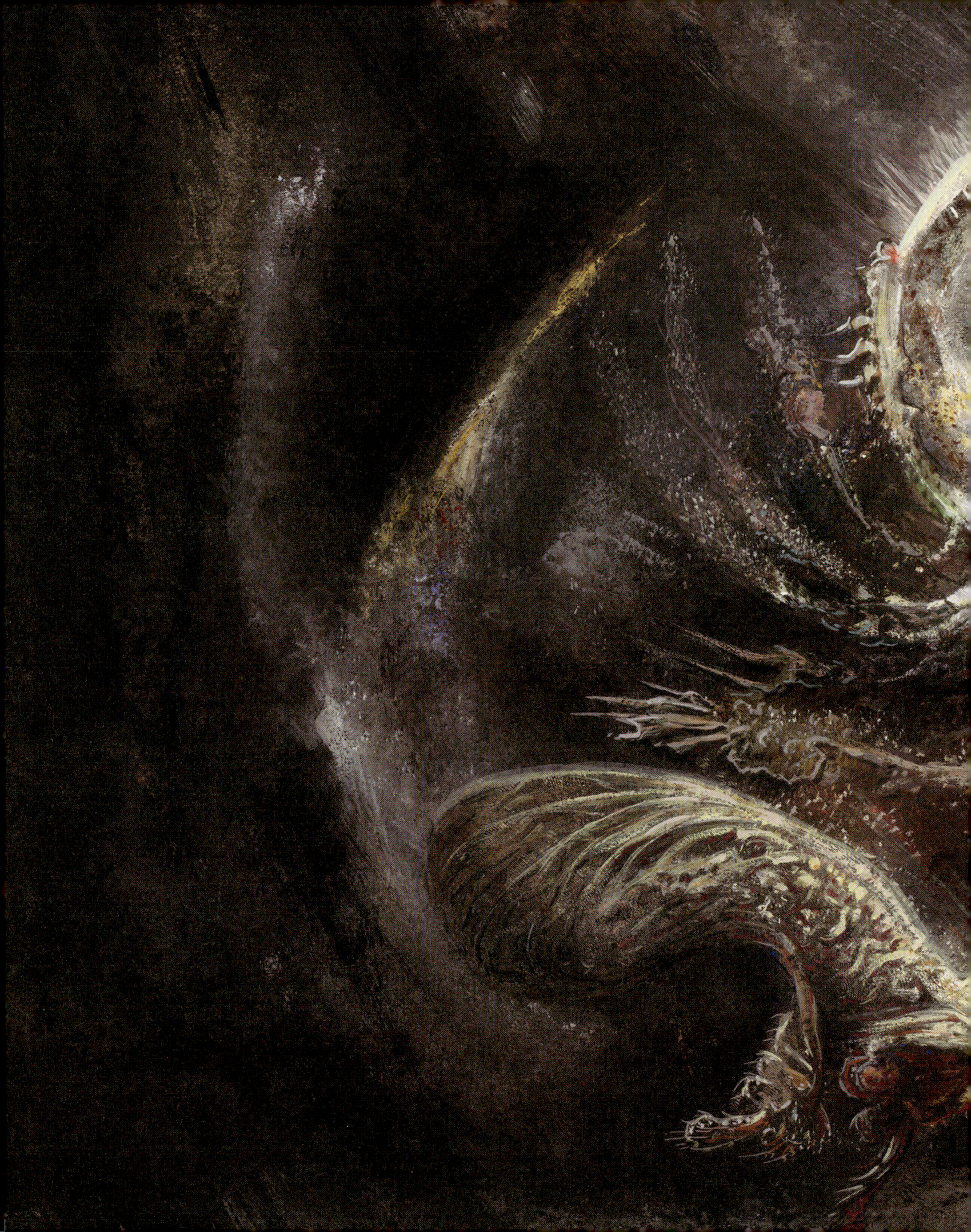

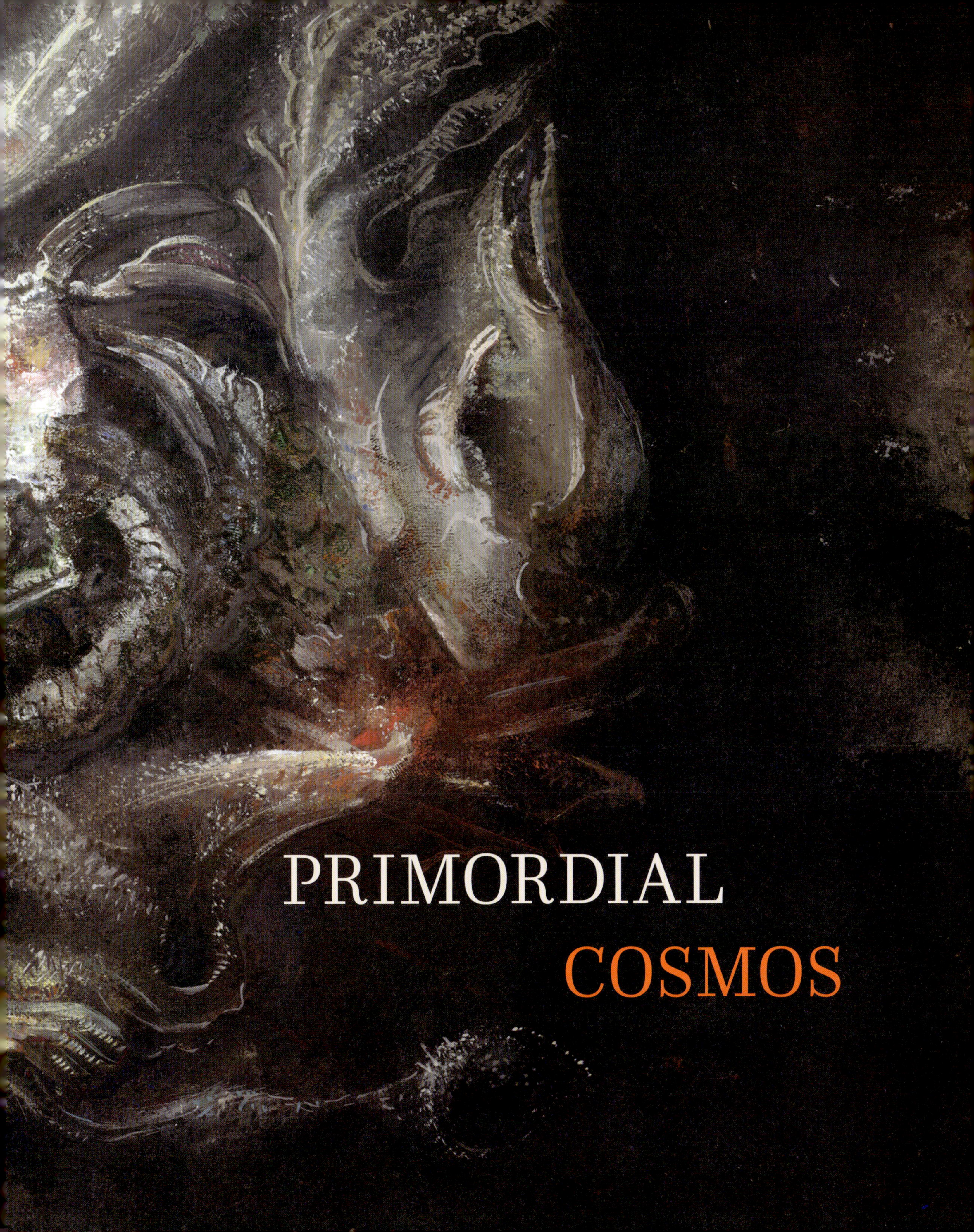
PRIMORDIAL
COSMOS

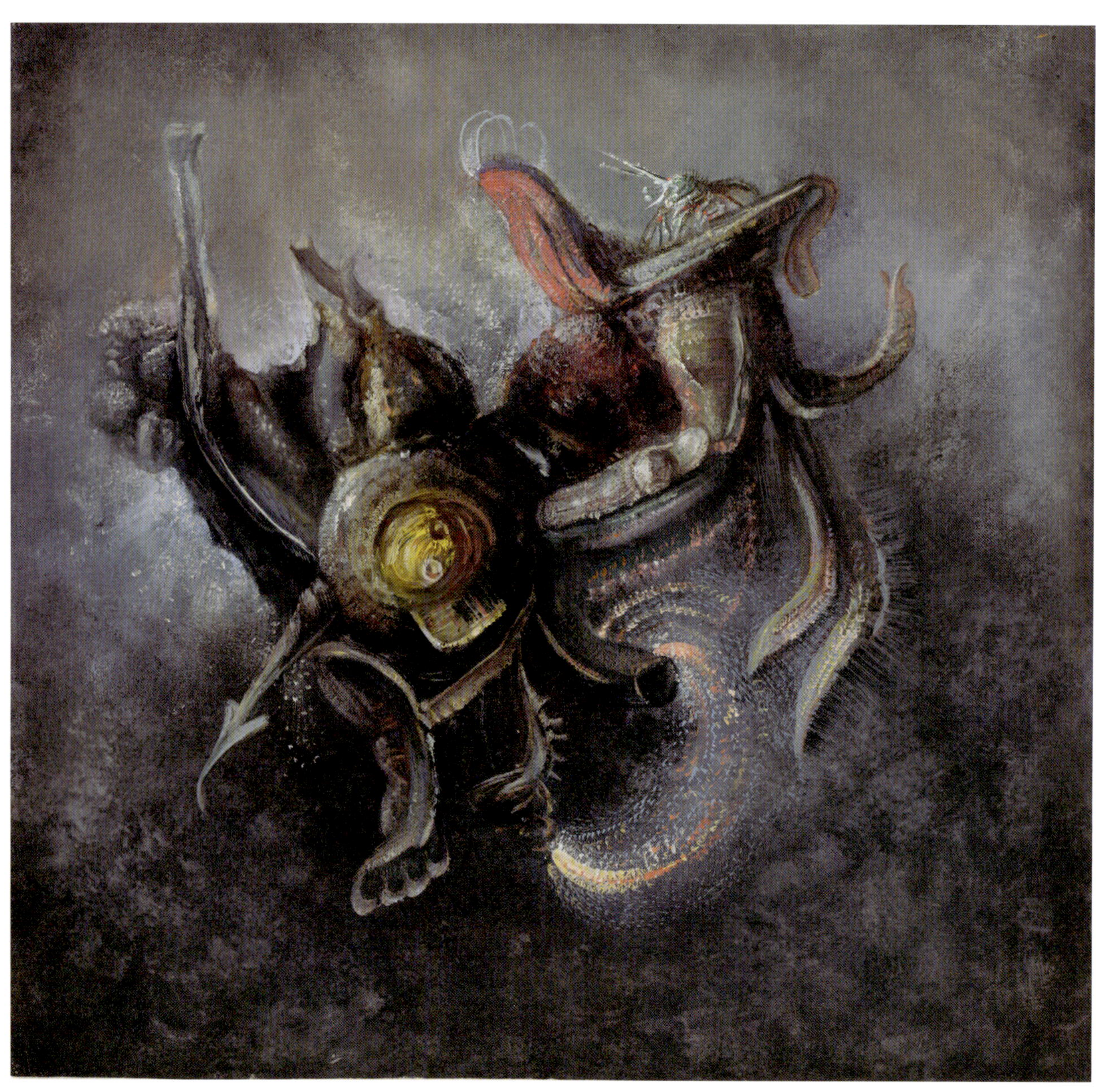

ALFRED KUBIN
The Saddle (Shell), c. 1906
Albertina, Vienna

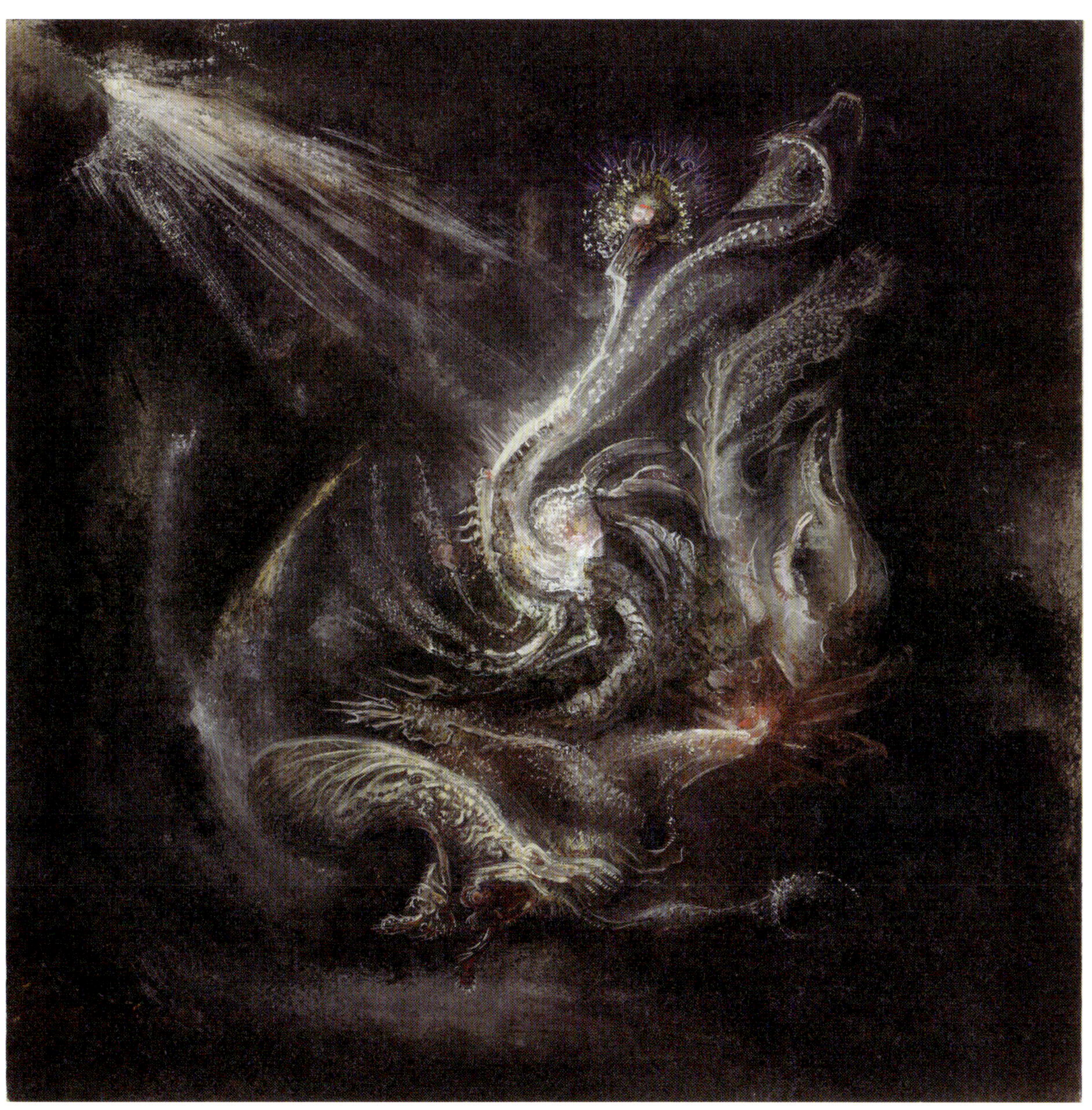

ALFRED KUBIN
Fireworks, c. 1906
Albertina, Vienna

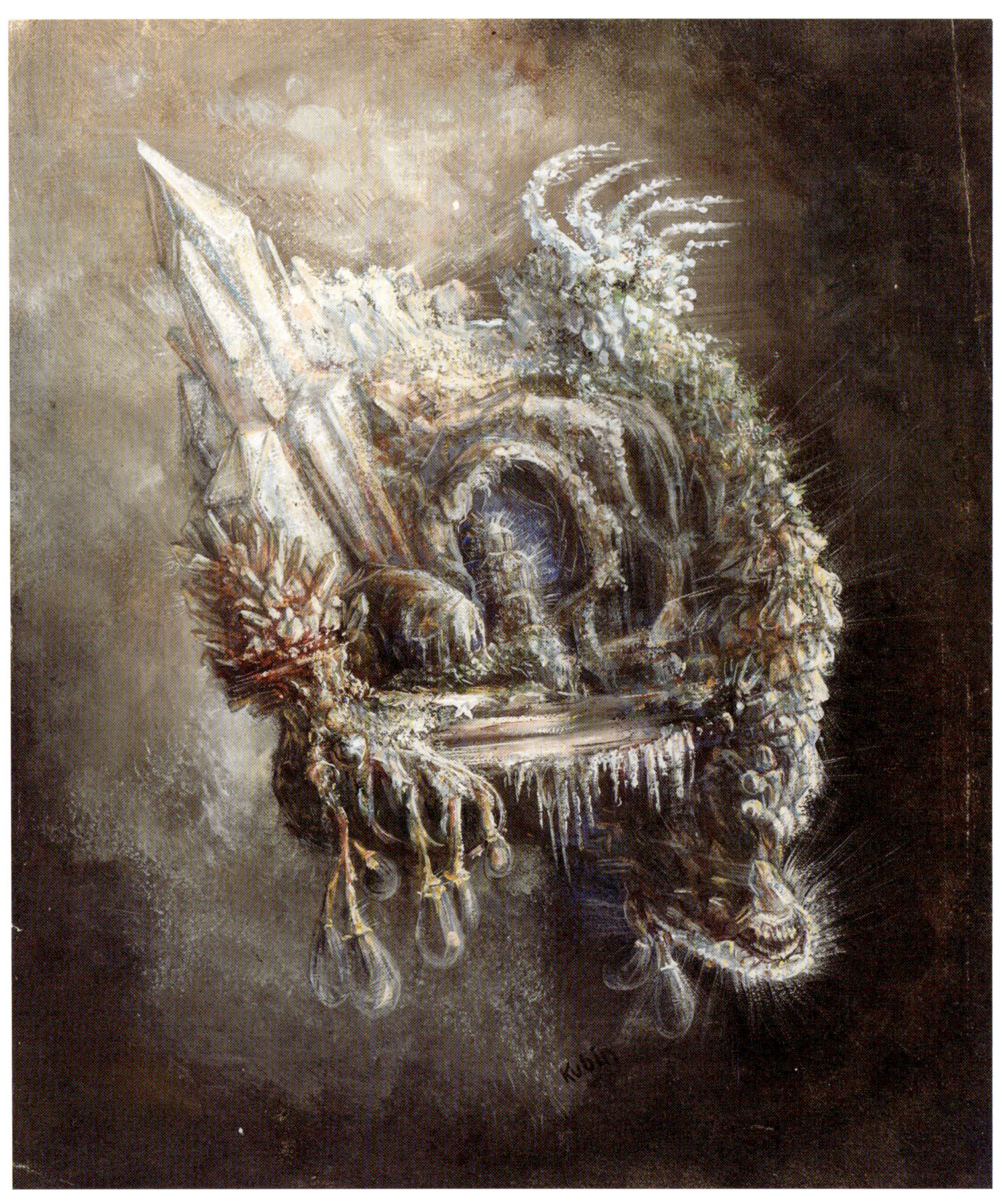

ALFRED KUBIN
Crystals, 1906
Lentos Kunstmuseum Linz

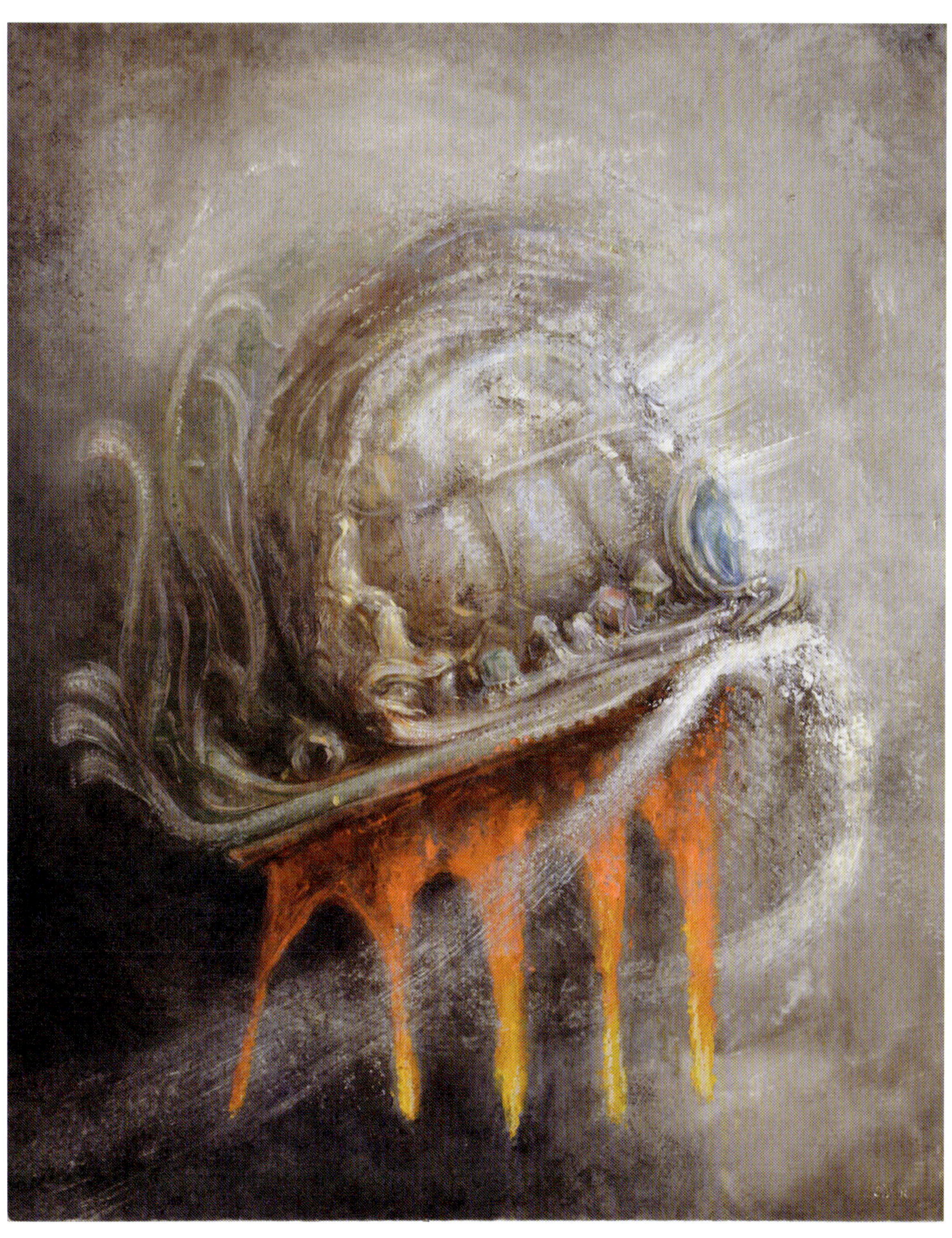

ALFRED KUBIN
Helmet in the Sea, 1906
Leopold Museum, Vienna

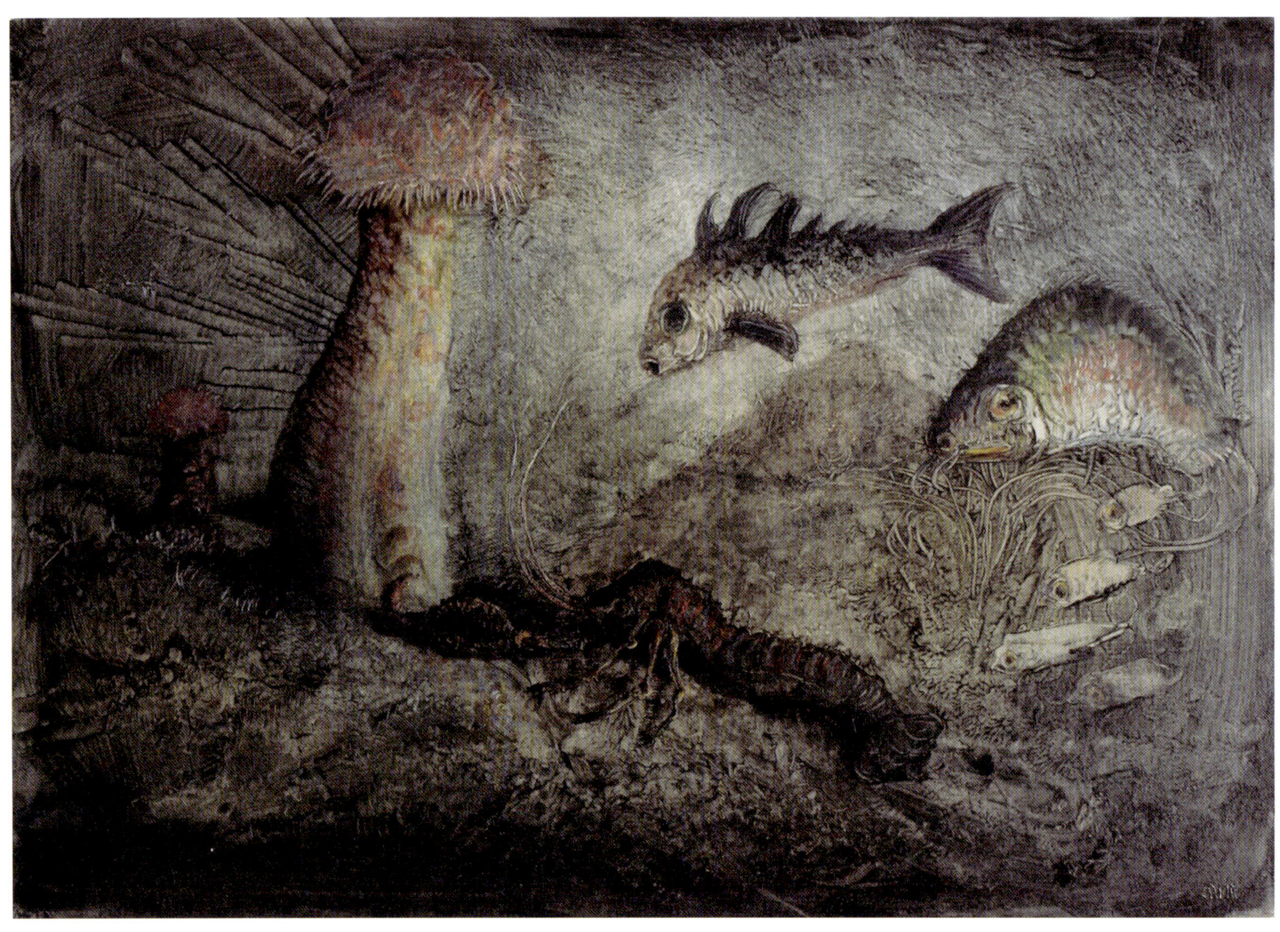

ALFRED KUBIN
Undersea Creatures, 1905
Leopold Museum, Vienna

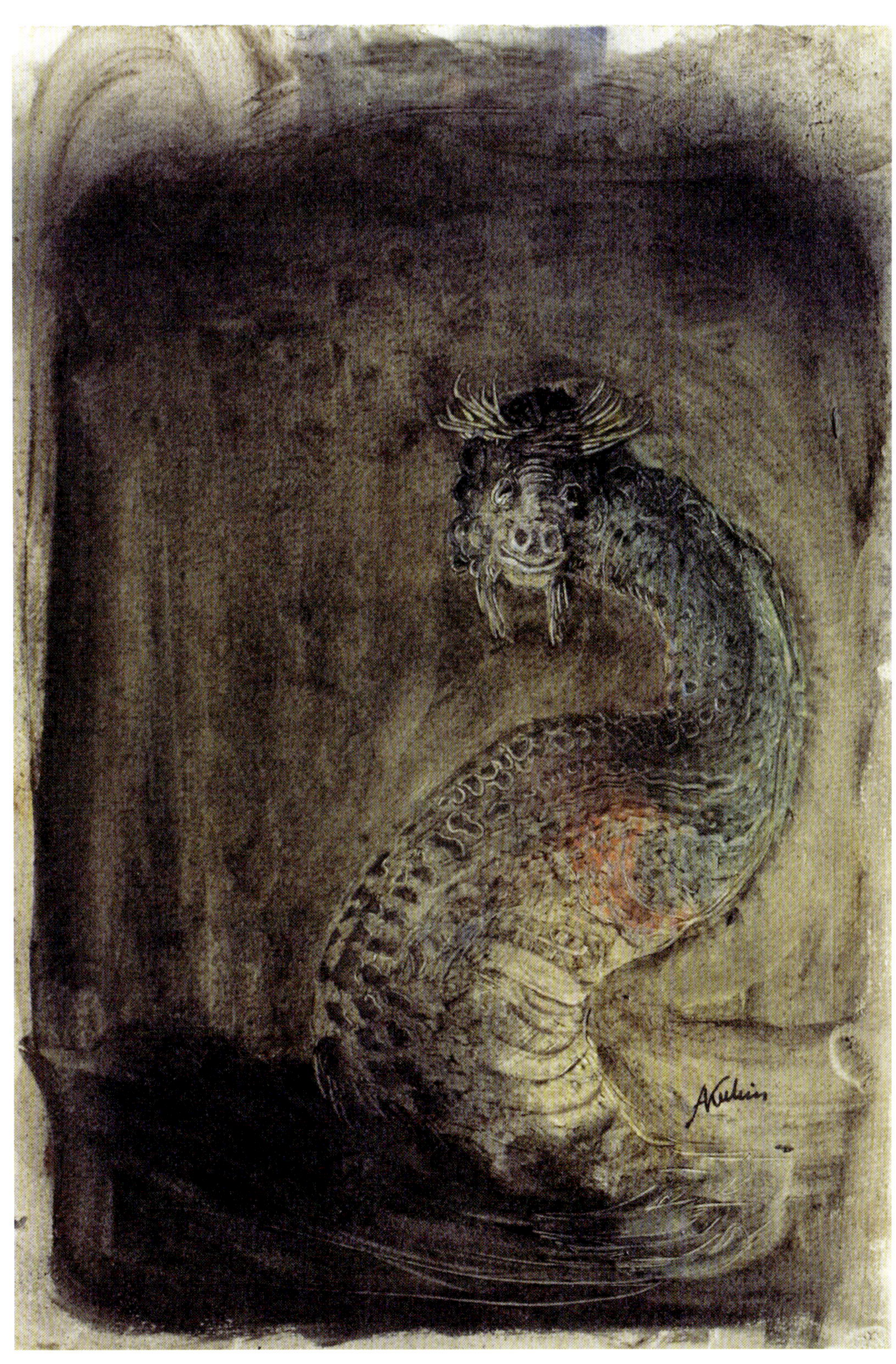

ALFRED KUBIN
The Sea Serpent, 1905/06
Leopold Museum, Vienna

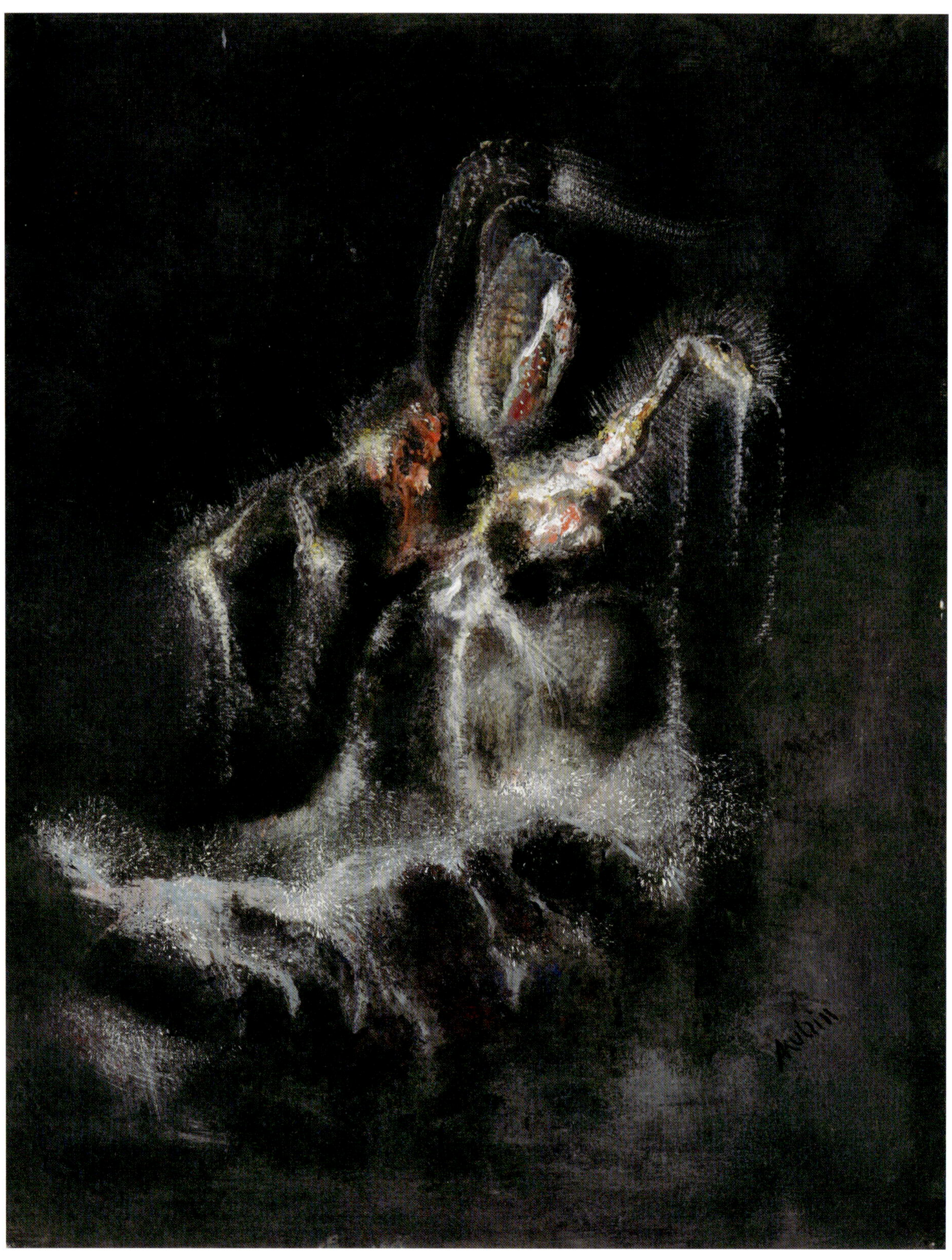

ALFRED KUBIN
Fabulous Creature, c. 1905/06
Albertina, Vienna. Forberg Collection (Inv. DL581)

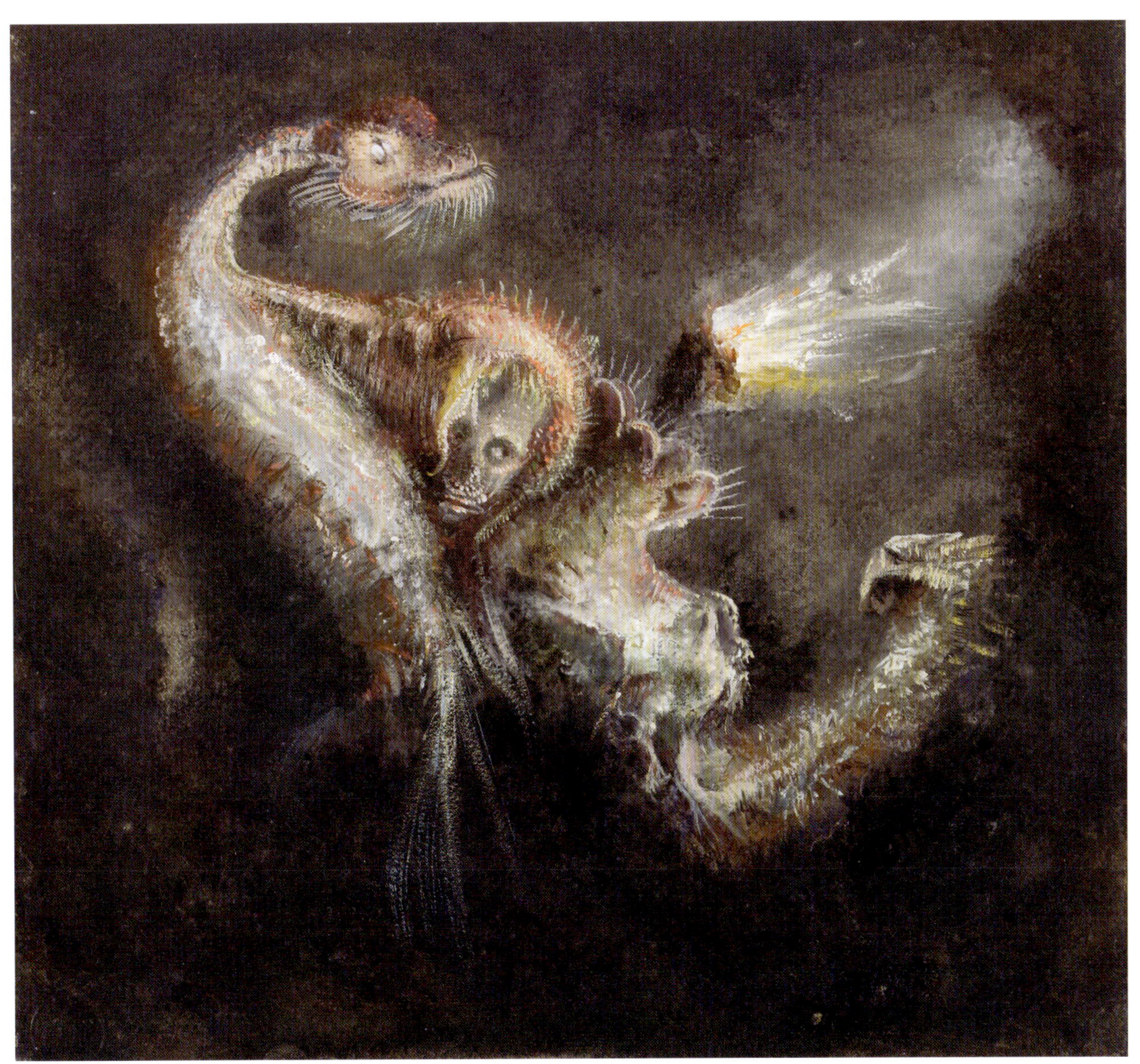

ALFRED KUBIN
Witch and Water Serpent, 1906
Leopold Museum, Vienna

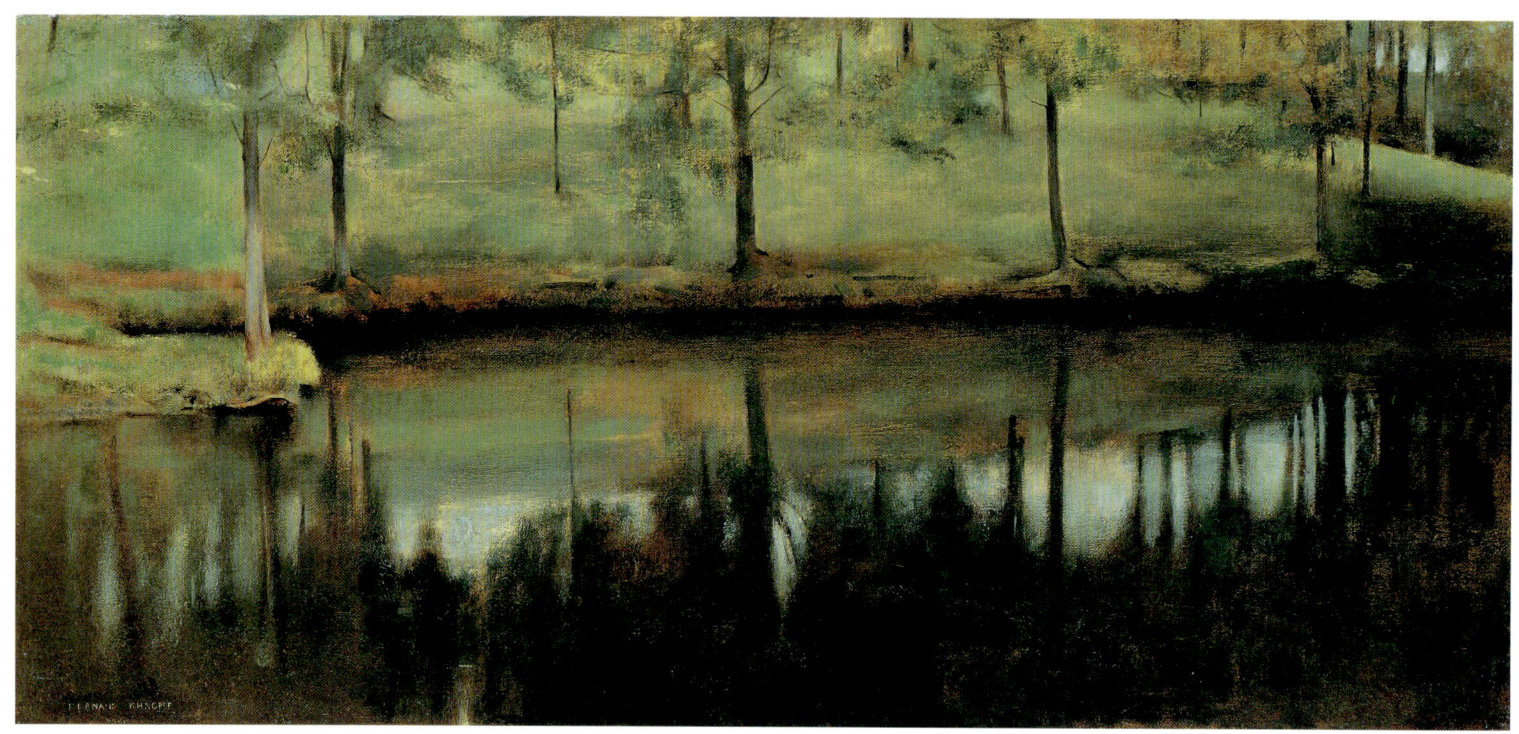

FERNAND KHNOPFF
Unmoved Water. The Pond of Ménil, 1894
Belvedere, Vienna

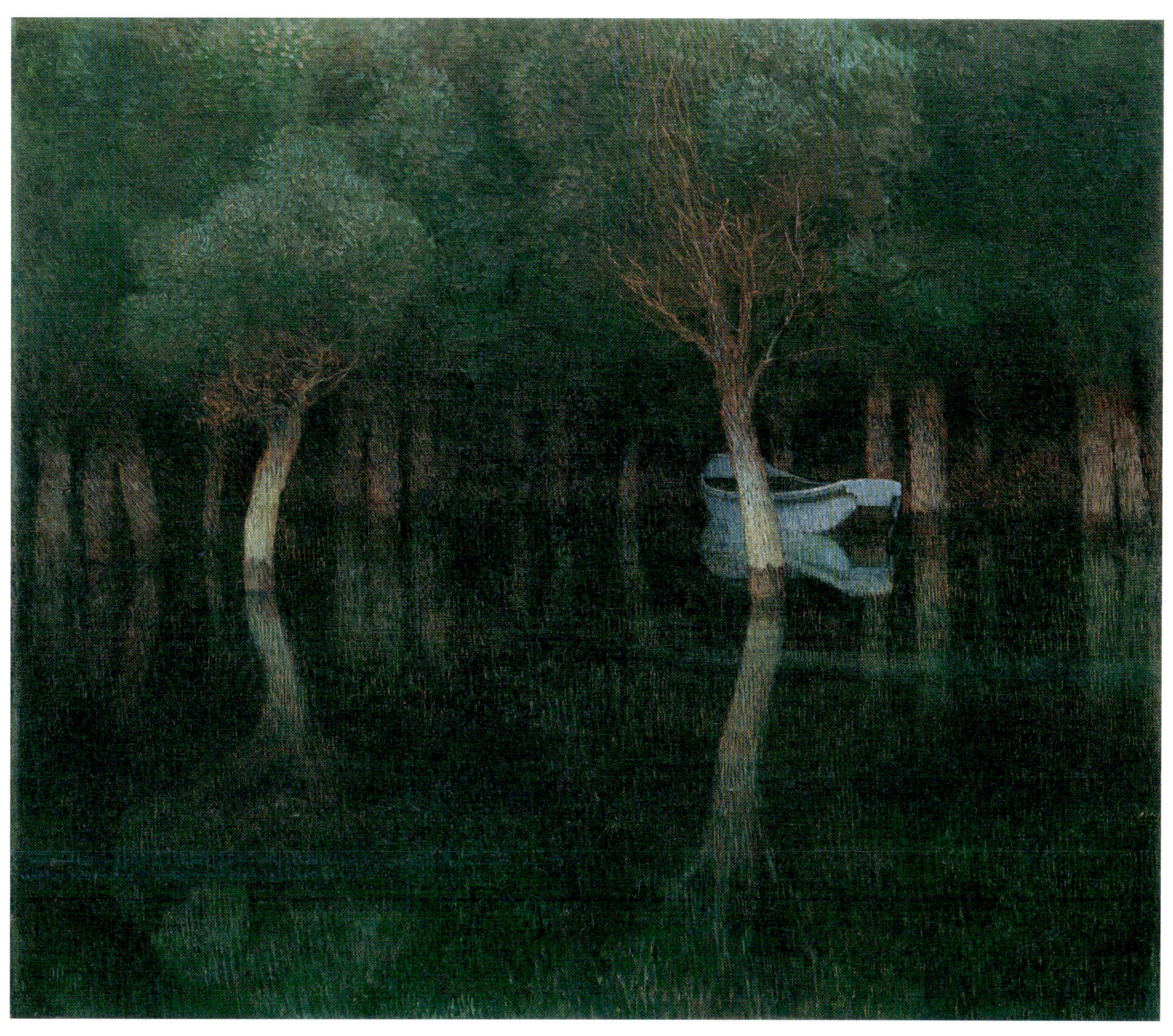

CARL MOLL
Twilight, 1900
Belvedere, Vienna

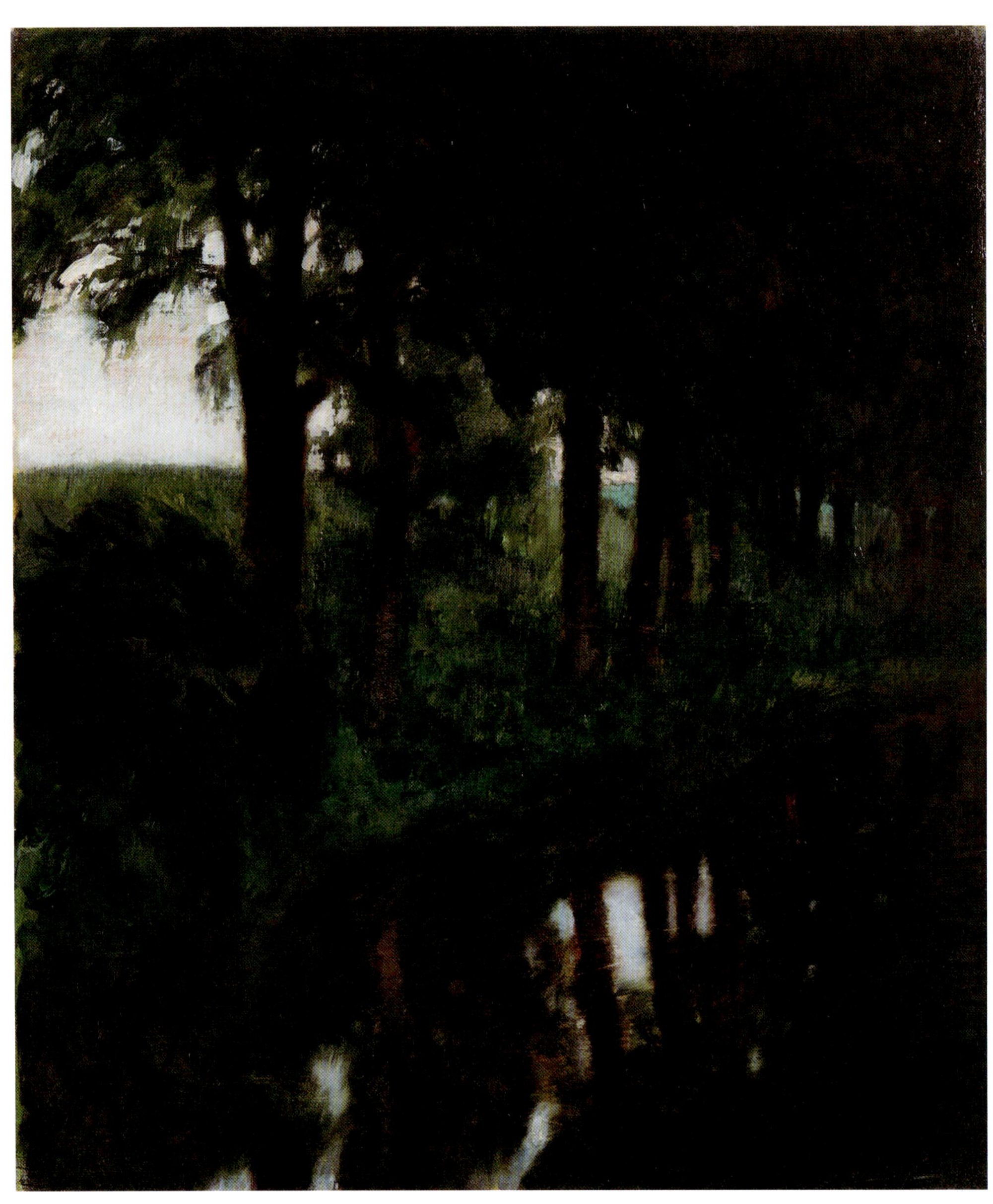

FRANZ VON STUCK
Trout Pond, 1890
Leopold Museum, Vienna

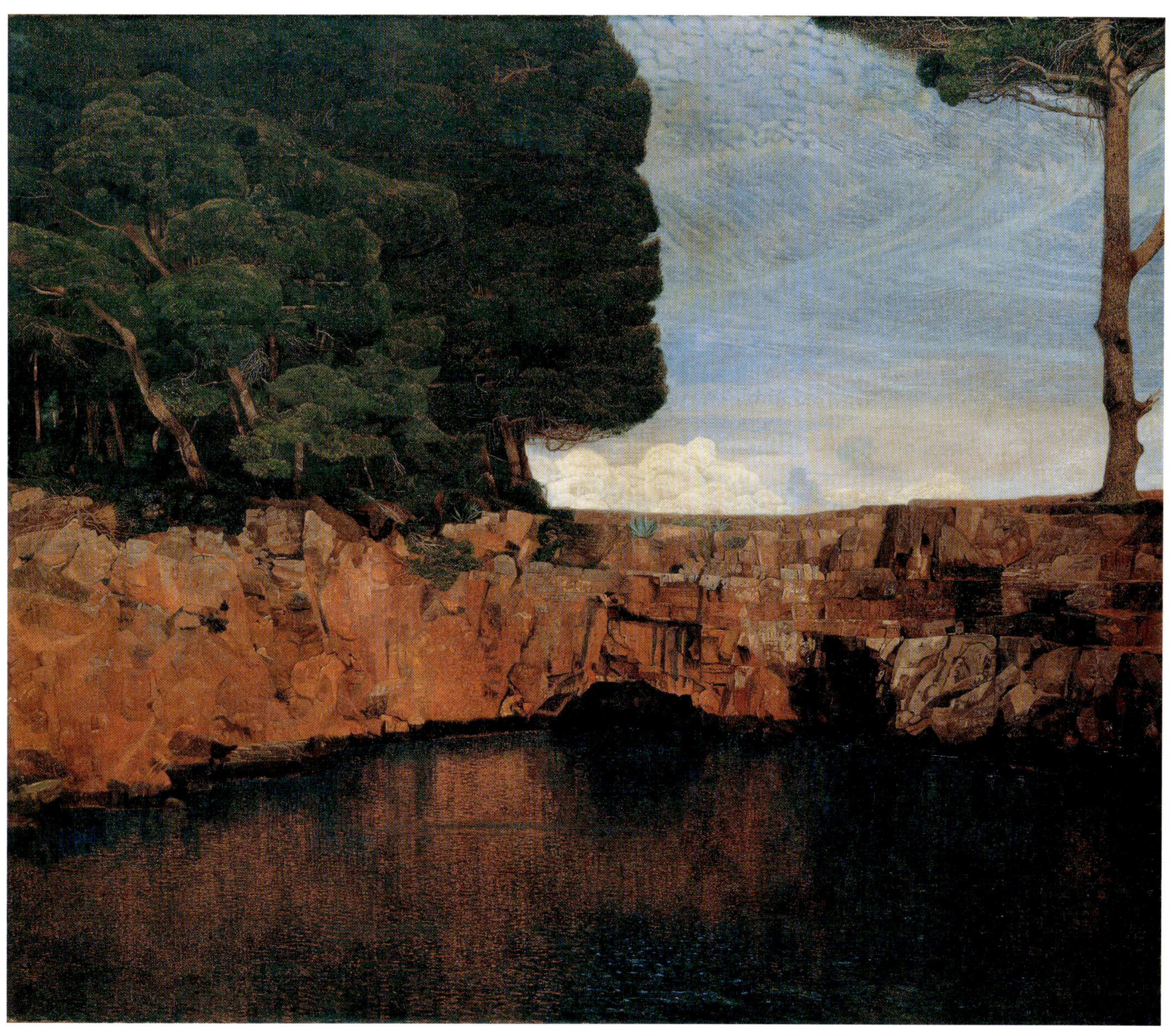

KARL MEDIZ
Solitude. Motif from Lacrona, c. 1902/03
Belvedere, Vienna

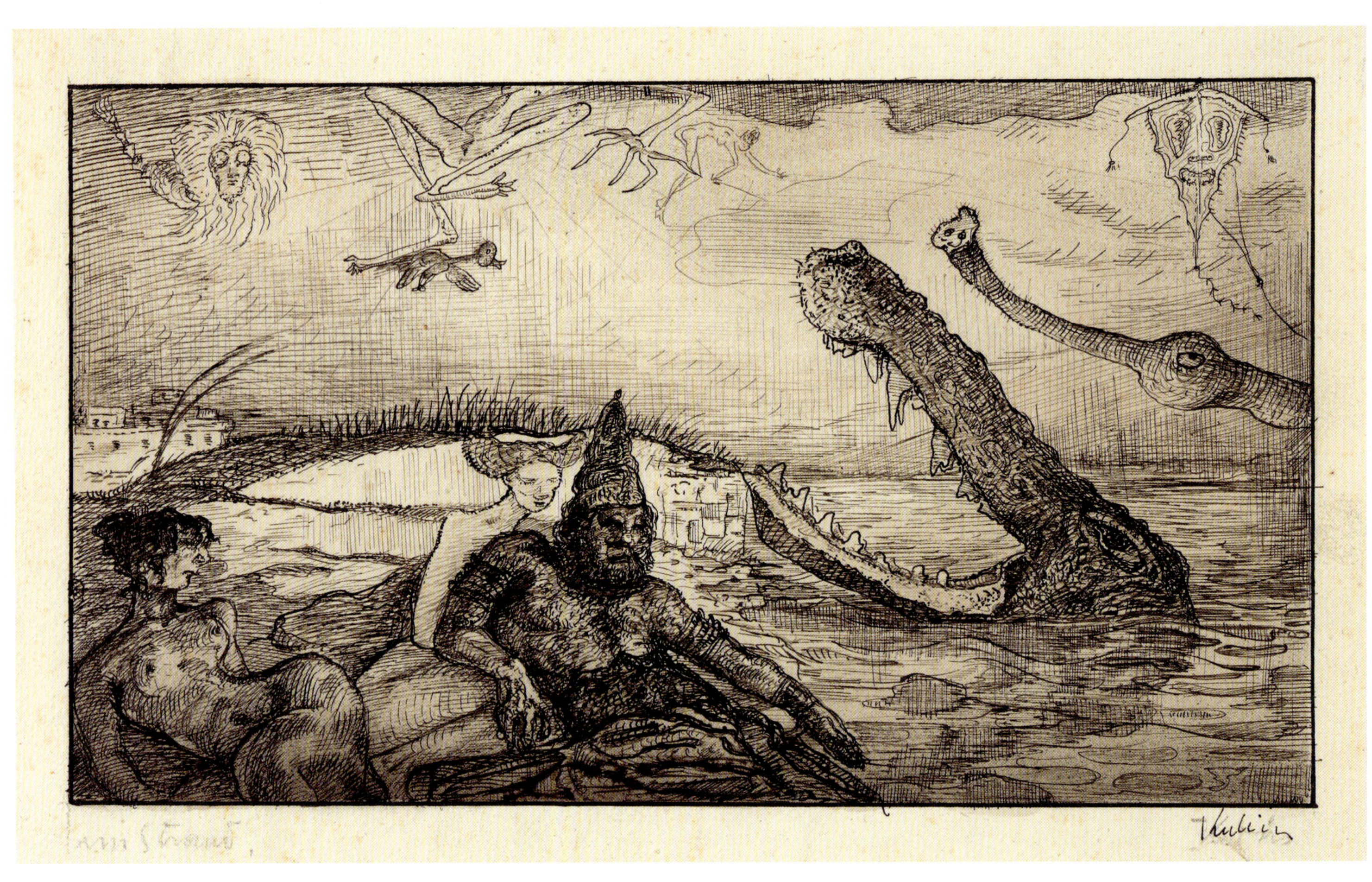

ALFRED KUBIN
On the Beach, Wreckage, c. 1918
Leopold, Private Collection

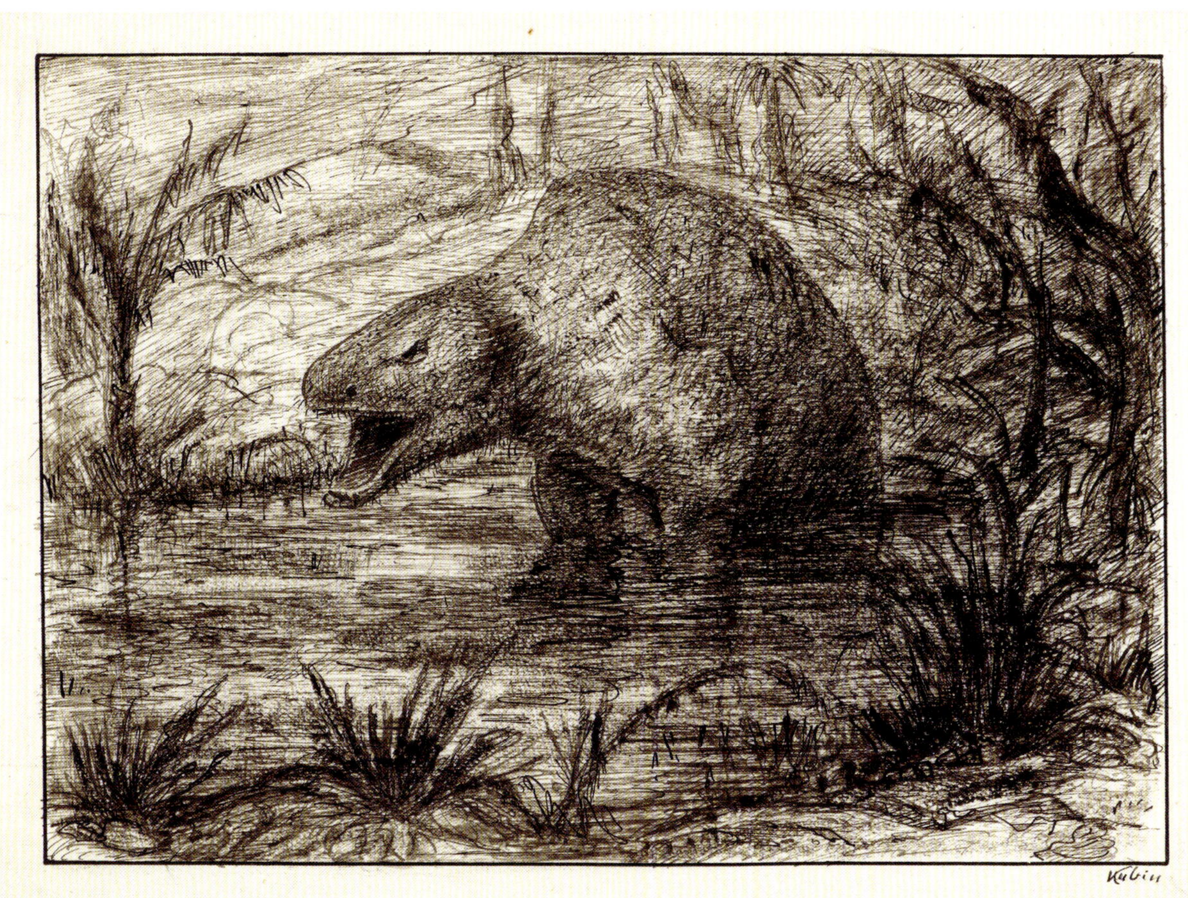

ALFRED KUBINS
The Animal in the Swamp, c. 1904
Leopold Museum, Vienna

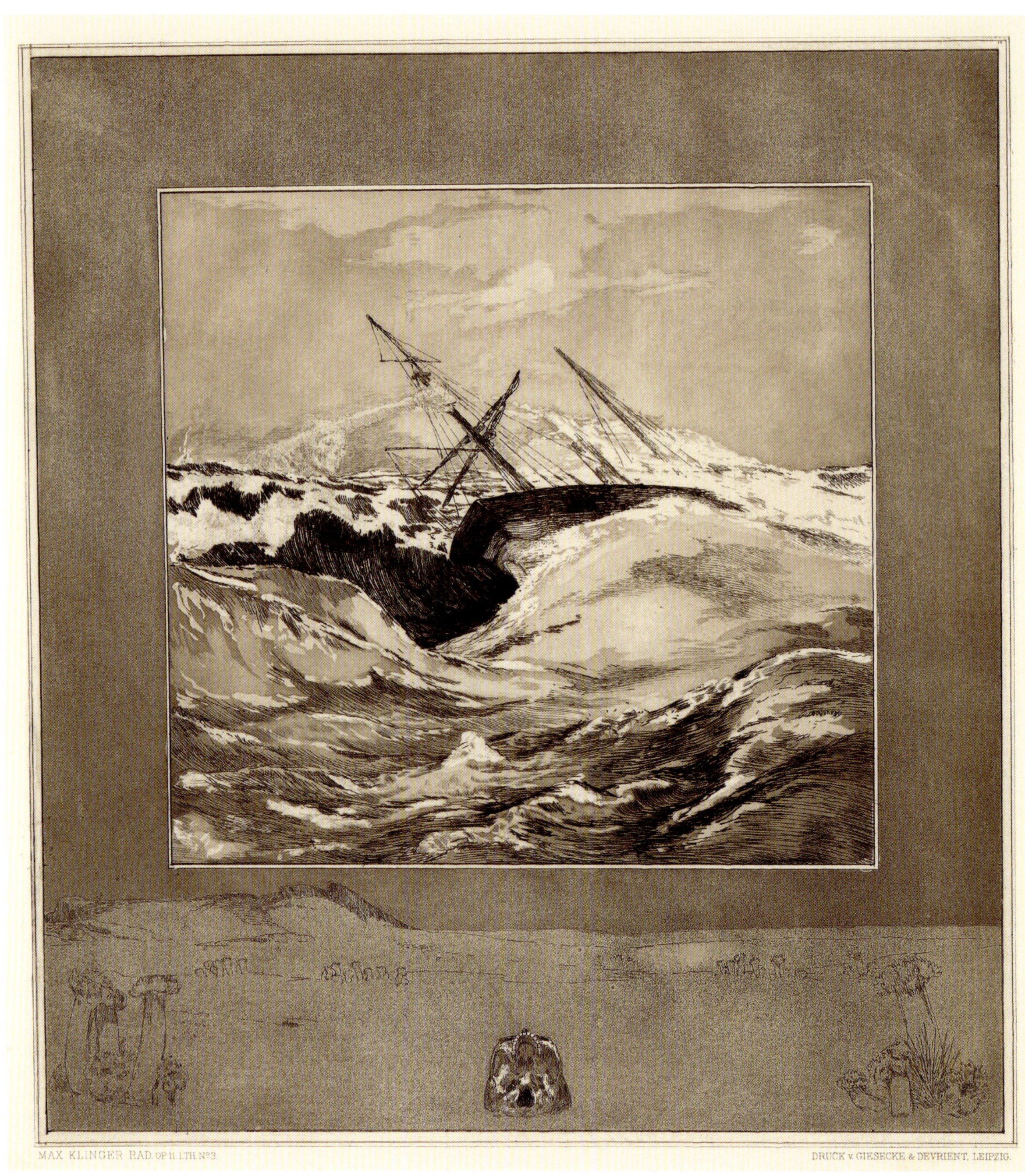

MAX KLINGER
Sea, from the cycle *On Death. Part 1,* 1897
Leopold Museum, Vienna

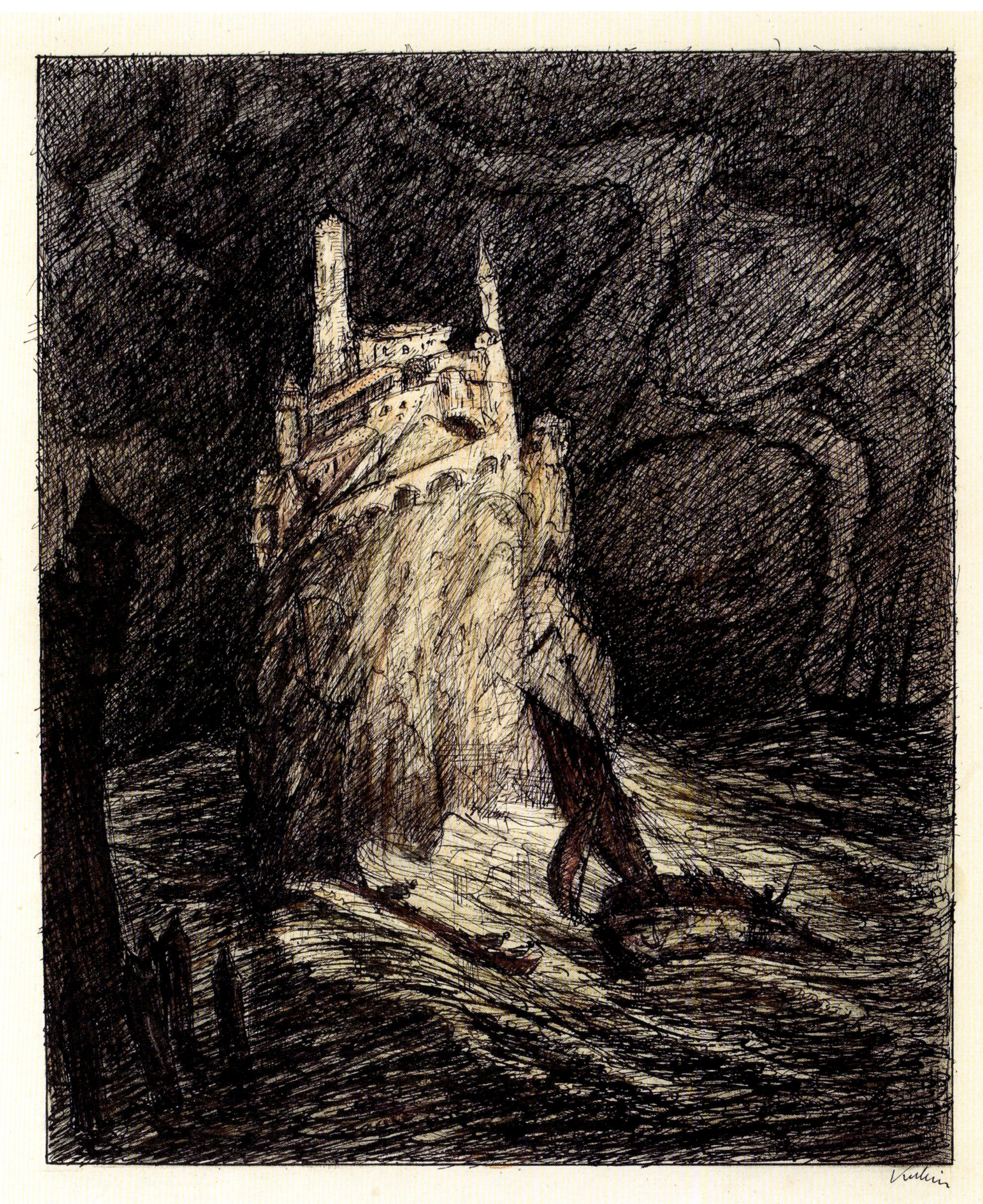

ALFRED KUBIN
The Castle in the Sea, 1910/11
Leopold Museum, Vienna

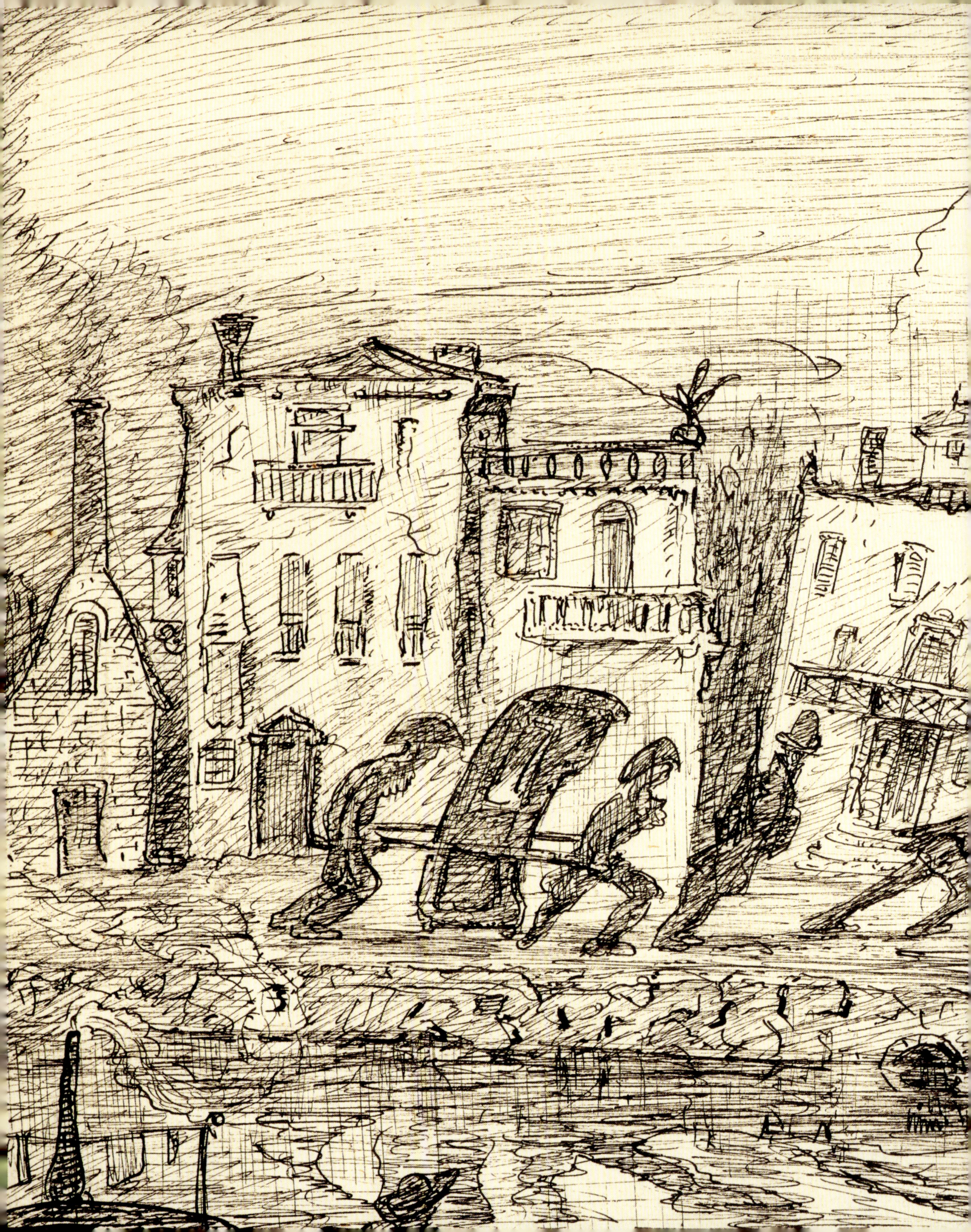

EERIE PLACES

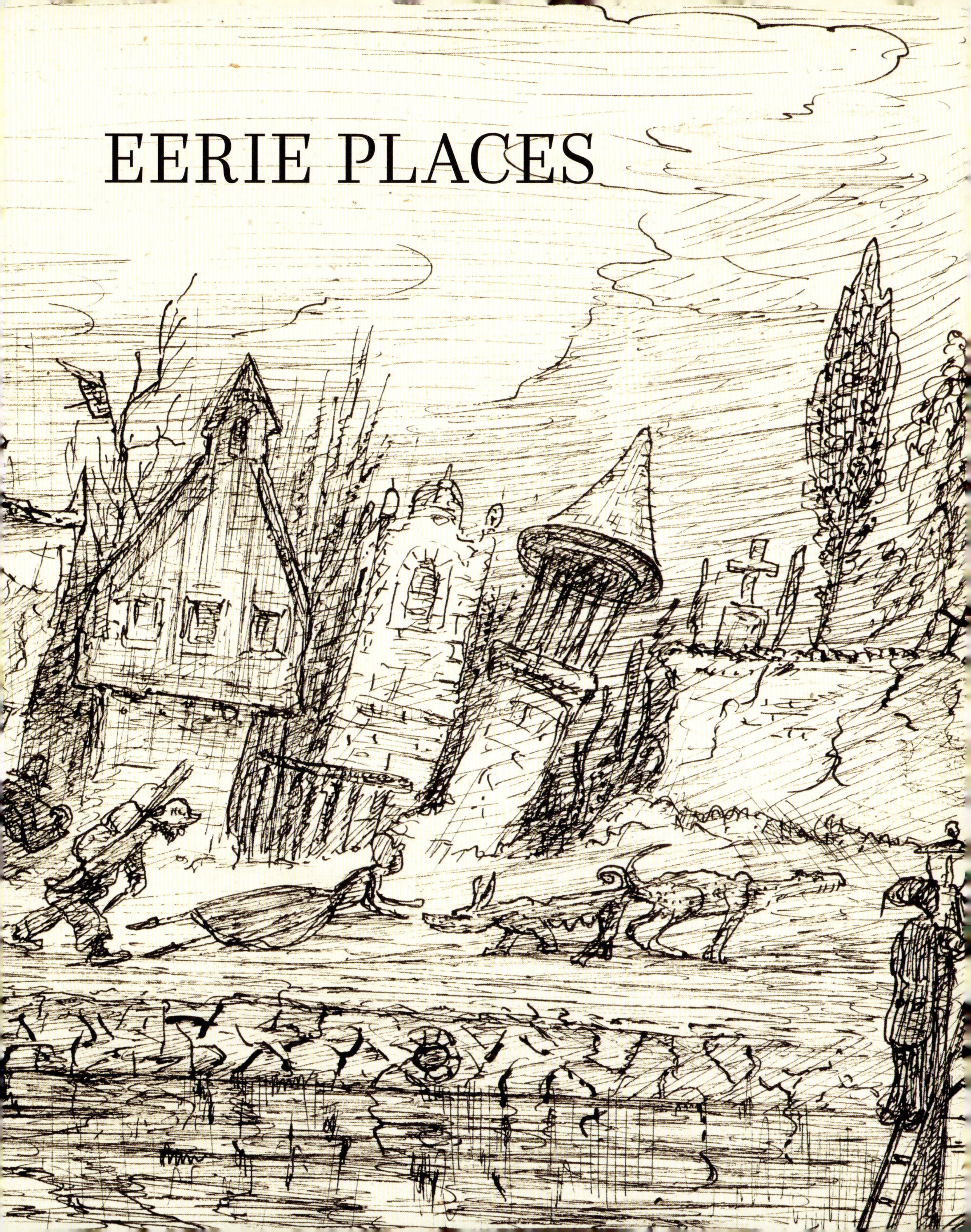

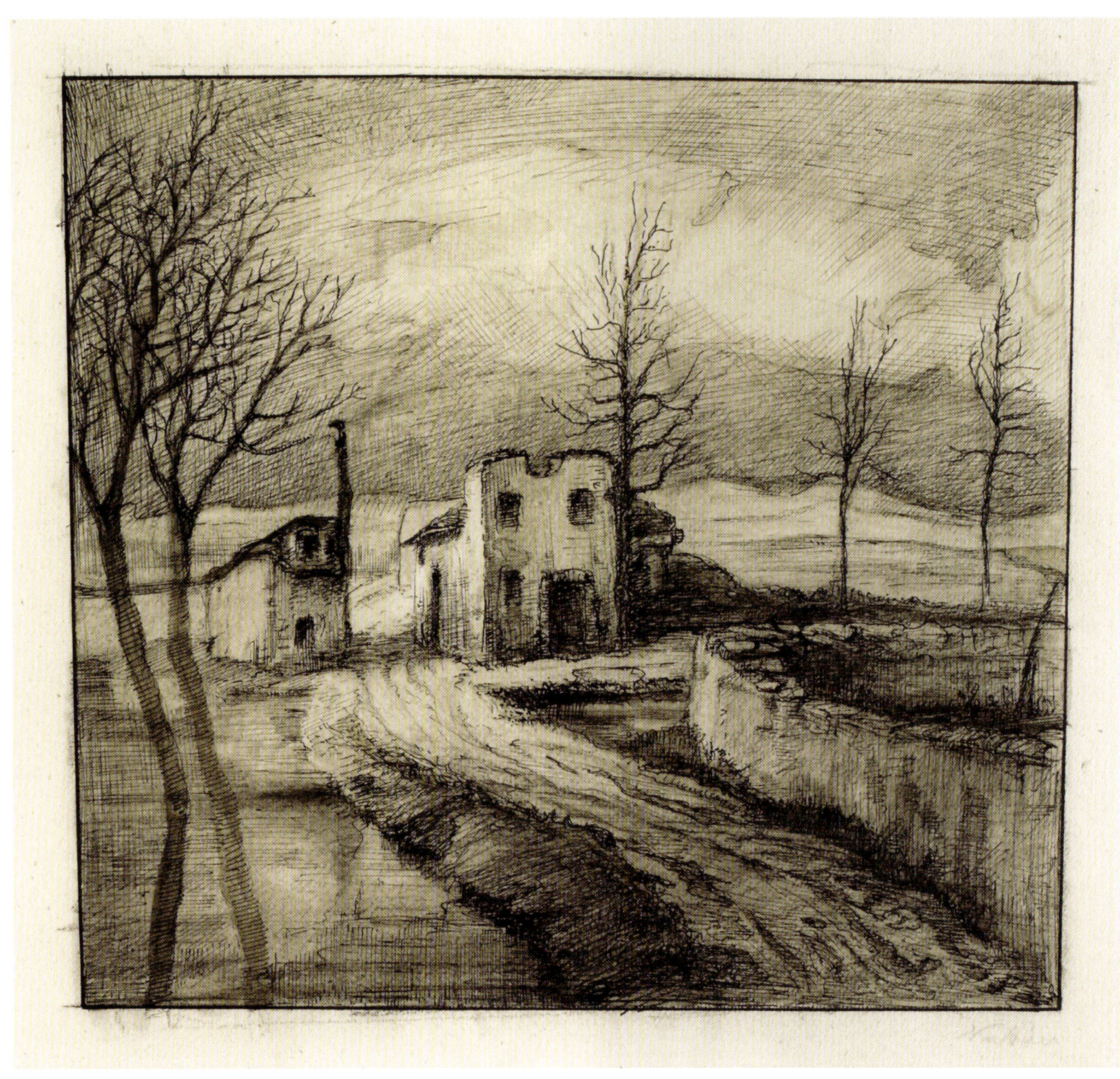

ALFRED KUBIN
Disreputable Place, 1903/04
Leopold Museum, Vienna

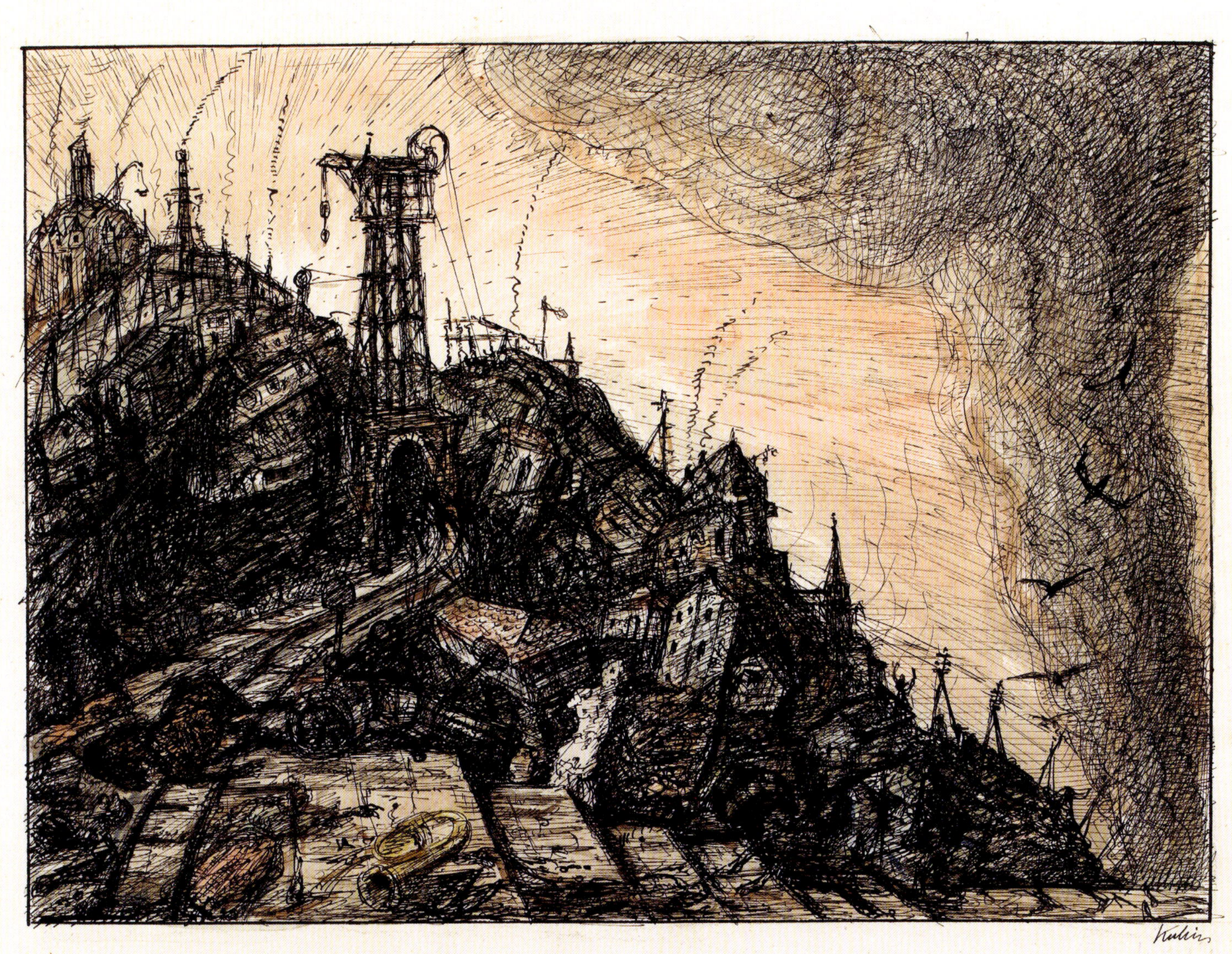

ALFRED KUBIN
Downfall, 1910/11
Leopold Museum, Vienna

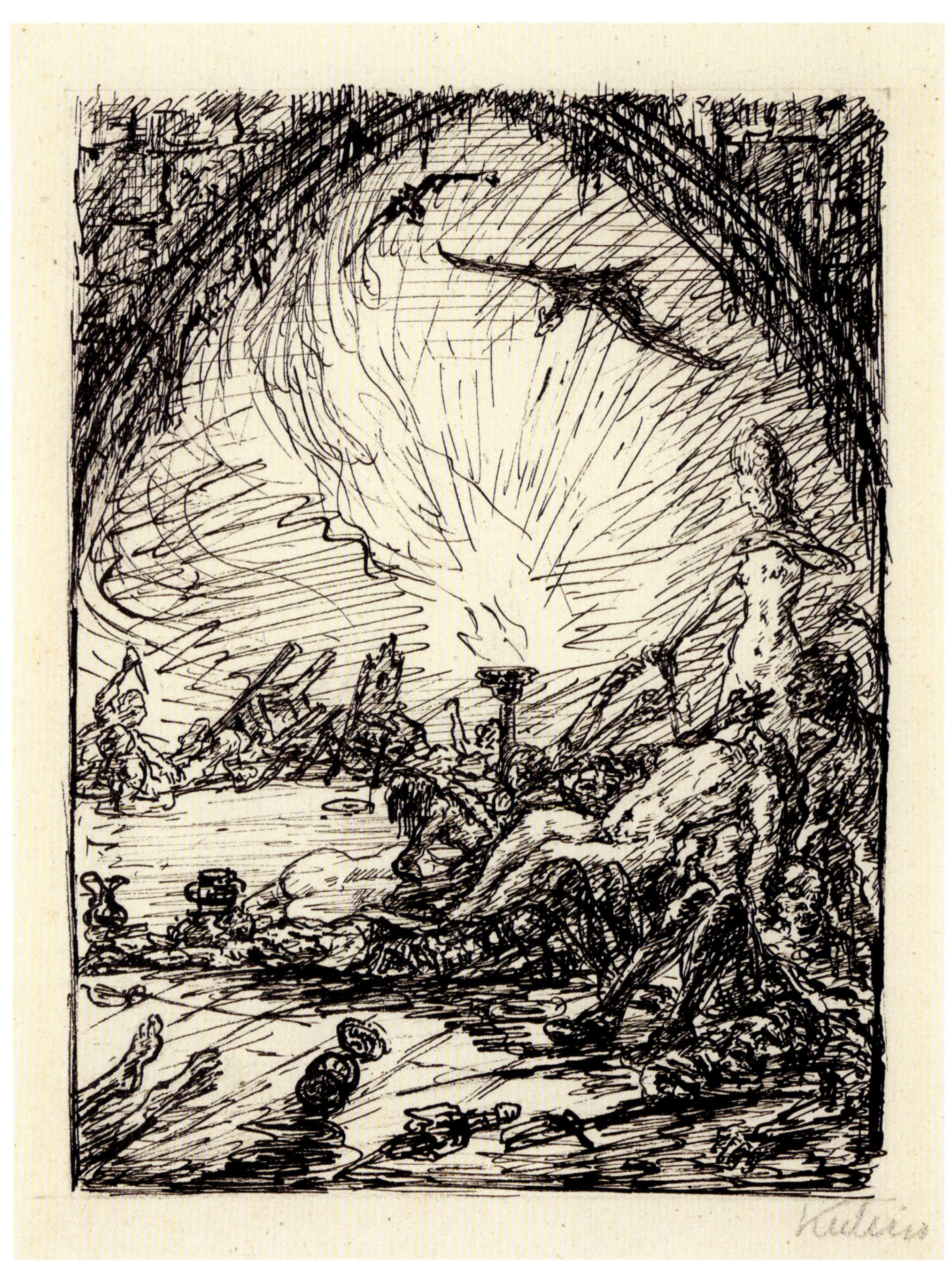

ALFRED KUBIN
Nighttime, 1913
Private Collection, Austria

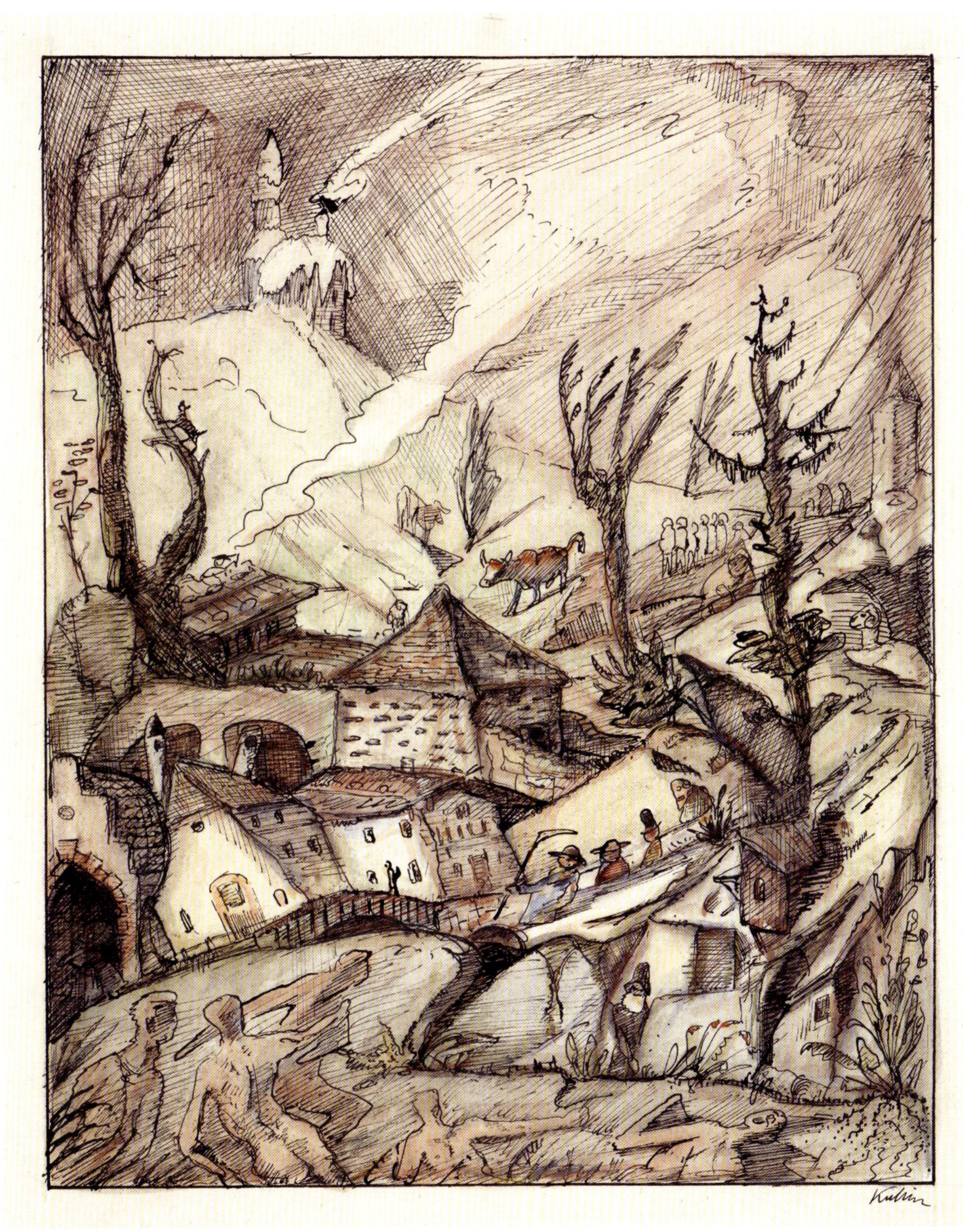

ALFRED KUBIN
The Earth Trembles, c. 1912
Leopold Museum, Vienna

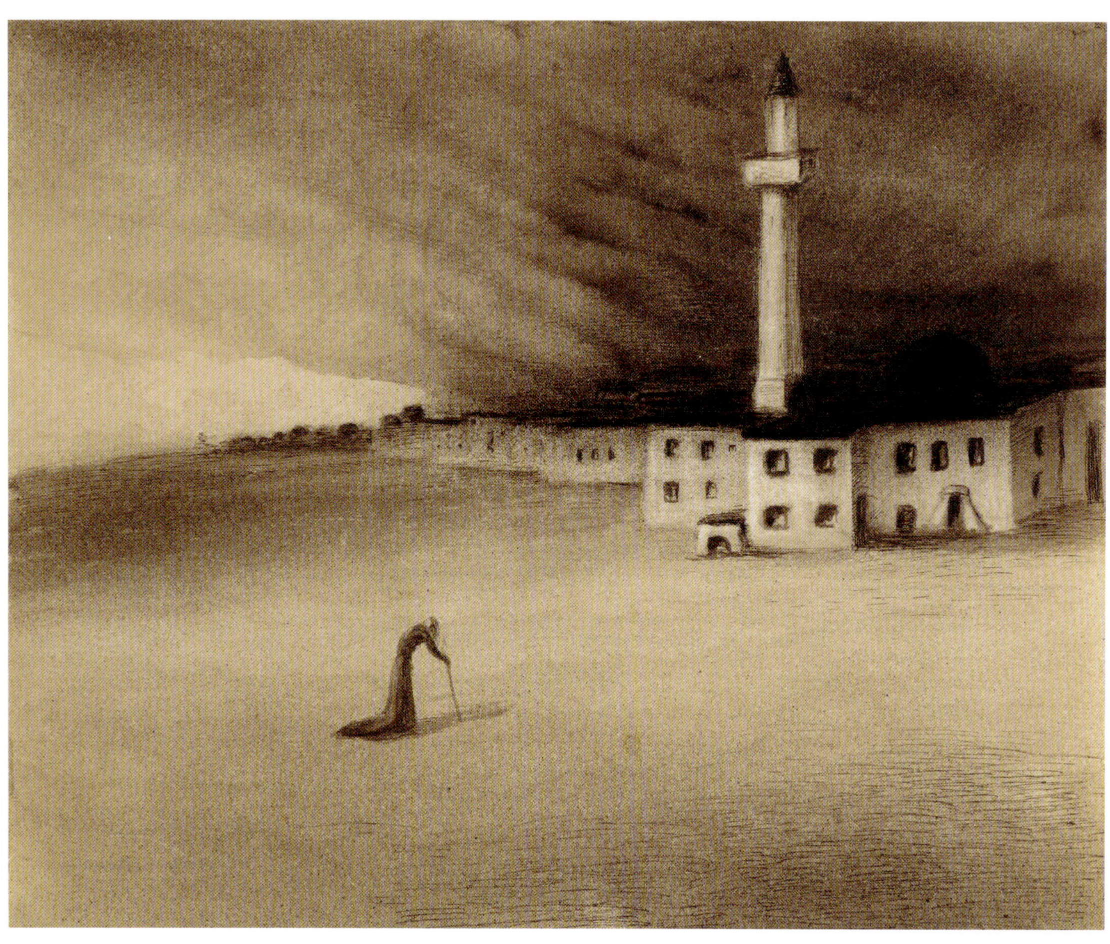

ALFRED KUBIN
The City Towards the East, 1903/04
Leopold Museum, Vienna

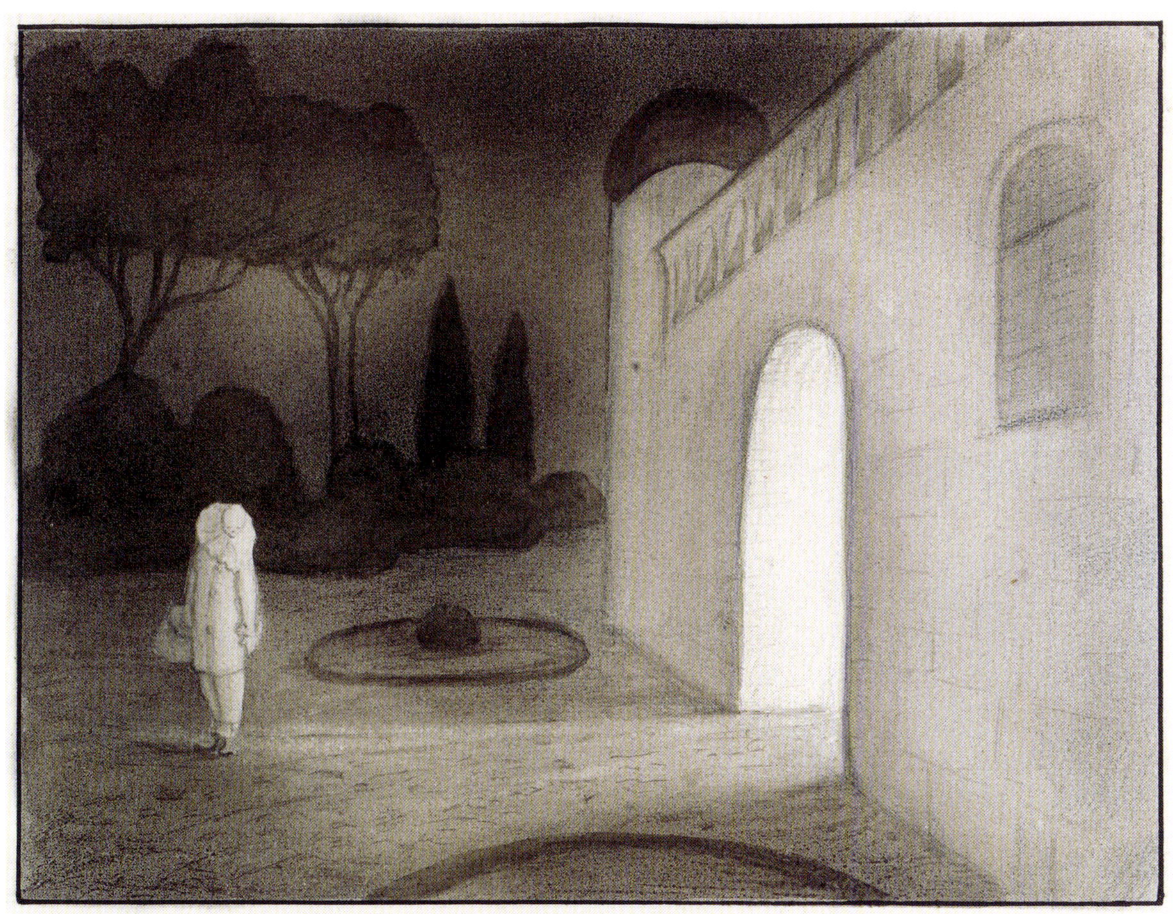

ALFRED KUBIN
Gallant Landscape, c. 1905
Leopold, Private Collection

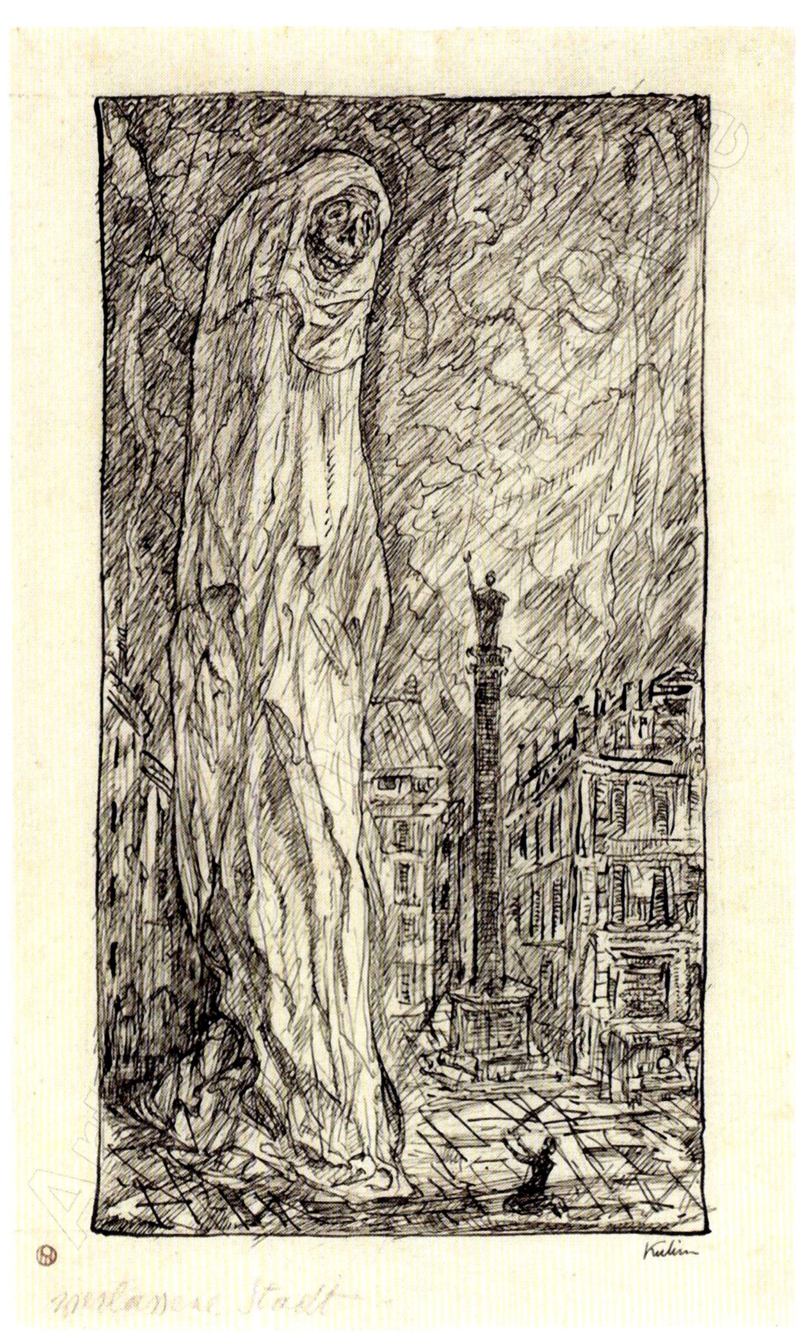

ALFRED KUBIN
Deserted Town, 1916
Private Collection

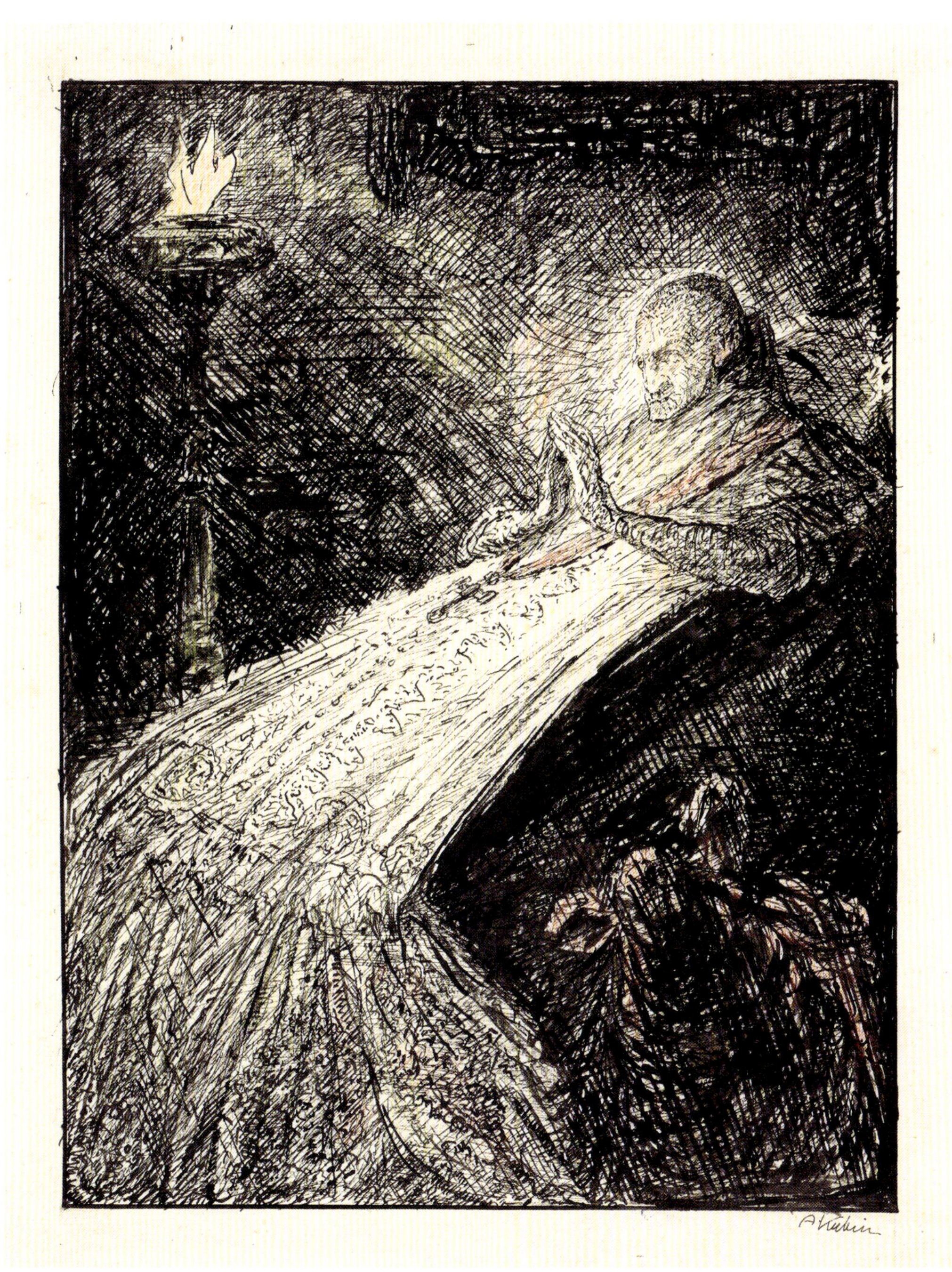

ALFRED KUBIN
The Cardinal, c. 1908/11
Lentos Kunstmuseum Linz

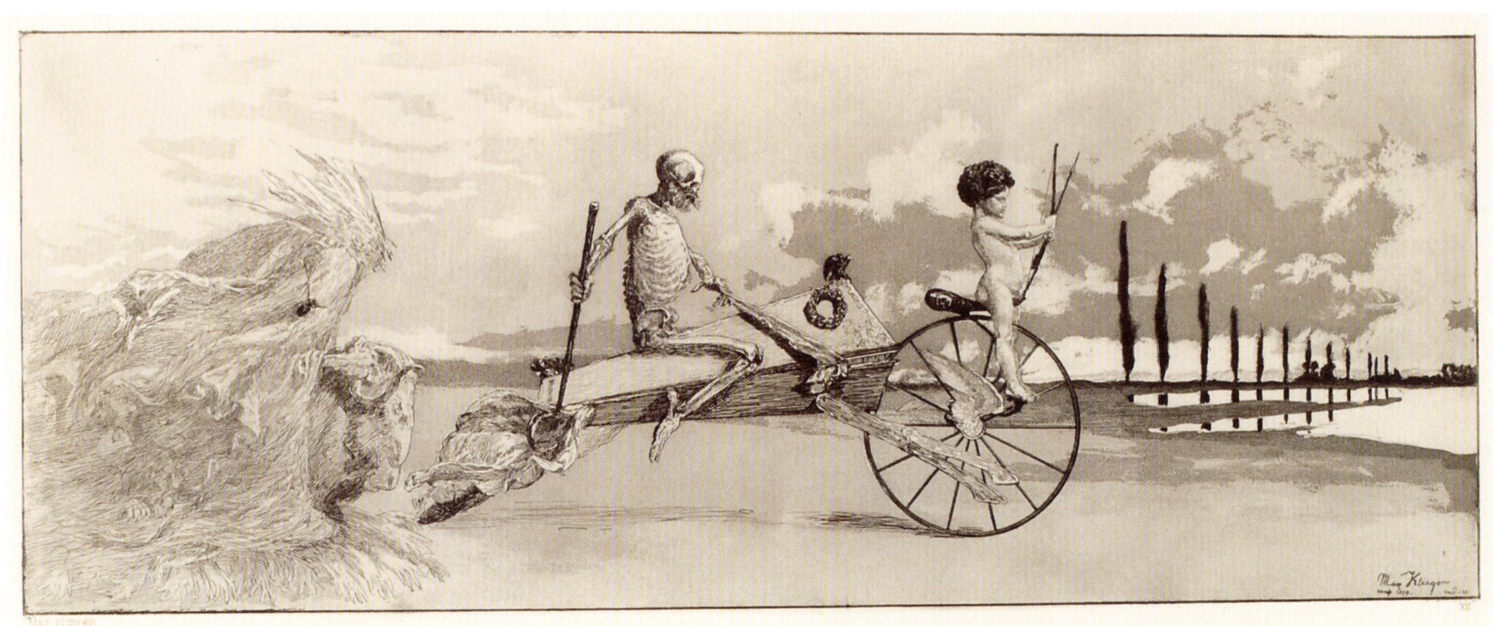

MAX KLINGER
Amor, Death and the Beyond, from the cycle *Intermezzi*, 1881
Private Collection Vienna

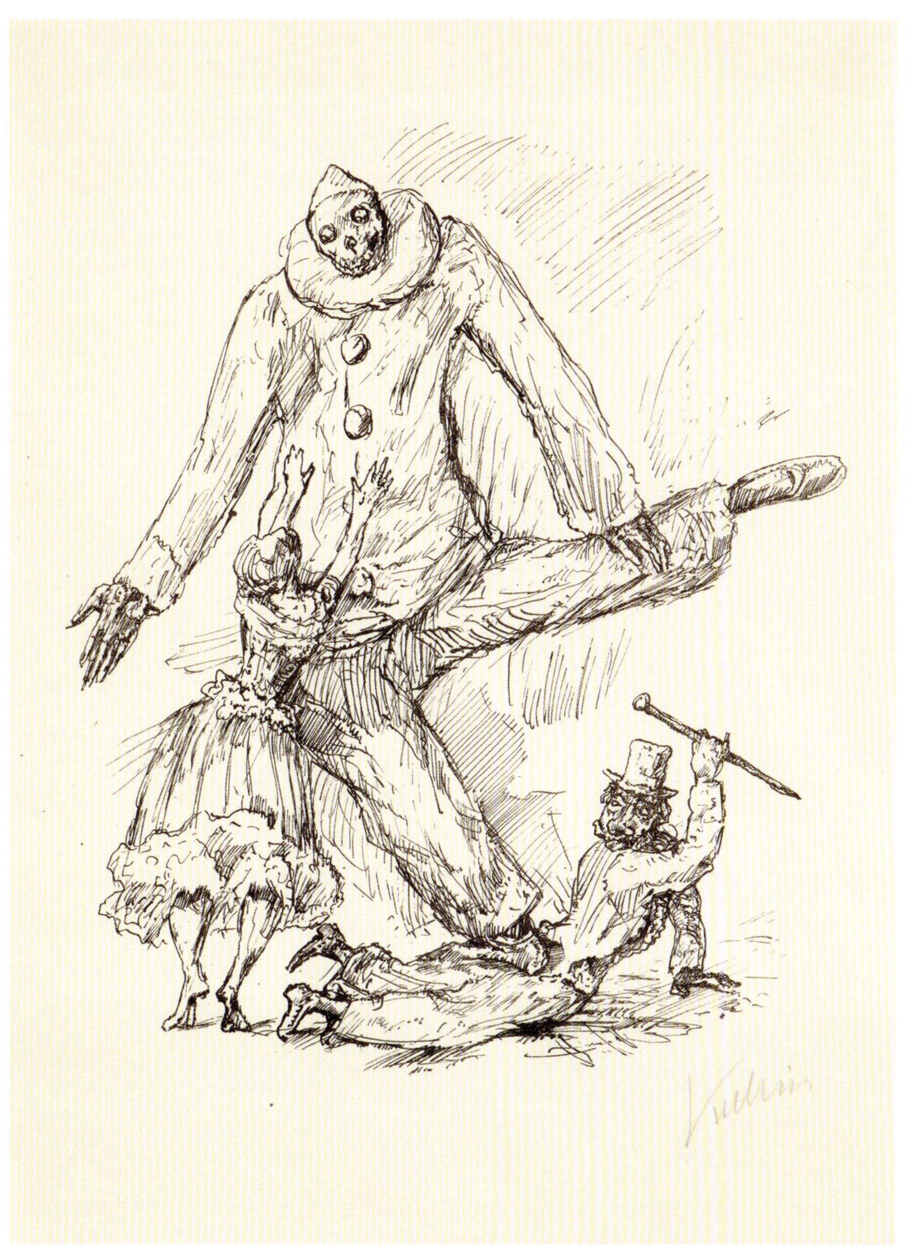

ALFRED KUBIN
Death as a Dancer, 1922
Leopold Museum, Vienna

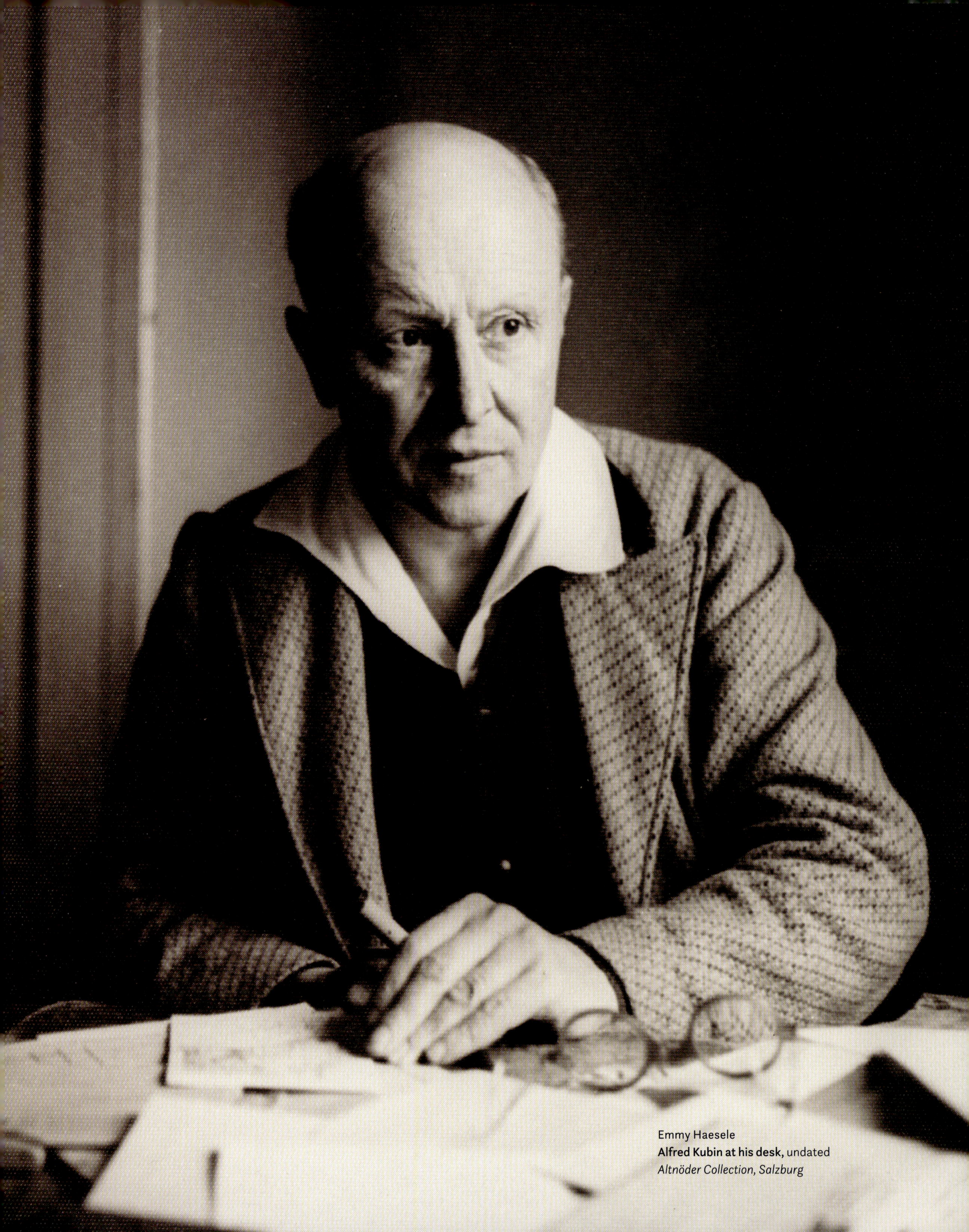

Emmy Haesele
Alfred Kubin at his desk, undated
Altnöder Collection, Salzburg

BIOGRAPHY

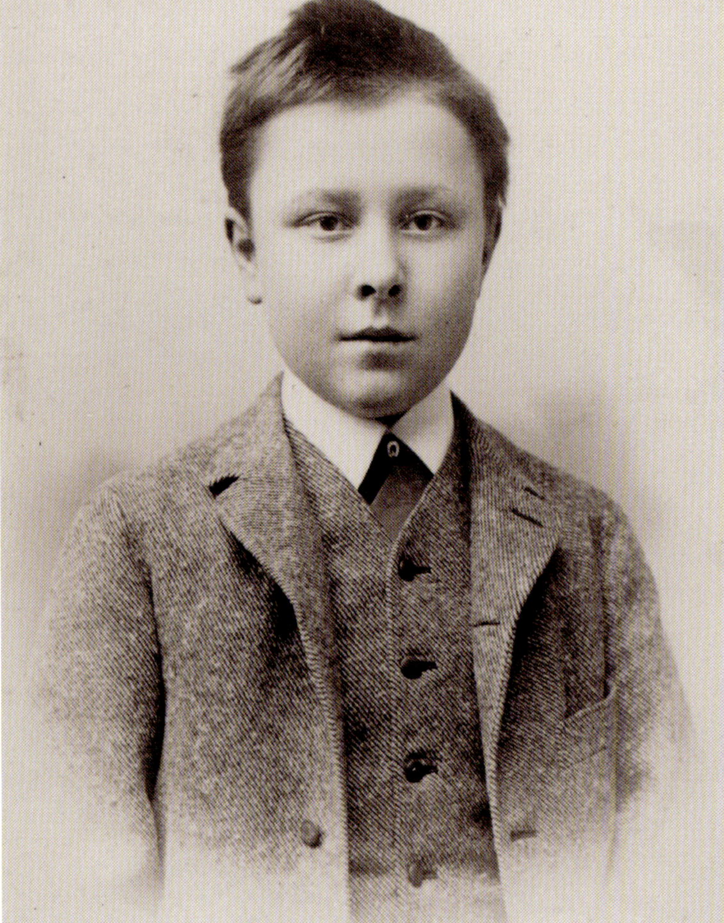

01

01 Anonymous photographer
Alfred Kubin, c. 1893
Städtische Galerie im Lenbachhaus und Kunstbau München

02 Anonymous photographer
Friedrich Franz Kubin, Alfred Kubin's father, May 1893
Städtische Galerie im Lenbachhaus und Kunstbau München

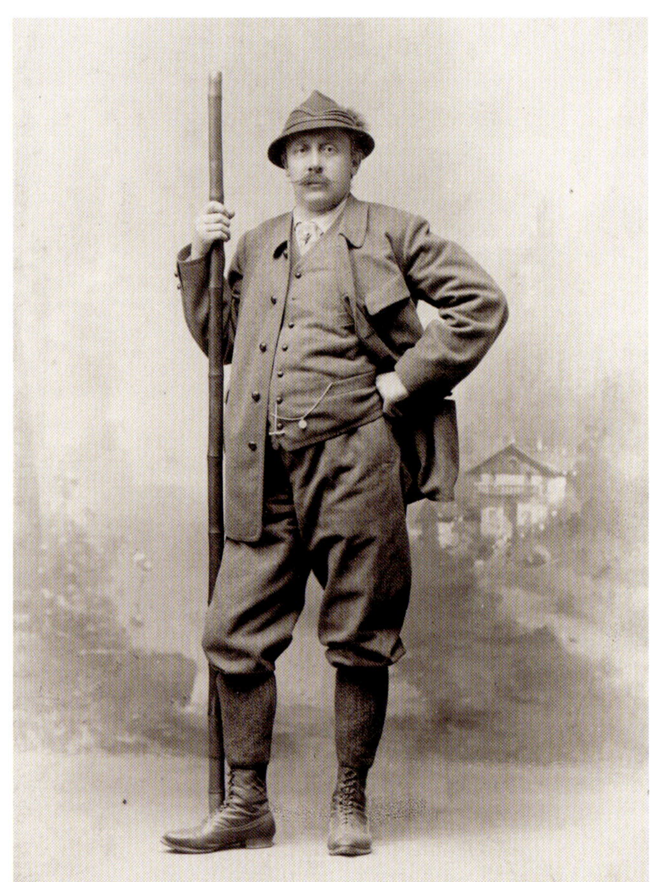

02

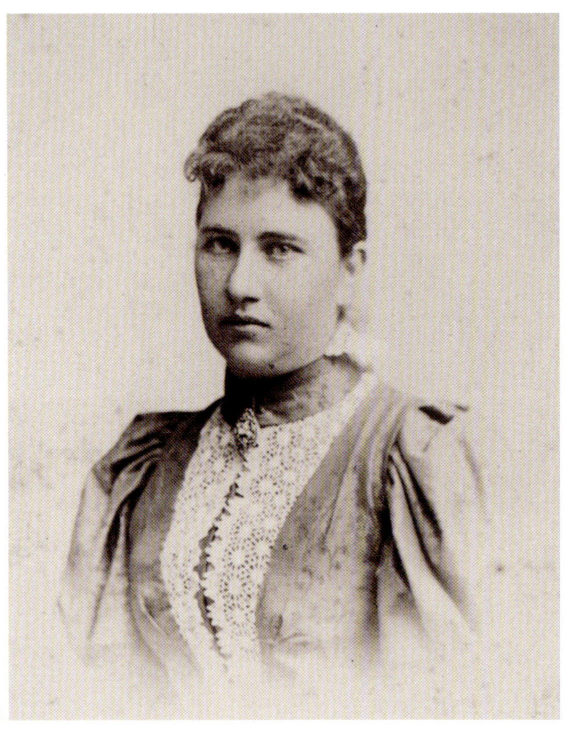

03

03 Alois Beer
Irene Kubin, one of Kubin's stepmothers, 1897
Altnöder Collection, Salzburg

Compiled by Lena Scholz

04 Anonymous photographer
The Kubin family: Alfred Kubin, his sister Maria (center), the stepsisters Rosalie and Friederike, the stepmother Irene and his father Friedrich Franz, 1902
Städtische Galerie im Lenbachhaus und Kunstbau München

1877

Alfred Leopold Isidor Kubin was born on April 10, 1877, as the first child of senior surveyor Friedrich Franz Kubin (1848–1907) and pianist Johanna Kubin, née Kletzl (1847–1887) in Leitmeritz (Litoměřice) in Northern Bohemia (today: Czech Republic). (01)

1879–1883

While Kubin's father went on to work as a land surveyor in Dalmatia, Johanna moved to Salzburg with her son, where Kubin's sister Marie was born in 1881. In 1883, the family relocated to Zell am See where Alfred Kubin also spent his elementary-school years. (02)

1887

In 1887, Kubin's sister Friederike was born. On May 8 of that year, the family suffered a heavy stroke of fate, when Johanna Kubin died from consumption (tuberculosis), leaving behind his father with three children. In the following September, he married his late wife's sister, Rosa Kletzl. She, too, died in childbed one year later, after giving birth to Kubin's half-sister Rosalie.

1888–1891

After two years of grammar school in Salzburg, with only moderate success, Kubin left school without qualifications to return to community school in Zell am See in 1891. His father married his third wife, Irene Kühnel (03 & 04). 14-year-old Alfred went back to Salzburg for an arts-and-crafts education at the State Trade School, but his grades remained poor.

1892–1897

In 1892, Kubin started an apprenticeship as a photographer with his uncle Alois Beer in Klagenfurt, Carinthia. However, conflicts ran high during his time of working for his uncle as an apprentice, culminating in a suicide attempt by his mother's grave that Kubin himself later described in his autobiographical writings. Kubin's father sent his son back to Klagenfurt, but his uncle fired him on the spot. He then tried to join the army as a volunteer and was accepted in 1897 despite his feeble physical constitution. Already three weeks after he had entered military service he suffered a severe nervous crisis during the funeral of a division commander and was treated for several months at the garrison hospital in Graz. Following his discharge, he was able to return to his father in Zell am See where he stayed for a year. In that time, he occupied himself making numerous drawings as well as copies of pictures from illustrated magazines.

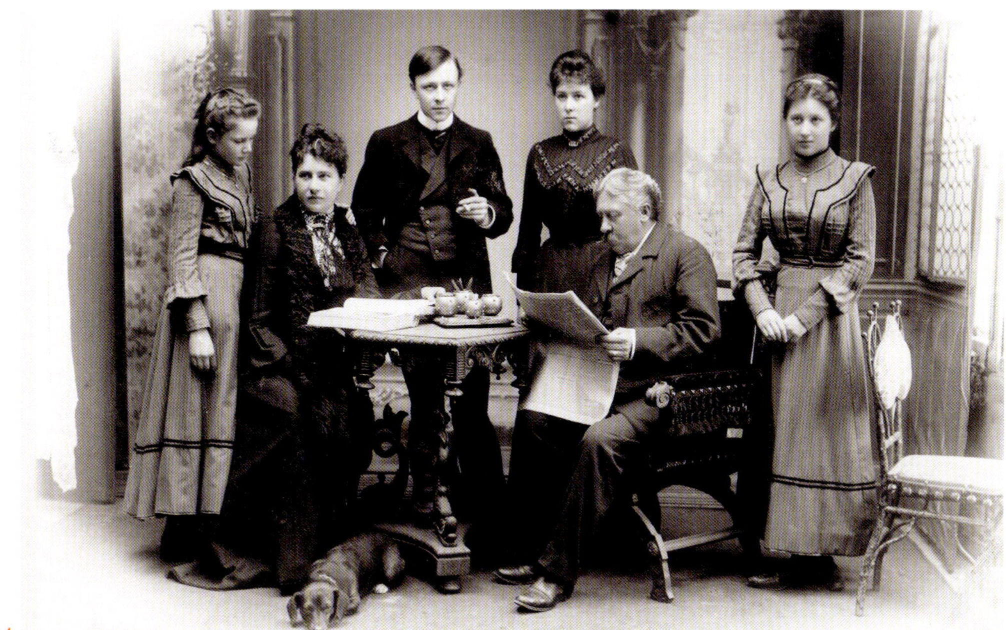
04

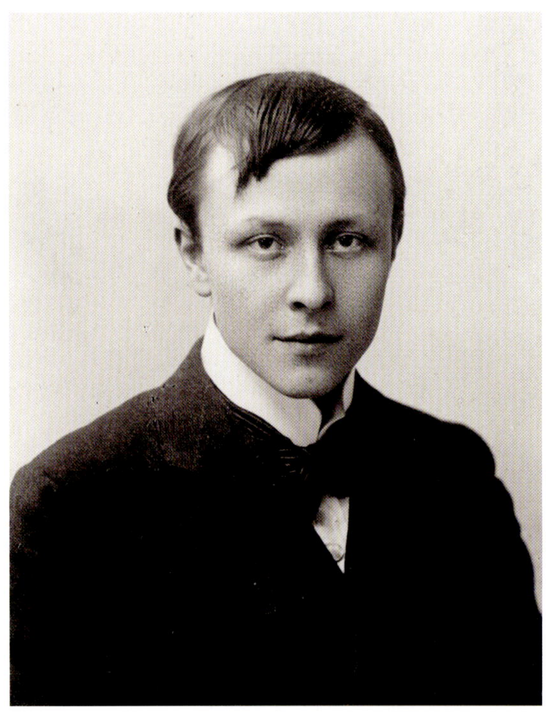

05

05 Anonymous photographer
Alfred Kubin in his first year in Munich, 1898
Städtische Galerie im Lenbachhaus und Kunstbau München

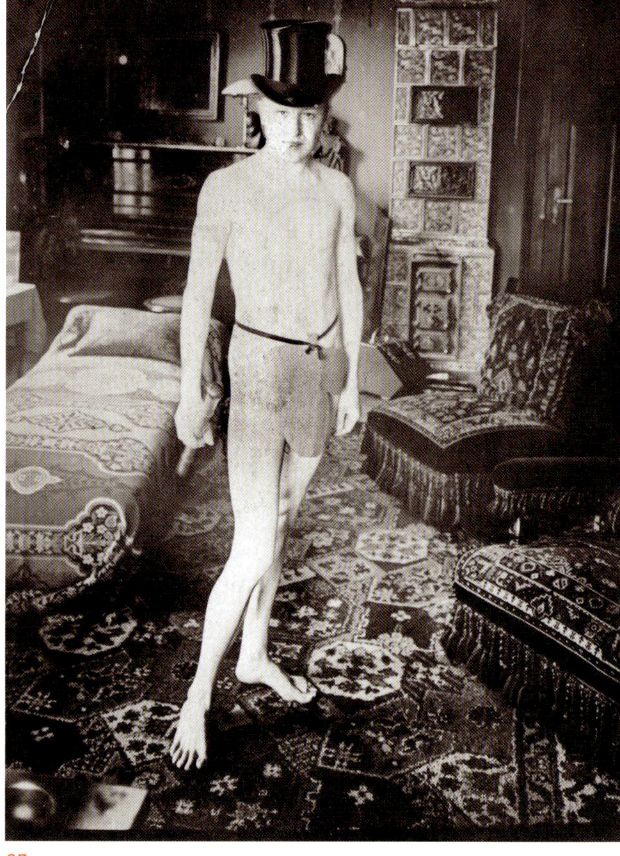

07

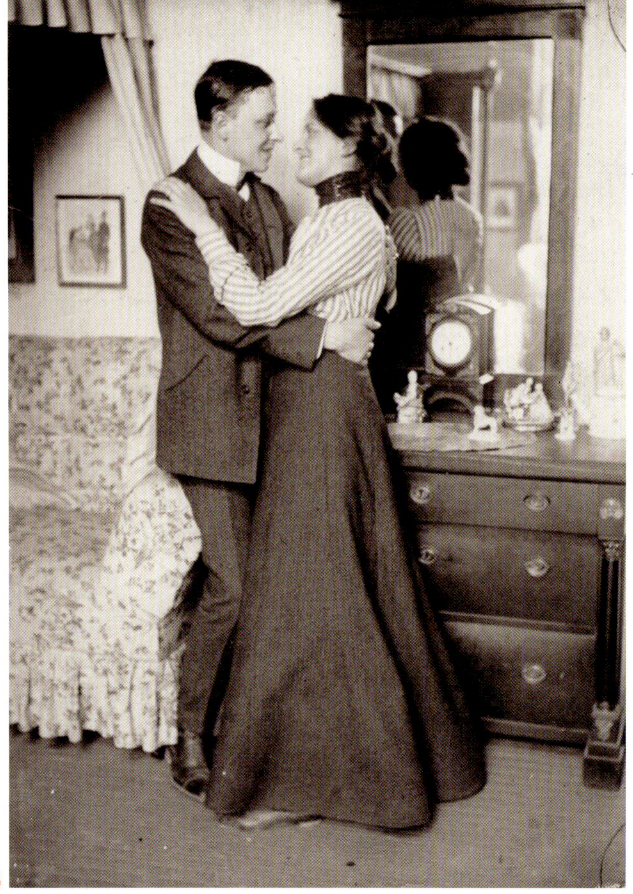

06

06 Anonymous photographer
Alfred Kubin and Emmy Bayer, 1903
Städtische Galerie im Lenbachhaus und Kunstbau München

07 Richard Ferdinand Schmitz
Alfred Kubin in Munich, 1904
Städtische Galerie im Lenbachhaus und Kunstbau München

08 Alfred Kubin
My Demon, early self-portrait, 1899
Private Collection, Austria

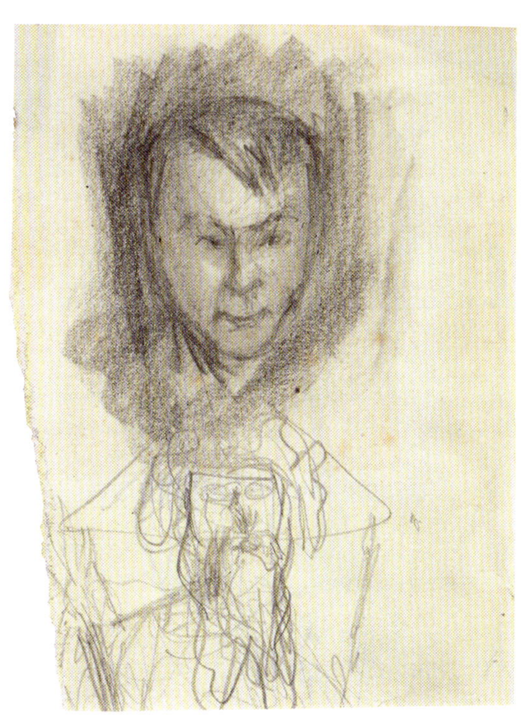
08

1898/99

On the advice of a friend of the family, Kubin was set up with a small inheritance from his grandparents and sent to Munich to study art (05). He first went to the private school of drawing of Ludwig Schmidt-Reutte and, from May 1899, enrolled for Nikolaus Gysis's drawing class at the Academy of Fine Arts. However, he attended class only sporadically and soon dropped out altogether. Visits to the Alte Pinakothek in Munich imbued him with great enthusiasm but also with massive doubt about his own artistic talent. His reading of Nietzsche and Schopenhauer further reaffirmed his pessimistic world-view. In 1899, Kubin first saw at the Munich Kupferstichkabinett (Print Room, today: State Graphic Art Collection) etchings by painter and graphic artist Max Klinger whose cycle *Paraphrase on the Finding of a Glove* left a lasting impression on him. Kubin experienced a critical "torrent of visions of black-and-white images" that he graphically captured in his notebooks. It was the kickoff of a frantic creative phase lasting several years in which he created hundreds of black-and-white sprayed and washed ink pen drawings that constitute Kubin's nightmarish-fantastic early work. Aside from the works of Klinger, he also became familiar with works by Francisco José de Goya y Lucientes, Félicien Rops, Edvard Munch, James Ensor and Odilon Redon at that time.

1900–1902

During his Munich years, Kubin became more and more involved in the local artist and literary scene, expanding his circle of friends and acquaintances in the bohemian milieu. He was a regular at Café Stefanie and Café Elite. His encounter with the poet Max Dauthendey, who was from Würzburg, marked the beginning of a lively exchange, and he also came in contact with Otto Julius Bierbaum and his newly founded Jugendstil journal *Die Insel*. In the fall of 1901, Kubin first met the art patron Hans von Weber who would later become his publisher and bring out a portfolio of facsimile prints of Kubin's drawings, which crucially helped establish him as an artist. In December 1901, on the recommendation of the Insel circle, Kubin for the first time exhibited his work at the renowned Berlin gallery of Paul Cassirer, causing quite a stir in the press.

1903

On January 3, 1903, the *Wiener Abendpost* ran an article by writer Richard Schaukal in which he called Kubin the "Austrian Goya", praising him as a "draughtsman of boundless imagination [...] and the most idiosyncratic creativeness." In the same year, Kubin was represented with twelve works in the annual spring exhibition of the Vienna Secession. During a visit in March to Schärding, where his family had relocated, Kubin met Emmy Bayer who he soon got engaged to (06). Back in Munich, he made the acquaintance of Oscar A. H. Schmitz, the author of a volume of stories entitled *Hashish,* which had recently created quite a furor. Through Schmitz, Kubin got access to the bohemian Schwabing circle around Karl Wolfskehl, Stefan George, and Ludwig Klages, which would later also include Countess Franziska von Reventlow. In September 1903, Kubin traveled to Dalmatia in the company of the Austrian writer-philosopher Fritz von Herzmanovsky-Orlando. Their continuing exchange of ideas is documented in a correspondence spanning almost fifty years. In December 1903, Kubin was dealt another heavy blow when Emmy died of typhoid in a Munich clinic.

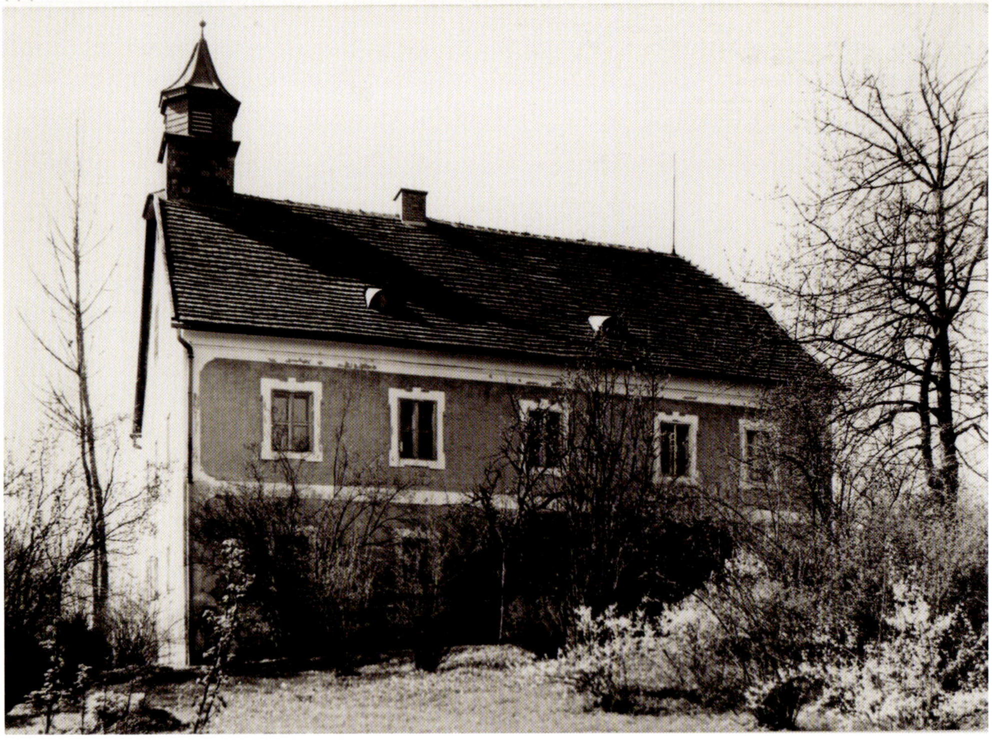

09

09 Anonymous photographer
View of the Kubin mansion in Zwickledt from the garden, 1966
Altnöder Collection, Salzburg

10 Alfred Kubin
German first edition of *The Other Side: A Fantastic Novel* with 52 Drawings by the Author, Munich, 1909
Altnöder Collection, Salzburg

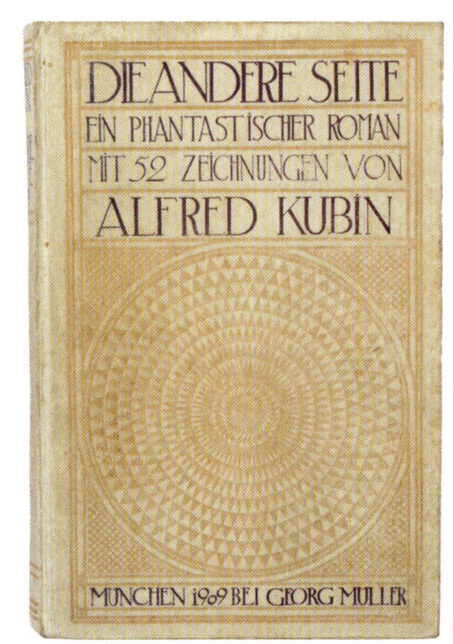

10

1904

In January 1904, more than 30 works by Kubin were included in the ninth exhibition of the Phalanx artist association headed by Wassily Kandinsky. In February, he first met Hedwig Gründler, the widowed sister of Oscar A. H. Schmitz, whom he married in September of that year. She brought her little son Otto into the marriage. Hedwig suffered from a painful facial neurosis. The treatments she needed necessitated numerous stays at hospitals and health resorts, which in turn meant extended periods of separation and loneliness for Kubin. Also, they entailed his wife's decades-long morphine addiction.

1905–1907

After the productive years of his early work, Kubin went through a prolonged creative crisis. In spring 1905, he traveled to Vienna where he met with artists of the Vienna Secession and received fresh artistic impulses particularly from Koloman Moser. From him he learned the technique of distemper painting in which watercolors are bound with glue. Kubin's change in motifs and style first met with reservation from his audience. In May 1906, the Kubin couple bought Schloss Zwickledt, the manor house of a secluded estate in Wernstein am Inn in Upper Austria where they moved to after having some refurbishment done (09). Kubin continued to have doubts about his artistic ability. From 1907, he increasingly focused his interest on book illustrations, which would become a major source of income for him. Among his first projects in this field were the illustrations for Gustav Meyrink's novel *The Golem,* although the book appeared in the following year without Kubin's drawings, as well as illustrations for a book of stories by Edgar Allan Poe.

1908/09

Kubin's fantastic novel *The Other Side,* written in only eight and illustrated in four more weeks, was brought out in 1909 by publisher Georg Müller and was received with great interest by the public (10). In fall of that same year, Alexej von Jawlensky invited him to join the New Munich Artists' Association. In the group's first exhibition at Thannhauser Gallery, Kubin was represented with several drawings.

1910/11

As a result of the publication of his illustrated novel, Kubin was increasingly receiving commissions for book illustrations, among others, for works of Edgar Allan Poe,

11 Alfred Kubin
Self-Portrait, c. 1910
Klewan Collection, Munich

Otto Julius Bierbaum, Gérard de Nerval, Fyodor Dostoyevsky, E. T. A. Hoffmann, Oscar A. H. Schmitz, and Wilhelm Hauff. Alfred Kubin's second portfolio, *Sansara. A Cycle Without End,* was published, containing reproductions of forty important original drawings of the preceding years, which visibly demonstrate his change of style compared to his early work. Enclosed in it was Kubin's first comprehensive autobiography, which he would continue in the decades to come. His meeting with the painter Paul Klee in 1911 marked the beginning of an intense artistic exchange. On the advice of Kandinsky and Gabriele Münter, Kubin left the New Munich Artists' Association and joined the newly founded group Der Blaue Reiter (The Blue Rider) as an external member. *The Munich Simplicissimus* and *Der Blaue Reiter Almanach (The Blue Rider Almanac)* first published reproductions of his pen drawings.

11

1912

In the second exhibition of the Blaue Reiter group at the Munich gallery of Hans Goltz, Kubin was represented with eleven works, among them the original drawings of the *Sansara* portfolio. In that year, he was in close contact with Klee and also received Klee's recently completed illustrations for Voltaire's *Candide*. Moreover, Klee suggested contributing to a portfolio of the Sema association of artists, established 1911 in Munich, for which purpose Kubin supplied his first-ever lithograph.

1913

Kubin had his first solo exhibition of fifty works at the Thannhauser gallery in Munich. Franc Marc invited him to contribute, together with Marc himself, Kandinsky, Klee, Erich Heckel, and Oskar Kokoschka, to an illustrated edition of the Bible. However, the outbreak of World War I came in the way of the finalization of this project. Still, Kubin's illustrations about the Prophet Daniel were published in 1918 in a special book edition. In September 1913, Kubin took part in the *Erster Deutscher Herbstsalon (First German Autumn Salon)*, held in Herwarth Walden's gallery Der Sturm in Berlin. It was the single most important gallery exhibition of the international avant-garde in Europe before the First World War.

1914

After Kubin's participation had previously been turned down, he was eventually included in the 1914 exhibition of the New Munich Secession next to Klee, Jawlensky, and Ernst Macke and also became an extraordinary member. From then on, he regularly exhibited in the *Graphische Ausstellungen (Graphic Art Exhibitions)*. With the beginning of the war, the Blaue Reiter circle fell apart and its members were dispersed. Macke and Marc fell at the front in the opening years of the war. Kubin was repeatedly deferred from military service.

1915–1921

In March 1916, also under the impression of Franc Marc's death in war, an outburst of long pent-up tensions and depressions occurred that Kubin referred to as a "Buddhist crisis," and which marked a turning point in his life. Kubin contacted the philosopher Salomo Friedländer (pen name Mynona) whose writings provided him with a central guideline in life. It was the beginning of a thirty-year exchange of letters. His brother-in-law Oscar A. H. Schmitz also became one of the people closest to Kubin. In 1917, Kubin took part in the annual exhibi-

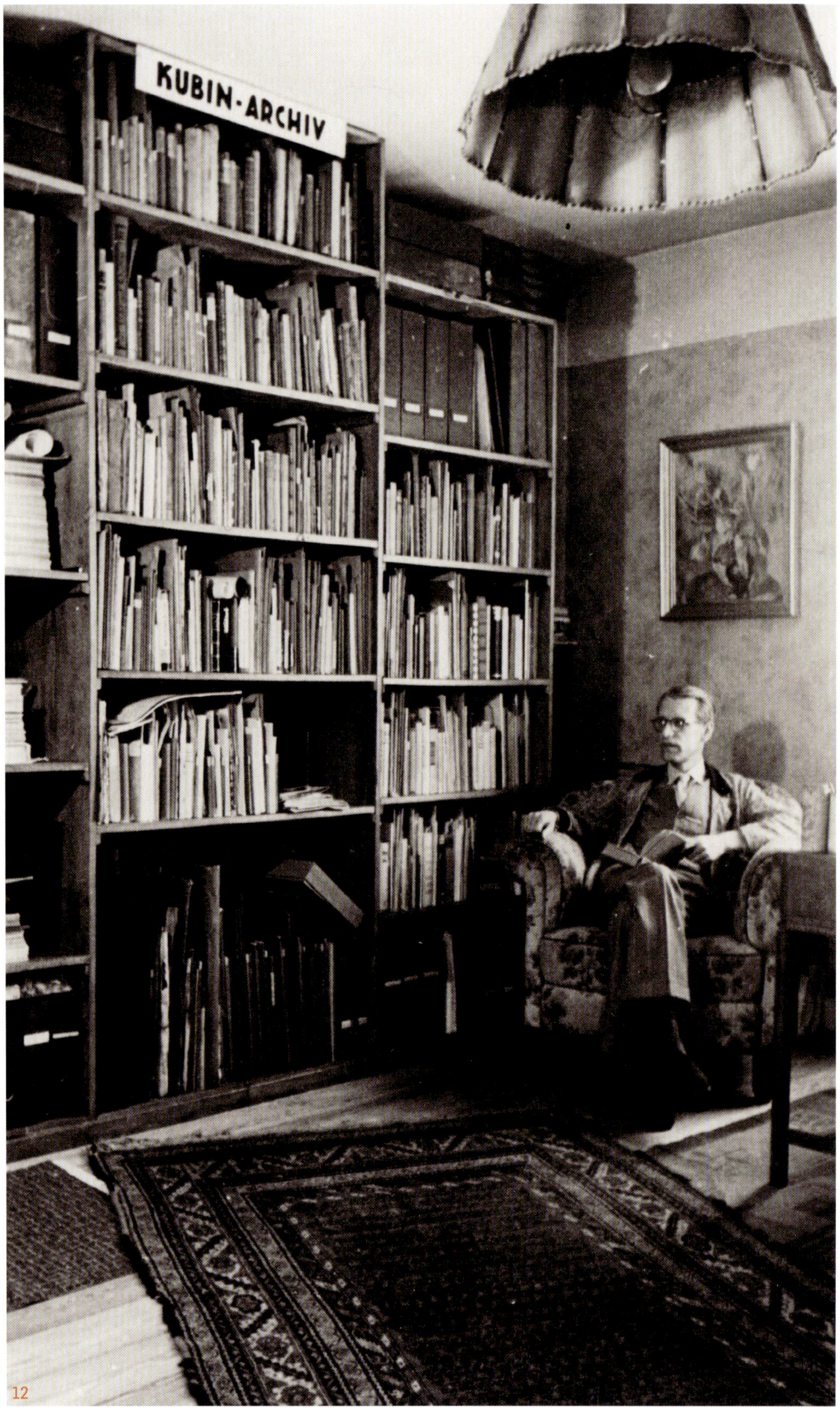

12

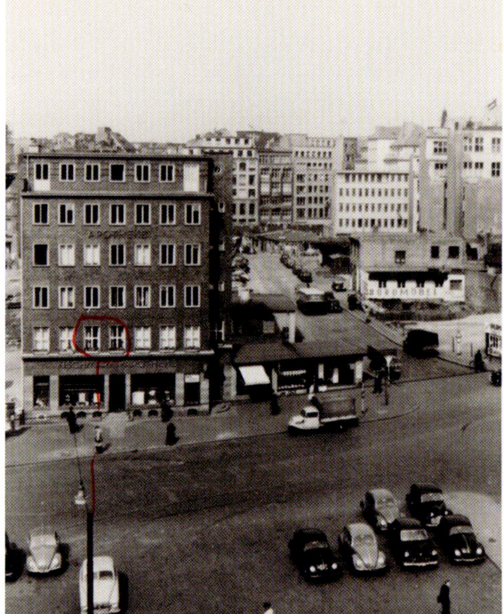

13

tion of the Munich Secession and the twelve-part special exhibition of the Kestner Society in Hannover and contributed six works to the 1919 comprehensive exhibition *Moderne deutsche Grafiken (Modern German Graphic Art)* at Thannhauser Gallery. In 1921, the Munich Goltz Gallery showed a first large retrospective of one-hundred works highly acclaimed by the press. He met the young Hamburg pharmacist Kurt Otte who later would be the founder of the Kubin Archive (12, 13). It was at this time that Hedwig Kubin was eventually cured from her morphine addiction, which caused Kubin to dedicate his portfolio *Strindberg, To Damascus* to the responsible physician, Dr. Laudenheimer.

1922–1926

At the Heidelberg Psychiatric University Clinic, Kubin first saw the Prinzhorn Collection; under the impression of it, he authored an essay entitled *Die Kunst der Irren (The Art of the Mad)*, which was published in Paul Westheim's *Kunstblatt*. The Berlin-based Fritz Gurlitt Publishers brought out another

12 Anonymous photographer
Archivist Dr. Kurt Otte at the „Kubin Archive" in Hamburg, undated
Altnöder Collection, Salzburg

13 Anonymous photographer
The „Kubin Archive" on Fischmarkt 3, Hamburg, undated
Altnöder Collection, Salzburg

14 Anonymous photographer
Alfred and Hedwig Kubin in front of their house in Zwickledt, 1925
Städtische Galerie im Lenbachhaus und Kunstbau München

important portfolio work under the title of *Traumland I und Traumland II (Dreamland I and II)*. Kubin met a married couple of painters, Reinhold and Hanne Koeppel, and paid them a first visit at their home in the Bavarian Forest. The Bavarian and the adjoining Bohemian Forest also provided him with a profound artistic experience. Until his old age, he would spend his holidays in the regions and also incorporated its legends and fairytales in his own artistic work, for example, in his illustrations of *Rübezahl* (1925) and his 1926 book *Dämonen und Nachtgesichte (Demons and Nocturnal Visions)*.

1927–1931

For his 50th birthday in 1927, the Neue Pinakothek in Munich showed a special exhibition of Kubin. In 1929, Ernst Jünger published a review of *The Other Side* in the journal *Der Widerstand*. It was the beginning of a twenty-year correspondence between Kubin and the writer. Featuring more than 250 works, the Munich-based gallery Graphisches Kabinett Günther Franke presented the largest Kubin exhibition in thirty years in 1930. A special issue of *Das Kunstblatt* dedicated to Kubin in 1931 published his essay *Fragment eines Weltbildes (Fragment of a World Picture)* in which he gave a fundamental outline of his worldview.

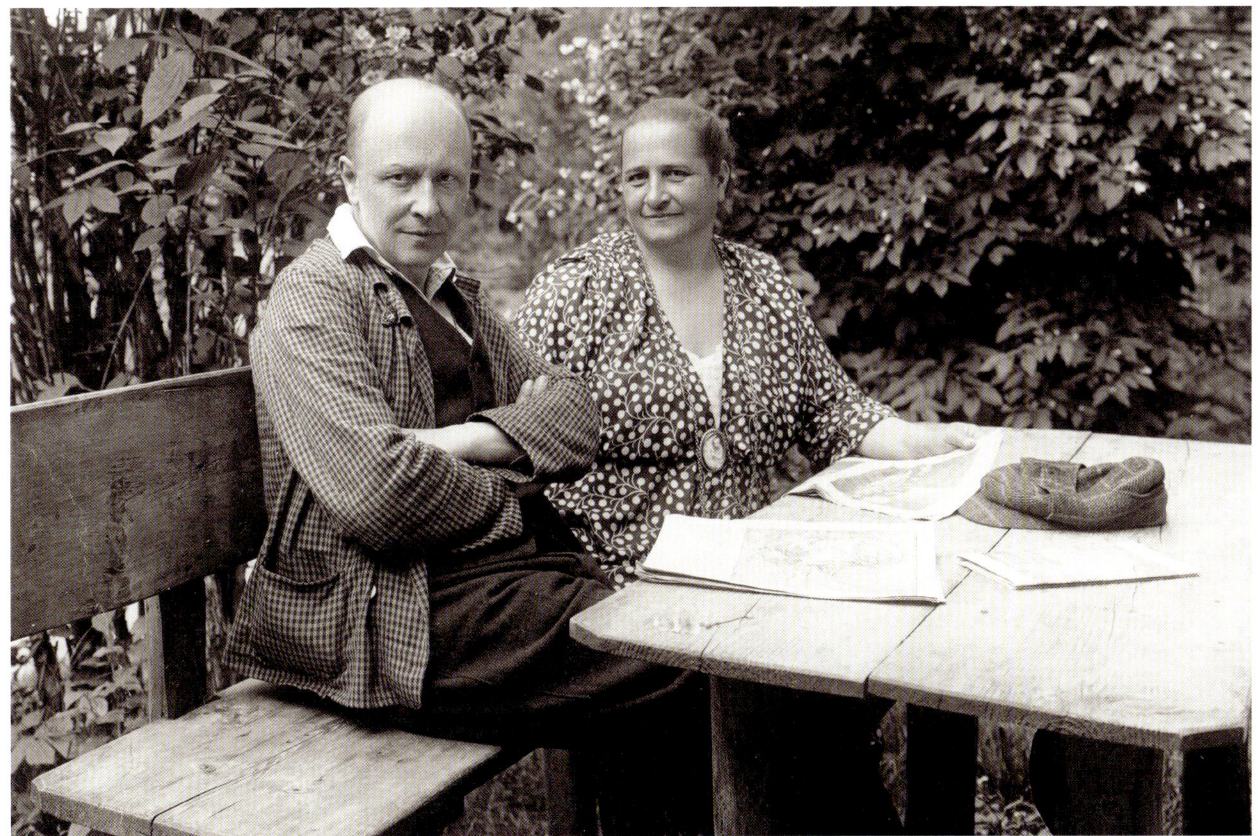
14

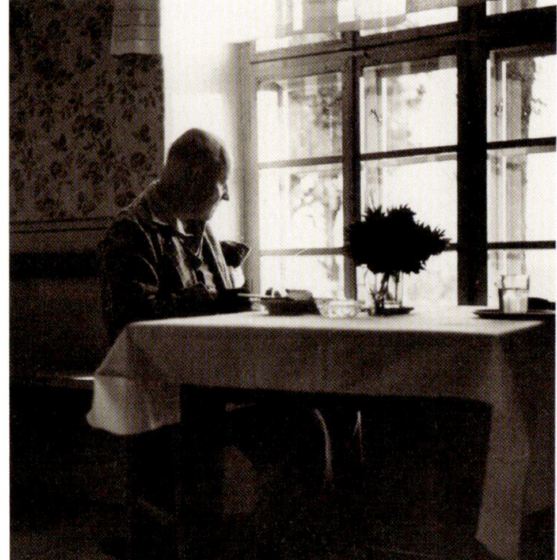

15

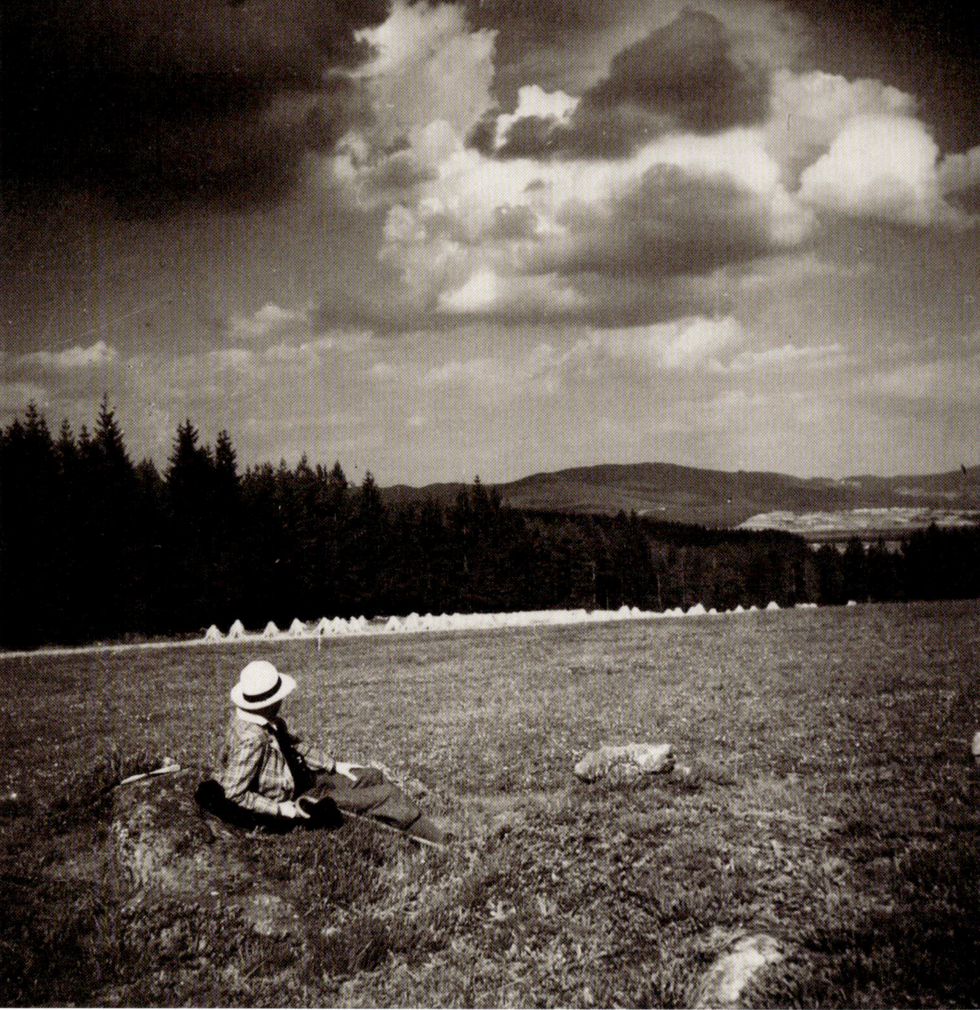

17

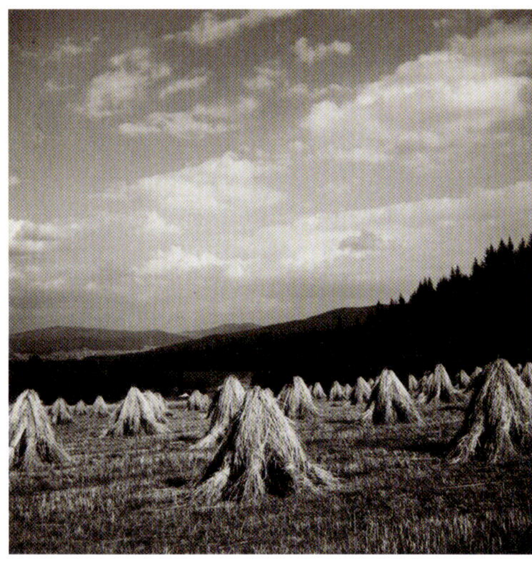

16

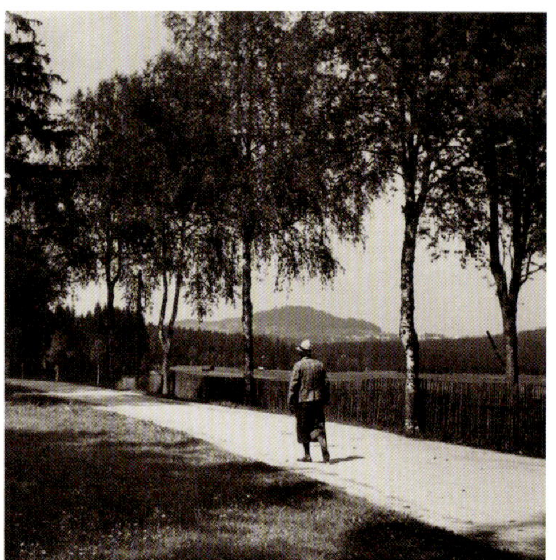

18

15 Emmy Haesele
Alfred Kubin sitting at the dinner table in Tusset, undated
Altnöder Collection, Salzburg

16 Emmy Haesele
Landscape with haystack, undated
Altnöder Collection, Salzburg

17 Emmy Haesele
lfred Kubin sitting in the grass, Tusset, August 1935
Altnöder Collection, Salzburg

18 Emmy Haesele
Alfred Kubin on a road lined with birch trees, undated
Altnöder Collection, Salzburg

19–22 Emmy Haesele
Alfred Kubin reading, at his desk, with a magnifying glass, all undated
Altnöder Collection, Salzburg

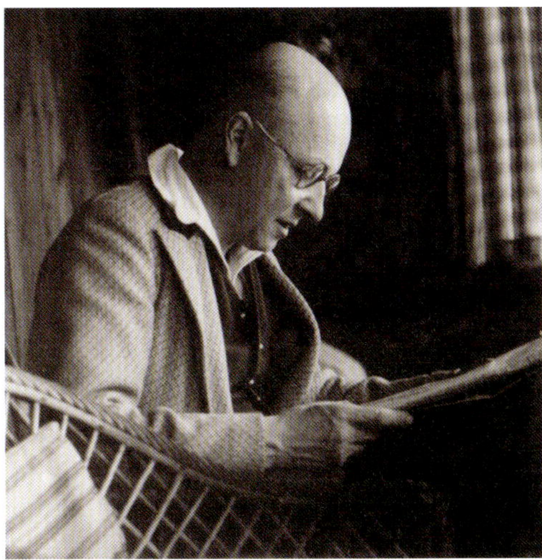
19

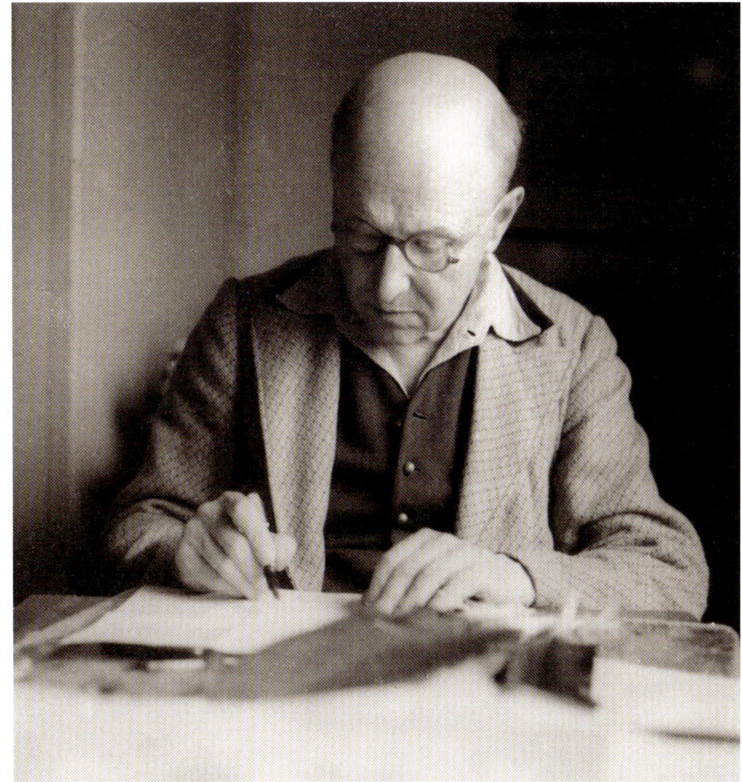
20

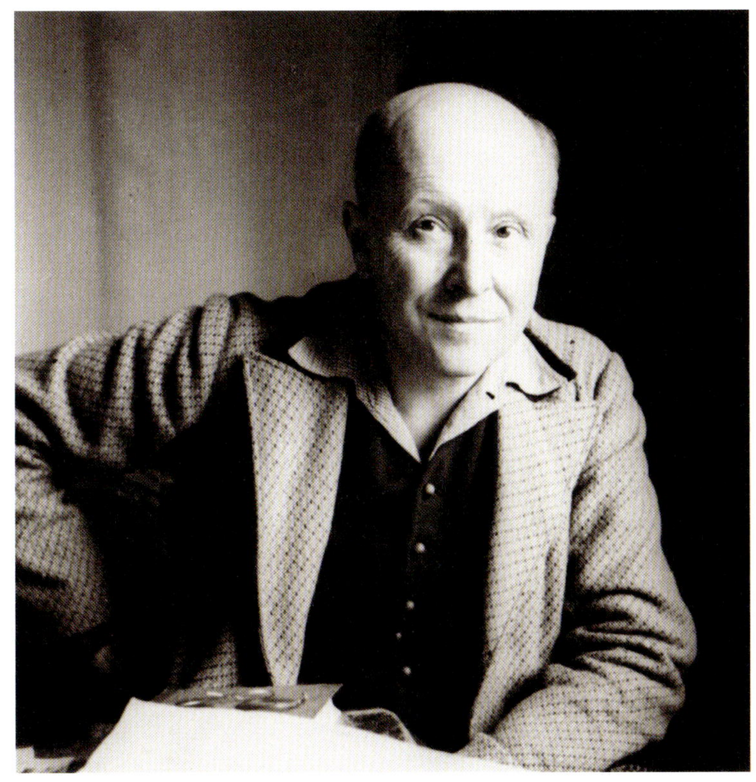
22

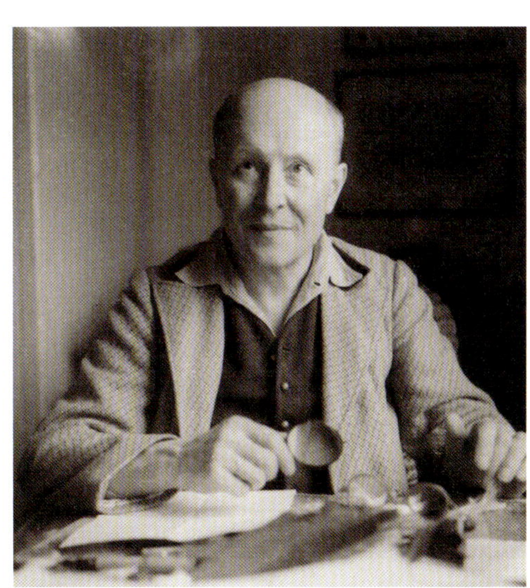
21

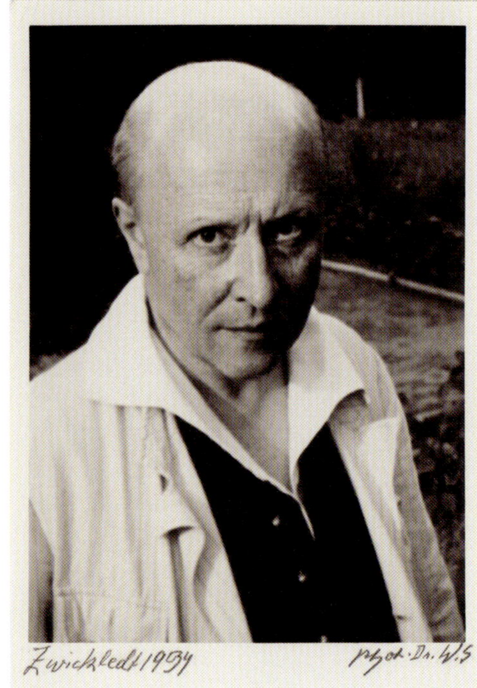

23

23 Wolfgang Schneditz
Alfred Kubin in Zwickledt, 1934
Altnöder Collection, Salzburg

24 Alfred Kubin/Otto von Holten
A Dance of Death, 1918
Leopold, Private Collection

1933–1939

For Kubin, the Nazi seizure of power in Germany at first meant a loss of income, border and money problems as well as worries about his wife Hedwig, who had Jewish ancestors. It became more difficult for him to find a publisher for his work. Some of his illustration drafts were only published after World War II. Kubin kept a low profile and spent his summers, some of them with different girlfriends, in the Bohemian Forest region. It was particularly his relationship with the artist Emmy Haesele that triggered a deep marital crisis. In 1937, Kubin's 60th birthday was celebrated by numerous, mostly Austrian galleries, among them the Graphic Collection of the Albertina in Vienna. In 1939, his anthology *Vom Schreibtisch eines Zeichners (From a Draughtman's Desk)* was published, which brought together several of his individual writings and became an important source for the reception of his work. After the outbreak of World War II, Kubin hurriedly traveled back to Zwickledt from the Bohemian Forest.

1940–1945

The death of his friend Paul Klee in 1940 shattered Kubin to the core. Despite difficulties, his volume *Abenteuer einer Zeichenfeder (Adventures of a Drawing Pen)* with numerous illustrations could be published in 1941. Kubin spent the war years in seclusion in his house in Zwickledt but remained in steady mail contact with friends and trusted acquaintances.

1946–1957

Kubin was getting more commissioned work as an illustrator again, among other things, for works by Ernst Jünger and Georg Trakl, and was awarded an Honorary Citizenship of the City of Linz in 1947. In summer 1948, his wife Hedwig died from the consequences of her long illness. Kubin worked on large-sized drawings about Arthur Honegger's oratorio *Totentanz (Dance of the Dead)*, which was his last portfolio to be published by Fritz Gurlitt Publishers (24). In 1950 and '52, he was present at the Venice Biennale, and in 1951, he was awarded the Grand Austrian State Prize for literature, music, and visual art. In 1955, Kubin bequeathed, in a donation agreement and against payment of a life annuity, his entire estate of drawings to the Republic of Austria and the State of Upper Austria.

24

1959

On August 20, 1959, Alfred Kubin died in Zwickledt after long sickness and was buried in Wernstein am Inn (28). His artistic estate was handed over to the Vienna Albertina and the Upper-Austrian State Museum. His library as well as his house in Zwickledt also went to the State of Upper Austria and were transformed in 1962 into the "Kubin Memorial Zwickledt," operated since 1992 by the State Museum of Upper Austria. The Kubin Archive curated by Kurt Otte was purchased in 1971 by the Munich Lenbachhaus and incorporated in its collections in 1983.

Compiled by Lena Scholz, with consideration of the Kubin biography drawn up by Annegret Hoberg: „Biografie", in *Alfred Kubin: Drawings*, ed. by A. Hoberg (Munich/New York, 2008), pp. 215–225 (exh. cat. Neue Galerie, New York, 25.09.2008–26.01.2009).

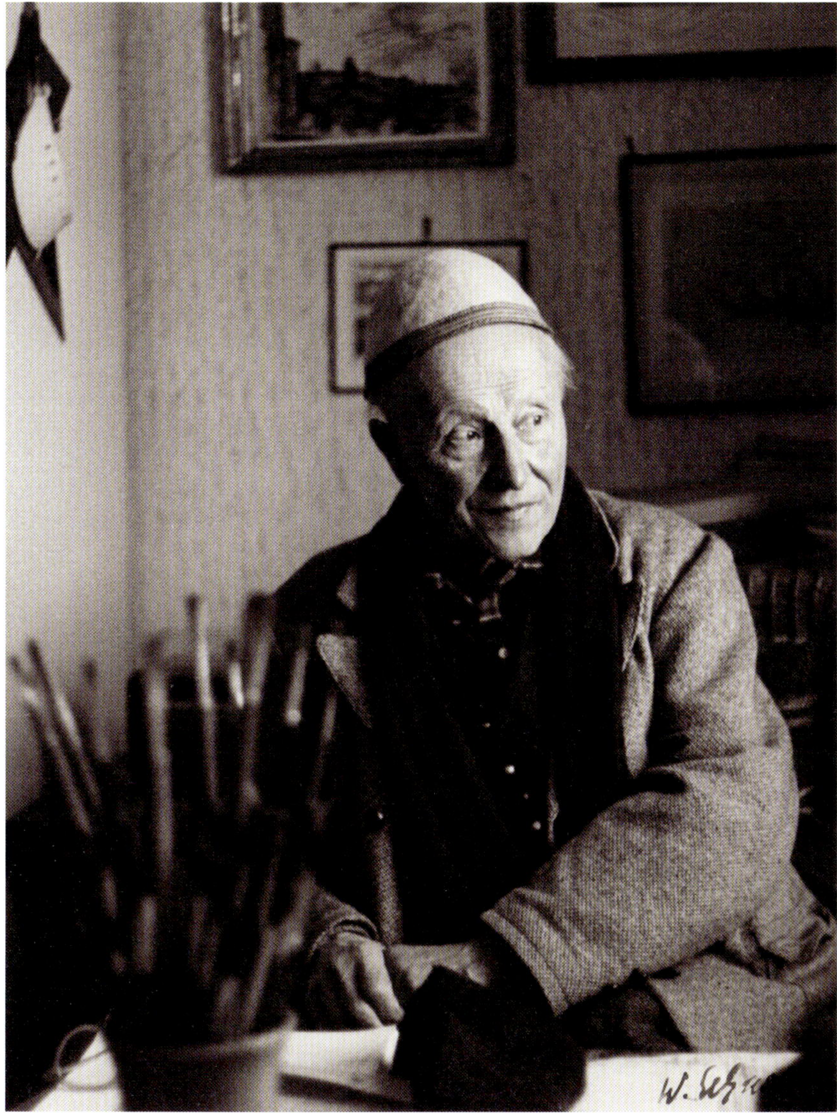

25

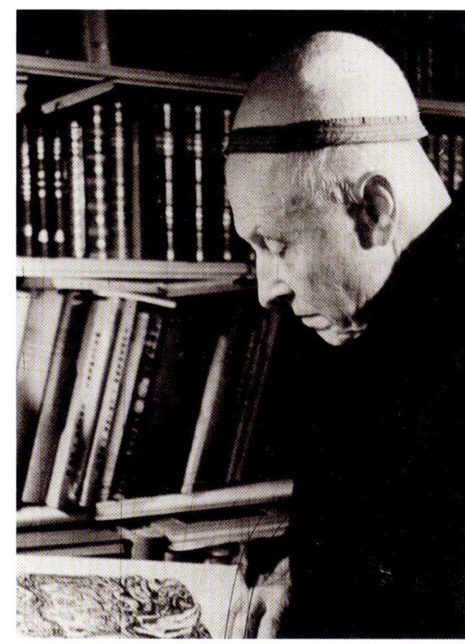

26

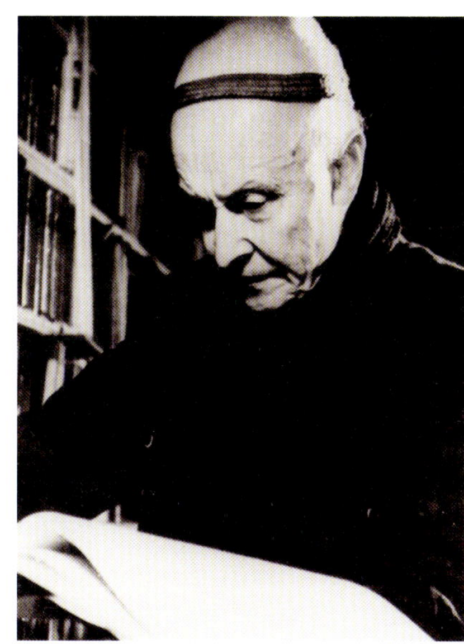

27

Worte Kubins auf dem Krankenlager im März 1959:

Ich habe
mein Leben lang
Angst gehabt . . .
Angst vor dem
was ich nicht wahr=
haben wollte
was ich verdrängen
wollte
nun habe ich
keine Angst mehr
weil ich die Wahrheit
erkenne

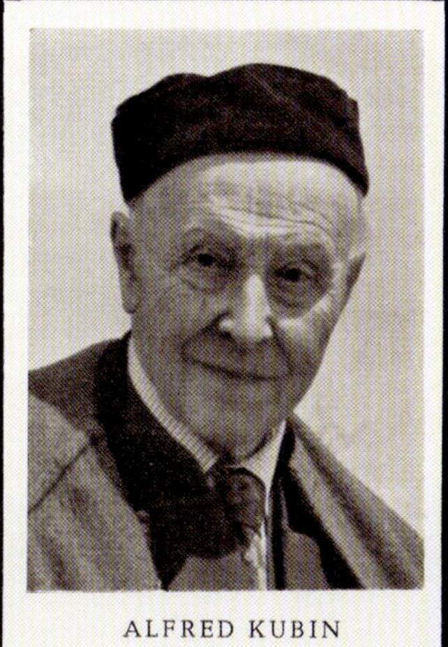

ALFRED KUBIN
geboren am 10. 4. 1877 in Leitmeritz
gestorben am 20. 8. 1959 in Zwickledt

28

25 Wolfgang Schneditz
Alfred Kubin sitting, 1952
Altnöder Collection, Salzburg

26 Wolfgang Schneditz
Alfred Kubin in front of a bookcase, c. 1952
Altnöder Collection, Salzburg

27 Anonymous photographer
Alfred Kubin with an open book, undated
Altnöder Collection, Salzburg

28 **Obituary notice for Alfred Kubin,** 1959
Altnöder Collection, Salzburg

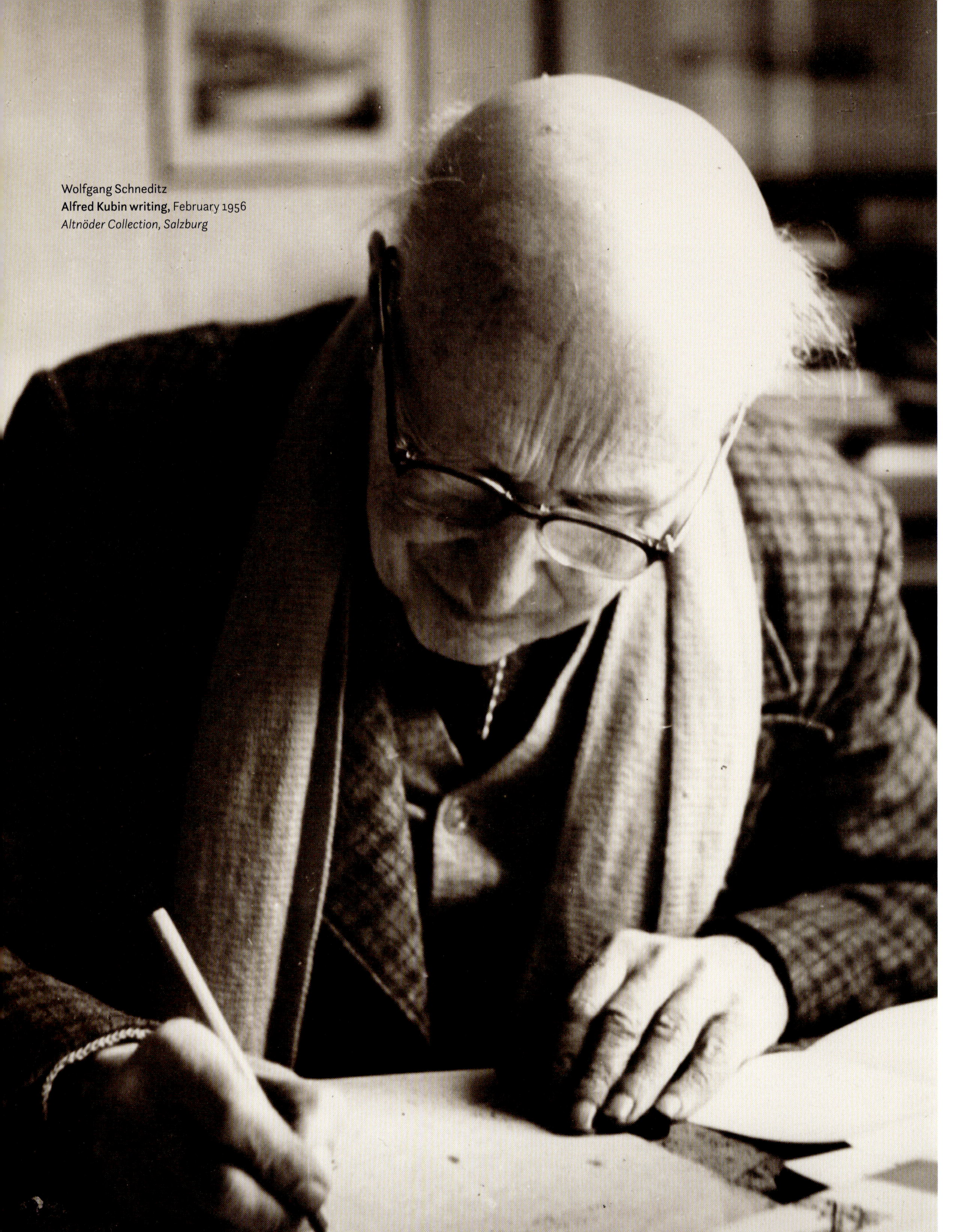

Wolfgang Schneditz
Alfred Kubin writing, February 1956
Altnöder Collection, Salzburg

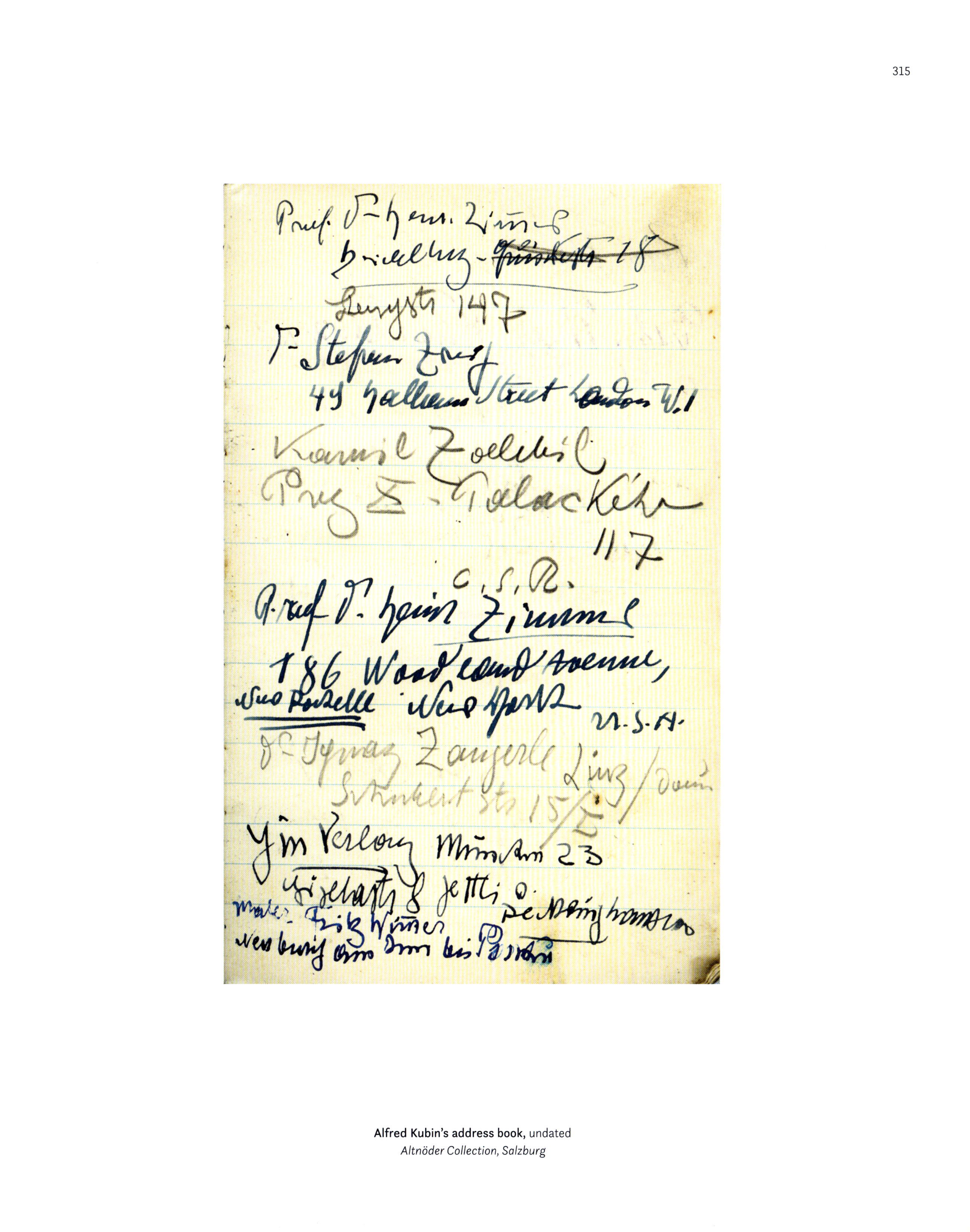

Alfred Kubin's address book, undated
Altnöder Collection, Salzburg

LIST OF WORKS EXHIBITED

ALFRED KUBIN
(Leitmeritz, Bohemia 1877–1959 Zwickledt, Wernstein am Inn)

Grotesque Animal World, c. 1898
India ink, washed, sprayed on cadastral paper
27.3 × 21.7 cm
OÖ Landes-Kultur GmbH, Land Oberösterreich, Graphic Collection, Ha II 7361
p. 83

Fortune, Page from Kubin's stepmother Irene Kubin's poetry album, c. 1898
Tempera on paper
22.3 × 14.6 cm
Private Collection, Austria
Not shown in the catalogue

My Demon, early self-portrait, 1899
Pencil on paper
11.8 × 9 cm
Private Collection, Austria
p. 305

The Prisoner's Dream, 1899
India ink, pen, pencil, chalk, washed, sprayed, border line on paper
30.7 × 25.6 cm
Städtische Galerie im Lenbachhaus und Kunstbau München
p. 68

My God, My God, What Are You Doing?, 1899/1900
India ink, pen, watercolor, spray technique on cadastral paper
31.6 × 39.8 cm
Leopold Museum, Vienna
p. 233

Nightmare, 1899/1900
India ink and pen on cadastral paper
16.4 × 20.4 cm
Leopold Museum, Vienna
p. 71

Ghostly Dancer, 1899/1900
India ink, pen, watercolor, spray technique on cadastral paper
31.2 × 19.6 cm
Leopold Museum, Vienna
p. 179

Cramp, before 1900
India ink, pen, watercolor, spray technique on cadastral paper
20.6 × 39 cm
Leopold Museum, Vienna
Not shown in the catalogue

The Good Lord, c. 1900
India ink, pen on cadastral paper
39.1 × 30.7 cm
Leopold Museum, Vienna
p. 77

Slaughterfest, c. 1900
India ink, pen, wash, sprayed, border line on cadastral paper
31.3 × 39 cm
Albertina, Vienna
p. 156

War Scene, c. 1900
Spray technique
7.5 × 20.7 cm
Private Collection, Austria
p. 97

Rape of a Moravian Peasant Woman, 1900
Pen, china ink, wash, spray technique on cadastral paper
20 × 31.5 cm
Private Collection
p. 180

From My Realm, 1900
India ink, pen, watercolor, spray technique on cadastral paper
37.9 × 30 cm
Leopold Museum, Vienna
p. 195

Starvation, c. 1901
India ink, pen, watercolor, spray technique on cadastral paper
31.2 × 39 cm
Leopold Museum, Vienna
p. 235

Monument, c. 1900/01
India ink, washed, sprayed on cadastral paper
31.5 × 19.8 cm
OÖ Landes-Kultur GmbH, Land Oberösterreich, Graphic Collection, Ha II 3177
p. 102

Pagan Sacrifice, c. 1900/01
India ink, washed, sprayed on cadastral paper
31.5 × 39.3 cm
OÖ Landes-Kultur GmbH, Land Oberösterreich, Graphic Collection, Ha II 3180
p. 185

The Lady on the Horse, c. 1900/01
India ink, pen, ink, washed, sprayed, border line on cadastral paper
39.6 × 30.9 cm
Städtische Galerie im Lenbachhaus und Kunstbau München
p. 157

Madame (also: Modern Chandelier Decoration), 1900/01
India ink, pen, watercolor, spray technique on cadastral paper
31.7 × 20.3 cm
Leopold Museum, Vienna
p. 178

Masturbation, 1900/01
India ink, pen, watercolor, spray technique on cadastral paper
39.5 × 31.9 cm
Leopold Museum, Vienna
p. 172

The Oppressive, 1900/01
India ink, pen, watercolor, spray technique on cadastral paper
38.2 × 30.7 cm
Leopold Museum, Vienna
p. 238

Into the Unknown, 1900/01
India ink, pen, watercolor, spray technique on cadastral paper
30.9 × 39 cm
Leopold Museum, Vienna
p. 245

Hysteria, c. 1901
India ink, pen, watercolor, spray technique on cadastral paper
23.8 × 32.6 cm
Leopold Museum, Vienna
p. 173

The Best Physician, c. 1901
India ink, pen, watercolor, spray technique on cadastral paper
27.1 × 38.6 cm
Leopold Museum, Vienna
p. 155

The Last Adventure, c. 1901
India ink, pen, watercolor, spray technique on cadastral paper
24.8 × 36.7 cm
Leopold Museum, Vienna
p. 143

Danger, c. 1901
India ink, pen, watercolor, spray technique on cadastral paper
29.3 × 32.6 cm
Leopold Museum, Vienna
p. 263

Suckers, c. 1901
India ink, pen, ink, washed,
sprayed on paper
26.6×19.8 cm
Städtische Galerie im Lenbachhaus und Kunstbau München
p. 215

After the Battle, 1901
Ink, sprayed, washed on
cadastral paper
19.7×31.4 cm
Museum Ortner, Vienna
p. 247

The Past (Forgotten—Sunken), 1901
India ink, pen, watercolor, spray
technique on cadastral paper
30.3×39.6 cm
Leopold Museum, Vienna
p. 261

The Egg, c. 1901/02
India ink, pen, gray, black,
brown wash, sprayed, border
line on cadastral paper
31.5×39.2 cm
Albertina, Vienna
p. 171

The Spider, c. 1901/02
India ink, pen on brownish
toned ground, sprayed, border
line on cadastral paper
32×39.7 cm
Albertina, Vienna
p. 141

The Symphony, 1901/02
India ink, pen, watercolor, spray
technique on cadastral paper
38.4×31.2 cm
Leopold Museum, Vienna
p. 239

Weakling, print 5 from the *Hans von Weber*-portfolio, 1901/02
Collotype on paper
33.3×43.6 cm
Leopold, Private Collection
Not shown in the catalogue

Sea Monster, 1901/02
Spray technique on cadastral paper
38.4×30.6 cm
Leopold, Private Collection
p. 223

Sleep, 1901/02
India ink, pen, watercolor and spray
technique on cadastral paper
36×29 cm
Leopold Museum, Vienna
p. 69

The Hour of Birth, 1901/02
India ink, pen wash, spray
technique on cadastral paper
25.5×30.6 cm
Leopold Museum, Vienna
p. 199

Fertility (1st Version), 1901/02
India ink, pen, watercolor, spray
technique on cadastral paper
37.2×27.2 cm
Leopold Museum, Vienna
p. 169 (1)

The Horror, c. 1902
India ink, pen wash, spray
technique on cadastral paper
32.6×31.1 cm
Leopold Museum, Vienna
p. 267

The Devil on the Chimney, c. 1902
India ink, pen, watercolor, spray
technique on cadastral paper
28.4×31.1 cm
Leopold Museum, Vienna
p. 236

Science, c. 1902
India ink, pen, watercolor, spray
technique on cadastral paper
36.8×30 cm
Leopold Museum, Vienna
p. 197

Man, c. 1902
India ink, watercolor, spray
technique on cadastral paper
38.5×31.4 cm
Leopold Museum, Vienna
p. 265

Untitled (Vulture Holding a Sword and Cowering Nude), 1902
India ink on cadastral paper
17.8×13.7 cm
Private Collection, Austria
p. 167

The Sign, 1902
India ink, pen, spray technique
on cadastral paper
30.8×36.4 cm
Lentos Kunstmuseum Linz
p. 249

Our All Mother Earth, 1902
India ink, pen, spray technique,
pencil on paper
15.4×34.8 cm
Leopold, Private Collection
p. 257

The Rat House, 1902
India ink, watercolor, spray
technique on cadastral paper
31.6×38.9 cm
Leopold Museum, Vienna
p. 269

The Blessed, 1902
India ink, pen, watercolor, spray
technique on cadastral paper
38.8×31 cm
Leopold Museum, Vienna
Not shown in the catalogue

Every Night a Dream Visits Us, c. 1902/03
India ink, pen, gray, black,
brown wash, sprayed, border
line on cadastral paper
39.3×31.9 cm
Albertina, Vienna
p. 73

The Orchid, 1902/03
India ink, pen, watercolor, spray
technique on cadastral paper
31.6×37.4 cm
Leopold Museum, Vienna
p. 147

Swift Ride, 1902/03
India ink, pen, watercolor, spray
technique on cadastral paper
31.4×19.9 cm
Leopold Museum, Vienna
p. 240

The Stairs, 1902/03
India ink, pen, watercolor, spray
technique on cadastral paper
38.8×29.3 cm
Leopold Museum, Vienna
Not shown in the catalogue

The Swellbelly, 1902/03
India ink, pen, watercolor, spray
technique on cadastral paper
19.6×31.4 cm
Leopold Museum, Vienna
p. 31

Memorial Work for My Bride Who Died in 1903, 1903
India ink, pen, watercolor, spray
technique on cadastral paper
38.1×31.3 cm
Leopold Museum, Vienna
p. 46

Unmasked, 1903
India ink, washed, sprayed on paper
28×30.3 cm
OÖ Landes-Kultur GmbH, Land Oberösterreich, Graphic Collection, Günter Rombold Collection, Ha II 13182
p. 217

The Male Sphinx, 1903
India ink pen, ink, brush,
washed, sprayed on paper
38.6×31.5cm
Städtische Galerie im Lenbachhaus und Kunstbau München
p. 111

Epidemic, print 7 from the *Hans von Weber*-portfolio, 1903
Print on paper
33.3×43.6 cm
Leopold, Private Collection
p. 268

Downfall, 1903
India ink, pen, washed,
sprayed on paper
37.2×31.5 cm
Staatliche Museen zu Berlin, Nationalgalerie, Scharf-Gerstenberg Collection
p. 138

The Hour of Death, print 14 from the *Hans von Weber*-portfolio, 1903
Print on paper
33.3×43.6 cm
Leopold, Private Collection
p. 255

Power, c. 1903
India ink, pen, ink, washed, sprayed on paper
37.3×31.3 cm
Städtische Galerie im Lenbachhaus und Kunstbau München
p. 222

The Fate of Mankind, print 1 from the *Hans von Weber*-portfolio, 1903
Print on paper
33.3×43.6 cm
Leopold, Private Collection
p. 259

The City Towards the East, 1903/04
India ink, pen, watercolor, spraytechnique on paper
24.5×30.3 cm
Leopold Museum, Vienna
p. 294

Disreputable Place, 1903/04
India ink, pen washed on cadastral paper
31.6×39.2 cm
Leopold Museum, Vienna
p. 290

The Swamp, c. 1903–1905
India ink, pen, spray technique on cadastral paper
23.3×31.4 cm
Lentos Kunstmuseum Linz
p. 188

Lady with Lace Panties, 1903/06
India ink, gouache, spray technique on cadastral paper
37×29.9 cm
Leopold Museum, Vienna
p. 124

Black Flowers (also: Salome), c. 1904
India ink, pen, watercolor, spray technique on cadastral paper
37.4×31.1 cm
Leopold Museum, Vienna
p. 145

Swarming Spirits, c. 1904
India ink, pen, watercolor, spray technique on cadastral paper
31.3×39.6 cm
Leopold Museum, Vienna
p. 248

The Animal in the Swamp, c. 1904
India ink, pen, watercolor on cadastral paper
31.2×39.2 cm
Leopold Museum, Vienna
p. 285

Memories of a Friend, 1904
India ink, watercolor on paper
24×32 cm
Leopold, Private Collection
p. 213

The Trojan Horse, 1905
India ink, pen, spray technique on paper
30×20 cm
Leopold, Private Collection
p. 241

Undersea Creatures, 1905
Distemper technique on paper
25.2×36.3 cm
Leopold Museum, Vienna
p. 276

Gallant Landscape, c. 1905
31.2×39.8 cm
Leopold, Private Collection
p. 295

Solitude, c. 1905
Spray technique on cadastral paper
31×39.3 cm
Leopold, Private Collection
p. 205

Fabulous Creature, c. 1905/06
Gouache, paste colors on cardboard
36.8×28.2 cm
Albertina, Vienna. Forberg Collection (Inv. DL581)
p. 278

The Sea Serpent, 1905/06
Gouache, paste paint technique on paper
35.5×25 cm
Leopold Museum, Vienna
p. 277

Crystals, 1906
Gouache on paper
43.8×38.6 cm
Lentos Kunstmuseum Linz
p. 274

Witch and Water Serpent, 1906
Gouache on paper
32.9×36.3 cm
Leopold Museum, Vienna
p. 279

Helmet in the Sea, 1906
Gouache on paper
35.8×29.4 cm
Leopold Museum, Vienna
p. 275

Death as a Horseman, 1906
Gouache on cadastral paper
28.7×47.2 cm
Leopold Museum, Vienna
p. 101

The Saddle (Shell), c. 1906
Tempera, gouache on black clay paper
37.5×39.9 cm
Albertina, Vienna
p. 272

Fireworks, c. 1906
Gouache on cadastral paper
37.2×36.3 cm
Albertina, Vienna
p. 273

The War, 1907
India ink, pen on paper
31.5×39.6 cm
Städtische Galerie im Lenbachhaus und Kunstbau München
p. 95

The Cardinal, c. 1908/11
India ink, pen, colored pencil on cadastral paper
33.1×25.4 cm
Lentos Kunstmuseum Linz
p. 297

Illustration of *Hop-Frog*, for Edgar Allan Poe's *The Tell-Tale Heart and Other Tales,* 1909
Line etching on paper
15.3×9.5 cm
Lentos Kunstmuseum Linz
p. 225

Uprising, from the *Sansara* portfolio, 1909/10
India ink, pen on cadastral paper
29.8×39.1 cm
Leopold Museum, Vienna
p. 96

Fertility (2nd Version), 1909/10
India ink, pen, watercolor on cadastral paper
38.8×31.7 cm
Leopold Museum, Vienna
p. 169 (2)

Gypsy Encampment, 1909/10
India ink, pencil on cadastral paper
33.3×39.6 cm
Leopold Museum, Vienna
S. 70

Goddess of Fate, c. 1910
Watercolor, india ink, washed on cadastral paper
19.5×13.8 cm
OÖ Landes-Kultur GmbH, Land Oberösterreich, Graphic Collection, Günter Rombold Collection, Ha I 15584
p. 144

Semi-Nude (Catwoman), c. 1910
India ink, watercolor on paper
13.7×12.5 cm
Leopold, Private Collection
p. 133

Funeral March, c. 1910
Ink, gouache on cadastral paper
31.2×39 cm
Leopold, Private Collection
p. 253

The World's Fool, c. 1910
India ink, pen on cadastral paper
39.7×31.6 cm
Leopold Museum, Vienna
p. 212

The Melancholy, c. 1910
India ink, pen on cadastral paper
31.5×39.3 cm
Leopold Museum, Vienna
pp. 231

Self-Portrait, c. 1910
Pen on paper
21.5×18.5 cm
Klewan Collection, Munich
p. 307

The Dancing Salome with Tambourine, c. 1910
India ink, watercolor on paper
13.7×8.7 cm
Klewan Collection, Munich
p. 112

The Angel of Death, 1910
India ink, pen on cadastral paper
19.7×31.7 cm
Leopold Museum, Vienna
p. 148

Downfall, 1910/11
India ink, pen, watercolor
on cadastral paper
30×38.9 cm
Leopold Museum, Vienna
p. 291

The Castle in the Sea, 1910/11
India ink, pen, watercolor
on cadastral paper
39.5×32.3 cm
Leopold Museum, Vienna
p. 287

God of Light, c. 1911
India ink, pen on cadastral paper
39.3×32.2 cm
Leopold Museum, Vienna
p. 149

The Earthshock, 1911/12
India ink, pen on paper
31.5×39.7 cm
Leopold Museum, Vienna
p. 288/289

The Earth Trembles, c. 1912
India ink, pen, watercolor
on cadastral paper
39.1×30.9 cm
Leopold Museum, Vienna
p. 293

Nighttime, 1913
India ink on cadastral paper
32.1×25.9 cm
Private Collection, Austria
p. 292

Vision of Death, c. 1914
Mixed techniques on cadastral paper
19.5×26.9 cm
Leopold, Private Collection
p. 216

The Malaysian Variety Show, c. 1915
India ink, watercolor on paper
28.6 cm
Private Collection, Austria
p. 88

Deserted Town, 1916
Pen, china ink on cadastral paper
31×19.7 cm
Private Collection
p. 296

On the Beach, Wreckage, c. 1918
India ink, watercolor on paper
15.9×28.1 cm
Leopold, Private Collection
p. 284

Anarchy, c. 1918
India ink on cadastral paper
39.8×31.4 cm
Private Collection, Austria
p. 99

The Fool, 1918/19
India ink, pen on paper
35.9×26.1 cm
Leopold Museum, Vienna
p. 209

Lord Devil, c. 1920
India ink on paper
32.7×26.5 cm
Leopold, Private Collection
p. 162

The Worm, c. 1920
India ink, pen, watercolor, spray
technique on cadastral paper
20.6×23.6 cm
Leopold Museum, Vienna
Not shown in the catalogue

Walpurgis Night III, 1920
Watercolor, india ink on
cadastral paper
31.2×39.4 cm
OÖ Landes-Kultur GmbH, Land Oberösterreich, Graphic Collection, Günter Rombold Collection, Ha II 13187
p. 151

The Hanged Man (Study), 1920/25
Pencil on paper
16.5×11.7 cm
Leopold Museum, Vienna
p. 208

Death as a Dancer, 1922
Lithograph on paper
34.7×25.5 cm
Leopold Museum, Vienna
p. 299

The Suicide (Dreamland I and II), 1922
Lithograph on tracing paper
29.3×34 cm
Leopold Museum, Vienna
p. 186

Death at Work, c. 1923
India ink, watercolor on paper
36.1×26.2 cm
Leopold Museum, Vienna
p. 187

Death [As a Woman] Comes for the Draftsman [Self-Portrait], 1930
Pencil on paper
29.1×28.5 cm
Leopold Museum, Vienna
p. 45

Narcissism, c. 1930
India ink, pen, watercolor on paper
23.4×17.8 cm
Leopold, Private Collection
p. 189

Witch's Apartment, c. 1932
India ink, watercolor on paper
44.5×35 cm
Klewan Collection, Munich
p. 150

Study for India ink drawing *Among Hyenas*, c. 1934
Pencil on paper
8.8×30 cm
OÖ Landes-Kultur GmbH, Land Oberösterreich, Graphic Collection, Günter Rombold Collection, Ha II 15877
p. 62

The Obedient Man, 1942
India ink, pen, watercolored on
cadastral paper
30.8×39.2 cm
Lentos Kunstmuseum Linz
p. 140

Lilith, 1948
India ink, pen, watercolor on paper
35.8×22.4 cm
Leopold Museum, Vienna
p. 160

People Love to Dance
Ink pen on paper
24×35 cm
Leopold, Private Collection
p. 87

Voracity and Self-Denial in Satan
Print on paper
20×30 cm
Leopold, Private Collection
p. 89

FRANZ VON BAYROS
(Zagreb 1866–1924 Vienna)

Sisters of Salome,
probably before 1920
Chalk, watercolor, charcoal,
pencil on paper
74.2×97.3 cm
The Daulton Collection, Los Altos Hills, California
p. 113

AUBREY BEARDSLEY
(Brighton 1872–1898 Menton)

Illustration for Oscar Wilde's *Salome*, published in *The Studio*,
vol.1, no. 1, 1893
Private Collection
p. 146

CHRISTIAN BEHRENS
(Gotha 1852–1905 Breslau)

Sphinx, 1880 (model)/1894 (casting)
Bronze, black-brown patinated
on contemporary wooden base
145.2×108.9×71.9 cm
Belvedere, Vienna, Permanent loan LETTER Foundation, Cologne
p. 134

ARNOLD BÖCKLIN
(Basel 1827–1901 San Domenico near Fiesole, Florence)

Shield with the Head of Medusa, 1887
Painted paper mache
61×61 cm
Private Collection
p. 130

KLEMENS BROSCH
(Linz 1894–1926 Linz)

The Artist's Bookplate, 1916
India ink on paper
27×12.2 cm
OÖ Landes-Kultur GmbH, Land Oberösterreich, Graphic Collection, Ha II 1422
p. 219

AUGUST BRÖMSE
(Franzensbad 1873–1925 Prague)

The Dream, c. 1901
Aquatint and drypoint on japan paper, trial proof
20.2×13.4 cm
The Daulton Collection, Los Altos Hills, California
p. 64

JOSEF ENGELHART
(Vienna 1864–1941 Vienna)

Salome, 1900
Watercolor, charcoal, pencil on paper
70.5×34.79 cm
Private Collection
p. 109

JAMES ENSOR
(Ostend 1860–1949 Ostend)

The Cathedral, 1886
Etching on paper
23.6×17.7 cm
Leopold, Private Collection
p. 227

The Infernal Procession, 1887
Etching on paper
8×11,5 cm
Leopold, Private Collection
p. 252

The Battle of the Demons, 1888
Etching, heightened with watercolor
28.5×39.9 cm
Albertina, Vienna
p. 80

Peculiar Insects, 1888
Etching on paper
11.9×15.9 cm
OÖ Landes-Kultur GmbH, Land Oberösterreich, Graphic Collection, KS II 844
p. 86

Wizards in the Wind, 1888
Etching on paper
17.9×23.8 cm
Leopold, Private Collection
p. 78

Doctrine Feeding, 1889
Copperplate on paper
17.6×24.5 cm
Museum voor Schone Kunsten, Gent (Belgium)
p. 79

The Destroying Angel, 1889
Etching on paper
12×15.5 cm
Leopold, Private Collection
p. 100

Demons Tormenting Me, 1895
Etching on paper
11.9×15.8 cm
Leopold, Private Collection
p. 66

Hop-Frog's Revenge, 1898
Etching, drypoint on paper
50×32.5 cm
Leopold, Private Collection
p. 224

Self-Portrait, 1898
Lithograph
53.5×37 cm
Klewan Collection, Munich
p. 67

The Deadly Sins Dominated by Death, 1904
Etching, watercolor on paper
19.6×30.7 cm
Leopold, Private Collection
p. 81

Baptism of Masks, 1925–1930
Oil on canvas
60×70 cm
Private Collection
p. 91

FRANCISCO JOSÉ DE GOYA Y LUCIENTES
(Fuendetodos, Aragon 1746–1828 Bordeaux)

Madhouse, after 1794
Oil on wood
44.5×69.5 cm
Belvedere, Vienna
pp. 210/211

Sprucing Themselves Up, from the series *Los Caprichos*, 1799
Etching, scraped aquatint and engraving on paper
31×21.1 cm
Albertina, Vienna
p. 229

The Sleep of Reason Produces Monsters, from the series *Los Caprichos*, c. 1799
Etching on paper
32.6×24.8 cm
OÖ Landes-Kultur GmbH, Land Oberösterreich, Graphic Collection, Ka II 634
p. 63

OTTO GREINER
(Leipzig 1869–1916 Munich)

The Devil Presenting Woman to the Folk, print 3 of series *Of Woman*, 1898
Pen-drawing lithograph on brownish simili-japan paper
79.3×56.6 cm
LETTER Foundation, Cologne
p. 163

Gaia, 1912
Etching on paper
57.5×40 cm
Leopold Museum, Vienna
p. 165

BERTRAM HARTMAN
(Junction City, Kansas 1882–1960 New York City)

The Embrace, 1912
Watercolor on paper
49.5×49.5 cm
Private Collection
p. 116

FRITZ HEGENBART
(Salzburg 1864–1943 Bayerisch Gmain)

The Plight, print 7 of portfolio *A Canon of Life*, c. 1910
Etching, roulette and aquatint on chamois-colored copperplate paper
49.7×38.2 cm
LETTER Foundation, Cologne
p. 218

THOMAS THEODOR HEINE
(Leipzig 1867–1948 Stockholm)

Devil, 1904
Bronze with brown patina
40.6×22.9×14.3 cm
Private Collection
p. 82

LOUIS CARL BRUNO HÉROUX
(Leipzig 1868–1944 Leipzig)

Pain, print 5 of portfolio *Vae Solis*, between 1909 and 1914
Etching on pink-brownish paper rolled onto chamois-colored thick moldmade paper
58.6×40.3 cm
LETTER Foundation, Cologne
p. 161

RUDOLPH HÖLBE
(Lemgo 1848–1926 Dresden)

Siren, 1885
Bronze, limestone pedestal with turntable
70×37×42.5 cm
LETTER Foundation, Cologne
p. 135

HUGO HÖPPENER (FIDUS)
(Lübeck 1868–1948 Woltersdorf)

Sphinx of Life, 1891
Charcoal on vellum paper, laid down on cardboard
101.5×75 cm
The Daulton Collection, Los Altos Hills, California
p. 121

FERNAND KHNOPFF
(Grembergen near Dendermonde, Flanders 1858–1921 Brussels)

With Verhaeren. An Angel, 1889
Ink, black chalk, graphite heightened with white and scratchings out on paper
33×19.5 cm
Private Collection
p. 117

Unmoved Water. The Pond of Ménil, 1894
Oil on canvas
53.5×114.5 cm
Belvedere, Vienna
p. 280

MAX KLINGER
(Leipzig 1857–1920 Großjena)

Witch and Bat, 1880
Aquatint on rolled china paper, trial proof
31×43.5 cm
The Daulton Collection, Los Altos Hills, California
p. 152

Night, from the cycle *On Death. Part 1,* 1897
Etching on paper
63.5×44.5 cm
Leopold Museum, Vienna
p. 196

On the Rails, from the cycle *On Death. Part 1,* 1897
Etching on paper
63.5×44.5 cm
Leopold Museum, Vienna
p. 256

Sea, from the cycle *On Death. Part 1,* 1897
Etching on paper
63.5×44.5 cm
Leopold Museum, Vienna
p. 286

Death as Saviour, from the cycle *On Death. Part 1,* 1897
Etching on paper
63.5×44.5 cm
Leopold Museum, Vienna
p. 251

Anxieties, print 7 of series *Paraphrase on the Finding of a Glove,* 1880 or 1881
Etching with slight tint on chamois-colored machine-made vellum, print 1924
31.9×48.7 cm
LETTER Foundation, Cologne
p. 72

Dreams, print 3 from the cycle *A Life,* between 1880 and 1884
Etching, aquatint, copper engraving on chamois-colored copperplate paper, print 1920
63.1×44.9 cm
LETTER Foundation, Cologne
p. 65

Amor, Death and the Beyond, print 12 from the cycle *Intermezzi,* 1881
Etching on paper
45.1×62.7 cm
Private Collection Vienna
p. 298

Temptation, from the cycle *A Life,* 1884
Aquatint on paper
41×21.6 cm
The Daulton Collection, Los Altos Hills, California
p. 126

Abandoned, from the cycle *A Life,* 1884
Aquatint in reddish-brown and black ink on paper
31.5×45 cm
The Daulton Collection, Los Altos Hills, California
p. 204

The New Salome, c. 1903
Bronze with black patina
47.2×29×20.4 cm
Leopold Museum, Vienna
p. 110

War, from the portfolio *On Death, Part 2,* 1909
Etching on japan paper
52.2×34 cm
The Daulton Collection, Los Altos Hills, California
p. 103

Philosopher, print 3 of portfolio *On Death, Part 2,* 1910
Etching, aquatint on chamois-colored simili-japan paper
62.1×46.5 cm
LETTER Foundation, Cologne
p. 201

HEINRICH KLEY
(Karlsruhe 1863–1945 Munich)

Inspiration (Self-Portrait), 1912
Pen drawing
25.5×36.5 cm
Museum Georg Schäfer, Schweinfurt
p. 200

GUSTAV KLIMT
(Baumgarten near Vienna 1862–1918 Vienna)

Thaleia and Melpomene, 1898
Pencil on paper
37.6×44.7 cm
Albertina, Vienna
p. 123

Bust Picture of a Woman With Her Hands in Her Hair, c. 1905
Black chalk on wrapping paper
44.7×30.6 cm
Museum Georg Schäfer, Schweinfurt
p. 128

JOSEF KUGLER
(Vienna 1867–1946)

Capriccio, 1913
Tempera on canvas
78×97 cm
Private Collection
pp. 84/85

LUCIEN LÉVY DHURMER
(Algier 1865–1953 Le Vésinet near Paris)

Danaë, c. 1900
Pastel on paper
59.6×87 cm
Private Collection
p. 175

WILHELM LIST
(Vienna 1864–1918 Vienna)

The Siren, print 9 of portfolio *Lithographs of Viennese Artists,* c. 1900
Chalk lithograph in yellow-brown, green and black on chamois-colored vellum
47.9×35.9 cm
LETTER Foundation, Cologne
p. 127

RICHARD LUKSCH
(Vienna 1872–1936 Hamburg)

The Insinuation, 1902/03
Ceramic (white glaze)
82×47×22 cm
Leopold Museum, Vienna
p. 122

KARL MEDIZ
(Vienna 1868–1945 Dresden)

Red Angel, 1902
Oil on canvas
172×185.5 cm
Archive Attersee
p. 115

Solitude. Motif from Lacrona, c. 1902/03
Oil on canvas
174×206 cm
Belvedere, Vienna
p. 283

CARL MOLL
(Vienna 1861–1945 Vienna)

Twilight, 1900
Oil on canvas
80×94.5 cm
Belvedere, Vienna
p. 281

GUSTAVE MOREAU
(Paris 1826–1898 Paris)

Perseus and Andromeda, 1882
Watercolour on paper
27.5×23.5 cm
Private Collection
p. 191

EDVARD MUNCH
(Løten, Hedmark 1863–1944 Ekely in Oslo)

Vampire II, 1895–1902
Color lithograph, lithographic crayon, india ink on paper
38.9×55.7 cm
Private Collection Vienna
p. 137

The Sin, 1902
Lithograph, lithographic crayon on paper
85.5×58.2 cm
Leopold Museum, Vienna
p. 131

Vampire, 1894
Drypoint etching
29.9×22.9 cm
Staatliche Museen zu Berlin, Nationalgalerie, Scharf-Gerstenberg Collection
S. 120

VIKTOR MÜLLER

(Frankfurt am Main 1830–1871 Munich)

Sphinx, 1906
Oil on canvas
82×86 cm
Belvedere, Vienna
p. 119

ADOLF MÜNZER

(Pleß, Upper Silesia 1870–1953 Landsberg am Lech)

Witch Riding, 1906
Mixed media
46.8×34.9 cm
Museum Georg Schäfer, Schweinfurt
p. 153

ODILON REDON

(Bordeaux 1840–1916 Paris)

The Gaze, 1910
Oil on canvas
73×73 cm
Private Collection
p. 202

Ecstatic Figures, 1910/11
Oil on canvas
38×46.5 cm
Klewan Collection, Munich
p. 203

FERDINAND FREIHERR VON REZNIČEK

(Vienna 1868–1909 Munich)

Salome
Gouache, opaque white on paper
44.5×39.8 cm
Museum Georg Schäfer, Schweinfurt
p. 108

GEORGES ANTOINE ROCHEGROSSE

(Versailles 1859–1938 El Biar)

War and Peace, 1886
Oil on canvas
170×114.9 cm
Private Collection
p. 105

FÉLICIEN ROPS

(Namur 1833–1898 Essonnes)

The Atheists' Dinner, illustration for *Les Diaboliques* by Jules Barbey d'Aurevilly, 1882
Etching
22×16 cm
Museum Georg Schäfer, Schweinfurt
p. 164

Street Corner, Four O'Clock in the Morning (Human Parody), 1878–1881
Pastel, coloured chalks, watercolour on paper
22.5×15 cm
Private Collection
p. 125

The Sacrifice, from the series *Les Sataniques,* 1878–1882
Pencil on paper
46×30 cm
Private Collection
p. 183 (2)

The Abduction, from the series *Les Sataniques,* 1878–1882
Pencil on paper
46×30 cm
Private Collection
p. 183 (1)

Satan Sowing Tares, from the series *Les Sataniques,* 1882
Heliogravure and vernis mou on simili-japan paper
27.8×20.4 cm
Museum voor Schone Kunsten, Gent (Belgium)
p. 94

Frontispiece for *Le vice suprême* by Joséphin Péladan, 1884
Heliogravure on paper
28.1×19.6 cm
Museum voor Schone Kunsten, Gent (Belgium)
p. 139

The Great Lyre, frontispiece for Stéphane Mallarmé's *Les Poésies,* 1899
Etching
24.5×17 cm
Leopold Museum, Vienna
not shown in the catalogue

The Cold Devils, 1905
Etching
25.7×19.5 cm
Leopold Museum, Vienna
p. 181

SASCHA SCHNEIDER

(Saint Petersburg 1870–1927 Swinoujscie)

Feeling of Dependence, c. 1893
Oil on canvas
250×165 cm
Private Collection
p. 207

FRANZ SEDLACEK

(Breslau 1891–1945 Poland)

Gate of Hell, 1916
Pen, brush, ink on paper
28.5×37.7 cm
Museum Ortner, Vienna
p. 98

THÉOPHILE ALEXANDRE STEINLEN

(Lausanne 1859–1923 Paris)

Dance of Death, c. 1900
Pen, ink on paper
27.5×21.1 cm
Private Collection
p. 230

FRANZ VON STUCK

(Tettenweis, Passau 1863–1928 Munich)

Trout Pond, 1890
Oil on canvas
63.8×56 cm
Leopold Museum, Vienna
p. 282

Paradise Lost, c. 1890
Oil on canvas
115.5×70.5 cm
Private Collection
p. 104

Mermaid, 1891
Oil on wood
28.2×82.3 cm
Private Collection
p. 176/177

Sensuality, ca. 1891
Oil on canvas
50.5×36.3 cm
Katharina Büttiker Gallery, Zurich
p. 129

Faun and Nymph, c. 1892
Oil on canvas
38.7×68.1 cm
Private Collection
p. 174

Amazon, 1897–1905
Bronze with black-brown patina
64.5×48×17.3 cm
Leopold Museum, Vienna
p. 132

Lucifer
Etching on paper
29.4×26.6 cm
Leopold Museum, Vienna
p. 237

PHOTOGRAPHS

ALOIS BEER
(Budapest 1840–1916 Klagenfurt)

Irene Kubin, one of Kubin's stepmothers, 1897
Altnöder Collection, Salzburg
p. 302 (3)

EMMY HAESELE
(Mödling near Vienna 1894–1987 Bad Leonfelden)

Alfred Kubin sitting in the grass in Tusset, August 1935
Altnöder Collection, Salzburg
p. 310 (3)

Alfred Kubin sitting at the dinner table in Tusset, undated
Altnöder Collection, Salzburg
p. 310 (1)

Alfred Kubin with a magnifying glass, undated
Altnöder Collection, Salzburg
p. 311 (4)

Alfred Kubin on a road lined with birch trees, undated
Altnöder Collection, Salzburg
p. 310 (4)

Alfred Kubin reading, undated
Altnöder Collection, Salzburg
p. 311 (1)

Landscape with haystack, undated
Altnöder Collection, Salzburg
p. 310 (2)

Alfred Kubin, undated
Altnöder Collection, Salzburg
p. 311 (3)

Alfred Kubin at his desk, undated
Altnöder Collection, Salzburg
p. 311 (2)

Alfred Kubin sitting at his desk, undated
Altnöder Collection, Salzburg
p. 300

RICHARD LEMP

Alfred Kubin's house in Zwickledt,1956
Altnöder Collection, Salzburg
p. 327

HERBERT RÖMER

Alfred Kubin's hands, 1949
Altnöder Collection, Salzburg
p. 52

WOLFGANG SCHNEDITZ

Alfred Kubin in Zwickledt, 1934
Altnöder Collection, Salzburg
p. 312 (1)

Alfred Kubin sitting, 1952
Altnöder Collection, Salzburg
p. 313 (1)

Alfred Kubin in front of a bookcase, c. 1952
Altnöder Collection, Salzburg
p. 313 (2)

Alfred Kubin writing, February 1956
Photograph
Altnöder Collection, Salzburg
p. 315

Alfred Kubin with an open book, undated
Altnöder Collection, Salzburg
p. 313 (3)

RICHARD FERDINAND SCHMITZ
(Gonzenhaim/Taunus 1876–1950 Munich)

Alfred Kubin in Munich, 1904
Städtische Galerie im Lenbachhaus und Kunstbau München
p. 304 (3)

ANONYMOUS PHOTOGRAPHERS

The "Kubin Archive" on Fischmarkt 3, Hamburg, undated
Altnöder Collection, Salzburg
p. 308 (2)

Archivist Dr. Kurt Otte at the "Kubin Archive" in Hamburg, undated
Altnöder Collection, Salzburg
p. 308 (1)

Friedrich Franz Kubin, Alfred Kubin's father, May 1893
Städtische Galerie im Lenbachhaus und Kunstbau München
p. 302 (2)

Alfred Kubin, c. 1893
Städtische Galerie im Lenbachhaus und Kunstbau München
p. 302 (1)

Alfred Kubin in his first year in Munich, 1898
Städtische Galerie im Lenbachhaus und Kunstbau München
p. 304 (1)

The Kubin family: Alfred Kubin, his sister Maria (center), the stepsisters Rosalie and Friederike, the stepmother Irene and his father Friedrich Franz, 1902
Städtische Galerie im Lenbachhaus und Kunstbau München
p. 303

Alfred Kubin and Emmy Bayer, c. 1903
Städtische Galerie im Lenbachhaus und Kunstbau München
p. 304 (2)

Alfred and Hedwig Kubin in front of their house in Zwickledt, 1925
Städtische Galerie im Lenbachhaus und Kunstbau München
p. 309

View of the Kubin mansion in Zwickledt from the garden, 1966
Altnöder Collection, Salzburg
p. 306 (1)

DOCUMENTS

Obituary notice for Alfred Kubin, 1959
Altnöder Collection, Salzburg
p. 313 (4)

Alfred Kubin's address book, undated
Altnöder Collection, Salzburg
p. 315

ALFRED KUBIN

German first edition of *The Other Side: A Fantastic Novel* with 52 Drawings by the Author, Munich, 1909
Book
Altnöder Collection, Salzburg
p. 306 (2)

ALFRED KUBIN/
OTTO VON HOLTEN

A Dance of Death, 1918
Book
Leopold, Private Collection
p. 312 (2)

PICTURE CREDITS

Albertina, Vienna: pp. 8/9 (detail), 28, 73, 80, 123, 141, 156, 171, 229, 270/271 (detail), 272, 273

Albertina, Vienna. Forberg Collection: p. 278

Aponem: pp. 230, 296

Attersee Archive: p. 115

Belvedere, Vienna: pp. 210/211, 280, 281, 283; **Belvedere, Vienna/Johannes Stoll:** pp. 119, 134

bpk/Hamburger Kunsthalle/Christoph Irrgang: p. 247

bpk/Kupferstichkabinett, SMB/Volker-H. Schneider: p. 120

bpk/Museum Georg Schäfer Schweinfurt: pp. 108, 125, 128, 153, 164, 200

bpk/Nationalgalerie, SMB, Collection Scharf-Gerstenberg/Jörg P. Anders: p. 138

bpk/Nationalgalerie, SMB/Andres Kilger: p. 56

Bröhan-Museum Berlin: p. 129

Dorotheum Wien, auction catalogue 31.05.2016: p. 91

Dorotheum Wien, auction catalogue 24.11.2020: p. 98

Grisebach GmbH: pp. 84/85, 174, 176/177

LENTOS Kunstmuseum/Reinhard Haider: pp. 140, 188, 225, 249, 274, 297

Leopold Museum, Vienna: pp. 4/5 (detail), 26, 31, 33, 44, 45, 46, 47, 49, 58, 60/61 (detail), 69, 70, 71, 77, 81, 92/93 (detail), 96, 101, 106/107 (detail), 110, 122, 124, 131, 132, 133, 137, 143, 145, 147, 148, 149, 155, 158/159 (detail), 160, 162, 169 (1&2), 172, 173, 178, 179, 186, 187, 189, 192/193 (detail), 195, 197, 199, 205, 208, 209, 212, 216, 220/221 (detail), 223, 227, 231, 233, 235, 236, 238, 239, 240, 245, 248, 253, 255, 261, 263, 265, 267, 268, 269, 275, 276, 277, 279, 282, 285, 287, 288/289 (detail), 290, 291, 293, 294, 295, 298, 299

Leopold Museum, Vienna/Photo: artscope: pp. 2, 10/11 (detail), 17, 19, 38 (detail), 52 (detail), 59, 66, 67, 78, 87, 88, 89, 99, 100, 112, 146, 150, 165, 181, 196, 203, 213, 224, 237, 240, 241, 242/243 (detail), 251, 252, 256, 257, 259, 284, 286, 292, 300, 302 (3), 305, 306 (1&2), 307, 308 (1&2), 310, 311, 312, 313, 314, 315, 326 (detail)

LETTER Foundation, Cologne: pp. 65, 72, 127, 161, 163, 201, 218

LETTER Foundation, Cologne/**Jean-Luc Ikelle-Matiba, Bonn:** p. 135

Courtesy of Ketterer Kunst GmbH & Co. KG: p. 43

Museum of Fine Arts Ghent, www.artinflanders.be: pp. 79, 94, 139

NEUMEISTER/Christian Mitko: p. 104

OÖ-Landes Kultur GmbH, Land Oberösterreich, Graphic Collection: pp. 63, 74/75 (detail), 83, 86, 102, 185, 219

OÖ-Landes Kultur GmbH, Land Oberösterreich, Graphic Collection, Günter Rombold Collection: pp. 6/7 (detail), 23, 62, 144, 151, 217

Private Collection: pp. 82, 105, 109, 116, 175, 202, 207

Private Collection, Austria: pp. 57 (1), 97, 167

Städtische Galerie im Lenbachhaus und Kunstbau München: pp. 57 (2), 68, 95, 111, 157, 215, 222, 302 (1&2), 303, 304, 309

Sotheby's London: pp. 117, 125, 130, 180, 183 (1&2), 191

The Jack Daulton Collection, photos Marty Kelly/Don Tuttle: pp. 64, 103, 113, 121, 126, 152, 204

For the works by Alfred Kubin: © Eberhard Spangenberg, München/Bildrecht, Wien 2022

For the works by Adolf Münzer: © Bildrecht, Wien 2022

For the works by Wolfgang Schneditz: © Ursula Rausch

For the works by Emmy Haesele: © Estate Emmy Haesele

Cover front page (detail): Alfred Kubin, *Into the Unknown,* 1900/01, Leopold Museum, Vienna (photo: Leopold Museum, Vienna)

Any suspected copyright claims, which could not be traced despite thorough investigation, should be addressed to the Leopold Museum.

INDEX OF FULL-PAGE ILLUSTRATIONS

LENDERS

Albertina, Vienna

Archive Attersee

Belvedere, Vienna

Katharina Büttiker Gallery, Zurich

Lentos Kunstmuseum Linz

Leopold Museum, Vienna

Leopold, Private Collection

LETTER Foundation, Cologne

Museum Georg Schäfer, Schweinfurt

Museum Ortner, Vienna

Museum voor Schone Kunsten, Gent (Belgium)

OÖ Landes-Kultur GmbH, Land Oberösterreich

Private Collection, Vienna

Private Collection

Private Collection, Austria

Altnöder Collection, Salzburg

Klewan Collection, Munich

Staatliche Museen zu Berlin, Nationalgalerie, Scharf-Gerstenberg Collection

Städtische Galerie im Lenbachhaus und Kunstbau München

The Daulton Collection, Los Altos Hills, California

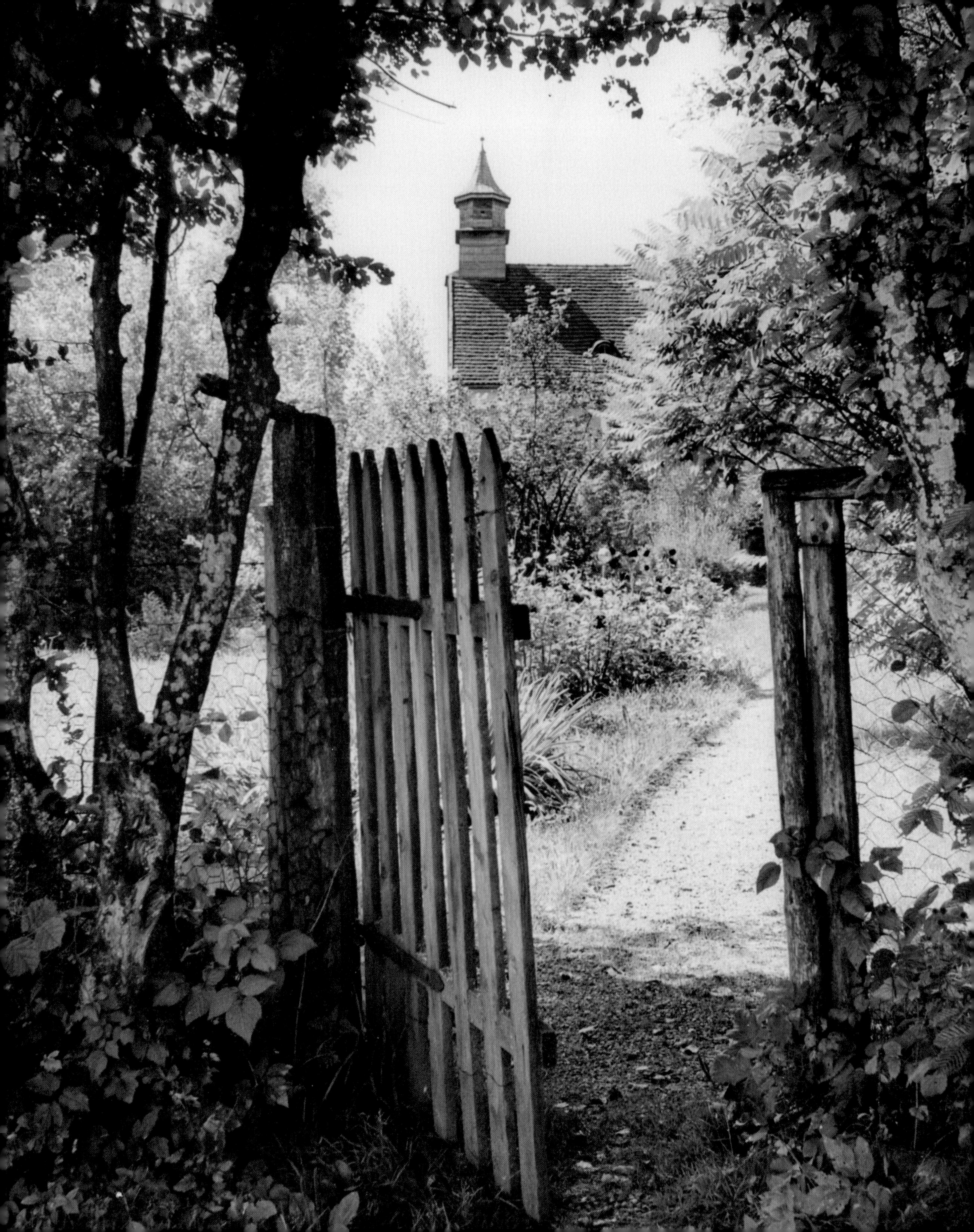

AUTHORS

ANNEGRET HOBERG

born in Düsseldorf, studies of art history, history, and archaeology in Tübingen, Hamburg, Paris, and Munich. Graduation with a doctoral dissertation on *Zeit, Kunst und Geschichtsbewusstsein—Studien zur Ikonografie des Chronos in der französischen Kunst des 17. Jahrhunderts.* 1984–1987 worked for the Bavarian State Collection of Paintings, Munich. 1987–2021 collection director for the Blauer Reiter department and the Kubin Archive at the Städtische Galerie im Lenbachhaus und Kunstbau, Munich. Numerous exhibitions and publication on the Blaue Reiter group, German Expressionism, and Alfred Kubin, among them *Alfred Kubin 1877–1959* (Lenbachhaus Munich/ Hamburger Kunsthalle, 1990/91), *Alfred Kubin—Das lithografische Werk* (Munich, 1999), *Alfred Kubin und der Blaue Reiter* (Lenbachhaus Munich, 2018), *Franz Marc – Werkverzeichnis,* 3 vols. (Munich/London, 2004–2011), *Der Blaue Reiter im Lenbachhaus München* (Munich, 2013), and *Gruppendynamik—Der Blaue Reiter* (Lenbachhaus Munich, 2021).

AUGUST RUHS

specialist in psychiatry and medical psychotherapy, psychoanalyst. Until 2011 deputy head of the Department of Psychoanalysis and Psychotherapy of the Medical University of Vienna. Between 2007 and 2015 chairman of the Vienna task force for psychoanalysis. Co-founder and chairman of "Neue Wiener Gruppe/Lacan-Schule", co-editor of the journal *texte. psychoanalyse. ästhetik. kulturkritik.* Numerous publications and translations in the area of clinical, theoretical and applied psychoanalysis. Most recent book publications: *Der Vorhang des Parrhasios—Schriften zur Kulturtheorie der Psychoanalyse* (Vienna 2003), *Unbewusstes Inszenieren—Symptom-Werk-Leben* (Vienna 2007), and *Lacan—Eine Einführung in die strukturale Psychoanalyse* (Vienna 2010).

BURGHART SCHMIDT

studied biology, physics and chemistry as well as philosophy and art history at Tübingen University. Received his doctorate in 1981 from Tübingen University and habilitated in 1984 at Hannover University. Acted as research assistant to Ernst Bloch (edition of complete works) at Tübingen University (1968–1977). Worked as lecturer for art philosophy at the University of Applied Arts Vienna (1977–1998), at the Vienna Academy of Fine Arts, as well as in Hannover, Graz, Klagenfurt, Linz and Salzburg. From 1997 to 2011 he worked as professor for language and esthetics at the Hessen State University of Art and Design and acted as the university's vice president. From 2001 till his death on the 13th of february 2022 he was a visiting professor at the University of Applied Arts Vienna.

HANS-PETER WIPPLINGER

studied art history, theater and media studies, as well as communication science at Vienna University. He has worked at the OK Centrum für Gegenwartskunst in Linz and at the New Museum of Contemporary Art in New York, as well as for the Vienna International Film Festival. He acted as director of the Museum Moderner Kunst in Passau (2003–2007) and as director of the Kunsthalle Krems (2009–2015). Since October 2015 he has been the Artistic Director of the Leopold Museum in Vienna. He has curated numerous thematic and monographic exhibitions on Classical Modernism as well as on contemporary art. He is the editor and author of numerous scientific essays on modern and contemporary art.

PUBLISHER'S NOTES

CATALOGUE TO ACCOMPANY THE EXHIBITION

Alfred Kubin. Confessions of a Tortured Soul
16.04.2022–24.07.2022
Leopold Museum, Vienna

TEAM

Artistic Director: Hans-Peter Wipplinger
Managing Director: Moritz Stipsicz
Curator: Hans-Peter Wipplinger
in cooperation with August Ruhs
Scientific Consultant to the Artistic Director and Project Coordinator: Dominik Papst
Personal Assistant to the Artistic Director: Paula Freisl
Personal Assistant to the Managing Director, Personnel Matters: Doris Molitor
Personal Assitant to the Managing Director, Project Coordinator: Miriam Wirges
Registrars: Johannes Semotan, Nicola Mayr
Restoration: Sandra Maria Dzialek, Monika Sadek-Rosshap, Stephanie Strachwitz, Beatrix Zeugswetter
Museology: Verena Gamper, Ivan Ristić, Nina Buchwaldt, Barbara Halbmayr, Aline Marion Steinwender, Simone Hönigl
Image Rights: Daniela Kumhala
Publication Management, Library and Archives: Lena Scholz
Digitization of the Collection: Anita Halbartschlager, Else Prünster
Provenance Research: Alfred Fehringer, Konstantin Ferihumer
Press and Public Relations: Klaus Pokorny, Veronika Werkner
Controlling: Doris Lex-Grabler
Strategic Organizational Development: Tina Zelenka
Marketing and Communications: Julia Kemetner, Christine Kociu, Regina Beran-Prem, Markus Hall
Event Management: Anna Suette, Valentina Scappi
Sponsoring, Fundraising: Dorothea Schellhorn, Regina Holler-Strobl
Cooperations: Anna Wagner
Art Education: Anita Götz-Winkler, Bianka Kalin
Graphic Design: Nina Haider, Ben Havlicek
Ticketing, Shop Management: Ulrike Köberl, Esther Moldovan, Jens Rogel, Michaela Kühr
Facility Management: Michael Terler, Johannes Becker, Wolfgang Benes, Rainer Petrat
IT and Media Engineering: Leonhard Gareiss, Luka Janicic
Office: Jasmin Hoffer
Accounting: Doris Lex-Grabler, Lena Smid

CATALOGUE

Editor: Hans-Peter Wipplinger
Authors: Hans-Peter Wipplinger, August Ruhs, Burghart Schmidt, Annegret Hoberg, Lena Scholz
Coordinating Editor & Image Rights: Lena Scholz
Graphic Design: Nele Steinborn
Copy Editing (German): Rainer Just
English Translations: Michael Strand, Agnes Vukovich (texts by Annegret Hoberg)
Printing and Binding: Gerin Druck GmbH
Image Editing: Pixelstorm Litho & Digital Imaging
Paper: Arctic Volume white, 150 g
Fonts: Questa & Questa sans

First Edition

Published by
Verlag der Buchhandlung Walther und Franz König
Ehrenstraße 4, D-50672 Köln

Bibliographic information published by the Deutsche Nationalbibliothek:
Die Deutsche Nationalbibliothek verzeichnet diese Publikation in der Deutschen Nationalbibliografie; detailed bibliographic data is available online at http://dnb.d-nb.de.

Printed in Austria

Distribution
Europe
Buchhandlung Walther König
Ehrenstraße 4 | D-50672 Köln
Tel: +49 (0) 221/20 59 6 53
verlag@buchhandlung-walther-koenig.de

Outside the United States and Canada, Germany, Austria and Switzerland by
Thames & Hudson Ltd., London, www.thamesandhudson.com

Outside Europe
D.A.P. / Distributed Art Publishers, Inc., 75 Broad Street, Suite 630, USA – New York, NY 10004, Fon +1 (0) 212 627 1999, orders@dapinc.com

ISBN: 978-3-7533-0198-3

Partner of the Leopold Museum

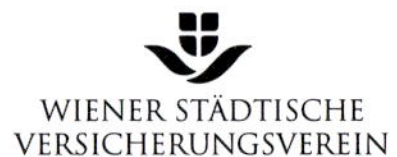

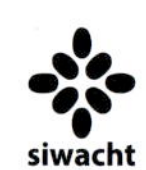

Benefactor

Bundesministerium
Kunst, Kultur, öffentlicher Dienst und Sport

With the kind support of